Handbook of Strengths-Based Clinical Practices

An interdisciplinary handbook about strengths-based clinical practices, this book finds the common factors in specific models from social work, psychology, and counseling. The book ends with a grounded theory-informed method that pulls together what each of the chapters report and posits a theory on the basis of that work. Comprising 23 chapters and written by leaders in the mental health fields, *Handbook of Strengths-Based Clinical Practices* shows how professionals and students can facilitate change and resiliency in those with whom they work.

Jeffrey K. Edwards, EdD, LMFT, is professor emeritus at Northeastern Illinois University and a past president of the Illinois Counseling Association.

Andy Young, MA, LCPC, is owner and director of New Prairie Counseling Center in Elmhurst, Illinois.

Holly J. Nikels, PhD, LCPC, ACS, is professor and program coordinator in the Department of Counselor Education at Western Illinois University-Quad Cities.

D1710213

"When people play to their strengths they exude a certain confidence that allows them to perform at their best, maximize social engagement, get the most out of life, and increase overall subjective well-being. This book effectively demonstrates the efficacy of current strengths-based models and concludes with a thoughtful assessment of how the best of each may come together toward a rational, unitary approach. This text is a must-read for anyone interested in strengths-based psychology."

—Matt Glowiak, PhD, LCPC, CAADC, NCC, Co-Founder of Counseling Speaks, LLC; Assistant Professor, Benedictine University; Contributing Faculty, Walden University

"The *Handbook* pulls together frameworks from a variety of helping professions and offers a tangible, succinct, and often challenging supervision model that brings into focus how a strengths-based approach can contribute to meaningful supervision experiences. Supervisors will experience continued substantial benefit from this handbook as they delve into the power of supervisee strengths as opposed to deficits, leading to empowered clinical practice."

—Vincent J. Walsh-Rock, MS, LCPC, Doctoral Candidate, Northern Illinois University

Handbook of Strengths-Based Clinical Practices

Finding Common Factors

Edited by
Jeffrey K. Edwards, Andy Young,
and Holly J. Nikels

Routledge
Taylor & Francis Group

NEW YORK AND LONDON

First published 2017
by Routledge
711 Third Avenue, New York, NY 10017

and by Routledge
2 Park Square, Milton Park, Abingdon, Oxon, OX14 4RN

Routledge is an imprint of the Taylor & Francis Group, an informa business

© 2017 Taylor & Francis

Library of Congress Cataloging-in-Publication Data
Names: Edwards, Jeffrey K., editor.
Title: Handbook of strengths-based clinical practices : finding common factors /
    edited by Jeffrey K. Edwards, Andy Young, and Holly J. Nikels.
Description: New York, NY : Routledge, 2016. Includes bibliographical references
    and index.
Identifiers: LCCN 2015046260 | ISBN 9781138897939 (hbk : alk. paper) |
    ISBN 9781138897922 (pbk : alk. paper) | ISBN 9781315708898 (ebk)
Subjects: LCSH: Clinical psychology. | Clinical sociology. | Counseling psychology.
Classification: LCC RC467 .H2925 2016 | DDC 616.89—dc23
LC record available at http://lccn.loc.gov/2015046260

ISBN: 978-1-138-89793-9 (hbk)
ISBN: 978-1-138-89792-2 (pbk)
ISBN: 978-1-315-70889-8 (ebk)

Typeset in Bembo
by Apex CoVantage, LLC

Printed and bound in the United States of America by
Edwards Brothers Malloy on sustainably sourced paper

Contents

Contents

Contributors

Mary Jo Barrett, MSW, executive director and co-founder, Center for Contextual Change, Skokie, IL

Matthew J. Beck, MSEd, LCPC, NCC, clinical faculty, Department of Counselor Education, Western Illinois University-Quad Cities

Tasia Buford-Howell, MA, DePaul University, Chicago, IL

Latifat O. Cabrirou, MA, LPC, doctoral student, Counseling Psychology Program, Loyola University

Tonya Davis, MSEd, LPC, NCC, PhD candidate, Counselor Education and Supervision, Northern Illinois University, DeKalb, IL

Louise Dimiceli-Mitran, MA, LCPC, MT-BC, FAMI, Rhythms Within LLC, Chicago, IL; Primary Trainer of the Bonny Method of Guided Imagery & Music, Therapeutic Arts Institute, Chicago, IL

Reade Dowda, PhD, assistant professor, Counseling Program, Fort Hays State University, Hays, KS

Jeffrey K. Edwards, EdD, LMFT, professor emeritus, Department of Counselor Education, Northeastern Illinois University, and past president, Illinois Counseling Association, DeKalb, IL

Linda Stone Fish, PhD, Syracuse University, Department of Marriage and Family Therapy, The David B. Falk College of Sport and Human Dynamics

Teresa B. Fletcher, PhD, LPC, professor of Sport & Health Psychology, Adler University, Chicago, Illinois

Trevor G. Gates, PhD, LCSW, assistant professor, Greater Rochester Collaborative MSW Program, College at Brockport and State University of New York, Rochester

Duane A. Halbur, PhD, Walden University

Susan Hurley, PhD, associate professor, Department of Clinical Mental Health Counseling, University of North Georgia

Sandra L. Kakacek, EdD, LCPC, Director of Training and Core Faculty Clinical Mental Health Counseling, Adler University, Chicago, IL

Brian L. Kelly, PhD, MSW, CADC, assistant professor, School of Social Work, Loyola University Chicago, IL

Megan Kelly, MA, school counselor, Adlai E. Stevenson High School, Lincolnshire, IL

Michele Kerulis, Adler School of Professional Psychology, Chicago, IL

David Kleist, PhD, professor, Department Chair, Idaho State University

Katie Kostohryz, PhD, assistant professor, Counselor Education; coordinator, Counseling Services & CEDAR Clinic; Department of Educational Psychology, Counseling, and Special Education, Penn State University

Michelle Marmé, PhD, CRC, LCPC, Cambourne Consulting, Riverwoods, IL

E. C. M. Mason, PhD, Department of Counseling and Special Education, DePaul University, Chicago

Michael Massengale, MA, doctoral student in Counseling Psychology, Georgia State University

Mary Nichter, PhD, Professor of Counseling and Chair, Education Leadership and Counseling Program, Sam Houston State University, Huntsville, TX

Holly J. Nikels, PhD, LCPC, professor, Western Illinois University, Macomb, IL

James Ruby, PhD, associate professor, Department of Human Services, California State University, Fullerton; core faculty, Department of School Counseling, Capella University

Lori A. Russell-Chapin, PhD, professor, EHS associate dean, and co-director of the Center for Collaborative Brain Research, Bradley University, Peoria, IL

Julie K. West Russo, EdD, LPC, program director, clinical coordinator, and assistant professor of counseling, Counseling Department, Trinity International University, Deerfield, IL

Jane Coe Smith, PhD, assistant professor, Department of Counseling, Idaho State University

Stephannee R. Standefer, LCPC, assistant director of Clinical Training and core faculty, Northwestern University, Evanston, IL

Anita Jones Thomas, PhD, dean and professor, School of Psychological Sciences, University of Indianapolis, Indianapolis, IN

Vanessa Whitnell, MA, DePaul University, Chicago, IL

Andy Young, MA, LCPC, New Prairie Counseling Center, Elmhurst, IL

Jessica Young, MA, LCPC, BC-DMT, GL-CMA, associate professor, Department of Creative Arts Therapies, Columbia College Chicago

Acknowledgments

The editors thank all of the authors and the many folks at Routledge Taylor & Francis for their contributions to this work that made this dream come true. Completing this book has been an interesting, long, and exciting adventure. During this time, we had many crises among the editors as well as the authors. We had deaths in families, issues with family members that scattered return dates, changes of jobs, as well as one author needing to take refuge due to a serious problem with a student. What all of this has taught us is how truly resilient we can be under stresses. Working with our strengths, and relying on each other to provide care, has made us all even stronger and has given us solid evidence of the power of our individual and collective strengths. We all hope you, the reader, find evidence of that in your own lives as well as in this book.

Section I

Introduction to Strengths-Based Practice

1

Strengths-Based Counseling 2.0

Continuing the Discussion

*Andy Young, Jeffrey K. Edwards, Holly J. Nikels,
and Stephannee R. Standefer[1]*

> There are two ways of spreading light: to be the candle, or the mirror that reflects it.
> Edith Wharton

This book is written from the perspective of many authors discussing their work as to what they believe to be a strengths-based model. Each has his or her own approach and view of how a strengths-based model fits their own unique work situation. Although the client populations and clinical settings may be different, two components remain constant: (a) the clinician's belief that using a strengths-based model is more effective than using the traditional medical model of pathologizing clients and (b) a rejection of the notion that the clinicians have more knowledge about the needs of the client than does the client him- or herself.

Strengths-based counseling has been in existence for many decades. Frequently, Carl Rogers (1961) and Abraham Maslow (1971) are credited with starting this movement. Rogers and Maslow both rejected the medical model of diagnosis and the notion of "fixing" problems. However, social worker Bertha Reynolds (1932) was a much earlier theorist in the mental health field and focused her work on the clients' strengths and the future. She opposed the psychoanalytic concepts of disease, which would eventually lead the way to what is known today as the *Diagnostic and Statistical Manual of Mental Disorders* (*DSM*; see American Psychiatric Association, 2013).

Modern day theorists Rapp & Goscha (2011) and Saleebey (2009, 2012) began with a team at the University of Kansas with ideas about a strengths-based model that was as broad as social work practice itself. Saleebey (2009) stated that

> practicing from a strengths perspective means this—*everything* you do as a social worker will be predicated in some way, on helping to discover and embellish, explore and exploit clients' strengths and resources in service of assisting them to achieve their goals, realize their dreams, and shed the irons of their own inhibitions and misgivings and society's domination. (p. 1).

Saleebey's (2009, 2012) work moves beyond a pure clinical model of therapy and/or counseling to a broader spectrum of case practice.

Social workers/family therapists Steve de Shazer and Insoo Kim Berg changed the problem-solving strategic family therapy model to one more solution focused. During their work at the Milwaukee Brief Family Therapy Center, they wrote many books, chapters, and articles, both together and separately (de Shazer, 1988, 1994, 2005; Berg, 1994, 1997; Berg & de Shazer, 1993). In the same postmodern vein, social workers Michael White and David Epston (1990) introduced their narrative therapy model to the world, which developed out of their belief that it is the stories we tell ourselves about our lives that create our individual realities. They argued that most of these stories could contain either marginalizing edits or wide gaps that leave out our times of fighting back against those stories that diminish our strengths (White & Epston, 1990).

In her book, *Normal Family Process*, Froma Walsh (2003a) argued that the work of clinicians has been taken over by the medical model in which clinicians are trained to look for deficits and problems rather than resiliencies. Former president of the American Psychological Association (APA) and evidence-based positive psychology/positive therapy founder Martin Seligman (2002) also believes that mental health professionals have been trained to look at weaknesses rather than strengths and overlook positive traits of personality. Seligman (2002) asserts that high levels of life satisfaction can be achieved by building and using one's signature strengths.

These ideas are vastly different than the problem-focused, diagnosis-driven view of the medical model. Some argue that the psychiatry, pharmaceutical, and insurance industries have "appropriated" the mental health field, making it wholly into a "sickness" model that is treated best by medication and provides limited access to talk therapy (Edwards & Heath, 2007). Walsh (2011) states

[o]ver the decades, family therapists have rebalanced the skewed perspective that long dominated the clinical field. In the many, varied approaches, therapeutic focus has shifted from deficits, limitations, and pathology to a competency-based, health-oriented paradigm, recognizing and amplifying family strengths and resources. (p. 43)

In modern mental health practice and training, there is a resurgence of strengths-based movement in the fields of family therapy, social work, counselor education, and counseling and clinical psychology. These programs typically include course work that introduces strengths-based and positive psychology ideas to their students as required content. Lopez and Louis (2009) provide a rich description of what it means to work from a strengths-based perspective, saying it "assumes that every individual has resources that can be mobilized toward success in many areas of life and is characterized by efforts to 'label what is right' within people and organizations" (p. 2). Thus, this handbook is designed to explore these important concepts.

This book consists of 23 interesting and varied chapters that we hope will add to the conversations about strengths-based work. By showing how these experts in the field use strengths-based ideas in their work, we hope to help the reader develop many ideas about what creates positive change in people. We examine a wide range of populations and settings from a clinical perspective as well as clinical training. Here you will read about how to gather, encourage, and use strengths of the economically disadvantaged, cultural minorities (from race to gender and the LGBTQ community), as well as those struggling with chronic illness, disabilities, and trauma. You will read about using a strengths-based philosophy with divergent modalities in group work, music and guided imagery, in schools and sports, and with those needing help with their substance abuse. Our strengths-based book looks at how the training of the next (and the current) generations of clinicians will be supervised and taught. Additionally, we will look at how strengths-based work is currently being used in leadership and organizational development because we believe that is the foundation of all we do. The old way, informed by a worldview that relies on a "broken-needs-fixing philosophy," is changing. Herein, we hope to give you a better way to work with many.

The Problem with Problems

The push by pharmaceutical companies, the American Medical Association, and managed care companies to marginalize nonpathologizing models has been a bone of contention for many clinicians. Bartlett and Steele's (2005) book, *Critical Condition*, reports these same industries have provided half a billion dollars to political campaigns, thus placing them in a position of influence with our legislators. For example, the latest edition of the *DSM* of the American Psychiatric Association has been rejected by the National Institute of Mental Health (NIMH) for research they call "bad science." However, the managed care industry requires a *DSM* diagnosis for reimbursement of clinical services, thus placing clinicians in a precarious professional and ethical position (Lane, 2013).

How can a clinician accurately diagnose bio-psycho-social-cultural-familial-spiritual issues using the *DSM* criteria? Mental health problems are most often multi-causal (Kiesler, 2000), and even in biological medicine the "concept of multi-factorial disease is fully accepted" (Schoenbach, 2001). Garcia and Petrovich (2011) propose an additional dimension to diagnosis that includes assessment of diversity and cultural strengths. Adding this dimension would provide for more accurate treatment planning tailored to the client's context and experience. The assumption that our varied and diverse culture demonstrates identical symptoms is faulty at best, invalidating at worst. It has even been suggested by some professionals that the recent *DSM-5* missed its chance to diagnose even those who do the diagnosing by not including a new disorder called *pervasive pathologizing disorder* (D. Epstein, personal communication, July 20, 2013).

In many ways, our culture has become a problem-focused malaise based on a medical model that works well with physical conditions, but often fails to accurately address human psychological and relational dilemmas. The medical model fails to take into account individual and multicultural differences in symptom assessment. The medical model ignores the most cost effective form of treatment available— individual strengths and resilience. Like the weather person on the news, we have been taught to believe that there is a 30% chance of rain (problems), rather than a 70% chance of staying dry (avoiding problems; Edwards & Heath, 2007). As anyone who has studied the mental health field knows, a problem can most often be an opportunity for change. Building on previous successes and optimizing resilience does not require medication and multiple costly visits to an overbooked psychiatrist.

Seligman (2005) suggested that an additional problem with the use of the *DSM* lies in the search for empirically validated therapies (EVTs). The quest for a quick solution runs the risk of encouraging clinicians to focus only on techniques that are problem-focused and designed to "fix" individuals that fit into *DSM* categories. As such, our mental health system is locked into problem saturation. Interestingly, the *DSM-4* (American Psychiatric Association, 2000) acknowledges this shortcoming by stating the following:

> In DSM-IV there is no assumption that each category of mental disorder is a completely discrete entity with absolute boundaries dividing it from other mental disorders or from no mental disorder. There is also no assumption that all individuals described as having the same mental disorder are alike in all important ways. (p. *xxxi*)

This disclaimer should give all mental health clinicians reason to pause and question the use of the *DSM* to diagnose and treat clients. Problem-focused interventions and labels often contribute to a client's perception of him- or herself and their experience. Ignoring the client's strengths and resilience creates a portrait of weakness and disease. This imbalanced and detrimental perspective promotes client illness rather than develops client strengths.

EVTs, as used in mental health care, are usually those that have been tested in a strict laboratory setting and differ from efficacy-based treatments, which are often considered to be more useful in real-world situations. In a clinical setting, each interaction is different than the one before. As such, it is not possible (or recommended) to apply the same treatment strategies every time to every client who exhibits the same symptoms. The results will be as varied as the clients themselves. Again, the *DSM* acknowledges this reality by stating that "[t]here is also no assumption that all individuals described as having the same mental disorder are alike in all important ways" (American Psychiatric Association, 2000, p. *xxxi*).

Bound by a system we inherited from physicians—which may carry the potential to cause more harm than good—many counseling professionals feel they are unable to move into more innovative models that their own practice-based evidence suggest are effective (Boisvert & Faust, 2002). Descartes was only partially correct; parts of our bodies may work like machines that break down and need fixing, but our mind (or soul) is another matter entirely. It is not biology in most cases that we are treating, but relational issues and issues of the mind's networks that create meaning.

Our beliefs about mental health are largely a product of ideas that are socially constructed, media driven, or formed by our own experiences. According to Seligman (2002), our perceptions regarding how positive most people are about their lives are severely skewed toward the negative. He found that people who are optimistic (i.e. those who have self-efficacy/personal agency) live better lives with less depressive features. Additionally, Seligman (2002) reported that surveyed Americans believe that the lifetime prevalence of clinical depression is about 49%, whereas it is actually somewhere between 8% and 18%. In a collaborative effort by leading experts in the field of depression (Forgeard et al., 2011), it was concluded that one of the primary issues for consideration in depression is the concept of learned helplessness.

One might guess that those reading this book already know of the work Seligman and Maier (1967) did on learned helplessness, its relationship to depression (Seligman, 1975), and how the concept was twisted around to present how one could then learn optimism (Seligman, 1991). From there, Seligman began to study and write about the connection of learned optimism to happiness (Seligman, 2002) and then evolved to flourishing (Seligman, 2012). All of that is connected to the notion of positive psychology Seligman and Csikszentmihalyi (2000) first rolled out in *Positive Psychology: An Introduction*. The evolving concepts of Seligman and his work have given birth to the strengths-based clinical work for the U.S. Military, when General George Casey, U.S. Army Chief of Staff, enlisted support of Martin Seligman to begin culturally transforming our military from focusing time and funding on pathology, to a focus on resiliency. Under Seligman's direction, the Global Assessment Tool (GAT) was developed that looked for soldiers' well-being. Because it is strength-based, the GAT introduced a common vocabulary for describing what is right with rather than what is wrong with soldiers. It is fascinating that the concept of something so close to our combat weary military as post-traumatic stress disorder can now be also thought of clinically as post-traumatic growth. Strengths-based modalities work to counteract learned helplessness by increasing self-efficacy and optimism. It is our belief that strengths-based work has evolved from the early work of many, and continues to grow and evolve, and it can be understood in common factors of many different ways of helping people. We are hopeful that all clinicians will someday work from a strengths-based model where needed. It is our position that a strengths-based model will develop those self-efficacious, optimistic, resilient, self-reliant, and healing changes in the clients we serve.

Our Strengths-Based Brain

As previously mentioned, there are several reasons why the use of evidence-based practices does not always fit the bill. The current volume of the *DSM*, the *DSM-5*, was met with the deafening sound of one hand clapping.

> For the first time, the National Institute of Mental Health (NIMH), the world's largest **mental health institute,** has shifted its funding support away from the DSM, citing a 'lack of validity'

and diagnoses based on 'clusters of clinical symptoms, not any objective laboratory measure'. (Donaldson James, 2013, n.p.)

The NIMH's focus has shifted from categorization to one of looking at the brain. "NIMH will put more of its research dollars into a new classification system, the Research Domain Criteria (RDoC), to incorporate genetics, imaging and cognitive science that focus more on neurological systems than just a collection of symptoms" (Donaldson James, 2013, n.p.). Strengths-based work is cognitive science with a subtle essence. Our understanding of two important measures of brain research has confirmed for us that working with strengths is a more efficacious way of helping people and groups get more from their experiences in a clinical setting.

Current research on the arousal of the sympathetic and parasympathetic nervous systems shows that focusing on a person's strengths instead of his or her faults contributes to a higher degree of agreement and goal attainment for both the clinician and client (Boyatzis & McKee, 2005). The core of what Boyatzis and colleagues (2013) demonstrated lies with their concept of the positive and negative emotional attractors. They believe that these attractors have the ability to pull individuals, couples, and whole organizations toward them. Positive emotional attraction happens when the parasympathetic nervous system is aroused. During this aroused state of the parasympathetic system, there is a focus on possibilities that include home and strength. This felt emotion works to create movement toward a desired goal. Clients see potential and possibilities of positive change. The opposite occurs when the negative emotional attractor is raised and happens when the sympathetic nervous system is aroused. The focus is then on problems, fear, and perceived weaknesses in a person, couple, team, or organization (Boyatzis et al., 2013). Focusing on negatives when talking with the group or individual potentiates the fight or flight condition and closes down the potential of looking at positives or hope.

We surmise that the same phenomenon occurs during counseling or supervision, when the focus is on what the person or group is doing wrong. Language has the potential of creating reality. In this case, a supervisor or clinician has the ability to close down conversation, hope, and future positive outlooks by moving in too quickly with negative comments or critical language. The potential for positive change can also be induced by beginning to focus on what has gone well during a session. This brain and nervous system science suggests that a culture of negativity and problem focus could create significant road blocks to mental health for clients. Conversely, a positive wellness perspective could potentiate a more successful outcome.

Brain research has proven that changing personal views can be very difficult, although not impossible, due to what psychiatrist and brain researcher Dan Siegel (2007) called a "top-down" way of operating. Siegel (2007) explained that

> [b]ecause the mind itself can be viewed as both embodied and relational, our brains actually can be considered the social organ of the body. Our minds connect with one another via neural circuitry in our bodies that is hard-wired to take in others' signals. (p. 45)

Siegel is referring to more than mirror neurons that connect us in things like mutual smiles between strangers and that occur almost automatically. Our brains are already encoded with preset conditions or values. These values are "loaded" into the narrative part of the brain and are set to reject new or novel input. The processing of stimuli is controlled by top-down influences that shape the dynamics of the thalamocortical networks and constantly create predictions about forthcoming sensory events based on previous experiences of present conditions. Culture, families, and groups all contribute to these presets, shaping our worldview of life. Additionally, they have the potential to provide positive stimuli and perception, as well as jamming any potential change in thinking and behavior. A client who was "taught" to be fearful of a specific type of person or event will have a difficult time changing those narrative presets. Political points of view, radical religious beliefs, or prejudicial opinions, as well as beliefs about ones' self are all preset over time in the grand narrative that resides in the thalamocortical networks and constantly informs us of our "reality" and how we make meaning of life and situations. This means that clinicians must pay attention to the language and manner in which they engage clients even more than previously believed. Strengths-based work relies on language as a means to support clients as they consider their attributes and to do more of what encourages their resiliency and positive change. Strengths-based counseling is based on what RDoC (National Institute of Mental Health, 2011) considers the cognitive part of NIMH's efforts, especially perception and language. It provides a more current way of understanding how to provide counseling/therapy to clients. Quite frankly, what we need more than RDoC or evidence-based therapy is a goodness of fit.

Accessing Strengths in Many Ways

Despite both systemic and personal roadblocks, there has been a resurgence of clinicians who choose to resist the gravitational pull of the status quo and work from a different perspective; one of encouraging strengths, looking for solutions, increasing happiness, and instilling resiliency. This "ordinary magic" of resiliency might last a lifetime and work for families as well as individuals (Masten, 2001; Masten & Curtis, 2000; Walsh, 1996, 1998, 2003a, 2003b, 2003c, 2006). Solution-focused therapy is evidence-based yet far less problem-focused than is most traditional counseling (Franklin, Trepper, McCollum, & Gingerich, 2011). The use of narrative therapy (White, 2007; White & Epston, 1990) either within a family context (Walsh, 1996, 1998, 2003a, 2003b, 2003c, 2006) or with individuals (Masten, 2001; Masten & Curtis, 2000) has solid evidence of positive outcomes without dwelling on negatives or pathological focus.

An article by Elsie Jones-Smith (2006) that appeared in a special issue of *The Counseling Psychologist* suggested that specific professions or movements contributed to the momentum of strengths-based ideas. Dennis Saleebey (2012), who authored *Strengths Perspective in Social Work Practice*, contributes to the discussion by stating that

> [p]racticing from a strengths perspective requires that we shift the way that we think about, approach, and relate to our clients. Rather than focusing exclusively or dominantly on problems, your eye turns toward possibility. In the thicket of trauma, pain, and trouble you see blooms of hope and transformation. (p. 1)

Strengths-based work is also present in the business world. Buckingham and Clifton (2001) wrote, "Casting a critical eye on our weaknesses . . . will only help us prevent failure. It will not help us reach excellence" (p. 3). The authors cite several statistics that paint a picture of prosperous organizations built by flourishing individuals. Building upon strengths exponentially increases employee engagement, job satisfaction, and corporate morale. When individuals perform using their strengths, they are 73% more likely to meet and exceed corporate objectives (Rath & Conchie, 2008).

A discussion about a strengths-based paradigm must include the work of Martin Seligman, the founder of positive psychology, whom we briefly discussed earlier, and his colleagues (Maddux, 2005; Mahoney, 2005; Peterson, 2006; Peterson & Seligman, 2004; Perloiro, Neto, & Marujo, 2010; Seligman & Csikszentmihalyi, 2000). According to its proponents, positive psychology is about living life fully with a good deal of happiness and how to flourish in many ways. When it is engaged in human living, positive psychology can move mountains of depression, anxiety, alienation, and despair. Knowing that happiness is a subjective phenomenon that has been discussed in many contexts, positive psychology scientifically investigates the components of happiness (Seligman, Parks, & Steen, 2004). These components are discussed more fully in other chapters of this book.

Since its inception, positive psychology has received both criticism and validation. Critics of positive psychology question the science behind the theory, suggesting that the study of psychology should only discuss the inherently problematic aspects of trauma, depression, and other perceived "negative" psychological experiences. We discuss some of these critics in the following text. Proponents of positive psychology research and tout the theories that emphasize identifying individual strengths and contributors to resiliency. Seligman's positive psychology names three elements that make up authentic happiness. The first is positive emotion or feelings such as comfort, pleasure, ecstasy, and warmth. The second element of positive psychology is engagement, which refers to a state of flow. Flow occurs when one is so connected to an activity that consciousness is completely absorbed by that activity. Sometimes we refer to this state as "being in the zone." The last element is meaning. When we live a meaningful life, we are connected to a sense of purpose greater than oneself. Seligman (2011) stated ". . . the gold standard for measuring well-being is flourishing, and that the goal of Positive Psychology is to increase flourishing" (p. 13).

Employing these elements of positive psychology during strengths-based work drastically reframes the lens through which we view clients, systems, and ourselves. Rather than diagnosing what is wrong with the client, system, or self we are highlighting what works well and move toward that. Rather than assuming the presenting symptoms are alike for every individual regardless of cultural and social differences, we are looking for and amplifying signature strengths and resiliency.

Strengths-based ideas also began to surface in the work of systems therapy models that began with the first- and second-order cybernetics of Margret Mead and her husband Gregory Bateson (Von Foerster, 1946) and culminated with the postmodern and social constructivist era. Atkinson and Heath (1990) wrote the following:

> From the perspective of second-order cybernetics, the living world is viewed as organized in recursive layers of autonomous systems that are related through feedback structures, and are self-generating by nature. If left alone, these systems will balance and heal themselves. The appearance of a symptom may be viewed as an indication that a system is adjusting itself, likely due to a disturbance created by an escalation of one of its variables. (pp. 145–146)

One can begin to understand the power of shifting perspective from believing people have a personal internal pathological problem, to one that is existing within the system, or family. Symptoms are then seen as the system's attempt to self-correct. It is only a short leap to move from this Batesonian thinking, where the feedback system is seen as language carrying messages about our worldview that regulates behavior and perception. Perception thus becomes our reality (Atkinson & Heath, 1990). The notion of a medical issue "within" the individual began to shift to one that considers that possibility of a problem-saturated feedback loop of language and internalized worldview.

Edwards (2013) collapsed strengths-based ideas and practices into two strains: those that include postmodern influences such as collaborative languaging systems (Anderson & Goolishian, 1988), evidence-based solution-focused therapy (de Shazer, 1994, 1988), narrative therapy (White, 2007; White & Epston, 1990; Freedman & Combs, 1996), and reflecting teams (Andersen, 1987, 1991a, 1991b, 1992a, 1992b, 2001; Stinchfield, Hill, & Kleist, 2007), and those whose roots are from psychology, such as positive psychology/positive therapy (Seligman, 1991, 1996, 2002; Seligman & Csikszentmihalyi, 2000), and from the work on resiliency (Masten, 2001; Masten & Curtis, 2000; Walsh, 1996, 1998, 2006). All forms of strengths-based work have a focus on a collaboration between the clinician and the client regarding what will make life better. A strengths-based perspective instills the belief that with action clients will increase their own effectiveness and thriving. We believe this more collaborative, less hierarchical method to be a far superior way to conduct counseling with most individuals, groups, or organizations.

Critics of Strengths-Based and Positive Psychology Movement

There are many critics of strengths-based work, and even more of the positive psychology move-ment. Most call for more empirical evidence (Ehrenreich, 2009; Held, 2004), criticizing the posi-tive psychology movement as "monolithic" and "unrealistic." Yet others fear the implementation of strengths-based perspectives minimizes reality and may feed delusional perspectives (Aspinwall & Staudinger, 2003). Critics of postmodern models accuse the movement of presenting a relativistic view of life. Fundamentalist groups have attacked those who espoused postmodernism chips away at the truths they hold as dear. Postmodern models are challenged as having an anti-enlightenment bent. Reason and empiricism that are important to the Enlightenment are pushed aside by post-modern thought, and the belief that people are like machines with parts that can be fixed, replaced, or remediated is challenged (Sokal & Bricmont, 1999). We will revisit this again later in this chapter in more depth.

Strengths-based work does not fit everyone. We are far too diverse a society to make that assump-tion. However, we posit there are many strengths inherent in our society that are minimized or ignored. We simply ask you to consider spending some time focusing on what goes right; seeing what happens when you explore the possibility. The following clients and their clinicians did just that.

Anecdotal Experiences

To illustrate the efficacy of strengths-based work, several chapters in this book include real-world examples from the authors' experiences. As editors, we offer here three scenarios about our own experience and perceptions of strengths-based clinical work.

> **Andy**: When working from a strengths-based perspective, one of the challenges we often meet is that many people have a very difficult time acknowledging that they have any strengths of their own. This self-doubt is typically heightened upon entering the counseling experience. After all, not only our clinical frameworks, but even our broader cultural narratives tend to equate the initiation of therapy with decreased functioning and organic personal deficits. Simply walking in the therapist's door, therefore, may actually serve to solidify one's self-perception as lacking in strength.

In helping my clients to resolve this resistance to acknowledging their own strengths, I find myself drawing from several clinical models as resources. As we have suggested, strengths-based counseling is more of a way of being than a discrete model unto itself. For example, I might utilize techniques from motivational interviewing, solution-focused therapy, narrative therapy, or even strategic family therapy. Regardless of the clinical source, however, the overarching goal is to help the person begin to notice his or her own intrinsic strengths that have been there all along.

A recent example of this occurred with a client whom I will call Diane. Diane had been seeing me for therapy after a contentious divorce that left her not only with self-doubt and condemna-tion, but also struggling with the judgment of other family members as well. After several months of avoiding a particular family member, she found herself in a conversation with this person discussing the rift between them. In describing this conversation to me Diane stated, "I needed their validation, and I got it." When I asked her what it meant for her to get that validation, she said that it gave her more inner peace. This led to a discussion of how the theme of the last week seemed to have been one of "moving on."

Diane's language and position seemed to suggest to me that all the positive progress that had occurred in the last week happened to her rather than by her. In this way, she presented herself as grateful yet helpless rather than as having personal agency. I asked her a question that was agentic in nature, meaning that it carried within it an embedded implication that Diane had intrinsic personal agency that affected the positive outcome she experienced. "What is it in you," I asked, "that gave you the strength to speak with this person and take hold of that inner peace?" I don't remember her exact response, but it was dismissive in nature, attributing the positive outcome to factors outside her control. Sometimes a simple agentic question like this is enough for someone to recognize their own inherent asset. However, as in this case, oftentimes the bait is left untaken.

At this point, I could have pressed the issue and challenged her view. It was, after all, she who initiated the conversation with her estranged family member. However, my guess is that simply countering her response with something more positive wouldn't have gotten very far. Rather, I chose not to challenge her position—that she was more a passive recipient than a source of the positive outcome—and to wonder aloud what it might be like if she were to internalize this theme of "moving on" into her own character. She immediately responded with a vivid, rich description of that future and how it would positively influence her children, her career, her relations with extended family, and even her future dating relationships. She offered this description with an ease and confidence in her voice that suggested she really believed what she was saying. My honest belief is that the strength she was now tapping into had been there all along. My hope was to help her uncover that strength and to help her notice that whenever she wants to she can draw from that strength. Whether she agrees with me that it was there all along, or sees it as a newly acquired trait, was of less concern to me, as long as she felt it was truly hers now.

Jeff: I like supervising students who already have clinical experience, and who need additional training and supervision to become licensed. Mona was one of those students, a seasoned music therapist who previously had been accepted in a local Psy.D. program, and who wisely left when she was told during her first week that what she already knew was not "real" clinical skills. A professor told her they would teach her to be a "real" clinician. How arrogant a statement this is to someone who already knew a great deal clinically! When Mona began to work with me, I worked with the skills she already had, and added to them, scaffolding new ideas and skills with her already capable and familiar ones. Together we set goals, and she was ready to add them to her repertoire. Talk therapy could be an adjunct to what she already knew. As I complimented her on her growth, she glowed, and I thoroughly enjoyed working with her. On our last day of working together in supervision, I asked her to evaluate our time together. She said: "The supervision with you has been fabulous. I have brought in all kinds of stuff, and some ethical stuff. And it's been really helpful that you could see me as a music therapist . . . and you've validated me in what I know already." What could be a better way to end this part of our relationship?

Stef: Fifteen-year-old Julia had recently confessed to her parents that she had a plan and means to commit suicide. They immediately admitted her to a local behavioral health hospital where she was treated for several weeks. Upon discharge, they sought family counseling to help them through Julia's continuing recovery. Mom and Dad were convinced they had failed Julia somehow; shell-shocked by what could have happened. Julia seemed to carry the weight of the family's tension; she was quiet and tearful during the intake. Mom and Dad displayed a superficial lightness intended to cover up their distress balanced with an authentic desire to gain skills to help Julia. The family emanated emotional wear, fear, and exhaustion. These were constant themes that surfaced throughout their intake. Once I had gathered the necessary intake information, I asked, "What stopped Julia from completing her plan?" The question caused them all to pause.

From my perspective, Julia displayed strength and courage from the moment she confessed her plan to her parents. Her parents displayed the same strength and courage when they took her to the behavioral hospital, admitting they did not know what to do and needed expert help in this situation. Last, their family was demonstrating great strength by choosing to come see me, willingly share their pain, hurt, and confusion, while looking for ways to move forward stronger, healthier. It was clear to me that they had not connected to their already existing resiliency and strengths in the situation. I was hopeful about their future simply because they were here ready to work.

After a lengthy silence, I posed the question directly to Julia, "Julia, why did you talk to your parents about your plans?" Slowly, she raised her eyes to meet mine and tearfully said, "I knew it would really hurt them if I left." I let the answer linger in the room for several seconds. Both Mom and Dad were openly shedding tears. "Looking back at it now, did you want to 'leave'?" Julia replied, "No, but I did not know what else to do."

Gently, I met her tearful eyes and said,

> I don't know if you have realized this yet, but I see a really strong and brave young lady here. It sounds like you were really, really sad and hopeless. You felt very alone and maybe even helpless. And while it was scary for you to tell your parents about your plans, you dug deep and found the courage to do so. That took great strength and courage.

I could tell instantly that Julia had not seen herself in this light. Her parents remained silent, allowing my words to sink in. "You are brave and strong, supported by brave and strong parents . . ." I continued to reflect to the family my insights on their unseen strengths. They seemed to tentatively ponder my words. I then began to outline a tentative plan on how we could move forward leaning into those strengths to enhance their family culture.

Six months into our work Dad and Julia came into session. There was a newfound hope in their relationship, one I had begun to take for granted until they shared the following story with me. Dad and Julia were invited to be panelists at a high school suicide prevention presentation. Both shared candidly their experiences and what they have since learned. One of the strengths-based practices they employed regularly was identifying what they liked in a situation as opposed to an extensive autopsy of what went wrong. Dad asked Julia, "What did you like about it?"

Julia replied,

> Dad, it was cool. I liked it, ok? It was a lot of fun because I saw how much I have grown. You don't need to do the strengths thing with me tonight. I know there is LOTS more good about me and my life than bad and when I focus on what's bad I got suicidal. I can talk to you, Mom, or Stef about stuff, I have all that support stuff goin' on. I am good—awesome, actually. So—can I get my nails done on Saturday? [Her "fee" for being a panelist.]

We continued to meet for a few more months and eventually terminated. They have kept me "on-call" when needed. And they have needed to come back in though not as frequently and for not as long. Strengths-based practice is not a magical cure-all technique or treatment. Neither is it a pithy reframe that minimizes hurt or trauma. We covered much in the time we were together. Sometimes I met with Mom and Dad, sometimes with just Julia, but most times with the entire family. At the core of our work we looked for ways to connect to individual and family resilience, strengths, and acceptance through life's challenges and triumphs.

These scenarios serve as an illustration of both the similarities and uniqueness of working within a strengths-based framework. We each practice our strengths-based orientation differently. This reflects the possibility that a strengths-based overlay may be successfully integrated with other theoretical frameworks that already exist within a clinician's repertoire. In this way, strengths-based counseling becomes trans-theoretical if not even a nonmodel.

From Models to Ways of Being

Similar to this movement away from thinking of strengths-based work as a standalone model, we also found ourselves focusing less on techniques and more on ways of being. Part of this notion grew out of the acknowledgment that when we thought of our own mentors who seem to most embody a strengths orientation, we noticed in those people not simply a skill set but an all-encompassing approach to life—an attitude that seemed to pervade their personalities both on and off the clinical stage. With this in mind, we have come to believe that as clinicians and supervisors a strengths-based orientation is much like a personal philosophy. It is not simply how we conceptualize our clinical cases, it is how we live our lives. It is personal in that it is about our commitment to nurturing our own strengths and assets. Looking for and encouraging our own strengths—like maintaining a zest for life, being good parents, enjoying the arts, savoring the beauty of nature and the world around us, staying current with new ideas, working on being a good human being, and forgiving our mistakes and those of others—helps us to be the best we can be, both personally and professionally.

Differentiating between strengths-based techniques and strengths-based ways of being may seem more like an exercise in semantics than anything else. After all, we have learned from experience that once you attempt to train other clinicians in ways of being you inevitably end up, at some point, talking about techniques. Although the semantic criticism may carry a grain of validity, it also may be that, inasmuch as language holds within it the power to construct meaning, such a nuanced and subtle difference in perspective may greatly shift the trajectory of one's clinical effectiveness. It may mean, for example, the difference between attempting to use over-rehearsed Rogerian statements of empathy to actually positioning oneself and one's feedback in the subjective experience of being with the client. This sort of subtle shift may allow the client to see the clinician less as just another professional helper and more as a unique human with gifts of healing to offer. In keeping with iso-morphic theory, this shift in perspective may, in turn, allow the client to see themselves as the unique human they are and to notice more therapeutically their own unique gifts of personal healing.

There are several strengths-based ways of being that we found useful in our own clinical and supervisory work. Being benevolently curious, for example, is a term that finds its roots in the reflect-ing team work of Tom Andersen (1991b). It suggests a position quite different from the expert stance we often espouse as clinicians, particularly (if not ironically) in our early years as professionals. As we become more benevolently curious we may find ourselves asking less direct questions of our clients in favor of simply wondering aloud in front of them. This verbal musing often includes embedded messages that seek to call the attention of both speaker and listener to the inherent strengths of each. For example, a counselor might say to a client, "I find myself wondering how it is that you managed to come in here today, despite the depression that seemed to want to stop you."

Similar to this idea of being benevolently curious, as strengths-based clinicians we also strive to be speculative rather than definitive. Solution-focused therapists often refer to this as the not-knowing position (Walter & Peller, 1992). This is a position of recognizing that simply being the one in the room with more letters behind one's name does not necessarily confer upon the counselor or supervisor the role of expert. In fact, strengths-based practitioners understand that the wealth of self-expertise brought into the clinical experience by the person they are helping may be just as important, if not more so, to the change process. At the very least, we strive to bring forth meaning and perception, and to avoid over-evaluative instruction or correction.

A third way of being that we notice in our strengths-based colleagues and ourselves is that of being self-reflective. As a clinician relinquishes the role of expert, and all the trappings that come with it, this frees him/her up to take on a very different role in the therapeutic relationship. We see variants of this in several different counseling modalities. In motivational interviewing, for example, the counselor appeals to the client's expertise in their own life and plays the part of an interviewer, matching the client's ambivalence. In the Rogerian approach we see perhaps one of the earliest examples of this transformation, as the counselor shifts from expert to empathic listener. Modern strengths-based practitioners may amplify this stance even further, positioning their feedback in the subjective experience of listening to and being with the client. This often includes becoming more self-disclosing or vulnerable where it is therapeutically valuable. An example of this might be a counselor saying, "As I sat listening to you just now, I felt both sad and grateful. It's hard to know how to reconcile that sort of emotional dichotomy but I knew as it happened in me that both those feelings were genuine." Consider the empowering difference between this emotional immediacy as compared to a more traditional statement of empathy like, "I can tell that you feel sad, and sometimes sadness is overwhelming. I do feel that once you get through this you will begin to see gratitude on the other side." Too often when we use statements such as the latter, we leave our own subjective experience out of the equation as though we were not in the room breathing the same oxygen as our client. In doing this, we continue a lopsided power structure in the clinical relationship—one that is evaluative at best and demeaning at worst—and inadvertently diminish the therapeutic impact of an otherwise valuable observation.

In the same way that musical notes on a page cannot do justice to the sounds of a room filled with the emotive reverberations of strings and brass and human voice, a set of techniques cannot capture those elusive qualities that certain clinicians bring to the counseling relationship through their own humanity. Yet, just as musical notation is necessary for the transfer of knowledge, so is the eventual codification of clinical techniques. Inevitably, in the chapters that follow we will explore and hear about specific techniques that help to elicit and amplify the strengths of our clients in the service of healing. Nevertheless, our hope with this volume is ultimately to reflect on those ways of being that go deeper than technique which we see, not only in those very pioneers of strength-based technique, but in our own mentors, our peers, and our very selves as well.

Now It Is Personal

It is evident that there are a number of clinicians who espouse the language of strengths-based work, yet continue to practice from a staunchly pathology-based approach. To truly promote, practice, and carry forward a strengths-based model often entails not simply a shift in language, but a radical upheaval in one's orientation. This includes a rejection of the traditional hierarchical stance toward one's clients and supervisees in favor of a more humanizing equanimity. In turn, this inherently brings about an increased respect for the dignity of the individual, even when the circumstances that initiate the clinical experience would seem to diminish that dignity. In the case of clinical supervision, the terminology itself (super-vision, I see better than you) falsely implies an innately hierarchical knowledge structure. Strengths-based work, therefore, also requires a commitment to the belief that even when a client's global functioning appears significantly decreased or when the supervisory structure of an organization suggests a top-down knowledge base, organic strengths exist within the person that may be unearthed and used toward sustained, positive change. It also requires an understanding that these strengths often occur in multifaceted contexts, including those related to family, culture, gender, personal historical events, and the negotiation of social narratives. It requires collaborating with our clients and supervisees as equals on a journey together.

Of course, as we noted earlier there are critics of strengths-based work. The postmodernism and social constructionism used in some of the "models" hijacked by those who use strengths-based ideas have been accused of presenting a relativistic view of life. Some fundamentalist groups believe that postmodernism chips away at the Truths (with a capital *T*) they hold dear. It has also been called *anti-enlightenment* because ideas such as reason, empiricism, and the belief that people are constructed like machines with parts that can be fixed or replaced is upsetting to some critics (Sokal & Bricmont, 1999).

Others critical of strengths-based work have mentioned that there are problems in the world that do need fixing, such as our recent financial crisis, or Bill Gates' work at multiple problems in Africa, and Al Gore's warnings on climate change. However, it is our position that there is a difference between the problems in the physical world (natural science) and that of a human's internal world (our minds). There are so many variables of what constitutes "mind" (see Bateson [1979] or Siegel [2007]). Because we are bio-social-psychological-spiritual-family-of-origin and cultural creatures—locally, nationally, and politically—our worldviews are unique. With such natural diversity among people who come to see us in a clinical setting, who has the right to make determinations of what is correct and what is not, and thus, deviant, pathological, or weak? By what collective authority have those who make these consensus opinions been awarded? The road to health most often has to be paved in an individual's worldview.

One must wonder why the literature about strengths-based models is growing so quickly or why professionals are using strengths-based counseling, supervision, and instruction more these days rather than the traditional method. We believe this shift of action and thinking is because the profession is ready for a change that empowers rather than points to deficits. Strengths-based approaches work without placing ideas of problems within the minds and heads of those with whom we serve. Anderson et al. (2008) at The Taos Institute stated the following:

> The meanings we assign to the world are not our private inventions. They do not originate in minds cut away from others. They are created within our history of relationships—from our early childhoods to our most recent conversations. . . . In transformative dialog, participants in a conversation are not the same at the conclusion of the conversation as they were when they began. (p. 14)

Your work with clients requires you to be strengths-based, so that dialogue is opened up, not closed down. It has been said that many people talk about using strengths-based work, but few really know how or when to use it (F. Walsh, personal communication, June 16, 2013). This may be accurate. After you have read all the chapters in this book, we encourage you to make up your own mind about this topic. We hope you will find the last chapter of the text to be useful, wherein we have synthesized what the common denominators and the differences are with a qualitative evaluation of the chapters.

Enjoy.

Note

1. Authors' names are given in a random order as there has been no hierarchy of contribution here.

References

American Psychiatric Association. (2000). *Diagnostic and statistical manual of mental disorders* (4th ed.). Washington, DC: Author.

American Psychiatric Association. (2013). *Diagnostic and statistical manual of mental disorders* (5th ed.). Washington, DC: Author.

Andersen, T. (1987). The reflecting team: Dialogue and meta-dialogue in clinical work. *Family Process, 26,* 415–428.

Andersen, T. (1991a). Reflections on reflecting with families. In S. McNamee, & K.J. Gergen (Eds.), *Therapy as social construction*. London, UK: Sage.

Andersen, T. (1991b). *The reflecting team: Dialogues and dialogues about the dialogues*. New York, NY: W.W. Norton.

Andersen, T. (1992a). Relationship, language and pre-understanding in the reflecting process. *The Australian and New Zealand Journal of Family Therapy, 13,* 87–91.

Andersen, T. (1992b). Reflections on reflecting with families. In Sheila McNamee & Kenneth Gergen (Eds.), *Therapy as social construction*. Thousand Oaks, CA: Sage.

Andersen, T. (2001). Ethics before ontology: A few words. *Journal of Systemic Therapies, 20*, 11–13.

Anderson, H., & Goolishian, H. (1988). Human systems as linguistic systems: Preliminary and evolving ideas about the implications for clinical theory. *Family Process, 27*, 371–393.

Anderson, H., Cooperrider, D., Gergen, K., Gergen, M., McNamee, S., Watkins, J.M., & Whitney, D. (2008). *The appreciative organization*. Taos, NM: The Taos Institute Publications.

Aspinwall, L.G. & Staudinger, U.M. (2003). *A psychology of human strengths: Fundamental questions and future directions for a positive psychology*. Washington, DC: American Psychological Association.

Atkinson, B.J., & Heath, A.W. (1990). Further thoughts on second-order family therapy—this time it's personal. *Family Process, 29*, 145–155.

Bartlett, D.L. & Steele, J.B. (2005). *Critical condition: How health care in America became big business—and bad medicine*. New York, NY: Broadway Books.

Bateson, G. (1979). *Mind and nature: A necessary unity (Advances in systems theory, complexity, and the human sciences)*. New York, NY: Hampton Press.

Berg, I.K. (1994). *Family-based services: A solution-focused approach*. New York: NY: W.W. Norton.

Berg, I.K. (1997). *Interviewing for solutions* (2nd ed.). Pacific Grove, CA: Brooks/Cole.

Berg, I.K. & de Shazer, S. (1993). Making numbers talk: Language in therapy. In Steven Friedman (Ed.), *The new language of change: Constructive collaboration in psychotherapy* (pp. 5–24). New York, NY: Guilford Press.

Boisvert, C., & Faust, D. (2002). Iatrogenic symptoms in psychotherapy: A theoretical exploration of the potential impact of labels, language, and belief systems. *American Journal of Psychotherapy, 56*, 244–259.

Boyatzis, R.E., & McKee, A. (2005). *Resonant leadership: Renewing yourself and connecting with others through mindfulness, hope, and compassion*. Boston, MA: Harvard Business Review Press.

Boyatzis, R.E., Smith, M.L., Van Oosten, E., & Woolford, L. (2013). Developing resonant leaders through emotional intelligence, vision and coaching. *Organizational Dynamics, 42*, 17–24.

Buckingham, M., & Clifton, D.O. (2011). *Now, discover your strengths hardcover*. New York, NY: Free Press.

de Shazer, S. (1988). *Clues: Investigating solutions in brief therapy*. New York, NY: W.W. Norton.

de Shazer, S. (1994). *Words were originally magic*. New York, NY: W.W. Norton.

de Shazer, S. (2005). *More than miracles: The state of the art of solution-focused therapy*. Binghamton, NY: Haworth Press.

Donaldson James, S. (2013). *Brain science upstages DSM-V, so-called mental health 'Bible'* [Television broadcast]. Retrieved from http://gma.yahoo.com/brain-science-upstages-dsm-v-called-mental-health-014118816-abc-news-health.html

Edwards, J.K. (2013). *Strengths-based supervision in clinical practice*. Thousand Oaks, CA: Sage.

Edwards, J.K., & Heath, A.W. (2007). *A consumer's guide to mental health services: Unveiling the mysteries and secrets of psychotherapy*. Binghamton, NY: Haworth Press.

Ehrenreich, B. (2010). *Bright sided: How positive thinking is undermining America*. New York, NY: Metropolitan.

Forgeard, M.J.C., Haigh, E.A.P., Beck, A.T., Davidson, R.J., Henn, F.A., Maier, S.F., Mayberg, H.S., Seligman, M.E. (2011). *Beyond depression: Toward a process-based approach to research, diagnosis, and treatment*. Hoboken, NJ: Wiley.

Franklin, C., Trepper, T.S., McCollum, E.E., & Gingerich, W.J. (2011). *Solution-focused brief therapy: A handbook of evidence-based practice*. New York, NY: Oxford University Press.

Freedman, J., & Combs, G. (1996). *Narrative therapy: The social construction of preferred realities*. New York, NY: W.W. Norton.

Garcia, B., & Petrovich, A. (2011). *Strengthening the DSM: Incorporating resilience and cultural competence*. New York, NY: Springer.

Held, B. (2004). The negative side of positive psychology. *Journal of Humanistic Psychology, 44*, 9–46.

Jones-Smith, E. (2006). The strength-based counseling model. *The Counseling Psychologist, 34*, 13–79.

Kiesler, D.J. (2000). *Beyond the disease model of mental disorders*. Westport, CT: Praeger Publishers.

Lane, C. (2013, May 4). *The NIMH withdraws support for DSM-5*. Retrieved May 24, 2016 from https://www.psychologytoday.com/blog/side-effects/201305/the-nimh-withdraws-support-dsm-5

Lopez, S.J., & Louis, M.C. (2009). *The principles of strengths-based education*. New York, NY: Taylor & Francis.

Maddux, J.E. (2005). Stopping the "madness": Positive psychology and the deconstruction of the illness ideology and the *DSM*. In C.R. Snyder & S.J. Lopez (Eds.), *Handbook of positive psychology* (pp. 61–70). Oxford, UK: Oxford University Press.

Mahoney, M.J. (2005). Constructivism and positive psychology. In C.R. Snyder and S.J. Lopez (Eds.), *Handbook of positive psychology* (pp. 745–750). Oxford, UK: Oxford University Press.

Maslow, A. (1971). *The farther reaches of human nature.* New York, NY: The Viking Press.

Masten, A.S. (2001). Ordinary magic: Resilience processes in development. *American Psychologist, 56,* 227–238.

Masten, A.S. & Curtis, W.J. (2000). Integrating competence and psychopathology: Pathways toward a comprehensive science of adaptation in development. *Development and Psychopathology, 12,* 529–550.

National Institute of Mental Health. (2011). *Proceedings of the RDoC Workshops.* Retrieved May 24, 2016 from http://www.nimh.nih.gov/research-priorities/rdoc/index.shtml

Perloiro, M.F., Neto, L.M., & Marujo, H.A. (2010). We will be laughing again: Restoring relationships with positive couples' therapy. In G.W. Burns (Ed.), *Happiness, healing, enhancement: Your casebook collection for applying positive psychology in therapy* (pp. 15–28). Hoboken, NJ: John Wiley & Sons.

Peterson, C. (2006). *A primer in positive psychology.* New York, NY: Oxford University Press.

Peterson, C. & Seligman, M. (2004). *Character strengths and virtues: A handbook and classification.* New York, NY: Oxford University Press.

Rapp, C.A., & Goscha, R.J. (2011). *The strengths model: A recovery-oriented approach to mental health services* (3rd ed.). New York, NY: Oxford University Press.

Rath, T., & Conchie, B. (2008). *Strengths-based leadership. Great leaders, teams and why people follow.* New York, NY: Gallop Press.

Reynolds, B.C. (1932). An experiment in short-contact interviewing. New York, NY: Taylor & Francis.

Rogers, C.R. (1961). *On becoming a person: A therapist's view of psychotherapy.* London, UK: Constable.

Saleebey, D. (Ed.). (2009). *The strengths perspective in social work practice* (5th ed.). New York, NY: Pearson.

Saleebey, D. (2012). *The strengths perspective in social work practice.* London, UK: Longman Pub Group.

Schoenbach, V.J. (2001). Multicausality: Effect modification. Retrieved May 24, 2016 from http://www.epidemiolog.net/evolving/Multicausality-EffectModification.pdf

Seligman, M.E.P. (1975). *Helplessness: On depression, development, and death.* San Francisco, CA: W.H. Freeman.

Seligman, M.E.P. (1991). *Learned optimism: How to change your mind and your life.* New York, NY: Albert Knopf.

Seligman, M.E.P. (1996). *The optimistic child: Proven program to safeguard children from depression & build lifelong resilience.* New York, NY: Houghton Mifflin.

Seligman, M.E.P. (2002). *Authentic happiness: Using the new positive psychology to realize your potential for lasting fulfillment.* New York, NY: Free Press.

Seligman, M.E.P. (2011). *Flourish: A visionary new understanding of happiness and well-being.* New York, NY: Free Press.

Seligman, M.E.P. (2012). *Beyond depression: Toward a process-based approach to research, diagnosis, and treatment.* Hoboken, NJ: Wiley.

Seligman, M.E.P., & Csikszentmihalyi, M. (2000). Positive psychology: An introduction. *American Psychologist, 55,* 5–14.

Seligman, M.E.P., & Maier, S.F. (1967). "Failure to escape traumatic shock." *Journal of Experimental Psychology, 74,* 1–9.

Seligman, M.E.P., Parks, A.C., & Steen, T. (2004). A balanced psychology and a full life. Philosophical Transactions of the Royal Society B: Biological Sciences, *359,* 1379–1381.

Siegel, D.J. (2007). *The mindful brain: Reflections and attunement in the cultivation of well-being.* New York, NY: W.W. Norton.

Smith, E.J. (2006). The strength-based counseling model. *The Counseling Psychologist, 34,* 13–79.

Sokal, A. & Bricmont, J. (1999). *Fashionable nonsense: Postmodern intellectuals' abuse of science.* Bloomsbury, UK: Picador.

Stinchfield, T.A., Hill, N.R., & Kleist, D.M. (2007). The reflective model of triadic supervision: Defining an emerging modality. *Counselor Education & Supervision, 46,* 172–183.

Von Foerster, H. (1946). *Cybernetics–Kybernetic 1: The Macy Conferences, 1946–1953.* Retrieved May 24, 2016 from http://www.asc-cybernetics.org/foundations/history2.htm

Walsh, F. (1996). Family resiliency: A concept and its application. *Family Process, 35,* 261–282.

Walsh, F. (1998). *Strengthening family resilience.* New York, NY: Guilford Press.

Walsh, F. (Ed.). (2003a). *Normal family process: Growing diversity and complexity.* New York, NY: Guilford Press.

Walsh, F. (2003b). Clinical views of family normality, health, and dysfunction: From deficit to strengths perspective. In F. Walsh (Ed.), *Normal family process: Growing diversity and complexity*. New York, NY: Guilford Press.

Walsh, F. (2003c). Family resilience: A framework for clinical practice. *Family Process, 42*, 1–18.

Walsh, F. (2006). *Strengthening family resiliency* (2nd ed.). New York, NY: Guilford Press.

Walsh F. (2011). Family therapy: Systemic approaches to practice. In J. Brandell (Ed.), *Theory and practice of clinical social work* (pp. 153–178). Thousand Oaks, CA: Sage.

Walter, J.L., & Peller, J.E. (1992). *Becoming solution-focused in brief therapy.* New York, NY: Brunner/Mazel.

Wharton, E. (1903). Vesalius In Zante. *The North American Review, 175,* 631. Retrieved May 24, 2016 from http://www.jstor.org/stable/25119328?seq=7#page_scan_tab_contents

White, M. (2007). *Maps of narrative practice.* New York, NY: W.W. Norton.

White, M., & Epston, D. (1990). *Narrative means to therapeutic ends.* New York, NY: W.W. Norton.

2

Strengths-Based Approaches
An Interdisciplinary Historical Account

Brian L. Kelly and Trevor G. Gates

In essence, the effort is to move away from defining professional work as the articulation of the power of expert knowledge toward collaboration with the power within the
individual or community toward a life that is palpably better—and better on the clients'
own terms.

(Saleebey, 2012, p. 15)

Strengths-based approaches have a long, rich, and varied history in social work, psychology, couple/
marriage and family therapy, and professional counseling. As early as the 1880s, American settlement
house movement pioneers Jane Addams and Ellen Gates Starr were conceptualizing and developing strengths-based services at Chicago's Hull House. This holistic approach was often critiqued
throughout the 20th century. Despite these critiques, proponents of strengths-based approaches continued their work throughout the 20th century and developed a rich theoretical, empirical, and
practice base. This base has included the works of social work theorist Bertha Capen Reynolds;
social group work advocate Grace Coyle; psychologist and developer of the humanistic approach
Carl Rogers; and the seminal work of Abraham Maslow's hierarchy of needs. Today, the work of
these practitioners and scholars manifests in Dennis Saleebey's strengths perspective, Charles Rapp
and Richard Goscha's strengths model for recovery, Steve de Shazer and Insoo Kim Berg's solution-
focused therapy, and others. This chapter explores the development of strengths-based approaches
in social work, psychology, couple/marriage and family therapy, and professional counseling, with
a particular attention to the historical contexts, tensions, and triumphs in its ultimately successful
establishment as a premier approach to working with and engaging others.

Pioneers of Strengths-Based Approaches

As early as the 1880s, settlement house workers on both sides of the Atlantic were conceptualizing
and developing strengths-based services for the communities they lived in and served. Settlement
houses, or settlements, as they are often referred to in historical literature (Skocpol, 1992; Woods &
Kennedy, 1922), were developed as a response to the charity organization movement, more formally
and historically known as the Charity Organization Society (COS). While settlements tended to
work from a strengths orientation, the COS worked from a "blaming the victim" model claiming,

"the apparatus of charity caused the 'pauperisation' of the poor" (Payne, 2005a, p. 35). COS organizers were concerned that too much charity would create social welfare dependence, an ideal with roots in the English Poor Law, which dates back to the middle ages and posits the notion that help for the poor should not inhibit their ability to work and help themselves.

While the COS was concerned with regulation of charity, and some would argue, of poor and working class families themselves (Axinn & Stern, 2005; Payne, 2005a), settlements and settlement house workers were concerned with promoting education for the poor and working classes, as well as sustaining Christian morals and values in developing European and American cities. Axinn and Stern (2005) provide a clear and succinct distinction between the two models of social welfare practice and what their workers and proponents stood for noting, "Whereas Charity Organization Societies assumed a well-functioning society with malfunctioning families as the starting point . . . [settlement houses targeted] the adequate functioning of the families" (p. 112).

Toynbee Hall, the first settlement, was established in 1884 in Whitechapel, London, England, by Canon Samuel Barnett (Woods & Kennedy, 1922). Inspired by the local missionary-like work of his acquaintance Arnold Toynbee, Barnett's idea was to have male university students live in poor and working class areas and utilize their educational and moral upbringing to engage community members in personal development. Early community engagement activities included the development of drama, literary, and youth recreation clubs as well as visual art exhibitions and rural holidays for young people (Payne, 2005a). Unlike the prescribed practitioner–client, top–down perspective of the COS, the settlement house movement promoted a symbiotic, strengths-based approach. This collectivist perspective is perhaps best represented in Woods and Kennedy's (1922) description of Toynbee himself in their analysis of the settlement house movement, *The Settlement Horizon: A National Estimate*. In it they state, "[Toynbee's] main contribution to the settlement lies in his insistence upon the spread of reciprocal first-hand contact between university and working men for fulfillment of the life of each as well as for salvation of the nation" (p. 25).

As word of Toynbee Hall spread, some Americans studying abroad journeyed across Europe to experience the settlement first hand and eventually brought the ideal of reciprocal, communal living for the betterment of society back to the States. After completing his undergraduate studies in Berlin in 1886, Stanton Coit traveled to London and resided at Toynbee for several months. While there, he envisioned a similar settlement for the residents of the poor and overpopulated tenements on the Lower East Side of New York City (Woods & Kennedy, 1922). Upon his return to New York City later that year he and several university men sought residence in the tenements and quickly established the first American settlement, the Neighborhood Guild (Alissi, 2009). Like Toynbee, the Guild was structured around social and educational clubs and events that fostered connection between settlement workers and tenement residents. While the Guild was geared toward placing university men, the College Settlement was quickly established to provide places for university women to engage in settlement work as well (Woods & Kennedy, 1922).

Meanwhile, from the American Midwest, Jane Addams and Ellen Gates Starr traveled across the Atlantic to London in 1888 and while there they visited Toynbee Hall (Lee, 2009). Impassioned and inspired by what they witnessed, upon their return to Chicago they quickly set about locating suitable property for a settlement and established Hull House in a predominantly Italian neighborhood on the west side of the city in 1889. Like their predecessors, Addams and Gates Starr promoted the use of social and educational clubs, including art- and music-based activities at Hull House (Addams, 1909; Glowacki, 2004). Addams in particular was concerned about urban dwellers' over exposure to vice and argued for the development of healthy, non-vice forming recreational activities. She believed that the role of art was "to preserve in permanent and beautiful form those emotions and solaces which cheer life and make it kindlier" and that exposure to the arts can "lift the mind of the worker from the harshness and loneliness of his task" and "free him from a sense of isolation and hardship" that she found to be so prevalent in the late 19th and early 20th century lives of urban residents (Addams, 1909, p. 101). A review of Hull House yearbooks and annual reports from this time period (Hull House, 1907; Hull House, 1910; Hull House, 1921) as well as Simkhovitch's (1938) description of daily life at Greenwich House, another settlement in New York City, suggests strong support for art- and music-based activities in settlement work as a means to not only engage tenement residents and bring them into relationship with each other and the worker, but also to do so in a way that engaged residents' talents, strengths, and interests.

Speaking directly to the role Addams played as an early and pioneering practitioner of strengths-based approaches, Lee (2009) notes, "It was Addams' clear purpose to not plan *for* but *with* and *in dialogue* with the neighborhood residents. Her philosophy was to encourage the abilities of the residents" and to "promote the work of others" (p. 15). Lee (2009) goes on to describe Addams as a "forerunner of the empowerment perspective" (p. 15) and a model for reciprocal, community-based practice. While Addams certainly was not alone in her efforts to promote empowerment-based practice within settlements, she was able to harness her efforts and raise Hull House and its programming to national and international attention.

While the Charity Organization Society's (COS) preferred method of intervention was fundamentally different than the strengths-based approach offered by the settlement movement, it found a home in the United States in Mary Richmond, a foremother of American social work, who conceptualized professional practice as, first, an individually-focused enterprise. Richmond began her career at the COS in Baltimore and eventually worked her way through the ranks to be the secretary general of COS (Murdach, 2011). Advocating for the professionalization of social work, Richmond conceptualized professional practice through social casework, an intervention that involved a structured *diagnosis* of individual and family problems, followed by an examination of community problems that contributed to the individual and family's difficulties (Turner & Jaco, 1996; Wenocur & Reisch, 2001). Social diagnosis sought "to learn the facts of what the *problem* [emphasis added] is as it exists, seems, and feels today" (Perlman, 1957, p. 116), and consisted of a series of systematic questions to gain additional information about an individual's history in order to arrive at a social diagnosis (Morris, 2000).

Richmond's (1917) orientation to diagnosing how social problems impact an individual and family's present functioning is perhaps best illustrated in her book *Social Diagnosis*. Richmond notes, "When a human being, whatever his economic status, develops some marked form of social difficulty and social need, what do we have to know about him and about his difficulty (or more often difficulties) before we can arrive at a way of meeting his need?" (p. 26). Social diagnosis was, thus, seen to serve a function of solving difficulties and meeting societal needs that may somehow go unmet without an intervention.

Though identifying family and community strengths was a natural extension of social diagnosis, early social casework and social diagnosis continued to be more like medically driven models of intervention than not. Part of the preoccupation with the medical model, which tended to be driven by assessment, diagnosis, and treatment of problems (Rapp & Goscha, 2006), was the need for a professional identity for social workers. The need for diagnosing and addressing problems necessitated the intervention of social workers. Richmond's model of social casework training provided a systematic way of intervening with a variety of individual and social problems across a variety of contexts (Margolin, 1997). Had the individual and family already had "strengths," there may have been less apparent need for intervention.

In considering the development of strengths-based and social casework approaches throughout the late 19th and early 20th centuries it is important to note the environmental and historical context in which they evolved. This was a time of great transition for the nation, as Ellis Island was flooded on a daily basis with the arrival of thousands of immigrants from many different and diverse cultures. While the communal, strengths-based approaches of the settlements often aligned with the indigenous cultural practices of many immigrants, naturalization policies and practices, which often included some form of social casework, often trumped more holistic and culturally inclusive strengths-based approaches in order to assimilate those seeking refuge and eventual citizenship in the United States.

Early and Mid-20th Century Strengths-Based Practitioners

Following the stock market crash of October 29, 1929, which is also known as *Black Tuesday*, the United States entered an economic depression of catastrophic proportions. Unemployment rates skyrocketed to previously unexperienced levels, resulting in the displacement of families and the loss of entire, previously thriving industrial communities. Estimates of the duration of the Great Depression vary, but it is clear that it lasted well into the 1930s, with some areas of the country not fully recovering until the end of World War II. It is hard to imagine the intense disillusionment and pressure individuals, families, communities, and the nation felt during this time. Despite the intense loss and clearly definable and diagnosable problems stemming from and evolving out of the Great Depression—and World War II for that matter—strengths-based practitioners continued to challenge the prevailing medically oriented, problem-based approach to services, which privileged the practitioners' expertise over the clients' experiences, well into the 20th century.

Instrumental in that fight was Bertha Capen Reynolds, a social work educator and activist from New England. Reynolds believed that social and economic justice issues had a significant influence on a person's ability to thrive and realize her or his potential. Through her work as an advocate and educator, Reynolds openly challenged the medical model, which assumed that the practitioner was the expert at solving the client's problems, and posited that treating clients as individuals who were capable of recognizing their own needs could lead to more effective social casework practice. In her influential monograph *Between Client and Community: A Study of Responsibility in Social Case Work*, Reynolds (1934) argued for services that recognized every human being's right to make her or his own mistakes and that every human being had the right to determine how much or how little help she or he would seek. Reynolds even noted that, "if [she or] he can get it from [her or] his own friends, so much the better" (1934, p. 35).

Reynolds believed that the social environment, including the person's social class, gender, and community, had significant impact on the person's ability to recognize their own strengths, assets, abilities, and resources. An advocate for shared partnership in which the practitioner, client, and community all have a stake, Reynolds taught a model of social casework that identified a client's resources and stimulated the client's confidence in herself or himself (Edward, 2009; Hartman, 1989; Hiersteiner & Peterson, 1999; Kaplan, 2002; Van Wormer, 2002). With that confidence supported, the client is able to make best use of the working relationship and to solve the problems that originally led her or him to seek services.

Although Reynolds advocated for strengths-based approaches through social casework primarily with individuals, Grace Longwell Coyle advanced strengths-based approaches within group work theory and practice. Group work developed out of an expanded national interest in recreational activities promoted by the leisure movement of the late 19th and early 20th centuries (Meyer, 1934; Pangburn, 1924; Reid, 1981) and more community-oriented forms of social work practice, such as settlement house work (Andrews, 2001). In discussing the nation's interest and investment in recreational activities throughout the early and mid-20th century, Coyle (1948) noted, "[there] is increasing acceptance by the public of the essential character of constructive leisure-time activities" (p. 5). Her statement along with the writings of other scholars at the time (see Dimock & Trecker, 1949; Kindelsperger, 1955) suggest that mid-century practitioners were supportive of the inclusion of recreational activities in their practice, thereby fostering acceptance of the whole person, or at least more than the troubled parts (Andrews, 2001).

Coyle (1955) believed that group work incorporated the "conscious use of social relations in performing community functions" (p. 340), and, not unlike Addams and Gates Starr and their work at Hull House earlier in the century, she was particularly interested in the potential for small groups to engage people in healthy forms of personal and civic development (Coyle, 1948). In addition, Coyle (1948) was interested in the potential for "interracial and interethnic understandings between Negro and white, between Christian and Jews, and between various nationality groups" (p. 14), within the membership of recreation and education groups and organizations. She believed that, "within the recreation and education agencies lie both occasion for friction and opportunities for experience and better understanding" (p. 14). Her thoughts highlight the potential for broader, systemic impact through inclusive group work practice, one that extends beyond the one-to-one casework model. Coyle's empowerment and strengths-based approach to group work suggest the potential for a broader, interpersonal understanding of strengths-based practice, one where clients are encouraged to not only engage and operationalize strengths within themselves, but to also recognize and celebrate the strengths that others bring to the group. Perhaps most significantly, she did so in a way that promotes racial, ethnic, and religious diversity in a time that was less tolerant (Walkowitz, 1999), thereby framing her ideas in much more of a progressive and strengths-based lens.

Whereas Reynolds and Coyle promoted strengths-based approaches within micro- and mezzo-level social work practice, and in doing so, at least from a systems perspective, at the macro level as well, Carl Rogers helped establish and develop strengths-based approaches in the psychology and professional counseling fields, specifically through the humanistic psychology perspective. Humanistic psychology promotes empathy within the therapeutic relationship, whereby the practitioner seeks to set aside their perception of the world to see the world through the client's eyes (Payne, 2005b). In employing empathy, the practitioner moves to a space of unconditional positive regard for the client by prioritizing the client in the therapeutic relationship and valuing whom the client was, is, and will become (Payne, 2011). Though not explicitly framed as a strengths-based approach, this holistic and non-pathological perspective was a seismic shift in the professional counseling and psychology fields. In many ways it worked as a critique and response to Freudian psychoanalytic theory and its regressive techniques as well as Watson's objective behaviorist approach, the latter of which is discussed in greater detail later in this chapter.

Often cited as one of the founders of the humanistic perspective, Rogers completed his undergraduate work in agriculture and turned his attention to more existential lines of scholarship during his graduate studies, including theology, education, and the highly influential post-Freudian work of Otto Rank (Kramer, 1995), all of which would play a significant role in the development of the humanistic perspective. It was the synthesis of these interests that led him to develop his own unique form of strengths-based, client-centered, or as it eventually became known, person-centered therapy. Within this practice model, Rogers (1957) asserts that there are six conditions that must be for a client to experience a beneficial and therapeutic change. These conditions include the following:

(1) A practitioner and a client are in relationship.
(2) The client experiences distress (e.g., anxiety, depression, etc.) and/or an incongruence in their experience and awareness.
(3) The practitioner is congruent and genuine; they are not "acting" as a "practitioner," rather they are fully present within the experience as themselves.
(4) Being fully present and genuine in the relationship, "the [practitioner] experiences unconditional positive regard for the client" (p. 96), whereby the practitioner accepts the client and their experience as is and judgment free.

(5) The practitioner also "experiences an empathic understanding of the client's internal frame of reference" (p. 96) and seeks to communicate it to the client.

(6) At least to a minimum degree, the client perceives and understands the practitioner's unconditional positive regard and empathy (Rogers, 1957).

In reviewing the model, it is clear to see elements of strengths-based approaches, including genuineness, unconditional positive regard, and empathy. It is also important to note that like Reynolds and Coyle, Rogers (1989) was interested in the application of his practice and theories to larger environmental and systemic issues, including international work, human rights work, and work for peace.

Abraham Maslow, an educator in Brooklyn, New York and another foundational psychologist in the humanistic perspective, argued that through the lifespan human beings have an innate curiosity, a desire to learn about the world, and a natural hierarchy of motivations (Coy & Kovacs-Long, 2005). He is best known for his hierarchical pyramid of needs, which posited that human beings are motivated by a variety of needs, including a need for safety, belongingness and love, esteem, self-actualization, and self-transcendence (a reflection of his beliefs later in his career as a psychologist [Koltko-Rivera, 2006]), and that lower needs on the hierarchical pyramid must be met before higher needs can be realized (Fisher, 2009; Hoffman, 2008). A central role of the practitioner is to help a person achieve a higher position on the hierarchy, thereby helping a person realize his or her "self-confidence, worth, strength, capability and adequacy" (Maslow, 1943, p. 382).

During this time, behaviorism in psychology also increased in popularity. John B. Watson (1913), one of the fathers of psychological behaviorism, argued that the field of psychology was not viewed as scientific because it tended to focus on introspection and conscious thought rather than targeting behavior. He believed that psychology could claim its place within the natural sciences if its attention shifted from the study of "speculative questions" of unseen phenomena to observable behavior. Strengths-based practitioners, however, did not focus on targeting behavior except perhaps by embellishing functional behaviors over behaviors that were dysfunctional. Asking the client to consciously consider her or his assets or possibilities would have also been antithetical to the scientific measurement of behavior that Watson believed was possible through behaviorism.

In his biography of Abraham Maslow, Hoffman (1988) noted that, though ultimately Maslow rejected behaviorism in favor of humanistic psychology, he was strongly influenced by his early career experiences and Watson's work, specifically his "optimistic belief in the nearly total malleability of human nature" (p. 34). Watson believed that we are all born equal and alike in our possibilities, influenced by only our environment. That belief in human possibility had a great influence on Maslow's understanding of self-actualization, a period in the hierarchy in which a person naturally focuses on their psychological growth, personal fulfillment, and life satisfaction (Maslow, 1943).

Throughout the early and mid-20th century, the fields of social work, psychology, couple/marriage and family therapy, and professional counseling all sought, to varying degrees, legitimacy as experts who were capable of solving problems of the human condition. Each profession sought to carve out a place in the mental health treatment industry by demonstrating that they had the unique training—one that was often absent in traditional psychiatric treatment—that could help them intervene in a way that was more humane. Social work, psychology, couple/marriage and family therapy, and professional counseling needed to justify the need for involvement of practitioners and were increasingly required by funders to show that their practices were scientific and evidence-based (Emener & Cottone, 1989; Hwang & Powell, 2009; Margolin, 1997; Rapp & Goscha, 2006; Robiner, 2006). For the most part, this led practitioners to favor the use of problem-based diagnosis and use of the *Diagnostic and Statistical Manual of Mental Disorders* became more widespread within the professions (Newman, Dannenfelser, & Clemmons, 2007). Thus, strengths-based approaches, though often part of the lexicon of practitioners, were less favored than were problem-based models.

Strengths-Based Approaches in the Late 20th Century and Beyond

Although the *Diagnostic and Statistical Manual of Mental Disorders* continued to dominate much of the social work, psychology, couple/marriage and family therapy, and professional counseling interventions well into the release of the third edition in 1980 and the fourth edition in 1994, some researchers and practitioners endeavored to continue and expand upon existing strengths-based approaches. Speaking to this movement, Dennis Saleebey (1996) noted,

> In part the impetus for the evolution of a more strengths-based view of social work practice comes from the awareness that U.S. culture and helping professions are saturated with psychological approaches based on individual, family, and community pathology, deficits, problems, abnormality, victimization, and disorder. (p. 296)

Through his research and work in mental health case management, Saleebey and his colleagues at University of Kansas School of Social Welfare developed the strengths perspective, which posits that regardless of any challenge, all individuals have inherent strengths and that it is the practitioner's duty to recognize and work with clients' strengths.

In his edited text *The Strengths Perspective in Social Work Practice*, Saleebey (2012) presents several principles of the strengths perspective, which include the following:

(1) Individuals, groups, families, and communities have strengths.
(2) Although trauma, abuse, and illness may be harmful, they may also be opportunities for growth.
(3) Never assume the upper limits of individuals, groups, families, communities, and their capacity for growth and change.
(4) Clients are best served through collaboration.
(5) All environments, regardless of perceived deficiencies, are full of resources.

Several researchers, scholars, and practitioners have built on and further developed the strengths perspective. Echoing Saleebey's (1996) initial sentiment of frustration with deficits-based approaches to practice, a decade later Rapp and Goscha (2006) critiqued the mental health field as "preoccupied with illness because of the dominance of the 'medical model'" (p. 56), which is largely geared toward an individual's problems. In response they developed an evidence-based, strengths-based case-management program for individuals with mental illness (Rapp, 1998; Rapp & Goscha, 2006). Working from a theoretical lens, Kemp, Whittaker, and Tracy (1997) developed the person–environment practice model, which posits that in any environment clients have strengths and it is the practitioner's task to work collaboratively with clients to explore their strengths and use those strengths for client change.

Building on the environmental aspect of the strengths perspective, Mattaini and Meyer (2002) note the inherent relationship between the strengths perspective and systems/ecological theories. They contend that strengths, when conceptualized from a systems perspective, "are not things that one carries" but "are realized in transactions in which a person has the skills to engage" (p. 15). This suggests that strengths are engaged and actualized through collaboration and active participation in the client–practitioner collaboration. Malekoff (2014) builds on the strengths perspective by applying it to group work, specifically evidence-guided practice principles for strengths-based group work with adolescents, which include forming groups for young people on the basis of their needs and wants, welcoming the whole person, and decentralizing authority by turning control over to young group members. Malekoff (2014) noted that the principles are "overlapping and interrelated" (p. 50) and that they are essential components of group work practice with young people "regardless of the practitioner's theoretical or ideological orientation" (p. 43). Practitioners of social work with groups have articulated additional models of strengths-based practice including empowerment (Hudson, 2009) and mutual aid models (Moyse Steinberg, 2009). Similar approaches have been extended to clinical supervision, whereby the supervising practitioner and supervisee work together to identify the supervisee's strengths and abilities prior to beginning and throughout the course of clinical supervision (Edwards, 2012).

Application of these strengths-based approaches, however, has been challenged by shifts in the environment. In particular, significant shifts in attitudes toward professional services occurred during the late 20th century, and these changes had direct impact on clients receiving services, especially clients from lower socioeconomic classes. The Personal Responsibility and Work Opportunity Reconciliation Act (1996) ended long-term welfare to needy persons by creating a responsibility to return to work as a condition for public assistance. The "problem" of needing public assistance was blamed on individuals and returning to work as a "responsibility" for receiving sustaining assistance reinforced that some clients were more deserving of help than others.

Despite these environmental challenges, a host of other counseling methods and theories emerged in the 20th century that were essentially grounded in empowerment and strengths-based approaches. Martin Seligman developed the concept of learned optimism and the field of positive psychology, somewhat ironically while studying depression and the idea of learned helplessness. Based on the premise that psychology is more than the study and treatment of deficits and pathology, it is also about "work, education, insight, love, growth, and play" (Seligman & Csikszentmihalyi, 2000, p. 7), positive psychology seeks to identify and nurture what is best in clients. It is based on the assumption that clients want to lead meaningful and fulfilling lives. The task of the practitioner is to be attentive to and value the subjective experience of individuals (e.g., sense of well-being, optimism, intra- and interpersonal skills and talents) and their roles and places within the various groups that constitute their lives (Seligman & Csikszentmihalyi, 2000); from that space the practitioner helps the client harness the strengths and resources that will enable the client to thrive (Seligman, 2007).

Postmodern therapists working from constructivist and social constructivist epistemologies made important contributions to the development of strengths-based approaches within the field of couple/marriage and family therapy. Seeking to shift the therapeutic focus from problems to solutions in ways that prioritize clients' livid experience, postmodern therapists developed counseling styles that prioritize collaboration and seek to empower clients' stories (Walsh, 2012). Narrative therapy, for example, posits that clients experience problems when the story of their lives, as told by themselves or by others, does not represent the world as the client sees it. Difficulties emerge when these stories become problem-saturated, and the task of the practitioner is to help clients retell the stories of their lives in ways that are more functional for them (White & Epston, 1990).

Working from a similar epistemological and theoretical base, de Shazer and Berg conceptualized the solution-focused brief therapy approach. Developed at the Brief Family Therapy Center after becoming dissatisfied with other brief therapy practices developed by clinicians at the Mental Research Institute (Nichols, 2013), solution-focused brief therapy was conceived to be a pragmatic, respectful, and hopeful approach to services that focuses on "what works" and holding clients accountable for making changes that they find most meaningful (de Shazer & Dolan, 2007; Lee, 2003; Thomas, 2013). De Shazer and Berg believed that the focus of the intervention should be entirely client-focused. They believed that clients have an inherent ability to know the nature of their situation and how to construct solutions for addressing the situation; in other words, clients know what they want (Berg & De Jong, 1996; Trepper, Dolan, McCollum, & Nelson, 2006). Solution-focused brief therapy sought to position clients as experts on their own lives and collaborators in the process of change (De Jong & Berg, 1998; de Shazer et al., 1986; Dolan, 2007).

Solution-focused interventions seek to engage clients in a conversation about finding solutions by employing the client as "expert" in the help-seeking process. Together the practitioner and client explore the client's perceptions about the situation, ask solution-oriented questions, and construct a new narrative that is free of the problem (Corcoran & Pillai, 2009; Lee, 2003; Miller & de Shazer, 1998; Trepper, Dolan, McCollum, & Nelson, 2006). During the first session of the solution-focused intervention, the practitioner attempts to elicit a statement of the solution to the presenting problem and to identify times in the client's life where the problem has been absent or where have been exceptions (Molnar & de Shazer, 1987). Most clients have had many exceptions to their problems, and it is the job of the practitioner to draw out those exceptions (de Shazer & Dolan, 2007). From those identified exceptions, potential solutions are identified. The focus of the remaining intervention is to help the client do more of what is working (or has worked in the past) and do less of what is not working.

Unfortunately, the expertise of the practitioner and problem-focused intervention continued to be favored during the late 20th century. This may have been driven by demands from insurance companies and other funders who demanded more accountability and incentivized treatment that was problem-focused, measurable, achievable, and short-term. Solution-focused brief therapy partially met the demands of funders insomuch as interventions tended to be short-term. However, solution-focused brief therapy was conceived to be an empowerment-based approach that challenges the traditional narrative of problems (Miller & de Shazer, 1998) and that was fundamentally different than problem-focused and measurable interventions that funders seemed to favor.

State of the Research and Literature

Although social work, psychology, couple/marriage and family therapy, and professional counseling have accepted, developed, implemented, and endorsed strengths-based practices over the last 130+ years, some scholars have noted that these practices lack empirical evidence of effectiveness (Gambrill, 2014; Gray, 2011; Staudt, Howard, & Drake, 2001). Despite these critiques and the ever pressing need to provide empirical evidence of efficacy and effectiveness from a predominantly positivist paradigm, some scholars continue to develop strengths-based theoretical work and conduct strengths-based research.

Current strengths-based empirical research is particularly well-developed in treatment programs for people with severe and persistent mental health diagnoses. For example, several Assertive Community Treatment (ACT) programs, which aim to reduce psychiatric hospitalizations and improve treatment outcomes for people with severe and persistent mental health diagnoses by providing case management, support, and rehabilitation within the community rather than institutional settings (Substance Abuse and Mental Health Administration, 2008), have demonstrated the operationalization and testing of strengths-based practices. Key components of the model include the client's engagement in identifying treatment outcomes that are meaningful and practitioners and clients actively working together in the client's recovery (McGrew & Bond, 1995). When there is high fidelity to the ACT model, ACT is effective at the stated goal of reducing psychiatric hospitalizations and improving treatment adherence for many clients (Bond, Drake, Mueser, & Latimer, 2001; Coldwell & Bender, 2007; Cuddeback et al., 2013; McGrew & Bond, 1995; Phillips et al., 2001; Scott & Dixon, 1995).

Additional strengths-based research has explored the use of audio documentary in group work with young people experiencing homelessness as means to engage their strengths (Kelly, 2015). Other researchers have explored strengths-based approaches and practices in school-based social developmental studies (Gleason, 2007), civil action training for young people (Atkinson, 2012), and youth homelessness services (Karabanow, 2003; Karabanow, Hughes, Ticknor, Kidd, & Patterson, 2010; Kidd & Davidson, 2007; Kidd & Evans, 2011). In terms of recent strengths-based theoretical work, the authors of this chapter have collaboratively proposed the implementation of the strengths-based social work interview with young people experiencing sexual abuse (Kelly & Gates, 2010) and a strengths-based, culturally anchored methodology for lesbian, gay, and bisexual research (Gates & Kelly, 2013).

Surely the push for and promotion of strengths-based approaches in theoretical and empirical work will continue. This is especially true for strengths-based treatment, such as ACT, which has easily measured program outcomes such as rate of psychiatric hospitalization and adherence to prescribed psychopharmacological treatment. Future research must continue to measure the application of strengths-based approaches in ways that meaningfully meet both client and programmatic outcomes.

Conclusion

This chapter highlighted the rich history of strengths-based approaches and reviewed how the work of pioneers such as Jane Addams, Mary Richmond, Bertha Capen Reynolds, Grace Coyle, Carl Rogers, Abraham Maslow, Dennis Saleebey, Steve de Shazer, Insoo Berg, and others have contributed to a practice ideal that values the assets, capacities, and skills that clients bring to the client–practitioner relationship. Clients are more than a set of problems to be solved and can be active participants in their own journey to wellness. Pioneers of strengths-based practice have applied this perspective to a variety of clients across a variety of practice settings and have found that the approach can be an effective way for responding to contemporary social issues affecting the people in our communities.

Great hope and possibility exists for strengths-based approaches in the 21st century. Though strengths-based practice has gained considerable popularity by practitioners and by funders of human service programs, opportunity exists for further empirical validation of strengths-based approaches. In particular, there are opportunities for demonstrating that adherence and fidelity to strengths-based approaches have positive client outcomes and that utilization of the approach helps improve the lives of the people being served.

References

Addams, J. (1909). *The spirit of youth and the city streets, Illini books edition.* Urbana, IL: University of Illinois Press.

Alissi, A. (2009). United States. In A. Gitterman & R. Salmon (Eds.), *Encyclopedia of social work with groups,* (pp. 6–13). New York, NY: Routledge.

Andrews, J. (2001). Group work's place in social work: A historical analysis. *Journal of Sociology and Social Welfare, 28*(4), 45–65.

Atkinson, K.N. (2012). *Education for liberation: A precursor to youth activism for social justice.* (Order No. 3551366, University of Illinois at Chicago). Retrieved on April 25, 2016 from http://search.proquest.com/docview/1293073764?accountid=12163. (1293073764).

Axinn, J., & Stern, M.J. (2005). *Social welfare: A history of the American response to need.* Boston, MA: Allyn & Bacon.

Berg, I.K., & De Jong, P. (1996). Solution-building conversations: Co-constructing a sense of competence with clients. *Families in Society, 77,* 376–391.

Bond, G.R., Drake, R.E., Mueser, K.T., & Latimer, E. (2001). Assertive Community Treatment for people with severe mental illness. *Disease Management and Health Outcomes, 9,* 141–159.

Coldwell, C.M., & Bender, W.S. (2007). The effectiveness of Assertive Community Treatment for homeless populations with severe mental illness: A meta-analysis. *American Journal of Psychiatry, 164,* 393–399.

Corcoran, J., & Pillai, V. (2009). A review of the research on solution-focused therapy. *British Journal of Social Work, 39,* 234–242.

Coy, D., & Kovacs-Long, J. (2005). Maslow and Miller: An exploration of gender and affiliation in the journey to competence. *Journal of Counseling & Development, 83,* 138–145.

Coyle, G.L. (1948). *Group work with American youth: A guide to the practice of leadership.* New York, NY: Harper.

Coyle, G.L. (1955). Group work as a method in recreation. In H.B. Trecker (Ed.), *Group work: Foundations & frontiers* (pp. 91–102). New York, NY: William Morrow and Company.

Cuddeback, G.S., Morrissey, J.P., Domino, M.E., Monroe-DeVita, M., Teague, G.B., & Moser, L.L. (2013). Fidelity to recovery-oriented ACT practices and consumer outcomes. *Psychiatric Services, 64,* 318–323.

De Jong, P., & Berg, I.K. (1998). *Interviewing for solutions.* Pacific Grove, CA: Brooks/Cole.

De Shazer, S., Berg, I.K., Lipchik, E.V.E., Nunnally, E., Molnar, A., Gingerich, W., & Weiner-Davis, M. (1986). Brief therapy: Focused solution development. *Family Process, 25,* 207–221.

De Shazer, S., & Dolan, Y.M. (2007). *More than miracles: The state of the art of solution-focused brief therapy.* Binghamton, England: Haworth Press.

Dimock, H.S., & Trecker, H.B. (1949). *The supervision of group work and recreation.* New York, NY: Association Press.

Dolan, Y. (2007). Tribute to Insoo Kim Berg. *Journal of Marital & Family Therapy, 33,* 129–131.

Edward, J. (2009). When social work and psychoanalysis meet. *Clinical Social Work Journal, 37,* 14–22.

Edwards, J.K. (2012). *Strengths-based supervision in clinical practice.* New York, NY: SAGE.

Emener, W.G., & Cottone, R.R. (1989). Professionalization, deprofessionalization, and reprofessionalization of rehabilitation counseling according to criteria of professions. *Journal of Counseling & Development, 67,* 576–581.

Fisher, E.A. (2009). Motivation and leadership in social work management: A review of theories and related studies. *Administration in Social Work, 33,* 347–367.

Gambrill, E. (2014). Social work education and avoidable ignorance. *Journal of Social Work Education, 50,* 391–413.

Gates, T.G., & Kelly, B.L. (2013). LGB cultural phenomena and the social work research enterprise: Toward a strengths-based, culturally anchored methodology. *Journal of Homosexuality, 60,* 69–82.

Gleason, E.T. (2007). A strengths-based approach to the social developmental study. *Children & Schools, 29,* 52–59.

Glowacki, P. (2004). Bringing art to life: The practice of art at Hull House. In C.R. Ganz & M. Strobel (Eds.), *Pots of promise: Mexicans and pottery at Hull House, 1920–1940* (pp. 5–29). Chicago, IL: University of Illinois Press.

Gray, M. (2011). Back to basics: A critique of the strengths perspective in social work. *Families in Society: The Journal of Contemporary Social Services, 92,* 5–11.

Hartman, A. (1989). Still between client and community. *Social Work, 34,* 387–388.

Hiersteiner, C., & Peterson, K. (1999). "Crafting a usable past": The care-centered practice narrative in social work. *Affilia: Journal of Women & Social Work, 14,* 144–161.

Hoffman, E. (1988). *The right to be human: A biography of Abraham Maslow.* New York, NY: St. Martin's Press.

Hoffman, E. (2008). Abraham Maslow: A biographer's reflections. *Journal of Humanistic Psychology, 48*(4), 439–443.

Hudson, R.E. (2009). Empowerment model. In A. Gitterman & R. Salmon (Eds.), *Encyclopedia of social work with groups* (pp. 47–50). New York, NY: Routledge.

Hull House Publishers. (1907). *Hull-House year book: September 1, 1906–September 1, 1907* [Annual report]. Chicago, IL: Author.

Hull House Publishers. (1910). *Hull-House year book: May 1, 1910* [Annual report]. Chicago, IL: Author.

Hull House Publishers. (1921). *Hull-House year book: 1921* [Annual report]. Chicago, IL: Author.

Hwang, H., & Powell, W.W. (2009). The rationalization of charity: The influences of professionalism in the non-profit sector. *Administrative Science Quarterly, 54,* 268–298.

Kaplan, C.P. (2002). An early example of brief strengths-based practice: Bertha Reynolds at the National Maritime Union, 1943–1946. *Smith College Studies in Social Work, 72,* 403–416.

Karabanow, J. (2003). Creating a culture of hope: Lessons from street children agencies in Canada and Guatemala. *International Social Work, 46,* 369–386.

Karabanow, J., Hughes, J., Ticknor, J., Kidd, S., & Patterson, D. (2010). The economics of being young and poor: How homeless youth survive in neo-liberal times. *Journal of Sociology & Social Welfare, 37*(4), 39–63.

Kelly, B.L. (2015). Using audio documentary to engage young people experiencing homelessness strengths-based group work. *Social Work with Groups, 38,* 68–86.

Kelly, B.L. & Gates, T.G. (2010). Using the strengths perspective in the social work interview with young adults who have experienced childhood sexual abuse. *Social Work in Mental Health, 8,* 421–437.

Kemp, S.P., Whittaker, J.K., & Tracy, E.M. (1997). *Person–environment practice: The social ecology of interpersonal helping.* New York, NY: Aldine de Gruyter.

Kidd, S., & Davidson, L. (2007). "You have to adapt because you have no other choice": The stories of strength and resilience of 208 homeless youth in New York City and Toronto. *Journal of Community Psychology, 35,* 219–238.

Kidd, S., & Evans, J.D. (2011). Home is where you draw strength and rest: The meanings of home for houseless young people. *Youth & Society, 43,* 752–773.

Kindelsperger, K.W. (1955). Common objectives of group work, physical education and recreation. In H.B. Trecker (Ed.), *Group work: Foundations & frontiers* (pp. 49−61). New York, NY: William Morrow and Company.

Koltko-Rivera, M.E. (2006). Rediscovering the later version of Maslow's hierarchy of needs: Self-transcendence and opportunities for theory, research, and unification. *Review of General Psychology, 10,* 302−317.

Kramer, R. (1995). The birth of client-centered therapy: Carl Rogers, Otto Rank, and "The Beyond." *Journal of Humanistic Psychology, 35*(4), 54–110.

Lee, J.A.B. (2009). Jane Addams. In A. Gitterman & R. Salmon (Eds.), *Encyclopedia of social work with groups* (pp. 13−16). New York, NY: Routledge.

Lee, M.Y. (2003). A solution-focused approach to cross-cultural clinical social work practice: Utilizing cultural strengths. *Families in Society, 84,* 385−395.

Malekoff, A. (2014). *Group work with adolescents: Principles and practices* (3rd ed.). New York, NY: Guilford Press.

Margolin, L. (1997). *Under the cover of kindness: The invention of social work.* Charlottesville, NC: University Press of Virginia.

Maslow, A.H. (1943). A theory of human motivation. *Psychological Review, 50,* 370−396.

Mattaini, M.A., & Meyer, C.H. (2002). The ecosystems perspective: Implications for practice. In M.A. Mattaini, C.T. Lowery, & C.H. Meyer (Eds.), *Foundations of social work practice: A graduate text* (3rd ed., pp. 3−24). Washington DC: NASW Press.

McGrew, J.H., & Bond, G.R. (1995). Critical ingredients of Assertive Community Treatment: Judgments of the experts. *Journal of Mental Health Administration, 22,* 113−125.

Meyer, H.D. (1934). Leisure. [Review of the books *Americans at play,* by J.E. Steiner, *Education through recreation,* by L.P. Jacks, *Leisure in the modern world,* by C.D. Burns, *The child and play,* by J.E. Rogers, and *The new leisure challenges the schools,* by E.T. Lies]. *Social Forces, 12,* 597−599. Retrieved on April 25, 2016 from http://www.jstor.org/stable/2569724

Miller, G., & de Shazer, S. (1998). Have you heard the latest rumor about . . .?: Solution-focused therapy as a rumor. *Family Process, 37*(3), 363–377.

Molnar, A., & de Shazer, S. (1987). Solution-focused therapy: Toward the identification of therapeutic tasks. *Journal of Marital and Family Therapy, 13,* 349−358.

Morris, R. (2000). Social work's century of evolution as a profession: Choices made, opportunities lost. From the individual and society to the individual (pp. 42−70). In J.G. Hopps & R.M. Morris (Eds.), *Social work at the millennium: Critical reflections on the future of the profession.* New York, NY: Free Press.

Moyse Steinberg, D. (2009). Mutual aid model. In A. Gitterman & R. Salmon (Eds.), *Encyclopedia of social work with groups* (pp. 50−53). New York, NY: Routledge.

Murdach, A.D. (2011). Mary Richmond and the image of social work. *Social Work, 56,* 92−94.

Newman, B.S., Dannenfelser, P.L., & Clemmons, V. (2007). The Diagnostic and Statistical Manual of Mental Disorders in graduate social work education: Then and now. *Journal of Social Work Education, 43,* 297−307.

Nichols, M.P. (2013). *Family therapy: Concepts and methods* (10th ed.). Boston, MA: Pearson.

Pangburn, W. (1924). Trends in public recreation. *Social Forces, 4,* 109−112. Retrieved on April 25, 2016 from http://www.jstor.org/stable/3004392

Payne, M. (2005a). *The origins of social work: Continuity and change.* Chicago, IL: Lyceum Books.

Payne, M. (2005b). *Modern social work theory.* Chicago, IL: Lyceum Books.

Payne, M. (2011). *Humanistic social work: Core principles in practice.* Chicago, IL: Lyceum Books.

Perlman, H.H. (1957). *Social casework: A problem-solving process.* Chicago, IL: University of Chicago Press.

Personal Responsibility and Work Opportunity Reconciliation Act. (1996). HR 3734. Retrieved on April 25, 2016 from http://www.gpo.gov/fdsys/pkg/BILLS-104hr3734enr/pdf/BILLS-104hr3734enr.pdf

Phillips, S.D., Burns, B.J., Edgar, E.R., Mueser, K.T., Linkins, K.W., Rosenheck, R.A., . . . & Herr, E.C.M. (2001). Moving assertive community treatment into standard practice. *Psychiatric Services, 52,* 771−779.

Rapp, C.A. (1998). *The strengths model: Case management with people suffering from severe and persistent mental illness.* New York, NY: Oxford University Press.

Rapp, C.A., & Goscha, R.J. (2006). *The strengths model: Case management with people with psychiatric disabilities.* New York, NY: Oxford University Press.

Reid, K.E. (1981). *From character building to social treatment: The history of the use of groups in social work.* Westport, CT: Greenwood Press.

Reynolds, B.C. (1934). Between client and community: A study of responsibility in social case work. *Smith College Studies in Social Work, 5,* 1–128.

Richmond, M. (1917). *Social diagnosis.* New York, NY: Russell Sage Foundation.

Robiner, W.N. (2006). The mental health professions: Workforce supply and demand, issues, and challenges. *Clinical Psychology Review, 26,* 600–625.

Rogers, C. (1957). The necessary and sufficient conditions of therapeutic personality change. *Journal of Consulting Psychology, 21,* 95–103.

Rogers, C. (1989). The rust workshop *1986.* In H. Kirschenbaum & V.L. Henderson (Eds.), *The Carl Rogers reader* (pp. 457–477). New York, NY: Houghton Mifflin Company.

Saleebey, D. (1996). The strengths perspective in social work practice: Extensions and cautions. *Social Work, 41,* 296–305.

Saleebey, D. (2012). Introduction: Power to the people. In D. Saleebey (Ed.), *The strengths perspective in social work practice* (6th ed., pp. 1–23). Boston, MA: Pearson.

Scott, J.E., & Dixon, L.B. (1995). Assertive Community Treatment and case management for schizophrenia. *Schizophrenia Bulletin, 21,* 657–668.

Seligman, M. (2007). *Positive psychology.* Retrieved from http://www.ppc.sas.upenn.edu/

Seligman M.E.P., & Csikszentmihalyi, M. (2000). Positive psychology: An introduction. *American Psychologist, 55,* 5–14.

Simkhovitch, M. (1938). *Neighborhood: My story of Greenwich House.* New York, NY: Norton.

Skocpol, T. (1992). *Protecting soldiers and mothers.* Cambridge, MA: Harvard University Press.

Staudt, M., Howard, M.O., & Drake, B. (2001). The operationalization, implementation, and effectiveness of the strengths perspective: A review of empirical studies. *Journal of Social Service Research, 27,* 1–21.

Substance Abuse and Mental Health Administration. (2008). *Getting started with evidence-based practices: Assertive Community Treatment.* Retrieved from http://store.samhsa.gov/shin/content//SMA08–4345/GettingStarted-ACT.pdf

Thomas, F.N. (2013). *Solution-focused supervision: A resource-oriented approach to developing clinical expertise.* New York, NY: Springer.

Trepper, T.S., Dolan, Y., McCollum, E.E., & Nelson, T. (2006). Steve de Shazer and the future of solution-focused therapy. *Journal of Marital and Family Therapy, 32,* 133–139.

Turner, J., & Jaco, R.M. (1996). Problem-solving theory and social work treatment. In F.J. Turner (Ed.), *Social work treatment* (4th ed.). New York, NY: Free Press.

Van Wormer, K. (2002). Our social work imagination: How social work has not abandoned its mission. *Journal of Teaching in Social Work, 22*(3–4), 21–37.

Walkowitz, D.J. (1999). *Working with class: Social workers and the politics of middle-class identity.* Chapel Hill, NC: The University of North Carolina Press.

Walsh, N. (2012). Clinical views of family, normality, health, and dysfunction. In N. Walsh (Ed.), *Normal family processes: Growing diversity and complexity* (4th ed., pp. 28–56).

Watson, J.B. (1913). Psychology as the behaviorist views it. *Psychological Review, 20,* 158–177.

Wenocur, S., & Reisch, M. (2001). *From charity to enterprise: The development of American social work in a market economy.* Urbana, IL: University of Illinois Press.

White, M., & Epston, D. (1990). *Narrative means to therapeutic ends.* New York, NY: W.W. Norton & Company.

Woods, R.A., & Kennedy, A.J. (1922). *The settlement horizon: A national estimate.* New York, NY: The Russell Sage Foundation.

Section II

Strengths-Based Clinical Practices with Varying Populations

3

The Collaborative Change Model

A Strengths-Based Blueprint for the Treatment of Relational Complex Trauma

Mary Jo Barrett and Linda Stone Fish

> Coming together is a beginning; keeping together is progress; working together is success.
>
> Henry Ford

When therapists walk away from a meeting with clients feeling good about their work, or a client reports satisfaction and change in their therapy and in their lives, we argue that strengths-based work is being done. When clients have experienced complex trauma, being strengths-based can be difficult. We define complex trauma as a pervasive mindset that often develops from historical and ongoing relationships of abuse, neglect, and violation. Many individuals, couples, and families who have a history of complex trauma come to therapy stuck in survival mindstates and desperately need help managing their lives. Clients with complex trauma often begin the treatment process having been traumatized in relationships that have similar characteristics to the ones they are entering into when they seek help. Clinicians, on the other hand, come to the relationship with the explicit understanding that they are to be helpful. In most psychotherapy training programs, we are taught to begin our therapy after a brief period of "joining" to move quickly into assessment followed soon after by interventions to challenge unproductive behaviors, thoughts, and feelings. We teach skills to extinguish symptoms and create positive behavioral cognitive and emotional changes. Unfortunately, this rapid movement towards challenge and change, in fact, can and often does trigger a survival mind state for clients who have experienced complex trauma. For us, the essence of a strengths-based model is the active and transparent use of collaboration. The client is an active member of the treatment team, as therapists call upon their strengths and resources to create change. We believe in the necessity of transparently using the clients' strengths and resources and integrating them into the creation of interventions.

Clinicians may be adept in a variety of effective treatment modalities and have an open heart but lack an effective blueprint for optimizing their relational skills and tools for interventions for those with complex trauma. Without a blueprint, when mental health practitioners are in challenging relationships with their clients they may unintentionally re-traumatize clients. Many of the clients who are seen in therapy have been emotionally, physically, sexually, financially, and/or spiritually violated and/or neglected by people who are supposed to be taking care of them. The therapeutic relationship runs the risk of repeating these traumatically stressful relationships. The use of a strengths-based model, integrating clients' strengths and resources into the treatment design, as well as the therapists' strengths, mitigates the possibility of becoming a therapeutic traumatic relationship. Armed with a blueprint that is explained step-by-step to our clients, practitioners and clients collaborate so that, as many clients have said about our model, "we are in this together." One client said, at an exit interview, "there is an order to putting my life back in order." Through full awareness and by collaboratively using our own strengths and integrating the strengths of the client, we create a non-traumatic healing context. This is the model for treatment we detail in this chapter.

The Collaborative Change Model (CCM; Barrett & Stone Fish, 2014) is a three-stage treatment plan for working with clients who have experienced complex trauma. Although our model is comparable to many other trauma-informed models of therapy, two main differences, which highlight its strengths-based footprint, are its transparent collaboration with clients and other professionals, and the emphasis we place on continuously returning to clients' resources as a matter of course in each therapy session and the entire therapeutic process. These two concepts are literally part of the CCM protocol.

We will be writing about the first stage of our CCM for working with individuals, couples, families, and communities who have experienced complex trauma, as this is the stage where we introduce strengths-based theory to the clients. The CCM is an organizational blueprint designed to help clients and therapists have a successful therapeutic experience. The first stage, "Creating a Context for Change," focuses on safety and transparent collaboration with clients. Stage 1 is practiced in every session and whenever a new challenge is introduced throughout therapy.

Developing a new relationship with a helping professional is stressful as is the change process. It can be disorienting and threatening. Clients often experience therapy as something that is happening to them. They have no idea what to expect and they do not understand the rules. Lacking a detailed blueprint for the process of therapy the therapist's actions may seem confusing, irrelevant, or critical. This stressful situation triggers survival mind states in which it is virtually impossible to achieve therapeutic growth. All of our clients' energies are focused on surviving while in this state and change is not an option. Neurobiological and developmental research has shown that we learn more effectively when our emotions are regulated and our information processing systems are functioning (Ford, 2009). When the brain is focusing on surviving as opposed to learning, therapeutic techniques and interventions are neutralized and become ineffective at best and re-traumatizing at worst.

Our model follows a clear sequence of stages (creating refuge, assessing vulnerabilities and the function of the symptom, assessing resources, exploring the positive and negative consequences of change, understanding and validating client's denial, availability and attachment, setting goals, and introducing acknowledgment) and is at the same time flexible and adaptive to therapist style, theoretical model, clinical setting, and client-presenting challenge. Helping others grow and change is a creative and sacred process. The CCM allows each and every client and therapist together to design the creative process of change that fits their strengths and styles. At the same time, the CCM holds that the natural cycle of change occurs in all good treatment for clients with a history of complex trauma. The beauty of the model is that it organizes a journey towards healing much like a blueprint organizes a creation, for all involved in a simple recursive loop that is creative, respectful, practical, client-centered, strengths-based, and effective.

Actually, all good trauma-informed practice has a strengths-based component. All good trauma-informed treatment follows a sequence that focuses on strength throughout its many stages. This has been eloquently articulated in Greenwald's (2007) fairy tale as an example of trauma-informed therapy. Greenwald tells the tale of a small town with a dragon and the town's desire to rid itself of the dragon by finding a hero. In the beginning, they find the hero and urge him to slay the dragon but he does not have the desire, courage, or the skills to do the work. The town, in its infinite strengths-based wisdom, finds him a place to work out. They hire a personal trainer and encourage him along as he works hard, experiences both defeat and success, gets ready to slay the dragon, and then, with a great deal of support, is successful. In the final phase of the fairy tale, the town's people discover why the dragon was attracted to their town to begin with and work constructively together to ensure that the dragon never returns. Our model follows the same sequence and we often tell our clients about Greenwald's fairy tale when explaining how therapy works to our clients.

Literature Review

There has been an explosion of resources for trauma-informed practice since Trepper and Barrett (1986, 1989) published their first books on the systemic treatment of incest, in which some foundational elements of our model were initially introduced. Some of these new resources have informed our work because they resonate with our model, with feedback from client exit interviews we have conducted, and because they focus on clients' resiliency and strengths. The trauma-informed practices that have significantly influenced our work focus on ways to create healing environments for clients (e.g., Bloom, 1997; Briere & Scott, 2012; Courtois & Ford, 2012; Herman, 1992; Van der Kolk, 2014; Miller-Karas, 2015). These practices empower clients with a history of complex trauma, value the dynamic interplay between trauma mind states and resiliency, and help therapists create environments in which the natural cycle of growth can be accessed.

Strengths-based trauma-informed practice is helped by information we have gathered by interpersonal neurobiologists (e.g., Badenoch, 2011; Siegel, 2010) and by those healers who take a somatic experiential approach (e.g., Levine, 2010; Miller-Karas, 2015). After studying the brain and the effects of trauma on the mind, Siegel (2012) has suggested that there are four essential ingredients for successful therapy: seen, safe, soothe, and secure. Siegel believes that clients must be seen by therapists, feel safe in the therapeutic environment, feel soothed by the process of therapy, and feel secure with the therapist's skills and competence. When clients experience the therapeutic encounter in this manner, their natural resources for growth and change are accessed.

Strengths-based trauma-informed practice is further enhanced when the mind is helped to focus on body sensations that enhance clients' access to resources. For example, many trauma-informed therapists are greatly influenced by the somatic experiencing approach (Levine, 2010), which helps explain how the body holds trauma and how the body can release it. Focusing on inner resources and a centered place of warm memories can help clients weather the negative effects of traumatic memories when they arise. Recognizing, honoring, and encouraging clients to attend to their body's wisdom is a strengths-based practice.

Last, trauma-informed practice that is attachment based (e.g., Hughes, 2006; Johnson, 2005; Muller, 2010; Siegel, 2015) can also be considered strengths-based practice. Hughes' (2006) work focuses on helping caregivers create loving environments for children who have attachment disorders. Although the term *attachment disorders* seems pathological, it actually helps parents make sense of a child's behavior in ways that engage them to experience their child in a positive light. Johnson's (2005) work with couples who have experienced trauma seems to have an effect similar to Hughes' work. Her work is strengths-based because she helps couples use their commitment, warmth, and inner resources to heal attachment based injuries and the impact of traumatic events. All of the above mentioned trauma-informed, strengths-based practices inform the CCM, which is detailed subsequently.

Application of the Strengths-Based Technique

The CCM blueprint divides treatment into three stages and each session has all three stages within it. These stages are modeled after the cyclical phases of natural growth and evolution: The contraction/pause phase is followed by an expansion/growth phase, which leads naturally into a consolidation phase (for more information about these phases, see Barrett & Stone Fish, 2014). The therapeutic healing process happens in these three stages over time, each session includes the three stages, and within each session the same cycle recurs again. This is the blueprint for therapy, both a visual map and a language that organizes the labor of everyone involved. The goal of the blueprint is to help all participants understand and envision the project and goals of the shared work and to help guide our clients into their own natural cycle of growth.

Stage 1 is Creating a Context for Change, Stage 2 is Challenging Patterns and Expanding Realities, and Stage 3 is Consolidation. Every session includes all three stages, which means in each session we create a context for change, challenge some patterns, and re-ground, helping clients center before ending the session, and engaging with their natural environment. For the purposes of this chapter, we focus on Stage 1.

The foundational work of Stage 1 is the most important stage of the evolving cycle and is actually crucial to the success of therapy. If you do not create a context for change with clients who have a history of complex trauma, they may experience therapeutic interventions from a survival mind state and treatment runs the risk of being re-traumatizing: In most instances, when individuals have difficulties controlling their emotions, cognitions, behavior, and relationships, we believe they are acting from a survival mindstate. They experience themselves as powerless, out of control, devalued, and disconnected and they react to stress from the survival mindstate of fight, flight, and/or freeze. When in a survival mind state, clients are not open to the change process and therapy may actually do more harm than good.

Unfortunately, for both clients and clinicians, Stage 1 seems to be the most misunderstood and least respected stage of therapy. It is skipped entirely or rushed and this undoubtedly creates therapeutic failures. Mental health practitioners see themselves as change agents, yet they risk re-traumatization, misalliance, and premature termination if they do not honor the importance of Stage 1. All clinicians have seen clients who have dropped out of other therapists' practices quite prematurely and though the ex-therapist may never receive feedback about the premature termination, it is often because the therapist failed to respect the importance of Stage 1.

Most of us are trained to begin our therapeutic relationship after a brief period of "joining" to move quickly into assessment followed soon after by treatment planning and interventions. This rapid movement towards challenge and change is stressful, it can be disorienting and threatening to clients who present in survival mind states. In fact, clients with a history of complex trauma, who are not in survival mind states when they begin treatment, can actually be triggered into survival mind states because something is happening to them that is completely unexpected and danger signals are set off. Without a strengths-based Stage 1 perspective, clients become labeled as resistant.

In Stage 1, we share our blueprint of therapy. We are collaborating with clients throughout the entire process, actively informing them of where we are and where we are going. As transparently as possible, we help clients understand that therapeutic change is a process of moving them from survival mind states to engaged mind states in which they are using all parts of their brains, not just those parts that have protected them in the past. Because repetition is crucial to growth, we repeat these concepts as much as possible in all stages of therapy. Our conversations about the therapy process and how we understand the nature of therapeutic change are deliberate and ongoing conversations. We partner in collaboratively designing the face of therapy.

Actually, when Stage 1 is minimized or rushed, clients with a history of complex trauma may simply stay locked in survival mind states, in some version of fight, flight, or freeze. Practitioners may unwittingly experience their clients as resistant and a negative cycle of interaction envelops the therapeutic context. When the blueprint for therapy follows a strengths-based and natural cycle of evolution, stress reactions are to be expected and can be managed collaboratively by creating a context for therapy and a context for change within each session. This stage of context creation might need to be repeated often in a session and during the overall therapy. When we look at growth and change in nature, we notice that the cycles are repeated, the sun, moon, and tide daily, whereas a tree repeats the same cycle annually. It is not therapeutic failure, nor a regression, it is the natural cycle of evolving—we call it *pause and ponder*. We pause and cocoon, taking time to recognize the pause and then we gently expand to new thoughts, behaviors, and feelings. Growth and change is a repetitive cycle. We cannot improve in any area of our life without repetition, thus we repeat the pause and ponder cycles over and over again within the session and throughout treatment.

In a recent first interview the following dialogue took place.

Therapist: Can you tell me everything about all your past therapy and treatment that worked and did not work for you? What did you like and what did you not like?

(At this point the therapist observes the client shutting down. Her skin became pale, she looked off into space, broke the previous eye contact, and did not say a word or make a move.)

Therapist: Remember when you told me that you often shut down as a coping skill? Did it just happen? You look like you might have shut down?

Client: Yeah. I did.

Therapist: Do you have any idea what might have happened? Do you know what I did that might have triggered the shut down?

Client: You asked me to make a decision.

In paying attention and asking questions, the therapist and the client learned important information about the client and their burgeoning therapeutic relationship. They learned that decision making, in the presence of this therapist at least, threatened the client and she shut down. Knowing this information allowed the therapist to create a context where the client would feel more empowered, safe, heard, understood, and secure before she was asked difficult questions.

Stage 1 has seven core components: creating refuge; assessing vulnerabilities and the function of the symptom; assessing resources; exploring the positive and negative consequences of change; understanding and validating client's denial, availability, and attachment; setting goals (which is not discussed in this chapter); and introducing acknowledgment. All seven components happen in Stage 1 though in an order that fits for each therapist and client encounter. For the purpose of a coherent narrative, however, each of these principles is described separately.

Creating Refuge

Strengths-based practice is grounded in encouraging clients to experience themselves as safe and secure enough to change. Safety has to come before evolving can take place. Similar to Siegel's four Ss (seen, safe, soothe, and secure) safety is part of the therapeutic context and relationship, and is practiced interpersonally and internally. We talk with clients at our first encounters about safe places, safe moments, and safe memories that they can access in therapy and outside of therapy when they experience stress. Creating refuge includes exploring safety, understanding the cultural and contextual variables that may interfere with experiences of safety, multidirected partiality (Bozsormenyi-Nagy & Krasner, 1986), and pretreatment planning.

We train thousands of practitioners in the CCM and spend as much time and energy on Stage 1 with practitioners as we expect them to spend with their clients. CCM therapists must experience safety, both physically and emotionally, in their offices as well. Although the metaphor is overused, reminding therapists to put their oxygen masks on before they help clients' put theirs on is an apt comparison. To do strengths-based work, therapists must be filled with hope. When depleted, frustrated, and/or experiencing yourself as useless, hope is often the first belief to go. To do good work, therapists must be ethically attuned to their clients (see Barrett & Stone Fish 2014 for further detail). Practitioners often experience profound satisfaction when their clients are making progress. When clients have more difficulty, which is often the case with clients who have experienced complex trauma, they may trigger uncomfortable thoughts and feelings for the practitioner. Without proper Stage 1 work on themselves (recognizing when they do not feel safe and secure and acquiring techniques for returning to their engaged mind states) practitioners may lose balance and end up being less helpful than they could be. Doing well with clients with complex trauma histories requires that therapists be grounded in the CCM, and be in supervision and/or consultation with other therapists so that they are always engaged in supportive and helpful environments.

Once we have created refuge within, it is time to consider safety with our clients. We ask clients about their internal and interpersonal harnesses. Harnesses are those resources which keep us grounded, calm, cool, and collected. We may explore these harnesses experientially with clients and/ or if grounded in somatic experiential theory and technique (e.g., Miller-Karas, 2015), may have clients go into their bodies to experience these resources. If we think it might be helpful, we might also ask clients to think about a time in their childhood when they felt safe and to draw that particular moment on a sheet of paper. We, again, are as transparent as possible, and always open to the possibility that no safe place arises. If they are able to access safety through such an exercise, we let clients know that this drawing is for them and that they do not have to share it with us, encouraging a sense of boundaries and empowerment.

We let clients know that our intent is to create this experience of safety within the context of the therapeutic relationship. We explain that the experience of safety is felt when we are calm, centered, and grounded, when we are in control and experience agency and the ability to be competent. We experience a sense of balance and serenity. When we feel safe, if we sense danger, we sense that we have harnesses in place to tolerate stress, we are capable of coping well, and we feel supported by other(s).

Contextual Variables

Strengths-based trauma-informed practice helps therapists and clients focus on creating refuge from contextual variables that dehumanize clients and leave them vulnerable to re-traumatizing events (Stone Fish & Harvey, 2005). Contextual variables that zap strength include but are not limited to variables such as gender, age, religion, race, class, and sexual and gender identity. In Stage 1, we ask about how the sociopolitical culture negatively and positively impacts our clients. Much of what mental health training teaches us is about how the majority culture pathologizes minority cultures and the effects of marginalization. These are real issues and we want to make sure these influences do not negatively impact the positive development of therapeutic relationships. So for example, when we train male therapists working with clients who have been traumatized, we help them acknowledge sexism and the undue privilege they experience based on their gender in the same way we urge white therapists to be cognizant of how their white privilege informs their therapeutic relationships. We ask about how clients feel powerless, damaged, out of control, or disconnected because of their sociopolitical contexts.

What training often fails to acknowledge, however, are the strengths inherent in many minority cultures and communities that offer great social support for our clients. When we have not been trained to see, we forget to ask and treatment may lack this important resource if the therapist does not make a deliberate effort to ask. For example, Rachel sought therapy because she had been sexually abused by her Rabbi as an adolescent. She discussed how the Rabbi traumatized her, not only through his abuse, but because she could not do anything associated with Judaism, nor walk into a temple, because of the impact and memories of what he had done. Rachel's therapist asked her to think about ways her religious practice was a resource, in what ways she felt connected, in control, and powerful in relation to religion and spirituality and how she could develop that now. Rachel found another synagogue, led by a progressive female Rabbi and developed community, that became a vital and important part of her healing context. Had her therapist not been curious about contextual resources, this may never have happened.

Multidirected Partiality

As part of creating refuge in the CCM, we discuss with clients who is or was in their social networks and how we might use those individuals as resources in the process of therapy. Boszormenyi-Nagy and Krasner's (1986) concept of therapeutic multidirected partiality is something we explain to clients. While in all clients' lives there are victims and perpetrators, the concept of multidirected partiality suggests that every member of a client's context is worthy of care and consideration. Although many clients cut off from or give up on multiple people in their social networks, it is our experience that there are untapped resources of social support that may not be mined unless the therapist has a strengths-based approach. There are relationships in our clients' lives that are toxic, dangerous, and unsafe. These are usually not relationships in which clients receive much in the way of love and support. There are, however, other relationships, sometimes tied to toxic relationships, that can be mined. Helping our clients develop a different understanding of their relationships, with the concomitant development from the guarded survival mind state to the more receptive engaged mind state, is a beginning conversation in creating a context for change.

Although we believe that every person in a client's life is worthy of care, strengths-based work requires safety consciousness, and we must always seek to determine the risk of harm to clients outside the therapy office. Part of creating a context for change is helping clients assess their current level of safety interpersonally and internally. We often create informal or formal safety commitment contracts that are continuously revisited throughout therapy. Safety contracts can be designed as casually or as detailed as the threat of harm demands. In many ways, Stage 1 can actually be conceptualized as designing an overall interpersonal and internal physical safety plan. One goal of therapy is for clients to find refuge and safety in their lives and to be able to access it when necessary. This is an important way to use the pause and ponder sequence. We help clients take a safety inventory in a pause moment, then re-engage and explore safety, then expand by designing a safety plan, which is examined in each subsequent session.

Pretreatment Planning

Pretreatment planning is a necessary and significant part of any strengths-based, transparent, and collaborative protocol and part of creating refuge. We often compare the CCM to a blueprint for building a house, once you have the blueprint then you communicate with the contractor and the subcontractor and make sure everyone is on board and properly tooled to complete the job. Pretreatment planning includes the collaborative measures taken to build a team with professional and personal people involved in our clients' lives. Strengths-based practice values influence from people who may be able to facilitate the metamorphosis from a reactive to a responsive environment. We begin this process by reviewing past experiences with helping professionals. We ask about other helping professionals: teachers, caseworkers, probation officers, physicians, nurses, alternative healers, psychotherapists, etc. We are interested in both the helpful and the unhelpful interactions and relationships, those that harness the natural cycle of growth as well as those that inhibit growth and development. If we discover, for example, that one of our clients had a positive relationship with a middle school teacher, we ask about the specific nature of that relationship and what was helpful.

Pretreatment planning introduces collaborative work with other professionals in our clients' lives. When possible, we talk to other professionals with our clients present to create a collaborative and transparent treatment plan. We also discover other professionals' expectations for our clients and their goals for treatment. We attempt to clarify roles so that duplication of services does not occur, and so that as many of the clients' needs are met as possible. Ideally, we meet periodically throughout the treatment process.

Pretreatment planning also considers clients' social network, family, and friendship connections. Many clients with a history of complex trauma have supportive relationships that are undervalued, under recognized and underutilized. We focus our curiosity around the nature of relationships that support engaged mind states contrasted with those in which clients are caught in interactional cycles of survival. Therapists and clients often focus exclusively on survival cycles and dangerous relationships that we forget to ask about the "angels" in our clients' lives. Of course, asking about safety and violence in all of our clients' relationships is important and needs to be done in individual sessions in a way that promotes self-disclosure. We discuss duty to report and informed, mindful, and engaged ways to probe clients about unsafe relationships in our book (Barrett & Stone Fish, 2014). Strengths-based trauma-informed practice is clear, transparent, and collaborative and clients are partners in keeping themselves and contexts as safe as possible.

Individual, couple, family, and group therapy are discussed in pretreatment planning as options for treatment at different stages of change so if violence makes it unsafe to see individuals together, the blueprint already accounts for individual treatment. Exploration of pretreatment variables may be threatening to clients with a history of complex trauma so that in-session behavior from clients may be from a survival mind state. When we notice clients react, it is time for the clinician to pause, and in the moment recreate safety through techniques that bring clients into a more engaged mind state.

Assessing Vulnerabilities and the Function of the Symptom

The second part of creating a context for change is assessing vulnerabilities and the function of the symptom. We introduce the idea that when people feel vulnerable, they act to feel powerful, in control, and/or to feel valued. We explore the connection between vulnerabilities and symptoms. We believe that the function of many symptoms that clients bring into therapy is to help them feel powerful, in control, and valued. When individuals in survival mind states feel fear and vulnerability, they act to feel powerful, in control, and valued. Because they act from survival mind states, the reactions often become symptoms. The function of the symptom is to help feel less fearful and vulnerable but symptoms end up not being helpful (which is why they are called symptoms). Rather than looking at symptoms as weaknesses, they are framed as attempts to cope with feelings that are experienced as unmanageable.

We assess vulnerabilities internally and interpersonally. Internally, we are curious about mind and body symptoms that make it difficult for clients to function. Flashbacks, states of disassociation, and nightmares are examples of symptoms as are body aches and pains, self-harm, anxiety, depression, suicidality, eating disorders, and/or drug and alcohol use and abuse. Abusive behaviors towards others in the form of emotional, verbal, physical, and/or sexual maltreatment are assessed. When acknowledging the functional and protective nature of the symptoms, we are accessing their strengths and resources. For these symptoms at one time "worked" for the client, helping them avoid painful feelings, memories, and dangerous situations. These symptoms no longer work, yet we can call upon other of the clients' strengths to create new behaviors that are less avoidant and potentially less harmful to the client. Some clients enter therapy already acknowledging that symptoms are used to cope with vulnerabilities while others experience feeling powerless, out of control, and devalued but have no insight into how or why this occurs.

Intimate relationships that are chaotic or avoidant are seen as vulnerabilities as well. Vulnerabilities and the function of symptoms are often two sides of the same coin in almost all vulnerabilities, particularly where relationships are concerned. When clients have been traumatized in intimate relationships they are likely to avoid or resist intimacy so the function of the symptom ends up making them more vulnerable. Pushing people away or alienating them with one's behavior serves to increase vulnerability. Strengths-based trauma-informed practice does not shy away from difficulties in our clients' lives, it helps make sense of them as coping strategies that have been helpful in the past.

Assessing Resources

Assessing resources is as important as assessing vulnerabilities because clients' strengths are the cornerstone to the healing process and to a strengths-based approach to treatment. Resources are the non-symptomatic behaviors that we use to help regain power, control, and value. Although clients often enter therapy in despair with the firm belief that they are continually experiencing symptoms they are not, in fact, always symptomatic. We explore resources as both a way to work towards safety and a means to effect change. An awareness of the clients' resources will help create a context of change while an awareness of their vulnerabilities will help design later interventions. For example, if a client is an introvert, we would not recommend group psychotherapy in the initial phase of treatment. Clients prone to introversion might have difficulty in a psychotherapy group because they have to engage with other people. While inability to engage in social support may keep them stuck in survival mind states, introversion is actually seen as a resource that is highlighted in Stage 1.

Resource assessment is similar to vulnerability assessment in that we are curious about internal and interpersonal resources. Internally, we ask about ways that clients have used resources to be able to experience being in control, powerful, and connected. We ask about psychiatric medication, and sometimes clients report that medication is the only thing that they can count on to calm them down and feel in control. We believe it is important to discuss our collaboration with the medical community and how useful it may be to have a thorough psychiatric evaluation in circumstances surrounding medication. Clients have told us that they really appreciate this discussion in the beginning stage of therapy. They contrast our approach with previous therapists who have suggested a psychiatric evaluation in a middle stage of therapy, causing clients to wonder whether their therapist believed they were mentally ill and what they said or did to alarm them. Terry's quote is a good example of assessing resources in therapy.

Terry is a 45-year-old teacher whose earliest memories include being in a car accident in which his father drove into a tractor-trailer and killed his mother and younger brother. Terry developed such severe anxiety symptoms whenever a school shooting occurred in another community that his survival mind state made it impossible for him to function in the classroom. He was interviewed after treatment about what he remembered being helpful:

> In the second or third interview, I had brought a cycling helmet into session because I was training for a half Ironman. My therapist asked me about the training and throughout therapy, which lasted about a year, she kept going back to something I said in that session about my confidence in my athletic abilities. Whenever I would feel defeated, fearful, anxious, or depressed, she would somehow bring it back to my confidence as an athlete, how I felt powerful and in control while biking and running and actually swimming as well. I guess I assumed therapy would be all about me opening up the past and learning new ways to focus on the present but instead it felt like she was encouraging me to hold onto what was good and build different kinds of muscles as well (Barrett & Stone Fish, 2014, p. 94).

Resources are interpersonal as well. Clients feel powerful, in control, valued, and connected in some of their friendship networks, extended family, and work or mentoring contexts. While there are many people in our clients' lives who have treated them horribly, there are often a few who have been angels and who have enabled and encouraged their progress in life. An integral aspect of strengths-based trauma-informed therapy is bringing these angels into the change process, figuratively or in reality. When inquiring about relationships in which clients feel valued, we often find themes that these relationships have in common and they can be highlighted in the therapeutic relationship. So, for example, in Terry's case, when he was asked about relationships where he felt powerful, in control, valued, and connected, he talked about friends and colleagues who shared his sense of humor. His therapist asked whether that was something he wanted to bring into their relationship and they talked about the use of humor as a resilient but sometimes delicate response to traumatic events.

Strengths-based trauma-informed practice also highlights the value of community as a resource for practitioners as well as clients. Working with clients who have a history of complex trauma is difficult work that is best done in collaboration with other professionals and gathering as much support as possible. None of us are expert at everything. Most communities are filled with practitioners who are experts in areas that a particular therapist is not and it is the expectation that practitioners consult with and refer clients to other strengths-based trauma-informed practitioners throughout the community.

Exploring the Positive and Negative Consequences of Change

The fourth component to creating a context for change is discussing the positive and negative consequences of change. When we discuss the positive and negative consequences of change for specific goals our clients are setting, we help them begin the process of using their engaged mind state. Thinking about change can be a trigger into survival mind states because change is uncomfortable, and breeds uncertainty, which may trigger fear and danger. When we are thoughtfully engaged in articulating some of the possibilities that the change process elicits, we help clients begin to experience some control over a process in which they have felt powerless in the past. Communicating and being mindful, which are two of the important components to engaged mind states, helps clients experience the possibility that they can indeed change and that their lives will improve.

In the process of engaging in creating a context for change, clients begin to understand that the symptoms they have been experiencing, which are incredibly painful, have their uses. They have come to recognize, for example, that cutoff keeps them from experiencing rejection or that anger outbursts keep them from getting hurt. What they are learning in this part of therapy is how these negative consequences keep them stuck in survival mind states and in interactional cycles of survival. Therapy, by its very nature, is intended to change clients' lives. In the change process, we may leave behind things that we may not be aware we will miss until we miss them. Preparing clients for what they will miss makes it easier when they come up against the negative consequence of embarking on the journey they are taking.

Many clients come to therapy to work on intimate relationships that they know are clearly destructive. Although clients can give you all the reasons they should leave these toxic relationships, they are often unable to extricate themselves, and if they do, they are pulled back in all over again. Family members and friends have told them they deserve better than this, that the person they are involved with is abusive, neglectful, not worthy of them, using them, and does not value them. It is obvious that clients and their communities clearly understand the likely positive consequences of change. They know that leaving this destructive relationship will please those who worry about them, free them to be available to meet someone who will treat them better, and will enable them to start living the life they deserve and had always imagined for themselves. It is much more difficult, however, for them to contemplate the negative consequences of leaving the relationship.

The negative consequences of leaving the relationship are often covert and avoided and become part of a negative interactional cycle. One negative consequence, for example, is fear of how the break up will affect the partner. They may fear that partners will harm themselves, the client, or other loved ones. Consequently they wrestle with their sense of responsibility for this aggression. This is a complicated dilemma because family and friends have told them repeatedly that they only have control over their own thoughts, feelings, and behavior. On the other hand, our clients have the lived experience of how other people have impacted—if not completely dominated—their thoughts, feeling, and behaviors. When we talk about the negative consequences of change, we must take into account the stark reality of destructive, toxic, and/or abusive relationships and how difficult they are to leave.

Another negative consequence of leaving a relationship that is toxic is the feeling that people have about themselves. Most people do not enter into a loving relationship with the motivation to hurt someone else. Even adult children in toxic relationships with their parents who may be angry at their behavior use their anger to protect themselves, not necessarily to hurt another. Most people do not like to think of themselves as perpetrators of others' harm. "I am not a bad person, I am a good person and it is not my intention to hurt anyone," is a mantra we hear over and over again when people think about their own behavior. The negative consequence of leaving a relationship is that it hurts others and flies in the face of our definition of self. This needs to be acknowledged as we move forward in the change process.

Self-destructive behavior provides another opportunity to explore the positive and negative consequences of change. Clients may come to therapy ready to acknowledge that overeating, for example, is starting to become problematic but they are unaware of how the negative consequences of stopping are going to be addressed. Overeating is a convenient way to relax and forget about your problems. Abstaining completely or even reducing frequency or quantity of average consumption may very well result in having to face problems that feel insurmountable. Discussing the negative consequences of change examines the specifics of how overeating helps clients cope, and helps the client project what losses will be experienced when this coping mechanism is no longer utilized.

The intent behind addressing negative and positive consequences is to acknowledge major behavioral patterns and minor ones. Each time a change is warranted, negative and positive consequences should be discussed. So, for example, if a partner states that she wants to spend more time with her partner, she is encouraged to identify what she would be losing. This ensures that the change process, when it occurs, becomes something that the client implements with full awareness. When clients examine both positive and negative consequences and recognize that the advantages to changing outweigh the disadvantages then they are ready to take the risk of the negative consequences. We often find, if we do not spend enough time discussing this component to creating a context for change, that we become more invested in the change process than the client.

Understanding and Validating Denial, Availability, and Attachment

The human brain allows us to function by compartmentalizing experiences, thoughts, and emotions. Although this is a highly successful survival strategy in everyday life, when our brains compartmentalize certain aspects of our experience, our engaged mind is less available. Many clients who have not had the experience of being able to self soothe when in distress adapt by compartmentalizing painful feelings. These feelings are then, often, unavailable for processing and therefore misunderstood. The feelings are there and clients react from them but they often do not have access to them in a way that is helpful.

Attachment style affects our ability to access emotional states, process memory, and understand responsibility in relationships. Clients who have attachment styles that tend to be avoidant, preoccupied, disorganized, insecure, or dismissive often have a difficult time directly accessing and controlling emotions and so are often unavailable to themselves and others. They may have trouble taking responsibility for their behaviors or acknowledging the impact of their behavior on self and others. They may also have difficulty acknowledging the impact of others' behaviors on them, or simply even remembering facts, or situations. Clients who are lucky enough to have lived with responsive caregivers have a mediating variable that is not present with clients whose attachment to caregivers is not secure. Responsive caregiving facilitates the capacity to stay present in the moment and incorporate new information and access most aspects of their experience, in other words, to be in an engaged mind state. In creating a context for change, we explore denial, availability, and attachment.

Our strengths-based perspective conceptualizes denial as a strategy formulated—consciously or unconsciously—while in a survival mind state. The process of compartmentalizing and denying material is a coping mechanism for surviving unmanageable stress. The problem, of course, is that in a survival mind state, most stress is perceived as dangerous and unmanageable. The survival mind is singularly focused on the perceived threat and lacks access to engaged mindfulness and feelings of control, power, value, and connection. Instead, in survival mind state, threat makes it so that we do not have available an awareness of the facts, the impact, and/or our relationship to what is occurring. This lack of availability is another way to look at dissociation and denial. We simply speak of what we have available to us in the real or perceived moment.

It may seem counterintuitive to validate a part of behavior that we have learned in our training is a defense mechanism that keeps people from being honest with themselves and others. In fact, this unavailability is alive and working in almost every situation of complex trauma. Part of creating a context for safety includes understanding the importance and the effects of unavailability in clients' lives. The unavailability exists internally and interpersonally. We experience this, as therapists, in the room with our clients, when they do not have an experience available to themselves or when we are aware they are no longer available in therapy or engaged with family members.

When clients are able to acknowledge the effects of complex trauma and how their behavior is affected by it, and how their behaviors and feelings affect others, they have integrated a strengths-based trauma-informed perspective. It is paradoxical that one way to survive a threatening thought, feeling, or action, whether triggered internally or interpersonally, is to avoid the facts of the trigger, the impact of the trigger, or to take responsibility for the threat. Yet it often occurs that, in order to survive a perceived threat, avoiding its existence allows us to survive. Although adaptive for a while, however, we often adapt by becoming unavailable to the narrative of our lives or the narrative becomes unavailable to us. When clients understand how the adaptation was useful, take responsibility for the ways in which it has outgrown its usefulness, and are open to the possibility of experiencing life differently, they are ready to move on with the change process.

Introducing Acknowledgment

We believe that the role of acknowledgment is one of the most powerful and most underutilized interventions in therapy with complex trauma. Acknowledgment is the burgeoning recognition of how clients understand their symptoms and how they contribute to their problem cycles. Acknowledgment is an increasing awareness of impact, facts, and responsibility, and clear statements about what they are committed to changing. Each acknowledgment in a session can easily be woven into the client's goals. So once again, just like the cycle of change and the stages of therapy, acknowledgments happen repeatedly during a session, and throughout the stages of treatment. When a client acknowledges a thought, a feeling, or a behavior during a session it is the practitioner's responsibility to capture that moment and integrate it into the process of change.

Client:	I just wish I knew how to handle my anger.
CCM Therapist:	Wishing that you knew how to handle your anger is a great start. Recognizing that you want that to change is incredibly important. Should we make that one of our goals?
Client:	Sure, sounds like a good idea.
CCM Therapist:	Let me share with you some of my ideas of how we might learn some skills that will help you meet your goal.

Following is another example:

Client:	I have absolutely no idea of how to handle my daughter's cutting. I just don't understand it! I am completely overwhelmed.
CCM Therapist:	You saying that and me knowing that is really helpful. I bet her cutting is triggering a lot for you, which makes it even harder to know what to do.
Client:	That is for sure.

CCM Therapist: You recognizing that gives me some ideas about the direction our sessions could go. You are acknowledging that you feel overwhelmed and you have acknowledged before that when you feel overwhelmed you retreat and, using your words, "go home and lick your wounds." You've also talked about wanting to be more involved in parenting her so we can work on different things for you to do when you are overwhelmed instead of retreating.

Acknowledgment sessions signal the end of Stage 1, and are the set-up for Stage 2. It seems as if, once people can acknowledge that what they have been doing is not working and that they have the power and control to change their behavior, we can move into Stage 2, which is the work of changing that behavior. Acknowledgment sessions are another example of the importance of an organized approach to treatment. They mark the delineation between stages when working on a specific goal.

Remember that a person can be in Stage 1 in one form of treatment and Stage 2 in another. For example, a couple may work all the parts of Stage 1 and then acknowledge how they contribute to their interactional cycle of survival and clearly be ready to start making changes, which is Stage 2 work. Although in Stage 2, however, when they begin to struggle with communication and deeper intimacy, one partner or both may realize that there are some individual or family of origin issues that they must address and for those issues, we pause and reorganize, utilizing Stage 1 language and interventions. Refocusing on safety, goals, assessment of needs, and resources is not conceptualized as a regression or set back to Stage 1. Rather, this oscillation is a simple and elegant part of the natural cycle of change, which includes pausing, regrouping, refocusing, and then moving into expansion. Like the blueprint for a house informs construction, we are forever running into unforeseen circumstances in which we must consult the blueprint, so that we can move forward in a constructive way that respects clients' needs for feeling valued, in control, and powerful.

Acknowledgment sessions can be formal or informal. Some of this depends on the practitioner's style and work environment, and some depends on the clients, their particular situation, and why they were referred for treatment. When practitioners work in formal environments where paperwork is completed at the end of Stage 1, then acknowledgment sessions are more formal. Acknowledgment occurs and a treatment plan is designed which begins Stage 2. In some agencies, acknowledgments and a treatment plan are written and signed by both clients and practitioners or even by the team that is working with the clients. In less formal settings, acknowledgments may not be formally documented but they nevertheless must occur for treatment to move to Stage 2.

When treatment is mandated by the judicial system then the acknowledgment sessions tend to be more formal as well. Probation officers, caseworkers, and judges may want a formal statement not only that their clients are following through on treatment but also that they have acknowledged problematic behavior and have established concrete goals towards working on change. When working with other professionals, the CCM practitioner can explain to all involved how Stage 1 sets the stage for helping clients reach treatment goals in Stage 2 so that everyone is working the model together.

Case Example

Jody Smith (21) and James Smith (22), a white, heterosexual couple, had their two daughters (a 3 year old and a 1 year old) removed from their home after a neighbor called the police because Jody and James left the girls home alone. The girls were staying with James' aunt and the couple was mandated to attend parenting classes and engage in family therapy. They were assigned to Kaylea, a CCM-trained practitioner. When Jody and James began treatment, they wanted the girls back and blamed the neighbor for them being removed. In the first session, James stated: "We are coming here to get the girls back and we will do anything you tell us but just to be clear, we did nothing wrong. The bitch who reported us did it for revenge. I called the police on her boyfriend last month because he pulled a gun on me and she wants me to pay. I'm thinking about calling a lawyer and suing her ass." Jody agreed with James. Kaylea appreciated the couple's perspective and their goals for therapy and explained how she could help them reach their goals. She understood, at this point, that they both felt powerless, devalued, and out of control, and she expected therapy to help them change this.

Creating Refuge

Kaylea talked with Jody and James about safety both outside and inside the therapy room. Both expressed a great deal of rage at their neighbor, Jody's mother, and James' parents for not taking the girls, and anger and blame towards each other for their current situation. They both acknowledged lots of yelling but a commitment to a non-violent relationship following an incident when they were first together that scared both of them enough to commit to, and to maintain, a pact to never touch each other or anyone else when they were mad. Affirming this tremendous accomplishment, Kaylea explored safety in the therapy room by talking with the couple about their experience of safety and by explaining the CCM stages and the change process. Following numerous conversations about safety, vulnerability, how the brain works, and survival mind states, Jody and James began to feel safe enough to explore some of their own behavior. They both acknowledged that they were quick to blame others for their problems, that they actually could use some parenting tips when they were overwhelmed, because everyone could, and that they did leave their children unattended on numerous occasions. They were not ready, however, to take responsibility for their behavior, nor for their children being taken from them.

Kaylea explored the couple's contextual variables that helped and hindered them. They shared experiences they both had had growing up feeling poor and "broken" compared with some of their peers, based on incidents that occurred in school and in their neighborhoods. Jody told a story about a school teacher that made her not trust the system to currently attend to her and her family's needs: "When I was in seventh grade, my family was evicted for like the tenth time and I came to school really tired and really late because we were sleeping on my auntie's couch and it was me and my sister and not a lot of room and we had to take two buses to get to school because she didn't live in the district. I walked into class one day, I'll never forget it, and this stupid teacher, in front of the entire class, looked at me with a huge scowl on her face and she said, 'what's the excuse this time Jody-girl, parents abandon you and run off to Vegas?' All the kids laughed, I turned bright red and slumped over to my desk. No apology, no nothing, the only notice I ever got was negative." Kaylea helped Jody make the connection between this and other horrific experiences as a child and teenager and her current experience of feeling powerless, disconnected, and devalued.

Assessing Vulnerabilities and Function of the Symptom

Because both Jody and James mistrusted authority, access to social support or outside help was threatening and dismissed. Child Protective Services had been called to their home on a few other occasions, and in-home family therapy was offered. The Smiths talked about how awful that experience was for them, they were angry and resistant and refused to try any of the techniques offered by the agency's puppet, which is what they called the in-home therapist. Kaylea and the Smiths discussed the function of their resistance. They felt powerless and devalued by Child Protective workers and the in-home therapist so they took whatever power they could muster to resist help. They both recognized, in fact, that this strategy was something they used with their families and their friends. They needed help with the children but when it was offered, it felt like criticism so they could not take it. Their coping mechanism, when dealing with unmanageable stress from trying to raise two small children on a limited budget and all alone, was to isolate and avoid anyone who might tell them that they were inadequate.

Assessing Resources

Jody and James, while alienated from family and neighbors, had created a united front against the world, which was a resource that Kaylea explored with them. They had never seen this as a strength and once they began to explore it, noticed that they had another untapped resource in their biking community that they could use. The Smiths were avid motorcyclists and were part of a community of cyclists who acted as family members to each other and many had offered on numerous occasions to help Jody and James with their daughters, yet Jody and James had never taken them up on their offers because of their avoidance of social support. The other untapped resources they had going for them was their work ethic. They were both employed full time and well respected at their jobs. Part of the reason they had left the children unattended had to do with work schedules that were inflexible so there were certain hours of the day when they both had to be at work. Because they had no help with the children and took their responsibilities seriously at work, the children were removed. Jody and James had taken their work ethic for granted until it was highlighted as a tremendous strength by Kaylea and offered up as a hopeful ingredient in putting their lives back together.

Exploring the Positive and Negative Consequences of Change

When Kaylea first introduced this concept to the Smiths, neither Jody nor James could think of any negative consequence to getting their girls back. Kaylea worked hard to help them see some of the negative consequences. For the Smiths to be the kind of parents they wanted to be, they had to acknowledge that they needed help from other people. The negative consequences of asking for help were many; they could be disappointed, they could get criticized, the children could get hurt by other people, the children could get close to other people, which might cause envy for the Smiths; that is, their united front might crumble, et cetera. Each of these consequences was explored in detail and discussions ensued about what they would do if and when any of these things occurred. The fear of facing what felt to both of them was unmanageable stress, if they let others into their lives, helped them recognize why change was so intimidating. In Stage 1, Kaylea made it clear to the Smiths that she was not asking them to change their behavior, just to acknowledge the complexity of the change process.

Understanding and Validating Client's Denial, Availability, and Attachment

Once safety was established and the Smiths began to trust Kaylea, they began talking about the consequences of leaving young children unattended. In the initial interviews, Jody and James denied leaving the girls alone. Once they felt safe with Kaylea, they were able to acknowledge that they did leave the girls alone but it only happened a couple of times and the girls were asleep and never noticed they were gone and they had no other options, and this was the best thing for their family, and more excuses ensued. As Kaylea explored the concepts of denial, availability, and attachment with the Smiths, they shared more about what actually happened. In fact, the girls had been left alone on numerous occasions when they had no babysitters and two to three hours of work overlap and a few times had been badly hurt. They left them in a pack-n-play once and came home to find the younger stuck under the equipment with a broken arm after the elder had gotten out by toppling it. Child Protective Services had been called once when the elder was found in the street, having been able to open the front door to their apartment and leave the building. They also came home once to find the elder daughter feeding the younger fried chicken wings with bones in them that she had found in the refrigerator. Jody shared this incident in therapy and James admitted that it was the first time he had heard it.

While Kaylea fully acknowledged that what the Smiths had done was troubling, illegal, and unsafe, she also explored with both Jody and James how these incidents could have occurred. She told them that the human brain has the ability to compartmentalize experiences, thought, reactions, and emotions so that we can function. While this is a successful survival strategy, when we compartmentalize certain aspects of our experience, our engaged mind state is less available. Because Jody and James believed that they had to leave their children alone to survive, they denied, not only that they were doing it, but also that it had severe consequences. In order for them to move into Stage 2 of treatment, and just as important, before they could be safe enough to parent their children again, they had to acknowledge that what they did was wrong and that it had profound and serious consequences for their children.

Introducing Acknowledgment

Many sessions ensued with Kaylea helping James and Jody acknowledge their behavior without blaming others. Kaylea, the caseworker, and the Smiths met together many times to discuss progress and unsupervised visits with the girls. They all agreed that unsupervised visits had to wait until both parents were able to acknowledge their behavior and its direct contribution to the girls' placement outside their home. Kaylea continued to explore the Smiths' understanding of their survival mind states, their vulnerabilities, and their resources. The Smiths saw danger, disappointment, and criticism everywhere and both responded by retreating, avoiding, and blaming. Kaylea continued to remind them that they knew how to work hard and help each other and that they could use these skills to be self-reflective and engage in mindful contemplation of how they could tolerate acknowledging that they had made mistakes and needed help. She reminded them of the cycle of change, that pause and ponder does not have to be frightening, and that they could practice self-soothing techniques and lean on and encourage each other to take responsibility for their behavior.

Acknowledgment is the acceptance and open admission that we have a problem and that we will address it. Acknowledgment involves taking responsibility for the impact of our behavior and is a process integral to change. Immediately after one supervised visit, James and Jody came to session depleted and withdrawn. When Kaylea gently probed into their drained expressions, Jody broke out in sobs of grief and James put his arm around her shoulder. When she was finally able to put words to her sorrow, Jody talked about how vulnerable her little girls are and how scared they must have been when they were left on their own. "No one saw how vulnerable I was growing up and so I guess I just figured I shouldn't see theirs but I was wrong. I am their mother and I should have protected them." "It is not too late," Kaylea said, "it is not too late." Slowly but surely, with enough encouragement, collaboration, and hope, both James and Jody were able to acknowledge that they could not leave the girls home alone and that they could not parent alone and that they needed help.

Mindfully following the natural flow of change by helping a client stay grounded and organizing the session through the use of a strengths-based model is in our experience the most effective way to create and sustain change both inside and outside of the office. The therapists use their own strengths to stay attuned to the client's trauma state and then to creatively design interventions to interrupt traumatic patterns, inside and outside of the office, and then to help the client develop alternative pathways to create and maintain healing. The interventions and therapeutic models used need to be based on the strengths of the clients and collaboratively designed and agreed upon between therapist and client. Together they are the treatment team. We believe and, through years of qualitative interviews with clients, have confirmed that change happens as a result of the strengths-based energy that comes from our minds, our hearts, and our souls. It is the exchange of this energy through our relationships, through our hope, our creative ideas, and our passion and compassion that we continue to create energy between us that will produce the desired change.

References

Badenoch, B. (2011). *The brain savvy therapists' workbook: A companion to being a brain-wise therapist.* New York, NY: W.W. Norton.

Barrett, M.J. & Stone Fish, L. (2014). *Treating complex trauma: A relational blueprint for collaboration and change.* New York, NY: Routledge.

Bloom, S. (1997). *Creating sanctuary: Toward the evolution of sane societies.* New York, NY: Routledge.

Boszormenyi-Nagy, I., & Krasner, B. (1986). *Between give and take: A clinical guide to contextual therapy.* New York, NY: Brunner/Mazel.

Briere, J.N. & Scott, C. (2012). *Principles of trauma therapy: A guide to symptoms, evaluation, and treatment.* New York, NY: Sage.

Courtois, C.A. & Ford, J.D. (2012). *Treating complex trauma: A sequenced, relationship approach.* New York, NY: Guilford Press.

Ford, J.D. (2009). Neurobiological and developmental research: Clinical implications. In C.A. Courtois & J.D. Ford (Eds.) *Treating complex traumatic stress disorders: An evidence-based guide.* New York, NY: Guilford Press.

Greenwald, R. (2007). *EMDR within a phase model of trauma-informed treatment.* New York, NY: Routledge.

Herman, J.L. (1992). *Trauma and recovery: The aftermath of violence-from domestic abuse to political terror.* New York, NY: Basic Books.

Hughes, D.A. (2006). *Building the bonds of attachment: Awakening love in deeply troubled children.* New York, NY: Jason Aronson.

Johnson, S. (2005). *Emotionally focused couple therapy with trauma survivors: Strengthening attachment bonds.* New York, NY: Guilford Press.

Levine, P.A. (2010). *In an unspoken voice: How the body releases trauma and restores goodness.* Berkeley, CA: North Atlantic Books.

Miller-Karas, E. (2015). *Building resilience to trauma: The trauma and community resiliency models.* New York, NY: Routledge.

Muller, R.T. (2010). *Trauma and the avoidant client: Attachment-based strategies for healing.* New York, NY: W.W. Norton.

Siegel, D.J. (2010). *The mindful therapist: A clinician's guide to mindsight and neural integration.* New York, NY: W.W. Norton.

Siegel, D.J. (2012, March). *Keynote address: The attuned therapist.* Psychotherapy Networker Conference, Washington, DC.

Siegel, D.J. (2015). *The developing mind: How relationships and the brain interact to shape who we are* (2nd ed.). New York, NY: Guilford Press.

Stone Fish, L., & Harvey, R.C. (2005). *Nurturing queer youth: Family therapy transformed.* New York, NY: W.W. Norton.

Trepper, T., & Barrett, M.J. (Eds.) (1986). *Treating incest: A multiple systems perspective.* New York: Haworth Press.

Trepper, T., & Barrett, M.J. (1989). *Systemic treatment of incest: A therapeutic handbook.* New York, NY: Routledge.

Van der Kolk, B. (2014). *The body keeps the score: Brain, mind, and body in the healing of trauma.* New York, NY: Penguin Books.

4

Uncovery

Beneath the Monolith of Addiction
There Remains a Human Being

Andy Young

Introduction

Jane looked at her husband on the other side of the couch in my therapy office and with utter res-ignation and palpable fear in her voice asked, "Why can't you just accept the fact that you can't ever drink again? That's what everybody says you have to do." Steve looked back at her in an impotent silence. The words he could not seem to access that moment in his wife's presence for fear of once again compounding her despair, he had shared with me earlier, as he had with her a thousand times before. Steve earnestly felt abstinence was not the answer to his problem. He was not ready to accept that he was powerless over his drinking and, in fact, he felt it was his duty to regain, rather than forfeit, power over this area of his life for the sake of his marriage, his children, and even his own health. He desperately wanted to try managing his drinking.

There was a time early in my career when I would have largely had only one general response as the clinician in this situation. Having been trained in traditional addictions counseling theories and methods, heavily influenced by the Minnesota model and 12-step recovery (White, 2014), my response would likely have included gently working with Steve to overcome his denial and accept the severity of his alcoholism; encouraging him to engage in support groups wherein he would be exposed to a rigorous, formulaic, yet time-tested philosophy regarding how to stay sober; and helping his wife set clear, consistent boundaries to preserve her own wellbeing, even if Steve chose to remain sick. This time, however, my approach was somewhat different. But we'll get to that later.

Had my approach with Steve been as I just described, it's possible, even likely, that he would not have engaged in treatment very long, refused to attend self-help meetings, and could have returned to his pattern of heavy binge drinking fairly quickly. As pessimistic as this may sound, there is a litany of studies that bears out the uncomfortable fact that traditional substance abuse treatment—the models of which were honed into homogeny throughout the 20th century and remain, by and large, the norm today—is not nearly as effective as we once thought (Currie, 1993; Glaser, 2013; Glaser, 2015; Foote, Wilkens, Kosanke, & Higgs, 2014).

In recent years, however, a new development known as the recovery movement, or recovery model, has been emerging in the fields of addiction and mental health with an emphasis on recovery-oriented systems of care. I must admit, when I first learned of this movement I was initially underwhelmed, assuming it had more to do with semantics than anything else. After all, hadn't traditional substance abuse treatment been oriented toward recovery since its inception? What was so new about this recovery movement, I wondered. Its growing popularity, however, has made strides in advancing the addictions field—a field that for decades had arguably been growing dusty from tired methodologies that have shown minimal effectiveness. The movement is, in many ways, a significant departure from traditional treatment precepts. Although it builds on many time-tested themes of recovery, retaining their value, it also repurposes them in novel, less than intuitive ways. In this way it has breathed new life into both the treatment industry and, more importantly, the recovery community.

Although this chapter is in no way meant to be a thorough overview of the recovery model, we explore how this emerging movement differentiates itself from more traditional, long-standing ideas of addiction treatment and recovery, taking on an important role in the progression away from a deficit-based model to one of a strengths orientation. We also investigate ways in which this model may carry with it those very legacies of pathology and deficit it attempts to shed, so that we may more fully integrate recovery informed treatment strategies into the broader, unified strengths-based clinical model. The chapter will conclude with a review of several techniques that may be used to approach clinical substance abuse work from an integrated recovery-oriented, strengths-based perspective.

A Word about a Word

The title of this chapter introduces a word that you won't find in any dictionary at present. To be clear, I have no intention of launching a new counseling model or self-help movement with the label *Uncovery*. Rather, while contemplating the historic, etiological definition of addiction recovery through a strengths-based lens, it occurred to me that even the term *recovery* itself expresses a sense of deficit. To *recover* is to acquire again that which has been lost. To *discover*, on the other hand, is to acquire that which was never possessed before. Both of these terms imply a present state of deficit. A strengths-based perspective suggests that honoring personal agency is not so much about discovering or recovering, but rather uncovering those natural, perhaps untapped attributes that have been present all along.

Use of the term *Uncovery* could very easily, and perhaps rightly, be dismissed as wordplay. That's really all it is and clinicians need not quibble over what terminology should be used in order for therapy to be effective. My goal in using such a novel term simply stems from my belief, informed by the likes of Anderson (1997), Combs and Freedman (1996), and others, that a new languaging can potentially jar previously held paradigms enough to open a new clinical awareness of important elemental strengths that were there all along and transform our operational understanding of recovery into a truly strengths-based perspective.

Literature Review

In 1784, Dr. Benjamin Rush, a signer of the Declaration of Independence, issued a tract in which he referred to excessive alcohol use as a progressive medical condition (White, 2014). Despite this historically influential, compassionate, yet relatively isolated reference to alcoholism being a disease, what characterized the earliest discussions across the American landscape regarding problematic use of alcohol was a morally derived language of deficit. From prominent abolitionist Anthony Benezet, who in 1774 referred to those addicted to alcohol as having "lost the power of delivering themselves from the worst of bondages" (as cited in White, Kurtz, & Acker, 2001, p.7) to University of Vermont professor William Sweetser's 1829 assertion that "intemperance enslaved one's moral faculties in shackles" (as cited in White et al., 2001, p.11), a pervasive narrative was born that has sustained the shifting sands of public perception regarding alcoholism and addiction for over two centuries. In 1820 J.J. Bounds in *The Means of Curing and Preventing Intemperance* stated that the drunkard's depravity should be "considered a vice, treated with ridicule and contempt" (as cited in White et al., 2001,

p. 9). Contrary to Rush's allusion to alcoholism being a disease, Bounds went on to explicitly state it is not a disorder and is out of the reach of medicine.

The early roots of the broader social work field within the United States were similarly bound to an understanding that the maladies we think of today as mental illness were a result of moral deficiency (Rapp & Goscha, 2012). Influenced by a Judeo-Christian concept of human frailty, Rapp and Goscha noted that the emphasis was on naming and conquering a problem through moral conversion or punishment of those who transgress moral norms. Such religious overtones can be heard in the language of Lyman Beecher, cofounder of the influential American Temperance Society, who referred to heavy drinkers as "addicted to the sin" or "the evil habit" (as cited in White et al., 2001, p. 9).

Also in the collective conscience of the time was a stark belief that abstinence was essential to solving America's problem of chronic drunkenness. Beecher (as cited in White et al., 2001), for example, suggested that "the plague is scarcely more contagious or more deadly" and that "there is no remedy for intemperance but the cessation of it" (p. 9). Even in Benjamin Rush's early disease formulation, as pointed out by Levine (1978), one finds not only the grim language of moral deficit, including loss of control, but the necessity of total abstinence in order to be cured.

The latter half of the 19th century and into the next saw the antecedents of what would become the modern addictions field shifting away from this moral-volitional language toward strains of the medical model that was emerging in the broader psychology and social work fields. Although undoubtedly a good thing, this transition was not without tumult and contradiction. In 1881, for example, prominent temperance lecturer John Gough (1881) stated that "drunkenness is a sin but . . . also a disease . . . a physical as well as moral evil" (p. 443). An 1873 annual report of the American Temperance Society regarded "drunkenness as a sin and a disease—a sin first, then a disease" (as cited in Levine, 1978, p. 153) As noted by Thombs (2006), there was little concern at the time for the inconsistencies and inevitable questions raised by this intermingling of moral and medical constructions.

In the broader mental health fields, however, this intermingling was less overt. Psychoanalytic theory, for example, may have simply disguised the emphasis on human weakness and deficit through the use of more sophisticated definitions (Rapp & Goscha, 2012). Underneath the surface there remained a perception that the problem is natural to the person, that positive change is implemented externally, and that the clinician, rather than the afflicted individual, was therefore the expert (Rapp & Goscha, 2012). This was the setting in which modern addiction treatment was born.

In my own early training as an addictions counselor, I learned that the disease framework of addiction was both enlightened and therapeutic. I remember many engaging debates both with peers as a student and later with professional colleagues, exploring and questioning the work of Milam and Ketcham (1984), E.M. Jellinek (1960), David Ohlms (1983), and others regarding the validity of the disease concept. But what most of us seemed to understand was that, regardless of any intellectual positions, framing addiction as a disease helped many of our clients free themselves from the weight of shame hanging over them. Even if the science lacked rigor—for example, Jellinek's groundbreaking research, designed to offer scientific credibility to the growing claim of alcoholism as a disease and long held as the holy grail thereof, consisted of a meager sample size of only 98 male Alcoholics Anonymous (AA) members (Glaser, 2015), and Ohlms' once influential paper on the presence of tetrahydroisoquinoline (also known as "THIQ") in the brain seems to have been relegated to the fringes of the digital information superhighway—it was clear that the disease concept was at the very least a useful narrative for many in early recovery.

In this way, providing a clinical label offers a sense of control, even relief. The very act of naming gives shape to something otherwise mysterious and incomprehensible. As pioneering narrative therapists White and Epston (1990) discovered, externalizing a problem—placing it outside of the person and giving it a name—enhances one's sense of agency and creates a dialectical opposition one can therapeutically push against.

The value of the disease concept notwithstanding, it nevertheless remains that a pathology-based approach bears inherent conflicts with a strengths approach. As White (2007) points out, self-understanding can be framed as a narrative map. A map inherently highlights or obscures certain data, and no map reveals everything about the terrain it represents. When the central function of the clinical narrative, as seen in a diagnostic impression for example, is to highlight pathology, what is often obscured is the individual's competence. A collaborative sense of curiosity is often obscured in favor of clinical certainty and expertise (Hoyt, 2000). Despite lip service being offered to the notion of focusing on client strengths—usually in the form of one question tacked on to the end of a pathology-driven intake assessment—one would be hard pressed to find a truly strengths-based initial assessment in clinical use (Cowger, 1992).

Furthermore, the act of naming a problem carries the potential of becoming less than helpful due to what it takes away from, or even adds to, the clinical equation. For example, the process of clinical diagnosis is inherently disempowering. Both the act and language of naming belong to the professional and, thus, power is taken away from the client. As Rapp and Goscha note, the minute you give a problem a name, the problem not only belongs to the person but also expresses important presumed facts about the person. Having a problem places one in a different group, set apart from the rest who don't have that problem (Rapp & Goscha, 2012). Or, put another way, labels belong to deviations, not normalcies. In fact, normalcy is often assumed by the perceived absence of a label.

Not only is power displaced, information is taken away as well. The reductive process of diagnostic labeling often fails to account for several important factors including the personal meaning behind a struggle, strengths that are hidden within the story, as well as familial, social, and environmentally contextual factors. As Foote et al. suggest (2014), explaining everything through the 'addiction' lens can lead to all other problems being explained through this singular prism, leaving out important clues to recovery.

What is potentially added to the clinical equation by diagnostic labeling is the presence of new layers that compound the problem and complicate treatment. In their seminal work outlining the foundations of strategic family therapy, Watzlawick, Weakland, and Fisch (1974/2001) suggested that the placing of behavioral difficulties such as addictive substance use into diagnostic categories can create the perception of the problem having some monolithic, magical power that is nearly impossible to resolve. More broadly put, their belief was that a problem-saturated view is often carried into the clinical process of solution finding to such a degree that attempted solutions often maintain or exacerbate, rather than resolve, the targeted problem. They saw the overuse of a pathology framework to describe normative behaviors as a chief example of this.

For the person struggling with addiction this monolithic narrative is experienced as a sense of hopelessness or impossibility of returning to normalcy. Interestingly, and rather paradoxically, this very point may simultaneously be the spark of hope for those who find recovery through 12-step programs and traditional treatment as well as the linchpin of despair for those who find such programs alienating and ineffective.

It is certainly this narrative upon which everything hinged at the onset of AA and the subsequent treatment industry it spawned (White, 2014). The central message of AA since its inception has been that one is powerless over this monolithic problem and recovery can only be accessed once one surrenders to this very fact. This simple, if perhaps ominous, narrative represented liberty from bondage for the earliest members of AA and the countless numbers who have followed their path for the better part of a century.

To suggest that the modern alcoholism treatment industry, including its prevailing philosophy and strategies, was spawned directly from AA and its simple narrative is far from an overstatement. As White (2014) describes, in 1948 the Minneapolis Board of Welfare sought consultation from Pat C., a recently sober member of AA, to assist in their new efforts at addressing alcoholism. With the explicit authorization of AA's governing board Pat accepted this role and, with only his burgeoning personal recovery experience as a blueprint, became the single most primary influence over what would become the most widely used addiction treatment model, the Minnesota model.

Several enduring techniques can be found in practice at countless treatment centers today that were initiated almost a century ago in Minnesota by Pat C. (White, 2014). These include the use of AA literature, lectures and discussions on the steps of AA, the completion of steps and acquisition of a sponsor as discharge contingencies, and alumni meetings as continuing care. Dr. Nelson Bradley, Superintendent of Willmar State Hospital at the time, remarking in 1975 on how quickly and wholeheartedly they replicated the model statewide, noted that the first programs had "scarcely celebrated their first birthdays when we so blithely accepted them as models of experience and skill" (as cited in White, 2014, p. 266). As the Minnesota model spread across the country so, too, did the authoritative influence of AA over the medical establishment. At Knickerbocker Hospital in New York City, for example, AA sponsors were granted admitting privileges over that of physicians—a practice that was also replicated elsewhere (White, 2014).

This narrative that sparked a revolution—that addiction is a permanent condition that can only temporarily be kept at bay through total abstention—may be just that: a narrative. As Foote et al. (2014) report, brain research on the neurobiology of addiction suggests that the image used in a public service announcement from the 1980s involving an egg frying in a pan was both a misnomer and a disservice. As the science now shows, your brain on drugs is less like a broken egg and more like a broken leg. The former suggests irreversible damage while the latter connotes the possibility of healing. On this point, contemporary treatment protocols that are based on recent brain science, including pharmacotherapies and harm reduction models, dovetail very well with the overarching strengths-based paradigm in their mutual provision of alternatives to status quo, pathology-oriented practices based on the "once an addict, always an addict" paradigm.

What the brain science suggests is that maybe the individual is not as powerless over the monolith of addiction as we have long believed and that maybe the brain can be retrained to resist problematic levels of use (Foote et al., 2014). As controversial as it sounds, it could be that even the brains of many who have maintained abstinence for years through long-term 12-step recovery could return to non-problematic moderate drinking as a result of changes that have taken place in their brains while sober. Although this is conjecture and there may be no reason to push such an idea on those for whom 12-step recovery is working, such questions become profoundly important for the great number of people for whom traditional 12-step based treatment doesn't seem to work.

In his book *Reckoning: Drugs, the Cities, and the American Future*, sociologist Elliott Currie (1993), against the backdrop of a long-held, widespread belief that traditional alcohol and drug treatment works, thoroughly annotates evidence to the contrary. Currie notes, for example, that the overwhelming majority of those who fit the criteria for substance dependence never step foot in treatment, a significant number of whom get sober without any professional help, and that even for those who enter treatment and get sober it is unlikely that the treatment itself made any significant difference. He points out that the very studies that gave way to the ubiquitous, uncritical assumption that treatment works were often circular and self-affirming in nature, inflating treatment effectiveness, and failing to account for treatment dropouts and other variables to which supposed successes may more accurately be attributed. Currie also notes a litany of longitudinal studies showing significantly high post-treatment relapse rates. Addressing the skepticism of those who support traditional treatment, Currie compellingly rules out hypotheses such as there not being enough treatment beds to meet demand or those accessing treatment having more severe disorders. In fact, his metadata bears out the opposite on both accounts. According to Currie, chief among reasons given by those with the most severe addictions (arguably the ones who need treatment the most) for not accessing treatment are reports that it is irrelevant, unhelpful, punitive, and overly regimented. Despite his warnings over two decades ago, it would be years before any substantial changes were seen in standard protocols of treatment.

Others have more recently made similar claims, challenging the efficacy of the traditional treatment and recovery model's most basic tenets, directly, if not inadvertently, bolstering the value of strengths-based possibilities. For example, a 2011 report by the Centers for Disease Control and Prevention found that 90% of heavy drinkers don't meet the criteria for alcohol dependence (Esser et al., 2014). A recent study by the NIAAA (National Institute on Alcohol Abuse and Alcoholism, 2012) found that 13% of people with alcohol dependence never receive treatment and that 75% of those who recover from the disorder do so without the help of either treatment or self-help programs such as AA.

Even more controversially, a number of studies suggest a return to moderate drinking is possible after having met the criteria for alcohol dependence. A series of studies by psychologists Mark and Linda Sobell throughout the 1970s describes how they were able to teach alcohol dependent individuals to drink moderately (Saladin & Santa Ana, 2004). As follow up studies revealed, not only were they able to drink moderately, they had more days of alcohol abstinence than a control group who were practicing abstinence. This suggests moderation may not only be a viable goal in itself but is an effective measure toward the eventual goal of abstinence. Abstinence-only proponents attacked the researchers' credibility, however, successfully stifling the influence of their findings. The Sobells were later exonerated by peer review, but the damage had been done (Saladin & Santa Ana, 2004). A 1976 study by the RAND Corporation similarly found that as many as 22% of alcoholics were able to return to moderate drinking. The study also found relapse was no more likely among controlled drinkers than among those practicing abstinence. The NIAAA, having funded the RAND report, subsequently repudiated it. Despite this, the RAND Corporation repeated the study on a bigger scale with similar results. Ironically, the NIAAA, in their own study three decades later, concluded that, twenty years after onset, over half of individuals with alcohol dependence were able to moderate their drinking without symptoms of dependence (Glaser, 2015).

Clearly the numbers of those for whom the traditional treatment routes don't work rank significantly high. Yet despite this evidence, for those same individuals a message of condemnation remains dominant in the halls of treatment centers, the rooms of self-help groups, and our culture at large, as echoed in these words of the Alcoholics Anonymous Big Book (Alcoholics Anonymous World Services, 2002):

> Those who do not recover are people who cannot or will not completely give themselves to this simple program, usually men and women who are constitutionally incapable of being honest with themselves. There are such unfortunates. They are not at fault; they seem to have been born that way. (p.58)

These words, still read aloud at self-help meetings worldwide today, crystallize a monolithic, dominant narrative of disempowerment. For those it helps it is a lived truth that need not be challenged. A case could be made that AA, for instance, was truly designed for chronic, severe alcoholics and that its principles were never meant for as broad a group as to whom it is now being pitched (Glaser, 2015). White (2014) noted that even among AA members a complaint has grown over time that the increasing number of mandated attendees has diluted the effectiveness of the program. For these and many other reasons, for those who experience this narrative as irrelevant, or worse immobilizing, we must capitalize on ways of dissolving its rigidity and replacing its influence with a more reflexive, strengths-based narrative.

William White proposed in 1998 that the popular slogan "Treatment Works" be dropped in favor of messages that shift the focus away from the treatment intervention itself to the desired outcome of recovery (White, 2014). Over the last decade or more this sentiment has taken hold in many arenas of both the addictions profession and the recovery community in the shape of what has been termed the new recovery movement. Within this movement there are two chief arteries through which change has taken place, one at the greater systems level and one at the direct service level. Transformations in culture and policy at national, state, and local levels have taken place to create what are termed recovery oriented systems of care, or greater systemic climates through which recovery can flourish. At the service delivery level—be it professional services or peer-led, volunteer community-based services—recovery management strategies are utilized to replicate approaches comparable to those which have effectively managed other chronic diseases such as diabetes and heart disease (White, 2014).

One core thrust of the recovery movement at the systemic level is to counter the public stigma that dehumanizes those suffering from addiction. The pioneers of this new movement have found the historic silence and invisibility of recovering addicts, codified in the AA principle of anonymity as a means to preserve safety, to largely further this public stigma (Kelly & White, 2011). To that end, the recovery movement challenges individuals and families to come forward and announce their presence in society, similarly to the advocacy campaigns of other previously stigmatized chronic conditions such as cancer. This effort provides living role models who depict not only the diversity of solutions available, but indigenous strengths as well (Kelly & White, 2011).

The recovery movement is, in many ways, inherently strengths-based, abandoning several long-held presuppositions of the traditional chemical dependence field. One of its core attributes is a departure from a pathology emphasis to one of long-term personal and family recovery. Recovery is seen as accessible via multiple, varied yet viable pathways, which are all cause for celebration, rather than the singular path model offered by traditional treatment (Kelly & White, 2011; White, 2014). Not only does this increase the availability and quality of services, it also increases one's personal agency through a greater emphasis on choice, which is understood as enhancing both motivation and subsequent outcomes. These diverse pathways of recovery, including abstinence, harm reduction, and moderation management models, are understood reflexively as each having optimal, partial, or, in some cases, no positive effect at all depending on the individual.

Kelly and White (2011) point out that we refer to addiction as a chronic disorder but largely treat it like an acute illness. They recommend that in order to cultivate a recovery orientation we should truly treat addiction as the chronic condition it is. Although focusing on a chronic disorder sounds pathology-driven at first, abandoning certain aspects of acute intervention in favor of a chronic care model appears to reinforce a strengths-based perspective. They recommend, for example, giving up practices such as viewing prior treatment episodes as predictions of failure, let alone punitively discharging clients when they simply confirm their diagnosis through continued use. Furthermore, they recommend that referring to addiction as a chronic disorder should include disclaimers to differentiate contemporary understanding from the outdated paradigm. Such disclaimers should specify that not all individuals have the same prolonged, progressive course requiring multiple treatments, or even need professional help at all (Kelly & White, 2011).

An example of recovery management at work at the community level can be found in the innovative recovery check-up phone calls initiated by the Connecticut Community for Addiction Recovery (CCAR; White, 2007). Statewide, everyone leaving a treatment facility in Connecticut is asked if they would like a weekly phone call from a peer in recovery for 12 weeks, regardless of whether their discharge from treatment is deemed successful or against staff advice. The resounding majority of people responded affirmatively, many requesting that the calls continue beyond the initial 12 weeks. What's more, this simple outreach from a peer has yielded sobriety rates of 88% as well as a 60% rate of reengagement for those who relapsed (Kelly & White, 2011; White, 2007).

This practice runs counter to an age-old tradition in 12-step recovery groups. When someone first attends AA they are often given a host of phone numbers from other members and directed to reach out for help if needed. Several facets of this dynamic make this sort of task difficult for anyone, let alone a newcomer to a sobriety group. For one thing, they are generally all strangers who are much more comfortable and familiar with the setting than the newcomer. He or she is also in a much more vulnerable position not just for being a newcomer, but also for being the one in need of help. The anxiety produced by this expectation may be enough to deter one from ever calling, if not giving up on meetings altogether. Nevertheless, many would see reversing that process as enabling an erosion of boundaries that threatens recovery.

What CCAR's example illuminates, however, in terms of the strengths-based nature of recovery management is how a relatively simple increase in external support, rather than enabling one's lack of motivation, actually elucidates his or her innate strengths. In the *Bateson-esque* language of strategic therapists (Gibney, 2006; Watzlawick et al., 2011), the paradoxical message of AA—that one must simultaneously admit powerlessness and yet muster up the willpower to reach out—becomes a double bind for many that impedes rather than expedites recovery. What CCAR has successfully done is revert the difficulty of reaching out for help back to what it really is, an ordinary difficulty rather than an indication of constitutional weakness or lack of readiness. Similar goals are reached more broadly throughout recovery management by making outreach practices, including linkages made by clinicians and even transportation to treatment, assertive rather than passive (Kelly & White, 2011).

Both in the clinical relationship and in the broader scope of recovery-oriented services, increased autonomy on the client's part is central to recovery management. Within sustained, collaborative partnerships, the client is empowered to assume responsibility for long-term management of their disorder while the professional takes on the role of a consultant. Professionally directed treatment plans are likewise replaced by client directed recovery plans (Kelly & White, 2011). In the recovery movement, as with a strengths-based orientation, we see an abandonment of medical rhetoric, such as the use of terms like *patient, diagnosis, disease,* and *prognosis* (White, 2014). This all aligns very well with strengths-based practices such as solution-focused therapy's "not-knowing" position (De Jong & Berg, 2012) and motivational interviewing's eliciting, rather than arguing for, change (Miller & Rollnick, 2013).

Although most literature pertaining to recovery management explores system change in greater detail than the specifics of the clinical relationship, signature features of this central aspect of service delivery, including the hierarchical, expert-driven, and fiduciary nature of clinical relationships, are clearly renounced (Kelly & White, 2011). Rather than rigidly defining what the clinical relationship should look like, what is stressed is implementing alternatives to the clinical relationship, or wrapping clinical services within a broader community-based, often peer-led support before, during, and after treatment episodes (White, 2014). Broadening the service delivery landscape is important, however we must also explore how to modify the clinical relationship itself to similarly abandon the top-down approach. This is where the strengths-based model integrates well with the recovery movement. The remainder of this chapter will explore specific strengths-based techniques that may be useful in reorienting the therapeutic relationship toward a more recovery-oriented, strengths-based position.

Applications

In my own clinical work, I find myself using several different strengths-based techniques that come from a variety of theoretical underpinnings, including solution-focused therapy, narrative therapy, strategic family therapy, positive psychology, motivational interviewing and others. In keeping with the plurality of pathways that can be found within the recovery model, some techniques may be better suited to a 12-step orientation whereas others may be more appropriate for the individual who does not find such an orientation useful. Similarly, some of these techniques may fit better within an abstinence-based model whereas others would be more constructive within a moderation management approach. Most of these techniques need not be confined to any one pathway. The overarching goals of these various techniques will generally fall into one or more of four general themes. These include counteracting therapeutic omnipotence, enhancing client competence, reframing narratives (particularly those regarding power), and broadening service menu and delivery. In most cases these goals are not discrete and will overlap across the various techniques.

Therapeutic omnipotence is a common, if not inadvertent, occurrence within traditional therapy generally and addictions counseling specifically, in which the therapist is seen as the expert, the more powerful one in the therapeutic relationship. One could say that it is the other side of the pathology coin—a paradigm in which the potency of one individual—be it therapist or client—is in direct inverse proportion to that of the other. Another way to think of it is that countering therapeutic omnipotence and enhancing client competence are complimentary if not, in many cases, one and the same. Counteracting therapeutic omnipotence, therefore, becomes central to any strengths-based work and neglecting to do so may render the relationship, in whole or in part, iatrogenic.

The very act of walking into a therapist's office implies a power imbalance in which one is the stronger, healthier, wiser helper and the other is the one in need. This inherent imbalance exists to varying degrees regardless of the therapist's orientation, intention, or experience. Strengths-based clinicians understand that this must be counterbalanced starting at the very beginning of therapy and that autonomy resides in a person's power to choose the course that follows. One of the first things a therapist can do, therefore, toward a strengths orientation is to hand as much of that power to choose the course of treatment over to the client. However, before even exploring the menu of treatment options, counteracting therapeutic omnipotence can take place in how the therapist structures or frames the therapy process itself.

One way I begin to do this is by distancing myself from any presumption that might suggest to my client an expectation of adherence or compliance to an agenda of mine. During our first meeting, for instance, I describe to nearly every one of my clients that one of three possibilities is likely to occur. I typically state, "Let's say we meet a few times . . ." (notice the non-coercive, almost hypothetical nature of the language).

One possibility is that you find our time useful and want to continue. I think that would be great. Another possibility is that you will find our time so useful that even after a few visits you feel like you've gotten what you need and no longer want to come in for therapy. I think that would be great too, perhaps even better. But a third possibility is that we meet for a few times and you don't really find it very useful.

This leads to a discussion of possible alternatives, which invariably include choosing a different therapist, trying something different in our therapy work, or even the possibility that therapy itself is not really what is needed. This last suggestion, made by a professional, has great potency in fostering client autonomy. I usually mention that many people are unsure how to break it to their therapist that their services are no longer needed, noting with humor that I look forward to getting fired. Using overtly non-coercive language, calling attention to the possibility that the client might not be satisfied with the therapeutic service, suggesting the client has the right to terminate treatment at his or her discretion whether it was helpful or not, and inferring that therapy might not even be necessary are all ways the therapist can use the very first words the client hears to begin counteracting therapeutic omnipotence.

For several years now, I have consistently made it a practice to end my first session with every client by benevolently and openly asking, "Do you want to come back?" I first witnessed this question being used by my colleague and coeditor Dr. Jeff Edwards in a clinical demonstration. As I write this I do not know if he used this question intentionally or if it came to him spontaneously during the demonstration. What I do know, however, is that it is what Edwards would refer to as a form of agentic questioning, or asking a question in such a way that it implies agency in the person, thus reaching the goal of enhancing competence. Again, language is important. "Do you want to come back?" has a different connotation, less expectant, than, "So when can we schedule our next appointment?" There is something about the colloquial nature of the question that I find even more agentic than asking "Would you like to schedule another appointment?" I've even had clients comment to me later that the question was empowering in that their right to decide whether to come back after the first session was truly respected.

Any question that implies personal agency—such as "how did you do that?" directed at some positive action on the client's part—can be considered an agentic question. But perhaps my favorite agentic question, which I also learned from Dr. Edwards, asks, "What is it about you?" Historically, for most people this question is usually the preface of something resoundingly negative. "What is it about you that you can never get your act together?" "What is it about you?" carries with it an implicit, "What's wrong with you?" Turning this pattern on its head by following with something positive can have significant agentic potential. I like to add a nice pregnant pause before finishing this question to increase the dramatic tension. "What is it about you . . . [pause] . . . that despite all the hardship you've been through, you are a survivor?" "What is it about you, that even though you relapsed over the weekend you managed to get yourself to my office today?" What ramps up the agentic nature of this question is that the positive action is not strictly attached to a behavior but to the person's identity. To ask it in a slightly different way, such as, "Why do you think you came to my office today despite relapsing over the weekend?" while not a bad question, loses a considerable amount of its agentic potential simply because it focuses the positive quality on the behavior choice rather than the person's identity.

Another technique that has significant potential for enhancing a client's sense of competence is the use of therapeutic compliments (Amendt, Wall, Kleckner, & Bryant, 1989). I learned while working under direct supervision of Amendt and his associates that sincere compliments can be found in almost any clinical situation. Being strengths-based is not simply pretending problems aren't there, but noticing agency within the context of the problem. I often verbalize what aspect of my client's behavior, attitude, or thought process impresses me, offering a comment like, "I'm really impressed with how well you handled that situation." Adding a comparison to some imagined others can help to enhance the sense of competence, "You know, a lot of people might not have put the brakes on a relapse as quickly as you did." Notice how I am hedging on this comparison just a bit with the phrase "might not have . . ." rather than "wouldn't have." In the language of strategic family therapy (Fisch, Weakland, & Segal, 1982), I am maintaining my therapeutic maneuverability here in case my client grossly disagrees with my assessment. This is similar to the concept in motivational interviewing of matching the client's ambivalence (Miller & Rollnick, 2013). Either way, if he or she were to balk at my suggestion that others might have handled it worse, I can easily follow up with something like, "Yeah, you might be right. But I'm still glad you handled it as well as you did." Even when a client is pointing out an overt fault or mistake, the therapist can receive the information with gratitude and embed a genuine compliment with a statement such as, "I really appreciate you having the confidence to share that with me. I know you're not proud of how you handled it, but you've really helped me to understand how difficult this is for you."

Another important strengths-based skill that has significant potential for both reducing therapist omnipotence and increasing client competence is simply avoiding the use of clinical terminology (Rapp & Goscha, 2012). Clinical terms tend to become hardened internalized identities and seldom provide much in the way of clues as to how to resolve problems. There are many reasons for this, not the least of which is that they rarely offer much regarding the specific context in which a problem occurs. Colloquial terms, on the other hand, have the potential to reinforce a narrative in which the problem and its correlates are smaller, less ominous, or perhaps even more conquerable. Even solutions can be de-stigmatized through the use of less clinical language. I remember some years ago listening to a BBC news story in which Londoners were interviewed regarding their use of pharmacological therapies for mental illness. Everyone in the piece referred to taking a *tablet*—a term not widely used in the United States where we often use the term *medication*. Outside of the fact I initially thought they were referring to an electronic reading device, I found that the notion of "taking a tablet" sounded so much less ominous, so much smaller than the notion of "being on medication." Taking something suggests you are in control, whereas being on something infers that you are along for the ride.

To think of it in narrative therapy terms, using non-clinical language is essentially a way of externalizing the problem (White and Epston, 1990). Referring to one's "drinking problem" rather than using terms such as *alcoholism, chemical dependence,* or *addict,* allows one to see the problem as something separate from oneself that can be pushed against, struggled with, even defeated. This non-clinical language can diminish a problem's sense of durability. This is a clear example of where a technique might fit for a particular individual on a particular recovery path, while not fitting for someone else. Many people in 12-step recovery, for example, don't find the term *alcoholic* as debilitating, but rather a liberating admission. In such cases there would be no reason to challenge the use of that term. However, for those who have not yet engaged, or perhaps never will engage, in that path, this simple language choice within the therapeutic relationship can make a subtle but significant difference. For many of those individuals, the term *alcoholic* has become so tightly cleaved to the cultural narrative of "once an alcoholic, always an alcoholic" that it creates an immobilizing double bind. Although these clients take strong objection to the idea of being an alcoholic they may be very amenable to the notion that they do, in fact, have a drinking problem of some sort. Sidestepping debatable clinical terminology then becomes a way in which they can avoid that double bind while still pursuing resolution of the problem, often through a broader array of potential solutions. Similarly steering clear of such debates with those who embrace the more pathologically driven language of AA may mean intentionally using, rather than avoiding, clinical language. Again, what is important here is determining what best meets the needs of a specific client. In either case, the use of non-clinical language is seldom problematic. What is often more in question is how much to use clinical language.

A similar example of how subtleties in language influence a strengths-based orientation is seen in the use of the term "useful" rather than "helpful." I am very intentional in my practice of rarely using the latter, in favor of almost exclusive use of the former. Asking a client, "How do you think today's session can be helpful for you?" is certainly worthwhile. However, the word "helpful" carries a subtle implication that the therapist or the therapy process is the active, empowered entity. Wording that question in a slightly different manner increases the potential for enhancing personal agency. "How do you think today's session could be useful to you?" implies that the client is using the therapy session as a tool at his or her own disposal. This language not only orients the view of the client but also that of the clinician toward client autonomy.

Another important technique, which may not immediately be thought of as strengths-based, is the therapeutic use of self-disclosure. This is more easily seen as countering therapist omnipotence than perhaps enhancing client competence. Nevertheless, some exploration may demonstrate its usefulness in that area as well. Early on in my career my clients knew virtually nothing about my personal life. They did not know that I was a musician as well as a counselor, or whether or not I had children. In an effort to maintain professional boundaries I intentionally left that data out of our clinical conversations. As I matured as a therapist over several years, I began exploring the use of self-disclosure as part of my therapeutic repertoire. My foray into strengths-based work began as I came to realize that if, when a client enters my office, I strip away most of the data regarding who they are—that which is not directly relevant to the problem area we are to address—then I am losing sight of a great deal of information regarding strengths that may be accessed in the service of problem resolution. I began inquiring into the broader, seemingly divergent contexts of my clients' lives in order to uncover those strengths. In a similar fashion, finding safe and ethical ways to disclose more of myself to my clients served as an isomorph opening up avenues to uncover client strengths.

Therapist self-disclosure allows a client to experience someone who "has it together" as vulnerable, perhaps even flawed. This carries with it enormous normalizing potential (Farber, 2006).

Self-disclosure could be a simple anecdote regarding an experience, or it could be an affective, or emotional, disclosure. One of the concerns regarding self-disclosure is that of problematic transference and countertransference. While I admit I am not an expert on psychoanalytic theory by any means, I find myself more concerned with interference than transference. If disclosing some aspect of my story interferes or gets in the way of my client's work, taking attention away from the therapeutic goals, then self-disclosure diminishes the quality of therapy. However, something human—some real emotion—must often transfer interpersonally in order for therapy to be effective. I will never forget teaching a graduate level addictions class in which two students were role-playing a therapy session. The student playing the role of therapist was very uncomfortable and stiff, trying hard to be therapeutic and having a difficult time finding her way in the conversation. After some time I paused the role-play and quickly said, "You're no longer a counselor, you're just a friend at a party." As they jumped back into the role-play, without thinking she instantly stopped trying to be a therapist and became quite therapeutic. When a client receives something authentic such as an affective disclosure from a therapist it is often transformative. I have, at times, allowed myself to shed a tear with a client or in response to a client's statement. Each time, my sense has been that this energized the positivity in the relationship as well as the motivation toward positive change within the client. Oftentimes, such emotional disclosure affords the client a deep sense of being understood.

An obvious factor in navigating the use of self-disclosure is finding the appropriate balance between disclosure and boundary keeping. I find the metaphor of a bicycle useful in understanding how those two aspects of the therapeutic relationship work together. If I were going on a long bike ride that included steep hills and other difficult terrain, I would opt for a multispeed bike rather than a single speed one. With a single-speed bike the only resource available is the energy in one's muscles. However, with a multispeed bike, one can leverage muscle energy through the use of gears. Appropriate use of those gears gives the muscles an opportunity to rest so they are recharged when needed for the occasional hill. Nevertheless, a multispeed bike without any muscles providing energy is not going anywhere. The muscles are just as necessary as the gears. In the therapeutic relationship, the muscles represent one's emotions, while the gears represent boundaries. Just like the bicycle, if there were no emotions present on the part of the therapist the relationship would be going nowhere. Likewise, without appropriate boundaries a therapist's emotions would quickly be depleted and in no way rested and ready for the more difficult terrain of the therapy process. However, when boundaries are effectively and frequently employed, much like gears on a bicycle, the therapist's emotional wellbeing may be recharged so that when those impactful moments come in a session, an extra dose of emotional disclosure on the part of the therapist can be very appropriate and effective.

One potentially awkward facet of self-disclosure that is very pertinent to the substance abuse field is therapist disclosure with respect to personal status regarding substance abuse recovery. I have heard many examples from colleagues over the years of how to navigate a client's inquiry into one's status and I have refined my own response as well. Many clinicians, when asked if they are in recovery themselves, respond to the question with a question. For example, a counselor might ask, "How would it be helpful for you to know?" There is nothing wrong with this. In fact, in the right context such a response can lead to a very therapeutic conversation. From a strengths-based perspective, however, I prefer to answer forthrightly before countering with such a question. This specific ordering—disclosure preceding the question—avoids an inadvertent power play and counters therapist omnipotence. To do otherwise suggests that I, as therapist/expert, will only answer your question once I have assessed the motivation, sincerity, or value behind it.

The standard response that I have honed over the years, prefaced with a forthright disclosure that I have not personally struggled with substance abuse, is usually something like, "Let's say we meet for a few sessions and you find it useful. If that's the case it won't likely matter whether I am in recovery or not. Likewise, it also won't matter if after a few sessions you find meeting with me not useful. In either case, whether I'm in recovery or not, if you don't find our meetings useful we should change course." I might add to this a few statements about how people often find value in having a variety of roles within their support network, including some in recovery and some who have never struggled with addiction. However a therapist responds to these sorts of inquiries from clients, one's level of comfort in responding is probably more important than the response itself.

There are other ways in which a therapist can pepper self-disclosure throughout therapy as a way to counter therapeutic omnipotence and enhance client agency. Given that I am not a recovering addict myself and that a stigma does exist regarding addiction, I am aware that the monolithic narratives around addiction often proscribe tacit assumptions that may be present in the counseling relationship. Examples of these may be that I, as the non-addict, have less to be ashamed of, that I have more willpower, or that I will thrust upon my client the same assumptions other non-addicts have. I often use self-disclosing anecdotes in subtle, indirect ways to counter these potential assumptions. I may, for example, talk about how when my wife bakes her delicious chocolate chip cookies—and she is in the room—I am hardly tempted to eat more than one, but when she runs to the store for an errand I find myself downing five of them hoping she never notices. This sort of anecdote does a few things. It establishes a point of humor, as clients often laugh when I describe a true story like this. The laughter is often mitigated, however, when I point out my father had diabetes and yet despite this I have at times continued to make poor eating choices on several occasions.

More importantly, these sorts of disclosures help to establish my own down-to-earth humanness in the relationship. This sort of anecdotal disclosure also has the potential to bring the problem of substance abuse back to where it belongs, in the broader realm of unhealthy mistakes that most humans make. I am very intentional in my use of the words *unhealthy* and *mistake* with clients in order to counter the stigmas around addiction. I prefer to frame addiction related choices as unhealthy or unwise, rather than bad. Similarly, I prefer to circumvent the monolithic narrative of failure with the more reflexive idea of mistakes. Tying the addiction experience to other less stigmatized, unhealthy mistakes can help dismantle the debilitating monoliths. Some may argue that using my experience with cookies as a parallel is an insult at best to the person wrestling with the gravity of drug addiction. It is important to emphasize that, rather than trying to make an overt one-to-one comparison or to water down my client's experience, my intention is to weave these anecdotes briefly into larger conversations in which we can collaboratively connect the dots between our choices as human beings, the brain processes they trigger, and the resulting outcomes. I have even admitted to my clients, as we laugh about the plate of cookies, that in all honesty, when we consider the impact of sugar, carbs, and fat on one's health, I'm not sure which would kill one of us first, my vice or theirs. With the right individual, playfully exploring such anecdotes can go a long way toward building rapport, normalizing, and enhancing agency. Or to put it more succinctly, a client's revelation that the therapist is just as human and feeble as they are can, as Fosha states (cited in Farber, 2006), "promote healthy differentiation and individuation while empowering patients to recognize their own ego strengths" (p. 129).

Early in his solution-focused therapy career, Bill O'Hanlon drew therapeutic techniques from his tutelage under Milton Erickson, many of which are suitable for a strengths-based framework. Linking and unlinking (O'Hanlon, 1987), for example, consists of joining strengths from one domain of life to the problem domain or splitting up sequential patterns within the problem domain.

Jared was a client of mine who was newly sober and struggling to figure out how to navigate social situations without drinking. I asked him if he could think of other situations, in a completely different area of his life or even a different time period, in which he felt uncomfortable or anxious due to being new to his role and not used to the situation yet. He quickly cited a few examples including starting a new job, dating, and becoming a father, spontaneously adding that he became comfortable in each of those roles over time, some rather quickly. This enabled him to more easily imagine himself getting comfortable in these new sober social situations and to employ strengths that had been present in him all along. I'll never forget the hopeful, confident way he stated, "I'd never thought about it that way." The language I used in this intervention normalized his current situation down to common elements that could then be related to other domains in which Jared had already exercised agency. Even my use of the word *yet* was intentional as a way to subtly infer that not feeling comfortable in this new sober role was temporary. Linking strengths from other, seemingly unrelated, domains is essentially reframing but with a strengths orientation.

Kevin was another of my clients, with whom I was discussing how to manage heroin cravings. I asked if he could think of times in which he somehow mustered up the will to successfully resist the urge toward an irresponsible or unhealthy choice. Again, I am using language to pare down relapse to an elemental definition that can then be linked to another domain where strength of character may be more accessible. Notice, I am also using the concept of willpower as a potential asset, rather than antagonist, of recovery. Kevin was quick to identify ways he had resisted very real urges to be irresponsible regarding both working out and eating right. As we talked he expressed more confidence that he could use these same strengths to resist drug cravings. His subsequent track record showed this to be the case. Some may rightfully argue that there are stronger neuropathways to be resisted in the realm of drug use than other domains. I would posit that this is exactly why it is important to harness the energy from previous success in those domains. It is the dominant, pathology-driven narrative of addiction that would have us believe accessing strengths across life domains is a matter of discrete apples and oranges.

A more indirect form of linking that is very Ericksonian in its subtlety of language would be to connect emotional states associated with addiction to innate strengths in the person's life, confounding previously established emotional patterns in understated ways. This certainly will not do any harm, and might influence the conversation in a positive, strengths-based way. An example of this might be fusing a term like craving to a positive motivator such as one's children: "You know, once people get sober, they often notice how much they crave time with their children, wanting to make up for lost time." Talking overtly about the value of spending time with one's kids as a means of displacing the reward of the drug high is certainly good, but according to Ericksonian principles communicating this indirectly through language choice may also prove effective (O'Hanlon, 1987). If nothing else, we must acknowledge that aspects of one's life, such as children, are powerful contextual strengths that have at times been overlooked by professionals and peers or seen as extrinsic and therefore less sincere motivations for change. Nothing could be further from the truth. Expanding the potential for recovery means recognizing these contextual factors as valid, motivating strengths.

For every linking that occurs an unlinking of sorts often follows alongside. In the above examples, for instance, when a strength from another domain is applied to the substance use arena there is great potential to unlink the powerlessness narrative from the substance use experience. Another example of this kind of link/unlink pairing is to differentiate one's narrative identities. A clinician may look for preferred identities—typically from other life domains—that conflict with the "alcoholic" identity. I might say to my client, for example, "As a business owner (or father/mother), how do you feel when you look back on these episodes of binge drinking?" This question implies the positive identity of *business owner* as the primary identity. However, it can also heighten ambivalence, increasing intrapersonal tension. Although this is often helpful in resolving ambivalence, attaching a compliment to the front end of such a statement can help to soften the blow. For example, "I'm really impressed with how honestly you are evaluating whether you want to continue drinking. I'm sure successful business owners have to make tough decisions based on honest evaluations all the time." Structuring communication in this way may help the client to dissociate their identity from the addictive behavior, positioning her or him in a more successful identity.

Counteracting the narrative of powerlessness is, perhaps, the most subversive yet liberating unlinking that can happen. The relief in the room has been palpable as I've suggested to some of my clients that maybe, in fact, they're not powerless—that maybe they can use their own willpower toward abstinence or moderated drinking. Steve, whose wife Jane couldn't understand why he wouldn't just admit all the things those people in AA admit, responded to me, "I really don't think I'm powerless. I don't think I should be. But every treatment center I've gone to has told me the only way to get better is to admit that." For some, hearing from a professional that maybe they can utilize their will-power toward recovery, rather than emboldening them to continue an unwinnable fight as feared, liberates them from shame and opens them up to recovery-oriented possibilities that fit for them.

From a purely philosophical standpoint, students of constructivism, which is the theoretical basis of narrative therapy (White & Epston, 1990), would suggest that the idea of being powerless over one's addiction is nothing more than a metaphor or construction. That is not to diminish its worth. As Gaiman states in the preface to his 2002 novella, *Coraline*, paraphrasing a quote from Chesterton, "Fairy tales are more than true—not because they tell us dragons exist, but because they tell us drag-ons can be beaten" (p. 2). This is not to say that concepts like recovery or powerlessness are fairy tales, but that as narrative constructions they are more than true for those who are able to utilize them in exorcising their demons. The skeptical bystander, however, may observe that for all the talk of surren-dering their willpower, members of 12-step groups actually seem to be using quite a bit of willpower.

Milton Erickson, in pioneering his brand of hypnotherapy, developed the hand levitation in which, through hypnotic suggestion, he directed people to use their muscles to lift their arm while simultaneously not realizing they were using their muscles to lift their arm. In this way, they accepted the construction that their arm was levitating without their power or will (Rossi, 2008). For all we know, this may be just what happens for many in 12-step recovery. They are using their willpower—for things like going to a meeting or calling a sponsor when craving a drink—while simultaneously believing they are not using willpower in recovery.

Perhaps the only people for whom this argument has any bearing are those who for whatever reason, like my client Steve, cannot get on board with the dominant recovery metaphors. In my collaborative work with Steve, we explored ways that he might leverage his will to resist cravings and endure opportunities to drink while remaining sober. Central to this was enhancing his motiva-tion, which was largely derived from career goals that he felt his drinking was getting in the way of. Working with someone outside of the dominant 12-step abstinence framework does not mean throwing out all aspects of that narrative. In many ways, Steve and I repurposed several popular 12-step principles, particularly coping skills such as living life on life's terms. Also repurposed was the nature of social support. Over time, Steve came to realize that even though he had no interest in formalized support groups or total abstinence, increasing his social support was vital to reaching his own recovery goals. Steve began therapy with a very dichotomized view of the abstinence/use con-tinuum. Having been told many times that he was either abstinent or actively alcoholic, he pushed hard against the notion of abstinence. Interestingly, as we softened some of these rigid narratives, depressurizing their dichotomous nature, not only did he begin to see controlling his drinking as exciting and possible, but he also decided on his own that practicing abstinence could and should be a reasonable part of his recovery plan. In many ways the older, polarizing view of addiction/recov-ery only inflated the significance of drinking for Steve, rendering stagnant his aspirations toward a better life. Introducing the broader, more reflexive, individualized, and strengths-based themes of the recovery movement put the wind back into his sails and, albeit not without some rocky seas, allowed him to move forward.

Conclusion

As a counselor working across a broad multicultural patchwork with many who struggle with addic-tion, I am excited about what the future holds for addiction treatment. With the scientific disciplines giving us new information about the brain and new medications to assist our behavioral efforts, and with the recovery community redefining what advocacy means at the systemic level, a broader and more integrated system of care looks promising. My hope is that we, the clinicians holed up in our offices and agencies, don't miss the boat. I have worked in abstinence-based treatment centers where moderation management was disavowed and I've worked in methadone programs where the 12 steps were scorned. In becoming strengths-based practitioners we have the opportunity to become bridges between divergent perspectives, finding the common strengths and refusing to carry forward the rigid, dichotomous narratives. In this way, we may do our part in broadening the possibility-laden future of recovery for many.

References

Alcoholics Anonymous World Services. (2002). *Alcoholics anonymous: The big book* (4th Ed.). New York, NY: Author.

Amendt, J.H., Wall, M.D., Kleckner, T., & Bryant, R.D. (1989). Therapeutic compliments: setting the stage for successful therapy. *Journal of Marital and Family Therapy, 15,* 159–167.

Anderson, H. (1997). *Conversations, language, and possibilities: A postmodern approach to therapy.* New York, NY: Basic Books.

Combs, G., & Freedman, J. (1996). *Narrative therapy: The social construction of preferred realities.* New York, NY: W.W. Norton.

Cowger, C.D. (1992). Assessment of client strengths. In D. Saleebey (Ed.), *The strengths perspective in social work practice* (pp. 139–147). New York, NY: Longman.

Currie, E. (1993). *Reckoning: Drugs, the cities, and the American future.* New York, NY: Hill and Wang.

De Jong, P. & Berg, I.K. (2012). *Interviewing for solutions* (4th Ed.). Belmont, CA: Cengage Learning.

Esser, M.B., Hedden, S.L., Kanny, D., Brewer, R.D., Gfroerer, J.C., & Naimi, T.S. (2014) Prevalence of Alcohol Dependence Among US Adult Drinkers, 2009–2011. *Preventing Chronic Disease, 11.* DOI: http://dx.doi.org/10.5888/pcd11.140329

Farber, B.A. (2006). *Self-disclosure in psychotherapy.* New York, NY: Guilford Press

Fisch, R., Weakland, J., & Segal, L. (1982). *The tactics of change: Doing therapy briefly.* San Francisco, CA: Jossey-Bass.

Foote, J., Wilkens, C., Kosanke, N., & Higgs, S. (2014). *Beyond addiction: How science and kindness help people change.* New York, NY: Scribner.

Gaiman, N. (2002). *Coraline.* New York, NY: Harper Collins.

Gibney, P. (2006). The double bind theory: Still crazy-making after all these years. *Psychotherapy in Australia, 12*(3), 48–55.

Glaser, G. (2013). *Her best-kept secret: Why women drink—And how they can regain control.* New York, NY: Simon and Schuster.

Glaser, G. (2015, April). The false gospel of Alcoholics Anonymous. *The Atlantic, 315*(3), 50–60.

Gough, J.B. (1881). *Sunlight and shadow.* Hartford, CT: Worthington.

Hoyt, M.F. (2000). *Some stories are better than others: Doing what works in brief therapy and managed care.* Lillington, NC: Taylor and Francis.

Jellinek, E.M. (1960) *The disease concept of alcoholism.* New Brunswick, NJ: Hillhouse Press.

Kelly, J.F. & White, W.L. (Eds.). (2011). *Current clinical psychiatry: Addiction recovery management, theory, research, and practice.* New York, NY: Humana Press.

Levine, H.G. (1978). The discovery of addiction: Changing conceptions of habitual drunkenness in America. *Journal of Studies on Alcohol, 39*(1), 143–174.

Milam, J.R., & Ketcham, K. (1984). *Under the influence: A guide to the myths and realities of alcoholism.* New York, NY: Bantam.

Miller, W.R., & Rollnick, S. (2013). *Motivational Interviewing* (3rd Ed.). New York, NY: Guilford Press.

National Institute on Alcohol Abuse and Alcoholism. (2012). Alcoholism isn't what it used to be. *NIAAA Spectrum, 4*(1).

O'Hanlon, W.H. (1987). *Taproots: Underlying principles of Milton Erickson's therapy and hypnosis.* New York, NY: W.W. Norton and Company.

Ohlms, D. (1983). *The disease concept of alcoholism.* Belleville, IL: Geary Whittaker Company.

Rapp, C.A. & Goscha, R.J. (2012). *The strengths model: A recovery-oriented approach to mental health services* (3rd Ed.). New York, NY: Oxford University Press.

Rossi, E.L. (2008). *The complete collected works of Milton Erickson, vol. 1.* Phoenix, AZ: The Milton Erickson Foundation.

Saladin, M.E. and Santa Ana, E.J. (2004). Controlled Drinking: More Than Just a Controversy. *Current Opinions in Psychiatry, 17*(3).

Sweetser, W. (1829). *Dissertation on intemperance.* Boston, MA: Billiard, Gray, and Company.

Thombs, D.L. (2006). *Introduction to addictive behaviors* (3rd Ed). New York, NY: Guilford Press.

Watzlawick, P., Weakland J., & Fisch, R. (2011). *Change: Principles of problem formation and problem resolution.* New York, NY: W.W. Norton and Company. (Original work published 1974)

White, M. (2007). *Maps of Narrative Practice.* New York, NY: W.W. Norton and Company.

White, M., & Epston, D. (1990). *Narrative means to therapeutic ends.* New York, NY: W.W. Norton and Company.

White, W.L. (2007). *Perspectives on systems transformation: How visionary leaders are shifting addiction treatment toward a recovery-oriented system of care.* Chicago, IL: Great Lakes Addiction Technology Transfer Center.

White, W.L. (2014). *Slaying the dragon: The history of addiction treatment and recovery in America* (2nd Ed.). Bloomington, IL: Chestnut Health Systems/Lighthouse Institute.

White, W.L., Kurtz, E., & Acker, C. (2001). *The combined addiction disease chronologies of William White, MA, Ernest Kurtz, PhD, and Caroline Acker, PhD.* Retrieved on September 15th, 2015 from http://www.williamwhite papers.com/pr/2001Addiction%20as%20Disease%20Chronology.pdf

5

Strengths-Based Culture and Family

Anita Jones Thomas, Michael Massengale, and Latifat O. Cabrirou

Darkness cannot drive out darkness, only light can do that. Hate cannot drive out hate: only love can do that.

Dr. Martin Luther King Jr., *A Testament of Hope: The Essential Writings and Speeches*

If one were to take a stroll through any amusement park in the United States on a sunny summer day, one would find families from all backgrounds with one goal, to have a fun and enjoyable time. For families with children, this includes creating lasting positive memories for the children; one would see smiles, laughter, and lots of picture taking and digital recordings, regardless of the cultural backgrounds of the families. This is the picture that is critical for mental health providers to bear in mind when working with families, especially diverse and/or marginalized families. We are defining a family as a set of two or more individuals, connected by blood or choice, who are defined by both internal and external boundaries, live by a set of rules (implicit and explicit) and shared norms, maintain a bond or emotional connection, operate according to roles and particular communication patterns, with the purpose of growth, connection, and intimacy.

The demographics in the United States are changing such that ethnic minorities or persons of color will become the numerical majority by the year 2035 (US Bureau of the Census, 2000). In order to provide effective services, psychologists, counselors, and social workers should be culturally competent (Arrendondo et al., 1996). Historically, culturally diverse clients were viewed as deviant and deficient (Katz, 1985). Ethnic minority clients were judged according to the genetic deficiency model to be pathological due to their physiological makeup and genes (Scharzbaum & Thomas, 2008). During the Civil Rights movement, ethnic minority psychologists highlighted the role of oppression and racism on the functioning of ethnic minorities, which shifted the lens from a genetic deficiency to cultural deficiency. Although the standard of comparison was still the Eurocentric mainstream perspective, psychologists began to view differences not from genetic factors, but due to environmental factors, particularly the ones related to poverty, gender socialization patterns, and racism. What both models failed to do was to explore the contextual and cultural influences on functioning of individuals, families, and cultural groups.

Mental health providers are increasingly working with diverse clients, clients who differ in background from the therapist on a number of factors, including race/ethnicity, gender, social class, immigration, spirituality, and sexual orientation. Families who appear for treatment are diverse in a number of ways as well as including single-parent, divorced, and same-gender parents. Each cultural group and by extension family has a set of adult competencies, goals, and outcomes for what a healthy adult contributing to society should be like. Socialization experiences transmit values, beliefs, and ideas around lifestyles based on cultural knowledge of the adult tasks and competencies needed for appropriate functioning in society (Harrison, Wilson, Pine, Chon, & Buriel, 1990). It is important for professionals to work with families from a strengths-based perspective and to be able to promote resilience in families. A strengths-based approach from our perspective includes using strengths, cultural values, and resources that families and people of color have. It assumes that cultural values are different and not deviant, that families and communities have the capacity for growth and development. Finally, the strengths-based approach assumes that cultural groups have adult competencies which define appropriate roles, values, beliefs, and lifestyle for members, and work collectively to foster competencies. Family clinicians need to better understand the importance and influence of culture on family functioning, and to learn to embrace the strengths and resilience factors in families and communities.

This chapter will describe strengths-based approaches to working with culturally diverse families and ways to promote resilience based on the literature. The chapter will then present a portrait of resilience for youth of color (American Psychological Association [APA], 2008) and provide ways for family clinicians to promote resilience. The portrait suggests that children and youth understand the importance of communalism, have flexibility to function within multiple settings, have critical mindedness (the ability to critically evaluate their experiences), and actively engage in their communities. Finally, ways to promote and strengthen cultural socialization processes in families will be discussed. Cultural socialization has been linked in the research to academic achievement and psychological well-being. The chapter will close with case examples, techniques and interventions, and tools for assessment.

Promoting Resilience and Strength in Families

Literature and research on resilience address the important role that parents and families play in fostering strengths and success in youth; this is particularly true for families of ethnic minority youth as work has primarily focused on understanding risk factors and developing interventions to reduce risk. Resilience has been defined as a dynamic process encompassing positive adaptation within the context of significant adversity (Luthar, Cicchetti, & Becker, 2000; Masten, 2001). Resilience incorporates individual level processes, and also entails contextual factors including family, community, and environment that contribute to the daily living experience of youth (Thomas & Rodgers, 2009). Models of resilience often include the notion of protective factors, characteristics, traits, or processes that help individuals to adapt to, become immune to, or overcome risks.

The notion of family resilience is a recent addition to social science research. Early studies on resilience focused primarily on innate qualities that make up an "invulnerable child" (Anthony, 1974) who can withstand numerous stressors and continue to thrive. As a result, most resiliency research that incorporated the influence of family units focused on how negative family environments such as parental mental illness (Garmezy, 1974) or maltreatment (Beeghly & Cicchetti, 1994) impacted individual resilience. The family unit, rather than a protective factor, was often something from which a child needed to be protected. However, this static notion of resilience failed to capture how even a remarkable individual successfully copes with a wide variety of environments. The use of longitudinal studies began to suggest that resilience is not a "'mantle' of fixed attributes, but rather a dynamic process that fluctuates across development" (Saltzman et al., 2011, 215). A process approach allows for nuance and better explains how resilience strategies may not be universally effective. This includes the notion that all families have resilience, but it is engendered less in some families (Masten, 2001). For example, a child who learned to "shut down" in order to cope with an emotionally volatile parent may have to unlearn this strategy as an adult to avoid creating stress in new relationships. As a result, researchers began to explore more complex adversity, such as chronic poverty, and began to identify how outside factors could mediate individual variability (Walsh, 2003; Walsh, 2006).

Notably, Werner's (1993) renowned study on indigenous individuals on the Hawaiian island of Kauai demonstrated that the quality of the caregiving environment mediated a variety of outcomes of children facing many stressors associated with poverty. The study demonstrated that despite adverse conditions, almost 33% of children had positive outcomes and additionally identified that resilience can ebb and flow for individuals over the course of the lifetime. This study supported the notion of a process approach as well as highlighted the need to also explore factors external to an individual. Due to some of the findings of Werner's study, Saltzman et al. noted that models of resilience should therefore focus more on "specific mechanisms of action that support or undermine resilient functioning" (p. 215). This will allow for skills and techniques that can be taught to foster resilience. Saltzman et al. further add that family factors should be prioritized by clinicians and researchers due to the "proximal determinants of child adjustment" (p. 215), as they allow for more specific targets for development.

Clinical Implications of Family Resilience

Since resilience encompasses factors external to the individual, family therapy seems to be an appropriate avenue to promote resilience in clients. It is important to note that family therapy traditionally has identified the family unit, and not necessarily individual members, as the client, and therefore family resilience itself becomes its own concept and it is worth exploring how the concept applies to clinical work.

Hawley (2000) advocates four clinical areas of particular importance when promoting family resilience: the need to focus on strengths, assess resilience as a developmental pathway, search for commonalities, and develop a useful family schema. Hawley's clinical implications highlight that strengths-based work, which often plays a central role in family therapy's constructionist approaches, promotes the coping and thriving essential to the concept of resiliency. It is essential to explore the coping strategies and successes already present to help formulate ways of coping with novel stressors. Secondly, Hawley stresses that family resilience is neither static nor works in all situations, and family therapists must explore factors that led to the current stressor(s) as well as explore a number of possible solutions. Additionally, this approach acknowledges that stressors are rarely "cured" and often need follow-up work to address lingering issues or new stressors.

Additionally, Hawley notes that while working with resilience can never be a "one-size-fits-all" approach, patterns of crisis and coping often emerge in a family's history. It is worth exploring these patterns to determine whether particular or even earlier interventions would help promote more consistent resiliency. Finally, Hawley briefly notes the necessity of exploring how a family defines a crisis. By exploring perception and coherence, work can be made to unify and focus the family members to find strategies to overcome the current stressor.

A second approach worth exploring is Walsh's (2003) family resilience framework. Walsh also takes a process approach and identifies three domains of particular importance: family belief systems, organization patterns, and communication processes. Taking a constructionist approach, Walsh promotes the exploration of the family's perception of the crisis, the approach to possible solutions, and larger existential concerns that inform the previous two. Similar to Hawley's notion of family schema, these three facets require challenging the very substance of the adversity and often reframing it in terms better grasped by the family. Secondly, this domain asks the family to promote optimistic outlooks by cultivating hope and taking steps to work towards any possible solution. Finally, exploring transcendent belief systems helps the family find purpose and strength to continue to strive towards potential resolution.

Walsh's second domain is focused on the families' organization patterns. By promoting structural strategies such as flexibility, a family becomes open to change and willing to begin taking steps in order to promote resolution. Additionally, resilience can be promoted in families by exploring the connectedness of individual members. A cornerstone of a resilient, unified response is the ability to rely on others in the family unit. This piece requires exploring a wide variety of issues including trust, openness, and even past transgressions that prevent trust and cohesion from building. Finally, it is important to explore what resources are already available in the community, both within governmental and non-profit agencies as well as broader resources available through family and other social networks.

Finally, Walsh identifies key communication and problem-solving processes crucial to promote solutions. By ensuring each member fully understands the adversity involved and promoting healthy emotional expression a family unit can work collaboratively to address the issue in question.

Family Strengths in Family Therapy

"The family strengths perspective. . . . does not ignore family problems but restores them to their proper place in life: as vehicles for testing our capacities as families and reaffirming our vital human connections with each other" (DeFrain & Asay, 2007, 3). Research around the world suggests that there are universal strengths for families, and that all families have strengths. DeFrain & Asay (2007) summarize research on families and outline these universal strengths. Research suggests that family strengths are not found in the structure of families (composition, types, members, etc.), but in the way that families function. Whitaker (1981), for example, suggests that it is the interpersonal process rather than a fixed set of outcomes that better represents family health. Strength in families develops over time, suggesting potential and malleability for families. Following this is the notion that families sometimes develop strengths from adversity and difficulties. Strong families are not perfect, but are always growing and changing.

Strengths-based family therapy approaches emerged as a result of focus on post-modern approaches, including solution-focused and narrative approaches (Allison et al., 2003). Post-modern approaches or social constructivist methods changed the field of family therapy to address the importance of meaning and interpretation of family members' experiences. Solution-focused therapy assumes that each person's perspective is equally valid and has to be explored in treatment. Therapists following this approach hold the premise that an individual's views on problems may enhance or diminish problems; seeing problems through a problem saturated lens may maintain or exacerbate the issues. Solution-focused therapists also believe that each individual has skills and resources to solve problems, and the therapist's responsibility is to help them to identify resources (O'Hanlon & Weiner-Davis, 1989), with the goal of evoking solutions, and strengths of the situation. Similarly, narrative family therapists believe that people create meanings from their experiences and people are influenced by discourses around them (Freedman & Combs, 1996; White & Epston, 1990). There is an assumption that people have good intentions, forcing therapists to have a positive perspective on clients. Individuals create stories (narratives) to organize their lives based on their interpretations and the socialization around both their experiences and their interpretations. The narrative approach has a philosophical foundation that people live in particular sociopolitical and historical contexts and these contexts also influence perceptions of experiences.

Both the solution-focused and narrative approaches to therapy help families and individual members to engage in reframing of the presenting problems from a problem-focused or negative interpretation to something that is more positive. The solution-focused therapists will focus on reframes and times of exceptions to the problem (O'Hanlon & Weiner-Davis, 1989). Focusing on the times in which the problem does not occur initially changes the way the family members perceive the problem, but will extend to the viewpoints on family structure, dynamics, and functioning. The shift to focusing on positives is believed to snowball into changes and natural reframes for the family. Solution-focused therapists will also explore the portions of previous solutions or coping methods and encourage families to engage in more of those behaviors. The narrative approach similarly steers the conversation to focus on positives by having families focus on unique outcomes, times in which the problem does not occur, or when expected negative behavior differs. The narratives or stories change as family members begin to focus on positive aspects and strength. Narrative therapists also encourage family members to find others to support their new or revised stories, to reinforce continued behavioral change (Freedman & Combs, 1996). This is particularly important for families of color whose experiences are often shaped by their sociopolitical contexts and experiences of oppression.

Cultural Resilience Models

The family resilience models and constructivist family therapy approaches have helped therapists to engage in a strengths-based approach. The narrative approach adds the importance of sociopolitical contexts in shaping individuals and families. Similarly, in addition to addressing families, resilience models are beginning to address larger contextual and systemic factors including culture, race, and ethnicity. For example, the phenomenological variant of ecological systems theory (PVEST; Spencer et al., 2006) is a model that attempts to account for the race/ethnicity and cultural experiences of African American youth by integrating social, historical, and cultural contexts within the normative developmental process. The model proposes that the perceptions individuals have of their experiences and their self-evaluation throughout the process are critical to functioning, health, and well-being. PVEST includes five components with bidirectional processes that operate in a recursive and cyclical way. Net vulnerability includes risk and protective factors present in the individual's life. Net stress includes challenges and available support systems. The third component, reactive coping processes, includes both maladaptive and adaptive coping styles, and the fourth component, emergent identities, includes positive and negative identity aspects. The final component is stage-specific unproductive or productive coping outcomes. The model is associated with racial and ethnic socialization, which would be a coping mechanism for families in supporting youth (Umaña-Taylor, Zeiders, & Updegraff, 2013). PVEST has been found to be a useful framework with immigrant families as well (Jacobs, 2009).

A second model on resilience with African American youth builds on the notion that children and youth should be considered to be "at promise" and not "at risk" (Boykin, 2000) and includes four intersecting components: communalism, critical mindedness, active engagement, flexibility. Communalism refers to a collective or communal worldview which emphasizes the connectedness of persons. Communalism comprises the high relevance of social bonds, obligations, and duties, reflecting a critical sense of interdependence to enhance well-being. The importance of collective relationships and extended and fictive kinship networks is seen in many cultural groups. Critical mindedness or critical consciousness helps protect against negative experiences of oppression; it is the process of critically evaluating and deconstructing social conditions and sociopolitical concerns. Critical mindedness is a developmental process which helps individuals to first recognize issues of inequity, then begin to develop strategies to address and eliminate inequities, and finally depersonalize experiences of oppression. The final stage of critical mindedness leads to action, and resilient youth engage in active engagement which includes agentic behavior in school, at home, and with peers. Resilient youth work to positively change and improve their environment. The final component, flexibility, includes bicultural skills and allows youth to adapt to a variety of situational demands. Bicultural skills allow children and youth of color to adjust behaviors, values, beliefs, and lifestyle concerns to match either the mainstream or traditional culture (APA, 2008).

Strengths of Families of Color

The literature advocates for the integration of therapy practices that are sensitive to the cultural experience, values, and needs of individuals and families, especially when working with clients from a racial or ethnic minority group. One of the basic assumptions of the strengths-based approach to therapy is that all individuals possess strengths that, if cultivated, can lead to an improved quality of life.

For clinicians providing therapy to racial/ethnic minority individuals and families, it is important to recognize and utilize the strengths and resources that the individuals and families possess. This section discusses strengths and characteristics of families of color.

Native Americans

Native Americans tend to value respect for nature, previous and future generations, silence and nonverbal communication, and a sense of communalism that includes all members of the extended family and the tribe. Tribes are interdependent systems, and individuals within the tribes are seen as a part of the tribe; there is not an emphasis on the individual unless it is related to how the individual is connected and related to tribal functioning. Decisions, behaviors, and values are derived from tribal membership. Native Americans value sharing and cooperation. There is a sense of shared resources, with the understanding that resources should be used as needed. Native Americans try to live in a harmonious and symbiotic relationship with nature. Their *being* worldview orientation, which differs from a Western *doing* orientation, allows them to choose behaviors to meet current needs for individuals or the groups, and to live in seasonal nature patterns. Traditional Native Americans also value noninterference, the importance of respecting others, and observing and responding thoughtfully. This translates into a more seemingly permissive parenting style, which allows freedom for the child, and promotes self-awareness. Spirituality is another important value, which includes the connection with all beings. Many believe that we are spiritual beings living within a particular time, and that noninterference helps individuals to grow and actualize (Schwarzbaum & Thomas, 2008).

African Americans

Boyd-Franklin (2003) outlines five strengths of African Americans that are a reflection the Afrocentric values. The first strength is the importance of extended family relationships, which includes family, friends, community members, important religious leaders. Family therapy is often recommended for African Americans due to the importance of social connections and communalism. The second strength is the importance of flexible gender roles. While many African Americans live in single-parent families or mother-headed households, there are not rigid stereotypes or expectations based on gender. Children are expected to contribute in multiple ways to the household, and are able to engage in a variety of roles. The third strength is spirituality. Clinicians should include religious leaders, pastors, or ministers in treatment, assess the importance of prayer as a coping mechanism, and the role of the church in providing resources for the client or family. The fourth and fifth strengths are the importance of education and hard work. Educational achievement is stressed in African American families and is often reinforced through religious institutions, and civic and community organizations. The communal nature of Africans requires that individuals contribute to the functioning and well-being of the group or tribe. This is reflected in valuing education and achievement as an adult competency for African Americans. African Americans are often seen as underachieving, are often disproportionately placed in special education classrooms, and have higher high school dropout rates than other groups. Social service providers need to work with clients around achievement, but also promote culturally relevant curriculums, work with teachers around expectations, and engage in programs that promote career development. Helping children and adolescents find mentors may also be effective for helping with achievement and career development.

Asian Americans

The term Asian American is used to describe a group of people whose origin can be traced back to countries within the geographic region of Asia. It includes individuals with Korean, Filipino,

Chinese, Japanese, Thai, Cambodian, Laotian, Indonesian, Indian, Pakistani, Vietnamese, Samoan, Guamanian, Hawaiian, Ceylonese, and other Pacific Islanders origin (Morishima, 1978). While each national group has its own cultural heritage, some generalizations can be made about their cultural strengths based on their similarities. Nguyen (1992), Ho (1987), and Berg and Jaya (1993) identified several strengths of Asian American culture. A cultural strength of Asian American culture is the value that is placed on family interdependence (Yee, Debaryshe, Yuen, Kim, & McCubbin, 2007). A strong emphasis is placed on the family with the belief that the extended family system is the most basic social unit. For this group, the needs and goals of an individual are placed below those of the group and younger family members are expected to be loyal to authority and give unconditional respect to adults. Despite how it may seem to a Western-minded clinician, many Asian American families experience inhibited emotional expression and authoritarian parenting styles as components of a harmonious relationship that is expected among family members.

For Asian Americans, a high value is placed on the context of the conversation when communicating such that nonverbal language—gestures, body language, eye contact, and voice quality—are as important as the words being spoken. Traditional Asian American cultures value rigid roles and status wherein each family member has a defined role and position in the family hierarchy. Each individual is expected to function within that role, regardless of their personal values and beliefs. With these values in mind, it is important for therapists working with Asian American families to be attentive to nonverbal cues, consider periods of silence as opportunities for reflection, and check often for understanding.

Latino Americans

Latino is a term used to describe people whose origin can be traced to any of the Latin American countries including Mexico, Puerto Rico, Cuba, Central and South America, and Spain. Ho (1987) and Marin and Marin (1991) identify family, spirituality, and fatalism as some cultural values of Latino families. The Latino family places emphasis on strong family loyalties, extended family networks, and interdependence among family members. Rotter and Casado (1998) highlight Latinos' regard for personalism, which differs from the American connotation of the term in that instead of an individualistic value of achievement, Latinos instead place emphasis on an individualistic value of self-worth. Instead of highlighting personal achievements, clinicians working with Latino families should focus on family members' evaluation of their own behaviors and attitudes.

Although the preceding passages provide a brief overview of some of the cultural strengths of Native Americans, African Americans, Asian Americans, and Latino Americans, it is imperative to be mindful that cultural identification is not mutually exclusive and instead exists on a continuum (Yoon, Langrehr, & Ong, 2011). Recent literature indicates that the cultural identity of racial/ethnic minorities may include a combination of more than one culture that is not necessarily equally salient at all times (Quintana, 2015). In considering the applicability of each cultural strength to the family, it is essential to be mindful of how other entities function as a part of the family's race. Each racial/ethnic minority family will differ in the extent to which the nuances of race/ethnicity, gender, class, religion, culture, and sexual orientation influence their strengths and values. For instance, a middle-class African American family may place a higher value on education while a lower class family may place a higher value on hard work.

Culturally responsive therapy should not be determined solely by broad knowledge of the culture. A culturally sensitive therapist must be aware of the intracultural differences that exist within each cultural group. The cultural strengths discussed are generalizations of each of the cultural groups and should not be seen as assets that every family that belongs to the cultural group ascribes to. Culturally responsive therapy should instead be tailored specifically to the family on the basis of the values and strengths with which it identifies. Because today's families are increasingly diverse, within the family, individual members may have different levels of cultural identification that may lead them to ascribe to different cultural values to different extents. Third generation Asian American families, for example, are more likely to be influenced by the dominant U.S. culture than the previous two generations. This may result in variability in the extent to which each family member values, for example, rigid roles and collectivist behaviors and attitudes.

Cultural Socialization Processes

Racial socialization is defined as the process by which African American parents raise children to have positive self-concepts in an environment that is racist and sometimes hostile and includes exposure to cultural practices, promotion of racial pride, development of knowledge of African American culture, and preparation for bias and discrimination (Hughes et al., 2006). Racial socialization processes have been linked to a variety of important outcomes in children and adolescents. Specifically, research suggests that parental racial socialization practices and messages are related to lower levels of depression and anxiety, and greater anger management, along with better school efficacy and achievement in children and adolescents (Bannon, McKay, Chacko, Rodriguez, & Cavaleri, 2009; Constantine & Blackmon, 2000; Davis & Stevenson, 2006; Marshall, 1995). Racial socialization processes serve as a protective factor against the negative psychological effects of racism (Neblett et al., 2008; Stevenson & Arrington, 2009) and as a way to bolster self-esteem (Harris-Britt, Valrie, Kurtz-Costes, & Rowley, 2007).

Clinical Vignettes

The following section includes cases of the authors which illustrate the use of culturally relevant strengths-based approaches.

Cultural Strengths

Katya was a 16-year-old girl whose family had recently integrated from Romania. Katya had developed a fear of going to school, which was so severe that she had missed nearly a month of school. Katya and her family lived close enough to the school for her to be able to walk. Unfortunately, Katya was accidentally hit by a snow plow one day while walking to school. She suffered from broken bones, and cuts and bruises, but was able to attend school shortly after the accident. The fear of going to school turned out to be a fear of walking to school, but the mother was also stressed and afraid to accompany her to school because of language issues and cultural differences. The father worked a late shift in a plant manufacturing cell phones and was unable to be present at home in the mornings to provide assistance. As only his income supported the family, they were anxious about him missing work to assist in the mornings, although all acknowledged that they felt the situation was grave as they feared that Katya would be expelled from school or fail. Every evening before he left for work, the father gave a prep talk to Katya and always felt reassured that she was going to be able to go to school the next day. When Katya tried to get ready, she would become extremely fearful, sometimes to the point of developing physical symptoms. She would become argumentative with her mother and often locked herself in the room. Truant officers and officials from the school tried to intervene but had limited success, as the mother did not speak English. It was arranged for the school to send assignments for Katya to complete at home.

Because of the nature of the presenting problem, the father's work schedule, and the mother's limited English proficiency, individual therapy was provided to Katya. It was determined to use systematic desensitization to overcome her fear. Katya and the therapist created a fear hierarchy that began with her getting up and getting ready for school to walking across the main road to the school entrance. We practiced this exercise for three weeks in individual sessions, but she had not been able to attend school despite engaging in relaxation activities in the morning. The mother attended the fourth session and watched as we engaged in the systematic desensitization. She became very excited and began to speak to Katya in Romanian. Katya translated for me, and began to describe a religious practice that her mother thought was similar to the systematic desensitization. According to their religious beliefs, fear is an emotion that can be handled by and replaced with the love of God. The mother began to describe a breathing exercise in which the person pictures his or her fear being swallowed by a warm ball of light, which represented God's love. The mother thought that Katya should begin to incorporate this religious practice with the therapy. We changed the systematic desensitization to include the image in which Katya, experiencing fear, would envision herself being enveloped by a warm ball of light. So for example, as she pictured herself approaching the street corner intersection to enter school, she took a deep breath and imagined the warm love of God covering her. This practice allowed her to overcome her fears and she was able to envision herself being accompanied by God to keep her safe all the way to school.

When asked why the family had not engaged in that exercise before treatment, Katya's mother explained that the practice includes lighting candles. Early when they arrived in America and rented their first apartment, they had an accident with a candle that burned a hole in the carpet. The landlord had prohibited them from burning candles again, and even though they felt they could do it safely, cultural issues and fears around immigration prevented them from engaging in the ritual. The treatment then focused on advocating for the family to be able to perform the ritual in the apartment with the landlord. They were able to find a safe place in the apartment to be able to light the candle and treatment ended shortly after that. Katya was able to re-enter school.

There are many lessons to be learned from this case. When working with families to empower them and foster resilience, clinicians need to initially assess for strengths, coping mechanisms, or cultural and/or religious practices of the family. Individual treatment was probably a poor initial strategy for Katya as it discounted the importance of the family in developing the treatment plan and selection of treatment interventions. A solution-focused family therapist would have worked with the family early on to look for exceptions for when Katya was able to overcome her fear or anxiety in other situations. The therapist would have also asked the family how they typically handled situations in which fear was present. A culturally sensitive therapist following a strengths-based approach that incorporated components to foster resilience would empower the family to select interventions based on cultural resources. Therapists need to ask if those practices or religious beliefs need to be incorporated into the treatment.

Therapists fostering strength also need to serve as advocates for the family with school, community agencies, or other organizations. It was important to serve as a cultural broker between Katya's parents and the school so that a plan could be developed to ensure that she was able to make academic progress at school. Part of this intervention was empowering Katya's mother to discuss her fears of cultural differences and language barriers. The school was more than willing to help assist Katya and the family, and mom became more comfortable interacting with school officials. It was also important in this case to advocate for the family to be able to engage in religious practices at home. The landlord experienced frustrations with the language barriers and decided to give a flat edict against lighting candles. Because of the parents' fears of being evicted, they did not try to negotiate with the landlord. Advocating and empowering the family allowed them to restore an important cultural practice.

Fostering resilience

Tony, Jr. (T.J.), is a 16-year-old African American young man who is the only child of Tony, Sr. (age 47) and Doreen (age 46). Tony works as a marketing executive for a major cellular company, and Doreen is an attorney. The family lives in an affluent suburb of a major metropolitan city and is one of five African American families in their area. T.J. attended public schools until high school. Although the public schools were among the best in the state, his parents felt that T.J. would need to be pushed and challenged to receive scholarships for top engineering schools. They enrolled T.J. in a private, predominantly White math and science academy outside of their neighborhood. During his freshman year, T.J. struggled to adjust; his parents believed he was having a negative reaction to the academic rigor of the new school, although T.J. protested that it was not the work but generally the negativity in the school. His grades were stellar at the end of the year. During his sophomore year, T.J. again complained about attending the school, and the family engaged in many fights about his desire to go to the public high school. T.J. complained that the students in the school were too "snobby" and that he was not making friends. Tony did not have much empathy for T.J. as his thoughts were that academics were more important than a social life. Doreen had more sympathy, but agreed that his school work and future were important. They "compromised" by becoming more involved in his school work and taking T.J. to more church social functions. His grades were also good at the end of his sophomore year.

During the summer before T. J.'s junior year, he became sullen and withdrawn. His parents became concerned and took him to his pediatrician who normalized the behaviors as part of changes from puberty. Shortly after school began, T. J. began to become more argumentative at home and at school. T. J. stopped turning in school assignments and his grades began to suffer. His parents became very concerned when T. J. was suspended from school after becoming involved in a fist fight over the basketball team. Therapy was recommended as part of the remediation program for school, and narrative therapy was selected as the approach for the family. During the initial session, both Doreen and Tony expressed their concern over his academics and getting into college. T. J. was quite withdrawn during the initial part of the session. When asked for his opinion about why his parents were seeking treatment for him, T. J. became quite animated and explained that while they were primarily concerned with his grades, college, and future, he was struggling in the present and he felt that they would not be able to hear his true feelings and complaints. The therapist decided to pursue a narrative approach to treatment for several reasons. It seemed clear that the stories and narratives that T. J. tried to tell his parents went unheeded and that their narrative regarding his grades and future did not meet his. The therapist also felt that there might be cultural and racial concerns and, given the importance of the developmental process at T. J.'s age, was concerned about the sociocultural and sociopolitical influence on the family's narratives.

The therapist engaged in psychoeducation with the family regarding using narrative therapy to address the family's concerns. The presenting problem was reframed to include important developmental tasks for T. J.; the family became united in constructing a narrative that would suit him and allow him to more clearly define his future. The therapist also engaged the family in a discussion on the APA resilience model for African American youth.

T. J.'s excitement over the model led the therapist to ask the family how often they spoke with T. J. about culture and race. Narrative therapy has an emphasis on sociopolitical factors, and eliciting discussions on race would also allow for attention to cultural strengths. Tony indicated that he felt the family was pretty open about discussing racism and oppression. Part of the reason, he explained, that they selected the math and science academy was to allow T. J. to be able to move forward as a Black man. Tony and Doreen had benefitted from the Civil Rights Movement and affirmative action, but they wanted T. J. to be able to achieve on his own, without the stigma of affirmative action. The family had been actively participating in an African American church and spent lots of time with their extended family. Doreen stated that they were sure that T. J. was secure in his identity. He seemed adept at handling multicultural settings and contexts. They were pleased that T. J. had both White and Black friends, although Tony noticed that he had been spending less time with friends. They had assumed this was because of the intensity of his school work.

T. J. seemed stunned by his parents' remarks. When addressed by the therapist, T. J. said that he felt that both parents had no idea about how he felt about his race, and that was part of his main concern with school. And contrary to what his parents believed, he felt totally insecure about what it means to be a Black man in America. The therapist asked if he had always had concerns, and T. J. responded that there were indeed new issues for him that started in high school. Although he knew he was Black during elementary and middle school, he had always been with the friends he had grown up with, and race was never discussed. The youth at the high school constantly talked to T. J. and asked questions about what it meant to be Black or made comments to him that they did not see T. J. as Black. It seemed as if T. J. experienced several incidents that the therapist categorized as *microaggressions*, remarks that were not intended to be overtly racist but had caused T. J. to spend a great deal of time reflecting. The fight that led to the suspension was over a statement that a White youth had made. He "jokingly" fussed at T. J. for not being a member of the basketball team. When T. J. indicated his lack of interest in basketball, the student continued that T. J. probably preferred playing with his "homies" on the court at home. T. J. snapped and hit him. The therapist noted T. J.'s interest in the resilience model and thought it might be a useful way for the family to help T. J. create a new narrative. The therapist and the family planned to use both the narrative approach and resilience model to address their concerns.

The next sessions were focused on examining the resilience model. The therapist began discussing communalism and the importance for T. J. feeling that he had a good source of social support with his extended family and peers. T. J. had normally spent part of the summers with his grandparents in the south, but had not done so this summer due to changes in Tony's work schedule. T. J. explained that being with his family was like a reprieve for him from dealing with racial issues at school. He has an older cousin, Robert, who lives and attends college near his grandparents. He was hoping to be able to discuss being a Black man with Robert, who, like Tony, was not interested in basketball and was pursuing a science career. T. J. thought that Robert could provide some tips since he seemed to have successfully made it through high school with his identity intact. T. J. reported that while he enjoyed some social activities at church, he was lately also receiving pressure from some of the youth regarding his identity. They often teased T. J. for speaking properly and "acting White" by being so focused on his school work. He felt he had less in common with his former school mates, and it all came to a head this summer when the trip to visit family was cancelled. He was very lonely during the summer, which led to the sullen and withdrawn behaviors. The family decided to let T. J. visit with Robert over a weekend. They also began to help him identify youth at church with whom he felt comfortable for social events outside of church.

The family engaged in discussions about the importance of T. J. becoming more flexible and bicultural in his interactions with others. T. J. was encouraged to find allies at school who were not likely to make microaggressions, and his social life at the school began to change. In one session, T. J. expressed his frustration at always having to represent Blacks at the school. The therapist encouraged Tony and Doreen to share their experiences with racism both at school and currently at work. T. J. was surprised that his parents also had oppressive experiences. The therapist encouraged both parents to help T. J. to find "comebacks" (Stevenson, 2014) to use when he felt racism was occurring. T. J. was able to come up with funny one-liners to respond to students he felt were not being racially sensitive. This approach was taken as humor helps to diffuse emotions and fits with the development and use of humor and sarcasm, a developmental strength for T. J.

T. J. then began to express his desire for race and culture to be more prominently discussed at school. The therapist discussed the need for both critical mindedness and active engagement as important skills that T. J. would need. T. J. felt that the school was superficial in acknowledging cultural issues, and wondered if the school would be open to developing a diversity club. The therapist encouraged T. J. and his parents to meet with either an administrator or teacher who they felt might be open to the idea. T. J. made a list of critical issues that he felt needed to be addressed, and with his parents' encouragement, he and some friends approached the social studies teacher to be a sponsor for the club. The therapist also encouraged the parents to take T. J. to other cultural events and activities to help him learn more about African American heritage and Afrocentric values. As T. J. began to change his narrative and to feel more comfortable with his identity, he became more engaged in school and his grades improved.

This case helps demonstrate the importance of helping families of color engage in processes of discussing sociopolitical and cultural concerns in treatment, especially as related to the presenting problem. Narrative therapy is quite effective in helping individuals to discuss the relevance of culture to their lives and functioning (Semmler & Williams, 2000). Often, family members are surprised to discover the role that culture and dominant values place on the development of meaning in their lives.

Challenges and Recommendations for Future Practices

The changing structure of families and the increase in diversity in our country make it critical that therapists who work with culturally diverse families engage in a strengths-based approach. Therapists cannot adopt a deficit approach or framework in working with ethnic minorities and must become educated on important cultural values. With that said, it must be acknowledged that providing culturally sensitive and relevant treatment can be quite complex and challenging. It is critical to acknowledge the importance of understanding systemic factors in treatment, and in working with culturally diverse families, this includes the intersection of family systems and cultural factors. Even in the organization of this chapter, models on strengths-based approaches and resilience were written individually without integration. Skilled therapists must balance family dynamics with cultural norms of family structure, roles, and function. This needs to include levels of acculturation to dominant norms and standards. It also needs to incorporate additional intersecting cultural factors, particularly social class. The complexity of the work almost requires constructivist approaches which allow clients to explore the meaning of their culture and identity.

The second set of challenges includes the stereotypes, assumptions, and hidden biases that clinicians bring to treatment. Media images of ethnic minorities, particularly of African Americans and Latinos, reinforces and exacerbates negative perceptions that people have. Therapists have to explore their biases and make concerted efforts to change them and increase their exposure to culturally diverse individuals. Language barriers need to be addressed in treatment, and therapeutic translators may need to be incorporated in treatment (Schwarzbaum & Thomas, 2008). Finally, therapists will need to become advocates and help families to address sociocultural and sociopolitical concerns.

Conclusion

Strengths-based approaches to working with culturally diverse families are quite effective in promoting resilience and positive functioning in individuals and families. Family and cultural resilience models provide an emphasis on promoting critical consciousness of families and advocating and empowering youth.

References

Allison, S., Stacey, K., Dadds, V., Roeger, L., Wood, A., & Martin, G. (2003). What the family brings: gathering evidence for strengths-based work. *Journal of Family Therapy, 25,* 263–284.

American Psychological Association, Task Force on Resilience and Strength in Black Children and Adolescents. (2008). *Resilience in African American children and adolescents: A vision for optimal development.* Washington, DC: Author.

Anthony, E. J. (1974). The syndrome of the psychologically invulnerable child. In E. J. Anthony & C. Koupernik (Eds.), *The child in his family: Children at psychiatric risk* (Vol. 3, pp. 3–10). New York: Wiley.

Arredondo, P., Toporek, R., Brown, S. P., Jones, J., Locke, D. C., Sanchez, J., & Stadler, H. (1996). Operationalization of the multicultural counseling competencies. *Journal of Multicultural Counseling and Development, 24*(1), 42–78.

Bannon, W. M., Jr., McKay, M. M., Chacko, A., Rodriguez, J. A., & Cavaleri, M., Jr. (2009). Cultural pride reinforcement as a dimension of racial socialization protective of urban African American child anxiety. *Families in Society: The Journal of Contemporary Human Services, 90*(1), 79.

Beeghly M, Cicchetti D. (1994). Child maltreatment, attachment and the self system: Emergence of an internal state lexicon in toddlers at high social risk. *Development and Psychopathology, 6,* 5–30.

Berg, I.K., & Jaya, A. (1993). Different and the same: Family therapy with Asian American families. *Journal of Marital and Family Therapy, 19,* 31–38.

Boyd-Franklin, N. (2003). *Black families in therapy: Understanding the African American experience.* New York: Guilford.

Boykin, A.W. (2000). The Talent Development model of schooling: Placing students at promise for academic success. *Journal of Education for Students Placed at Risk, 5,* 3–25.

Constantine, M. G., & Blackmon, S. M. (2002). Black adolescents' racial socialization experiences: Their relations to home, school, and peer self-esteem. *Journal of Black Studies, 32,* 322–335.

Davis, G., & Stevenson, H. C. (2006). Racial socialization experiences and symptoms of depression among Black youth. *Journal of Child and Family Studies, 15,* 303–317.

DeFrain, J., & Asay, S.M. (2007). Strong families around the world: An introduction to the family strengths perspective. *Marriage & Family Review, 41*(1–2), 1–10.

Freedman, J., & Combs, G. (1996). *Narrative therapy: The social construction of preferred realities.* New York, NY: Norton.

Garmezy, N. (1974). The study of competence in children at risk for severe psychopathology. In E. J. Anthony & C. Koupernik (Eds.), *The child in his family: Children at psychiatric risk* (Vol. 3). New York: Wiley.

Harris-Britt, A., Valrie, C. R., Kurtz-Costes, B., & Rowley, S. J. (2007). Perceived racial discrimination and self-esteem in African American youth: Racial socialization as a protective factor. *Journal of Research on Adolescence,* 17, 669–682.

Harrison, A. O., Wilson, M. N., Pine, C. J., Chon, S. Q., & Buriel, R. (1990). Family ecologies of ethnic minority children. *Child Development,* 61, 347–362.

Hawley, D. R. (2000). Clinical implications of family resilience. *The American Journal of Family Therapy,* 28, 101–116.

Ho, M.K. (1987). Family therapy with Asian/Pacific Americans. In M.K. Ho (Series Ed.), *Family therapy with ethnic minorities* (Vol. 5, pp. 24–68). Newbury Park, CA: Sage.

Jacobs, C.Y. (2009). A study of the influence of political, school, and family contexts on the relationship between immigration status and immigrant generation status and educational outcomes among low-income urban adolescents. *ProQuest Dissertations.* Paper AAI3363371. Retrieved on April 14, 2015 from http://repository. upenn.edu/dissertations/AAI3363371.

Katz, J.H. (1985). The sociopolitical nature of counseling. *The Counseling Psychologist, 13,* 615–624.

Luthar, S.S., Cicchetti, D., & Becker, B. (2000). The construct of resilience: A critical evaluation and guidelines for future work. *Child Development, 71,* 543–562.

Marin, G., & Marin, B.V. (1991). *Research with Hispanic populations.* Newbury Park, CA: Sage.

Marshall, S. (1995). Ethnic socialization of African American children: Implications for parenting, identity development, and academic achievement. *Journal of Youth and Adolescence, 24,* 377–396.

Masten, A.S. (2001). Ordinary magic: Resilience processes in development. *American Psychologist, 56,* 227–238.

Morishima, J. (1978). The Asian American experience. *Journal of the Society of Ethnic and Special Studies, 2,* 8–10.

Neblett, E.W. Jr., Philip, C. L., Cogburn, C. D., & Sellers, R. M. (2006). African American adolescents' discrimination experiences and academic achievement: Racial socialization as a cultural compensatory and protective factor. *Journal of Black Psychology, 32,* 199–218.

Nguyen, N.A. (1992). Living between two cultures: Treating first-generation Asian Americans. In L.A. Vargas & J.D. Koss-Chioino (Eds.), *Working with culture* (pp. 204–222). San Francisco, CA: Jossey-Bass.

O'Hanlon, W., & Weiner-Davis, M. (1989). *In search of solutions: A new direction in psychotherapy.* New York, NY: Norton.

Quintana, S. (2015). Forward. In C.E. Santos & A.J. Umaña-Taylor (Eds.), *Studying ethnic identity: Methodological and conceptual approaches across disciplines* (pp. *xi–xiii*). Washington, DC: American Psychological Association.

Rotter, J.C., & Casado, M. (1998). Promoting strengths and celebrating culture: Working with Hispanic families. *The Family Journal: Counseling and Therapy for Couples and Families, 6,* 132–136.

Saltzman, W. R., Lester, P., Beardslee, W. R., Layne, C. M., Woodward, K., & Nash, W. P. (2011). Mechanisms of risk and resilience in military families: Theoretical and empirical basis of a family-focused resilience enhancement program. *Clinical Child Family Psychology Review, 14,* 213–230.

Schwarzbaum, S., & Thomas, A. J. (2008). *Dimensions of multicultural counseling: A life story approach.* Thousand Oaks: Sage.

Semmler, P.L., & Williams, C.B. (2000). Narrative therapy: A storied context for multicultural counseling. *Journal of multicultural counseling and development, 28,* 51–62.

Spencer, M.B., Harpalani, V., Cassidy, E., Jacobs, C.Y., Donde, S., & Goss, T.N. (2006). Understanding vulnerability and resilience from a normative developmental perspective: Implications for racially and ethnically diverse youth. In D. Cicchetti & D.J. Cohen (Eds.), *Developmental psychopathology: Vol. 1. Theory and method* (2nd ed., pp. 627–672). Hoboken, NJ: Wiley.

Stevenson, H. C. (2014) *Promoting racial literacy in schools: Differences that make a difference.* New York: Teachers College.

Stevenson, H. C., & Arrington, E. G. (2009). Racial/ethnic socialization mediates perceived racism and the racial identity of African American adolescents. *Cultural Diversity and Ethnic Minority Psychology, 15,* 125–136.

Thomas, A.J., & Rodgers, C. (2009). Resilience and protective factors for African American and Latina girls. In J. Chin (Ed.), *Diversity in mind and action* (Vol. 3, pp. 117–128). Westport, CT: Praeger Press.

Umaña-Taylor, A.J., Zeiders, K.H., & Updegraff, K.A. (2013). Family ethnic socialization and ethnic identity: a family-driven, youth-driven, or reciprocal process? *Journal of Family Psychology, 27,* 137–146.

U.S. Census Bureau. (2000). http://www.census.gov/PressRelease/www/releases/archives/hispanic_origin_ population/000490.html. Retrieved November 2004.

Walsh, F. (2003). Family resilience: A framework for clinical practice. *Family Process, 42*(1), 1–16.

Werner, E. E. (1993). Risk, resilience, and recovery: Perspectives from the Kauai longitudinal study. *Development and Psychopathology, 5,* 503–515.

Whitaker, C.A. (1981). Process techniques of family therapy. In R.G. Green & J.L. Framo (Eds.), *Family therapy: Major contributions* (pp. 419–444). Madison, WI: International Universities Press.

White, M., & Epston, D. (1990). *Narrative means to therapeutic ends.* New York, NY: Norton.

Yoon, E., Langrehr, K., & Ong, L. Z. (2011). Content analysis of acculturation research in counseling and counseling psychology: a 22-year review. *Journal of Counseling Psychology, 58,* 83–96.

6

Strengths-Based Approaches and Strategies in School Counseling

E. C. M. Mason, Tasia Buford-Howell, Megan Kelly,
and Vanessa M. Whitnell

> A teacher's purpose is not to create students in her own image, but to develop students
> who can create their own image.
>
> Author Unknown

In recent years, there have been philosophical and applied shifts in the practice of counseling, couples/marital and family therapy, and psychology. Many practitioners have moved from the medical model, which highlighted pathology, to one that encourages the development of assets (Smith, 2006). Strengths-based work, which historically dates back to several early social workers (Healy, 2005; Rapp, 1997; Saleebey, 2002), is representative of this shift as it is concerned with focusing on individuals' strengths instead of deficiencies. The goal of the strengths-based approach is for the individual to identify and apply the skills and strengths he, she, or they currently possesses to areas of life that pose challenges.

Strengths-based work is set apart from other techniques because it is asset-oriented. Using a strengths-based practice, clients are tasked with using the counseling session as an opportunity to brainstorm how they can use their inherent and learned strengths and skills to solve problems. Not only does strengths-based counseling help clients solve seemingly unsolvable situations in the present, but it also provides a foundation of skills to draw from in the future. This chapter discusses the significance of strengths-based work as it applies to school counseling and fits with the role and responsibilities of the school counselor.

The practice of strengths-based work in the context of the specific field of school counseling is a natural fit (Galassi & Akos, 2007). The role of the school counselor, by definition, includes imparting students with skills that they can apply throughout life as well as helping them to identify the tools and strengths they already possess. In the strengths-based framework, school counselors have the opportunity to help students develop positive characteristics such as resiliency and higher levels of self-esteem.

This chapter will present a theoretical basis for using a strengths-based approach in school counseling. Strengths-based approaches and strategies will be presented as they connect to other relevant theories and practices. In addition, this chapter will demonstrate specific ways in which school counselors can utilize strengths-based strategies in individual counseling, group counseling, classroom guidance, school wide programming, and in consulting with families and school staff.

Objectives

The purpose of this chapter is to introduce the reader to the practice of using strengths-based strategies in school counseling. Work with children and adolescents, families, and school staff lends itself quite naturally to strengths-based approaches. The school setting is unique and thus presents some particular opportunities and challenges for strengths-based counseling.

The objectives of this chapter are for the reader to:

- Understand the school counselor's use of strengths-based approaches and strategies
- Understand strengths-based counseling with various school-based populations
- Understand strengths-based counseling in the school setting
- Consider the theoretical underpinnings and research support of strengths-based counseling in schools and school counseling
- Examine practical applications of strengths-based counseling in school counseling

Review of Literature

A strengths-based approach involves building on the positive skills and characteristics of students as opposed to targeting problem behaviors. Its globalized mission statement and proclivity towards cultural sensitivity makes it an ideal approach for any student population (Galassi & Akos, 2007). Implementing this approach into the school setting has been proven to be beneficial for children and adolescents (Madden, Green, & Grant, 2011). Positive effects of the strengths-based approach for children and adolescents can include increased levels of autonomy, self-esteem, life satisfaction, and resilience, as well as a lower likelihood of substance use, truancy, and conduct problems (Madden et al., 2011; McCammon, 2012; Proctor et al., 2011).

According to Galassi and Akos (2007), strengths-based work views "personal/social, academic, and career development as interrelated and overlapping," which makes it a powerful, effective, and multifunctional approach (p. 193). If school counselors and other school staff members can help students to improve personal life through strengths-based work, then students' academic and career development aspects should be positively affected as well. An aspect that makes strengths-based work so unique is its universal interventions and ideology. Strengths-based work allows school counselors to apply its techniques and principles into their schools given its appreciation for "cultural [e.g., ethnic identity] and other contextual factors [e.g., urban versus rural environments] that affect the acquisition and development" of students' strengths, which allows it to reach an even greater audience compared to many other developmental interventions (Galassi & Akos, 2007, p. 296).

Numerous studies have been conducted over the last decade to test the efficacy of strengths-based interventions on individuals. One study in particular by Madden et al. (2011) set out to determine whether or not there was a correlation between strengths-based coaching and overall well-being in adolescent males. The researchers implemented a strengths-based coaching program with 38 males between the ages of 10 and 11 years of age in a private school in Sydney, Australia. The participants in the program had a series of face-to-face coaching sessions in which they identified personal character strengths, resources to help them achieve their goals, and created a self-regulation cycle that involved setting goals, developing action plans, and monitoring and evaluating progress. According to Madden et al. (2011), results from this study found significant increases in the students' self-reported levels of engagement (i.e., their ability to handle challenges) and hope, which support the notion that strengths-based work has a positive impact on students' general welfare (p. 77).

Related to strengths-based work, the practice of positive psychology involves "intentional activities that aim to cultivate positive feelings, behaviors, or cognitions" (Proctor et al., 2011, p. 387), which has been researched extensively by Seligman, Steen, Park, and Peterson (2005). These researchers found that students' depressive symptoms subsided for six months after they were given a positive psychological intervention wherein they were asked to identify different strengths they possessed each day over the course of one week (Proctor et al., 2011). As an expansion of the work conducted by Seligman et al. (2005), Proctor et al. (2011) set out to find the effects of a positive psychological program on 319 students between the ages of 12 and 14 years. This study found that the participants who were exposed to the positive psychology intervention program reported an increase in life satisfaction and self-esteem compared with the participants who were not exposed to the positive psychology intervention program.

McCammon (2012) mentioned in her article that students who are counseled through a problems-based lens are likely to lose their sense of autonomy as well as any connection to their community, which can prevent them from taking on leadership roles and assuming responsibilities within their communities. Conversely, McCammon (2012) explained that those who are exposed to a strengths-based framework feel higher levels of affirmation, empowerment, and intrinsic motivation. McCammon (2012) stated that positive youth development requires practitioners to identify individual strengths of the adolescent, sufficient community support for its adolescents, and protective factors that help adolescents to have a positive outlook despite living in high-risk contexts. McCammon (2012) identified a series of social and emotional benefits that come from social and emotional learning (SEL) programs, which are designed to promote youth's strengths while inhibiting problem behaviors. These benefits include "self-awareness, social awareness, self-management, relationship skills, and responsible decision making" (McCammon, 2012, p. 563). The author noted that research findings showed the combination of a strengths-based approach with SEL programs decreased the likelihood of students dropping out of school, improved attendance rates, and reduced the likelihood of substance use and conduct problems.

For strengths-based interventions to have a beneficial effect on adolescents, educators need to reframe the way school counselors work with students when they are struggling. Hewitt (2005) noted that many school staff members are quick to focus on students' faults, which oftentimes inhibits solution-finding because they can be so preoccupied with what students have done wrong. Hewitt (2005) stated that "[i]f you focus on the negative, the negative grows. If you focus on the positive, the positive grows," which is the underlying basis of strengths-based work (p. 24). She supports this theory by explaining that if children are to exude optimism and resilience then school staff must first model it for them. The author provided eight behaviors of teachers who incorporate strengths-based work into their classrooms. These behaviors include the following: (1) focusing on what the student can do; (2) making realistic appraisals and avoiding the use of generalizations; (3) looking for and giving credit for evidence of progress, without minimizing or discounting the positive; (4) positively reframing behavior; (5) looking for the "silver lining" in a student's behavior and starting there; (6) working with the factors that you can control; (7) looking at the whole picture—it is as important to focus on the factors that are present when the misbehavior does not occur as when it does; and (8) being aware of the labels that you use and the projections that you make" (Hewitt, 2005). Hewitt explained that these eight behaviors allow the educator to place emphasis on students' positive attributes, which in turn makes a positive impact on students. Hewitt (2005) stated that taking an optimistic view does not mean that the educator avoids problems, but rather, "It means that you look for what you are able to nourish in order to overcome those problems" (p. 25).

Academic Achievement

Strengths-based school counseling is effective with school-aged youth and can be a means to increasing academic achievement. The findings of research conducted by Park and Peterson (2008) show that students' academic achievement is influenced by more than just individual intelligence. Achievement is impacted by a set of character strengths including perseverance, gratitude, and hope, which should be recognized, celebrated, and encouraged. These strengths should be cultivated in students who already possess them and individual and group interventions should be designed to develop and strengthen them (Park & Peterson, 2008).

Dixon and Tucker (2008) discuss how "mattering" can have an impact on students' academic success. A student's ability to feel he or she matters (i.e., feels needed), is wanted and valued is an integral part of his or her social and emotional development. If the student successfully achieves the task of belonging and mattering in his or her identity development, the positive attributes associated with this achievement can result in the desire and need to succeed.

It is relatively simple to make students feel as though they matter in individual counseling work by using basic counseling skills such as active listening and unconditional positive regard. Dixon and Tucker (2008) outline how school counselors can apply mattering in individual work:

> (a) verbally and nonverbally attending to students; (b) demonstrating how important students are to school counselors and to the counseling process by acknowledging students' continual attendance, participation, opinions/ideas, and completion of out-of-counseling goals and homework; and (c) illustrating to students that school counselors actually rely on them for successful counseling goals and outcomes because it is up to them to apply what they are learning from their counseling experiences. (p. 124)

In classroom guidance lessons, school counselors should make a point to ensure every student has a role. The counselor should allow each student to have meaningful participation, creating a sense of mattering to the group and the lesson. This practice can also be impactful for the teacher as the school counselor demonstrates how critical it is to show students they matter in the classroom (Dixon & Tucker, 2008).

Similarly, teachers' expectations of students are a reliable indicator of academic achievement. In a study conducted by Rosenthal (as cited in Aronson, 2002), results showed that students who were predicted to show academic gains throughout the school year on the basis of their performance on a non-verbal test of intelligence had greater intellectual gains as their teachers had been led to expect them. When teachers were asked about the classroom behavior of the students, they reported "the children in whom intellectual growth was expected became more intellectually alive and autonomous, or at least were so perceived by their teachers" (Aronson, 2002, p. 30). Conversely, students who were in the control group and were not expected to grow intellectually, but did, were regarded by the teachers as "less-well adjusted, less interesting, and less affectionate" (Aronson, 2002, p. 30).

It is very clear that when students believe they have an important role in their school community, they feel valued. As a result, they have higher self-esteem and acquire some of the characteristics required to be successful as well as the desire to succeed. Likewise, teachers' expectations of students influence their perception of and behavior towards the students, which in turn positively impacts students' performance.

Minority Groups

Strengths-based school counseling can be especially impactful for students who come from groups who have been historically discriminated against, marginalized, and have often already been led to believe they have deficiencies. Educators are well positioned to train students to reframe this negative thinking by highlighting their strengths through celebrating their culture. For example, first generation Latino/as enrolled in U.S. schools often have trouble becoming familiar with the school environment, have lower test scores than their peers, and higher dropout rates (Villalba, 2007).

Strengths-based work with this population frames cultural traits, traditions, customs, and language as assets instead of deficits and engages personal assets for confronting stressors.

Villalba (2007) suggests that counselors highlight three culture specific assets—bilingualism, biculturalism, and the strength they gain from family bonds. Some Latino/as have the advantage of speaking two languages fluently upon graduation from high school. Being bilingual is an advantage in the increasingly global society and many Latino/as are unaware of how this may work to their advantage in the job marketplace. However, in an attempt to acculturate, they often neglect their Spanish fluency in order to learn English (Villalba, 2007). In the strengths-based framework, this is an opportunity for the counselor to make the student aware of opportunities that come along with bilingualism instead of focusing on limited language proficiency. This shift could result in increased self-esteem, self-efficacy, and post high school expectations (Villalba, 2007).

Although some Latino/as may find biculturalism difficult, the ability to maintain their native culture as well as understand and navigate U.S. culture, is an asset. The fact that they are able to balance two or more cultures shows resiliency and resourcefulness, and can be used to reduce the effects of stress related to acculturation. This ability can also be indicative of success in navigating in a variety of systems such as schools (Villalba, 2007).

Family bonds can be just as important to Latino/as as language and culture. The school counselor's main focus when working with these students through a strengths-based lens should emphasize family closeness, unit, and resilience. The school counselor can work with the individual student to identify individuals within the family who may be able to assist with current problems in a similar manner in which they have helped in the past. This approach can also be extrapolated so as to build a sense of community through a psychoeducational group for Latino/a students, in which they can share stories of their families' experiences and how they may have worked through challenges (Villalba, 2007).

It is important to note that whereas all cultures value strengths, strengths may not look the same across groups as culture plays a major role in how strengths are expressed. Moreover, characteristics valued as strengths in one culture could be viewed as weaknesses in another. For instance, in individualistic cultures autonomy is a highly regarded strength. However, in collectivist cultures social competence and connectedness are valued (Smith, 2006).

Resilience

"Resilience refers to a class of phenomena characterized by good outcomes in spite of serious threats to adaptation or development" (Masten, 2001, p. 228). Most at-risk students possess an innate strength to overcome the adversity they face. It has consistently been shown that youth from families with high dysfunction and who lack resources are able to not only survive, but also create adequate lives for themselves (Smith, 2006). They cite their exposure to protective factors as buffers. Benard (as cited in Smith, 2006) listed three key protective factors for children: (a) a caring and supportive relationship with at least one person, preferably an adult; (b) consistently clear, high expectations communicated to the child; and (c) sufficient opportunity to contribute meaningfully to one's social environment (p. 51).

Protective factors can be either internal or external. The family, school community, peers, and society are external factors. School-related protective factors for students include commitment to school, positive relationship with at least one teacher, academic achievement, college aspirations, high expectations for success, and leadership and decision making at the school. In many ways, resiliency lays the groundwork for strengths-based work because clients/students can look back on situations they have overcome and identify the strengths that may help them continue to overcome. "Resiliency provides the process by which strength is developed" (Smith, 2006, p. 32).

Application

Common Applications in School Counseling

Strengths-based approaches and techniques in school counseling are common. Given the developmental nature of working with school-aged populations, the practice of identifying strengths in students is a highly productive strategy for school counselors in assisting with student growth in a variety of areas. The American School Counselor Association's (ASCA, 2012) national model recommends that school counselors serve students in three general domains: academic, career/college, and social/emotional. A strengths-based approach to all three of these domains can be the theoretical and practical foundation of a school counselor's work and the school counseling program as a whole (Galassi & Akos, 2007).

One particular model of strengths-based beliefs and strategies that is frequently used in school counseling is the solution-focused counseling (SFC) or solution-focused brief counseling (SFBC) model (Berg & Steiner, 2003; deShazer & Dolan, 2007; Sklare, 2014). This model suggests, at its core, that students have the skills they need to solve most problems on the basis of inherent strengths and skills developed from previous experiences. The role of the school counselor is to help students gain insight into their strengths and skills and to apply them to novel situations. Interactive SFBC activities such as goal setting, the use of rating scales, and "the miracle question" help the school counselor to draw out this insight and move towards a plan of action. The targeted, problem-solving, and positive nature of the solution-focused model, particularly the brief version, lends itself well to school counselors who often have large caseloads and thus abbreviated time with students (Sklare, 2014).

Individual applications

Strengths-based approaches and strategies, including the solution-focused model, are most often associated with working with individual students in school counseling (Berg & Steiner, 2003; Sklare, 2014). Examples of this might include assisting students in the domains mentioned earlier such as working through grief and loss (social/emotional), creating a plan to improve a grade in a class (academic), or drafting a college application essay (career). For example, in the case of grief and loss, the school counselor can assist a student in identifying coping strategies and resources that were used in previously challenging situations and help him or her translate those to the current grief and loss experience. The hope of using such a practice is that students begin to internalize the strengths-discovery process on their own so that they become more independent in finding solutions to common problems.

School counselors can be intentional in individual counseling about using strengths-based language when referring to students, themselves, or others. In this way, school counselors can teach students strengths-based vocabulary, words, and phrases such as *resilience, positive self-reflection*, and *affirmation*. Teaching students this language provides them with alternatives to the deficit-based language they may hear throughout the day and from other sources, supports their positive self-talk, and assists them in being able to reframe seemingly negative challenges as opportunities for growth.

Group counseling applications

In a group counseling setting, school counselors can draw upon strengths-based techniques to encourage vicarious learning among group members. For example, in a group designed to help students recover from and/or prevent dating violence, school counselors can ask members to identify their individual coping skills, strengths, and resources. This can be done in a variety of ways such as simple discussion or in using creative techniques like constructing vision boards, collage, or having students write notes of affirmation to themselves or others in the group. In hearing, seeing, or witnessing the skills, strengths, and resources of others, members may gain new insights into themselves as well as learn new strategies that they can also adopt.

Further, as in individual counseling, the school counselor him- or herself can also be a strengths-based model for students in the way that he or she speaks and acts if confronted with a challenge. Minimal but strategic self-disclosure of personal experiences working through common problems using a strengths-based framework can help students normalize their own concerns while also building hope.

Large group or school wide applications

Mentoring programs and anti-bullying campaigns coordinated by school counselors are just two examples of large group or school wide interventions that constitute strengths-based work. At this level, the power of a strengths-based approach is systemic, impacting many, and, if successful, can help to create a strengths-based culture in schools. School counselors can be uniquely instrumental in helping create a strengths-based culture by implementing such programs with intentionality and a data-driven design. For example, school counselors can conduct classroom or grade level presentations, distribute materials, provide trainings and information to parents and staff that outline the school's value of diversity and how to engage in learning about various cultures both in class as well as at home. Further, when school counselors include all staff and families to join in on such activities, and also engage the residential and retail community in which the school resides, the strengths-based efforts can have exponential impact well beyond the original goals of the school counseling program.

Special populations

School counselors' awareness of and response to special populations, particularly those who may be marginalized by school policy, are important indicators of a school counseling program grounded in a strengths-based approach. Such populations may include, but are certainly not limited to the following:

- Ethnic or racial minority students
- Students in temporary living situations or those in poverty
- Students with disabilities
- English language learners
- Third culture students
- Refugee students
- First generation college students
- Students who are non-gender conforming
- Gender identity or sexual orientation minority students

Providing in-school counseling services and special programs, as well as connecting these populations with external resources, capitalizes on a strengths-based approach. Whether working with the students or school staff, school counselors can help identify the unique strengths of these student populations. This is especially important if the strengths and skills of a group are not necessarily valued by the school or community culture. In doing this work, a school counselor's role as an advocate becomes a critical element in manifesting a strengths-based approach. For example, examining and challenging data that suggests minority students are less often enrolled in honors and Advanced Placement courses in a school demonstrates an equity-focused and strengths-based approach of a school counselor.

Fit with the ASCA model

The ASCA (2012) national model itself can be seen as a strengths-based document and one that promotes strengths-based school counseling practices and programs. Given that the four themes of the model are leadership, advocacy, collaboration, and systemic change, the model assumes a positive role for school counselors on behalf of the work they do for students. While the ASCA model does not outline or reference specific techniques or approaches, it stands on the premise that school counselors serve all students, thus acknowledging the strength of a program lies in its ability to honor the unique needs of each and every student, individually and as they belong to various groups. Further, the ASCA model empowers the school counselor as a change agent whose origin of professional identity as such is elemental to the delivery of a program that is grounded in serving all students (Mason, Ockerman, & Chen-Hayes, 2013).

In addition, the ASCA national model encourages other practices that support a strengths-based framework for serving students. These other practices include the use of an advisory council with diverse stakeholders to provide input and feedback for the school counseling program, visioning and goal setting by the school counselor(s), a data-driven approach to providing services to students through the school counseling program, and the examining and sharing of positive outcomes of the program via evaluation and communication tools.

Case Studies

School-Based Case Study: Brave Bucks

In an effort to reinforce positive behaviors among adolescents, one urban high school's school counseling program has helped to implement a program called *Brave Bucks*, which aims to instill the school values of responsibility, team work, leadership, loyalty, and determination among all members of the student body. Each week, school staff members are provided with ten yellow tickets, which are awarded to students when they are observed modeling one of the school values. Students are recognized for a host of behaviors, including being on time to class, dressing in the proper uniform, turning in assignments on time, helping others, et cetera. Students who receive brave bucks can redeem their tickets for a prize at the end of each week (e.g., gift-card, out of uniform pass, free homework pass, snacks, etc.) and are recognized on television monitors across the school. This proactive and strengths-based approach has helped the school to increase academic performance and attendance, to decrease discipline concerns, and to promote a positive school culture among both faculty and students.

Group-Based Case Study: Peer Council

In a school district with one of the highest in-school and out-of-school suspension rates in the country, one high school uses a program called *Peer Council* to aid in addressing discipline concerns among referred students. Although organized by the school counselor and teacher advisors, the program is driven by a group of students who are trained in conflict resolution, mediation, and solution-focused techniques.

Students who are referred to the discipline office are given the option of voluntarily participating in a meeting with the Peer Council to acknowledge the concerning behavior and who was harmed by it, or of taking a traditional consequence (e.g., detention, parent conference, suspension) to devise a strategy to prevent repeated behaviors. Peer Council student members teach the referred student productive alternatives to maladaptive behavior and highlight the strengths and skills of the student that he or she can draw upon in future situations. Working collaboratively, the Peer Council and the referred student complete a contract that identifies strengths of the referred student and a plan to utilize those strengths to repair the harm that was done. The goal of Peer Council is not to assign blame, but rather to promote a positive culture within the school where students feel heard, respected, and honored for their unique strengths.

Olivia, for example, is a freshman student with average grades and no previous significant behavior concerns. She was referred to the discipline office for repeatedly talking out of turn and being out of her seat during English class after multiple daily redirections by the teacher. The discipline office and the Peer Council faculty advisor determined it was appropriate to extend an invitation to Olivia and her teacher for Peer Council and both agreed. During the 40-minute session, Peer Council members, Olivia, and her teacher discussed the incidents and classroom rules but also identified individual student strengths and talents that might be used as part of the Peer Council contract. Through this open dialogue it was determined that Olivia found the assigned work to be too simplistic and that her behavior was partially a result of not feeling academically challenged. As part of the contract, Olivia agreed to accept more rigorous assignments from her teacher. To further combat the issues of talking and being out of her seat, the Peer Council suggested that the teacher provide Olivia with leadership opportunities that would allow her to move around the class to help her peers with the assigned tasks at designated times. Council members checked in with both Olivia and the teacher and found that since the implementation of the contract created at the Peer Council meeting, Olivia had been much more focused and had utilized her individual assets and skills for the betterment of both herself and the class as a whole.

Individual-Based Case Study: Marie

Marie is a 16-year-old junior who has above average grades, is a member of her high school basketball team, and has an active social life. However, Marie has recently exhibited extreme anxiety because she aspires to go to college but fears she will not get accepted anywhere because of her low ACT score. Marie explains this to her school counselor, Mr. Whit, to get advice about how to handle her dilemma. During the discussion, Mr. Whit focuses on Marie's personal strengths, such as her athleticism, work ethic, and likeable personality. Now that Marie is feeling more confident and less worried, Mr. Whit asks Marie to identify a goal that she wants to work towards. Marie tells Mr. Whit that her primary goal is to get into college. From there Mr. Whit works with Marie on a solution that will help her achieve her goal. Mr. Whit advises Marie that when writing her college application essays she can emphasize her dedication to the basketball team, her persistence in training, her mature work ethic, and her strong grades. These suggestions inspire Marie to utilize her social skills by recruiting her friends to start a volunteer club at school, which she believes will strengthen her college applications. After meeting with Mr. Whit, Marie no longer feels anxious or incompetent, but rather filled with optimism and determination to succeed in achieving her goal.

Implications

The end goals of school counseling for prekindergarten to 12th grade students are generally positive self-concept, productive social relationships, evidence of academic achievement, and the development of future aims (Wittmer & Clark, 2007). All of these goals are well-suited for a strengths-based approach to school counseling. However, school counselors must be very intentional about using a strengths-based framework, as this requires approaching situations from several angles.

First, the school counselor must actively believe in the inherent strengths of students regardless of family origin, school attendance, academic performance, disciplinary record, disability, or any other variable. This can sometimes be difficult given the large caseloads that school counselors have, the conditions in which they may work (e.g., as a single school counselor, with many non-counseling responsibilities, with little or no budget or resources for support, with administration who does not understand or value the role of the school counselor) or the state of the surrounding community (e.g., poverty, unemployment, social discord, or upheaval). When, for any individual student, there is a long period of struggle with behavior, school performance, relationships with self or others, even a well-trained, well-meaning school counselor can lose sight of a student's strengths. At this point, exercises in self-reflection and consultation with other strengths-based-minded professionals are a necessity to help regain the strengths-based perspective. The practice of ongoing professional, clinical supervision is not common in school counseling as it is in some other helping fields (Oberman, 2005; Page, Pietrzak, & Sutton, 2001; Rutter, 2006; Wachter, Minton, & Clemens, 2008; Wilkerson, 2006). However, school counselors would most certainly benefit from clinical supervision that helps them in maintaining a strengths-based perspective, not only on their students but on their own work as well. Because of the often large caseloads and variety of responsibilities that school counselors have, the nature of the day may necessitate making significant decisions quickly, including those that are in the midst or the wake of a crisis. Wachter, Minton, and Clemens (2008) proposed a peer-supervision model for school counselors to address crises that provides the school counselor with the type of affective support and evaluation process that match well with a strengths-based approach. This P-SAEF model emphasizes first the strengths of the school counselor in handling the crisis as well as the actions taken by the school counselor that worked well. Although this model was developed to accommodate the practicing school counselor, it could be modified for use with school counselors in training or could be adapted to a group supervision format.

Second, the school counselor must advocate and highlight the inherent strengths of students to others including school staff, peers, and families. This might be done in parent-teacher conferences, when consulting with teachers about students, during classroom or group activities, in and around the school building, or when examining school policies that are inequitably punitive towards certain groups of students. Others can lose sight of students' strengths too when times are difficult and the focus seems to be solely on the negative aspects of a student's (or group of students') behavior or performance. During these times, the school counselor can be the one to provide objectivity, help others reframe their perspective, highlight the strengths a student or group of students has, and provide a sense of hope. This becomes imperative when school staff and families are collaborating together for the benefit of a student and his or her future.

Third, the school counselor must help the individual student value his or her own inherent strengths. For students who feel undervalued, have been abused or neglected, experienced significant crisis or trauma, or who have been taught that love is conditional, this can be an extremely challenging task. For such students with low self-concept or self-efficacy, identifying personal strengths takes more time and effort, most likely through individual counseling. School counselors with a strengths-based and whole-child approach understand that assisting in generating insight around students' own strengths can further empower them to make improvements in school.

Conclusion

The varied developmental issues of students often faced by those working as school counselors present a prime opportunity to utilize an approach and a skill set that engender positive self-worth in students so as to maximize their academic, career/college, and social/emotional-ready success. Strengths-based techniques are practical, empathic, and justice-oriented, and integrate easily into most all school counseling activities across all domains. Moreover, strengths-based techniques are ones that school counselors can model and teach to students with the aim of life-long use.

The significance of the role the school counselor plays in contributing to an overall positive school climate is also elemental to strengths-based work on a macro level. This need for a strengths-based approach at multiple levels within schools and on behalf of many types of students ties back to the primary goal of the ASCA national model, which is to serve *all* students. Over the decades the role of the school counselor has evolved and this growth is expected to continue as the needs of schools and students change. Despite whatever the issues of the time may be or what the current trends may indicate, strengths-based work is timeless and never out of date. School counselors who use strengths-based approaches and techniques will remain relevant and valuable in our ever-changing global society.

References

American School Counselor Association. (2012). *ASCA national model*. Alexandria, VA: Author.

Aronson, J. (2002). *Improving academic achievement: Impact of psychological factors on education*. Amsterdam, The Netherlands: Academic Press.

Berg, I.K., & Steiner, T. (2003). *Children's solution work*. New York, NY: W.W. Norton & Co.

deShazer, S. & Dolan, Y. (2007). *More than miracles: The state of the art of solution-focused brief therapy*. Binghamton, NY: Haworth Press.

Dixon, A.L., & Tucker, C. (2008). Every student matters: Enhancing strengths-based school counseling through the application of mattering. *Professional School Counseling, 12,* 123–126.

Galassi, J., & Akos, P. (2007). *Strengths-Based school counseling: Promoting student development and achievement*. Mahwah, MJ: Lawrence Erlbaum Associates.

Healy, K. (2005). *Social work theories in context: Creating frameworks for practice*. Basingstoke, UK: Palgrave Macmillan.

Hewitt, M. (2005). The importance of taking a strength-based perspective. *Reclaiming Children & Youth, 14,* 23–26.

Madden, W., Green, S., & Grant, A.M. (2011). A pilot study evaluating strengths-based coaching for primary school students: Enhancing engagement and hope. *International Coaching Psychology Review, 6,* 71–83.

Mason, E.C.M., Ockerman, M.S., & Chen-Hayes, S.F. (2013). The change-agent-for-equity (CAFE) model: A framework for school counselor identity. *Journal of School Counseling, 11*(4), 1.

Masten, A. (2001). Ordinary magic: Resilience processes in development. *American Psychologist, 56,* 227–238.

McCammon, S. (2012). Systems of care as asset-building communities: Implementing strengths-based planning and positive youth development. *American Journal of Community Psychology, 49*(3/4), 556–565. doi:10.1007/s10464–012–9514-x

Oberman, A. (2005). Effective clinical supervision for professional school counsellors. *Guidance & Counseling, 20*(3/4), 147–151.

Page, B.J., Pietrzak, D.R., & Sutton, J.M. (2001). National survey of school counselor supervision. *Counselor Education and Supervision, 41*, 142–150.

Park, N., & Peterson, C. (2008). Positive psychology and character strengths: Application to strengths-based school counseling. *Professional School Counseling, 12*, 85–92.

Proctor, C., Tsukayama, E., Wood, A.M., Maltby, J., Fox Eades, J., & Linley, A. (2011). Strengths Gym: The impact of a character strengths-based intervention on the life satisfaction and well-being of adolescents. *The Journal of Positive Psychology, 6*, 337–388.

Rapp, C. (1997). *The strengths model: Case management with people suffering from severe and persistent mental illness.* New York, NY: Oxford University Press.

Rutter, M.E. (2006). Group supervision with practicing school counselors. *Guidance & Counseling, 21*, 160–167.

Saleebey, D. (2002). *The strengths perspective in social work practice.* Toronto, Ontario, Canada: Allyn & Bacon.

Seligman, M. P., Steen, T. A., Park, N., & Peterson, C. (2005). Positive psychology progress. *American Psychologist, 60*(5), 410–421. doi:10.1037/0003-066X.60.5.410

Sklare, G. (2014). *Brief solution-focused therapy that works. A solution-focused therapy approach for school counselors and other mental health professionals* (3rd ed.). Thousand Oaks, CA: Corwin/Sage.

Smith, E. (2006). The strength-based counseling model. *The Counseling Psychologist, 34*, 13–79.

Wachter, C.A., Minton, C.B., & Clemens, E.V. (2008). Crisis-specific peer supervision of school counselors: The P-SAEF model. *Journal of Professional Counseling: Practice, Theory & Research, 36*, 13–24.

Wilkerson, K. (2006). Peer supervision for the professional development of school counselors: Toward an understanding of terms and findings. *Counselor Education and Supervision, 46*, 59–67.

Wittmer, J. & Clark, M.A. (2007). *Managing your school counseling program: K-12 developmental strategies* (3rd ed.). Minneapolis, MN: Educational Media Corporation.

Villalba Jr., J.A. (2007). Culture-specific assets to consider when counseling Latina/o children and adolescents. *Journal of Multicultural Counseling & Development, 35*, 15–25.

7

The Economics of Developing Resilience with Families in Need

A Strengths-Based Approach

Tonya Davis

No family is problem free; all face serious challenges over the life course.

Froma Walsh

Since the beginning of time, many families have undergone trials and tribulations but not all are easily broken. In fact, despite hardships, many families will rise above the ashes of despair and thrive like never before. This chapter looks at noteworthy occurrences related to a high or low familial resilience contingent upon having access to strengths-based interventions such as positive psychology. Subsequently, this approach can take place by way of psychotherapy, mentoring, and/or community support. These examples inherently speak to the idea of social justice related to equal and sufficient access to resources (Kincaid, 2008).

An additional goal of this chapter is to provide examples of a strengths-based approach pertaining to positive psychology theory. The proposed idea is "moving away from a search for deficits or pathology in families in favor of seeking its strengths and potentials—familial resiliences—is part of the evolving movement of positive psychology" (Goldenberg & Goldenberg, 2008, p. 10). There are a number of families who experience adversities yet prosper despite them. Peterson (2009) posits that many families are more apt to flourish when helping professionals are available and able to concentrate on what is going well in their clients' lives. When collaborating with clients to uncover current and previous triumphs, strength and resilience are likely to emerge. Positive psychology lies within the ideals of social justice and equal access to systemic resources. Providing an evenly balanced and adequate arrangement of resources to families across communities invariably addresses the notion of creating systemic change within communities. When individuals can identify and build upon their strengths instead of weaknesses, they are more apt to experience empowerment and be motivated. This rationale is the basis for the foundational ideologies pertaining to the economics of developing resiliency from a strengths-based approach with families in need.

Review of the Literature

As previously mentioned, understanding that many families undergo adversity and social injustices, the implication for the need of community wide systemic change potentially exists. Primarily this is because of a lack of support that speaks to fairness and access, which can enable families across communities to thrive despite hardships. The literature shows a specific correlation between observable facts related to how familial resilience and the eradication of social inequalities can affect systemic change. This correlation provides a working knowledge of familial resilience, social justice, systemic change, and how these interconnect. The literature also examines the connection between families experiencing adversities and their ability to get beyond hardships by way of positive psychology (i.e., instillation of strengths).

Familial Resilience: Framework, Concept, and Application

Throughout the literature, definitions of familial resilience are generally defined as a vast understanding and recognition of quintessential elements that permit families to overcome the assiduous pressures of life (Benzies & Mychasiuk, 2009; Black & Lobo, 2008; Walsh, 1996, 2003). Familial resilience is fostered by a solid structural design, trouble shooting, sharing of community resources, an exchange of ideas, and validating convictions. The art of constructing familial resilience lies in strengthening the family as a cohesive unit (Walsh, 1996).

The literature also provides a collective idea of familial resilience with regard to possessing key features which may include but are not limited to flexibility, optimistic viewpoint, faith and spiritual belief, harmony and unity, family customs, fiscal responsibility, balance, familial restitution and encouragement, collaboration, and validation. If these factors are in place, families are more apt to experience a solid familial foundation and an imbued sense of prosperity (Black & Lobo, 2008). Today the answer that remains elusive is why some families can experience this notion called familial resilience, while other families continue to dissipate. Important to note is the idea that while families were not the intended area of focus in many of these studies regarding resilience, they have been included in the literature within recent years as a critical area to expound upon (Black & Lobo, 2008). Table 7.1, adapted from Black and Lobo (2008), addresses specific aspects of resilience as well as household attributes. Equally noted here is the importance of recognizing the application of assistance relating to familial resilience and the notion that one size does not fit all. Moreover, support may be viewed as a contingency based on needs. Whether a newly identified problem of concern is producing intense challenges or an indeterminate worry or complication, a global outlook is vital regarding whole attempts to promote healing, hope, and restoration (Walsh, 1996).

Table 7.1 Resilient family prominent protective and recovery factor characteristics

Resilience factor	Family characteristic
Positive outlook	Confidence and optimism; repertoire of approaches; sense of humor
Spirituality	Shared interval value system that gives meaning to stressors
Family member accord	Cohesion; nurturance; authoritative discipline; avoidance of hostile parental conflict
Flexibility	Stable family roles with situational and developmental adjustments
Family communication	Clarity; open emotional expression; collaborative problem solving
Financial management	Sound money management, family warmth despite financial problems
Family time	Makes the most of togetherness with daily tasks
Shared recreation	Develops child social and cognitive skills; cohesion and adaptability
Rituals and routines	Embedded activities that promote close family relationships; maintenance during family crisis
Support network	Individual, familial, and community networks to share resources

Notes: Adapted from "A conceptual review of family resilience factors," by K. Black and M. Lobo, 2008, *Journal of Family Nursing, 14*, p. 38. 2008 by SAGE Publications. Adapted with permission.

Considerations

A major tenet of familial resilience is social support, and it has proven beneficial to many families experiencing intense hardships as it can provide an overall sense of comfort and security (Benzies & Mychasiuk, 2009). It is clear that if organizations and communities are able to provide assistance to families with basic needs as well as with emotional and physical needs, more families are likely to experience the concept of resilience and at higher proportions (Benzies & Mychasiuk, 2009).

An essential aspect of resilience is building on the existing strengths of families as well as continuing to support the efforts in the development of new strengths and this can be done by way of quantification (Trivette & Dunst, 1990). The thought lies within the concept of recognizing existing strengths and how that knowledge can be captured and duplicated to conceivably close the disparate gap of the deteriorating family thereby inducing benefits for the masses (Trivette & Dunst, 1990). Through an examination of the family strength considerations available (i.e., family strengths scale, family functioning style scale, family strengths inventory, and family hardiness index), there are known assessments that can be used as a means for measuring strengths that families either have or can be empowered toward achieving (Trivette & Dunst, 1990).

Social Justice: Perspective and Diversity

Once strengths are measured and understood, making sure that families have equal opportunities to gain access to said resources while building upon strengths can be a potential hurdle. This is where social justice comes into play. Largely agreed upon by the literature, it is defined here by Miller and Engel (2011) as a "condition whereby all people are afforded fair opportunities to enjoy the benefits of society" (p. 25). This concept is talked about in schools under the guise of reform, and of funding or achievement gaps, in workplace settings by way of diversity trainings and/or equal employment opportunities, and in churches that can have significant community stature regarding social justice as well as through songs crooned by well-known song writers (Loewen & Pollard, 2010; Miller & Engel, 2011).

As a result, it has become increasingly clear that at the heart of every social justice movement is a matter of self-worth (Loewen & Pollard, 2010). Family types are all-encompassing and ever-changing, no matter the variable at play. Regardless of socioeconomic status (SES), two/single parents and/or guardians, same sex parents/guardians, ability or disability, varied racial or ethnic make-up, et cetera, everyone is deserving of fairness and equality (Erford, 2011). To deny individuals and families access to services on the basis of a partiality of any kind is erroneous thinking (Loewen & Pollard, 2010). Kincaid (2008) defined social injustice as: "inadequate access to resources [which] is correlated to demographics of diversity including race, gender, ability, age, and culture. The overrepresentation of these groups in homeless, undereducated, impoverished, imprisoned, and otherwise disadvantaged populations is an [immense] issue of social justice issue" (p. 1). As a direct result, social justice has become increasingly hard to delimit and more specifically, while a general consensus needs it to exist, the tangible functioning of egalitarianism is often entwined under the auspices of governmental ideologies (Kincaid, 2008). This impression moderately speaks to increasing and sustaining individual and familial resilience.

Considerations

As the field of counseling evolves, so do the needs of counselors and counselor educators. To keep up with the changing times, the profession as a whole may want to consider where it all began (i.e., programs preparing counselors and counselor educators). Whether the profession is thoughtful about providing instruction through a social justice lens or whether it is mere hypocrisy is a legitimate non-rhetorical question (Moule, 2005).

On the other hand, there is a potential trickle-down effect. The phenomenon stems from what counselors and counselor educators may or may not learn or may or may not teach. That philosophy undergirding this phenomenon becomes vital to the inputs of society. Consequently, the concern of "lack" with regard to knowledge collected through a social justice lens may theoretically have potential ramifications on familial resilience. As stated this review seeks to connect the apparent truths regarding how familial resilience is obtained, sustained, and how advocating for social justice can aid in familial resilience while simultaneously challenging social injustices. The proposed concept of progressing past the pursuit of insufficiencies within the family unit in support of tracking promise, strengths, and efficacy (i.e., familial resilience) is part of an evolving movement toward systemic change (Goldenberg & Goldenberg, 2008).

Positive Psychology: Economics of Resiliency and a Strengths-Based Approach

A proposed concept that should be used for the exploration of familial insufficiencies while in pursuit of familial resilience is a rapidly developing movement called positive psychology (Goldenberg & Goldenberg, 2008). Understanding the world as revolving around tragedies and adversities makes it difficult for families to perceive that they can actually develop an ability to experience personal growth and prosperity. The reason why some families thrive in the midst of suffering whereas others deteriorate is quite elusive. Positive psychology is useful particularly with familial resilience and those experiencing a needs deficit. Seligman (2001) defined positive psychology as "the scientific study of what goes right in life" (p. 3).

Positive psychology can be viewed as a step in the right direction. There are three main tenets that focus on positive psychology. Used in the helping professions, the first tenet is based on the concept of restricted or limited understandings of safety, contentment, and pleasure (Harris, Thoresen, & Lopez, 2007). The second stems from personal characteristics that are found in the abilities to care for others and to exhibit bravery, optimism, appreciation, tolerance, good judgment, and wit (Harris et al., 2007). Last, the helping professional should possess a capacity to establish relationships to sustain intrinsic worth via courteousness, cultivate selflessness, and to maintain a connection with society and its subcultures (Harris et al., 2007).

Having an awareness and understating of a strengths-based intervention such as positive psychology can potentially bring about a broadening of unrealistic views regarding familial resilience. Positive psychology begins to gently shift the focus from looking at what is wrong to what is right. By transferring these theoretical areas of focus while assisting families amid adversity and trials, a systemic change may occur.

A great deal of scholarship has been devoted to strengths-based interventions, much like the theory of positive psychology and its study. Although the pool of research is increasing, more strategies (e.g., intervention strategies and treatment plans alike) provided to enhance the learning of future helping professionals will be a necessity. In fact, Harris et al. (2007) acknowledged insignificant consideration toward approaches and evolving validations connecting personal psychology and counseling efforts. A permanent or temporary reprieve from intense turmoil could be a consequential experience, nonetheless. It is appropriate to place a much deeper emphasis on investigating this type of implication (i.e., the direct connection between familial resilience and positive psychology). The goal is to establish acceptable results in applying theory to practice and this transformation can be expressed in three ways. The first is an intentional infusion of positive psychology in the counseling process. The second approach is shifting the focus from the problem (i.e., what is wrong and not working) to the solution (i.e., what is right and working well). The third approach speaks to the family's ability to experience interpersonal growth and prosperity during and after a perceived hardship (Harris et al., 2007). This notion blends nicely with the wellness model of counseling. Remley and Herlihy (2010) described it as follows: "[C]ounselors take a developmental perspective and regard people's personal and emotional concerns as normal and natural, not pathological; it's believed that prevention and intervention is far superior to remediation" (p. 55). This idea speaks directly to the correlation between positive psychology and what it can do for families and their ability to bounce back from life's adversities.

Considerations

Beavin-Bavelas and Segal (1982) described a family system as a "special set of people with relationships between them; these relationships are established, maintained, and evidenced by the members communicating with each other, hence the key word being communication" (p. 102). The systems approach did not originally derive from the sector of ordinary sciences or the branch specially geared toward interpersonal relationships but more so from the aspect of remedying psychological hindrances (Beavin-Bavelas & Segal, 1982). Generally, the perception of systems theory cleverly corresponds with the classification termed "family," and it becomes useful to understand how a family tends to function, interact, and thrive with all of its collective components (Beavin-Bavelas & Segal, 1982). When helping professionals consider the family unit regarding what makes a family thrive from a systems perspective, it is reasonable to view familial resilience and the prevention of social injustices synchronized with creating systemic change.

When contemplating a systems view with regard to familial resilience and eliminating social injustices, there are simply no guarantees. Although some would argue that the inevitability is too great, helping professionals would contend that with fundamentals (i.e., communication and/or cohesion) familial resilience can continue to increase and social injustices can be purged from our society, lending a hand toward systemic change. Authors like Beavin-Bavelas and Segal (1982) believe that communication is a vital piece to the puzzle called familial resilience. Without a working communication paradigm families would be left disarmed. Varied types of communication have been studied. Authors like Alexander (1973) more specifically studied defensive and supportive communication, which has been known to have an effect on family cohesion. Olson (2000) defined family *cohesion* as "the emotional bonding that family members have towards one another and [it] has four levels: disengaged, separated, connected, and enmeshed" (p. 145). The idea is to keep in mind that a long-term balanced familial commitment is contingent upon the level of cohesive functioning, as well as the quality and quantity of communication (Olson, 2000; Peterson, 2009). This level of functioning may or may not be helpful for helping professionals to know when they are attempting to understand familial resilience, longevity, and balance regarding all systems which play a role toward eliminating social injustices, thus allowing the helping professional to become a major conduit for systemic change.

Application of Positive Psychology: a Strengths-Based Approach

One of the concepts necessary to consider when using a strengths-based technique is what you are doing and how you go about doing it. The following case demonstrates my use of positive psychology with a client (i.e., client is subsequently defined as a family unit made up of four individuals). Note that I view the client in this case as a microcosm of a larger system (i.e., extended family and friends that provide outside emotional, mental, spiritual, and physical support). It is important to share that ideas and concepts uncovered via these sessions aid in the client's awareness of self within the system they live in and their ability to identify emotional, mental, spiritual, and physical needs in order to thrive. As seen in this case, you will observe a multi-dimensional point-of-view and how a family can significantly bring about change within their system. This client is experiencing an evolution within their family system and that familial resilience can be seen here as the correlation between the support of individual family members who construct a single family unit thereby establishing opportunities for all of them to thrive.

Case Study

Client Background

Carol and Douglass are both 45 years old. She is an account executive, he worked in construction, and was an assistant high school basketball coach. Both were seemingly healthy individuals as evidenced by recent exams. They each have an adult child from previous relationships. His son is 24 and in his third year of college, and her daughter is 22 and in her fourth year in the armed forces. Carol and Douglass also have three children together (one daughter age 14 and two sons ages 10 and 12). They were married for 15 years. Douglass was well known in the community, was a former high school basketball standout, and had a lot of friends and acquaintances; Carol was more reserved but felt comfortable around his friends, and Douglass felt comfortable around her friends as well. Other than an occasional glass of wine during social outings with friends, there was no remarkable history; there was no history of drug usage either. Carol and Douglass dated in high school, went their separate ways, and had previous relationships that produced children. When those relationships failed, both of them ironically found themselves at the same event where they reconnected and reminisced about old times. Their love was rekindled and they married 1 year later. Their first child together was born 1 year after they were married. Douglass was laid off from his construction job about 1 year ago. He began working two part-time jobs to make ends meet. In addition to working two part-time jobs, Douglass found himself assisting the head coach of his alma mater with the basketball team, a long lost love of his. Carol had health care benefits through her job, and together they were making things work. Douglass would often take the children to basketball practice with him. As a result of attending frequent practices, all three children took such a liking to basketball, they began playing with their own age appropriate teams. A major familial goal for Douglass and Carol had involved Douglass obtaining a full-time position with hopes of earning more money to pay for the children's basketball teams and training camps. When Carol and Douglass had disagreements they relied heavily on their belief in God. Their faith was extremely important to them, their marriage, and how they raised their children. They went to church weekly and both were very active serving in various ministries within the church. The children were also active in the children's ministry. It was not uncommon for the family to be in church a few days per week. Carol and Douglass were happy in their marriage, and they enjoyed being together as a family. A skill that Carol and Douglass developed for themselves and as a family unit was humor. Whenever they may have been worried about finances, both would use humor as a way to keep the concern at bay. Carol and Douglass were not the arguing type and if by chance humor did not work, they would call a truce, go to their separate corners, and allow cooler heads to prevail. They co-parented in the same humor filled way. Humor was used throughout the home and the children thrived within the environment. The three younger children were on the high honor roll at school, highly functioning and respectful in the home, and well-adjusted socially.

Description of the Presenting Problem

Six days before Christmas, Carol was attending an out-of-town business trip. She checked in with her family that evening as she normally would. Douglass had reported things were fine; the children were excited about Christmas Day and eager to open the presents he had purchased that day. Carol and Douglass said goodnight and shared their normal evening pleasantries (i.e., "I love you, rest well, and goodnight honey") with one another. At approximately 8:30 a.m. the next morning Carol received a phone call from a police officer calling from her home. He explained to her that their 14-year-old daughter called 911 because her father was on the floor and was not breathing. The police officer proceeded to explain that Douglass had been treated by the paramedics, but it was determined that Douglass had passed away at the home before he could be transported to the hospital. The police officer asked Carol if she understood what he said. Carol recalled feeling numb, unable to answer him, and had a hard time breathing. After what Carol described as an "eternity," she managed to ask the police officer where her children were, and he stated that the children were with other helping professionals on the scene. He also stated that their daughter was visibly shaken up. Carol recalled that the officer inquired about the length of time before she could get back home or get other family members to their home. Carol mentioned that she called Douglass' mother and sisters to inform them of his passing and was able to catch an early flight home. Douglass had a massive heart attack and died 5 days before Christmas at the age of 45.

Family Affected

All of the members of Carol and Douglass' household experienced emotional turmoil as would be understandably expected with the sudden loss of a loved one. Because money had been an issue in the past, Carol was faced with managing the household on one income in addition to the emotional unrest. With the loss of her husband and the father of her children, Carol felt like her problems were magnified. Thoughts of how they would survive this loss emotionally, mentally, and financially consumed Carol and the children. Carol was grateful for having enough money from the life insurance to at least pay for Douglass' funeral expenses, but the thought of not being able to replace his salary was wearing on her. Carol also knew that she needed to enlist the help of professionals to better focus her attention on her needs as well as the needs of their children.

Client's Symptoms and Diagnosis Criteria

Family disruption due to death of family member (V61.07) is the official diagnosis for the overall family unit. Carol showed remarkable strength during her loss as she navigated her thoughts and feelings as well as those thoughts and feelings of their children. All family members experienced sadness and actively visited the five stages of grief (denial, anger, bargaining, depression, and acceptance). Everyone within the family unit did not experience each stage at the same time nor in the same way. Carol and her children experienced loss very differently, but they supported each other through the process. While Carol was concerned for all of their children, she was able to recognize that their two youngest sons seemed to be experiencing a disinterest in the sport that they had previously so enthusiastically enjoyed with their father. Not wanting to see them lose interest in one of the few things they had previously enjoyed, she decided to seek emotional support for everyone in the household.

Intervention

Carol was referred to me 4 weeks after Douglass passed away. We met for three individual sessions where we identified her concerns and struggles (i.e., loss of her lover and best friend, how she would make ends meet, how she would raise the children without Douglass), made sense of them, and spent time resolving them. I also met with Carol with her three younger children to identify, understand, and resolve their concerns (i.e., what does life without Daddy look like, missing him and how to cope with that, wondering if they were still a family without Daddy) for five additional sessions. I used a person-centered approach in addition to the tenets of Martin Seligman's positive psychology (i.e., meaningfulness, signature strengths, authentic happiness, learned optimism). The identified therapeutic goal was to strengthen the family unit as a whole by enlisting the help of the aforementioned tenets. The tenets of positive psychology work to address all of the family's concerns and bolster an imbued sense of contentment and overall well-being within the family unit. The significance of infusing this strengths-based approach (i.e., positive psychology) speaks to the importance of minimizing, if not eliminating, psychological pain and the development of resilience within the family unit.

Therapeutic Peak

I noticed a peak midway through our last family session (i.e., 12 weeks after Douglass passed away). Carol and the children came into the last session energetic. Carol stated that the sessions helped her feel "stronger, empowered, and prepared to face her concerns based on her new frame of thinking." When asked what stood out the most during the family sessions, Carol noted how we focused our work on what was going well in their lives, the many positives that they began experiencing daily, and how to start looking forward to life with her children and being able to love each other through their loss. Carol noticed that she had developed a sense of personal strength and resolve to thrive. Her evidence was based on her new ability to reframe her negative thoughts, be genuinely happy and optimistic, re-branding the meaning of life by living life in honor of Douglass, and living life on purpose. Carol planned to take these lessons learned in counseling and distribute them to her family.

Results and Supporting Evidence from Counseling Relationship

Carol and the children still have a long road of healing ahead of them. They all understand that Douglass can never be replaced, healing will look differently for each of them, and healing will likely require more time. Carol and the children are optimistically hopeful for a future full of happiness and a sense of healing and restoration. Carol and the children had vastly different demeanors from the first few sessions but have effectively begun a promising new journey as evidenced by their smiling and laughter throughout the last couple of sessions. They felt encouraged about the future and have found great support in their family and friends. Carol shared that using what she learned and reinforcing that with the children will help her family look at "what's going right within their family" and would help them experience a happier, more cohesive family dynamic.

Example of Strengths-Based Interventions

Being supportive, providing encouragement, and challenging Carol and the children during the appropriate times were critical factors in maintaining the authenticity of the therapeutic relationship. The power of relationship building fully allowed Carol, the children, and me to move genuinely throughout our sessions. Aside from the basic listening sequence (i.e., reflection of feeling, paraphrasing, summarizing, encouraging, client observations, attending behavior, open and closed ended questions), it was also necessary to use advanced skills when Carol or the children needed more of a directive approach (i.e., confrontation, skill integration, focusing, reflection of meaning). An example of a strengths-based intervention began when I asked Carol and the children, "What does it mean to not be able to see Douglass/Daddy anymore?" The 12-year old, Brian, replied, "Daddy being gone means that we are not a family anymore." I used a gentle challenge here and asked him (already knowing that in a previous session he said, "Daddy will always be with us because he lives in our hearts."), "Do you remember telling me that Daddy will always be with you because he lives in your heart?" Brian replied, "Yes, I remember." I asked Brian, "What does it mean for Daddy to live in your heart?" Brian said, "It means that we will always be a family because if Daddy lives in my heart he can never leave me or us." Carol and Brian became tearful at the realization that they would always be a family and they all had a family hug. Helping this family reframe the way they viewed their family dynamic was most important for them.

Developing Familial Resilience

The economics of developing resiliency with families in need takes on a multi-tiered approach. Taking great care to make sure that equal distribution of community resources is afforded to all families in need is essential to sustaining a family's ability to be a healthy cohesive unit (Kincaid, 2008). Ensuring that resources necessary to survive as well as thrive are at their disposal is imperative to prevent deterioration of the family unit. This family faced abruptly occurring emotional, mental, and financial concerns all because of the sudden death of a father and husband. The goal was to be sure that all of these concerns were addressed. Providing individual counseling for Carol and family counseling for the three younger children was just a step in that direction. Additional adjunct services provided were establishing mentoring for the children through a local nonprofit organization and community sponsorships that paid for the children's basketball camps and fees for their travel basketball teams. Carol continued counseling and was also referred to a financial planner that agreed to help her with her concerns pertaining to her financial situation and how to budget effectively. Carol and her children were referred to a family grief support group where they attended together. To effectively establish familial resilience for this family, many resources were necessary in maximizing their potential for optimal growth.

Implications

As the field of counseling evolves, so do the needs of counselors in training, counselors, and counselor educators. To keep up with the changing times, the profession as a whole may want to consider where it all begins: the programs preparing counselors and counselor educators. Whether the profession can be intentional about providing instruction through a strengths-based lens by way of positive psychology, social justice, and resilience is a legitimate concern. This concept stems from what counselors and counselor educators learn, teach, or do not learn or teach. The lack of knowledge collected through a social justice lens may theoretically have potential ramifications on familial resilience. The proposed approach of tracking promise, strengths, and efficacy rather than insufficiencies within the family unit is part of an evolving movement toward systemic change (Goldenberg & Goldenberg, 2008).

Harris et al. (2007) acknowledged that "little attention has been given to developing rationales or strategies that link positive psychology to the daily work of counselors; work that often involves the relief of acute suffering" (p. 3). It is because of this lack of awareness that it is appropriate to place a much deeper emphasis on investigating this type of implication (i.e., the direct correlation between familial resilience and positive psychology.

Little has been written about familial resilience and the parallel pertaining to the lack of social/communal support and resources available. The equal distribution of this type of support may be nonexistent. This support is likely to provide benefits to many families experiencing intense hardships an overall sense of comfort and security (Benzies & Mychasiuk, 2009). On the other hand, this type of support could also provide a false sense of comfort and security. It is thought that if organizations and communities are able to provide assistance to families with basic needs, as well as emotional and physical needs, this could potentially allow more families to experience the concept of resilience at higher proportions (Benzies & Mychasiuk, 2009).

Consultation

When considering consultation, Caplan's consultee-centered model is used most often. The model is to train the counselor and/or agency with the hopes of equipping professionals and organizations with the tools and resources necessary to affix positive psychology to the family (Sears, Rudisill, & Sears, 2006). The end result is built upon existing strengths by way of practical application for families experiencing tragedies.

Another spin on positive psychology comes from a broader scope. Seligman (2001) argued that there are too many resources being manipulated to manage disorders and this is inherently a waste in the face of potential for research driven prevention. Hence, Seligman (2001) posited that "... the productive task of prevention research will be to create science, taxonomy, measurement, causal analysis and inventions, and human strengths" (p. 3). This is where familial resilience and social justice meet systemic change. The primary focus of this study will be to provide data that will establish a fundamental measure of knowledge pertaining to the characteristics that enable families to thrive. These factors provide the facilitators and participants with the ability to readily identify the characteristics that contribute to awe-inspiring familial resilience.

A thoughtful evaluation of the literature regarding familial resilience, social justice, and a need for systemic change is provided through within this review. There is more information to be unveiled about the aforementioned domains. This information may possibly lie within the following questions: Are all families equally afforded the same opportunities and resources in the same capacity and consistency? Do all families have equivalent access to the resources that make them unbreakable? Are counselors and counselor educators adequately equipped and prepared to dispense services and resources that speak to disavow social injustices? Does the solution lie in the science of positive psychology?

Families remain intact and thrive despite access to nontangible services and resources. Understanding and fostering a family's ability to remain persistent may be the difference between familial resilience and familial dissolution. When referring to family systems, realistic considerations like what makes a family a resilient one are fair ones and inevitably include a systemic point-of-view. Additional research is essential in determining the synchronicity of familial resilience and the prevention of social injustices.

Positive psychology can effectively contribute much to the enhancement of familial resilience. The Department of Health and Human Services funding for positive psychology research could aid in familial resilience and possibly address the need for systemic change.

Final Thoughts

Further studies should look into answering some additional questions that helping professionals may want to consider, such as whether there is a significant difference between possessing high or low familial resilience on the basis of having access to positive psychology via talk therapy, mentoring, and/or community support. Does that speak to disavow social injustices? Are all families equally afforded the same opportunities and resources in much the same capacity and consistency? If not, then what is the smallest action that can be done to ensure the scales are balanced? What happens to whom if these questions are not answered? These questions are not an exhaustive list of considerations, but they are merely a starting point for helping professionals to begin the process of pondering such concerns to evoke change.

References

Alexander, J. F. (1973). Defensive and supportive communication in family systems. *Journal of Marriage and Family, 35,* 613–617.

Beavin-Bavelas, J.B., & Segal, L. (1982). Family systems theory: background and implications. *Journal of Communication, 32*(3), 99–107.

Benzies. K., & Mychasiuk, R. (2009). Fostering family resilience: a review of the key protective factors. *Child and Family Social Work, 14,* 103–114.

Black. K., & Lobo. M. (2008). A conceptual review of family resilience factors. *Journal of Family Nursing, 14,* 33–55.

Erford, B.T. (2011). Transforming the School Counseling Profession (3rd ed.). Upper Saddle River, NJ: Pearson Education.

Goldenberg, H., & Goldenberg, I. (2008). Family therapy: An overview. Belmont, CA: Thomson Brooks/Cole.

Harris, A.H.S., Thoresen, C.E., & Lopez, S.J. (2007). Integrating positive psychology into counseling: Why and (when appropriate) how. *Journal of Counseling & Development, 85,* 3–13.

Kincaid, S. (2008). Diversity and social justice dynamics: an analysis of the national standards for human services education. *Human Services Today, 5,* 1–8.

Loewen, G. & Pollard, W. (2010). The social justice perspective. *Journal of Postsecondary Education and Disability, 23,* 5–18.

Miller, P.M., & Engel, M.T. (2011). Forging vertical linkages in the public sphere: School-church engagement for social justice. *Educational Foundations, 25,* 25–42.

Moule, J. (2005). Implementing a social justice perspective in teacher education: invisible burden for faculty of color. *Teacher Education Quarterly, 32*(4), 23–42.

Olson, D.H. (2000). Circumplex model of marital family systems. *Journal of Family Therapy, 22,* 144–176.

Peterson, C. (2009). Positive psychology. *Reclaiming Children and Youth, 18*(2), 3–7.

Remley, Jr., T.P., & Herlihy, B. (2010). *Ethical, legal, and professional issues in counseling.* Upper Saddle River, NJ: Pearson Education.

Sears, R.W., Rudisill, J.R., & Sears, C.M. (2006). Consultation skills: For mental health professionals. Hoboken, NJ: John Wiley & Sons.

Seligman, M.E.P. (2001). Commentary on priorities for prevention research at NIMH. *Prevention and Treatment, 4,* 1–3.

Trivette, C.M., & Dunst, C.J. (1990). Assessing family strengths and family functioning style. *Topics in Early Childhood Special Education, 10,* 16–36.

Walsh, F. (1996). The concept of family resilience: crisis and challenge. *Family Process, 35,* 261–281.

Walsh, F. (2003). Family resilience: a framework for clinical practice. *Family Process, 42,* 1–18.

Walsh, F. (2006). *Strengthening family resilience* (2nd ed.). New York, NY: The Guilford Press.

8

Strengths-Based Affirmative Advocacy

School Counselor Strategies to Help LGBT Youth Become More of Who They Are

Matthew J. Beck

To address the needs of lesbian, gay, bisexual, and transgender (LGBT) student populations, the field of school counseling must expand its attention from the negative outcomes to the protective factors that foster growth and development of this underserved student population. Prior research has clearly documented the struggles and barriers that LGBT students face in hostile and unwelcoming school climates (Kosciw, Greytak, Palmer, & Boesen, 2014). For example, the *2013 National School Climate Survey* (Kosciw, Greytak, et al., 2014) conducted by the Gay, Lesbian, & Straight Education Network (GLSEN) found that LGBT youth encountered anti-LGBT language (71.4% of students heard the term *gay* derogatorily used), reported victimization (74.1% of students were verbally harassed), and experienced discrimination (17.8% of students were not allowed to establish a Gay−Straight Alliance [GSA]) at school (Kosciw, Greytak, et al., 2014).

Scholars have begun to address the lack of focus on the positive development of LGBT youth (Toomey & Russell, 2011) and an increased attention to the role that supportive resources and personnel have on students' educational success (Kosciw, Palmer, Kull, & Greytak, 2013; Kosciw, Greytak, et al., 2014). For example, according to the *2013 National School Climate Survey* (Kosciw, Greytak, et al., 2014), when schools have 11 or more supportive personnel to LGBT youth, students had higher grade point averages (GPAs) than do other students with scant supportive staff (3.3 vs. 2.8), thereby indicating more connection to the school campus (Kosciw, Greytak, et al., 2014). Additionally, LGBT inclusive curricular resources can positively impact student experiences. For example, GLSEN's 2013 (Kosciw, Greytak, et al., 2014) study found that 78.5% of LGBT students in schools with inclusive curriculum reported hearing fewer anti-LGBT remarks compared with 54.7% of youth without an inclusive curriculum.

These findings highlight the critical role that LGBT-related school resources can have in creating a positive, safe, and healthy learning environment for all students. Thus, from a strengths-based advocacy lens, these positive findings further demonstrate how school counselors can provide service and advozate for and with LGBT student populations. Moreover, these perceived benefits could impact the role of the school counselor, as both an ally and social justice advocate, when communicating with educational stakeholders for implementation of affirmative services for LGBT youth (Beck, Rausch, & Wood, 2014).

When making efforts to move in this direction, school counselors should first self-assess their own perspectives and worldviews of what strengths-based counseling means. This author believes that the strengths perspective offers a framework through which school counselors believe and model that all of their students have capacity, potential, and resilience (Saleebey, 2008). In this regard, a strengths perspective fosters youth empowerment through meaningful relationships, cultural connections, and the promotion of positive academic, social-emotional, and college and career development (Saleebey, 2008). In comparison to other problem-focused approaches, where diagnostic labels and deficits carry from classroom to classroom with students, a strengths perspective offers a more hopeful lens through which school counselors "think differently about the children you counsel and teach—even those who seem awash in trouble" (Saleebey, 2008, p. 69).

As specific to working with LGBT students, using a strengths-based approach can assist school counselor advocates when addressing the academic, social-emotional, and college and career development of LGBT youth. For example, research has found that LGBT students report more favorable school experiences and educational outcomes when affirmed with LGBT-related supports such as supportive school personnel, GSA clubs, and inclusive curricula (Kosciw, Greytak, et al., 2014). Thus, by highlighting the strengths enhancing school environments where LGBT students thrive and can be more of themselves, school counselors may be in a more influential position to improve the learning environment for all students, including LGBT youth.

An additional and critical component in strengths-based work for LGBT students also involves self-reflection and how school counselors view change and advocacy for this underrepresented population. In my work as a former school counselor, the facilitation of self-reflective questions helped to guide my perspective of strengths-based work regarding LGBT topics. Helpful questions included the following:

(a) Do I believe all students have the skills, assets, and talents to rise above challenging situations?
(b) How do I visualize and advocate for school environments that can be different and better for LGBT youth?
(c) How can I enlist the voices of LGBT youth within my school, to develop more sensitivity and appreciation to student differences?

Additionally, school counselors should be reunited with their personal beliefs, passion, and values that brought them to the field of school counseling.

While writing this chapter and reflecting upon my own perspectives of strengths-based work with LGBT youth in K−12 settings, three unanswered questions became clear to me:

(a) What evidence-based programs and protective factors have been successful in supporting LGBT youth resiliency and development within the context of school systems?
(b) How might school counselors combine strengths-based counseling and social justice work, to provide a richer framework and language to communicate with educational stakeholders for enhancing LGBT programs and services?
(c) How might highlighting and sharing more LGBT success stories within the school counseling literature serve as an inspiration for other school counselors to remain fearless, elicit change, and infuse more affirming resources and programs into developmental school counseling programs?

The purpose of this chapter is to answer these critical questions and discuss how the combination of strengths-based school counseling (Galassi & Akos, 2007) and social justice work into strengths-based affirmative advocacy (SBAA) can inform the work of school counselors with LGBT students. This can serve a frame of reference with respect to specific language and interventions that support school counselors when advocating for and with LGBT youth. A clear format for working with this realm is especially important in resistant school systems where change is clearly needed, but not always welcomed. Specifically, this chapter provides application for school counselors to strengthen their advocacy efforts through the promotion of positive outcomes from affirming programs, services, and holding environments that enrich and foster the well-being of LGBT youth. As such, SBAA could be an intended mechanism for change that school counselors could use when working with educational stakeholders to create more affirming spaces (i.e., GSAs, inclusive curriculum, etc.).

This chapter begins with a short discussion regarding how school counselors can use and combine strengths-based school counseling and social justice work. Next, the author will provide a rationale in how the combination of these two approaches into SBAA could be an influential framework for school counselors to utilize when addressing the aforementioned LGBT problem areas. A brief review of literature for strengths-based work with LGBT populations will follow this justification. I will also highlight my story as a former school counselor advocate for LGBT youth and how this experience has motivated me to develop additional recommendations for school counselor practice, especially for helpers to use SBAA when working to create and sustain inclusive programs and services into developmental school counseling programs. Last, I will outline strategies for school helpers to utilize SBAA when advocating for LGBT-inclusive programs and services, across multiple levels within a school community (i.e., individual, school-wide, administrative, etc.).

The Strengths-Based Approach and Application in School Counseling

Strengths-Based School Counseling

Authors Akos and Galassi (2008) discussed how the role of school counselors has evolved from providing reactive-based strategies to the promotion of more strengths-based principles. Specifically, Galassi and Akos (2007) outlined the following six roles a strengths-based school counselor has:

(a) to promote context-based development for all students,
(b) to promote individual student strengths,
(c) to promote strengths-enhancing environments,
(d) to emphasize strengths promotion over problem reduction and problem prevention,
(e) to emphasize evidence-based interventions and practice, [and]
(f) to emphasize promotion-oriented developmental advocacy at the school level. (p. 3)

These recommendations synchronize with the vision of school counseling and how the profession continues to evolve over time in response to student and societal needs (American School Counselor Association [ASCA], 2012). According to Akos and Galassi (2008), "[t]he shift involves a movement away from a primary emphasis on pathology and deficits that impede development in a small percentage of students to a primary focus on personal strengths and environments that facilitate positive development for all students" (p. 66). Therefore, fostering the development of all students and environments that support autonomous growth rather than employing reactive procedures (Galassi & Akos, 2007) is an important paradigm shift of which the school counselor should be mindful. According to Akos and Galassi (2008), "it is difficult to imagine school counselors impacting development for all students without operating from a strengths-based perspective" (p. 66). Given that school counselors advocate for programs that impact positive development for all students, it stands to reason that social justice work is a necessity when working to create change for underserved student populations, especially LGBT youth.

Social Justice Advocacy

According to Akos and Galassi (2008), acknowledging strengths-enhancing school climates is an essential component of strengths-based school counseling. Often, school counselors incorporate social justice advocacy into their role as change agents, directed to advance services and further promote enhancing environments (Akos & Galassi, 2008; Ratts, DeKruyf, & Chen-Hayes, 2007). Moreover, several researchers have defined the role of school counselors as social justice leaders. According to Akos and Galassi (2008), "the school counselor functions as an agent of systemic change who engages in leadership, advocacy, collaboration, and teaming with other professionals" (p. 66). Singh, Urbano, Haston, and McMahon (2010) stated the role of a school counselor with social justice work as one who addresses "educational inequities and differences in academic achievement that may be grounded in issues of race/ethnicity, gender, class, disability status, and sexual orientation, and that may prevent many students from maximizing their academic, social, and personal potential" (p. 135). According to Ratts et al. (2007), "[s]ocial justice advocacy is warranted to right injustices, increase access, and improve educational outcomes for all students" (p. 90).

Professional counseling organizations have outlined the ways in which school counselors serve as social justice advocates. For example, the ASCA ethical guidelines (2010) demonstrate that school counselors "work as advocates and leaders in the school to create school counseling programs that help close any achievement, opportunity and attainment gaps that deny all students the chance to pursue their educational goals" (p. 6). Within these mentioned definitions, the themes of advocacy, leadership, and collaboration align with the current vision of the school counseling profession (ASCA, 2012). In addition, ASCA's (2014) position statement strengthens school counselors' role and responsibilities in providing services with LGBTQ youth, which include to (a) support youth with feelings about their sexual orientation and/or gender identity; (b) advocate for equitable and inclusive curricula and safe spaces (i.e., GSAs); (c) work with educational stakeholders for adoption of inclusive policies and procedures; (d) advocate for staff training on LGBTQ-inclusive practices; and (e) create an inclusive environment that addresses the risk factors that LGBTQ students face. Last, the American Counseling Association (ACA; 2014) Ethical Code C.5. clearly articulates that professional counselors cannot discriminate on the basis of gender, gender identity, sexual orientation, marital or partnership status.

Although the literature clearly outlines the ethical and fundamental responsibility in school counselors' work with LGBT students, advocacy attempts are inconsistent, especially in school districts where changing the status quo is challenging. Authors Bemak and Chung (2008) outlined factors that may coincide with the ability of school counselors to devise social justice change. They have suggested the term "nice counselor syndrome" for a professional who is characterized as a kind-hearted spirit who strives to be liked by everyone, and thus avoids taking a stand on social justice issues (p. 374). Additional challenges have been cited such as (a) the transformed role of the school counselor as a school-wide change agent is a recent initiative for the school counseling profession (Galassi, Griffin, & Akos, 2008), (b) fear of risk taking (Beck et al., 2014), (c) LGBT topics may be taboo in some school communities (Goodrich, Harper, Luke, & Singh, 2013), (d) lack of tenure status (Valenti & Campbell, 2009), and (e) absence of advocate efficacy (Beck et al., 2014).

It is apparent that creating LGBT-friendly programs and services may be challenged from resistant school-systems, which may ultimately interfere with the ability of school counselors to speak up as influential change agents for LGBT student populations (Jennings, 2014). This may suggest that the field of school counseling needs additional avenues besides the focus on problem reduction for school counselors to consider when advocating for programs and services. Consequently, when school counselors identify supportive services and environments that are working well for students, using a social justice framework to inform educational stakeholders of these benefits can be very instrumental, uplifting, and perhaps more comfortable.

Strengths-Based Affirmative Advocacy with LGBT Youth

SBAA unites the aforementioned competencies from both strengths-based school counseling and social justice advocacy, in an effort to promote affirming services and environments that empower LGBT youth to be more successful in their academic, personal/social, and career development. SBAA recognizes the developmental pathway and positive assets of LGBT youth and how their meaning-making experiences from more affirmative school climates can serve as an imperative advocacy tool for school counselors. The implementation of SBAA can help to strengthen the coping skills of LGBT youth through acknowledging the ways in which enhancing environments can contribute to internal and external coping mechanisms. For example, researchers have documented that more inclusive and affirming school environments correlate with more academic, personal/social, and career success for LGBT students (Kosciw, Greytak, et al., 2014). As such, SBAA blends these protective factors, along with school counselor advocacy interventions, to challenge the inequities that are still predominant for LGBT youth.

This collaborative approach aims to support the strength, resilience, and healthy development of all students, including LGBT youth, and aligns within the aforementioned standards upheld by the field of school counseling. For example, ASCA's (2014) recommendation for school counselors to "promote affirmation" and create "equal opportunity" for students can provide direction and support regarding how school counselors can use strengths-based advocacy to build, highlight, and celebrate inclusive programs that are making a difference in the lives of LGBT students (pp. 36–37).

Review of Literature

Several researchers have called for a paradigm shift away from problem reduction and an increased attention directed to how the protective factors and enhancing environments help LGBT youth thrive more at school (Kosciw et al., 2013; Toomey & Russell, 2011). However, only a few published studies have utilized a strengths-based perspective where the intervention focus was on the positive growth and development of LGBT youth and programs (Asakura & Craig, 2014; Craig, 2013; Craig, Austin, & McInroy, 2014; Kosciw et al., 2013; Kosciw, Greytak, et al., 2014; Kosciw, Palmer, & Kull, 2014; Toomey & Russell, 2011).

In general, scholars have reported strengths-based outcomes for LGBT-interventions in K–12 settings, including GSAs (Craig et al., 2014; Kosciw, Greytak, et al., 2014; Kosciw, Palmer, et al., 2014; Lee, 2002; Szalacha, 2003; Toomey & Russell, 2011) and LGBT-inclusive curricula, anti-bullying policies, and supportive school personnel as meaningful contributors to the development of safer school climates for all students (Kosciw, Greytak, et al., 2014; Kosciw, Palmer, et al., 2014). Specifically, GLSEN's *2011 National School Climate Survey* (Kosciw, Greytak, Bartkiewicz, Boesen, & Palmer, 2012) reported for the first time in over a decade of national surveys a decrease in victimization for LGBT youth (Kosciw et al., 2012). According to GLSEN's Executive Director, Dr. Eliza Byard, "[w]ith this report, we are beginning to be able to discern real impact of our efforts" (GLSEN, 2012a). These findings provide a brief snapshot on how strengths-based resources and interventions can benefit LGBT student populations and potentially strengthen school counselor advocacy efforts to create more inclusive environments. In later sections of this chapter, I provide the specific strengths-based findings from the aforementioned studies, to support and strengthen the suggested applications for school counselor practice.

As a method to introduce SBAA to school counselors, helpers may need to hear relevant stories from affirmative advocates, as a method for inspiration and motivation towards taking more of a stand on LGBT topics. Thus, in this next section, I will share a critical incident that has served as an influential turning point in my professional career as a strengths-oriented and affirmative advocate for LGBT youth and families.

Case Example: My Journey as a Fearless and Strengths-Based LGBT Advocate

During my fifth year as an elementary school counselor, the administration enlisted my services to help address an increasing problem of students using anti-LGBT language, such as "that's so gay," in negative and harmful manners. In efforts to create a more respectful and empathic school climate towards LGBT populations, I incorporated the GLSEN (2012b) anti-bullying curriculum *Ready, Set, Respect!* and the children's story *The Family Book* by Todd Parr (2003). I was unaware that the implementation of these imperative resources would be perceived and challenged by harsh, conservative, and unsupportive feedback.

After an abundance of phone calls and e-mail messages, my initial advocacy efforts directed me to attend the first school board meeting, where I witnessed community members participate in a prayer vigil and voice their opposition to one page in the children's book that stated, "[s]ome families have two moms or two dads."

As a result, my strengths-based advocacy endeavors prompted me to educate and clarify inaccurate information that was circulating within this small community. I presented my rationale and the positive research findings to the school district's formal curriculum committee, where parents and educators voted and voiced that the challenged materials were age-appropriate, research-based, and necessary to address the documented bullying problems. In response, the opposition disagreed, grew louder, and even began to request that their children be removed from my classroom social and emotional lessons. As the opposition continued to evolve, the administration began to distance themselves from my respect-for-all efforts.

After several months of debate at heavily attended board meetings, school officials issued a directive to all school personnel in my building, stating that "all resources and conversations with students depicting two moms/two dads, gay/lesbian families, same-sex parents, LGBT materials, and sexual orientation were not allowed". This alarming and sweeping ban of LGBT resources ignited my voice for change and was counter-productive to the protective factors I was striving to build within my school counseling program. I could not sit back and allow this injustice to continue. My advocacy efforts partnered with other supportive allies, within and outside of the school district. For example, our collaborative coalition developed a family reading night outside of school hours, where children and families could gather and still hear these affirming messages. I received invaluable support from local, state, and national LGBT organizations and the story generated national media attention around this important issue. Although the ban which disallowed me to use these materials in future classroom lessons was not lifted, my vision to impact change and incorporate LGBT-inclusive programs and protective factors was not extinguished. This critical incident has directed me to become a School Counselor Educator, where my passion and energy is focused on the training of future school counselors as strengths-based allies and advocates for LGBT youth.

As my personal story indicated, ensuring that LGBT students receive equal services and programs, especially when there is a clear need for affirmative change within a school system, can be complex and challenging. Therefore, in the following section, my personal example will be intertwined to provide practical and relevant real-life examples regarding how strengths-based affirmative advocacy (SBAA) benefitted my advocacy efforts.

You will also find that several of my recommendations and research findings are derived from the GLSEN, the leading national education organization that works to create respectful and safe school climates for all students, regardless of sexual orientation, gender identity, or gender expression (GLSEN, n.d.a.). For the purpose of this chapter on strengths and advocacy with LGBT youth, it is appropriate to use GLSEN materials for several reasons. First, GLSEN's programs have been extensively researched and provide K–12 educators with developmentally appropriate materials. Second, these resources have been endorsed by several national educational organizations such as the National Association of Elementary School Principals (NAESP) and the National Association for the Education of Young Children (NAEYC). As such, school counselors can utilize SBAA when working with stakeholders and other educational groups with the shared goal of creating safer school environments for LGBT youth. Third, GLSEN focuses on student-led initiatives that aim to transform change for LGBT youth and overall school climates (Kosciw, Greytak, et al., 2014). As a result of my experience with instituting GLSEN programs, I am more able to "walk the talk" in how these programs have truly made a difference in the lives of the students and families for whom I served as a school counselor.

Additional examples of this case can be found within Beck et al. (2014) and Beck, Davis-Gage, & Butler (in press).

Applications for Strengths-Based Affirmative Advocacy in K–12 Settings

The remaining section provides strategies for school counselors to use SBAA when working to create more affirming spaces for LGBT youth. These strength-enhancing recommendations aim to shift the focus from reaction to prevention that was found within the school counseling literature and to increase the understanding in how affirming programs can help LGBT youth feel safer, supported, and connected at school. These suggestions for school counselor practice are infused at multiple levels throughout, given that change can be non-linear and occur at different levels simultaneously (Beck et al., 2014). For example, school counselors may find that they are working with an LGBT youth individually on protective factors only to find that they are advocating with the student on a much larger systemic level such as the implementation of affirmative safe school policies (Beck et al., 2014).

Promoting Youth Self-Advocacy

There are several ways school counselors can foster the strengths, assets, and resiliency when working individually with LGBT youth. First, it is important for school counselors to have specific grasp of the knowledge and skills for intervention with LGBT youth (Beck et al., 2014). As such, school counselors must realize the need for preventative action and services within their own school counseling programs. Research has suggested that LGBT youth experiences can be understood in the context of *minority stress theory*, which is defined as the stress resulting from the conflict between a school's expectations and the student's identity (Meyer, 2003).

In anticipation of this perceived mismatch, school counselors can adjust their questioning techniques and rehearse proactive coping and self-advocacy skills to create more stress-resistant qualities in LGBT youth. Specifically, school counselors can practice role-playing situations such as the utilization of positive self-talk and standing up for oneself. Also, school counselors should tailor their questions with LGBT youth to reflect more support and self-esteem, in efforts to discern the positive strengths youth may employ when faced with adversity. For example, school counselors can ask youth to describe a time in which they found support from others (teachers, peers, family, community members, etc.) and how these individuals may have provided strength, courage, and hope.

Additionally, school counselors can use the voice of LGBT youth as a method to promote self-advocacy. Empowered-based questions may help LGBT youth identify supportive allies and resources, increase their self-confidence, and foster empowerment through connectedness with others. These insights may also provide an increased awareness for the school counselor to realize the change that needs to happen outside of the individual counseling session and within the school community. School counselors may realize from their individual work with youth that collaborative partnerships with the student and others may be necessary to impact injustices found at the systemic level. For example, the youth and school counselor may work on strategies such as inviting an LGBT guest speaker on bullying. Therefore, this discussion aims to direct change within the individual session for the student and also impact the larger school audience by helping more youth feel less isolated and more hopeful that resources and supports are there to help.

School counselors can also bring a strengths-based perspective into their individual sessions through the use of LGBT-inclusive books such as *The Family Book* by Todd Parr (2003) and *And Tango Makes Three* by Justin Richardson and Peter Parnell (2005). These stories and the representations of inclusive characters may help LGBT youth feel more wholly accepted and experience an increased sense of belonging to school. It is important for LGBT youth to receive nurturing messages that they and their families share many common values and worldviews with other children. Therefore, school counselors should familiarize themselves with inclusive-themed children's books for their individual and classroom-level guidance work.

As you learned in my case example, I was asked by the administration to locate resources that fostered more respect and tolerance towards diverse populations, with the shared goal to combat the anti-LGBT name-calling concerns in my elementary building. Therefore, I referenced the annotated bibliographies on diverse children's books from the Welcoming Schools (n.d.), a project of the Human Rights Campaign. These stories helped me teach more inclusively about respecting differences towards marginalized populations. Specifically, I used many of these suggested books individually to orient youth to diverse characters and role models.

School counselors can also promote a strengths-based perspective when supporting youth in their sexual identity development. According to Kayler, Lewis, and Davidson (2008), school counselors should be mindful that not all LGBT youth may want to discuss their sexual orientation or feel comfortable to come out to others. Therefore, a critical component for school counselors is to create a safe, nurturing, and confidential environment, where all youth feel comfortable to be their authentic selves. Additionally, it is crucial for school counselors to meet LGBT youth at wherever they may be in their sexual identity developmental journey.

To support the role of school counselors when working with youth individually and within systemic levels, one must first understand and be able to assess the sexual identity development of students (Kayler et al., 2008). Researchers have emphasized that school counselors should utilize the sexual identity development models in their work with LGBT youth such as Cass's strengths-oriented model (1983) that offers a positive light in conceptualizing the six sexual identity stages that LGBT youth may encounter in their journey, such as confusion, comparison, tolerance, acceptance, pride, and synthesis (Helton & Smith, 2004). However, given that stage models tend to be more linear in scope, school counselors need to be mindful that the coming out process is different for all youth, often life-long, and that one model cannot truly define how LGBT youth make meaning from their sexual identity experiences. Therefore, school counselors must ensure that LGBT have safe, supportive, and trustworthy resources and allies when deciding to share their sexual orientation and gender identity with others beyond the school counseling office.

To help bolster imperative self-advocacy skills when providing individual counseling to LGBT youth, school counselors should familiarize themselves with current success stories where LGBT youth work to make schools safer for themselves and their peers. Recently, Jake Stallman, a high school student from Tipton, Iowa, encountered resistance after disclosing his sexual orientation at school. Jake's perseverance to overcome homophobia, to be the first male cheerleader, and to inspire others through his personal stories and experiences found on the blog Matthew'sPlace.com, earned him the 2013 Spirit of Matthew award from the Matthew Shepard Foundation (Matthew Shepard Foundation, n.d.). Therefore, youth stories can serve as a powerful and inspirational strategy for school counselors in helping to empower LGBT youth. School counselors can utilize Jake's blog to connect LGBT youth to other affirmative supports and services that share a common vision of ensuring that all youth are safe at school (Matthew Shepard Foundation, n.d.). Additionally, these inspirational stories can serve as important discussion starters between the school counselor and student. For example, the school counselor can lead a conversation in how the power of Jake's voice not only created change for himself, but for other youth who may have been denied equal opportunities as a result of their sexual orientation and gender identity. Jake's voice can be a powerful example for school counselors to demonstrate hope, encourage self-advocacy skills, and for LGBT youth to envision a school environment where things can be different.

Creating Student Organizations

Perhaps central to fostering the growth and development in LGBT youth is the importance of creating safe spaces at school where students can increase their connections with peers like themselves, straight allies, and supportive school personnel (Frank & Cannon, 2009). Opportunities for group engagement may provide an outlet for LGBT youth to be more of themselves and bolster the needed resiliency skills from unwelcoming school climates. School-based groups can serve as an additional delivery component within school counseling programs to help facilitate LGBT youth's sharing of feelings and experiences. Furthermore, on a larger systems level, strengths-based groups may also send an influential and visible message to youth that their school is affirmative and will not tolerate discrimination of LGBT populations (GLSEN, 2007).

School counselors are strengths-based leaders who need to advocate for the creation of affirmative student clubs such as GSAs. GSAs provide a safe environment that fosters the self-acceptance of all students regardless of their sexual orientation (GLSEN, 2007). According to GLSEN (2007), "GSAs often advocate for improved school climate, educate the larger school community about LGBT issues, and support LGBT students and their allies" (p. 1).

There has been significant evidence to support how strengths-oriented GSAs offer more meaningful and protective benefits for LGBT youth and impact the inclusive level of the entire school. Specifically, GLSEN's 2013 National School Climate Survey (Kosciw, Greytak, et al., 2014) found that schools with a GSA correlated with more positive experiences for LGBT youth, including hearing fewer homophobic remarks, a decrease in incidence of anti-LGBT victimization, being less likely to feel unsafe because of their sexual orientation (46% of students with a GSA vs. 64.4% of other students), and experiencing an increased connection to their school (Kosciw, Greytak, et al., 2014). On a school-wide level, Griffin, Lee, Waugh, and Beyer (2004) reported that GSAs offer systemic support through the promotion of a visible and safe place for all youth and an increased awareness of school-wide inclusive efforts for LGBT change. Other strengths-based findings with GSAs include increased self-pride (Lee, 2002), increased school belonging (GLSEN, 2007; Lee, 2002), access to supportive school staff (GLSEN, 2007; Kosciw, Greytak, et al., 2014; Szalacha, 2003), less absenteeism (Szalacha, 2003), higher GPA (Toomey & Russell, 2011), decreased sense of isolation (Craig et al., 2014), and school personnel who use positive statements about LGBT people (Szalacha, 2003). It stands to reason that school counselors have invaluable positive outcomes to utilize when advocating how GSAs support the positive development for LGBT youth.

As part of their social justice advocacy role, school counselors are in a leading position to implement GSAs as a prime method to increase school safety and to bolster a sense of school belongingness for LGBT youth. Still, several authors noted that the implementation of a GSA could present school counselors with additional obstacles and barriers in their advocacy efforts. For example, school counselors might be inaccurately accused of bringing up topics on sexuality within a GSA (Jennings, 2014). In addition, Curry and Hayes' (2009) manuscript shared the first author's experience with school officials when one school counselor tried to create a small group for her LGBT high school students and was told, "We can't do that. Parents will think we are turning their kids gay" (Curry & Hayes, 2009, p. 11). Therefore, school counselors need to be prepared to utilize a strengths-based approach to counter the exclusionary practices found in resistant school systems.

School counselors can establish the SBAA framework in speaking out how GSAs make a difference in the lives of LGBT youth. First, school counselors can work to change the status quo by using the mentioned positive outcome-focused research that documents how GSAs offer an opportunity for increased positive youth development and school connectedness for LGBT youth. Second, school counselors often find themselves in leadership roles, as group facilitators, for school-based clubs. As such, school counselors can volunteer to lead, organize, and monitor the GSA. As a result, LGBT youth and school personnel gain exposure regarding how school counselors model appropriate risk-taking and fearless advocacy in their development of programs that enrich the lives of all students.

Incorporating Inclusive Curricula

In addition to highlighting the protective factors for LGBT youth within individual and small groups, school counselors can also extend their SBAA efforts to enhance the school-wide culture. Helpers can utilize the SBAA framework at the classroom (i.e., developmental, social, and emotional lessons) and school-wide levels (i.e., year-round programs) through representation of positive examples of inclusive individuals, families, and historical figures (GLSEN, 2011). The use of affirmative curricula and programming can be strategies for school counselors to help foster the protective factors for LGBT students. For example, infusing inclusive classroom lessons into a school counseling curriculum can be an effective time-management strategy for school counselors to message how LGBT people and events continue to positively impact society. These enriching and inclusive messages can help school counselors teach students imperative life skills such as the appreciation of differences among multicultural populations and insight-oriented reflection exercises that assess for biased attitudes and stereotypes.

Researchers (Kosciw, Greytak, et al., 2014) have indicated how the use of inclusive curricula for LGBT students can provide purposeful and essential protective factors. GLSEN's *2013 National School Climate Survey* (Kosciw, Greytak, et al., 2014) study found that when students were exposed to positive examples of LGBT individuals, history, and events, there was less victimization and an increase in academic outcomes such as higher reported GPAs for LGBT youth (Kosciw, Greytak, et al., 2014). In addition, Kosciw, Greytak, et al. (2014) found that as a result of inclusive curricula, LGBT youth felt an elevated sense of connectedness within their schools. Specifically, these researchers indicated that LGBT youth who attended schools with an affirmative curriculum were more likely to report that other students were more accepting of LGBT students (75.2% vs. 39.6%) and less likely to feel unsafe at school (Kosciw, Greytak, et al., 2014).

It stands to reason that school counselors should utilize the SBAA framework when developing a social and emotional curriculum, which includes positive LGBT topics. Specifically, to cultivate more respect and acceptance towards diverse student populations, school counselors must advocate and work to infuse inclusive programming at the elementary level. The primary years serve as a critical time to plant the seeds of respect and to develop strengths-based interventions that challenge the harmful attitudes, biases, and stereotypes that often form at early ages. For example, school counselors can utilize a free curriculum such as GLSEN's (2012b) *Ready, Set, Respect!*, which aims to teach more inclusive attitudes and respectful behaviors to children. School counselors can combine their strengths-based advocacy with the aforementioned positive research findings to demonstrate how inclusive programming helps LGBT youth thrive more at school.

As the example of my story illustrated, I incorporated GLSEN's (2012b) *Ready, Set, Respect!* into my developmental guidance curriculum to counter the documented anti-LGBT language found within the hallways of the elementary school. Specifically, I used GLSEN's lesson entitled *Words Do Matter*, where students created lists of more respectful put-ups as compared to put-downs (GLSEN, 2012b). In my case, the resistance from the community did not inhibit my ability to provide positive examples of diverse families and LGBT representations to all my students. I observed how these resources worked to increase peer support, foster authentic conversations, and create more positive interpersonal communication strategies among students. Although a small majority of school community members did not want to hear these positive examples, I continued to share my message.

In addition to inclusive curricula at the elementary level, school counselors can seek school-wide comprehensive prevention at the middle and high school levels, such as GLSEN's *Day of Silence* and *No Name Calling Week*. School counselors can use the SBAA framework when recommending the activities and lessons from *No Name Calling Week*. Helpers can demonstrate that over 60 national partner organizations, such as The National School Boards Association, The National Association of Elementary School Principals, and the American Counseling Association, among others, have joined together in support of these affirmative programs (GLSEN, n.d.b.).

School counselors can combine the previously mentioned strengths-findings to support their advocacy with recommendations of LGBT-related themes in all school subjects. Given that school counselors may only visit a classroom a couple times a month for a developmental lesson, all students need to hear these positive and affirmative messages daily. As a result, school counselors should collaborate and serve on curriculum committees, where school personnel discuss, collaborate, and select textbooks and materials (GLSEN, 2011). In addition, working with stakeholders to revise curriculum standards may serve as another avenue for school counselors to highlight how an inclusive curriculum aims to support the protective factors for LGBT student populations (GLSEN, 2011).

Strengthening Ally Support

SBAA perspective also implies that school counselors have additional allies who support their strengths-based mission to help LGBT youth become more of who they are. According to GLSEN (2013a) an

> ally is an individual who speaks out and stands up for a person or group that is targeted and discriminated against. An ally works to end oppression by supporting and advocating for people who are stigmatized, discriminated against or treated unfairly. (p. 5)

Therefore, the role of supportive and visible school personnel may be influential in helping to transform change on all ecological levels within the school community. For example, an unidentified LGBT youth cited in GLSEN's *Safe Space Kit* claimed, "[w]hen teachers are accepting of you, it means the world to you. You know that things will be OK and that they are there for you" (GLSEN, 2013a, p. 1).

Scholars have demonstrated the ways that supportive personnel can impact LGBT school experiences including: greater self-esteem (Kosciw et al., 2013), higher GPA (Kosciw, Greytak, et al., 2014), and diminished victimization (Kosciw et al., 2013). These findings support how valuable the affirmative partnerships with additional school personnel can be for LGBT youth, especially in support of their academic and social development. As such, the mere presence of affirming allies at school can be a powerful protective factor for LGBT youth.

Promoting partnerships that foster strengths-enhancing environments is an essential principle not only within the SBAA framework, but also for the role of a school counselor as an effective collaborator. School counselors can take on a leadership role when working to increase and strengthen ally support. As a starting point, school counselors can utilize GLSEN's (2013a) *Safe Space Kit*, designed to inform educators on the positive impact their role as an ally can have for LGBT youth. School counselors can emphasize the aforementioned findings during in-service trainings, in generating interest and support from staff. Additionally, school counselors can symbolize the need for visibility of educator support by distributing Safe Space posters or stickers to all school personnel (GLSEN, 2013a). Recently, GLSEN launched a campaign from 2010 to 2013, where all middle and high schools in the United States received a free Safe Space Kit (GLSEN, 2013b). Using the resources already at their disposal, school counselors can utilize SBAA to demonstrate how national education organizations such as GLSEN are uniting through conversation and action, to promote the need for visibility of support and safety for LGBT youth. School counselors can emphasize this strength-in-numbers approach from GLSEN's campaign to inspire more school personnel to become active and visible allies for LGBT youth.

Strengths Enhancing Safe School Policies

School counselors may find themselves advocating for affirmative policies and procedures that enhance the growth and development of LGBT youth. Instead of speaking out on policies that inhibit opportunities, as often found in a traditional and reactive approach, school counselors can use the SBAA framework to showcase how inclusive practices and policies are helping LGBT youth thrive more at school. For example, GLSEN's *2013 National School Climate Survey* (Kosciw, Greytak, et al., 2014) found that LGBT students who attended a school with a comprehensive anti-bullying policy reported hearing fewer homophobic comments and were more likely to indicate that school personnel intervened when an anti-LGBT bullying situation had occurred.

These findings call for school counselors to advocate that comprehensive policies, which protect and promote the safety and well-being of LGBT youth, indeed make a difference. As such, school counselors need to be active participants at all levels (i.e., district, state, and national) when policy makers are at the table. School counselors should be visible and vocal within counseling associations in efforts to develop position statements and revise ethical standards that outline school counseling practice with LGBT youth.

Within the SBAA framework, school counselors need to be informed about how current strengths-based movements are affecting change for LGBT youth. For example, in April 2014 the state of Massachusetts became the 17th state to pass legislation that incorporated language that specifically protects LGBT youth from bullying and harassment (GLSEN, 2014). As a result, school counselors should build upon this momentum when lobbying with stakeholders on policies that include language that specifically protects LGBT students against bullying.

Instilling Hope

Last, it is essential that school counselor advocates maintain hope and empowerment in their work with LGBT youth. It is imperative for helpers to give voice to LGBT youth and to use their influence as a vehicle for change. School counselors can facilitate hopeful conversations that strive for LGBT youth to envision a better future. School counselors need to demonstrate that not only do things improve, but that things can be different. According to Chung and Bemak (2012), "part of being a motivator is instilling hope and belief in a promising and hopeful vision, so a social justice leader helps stakeholders move from accepting 'what is' to believing in 'what could be'" (p. 165). Therefore, it is critical for school counselors to have interventions that provide empowerment when working to help LGBT youth thrive despite adversity within unwelcoming environments.

As a starting point, school counselors can use social media as a creative outlet to support the positive protective factors for underserved students. For example, helpers can use a resource such as *It Gets Better Project*, started by Dan Savage in 2010, that was developed as a preventative method to address the increase in youth suicides from incidents of anti-gay bullying (It Gets Better Project, n.d.). Specifically, this project began as a single video where Savage and his partner disclosed their personal struggles in growing up gay and how things got better for them (It Gets Better Project, n.d.). In response, there have been over 50,000 self-made videos posted on the website from allies all around the world such as politicians, celebrities, teachers, et cetera. To date, more than 50 million viewers have watched these inspiring narratives (It Gets Better Project, n.d.).

These hope-inspiring stories can be an invaluable resource for school counselors in their advocacy to promote change for LGBT youth. School counselors are encouraged to access these video clips during individual counseling sessions with LGBT students, as a strategy to instill hope. Additionally, these videos can also serve as a springboard for conversations about supports, resources, and safety plans for LGBT youth. Furthermore, these inspirational stories can help to normalize youth experiences and validate that LGBT youth are not alone in their experiences.

When working to promote change on a larger systems level (i.e., school district), school counselors can use the It Gets Better Project to showcase the number of responses from celebrities, educational organizations, and politicians, et cetera. This strategy may encourage stakeholders to take more action (i.e., to develop safe school policies to protect LGBT youth) and consider how their own position statements can positively influence the lives of LGBT students within and outside of the school district.

School counselors may discover that sharing their own stories about LGBT family members and friends is useful in their work with students. These strengths-promoting disclosures may provide additional avenues for school counselors to consider when working to build more trust within the counseling relationship, model appropriate risk-taking skills, and to acknowledge an invested interest as a school counselor in advocating for human rights. Last, a school counselor's personal disclosure of their family, friends, or even own journey towards resiliency may help to create a more collaborative and authentic partnership. Although this level of immediacy sharing may require much consideration, this personal sharing may serve as another method for school counselors to connect more with LGBT youth.

Future Directions for Strengths-Based Affirmative Advocacy in K–12 Settings

Upon writing this chapter, there was one obvious barrier facing strengths-based work with LGBT youth. More specifically, this strengths-based perspective continues to lag behind the reaction focus found within the literature. That is, the ASCA publication *Professional School Counseling* released a special issue in 2008 about strengths-based school counseling. However, there were no articles that explicitly examined how strengths-based school counseling could apply with LGBT youth. As a result, researchers and authors need to acknowledge this gap and provide scholarship that can support the role of school counselors in utilizing a strengths-based perspective to support LGBT youth development and to bolster their advocacy efforts in the creation of more LGBT-inclusive spaces at school.

Cultivating an SBAA approach as a method of creating a more promising future for LGBT youth acknowledges the direction and action that the school counseling profession needs to act upon. As Martin Luther King, Jr. once stated, "You don't have to see the whole staircase—just take the first step" (Chung & Bemak, 2012, p. 265). As such, we must work collaboratively and purposefully at taking these next steps. We must work together, at the practitioner and school counseling preparation levels, and across interdisciplinary departments on future research and evidence-based strategies to support how strengths-based advocacy is creating more success for LGBT youth. Thus, we need to capture more narratives and stories from current school counselors in how they navigate their own journey as LGBT advocates.

Finally, school counselors need to be the trailblazers, leaders, and visionaries of change for LGBT youth. Every day our society around us is becoming more accepting and affirming to the rights and equality of LGBT populations. Therefore, these advancements towards justice call for action and attention in how we advocate for change within our school systems. Now is the time to take this step forward!

Final Thoughts

This chapter addresses the need for school counselors to step outside of traditional advocacy approaches that have focused more on the negative outcomes that LGBT student populations face. I have encouraged readers to look beyond these reactive approaches and to consider how blending strengths-based school counseling and social justice work into SBAA can be a positive, creative, and richer strategy in working to promote change for LGBT youth within multiple advocacy levels. The information presented in this chapter, including my personal advocacy story, is intended to inspire, enlighten, and encourage school counselors to use the SBAA framework in their advocacy work with educational stakeholders in the development of more affirming and inclusive spaces. As such, specific recommendations for school counselors in using this SBAA approach to cultivate more change and to help LGBT youth thrive in adverse school environments were suggested.

References

Akos, P., & Galassi, J.P. (2008). Strengths-based school counseling: Introduction to the special issue. *Professional School Counseling, 12,* 66–67. doi:10.5330/PSC.n.2010–12.66

American Counseling Association. (2014). *Code of ethics and standards of practice.* Retrieved on June 10, 2014 from http://www.counseling.org/resources/aca-code-of-ethics.pdf

American School Counselor Association. (2010). *Ethical standards for school counselors.* Alexandria, VA: Author.

American School Counselor Association. (2012). *The ASCA national model: A framework for school counseling programs* (3rd ed.). Alexandria, VA: Author.

American School Counselor Association. (2014). *The professional school counselor and LGBTQ youth.* Alexandria, VA: Author.

Asakura, K., & Craig, S.L. (2014). "It gets better" . . . but how? Exploring resilience development in the accounts of LGBTQ adults. *Journal of Human Behavior in the Social Environment, 24,* 253–266. doi:10.1080/1091135 9.2013.808971

Beck, M. J., Davis-Gage, D., & Butler, S.K. (in press). Diversity and advocacy: "Where all children come first" LGBT advocacy and community resistance. In C. Wood, T. Portman, and L. Tyson (Eds.), *Critical incidents in school counseling, 3rd Ed.* American Counseling Association: Alexandria, VA.

Beck, M.J., Rausch, M.A., & Wood, S.M. (2014). Developing the fearless school counselor ally and advocate for LGBTQIQ youth: Strategies for preparation programs. *Journal of LGBT Issues in Counseling, 8*(4), 361–375. doi:10.1080/15538605.2014.960126

Bemak, F., & Chung, R. (2008). New professional roles and advocacy strategies for school counselors: A multicultural/social justice perspective to move beyond the nice counselor syndrome. *Journal of Counseling & Development, 86,* 372–381. doi:10.1002/j.1556–6678.2008.tb00522.x

Cass, V.C. (1983). Homosexual identity: A concept in need of definition. *Journal of Homosexuality, 9*(2–3), 105–126. doi:10.1300/J082v09n02_07

Chung, R., & Bemak, F.P. (2012). *Social justice counseling: The next steps beyond multiculturalism.* Los Angeles, CA: SAGE Publications.

Craig, S.L. (2013). Affirmative supportive safe and empowering talk (asset): Leveraging the strengths and resiliencies of sexual minority youth in school-based groups. *Journal of LGBT Issues in Counseling, 7,* 372–386. doi :10.1080/15538605.2013.839342

Craig, S.L., Austin, A., & McInroy, L.B. (2014). School-based groups to support multiethnic sexual minority youth resiliency: Preliminary effectiveness. *Child & Adolescent Social Work Journal, 31,* 87–106. doi:10.1007/s10560–013–0311–7

Curry, J.R., & Hayes, B.G. (2009). Bolstering school based support by comprehensively addressing the needs of an invisible minority: Implications for professional school counselors. *Journal of School Counseling, 7*(7), 1–20. Retrieved on June 25, 2014 from http://www.jsc.montana.edu/articles/v7n7.pd

Frank, D.A., II, & Cannon, E.P. (2009). Creative approaches to serving LGBTQ youth in schools. *Journal of School Counseling, 7*(35), 1–24. Retrieved on June 17, 2014 from http://www.jsc.montana.edu/articles/v7n35.pdf

Galassi, J.P., & Akos, P. (2007). *Strengths-based school counseling: Promoting student development and achievement.* Mahwah, NJ: Lawrence Erlbaum.

Galassi, J.P., Griffin, D., & Akos, P. (2008). Strengths-based school counseling and the ASCA national model. *Professional School Counseling, 12,* 176–181. doi: 10.5330/PSC.n.2010–12.176

Gay, Lesbian, & Straight Network (GLSEN). (2007). *Gay-Straight Alliances: Creating safer schools for LGBT students and their allies (research brief).* New York, NY: Gay, Lesbian and Straight Education Network. Retrieved on July 18, 2014 from http://glsen.org/learn/reasearch/national/gsa-brief

Gay, Lesbian, & Straight Education Network. (2011). *Teaching respect: LGBT-inclusive curriculum and school climate (research brief).* New York, NY: Gay, Lesbian and Straight Education Network. Retrieved on July 18, 2014 from: http://glsen.org/learn/research/national/teaching-respect

Gay, Lesbian, & Straight Education Network. (2012a). 2011 National School Climate Survey [Press release]. Retrieved on July 18, 2014 from http://glsen.org/press/2011-national-school-climate-survey

Gay, Lesbian & Straight Education Network.(2012b). *Ready, set, respect! GLSEN's elementary school toolkit.* Retrieved on July 18, 2014 from http://glsen.org/readysetrespect

Gay, Lesbian, & Straight Education Network. (2013a). *The safe space kit: Guide to being an ally for LGBT students.* Retrieved on June 4, 2014 from http://www.glsen.org/sites/default/files/SSK_2013_book.pdf

Gay, Lesbian, & Straight Education Network. (2013b). *Can you #SpotTheSticker?* Retrieved on June 4, 2014 from http://blog.glsen.org/blog/can-you-spotthesticker

Gay, Lesbian, & Straight Education Network. (2014). *GLSEN applauds Massachusetts for passage of LGBT-inclusive anti-bullying law* [Press release]. Retrieved on June 4, 2014 from http://glsen.org/article/glsen-applauds-mass-lgbt-inclusive-anti-bullying-law

Gay, Lesbian, & Straight Education Network. (n.d.a.). *Improving education, creating a better world.* Retrieved from on July 19, 2014 http://glsen.org/learn/about-glsen

Gay, Lesbian, & Straight Education Network. (n.d.b.). *No-name calling week elementary school (K-5) lessons.* Retrieved on July 19, 2014 from http://glsen.org/nonamecallingweek/elementary

Goodrich, K.M., Harper, A.J., Luke, M., & Singh, A.A. (2013). Best practices for professional school counselors working with LGBTQ youth. *Journal of LGBT Issues in Counseling, 7,* 307–322. doi: 10.1080/15538605.2013.839331

Griffin, P., Lee, C., Waugh, J., & Beyer, C. (2004). Describing roles that gay–straight alliances play in schools: From individual support to school change. *Journal of Gay & Lesbian Issues in Education, 1*(3), 7–22. doi:10.1300/J367v01n03_03

Helton, L.R., & Smith, M.K. (2004). *Mental health practice with children and youth: A strengths and well-being model.* New York, NY: Haworth Social Work Practice Press.

It Gets Better Project. (n.d.). *What is the It Gets Better Project?* Retrieved from http://www.itgetsbetter.org/pages/about-it-gets-better-project/

Jennings, T. (2014). Sexual orientation curriculum in U.S. school counseling education programs. *Journal of LGBT Issues in Counseling, 8,* 43–73. doi:10.1080/15538605.2014.853639

Kayler, H., Lewis, T.F., & Davidson, E. (2008). Designing developmentally appropriate school counseling interventions for LGBQ students. *Journal of School Counseling, 6*(6), 1–22. Retrieved on September 7, 2014 from http://www.jsc.montana.edu/articles/v6n6.pdf

Kosciw, J.G., Greytak, E.A., Bartkiewicz, M.J., Boesen, M.J., & Palmer, N.A. (2012). *The 2011 National School Climate Survey: The experiences of lesbian, gay, bisexual, and transgender youth in our nation's schools.* New York, NY: Gay, Lesbian, & Straight Education Network.

Kosciw, J.G., Palmer, N.A., Kull, R.M., & Greytak, E.A. (2013). The effect of negative school climate on academic outcomes for LGBT youth and the role of in-school supports. *Journal of School Violence, 12,* 45–63. doi:10.1080/15388220.2012.732546

Kosciw, J.G., Greytak, E.A., Palmer, N.A., & Boesen, M.J. (2014). *The 2013 National School Climate Survey: The experiences of lesbian, gay, bisexual and transgender youth in our nation's schools.* New York, NY: Gay, Lesbian, & Straight Education Network.

Kosciw, J.G., Palmer, N.A., & Kull, R.M. (2014). Reflecting resiliency: Openness about sexual orientation and/or gender identity and its relationship to well-being and educational outcomes for LGBT students. *American Journal of Community Psychology, 55*(1–2), 167–178. doi: 10.1007/s10464-014-9642-6

Lee, C. (2002). The impact of belonging to a high school gay/straight alliance. *The High School Journal, 85*(3), 13–27. doi: 10.1353/hsj.2002.0005

Matthew Shepard Foundation. (n.d.). *Jake's place.* Retrieved on May 19, 2014 from http://www.matthewsplace.com/blog/jakes-place/

Meyer, I.H. (2003). *Minority stress and mental health in gay men* (2nd ed.). New York, NY: Columbia University Press.

Parr, T. (2003). *The family book.* New York, NY: Little, Brown & Company.

Ratts, M.J., DeKruyf, L., & Chen-Hayes, S.F. (2007). The ACA Advocacy Competencies: A social justice advocacy framework for professional school counselors. *Professional School Counseling, 11*(2), 90–97. doi: 10.5330/PSC.n.2010–11.90

Richardson, J., & Parnell, P. (2005). *And tango makes three.* New York, NY: Simon & Schuster.

Saleebey, D. (2008). Commentary on the strengths perspective and potential applications in school counseling. *Professional School Counseling, 12,* 68–75. doi: 10.5330/PSC.n.2010–12.68

Singh, A.A., Urbano, A., Haston, M., & McMahon, F. (2010). School counselors' strategies for social justice change: A grounded theory of what works in the real world. *Professional School Counseling, 13,* 135–145. doi: 10.5330/PSC.n.2010–13.135

Szalacha, L.A. (2003). Safer sexual diversity climates: Lessons learned from an evaluation of Massachusetts safe schools program for gay and lesbian students. *American Journal of Education, 110,* 58–88. doi:0195–6744/2004/11001–0003

Toomey, R.B., & Russell, S.T. (2011). Gay-straight alliances, social justice involvement, and school victimization of lesbian, gay, bisexual, and queer youth: Implications for school well-being and plans to vote. *Youth and Society, 45,* 500–522. doi 10.1177/0044118X11422546

Valenti, M., & Campbell, R. (2009). Working with youth on LGBT issues: Why gay–straight alliance advisors become involved. *Journal of Community Psychology, 37,* 228–248. doi:10.1002/jcop.20290

Welcoming Schools. (n.d.). *Excerpts from Welcoming Schools bibliographies of recommended books for elementary students: Family diversity, gender, and bullying.* Retrieved on September 9, 2014 from http://hrc-assets.s3-website-us-east-1.amazonaws.com//welcoming-schools/documents/WS_Recommended_Bibliographies_Excerpts.pdf

9

Strengths-Based Theory and Practice

Perspectives and Strategies that Enhance Growth, Hope, and Resilience for People Living with Chronic Illness and Disability

Michelle Marmé

Disability is a social experience, not simply a medical impairment or disorder. [People] aren't truly disabled until they enter a world filled with stairs instead of elevators, or workplace discrimination that prevents them from getting a job.

Elizabeth Heideman (2015)

Disability need not be an obstacle to success.

Stephen Hawking (2011)

As the 21st century reaches its adolescent years, people with chronic illness and disability are more likely than ever before to be participants in classrooms, in employment settings, and in counselor offices seeking assistance in working toward meaningful lives. Many factors contribute to the increasing numbers of people with chronic illness and disability (CID) finding themselves in the mainstream of life. People are able to survive injuries, such as spinal cord and acquired brain injuries, HIV/AIDs and cancers that were life-ending previously. Advances in medicine, health care, and technology allow people with CID to manage symptoms and complications, allowing them to engage more fully in the world. Enhanced awareness, identification, and supports for children with sensory processing issues, autism spectrum disorders, and nontraditional learning requirements afford children more meaningful participation and success in academic settings. By succeeding in primary and secondary schools, these young adults are then able to participate successfully in postsecondary education and work environments. Legislation supporting increased physical and programmatic accessibility in schools, governmental, commercial, recreational settings, and places of worship has paved the way for fuller participation of people with chronic illness and disabilities in the mainstream of life (Welch & Palames, 2015; American Association of Persons with Disabilities, 2015; Bruyere & Reiter, 2012; Jenkins, Patterson, & Szymanski, 1992).

Increasingly, the life issues for people with CID are being recognized as components of diversity and multicultural concern in counselor training and practice. The attention given to *Older Adults*, *People with Disabilities*, and *Deaf Children and Their Families* among the chapter titles in Courtland Lee's

125

2013 book, *Multicultural Issues in Counseling: New Approaches to Diversity, Fourth Edition*, is encouraging. For counselors to become culturally competent professionals, it is vital to develop an understanding of the many perspectives in conceptualizing the "evolving concept" of disability (WHO, 2011, p. 4; Eddey & Robey, 2005; Wehmeyer & Shogren, 2014). Developing agility in working effectively with people with CID must become a priority in professional counselor development.

Strengths-based approaches are essential to the mobilization of resources for people with CID and those in their spheres of influence as they incorporate the added complexity in living linked to integrating CID into their lives. Intuitively, individuals with chronic illness and disability, as well as those close to them, understand that developing lives of meaning must be built upon an exploration, identification, and refinement of one's strengths. Experience has taught us that focusing on labels, deficits, and mistakes is self-defeating and non-productive with regard to crafting engaging, satisfying lives.

Rehabilitation counseling research, literature, and counselor education have been anchored in the seminal work of Beatrice Wright. Among her conceptual contributions are the following: an emphasis on the individual rather than the disability; in mining the positive resources within the person and the situation (specifically, guiding the individual to draw upon the strengths in his or her relationships, his or her community, and resources such as education, technology, aptitudes, and interests not previously tapped); an emphasis on the assets of the individual rather than the limitations; the value of hope in adjusting to disability, illness, misfortune, or suffering; the belief that a disabling condition does not spell the end of a life worth living (Dembo, Ladieu-Leviton, & Wright, 1956; Wright, B., 1958, 1960; Wright & Lopez, 2005; Wright, B., 1983; Maki & Tarvydas, 2012; Wright, G., 1980; McCarthy, 2014). Each of these positions is addressed briefly in this chapter. To enjoy the richness of Dr. Wright's work, the reader is encouraged to spend some time with the references listed. Additional foundational work has been provided to counselor education for nearly 40 years by Ivey, Ivey, and colleagues. Their emphasis on the principle that people grow from their strengths (Ivey, Ivey, & Zalaquett, 2014, p. 202; first edition published in 1983) has long guided rehabilitation/ counselor training and practice. Strengths-based approaches flow from these early professional roots.

Seligman's recent enhancement to positive psychology as presented in his 2011 book *Flourish: A Visionary New Understanding of Happiness and Well-Being* provides an exciting, even more exacting template for consideration of strengths-based approaches to working with people with CID. His redirection of positive psychology from the topic of happiness to the construct of well-being is powerful. He states that "the gold standard for measuring well-being is flourishing, and the goal for positive psychology is to increase flourishing, in the individual and in the world" (Seligman, 2011, p. 13). As he alludes, his earlier focus on happiness and life satisfaction proved to be more reflective of moment-dependent assessments than enduring factors, and too closely associated with the notion of a cheerful mood. For those grappling with catastrophic loss, references to anything that might seem to promote a superficial look-on-the-bright-side line of thinking was generally received as condescending and had great potential to be detrimental to building a relationship with the client.

This shift in theory has set in motion an important refinement in therapeutic goals. The goal of well-being theory is to enhance the elements of well-being. In turn, this enables the individual to be more resilient and more adaptable to the demands of life. The elements of well-being are represented in the pneumonic PERMA. They are positive emotions, engagement, relationships, meaning, achievement. These in turn are the criteria for flourishing (Seligman, 2011, p. 239). By engaging in and developing each of these elements, people construct deeper, more engaged, and more meaningful experiences, more of the time. Living within the context of these elements, one is capable of responding to whatever happens with the capacity to respond and to grow. Thus, they will flourish. Well-being theory is empowering. Particularly for those who have experienced traumatic onset of disability, opportunities for turning trauma into growth (Seligman, 2011, p. 152) must be captured and embraced. This emphasis away from minimizing negative states to enhancing positive ones provides a path to a healthier, more balanced, more resilient life.

In following a strengths-based approach to collaborating with persons with CID, I find the opportunity to incorporate the most productive and appealing aspects of other theories, such as client-centered (receiving/accepting clients as they are, actively listening), Adlerian (social interest, drive for people to be their best selves), and cognitively oriented approaches (recognizing, exploring, and re-teaching the associations between thoughts, feelings, and actions). With a strengths-based focus at the heart of my work, I find greater coherence. The search for well-being succinctly encompasses what I believe people are seeking. While many of the discrete skills involved can be taught, strengths-based approaches are far more than a handbook of exercises. I regard strengths-based approaches as anchored in the counselor developing a personal belief and commitment to embrace that framework. It is a way of being, a way of seeing the world and others. To meet the individual where he or she is, as we know we intend to do, we must do our own work in embracing positive emotions, optimism, and be able to focus on the other while remaining present in our own skin. If we have not embraced and searched for well-being in our own lives then our efforts to assist the other will be compromised. We will not understand, really understand, the "GRIT" (Seligman, 2011, p. 118: very high persistence and high passion for an objective) required to develop these skills and strengths.

Developing a true appreciation of well-being theory and applying a strengths-based approach to our work as clinicians requires attention and commitment. These perspectives are not consistent with the mores of a society that favors rapid insight and solutions. To adopt, practice, and embrace a strengths-based approach to our work, we must live within that framework. While ultimately liberating, the challenges of life put our beliefs and skills to the test at every turn. Even these personal struggles, if savored (Froh & Parks, 2013, pp. 149–152), become helpful in our work to invite others, our clients, into this schema for approaching the world. In order to appreciate the beauty in the moment, the power of a kind word, the relishing of incremental successes, the counselor must live these experiences. We can be better educators of the theory if we have struggled to apply it to our own lives. Our ability to connect with the client will be enhanced if we are following our own paths toward PERMA, toward flourishing.

Strengths-based approaches guide counselors both in their disposition toward the individual and in the array of responses to provide to the individual. At their heart, strengths-based approaches conceptualize the individual seeking assistance (the client) and the individual providing assistance (the counselor) as collaborators in a relational process, directed toward the exploration and identification of issues, concerns, assets, supports, obstacles, strategies, opportunities for growth, and clarification of goals. In the context of this relationship, the counselor and the client reflect upon thoughts, feelings, and behaviors in positive, affirming ways. The relationship itself is an element of PERMA.

The subtle and immensely powerful effect of language and its ability to shape our reality must be mentioned here, with respect to strengths-based approaches. Think for a minute about the difference between speaking of a situation with respect to the potential it offers rather than the risk involved. The impact on the listener is substantial. The engagement with thinking about potential is far stronger than focusing on the real/imagined risks.

Although a mainstay of good therapeutic intervention in general, homework and assignments to be carried out in the real world are essential. Processing the enactment of these and results of homework follow. Attempts to complete assignments are recognized for the strength and commitment it takes to venture outside one's comfort zone. Mistakes are reframed as the individual's best efforts to move toward a desired situation or result. The individual's insights to his or her strengths, relationships, achievements become a vital focus for counseling and growth. As such, the effort can be evaluated for its potency and assessed for alternatives that might lead to more desirable, productive outcomes.

Harris, Thoreson, and Lopez (2007) presented the core concepts of positive psychology, in the context of Seligman's original model, as incorporating subjective experiences, individual traits or dispositions, and interpersonal/group level virtues that would enhance the quality of the community (p. 3). Following a strengths-based perspective, essential elements also include encouraging optimism, mindfulness, creativity, resilience, interpersonal skills, relating to others, humor, responsibility, and work ethic in those seeking to incorporate CID into their lives.

The primary goal in rehabilitation/counseling education has been to assist individuals in exploring and moving toward what makes life most worth living. In the company of an accepting collaborator, who joins with the individual on a process of discovery and change, a strengths-based counseling relationship can be the catalyst for the individual to find and embrace a fulfilling life.

This chapter provides a context for considering your work with individuals who have chronic illness and disabilities. The reader is challenged next to consider that being a multiculturally competent mental health practitioner requires understanding (1) the social construction of disability and chronic illness; (2) the societal/historical assumptions, attitudes, and expectations of people with CID; and (3) a brief overview of the literature that exists among rehabilitation counseling and psychology research with respect to strengths-based approaches to working with people with CID. Once this foundation has been laid, readers will be provided with an invitation to understand how well suited the premises of positive psychology and strengths-based approaches are in their work with children and adults with chronic illness and disabilities, and their significant others, as clients create lives of meaning, growth, and happiness.

Review of the Literature

To provide a context for the reader to best understand the utility of strengths-based approaches in counseling people with CID, traditional assumptions and attitudes, key terms, concepts, and compounding social factors must be examined. Given that the scope of this book focuses on strengths-based approaches for working most effectively with people with CID, only a few topics under the general theme of social psychology of disability will be addressed at this time: definitions of terms that help frame a foundation for your work with people with CID, data regarding the prevalence of disability, and models for understanding people with CID.

Definitions: Impairments, Disabilities, Handicaps, and Equalization of Opportunities

The definition of terms presents a challenge to the reader because much controversy, some friction, and considerable political significance surrounds the definition and terminology favored by various stakeholders in the definition of disability and related concepts. Although variations and disconnects exist among the definitions endorsed by social security, school systems, insurance companies, state vocational rehabilitation agencies, disability studies, and disability rights groups, it is far outside the scope of our work in this text to address the intricacies of those debates. Suffice it to say that the lack of consensus in the definitions of terms central to qualifying for each of these programs is the source for substantial confusion and consternation among individuals with CID and those close to them.

Actually, the notion of referring to people with CID as a group is a highly flawed concept. People with CID are profoundly heterogeneous, by diagnosis, by level of function, by interests, by financial and social opportunities readily available to them, by who determines whether a person is/is not a person with CID. Also, it is essential to remember that many people have multiple chronic illnesses and disabilities. Again, for expediency, the complicating factors of managing multiple chronic illnesses and disabilities will not be addressed in this chapter. Despite the inexactitude of its use, for the purposes of this chapter, I will default to referring to people with CID as a group.

For ease of communication, the definitions provided by the World Health Organization (WHO, 2011), in its International Classification of Impairments, Disabilities and Handicaps, are offered as bench marks for your work with children and adults with CID. The WHO makes distinctions among impairment, disability, handicap, and equalization of opportunities. The perspective of the WHO represents the medical model of disability. To aid in understanding the separation in perspectives between the medical model and the social model of disability, as available, definitions from Shakespeare (2006) will also be offered. These concepts are defined as follows:

(a) *Impairment* is "any loss or abnormality of psychological, physiological, or anatomical structure or function." Impairments are disturbances at the level of the organ which include defects in or loss of a limb, organ, or other body structure, as well as defects in or loss of a mental function. "Examples of impairments include blindness, deafness, loss of sight in an eye, paralysis of a limb, amputation of a limb; mental retardation, partial sight, loss of speech, mutism" (WHO, 2011, p. 3). The social model of disability offers a complimentary definition in explaining impairments as "individual and private" (Shakespeare, 2006, p. 198).

(b) *Disability* is "complex, dynamic, multidimensional, and contested" (WHO, 2011, p. 3). According to the WHO, the term refers to any "restriction or lack (resulting from an impairment) of ability to perform an activity in the manner or within the range considered normal for a human being." It describes a functional limitation or activity restriction that is caused by an impairment. Disabilities are descriptions of disturbances in function at the level of the person. Examples of disabilities include difficulty seeing, speaking, or hearing; difficulty moving or climbing stairs; difficulty grasping, reaching, bathing, eating, toileting.

In contrast, Shakespeare (2006) offered the following definition from a social model perspective: Disability is a "structural and public concept; a social creation, a relationship between people with impairment and a disabling society" (p. 198). The reader can readily see where conflicts and miscommunications arise when disability is considered by some to be a deficit in functioning in the individual, whereas others in the conversations understand it to be deficits in society's ability or flexibility to respond to the individual.

Hill and Goldstein (2015) have drawn attention to the equating of disability with the "inability to work, parent, or live independently" (p. 2227). Within this context, people were to accept their marginalization from typical adult roles and to be content to be the objects of charity and pity. An outgrowth of this was the seemingly logical belief that if one was not expected to work as an adult, ensuring a rigorous education for that person during formative years was not a priority.

As adults, many people with CID live outside the economic and societal mainstream. Consequently, they were largely invisible in their communities. "Those who were able to work, live on their own, or raise a family were seen as inspirational outliers" (Hill & Goldstein, 2015, p. 2227). The use of these images in advertising and feel-good television specials has alarmed those who regard such imaging as disrespectful, stigmatizing, and condescending to people with disabilities. Heideman (2015) referred to this use of images of people with disabilities engaging in typical societal expectations, such as having friends, going to school, enjoying a concert, as heroic, inspirational, or tear-generating: "inspiration porn." Specifically, this term refers to the portrayal of people with CID as triumphant or inspiring when they are merely living their lives. On one hand, the underlying assumption of the medical model is that having CID equates to hardship, to marginalization from traditional adult roles, and to tragedies that must be overcome. This perspective incorrectly supports the notion that disability can be overcome with a smile and determination. Such beliefs serve to comfort us from the threat of our own vulnerability and mortality. The result is that disability is reinforced as being connected to a problem in the person and not as the social experience related to oppressive policies and inaccessibility.

(c) A *handicap* is a "disadvantage for a given individual, resulting from an impairment or disability that limits or prevents the fulfillment of a role that is normal (depending on age, sex and social and cultural factors) for that individual." (WHO, 1980, p. 29)

The term is also a classification of "circumstances in which people are likely to find themselves" (WHO, 2011, p. 5). Handicap describes the social and economic roles that place people with CID at a disadvantage compared with other persons. These disadvantages are brought about through the interaction of the person with specific environments and cultures. Examples of handicaps include living in an inaccessible home, lack of accessible transportation, being socially and physically isolated.

Handicaps are "concerned with the disadvantages experienced by the individual as a result of impairments and disabilities; thus, handicaps reflect the interaction with and adaptation to the individuals' surroundings" (WHO, 2011, p. 5).

(d) *Equalization of opportunities* is the process through which the general system of society, such as the physical and cultural environment, housing and transportation, social and health services, educational and work opportunities, cultural and social life, including sports and recreational facilities, are made accessible to all. Equalization relates to the process of building a suitable environment to reasonably accommodate those needs (WHO, 2011, p. 5).

The underlying concept is that physical and attitudinal aspects of accessibility be incorporated into the planning of all arenas of life. Its significance rests on the belief that "special" or "separate" access and "accommodation" are not sufficient goals. Systems need to be (re-) designed to enhance life opportunities for any person to access freely. Most "accommodations" benefit many other constituent groups. One example would be curb cuts for sidewalk accessibility. While these are a great improvement for people with mobility impairments, you have surely noticed the advantage that these offer to workers with trolleys, parents with strollers, skate boarders, and bicyclists.

Prevalence of People with Disability

The Bureau of Labor Statistics (2015) estimates that

> people with disabilities represent 19 percent of the total civilian noninstitutionalized population. 12 percent of the total population reported having a severe disability. People with a disability have a physical or mental impairment that affects one or more major life activities, such as walking, bathing, dressing, eating, preparing meals, going outside the home or doing housework. (p. 2)

Please note that this estimation of approximately one in five people in the United States reporting a disability should be considered a substantial under-evaluation of the population of interest for this chapter. This number does not include those people with CID who are in the military, who are incarcerated, who did not self-report as having a disability; neither does it include individuals with chronic illness who may not regard themselves as "having a disability." Just imagine what the real numbers must be!

The Bureau of Labor Statistics (2015) further reported that

> 11 percent of those people, age 25 to 64 with a non-severe disability, live at or below poverty level income standards; while 26 percent of those people, aged 25 to 64 with a severe disability, live at or below poverty level as compared to 8 percent of those without a disability, aged 25 to 64, who live at or below poverty level. (p. 4)

People who live in poverty may have diminished access to health care, sanitary living conditions, and educational opportunities. With this combination of factors in play, people are thought to be at greater likelihood for joining the ranks of CID sooner. As the population ages, membership in CID is nearly guaranteed (WHO, 2011). A circular relationship appears to exist among those who live in poverty/restricted financial situations and disability: those who are members of one group are likely members of the other.

As Gostin (2015) remarked, "the marginalization of people with CID is in one sense remarkable because so many individuals have been, or will become, disabled at some point in the life course" (p. 2231). Thus, in the mid-1980s, the expression "temporarily able bodied" came into general use among people involved in disability rights groups. Although disability can occur at all ages, it is eight times more likely in old age; one-fourth of Americans in their mid- to late 60s have a severe disability, such as major impairments in mobility, vision, hearing, and/or the ability to care for themselves. As the population ages, the prevalence of disabilities will continue to increase with enormous personal consequences as well as health and social costs (Bureau of Labor Statistics, 2015). At present, this dynamic exists: People with CID are at greater risk of living in poverty, and living in poverty appears to increase the risk of having CID. Additionally, people with CID are likely members of numerous marginalized groups.

Social Psychology of Disability

The social psychology of disability is a fascinating academic discipline. Areas of inquiry include societal-level issues such as the following: societal views and perspectives on people with CID, stigma, stereotypes, prejudice, legislation, social movements, disability rights movements, and the power of language to set the boundaries of our thoughts. Additionally, within this area of study, interactional responses to disability are considered from interpersonal and intrapersonal perspectives. The interested reader is encouraged to consult Stano (2009), Dunn (2015), Livneh and Antonak (2005), Olkin (2009), or Nagler (1993) to learn more about the social psychology of disability and the psychosocial aspects of identity formation and social interaction.

The Social Construction of Chronic Illness and Disability

Think about a recent contact that you have had with a person with CID—a family member, a friend, co-worker, neighbor, or person on the street. What were your thoughts and feelings when you interacted with that person? How did these affect your behavior when you interacted with that person? Despite the substantial advances in access and opportunity in recent decades, *interaction strain*, arising from not knowing how to interact in a "normal" way, remains an important factor affecting the ease of communication between people with CID and others. As counselors, it is essential to understand the dynamics underlying your response to your clients so that you are able to provide the kind of support and assistance that your role demands. Proximity to those perceived as different from you can violate your sense of ego safety, because if this could happen to the other, why are you not similarly disposed? If we, as counselors, cannot imagine a meaningful life for the person with whom we are working, how can we authentically support them in their work toward that end?

Disability is a universal experience of humanity (Zola, 1989, p. 401). Disability is also a sociopolitical construct and, as such, identification as a person with disability is a nuanced situation. A person may be disabled in one setting, given its requirements, and not in another setting. For example, a 20-year-old college student diagnosed with attention-deficit/hyperactivity disorder may be significantly disabled in a classroom without accommodations but not at all disabled in his part-time job coaching middle-school basketball players in an afterschool program. The student is the same; the requirements of the environment, in a sense, create the disabling situation.

The etiology of CID may be from many sources—the result of genetic or hereditary conditions; birth trauma; accident or injury; diseases, illnesses, or conditions associated with aging or lifestyle. Onset may be early in life or at any point in the course of one's life (Luse, 2009). Families may share a predisposition to disabilities, such as hemophilia, diabetes, or heart disease. Disabilities may appear suddenly or gradually, may follow a progressive course, remain rather static after a period of initial physiological recovery (as with stroke or spinal cord injury), or present periods of exacerbation and remission (as sometimes happens with multiple sclerosis or lupus erythematosus).

When one has experienced a traumatic injury, the individual may be the only one in his or her social system to have the experience of disability. Traumatic injuries often threaten the sense of ego integrity among all involved. Mechanisms for coping, both for the person with CID and those close to him or her, factor greatly into the adjustment process, for everyone. Particularly for those with traumatic or adult onset disabilities, you may find that the individual has not been "socialized" into a role as a person with disability. As such, although you may understand the individual to be part of a group, the individual and those close to him or her may not share your perception. The individual or that person's support system may hold widely divergent, rapidly vacillating understandings of what is and what may be. Each person in that family or social support constellation follows their own path in responding to the individual's disability.

One's CID may be visible or invisible. The distinction here is a significant one. A person with a *visible disability* presents with a concrete sign of their differentness; that is, he or she may be seated in a wheelchair or using an assistive device for ambulation, missing a limb, or accompanied by a service dog. The counselor has some context for approaching and interacting with the individual. Although the counselor's assumption about the client's world may be inaccurate, there is an opportunity for the counselor to think "Because I see _____, I will expect the person to think/feel/believe_____." Though the dynamics of communication are always complicated, both individuals in the interaction have some information to frame how they respond to each other.

A person with *invisible disabilities*, without external markers of disability, may present a contradiction of expectations for the observer. Examples of invisible disabilities that individuals may present include delusional thinking patterns, impulse control/over control with respect to food and exercise, ritualistic behaviors and speech characteristics, receptive and/or expressive language issues, reduced hearing, expressive speech problems, or other cognitive processing issues. Without an expectation as to why the individual is not behaving/responding as the observer anticipates, the observer is left adrift. Contradictions without context most often lead the observer to feelings of confusion, frustration, and irritation, which are powerfully communicated back to the person with CID. This miscommunication generates stress and discomfort in both the observer and the observed.

Some believe that those with invisible disabilities, such as learning disabilities, attentional and processing issues, and reduced hearing, may be at greater disadvantage when interacting with strangers as the responder has no marker for evaluating and responding to the disconnects in communication. A typical response by the observer is to minimize contact and interaction with the person whose behavior is confusing. Too often, rather than inquiring about the source of the communication disparities, the observer merely assigns a negative explanation to the individual (e.g., someone with speech difficulties might be assumed to be intoxicated) and avoids contact.

Each individual must be considered for his or her uniqueness. Although this statement sounds obvious, when interacting with a person who appears to be a member of a group unfamiliar to you, it is essential to examine your beliefs and expectations of the individual and of that group.

Designation of one's membership as a "person with disability" is often made by others. That is to say that, given the political implications of language, the medical system may deem an individual as having a disability, whereas the individual him- or herself may not share this characterization. This, in part, is foundational to the resistance to medical and educational models that label people. Individuals may or may not self-identify as being a person with disability. You are encouraged to recognize this factor and to defer to the individual's self-designation. Remain mindful that that person's world view may be very different from the one that you imagine for them.

CID is all-inclusive in its membership: people of any age, gender, ethnic/racial identity, education, work experience, financial situation/economic background, religious/spiritual identity, or political viewpoints of every description are eligible. Individuals may be balancing the medication and treatment protocols of multiple CIDs.

Disability and chronic illness are regarded variously from medical models in which one's body is dis-abled, defective, and in need of repair. Other models for conceptualizing disability are from psycho-socio–political and historical perspectives which consider disability as a social justice issue and a human rights issue. Key descriptors for learning more about various models for conceptualizing disability include the following: oppression; social construction of disability; disability studies; history of disability.

Assumptions, Attitudes, and Expectations of People with CID

Through the years and across cultures, people with disabilities have been regarded variously as chosen by God as messengers; punished for wrongs or sins committed by the individual or that person's family or tribe; and as the objects of pity, fear, scorn, charity, inspiration, and medical intervention (US Holocaust Memorial Museum, 2015; Pryor, 2015). Social responses have ranged from adoration and respect (for being closer to a deity) to marginalization, isolation, objectification, and slaughter.

Throughout the first half of the 20th century, the *best practice* in the United States with respect to people with disabilities was considered to include isolation within the family home, removal from the home community to state hospitals and state run schools, where people with disabilities could be "with others like them." Models of fear and distancing were gradually replaced by models of charity and pity (Nagler, 1993). By the 1970s, advancements in health care propelled the medical model and its emphasis on repair and remediation, driven by experts, and requiring those *afflicted* to embrace idealized standards of physical function in the search to be cured. People were defined by what they lacked: dis-abled; in-valid; victim; ab-normal. They were expected to take a passive role in response to the medical experts who would guide them to what was best for them (Linton, 2006).

By the late 1970s, push back to the medical models was building strength with the consumer-driven invocation of "nothing about us without us" (American Association of Persons with Disabilities, 2015; Charleton, 1998). People with CID assumed leadership and direction of political actions to change the dialogue. With increased energy and action toward independent living, this movement grew into the social model of disability in which disability was regarded as points along the continuum of human variation, rather than a categorical variable of acceptable/unacceptable. The social model recognized that the source of one's limitations and encumbrances rested outside the individual, in attitudes and society (WHO, 2011, p. 4). Subsequently, the emergence of universal design, legislation emphasizing the value of interdependency, as well as independence, consumer-driven self-advocacy, increased political, physical, and programmatic access, and deinstitutionalization shifted the conversation from medical and educational professionals to people with CID setting the terms and parameters of the discourse, actively involved at local, state, national, and international levels of political influence.

Values have shifted from insistence of independence as the sanctioned goal to acknowledgement of interdependence as a satisfying and realistic target. In part, this transition mirrors the cultural values, beliefs, and traditions of a multiethnic population. This shift also recognizes greater inclusivity of one's family, community, and larger society as participants in the person's life (Eddey & Robey, 2005).

Throughout this time, however, attitudes have been slower to change. Societal responses have continued to result in "exclusion, lowered expectations, and limited opportunity to participate fully and meaningfully in all the US has to offer" (Hill & Goldstein, 2015, p. 2227). The results have been continued stigma, discrimination, and isolation.

For those who hold joint membership in other marginalized groups as well, the results are multifactorial. Attitudes and lowered expectations for membership in one group are compounded when an individual is assumed to hold membership in multiple marginalized groups. The intentional and unintentional beliefs of the gatekeepers of educational, economic, and social institutions add to the challenges of succeeding in school, participating in the workforce, and being able to contribute to the larger community (Bureau of Labor Statistics, 2015).

Inconsistencies in data collection with respect to disability among people of color restrict clear understanding of the real incidence of disability in the United States. The Disability Rights Education and Defense fund (Yee, 2011, p. 1) indicates that disability prevalence is highest among African Americans who report disability at 20.5 percent compared to 19.7 percent for non-Hispanic whites, 13.1 percent for Hispanics/Latinos and 12.4 percent of Asian Americans. In raw numbers, over 10.8 million non-institutionalized persons with disabilities (PWD) aged 5 and over are estimated to be members of ethnic minorities.

Expectations of People with Chronic Illness and Disability

What is it that society expects of people with CID? Acceptance of their disability? Adjustment? Adaptation? Adherence to the Kubler-Ross stages of grief? Each term brings along its own aura of inferences and controversies. For the purposes of this chapter, Stano's (2009, p. 98) concept of "meaning reconstruction" seems to hold the greatest significance in conceptualizing the experience of disability. He describes the individual's need to "make sense of the world and one's place in it; making sense of the loss and/or the required changes in one's way of being." Implied in "meaning reconstruction" is the notion that one searches to find benefits in the changes that have occurred. The impact of CID is "highly subjective but incorporates views of others, societal expectations, and degree of importance that is placed on the body part(s) that have changed" (Olkin, 2009, p. 10).

For both the study of the social psychology of disability and to provide a context for counseling people with disabilities, a brief comment about identity development is warranted. Identity is a dynamic, fluid experience for all humans. For all people, one's identity has both enduring factors, as evidenced by self-statements as to "who I am" and "what I stand for," and more malleable aspects as happen continually when one encounters a world that either confirms/reconfirms one's beliefs about oneself or challenges those beliefs.

One application of Kurt Lewin's Field Theory (Lewin, 1939) offers the notion that a person develops a sense of who one is and goes into the world/society/interactions with that sense of identity. Each interaction with the environment, structural or attitudinal, then serves to either confirm or challenge that sense of self. After reaching a threshold of contradictory feedback, likely unique and relatively variable for the individual, one may question and revise those beliefs about oneself. Therefore, some aspects of one's identity are tweaked and refined.

As we enter new environments (think of your transition from high school to college, for example) or as we face new life roles (from individual/couple to parent, for example), we enter each situation with some sense of who we are and how we think, feel, and behave. The challenges of each transition set in motion a dynamic in which we are searching to redefine and similarly reclaim what we know about "ourselves."

For people who have experienced and are experiencing chronic illness and disability, this process is also part of the human condition. Nosek (2012) deepens this position in defining it as *response shift* (p. 117) saying, "Living with a disability is a process of constant change and constant adjustment, a process that is difficult to measure and to categorize" (p. 116). The individual who comes to see you for counseling will be experiencing these cognitive/emotional/behavioral calisthenics, heightened by the presence of a CID. Remember that this is part of the portrait that each client will present and, as such, deserves sensitive examination and support as one searches to re-establish a balance.

Power of Language in Shaping Beliefs about People with CID

The language one uses is powerful in conveying beliefs about the centrality of CID in one's life. With respect to people with disabilities, "people first language" maintains that respect and sensitivity for the individual are best expressed by speaking of the individual as separate and primary to any other reference, either one's medical diagnosis or physical characteristic. References to one's disability are made only as is necessary or appropriate for conveying the intended message, since one's disability is one aspect of that person and need not be mentioned in every context.

Many guides exist to flesh out this concept and to help guide you in reconsidering how to address, directly or indirectly, people with disabilities, without depersonalization, or endorsing stigma and stereotypes: one example is posted at Temple University [follow the link to tucollaborative.org; select Community Inclusion from the drop down menu; then, select Language to find the information about person first language] (Temple University Collaborative on Community Inclusion of Individuals with Psychiatric Disabilities, 2015). This site explains several key concepts, such as: avoid labeling the person by naming the specific diagnosis (e.g., refer to a "person diagnosed with schizophrenia" rather than "the schizophrenic"); avoid generic stereotypes, such as "the mentally ill," instead referring to *a person with depression* (a specific definition); realize that people with the same diagnosis may well have little in common, beyond their diagnosis and the prejudice and discrimination that they experience; and, last, your responsibility to speak with respect when referring to any of your clients or the people you represent. Listen closely to your client, however, for guidance as to how the individual chooses to self-reference.

Since this is a politically charged topic among rehabilitation counseling, disability studies, and disability rights advocates, rich with varying positions and controversy, you may be interested to read more on this topic. For more on this, refer to the Olkin (2009) book referenced in this chapter.

Strengths-Based Approaches to Working with People with Chronic Illness and Disability

Despite the intimate and long-standing connections between rehabilitation counseling education, literature, and practice (Wright, 1958, 1960; Wright & Lopez, 2005) and the core beliefs of strengths-based approaches, research seeking empirical validation of these approaches to people with CID has taken form largely in recent years. Since Elliott, Kurylo, and Rivera (2002) noted the lack of empirical evidence to support the efficacy of assessing and enhancing the strengths and unique qualities of people with disabilities in facilitating their adjustment to disability, research attention and funding have shifted to testing these concepts and instruments.

In recent years, researchers have responded to that claim pursuing two general avenues of research: the applicability of strengths-based constructs for people with disabilities, and the reliability and validity of instrumentation to measure the outcome of strengths-based approaches.

The application and efficacy of strengths-based approaches have been investigated with the following subject groups: people with spinal cord injuries (Kalpakjian et al., 2014), people with traumatic brain injury (Hayden, Green, & Dorsett, 2012), people with eating disorders (Barskova & Oesterreich, 2009; Chan, Chan, Ditchman, Phillips, & Chou, 2013); people with mental health issues (Song & Shih, 2014). The interested reader is encouraged to consult these articles to explore confirmatory evidence as to the relevance of strengths-based approaches to people with various chronic illnesses and disability.

For the purposes of this chapter, the research conducted on key strengths-based constructs will be addressed briefly: optimism; hope; post-traumatic growth and resilience. The research addressing the reliability of established scales related to these constructs will be reviewed as well.

Optimism

Optimism is associated with increased persistence and enhanced goal attainment. Optimistic people are likely to see problems as both expected and solvable, so they are likely to use coping strategies that deal directly with the stressors as they arise and to approach solutions with greater flexibility. Rand & Shea (2013) found that optimistic people demonstrated higher sense of locus of control and reported higher qualities of life. For those admitted to a rehabilitation hospital for care, those who identified as being optimistic at admission were found to be less likely to experience post-traumatic stress and depression, at discharge. A question that remains to be investigated is the effect of prolonged challenge to one's optimistic outlook, on multiple life fronts.

Rand and Shea (2013) share a number of interesting conclusions from their investigations of optimism. They define optimism as "the general tendency to focus on the positive aspects of life and events" for people in general, although not specifically with respect to people with CID. Additionally, they report evidence of a self-fulfilling component between one expecting to find good things to happen and an increased likelihood that one will find just that.

Seligman (2011) writes extensively about optimism, its effect on human physiology and health. He offers the idea that positive mental health requires the presence of positive emotion, engagement, meaning, good relationships, and accomplishment, not just the absence of disorder. Then, he examines ways that optimism affects both susceptibility to chronic illness and infection, as well as its influence on survival from on-going physical challenge. Optimists approach compromised situations differently than pessimists. An optimist will respond to adversity with the belief that such setbacks are temporary, changeable, and local, confident that he or she will be able to handle what comes next. More optimistic people have been found to have better outcomes from cancer, cardiovascular disease, and infections. Perhaps most reassuring is the fact that optimism can be learned, by those who are not inherently so inclined. Learning to find small blessings in each day and writing them down is a helpful activity for enlarging one's ability to appreciate the smaller gifts of a kind word, of someone following through on a promise, or getting to sit down on the bus at the end of a long day.

Hope

Chan et al., (2013) investigated the applicability of Snyder's hope theory to the reported life satisfaction among people with spinal cord injuries. They found support for the construct of hope as promoting participation in meaningful life activities and life satisfaction among those who participated in their study. Smedema, Pfaller, Moser, Tu, and Chan (2013) investigated the psychometric validity of the two-factor structure (pathways thinking and agency thinking) of the Adult Trait Hope Scale for people with spinal cord injuries. Researchers found a moderately high level of internal consistency and reliability on both subscales. Agency thinking and pathways thinking were both found to be positively associated with hope-related constructs such as self-esteem, self-efficacy, acceptance of disability, and life satisfaction. These findings suggest that the use of this instrument is warranted in assessing people with disabilities, particularly those with spinal cord injuries.

Rand and Shea (2013) suggest that research in the utility of these constructs with regard to positive adaptive coping and life satisfaction are limited by a number of factors: the lack of longitudinal research; lack of inclusion of subjects experiencing progressive, chronic illnesses and disabilities; lack of measures addressing the social/environmental context of CID; non-inclusion of those with cognitive deficits; lack of proper instrumentation in the measurement of various factors involved in the construct of "optimism" (p. 91). While intuitively appealing, additional research in these areas is clearly desired to better understand the complex interplay among these factors for people with CID.

Post-traumatic Growth and Resilience

Post-traumatic growth (Seligman, 2011), growth following adversity (Joseph, 2009; Tedeschi & Calhoun, 2004), and positive growth following acquired physical disability (Elliott, Kurylo, & Rivera, 2002) are discussed in the professional literature. Seligman (2011, pp. 161–162) provides a model for conceptualizing how people, particularly soldiers, can draw on the trauma in their lives to set the stage for growth. At the onset, the individuals respond to the trauma itself, grappling with shattered beliefs about the self, others, their future. They develop techniques for controlling the intrusive thoughts and images that fuel anxiety. From thought stopping to other strategies are developed for containing the spread of these concerns into their daily lives. Perhaps by limiting the amount of time each day one allows him/herself to "think about questions about the future," one can gain a greater sense of control over the uncontrollable. By using strategies such as direct thought stopping, making lists of tasks that need to be completed that day and which can be delegated to others or to another day, one asserts a sense of control and mastery in accomplishing daily responsibilities.

The next stage involves facilitating the constructive disclosure of events that led to the traumatic event. By helping individuals tell their story in such a way that they describe the experience with appreciation for who/what was helpful in the experience, and what was unavoidable. This then builds toward "creating a trauma narrative," where individuals reframe events, characterizing the trauma as a significant decision point, a fork in the road. This story then enhances the appreciation of the paradox of the situation: that both loss and gain happen. One identifies what strengths surfaced in the situation and life, how relationships improved, perhaps how their spiritual life deepened, and doors/opportunities opened.

Finally, individuals explore and articulate new ways of living, of contributing to the welfare of others, of accepting growth while still reconciling with the experiences of loss/guilt/sadness related to what has been lost. This culminates with the crafting of a new identity that recognizes both who one was, as well as the self that has been discovered.

Seligman shares the position that "substantial numbers of people experience something horrific—torture, grave illness, death of a child, rape, imprisonment—and respond with intense depression and anxiety and then they find meaning in what has happened and grow" (2011, p. 159). The enigma of such occurrences is that those who have experienced one awful event are found to display more intense strengths after the event than those who have not been similarly challenged. Those who have sustained two such awful events have been found to be stronger than those who had one horrific event happen.

Applying this information to soldiers, Seligman (2011) found that if soldiers know about post-traumatic stress disorder (PTSD), which of course they do, but not about resilience and growth, a self-fulfilling downward spiral can be created. If, however, soldiers are educated about the symptoms of normal grief and mourning to avoid amplifying the intensity of their emotions, they are freed to experience their emotions as they surface, recognize them for what they are, and not make rash self-diagnoses of PTSD. People who are inclined to catastrophize are found to be more susceptible to PTSD.

Although references to the potential for positive growth to come about as a result of suffering have been found throughout human history. Tedeschi and Calhoun (2004, p. 341) emphasize considering the trauma as a "springboard to a greater level of psychological functioning," without implying that the trauma itself was a good thing. Resilience refers to the ability to respond productively to situations and circumstances as they present themselves.

Strategies for Applying Strengths-Based Approaches to Working with People with Chronic Illness and Disability

With these points in mind, the reader is urged to prepare for working with people with CID by considering tangible ways that she/he can engage the client in a positive way from the first moments of contact, emphasizing the enthusiasm with which s/he anticipates working with the client, the expectation that this will be a collaborative relationship, and setting expectations for free and open discussions early in the relationship. The counselor must express attitudes of acceptance, openness, and curiosity, both verbally and nonverbally. Your verbal and nonverbal language expresses your beliefs more than you may be aware. By your posture, your eye contact, the tentativeness of your speech, your openness to being physically close to the client with CID will all set the tone for the interactions ahead. You will be communicating your comfort with the other, as well as with the topics addressed and avoided, and your beliefs about the person.

As obvious as it may sound, you must believe in your client's right and power to construct a happy and fulfilling life. You must believe in the possibility that your client has the capacity to assess his/her situation, set goals, and achieve them. If you don't believe these things, your nonverbal behavior will betray you and the client's work will be compromised. The best way to explain and encourage your client on techniques as presented in *Flourish* (Seligman, 2011) is to practice the techniques yourself (Froh & Parks, 2013).

Rather than asking the client to describe the details of the traumatic event or the prolonged process of diagnosis and treatment thus far, help the individual explore various aspects of post-traumatic growth that may have occurred. Ask the person to focus on what is going well in his/her life, how his/her outlook on life has changed since the time of injury, how priorities may have shifted, what he/she has discovered about him/herself in the course of this experience, how his/her thoughts about spirituality may have changed, and what his/her hopes are for the future. By asking questions about faith, hope, personal strengths, spirituality, mindfulness practices, social engagement, and contributing to one's community, the counselor sets expectations in place that these are opportunities for the individual to consider, even if they are not current practices. Additionally, by opening the conversation on these topics, reasonably associated with mental health and community integration, both the counselor and client are more likely to visit them at a later time.

If the initial focus of your sessions rests in the details of one's injury or the (likely) circuitous route to diagnosis and treatment, the dynamic of your sessions will be more likely to lead in the direction of focusing on losses, betrayals, disappointments, and frustrations. The person is coming to see you, most likely to discuss relationship issues or career concerns or some other matter that is anchored in the future. Rather than establishing a dynamic focusing on the wrongs that have occurred, you guide the individual to share with you what strengths they have seen in themselves, what surprises they found, how these may help them in moving forward, then you have a direction and substance to ignite the process. Your *positive asset search* (Ivey, Ivey, & Zalaquett, 2014) may disarm the individual and some resistance may surface. You need to meet the client where she/he is and move from there, of course.

At a later time, after a positive dynamic has been set, the mandatory history taking can be completed. It may be that much of the background information may be sourced from other documents and/or that the client can provide that information to you as a homework assignment. Then, together, you can process the thoughts and feelings associated with "sharing one's story," guiding an exploration of the strengths that the client found in him/herself in the course of those experiences.

With respect to the person's medical diagnosis, you are urged to do your own research on the nature of the illness or diagnosis, on your own time. After you have some familiarity with the diagnosis, treatment, and prognosis, as pertinent, you can ask the individual for clarification or confirmation of relevant aspects. For example, if you are seeing the person for relationship issues and a medication that the person is taking may affect one's behavior or physiology, you may want to discuss this with him/her. However, avoid requiring the individual to be your "guide" to life with a chronic illness and disability.

Anecdotally, many individuals have indicated to me that their largest grievance with the mental health workers with whom they have sought assistance has been just this: They seek assistance on a non-disability, just-trying-to-sort-out-life related conflict in their lives only to have the counselor set an agenda requiring the client to describe the circumstances surrounding the onset of their disability, the process of diagnosis, and treatment. And, then, requiring the client to answer endless "so, what is it like to be *like you?*" sorts of questions, apparently of interest to the counselor but not related to the client's goals for counseling. The individuals are left feeling as though they have not been heard, or helped. The issues for which the individual is seeing you must be the focus of the sessions. The person with whom you are working may or may not *identify* him/herself as a *person with disability* nor as a member of the *disability community*. Consequently, do not attempt to convince them of their membership.

For many people, especially by the time that you see them, their CID may be new to you but well integrated into their reconstructed identities. The client may have no need to address CID issues with you. If clients say that they want "to sort out their relationship with a parent or career," then follow their lead, focus on the issue that they have identified. Their disability may or may not be directly relevant in your work together. Listen to the client and respect his/her ability to identify the life issue for which they seek your assistance.

Disability is part of the human condition. However, given the reticence that children and adults with non-obvious disabilities such as attention deficit disorders, learning disabilities, or debilitating social anxieties (list is much longer) likely experience, individuals may be reluctant to self-identify as a person with disability. From a chronic-illness-and-disability-centric perspective, the reader should assume that the government estimates of 20 percent prevalence of disability among people in the United States far underestimate the scope of the population of interest in this chapter.

In view of this, think about how you can make your office welcoming to people with disabilities. This may involve considering the layout of your office to be welcoming to someone with accessibility needs, so that entry into your space does not require the movement of furniture. Brighter lighting available to augment communication with individuals with reduced vision or hearing. Signage or artwork that subtly convey an awareness and an openness to topics of disability.

McCarthy (2011) reminds us of Beatrice Wright's notion of *status substitution* as a solution for connecting with a client when time and workload pressures might strain the counselor's sense of compassion for the client: "If you like Elvis Presley or Marilyn Monroe [to update: Tom Hanks or Sandra Bullock? Emma Watson or Daniel Radcliffe?] or a particular politician, relative, or friend, just pretend your client is that person, someone you like and want to do a lot of good things for . . ." (p. 68). Our clients are learning about acceptance from us. Each deserves our attention and focus. Any client will benefit from your trying *status substitution* if you sense your attention or compassion lagging.

Several other critical concepts of Wright's are reviewed by McCarthy (2011), as well: the theory of *value changes in acceptance of loss or disability*, as well as the *emphasis on the person and not the disability*. She cautioned against *idolizing normalcy* and the *requirement of mourning* (p. 70). Each will be explained briefly here.

When she spoke of a theory of *value changes in acceptance of loss or disability*, she and her colleagues (Dembo, Ladieu-Leviton, & Wright, 1956/1975), described the process of value change in response to one's disability that includes

(a) enlarging the scope of values,
(b) subordinating physique relative to other values,
(c) containing disability effects, and
(d) transforming comparative-status into asset values (p. 70).

In this, Wright and colleagues assert that in reconstructing meaning after disability and/or in response to chronic illness, individuals grapple with elemental questions of existence, i.e., what really matters in life?, and discover a wider range of values than were held previous to this challenge to their sense of identity and meaning. The physical aspects of one's existence, by necessity, come to hold less meaning than other emerging values. One seeks to focus on the moment more, on key aspects of life that may have been accomplished previously virtually unnoticed, such as brushing one's teeth or getting out of bed. From a strengths-based perspective, this is conceptualized as "savoring," noticing and appreciating the beauty/delight/grace of the moment (Seligman, 2011, p. 42). By learning other ways to accomplish essential life tasks, either independently or with the assistance of another person or technology, the effects of the impairment/disability are contained. Last, perhaps over a longer period of time, one comes to appreciate what one can do and can enjoy in its own way, without a continual comparison between how life is now and how life was before. With this model in mind, counselors can meet the client with the expectation that some important work is to be done. The counselor helps identify where the client is along these non-sequential steps and works with them toward discovery of the newness of life experience.

This model complements the second issue: *focusing on the individual and not the disability*. This concept has several facets: mining the positive resources within the person and the situation, including emphasis on the assets of the person rather than the limitations; focus on the similarities among people, both those with CID and those without, rather than the differences between those without disabilities and those with CID; discuss and model the value of hope in adjusting to disability or misfortune or suffering; and reinforce the belief that a disabling condition does not spell the end of a life worth living (McCarthy, 2011, p. 70).

Idolizing normalcy sounds obvious and deserves some consideration in order to appreciate it fully. This might also fall under the term ableism. Both terms refer to the process in which one assumes, without reflection, that there is a "right" way for tasks to be accomplished; the implication is that to attempt the task in another way is demeaning, inadequate, or wrong. Messages of inferiority (for the person who has to complete a task in a non-standard way) are clearly communicated to the individual who is left to attempt life tasks in a "lesser" manner. Consider how your office, your interests, your assumptions, and your language may emphasize your beliefs, values, assumptions, and biases.

An example of this would be academic accommodations for a student with attentional issues who requires a quiet environment for her math tests. Teachers and administrators can clearly, albeit indirectly, communicate to students that this is really not acceptable. For those who can calculate math problems while walking through a shopping mall, the need for a low stimulus environment may be difficult to understand. It may be bewildering to the adult in this situation to understand that this accommodation is merely equalizing the student's opportunity to demonstrate the target skill, solving the math problems.

However, for the 5th grader who understands her math work but is unable to complete the computation and demonstrate her competence during a test when the child next to her is tapping her foot vigorously throughout the testing, this accommodation is not an indulgence or a favor. It is necessary to ensure that the test truly is measuring her math skills. Frequently, the subtle and not-so-subtle responses from the adults in the school environment seem to imply to the student that she shouldn't inconvenience people and just *be like everybody else*. Children with disabilities don't necessarily need a great deal of help to succeed in school. They do need and deserve to have the appropriate help.

The last concept McCarthy (2011, p. 70) asks us to examine is that of the *requirement of mourning*. This construct involves the requirement by those who value a specific attribute, such as walking, to assume that anyone who does not possess that attribute must be suffering or, if they are not suffering/ashamed/devastated, they should be. If they should be suffering and are not, then they should be devalued for not suffering as would be expected. This thinking is related to the model based on pity mentioned earlier. The person who has the "lack" or the disability is caught between being expected to feel badly for not being able to walk or, if they have made peace with that, they should be ashamed/devalued in some way for not feeling badly. Keep these concepts in mind as you read the remainder of the chapter.

Some general considerations about working with people with CID merit your attention. Do not offer false reassurances. They are hollow and will diminish trust. Do not attempt to counsel toward "things will be alright," when the issue at hand is not "alright." There is much that rests outside our control; you can share that that is a universal experience and the feelings associated with being in that position. Be mindful that the "limitations" that you may see or the grim future and outcomes that you may imagine may be more a function of the limitations of your knowledge, imagination, or present level of what is known to be available. By definition, any added factor has potential to reduce or remove "limitations" thought to be absolute. That message is vital to share with the client, as well as the necessity for the client's vigilance in exploring assets in him/herself and in his/her social and physical environment. Who would have expected that there are now wheelchairs that climb stairs for people who cannot stand or walk? Who would have expected that there are echolocation strategies for navigating new environments for people who are blind? Who might have predicted that my father would survive stage 4 non-Hodgkin's lymphoma for 17 years because the right doctors, treatments, medicines, and persistent family members would be in place as he needed them? There is always reason for optimism: so much is far beyond our control and knowledge.

With that, however, strengths-based approaches do not ignore obvious or negative issues in the person's life. The counselor must respond compassionately to the client's needs to be heard and to be validated. In the course of helping the client to embrace the present, the counselor can help the individual shift away from then-versus-now thinking to now-and-beyond thinking, once attention has been given to exploring what the client now values, how life works for him/her at this point, and what he/she has learned about him/herself in the process. By exploring strategies that the person has developed for managing challenging situations, the client can identify the strengths she/he found in being able to handle those situations. Tedeschi & Calhoun (2004) caution that counselors must clearly understand and communicate that the personal growth after trauma originates from within the individual and the person's search for positive emotions, engagement, relationships, meaning, and achievements, subsequent to the trauma. Any implication to an inherent value to the trauma itself must be avoided.

Case Studies

Jacob

Jacob was 18 years old when he came to the rehabilitation hospital for treatment after an electrical accident. He and his brother had gotten too close to a live wire. The shock killed his brother. Jacob walked away from the accident with a hemiparesis and cognitive functioning issues. We worked together, at varying intensities, for 4 years, through his hospitalization and once he returned to the community. We worked well together. He was bright, clever, and unruly; these were strengths that I suspect he had nurtured since birth. He tested every boundary, at every turn. Sharing a part of his journey to maturity, to making his place in the world, was both an honor and a challenge. Toward the end of our work together, he told me that he hadn't understood why I believed he would create a life worth living. He said that my consistency in telling him this had baffled him. Gradually, though, he had "borrowed my belief that he would re-construct his life and be okay, until he was able to believe it himself." He gained faith in himself. By 10 years after his injury, he had finished college, had a good job with the city, had married, and they were expecting their first child. He had fashioned the life that he wanted.

Anecdotally, there is much to support the premise that clients look to their counselors for faith in making their lives work out, for encouragement, for hope, for persistence, for optimism, for new ways of thinking and responding to setbacks and disappointments. While there may be little empirical evidence to support these claims, there are many client examples to support this belief: Counselors must believe in their clients, have hope for their capacities to garner their strengths, and build on that foundation to make their lives work. Sometimes, that may be the greatest skill that we have to offer.

Healing Environments Can Support PERMA

My first professional rehabilitation counseling positions were in hospitals, a veterans hospital and a rehabilitation institute. In the large, urban rehabilitation hospital, people were admitted within days or weeks of traumatic injuries. Those with spinal cord injuries generally stayed for inpatient services for 6–10 months for their first admission. Patients were in rooms of four individuals, varying in ages, education, social, economic experiences, and every imaginable way, with the exception of their shared encounter with a life-changing event, often a spinal cord injury. They worked hard, from the moment they opened their eyes in the morning until they fell asleep. They participated in therapies together. They ate meals together in the cafeteria or on the unit. No televisions or telephones were allowed in patient rooms. [This was long before cellular phones.] So, at night and on weekends, people talked to each other. They met each other's families. They talked about their days, their hopes, and their disappointments. They found common ground. They bolstered each other. They encouraged each other with stories of how other people had "made it," made progress no one would have predicted. They reminded each other that you just have to keep trying. Optimism bred optimism.

The "ordinary magic" (Masten, 2001) that happened every day there was stunning. Although the staff were highly talented and dedicated to their professions and providing the highest levels of service to their clients, I think the structure of the environment was a great catalyst for flourishing, for PERMA to take place. Moments of effort, successful or not, took on value (savoring). People listened. People cared. People remembered.

People were thrown together by happenstance. They became friends, confidants, family. PERMA flourished as they helped each other through some of the most challenging moments of their lives. They found a strength of spirit, a resilience that they had not anticipated. Each act of kindness, of listening and responding authentically, shared with others who understood their situation as no one else could, offered the sense of well-being described by Seligman (2011, p. 20). The sincere levels of caring for each other were palpable; these relationships offered reassurance of their "capacity to be loved," as well as allowing deeper relationships than many may have known previously, so fundamental to well-being (p. 21).

Being able to share accomplishments, such as brushing your teeth with adaptive equipment or making a safe transfer from the wheelchair to the therapy mat, with others who could truly appreciate the surge of independence that each offered, allowed each one to be their best self. Sharing their thoughts, feelings, fears, and hopes with others, perhaps as they never had before, built a closeness that was priceless. This intensity, these opportunities to trust and be trusted, allowed people to *flourish* in the midst of the most challenging days of their lives.

PERMA was at work in the lives of these (as it happened) men: positive emotions, engagement, relationships, meaning, and achievement. At this time of great uncertainty in their lives, they also found absolute acceptance from people (peers and staff) who cared about them and were fully focused on now-and-future as opposed to comparing now-and-then. The companionship, intimacy, and understanding of each other, living in such close circumstances, added a most likely unintended intensity to their situation. Being able to accomplish activities of crucial importance to you and having them appreciated by those around you, who understood the effort, the grit, involved in those accomplishments, enriched the relationships, the meaning of the accomplishments, and the achievements themselves. For some, this was the first time in their lives that they were asked and seriously considering *what do I want to do with my life?* And people were really listening to their questions, concerns, and answers. In the most paradoxical of ways, this was flourishing.

Jessica

Jessica was 27 years old when she first called for an appointment. She reported that she was university educated, an employed writer, and married for 3 years at the time of our first meeting. She came to the first appointment, sat on the edge of her chair, and kept her coat on for the entire meeting. She stated that she was concerned about her eating, purging, and exercise behaviors and the way that they interfered with her daily life. She stated that she had never spoken about these behaviors or concerns with her husband and did not believe that he had any awareness of them. She stated that she had started these behaviors at approximately age 10. She linked her concerns to having *perfectionistic tendencies* and the bullying she experienced from the 4th grade throughout high school.

In some ways, Jessica was far from an "ideal" client at the start. Although exceptionally intelligent and highly articulate, she was resistant to acknowledge connections between events, thoughts, and feelings that she had about the events in her life and her behaviors that followed. For the first 8 months that she came to sessions, she continued to sit on the edge of the chair and keep her coat on, despite the provision of an immaculately clean office, modern furniture, and comfortable levels of climate control. Sometimes to my surprise, she kept making and keeping the next appointment. She came to each appointment with the check written to me and carefully tucked in an envelope. She was meticulous in her manner, appearance, and behaviors.

I attempted to maintain a consistent level of warmth, support, and encouragement throughout our work together. We focused on her persistence in therapy, her dedication to exploring what needs her behaviors were serving, and identifying other strategies for meeting those needs. We did not talk about *forbidding behaviors* or *setbacks* or *failures*. Instead, her exercise and food behaviors were redefined as strategies for satisfying her needs. As such, we agreed that they would always be available to her. Over time, Jess became increasingly comfortable sharing her humor, risking disclosures, and, albeit tentatively, engaging in mindfulness exercises. These led to her allowing that her behaviors might serve several levels of protection for her. With some reluctance, she agreed to define other behaviors that might meet her needs—of self-soothing, control, to amend her frustration with her career and faltering communication with her spouse, her long-standing distrust of people, and limited patience and tolerance of herself. The emphasis, of course, was to identify behaviors that didn't involve food rituals, extreme exercise, or purging. With steady support, encouragement, non-shaming strategies, and emphasis on hope, mindfulness, forgiveness, she was able to find ways to identify when she had needs not being met, identify an array of behaviors that she could choose and execute other than those identified initially, and to choose to make choices and act in her life in ways that resulted in greater comfort and happiness.

The strengths-based strategies and behaviors illustrated in this brief scenario are (1) expressing firm and unwavering support for the client's capacity to choose her best path; (2) patience to move at the pace that the client could tolerate; (3) offering hope, encouragement, structured strategies for problem conceptualization and problem solving in non-self-deprecating language; (4) non-shaming responses to setbacks, when the food /exercise-related strategies were chosen; and (5) modeling optimism, acceptance, hope, forgiveness, and gratitude. Reliance upon binging/purging/excessive exercise were reframed as choices made that were then objectively processed for their suitability going forward.

Upon reflection, Jess developed a confidence in herself, in her ability to speak out, to look more to the future than being dominated by the past. Or, as Seligman (2011, p. 104) suggests, "drawn by the future, not driven by the past"? Yes. PERMA? Yes. She increased her positive emotions dramatically, shifting from a somewhat fatalistic stance to one in which opportunities were welcomed, strangers considered, possibilities enlarged, risks cautiously approached. Although her involvement in counseling ended some years ago, she is now in a high management position in her work, has greatly enriched her communication and relationship with her husband and is enthralled in her role as mother to their young son. The transformations that she has made in her life have been thrilling to watch. An emphasis on strengths-based assets and creating a future worth living, a leap of faith, and grit on all sides can yield startling results.

Final Thoughts

By this point in the text, the reader is well aware that strengths-based practice does not support a Panglossian romp through life, concluding that "All is for the best in this best of all possible worlds." Providing meaningful assistance to people with chronic illness and disability demands each of us to carefully study the cultural issues for people with CID, realizing that entry into this group is open to each of us. That the complexity of each individual's life is compounded by the addition of the personal/social implications of CID.

As with all clinical encounters, the success of the interaction and therapeutic process begins with the counselor: your perceptions, your assumptions, your expectations of the other, and your expectations of yourself in supporting the choices of the other. If you don't believe in the opportunities/ aspirations/goals of the other, chances are great that the client will not either. Supervision is essential to help counselors process the veracity of their beliefs in the potential for clients to benefit from this approach.

The challenge to drawing on strengths-based approaches in working with people with CID is that the counselor must believe in the process. Meeting people who have sustained significant loss or are in the midst of continuing loss can be threatening to the counselor's personal sense of safety in the world. You must do your own work in order to maintain emotional balance for establishing close connections with people whose lives have encountered such change.

People who have been marginalized historically and economically often have limited access to healthcare, proper nutrition and education, or environmentally healthy living environments. As a result of these disparities, people in such situations are likely at greater risk for developing chronic illness than those with robust healthcare, varied and healthy diets, and access to environmentally safe living environments. The effects of sustained health concerns and disability likely result in compounding effects for the individual and add to the complexity of the individual's work in crafting a meaningful life. Working with people with CID compels you to stretch yourself professionally to be multiculturally competent, to identify and process through supervision your own issues related to loss, the capriciousness of situations outside our control, and the energy required to meet the client where he/she is rather than giving in to the frustration one may feel when the client is not moving *fast enough*. That is, not moving as we would wish them to do. At the same time, sharing the journey with people as they find strength, hope, new understandings of themselves and others can be exhilarating.

Infusing a focus on strengths into counseling need not take substantially more time or require the use of explicitly strength-promoting interventions (Harris, Thoreson, & Lopez, 2007, p. 10). From the initial meeting, drawing upon both strengths-based beliefs and strategies, the accepting, forward looking, hope-supporting encounter of the counselor with the client will set in motion a sequence of interactions that will remain with the client, even if that is your only meeting. By being goal focused and change oriented, in the context of an accepting and supportive relationship, the client as collaborator is able to move ahead, gaining skills in that first encounter. Since, from that first encounter, the client is invited to identify and recognize internal and external strengths, this cognitive framework will have enduring effects. Critical aspects of the relationship that people experience in counseling— acceptance, clear communication, courage to risk talking about what is important, learning how to assess safety in situations—become a model that they seek to recreate outside your office.

People with disabilities and chronic illness will be in your classrooms, in your offices, and among those referred by their health insurance companies. If you choose to seek out working with people with CID, make sure that you are properly educated and supervised. You may contact the Commission on Rehabilitation Counselor Certification (CRCC; Commission on Rehabilitation Counselor Certification, 2015) to identify recommended content areas and academic training for working with people with CID. Additionally, CRCC may assist you in locating certified rehabilitation counselors in your area that may be available to provide you with consultation and supervision.

Even now, as you think about the clients that you are now seeing, you are likely to find that the issues addressed in this chapter are relevant to more than a few of the people you are currently seeing. If you are interested in working with people who have CID, you may consider contacting local medical rehabilitation centers and the state departments of vocational rehabilitation, centers for independent living, college offices that serve students with disabilities. Levels and sources of reimbursement for your counseling will depend upon the funding source and/or the individual's ability to pay. Holding a clinical level of licensure in your state is recommended.

In this chapter, I have highlighted the belief that the impact of following strengths-based approaches rests with the perspective that the counselor embraces and shares with the client. The potency of the specific techniques and strategies largely depends upon the counselor's preparation. What you do as a strengths-oriented counselor flows from your belief system as to what helps people find their better, stronger, more confident selves. While the strategies can be powerful in their own right, without striving to embrace a respect for the individual's capacity to create a happy, fulfilling life, their power seems greatly diminished.

From the initial meeting with individuals with CID, counselors must reflect upon their own experience of chronic illness and disability, embrace the client with an accepting and supportive presence. You must research the latest information on the nature of the chronic illness and/or disability that the client presents. Questions to the client about the client's CID should be restricted to those pertinent to your work with the individual. Remember: the reason they have come to see you may have little to do with their CID. Also, it is not their responsibility to educate you about their diagnoses, treatments, unless this information is specifically relevant to your work together.

In this chapter, I assert that strengths-based approaches complement the philosophy and strategies of those requisite counseling skills that provide the individual with a safe place in which to raise, examine, and consider issues in living that lead to the creation and enjoyment of living the life one chooses. In closing, I offer the following quote:

> Hope is what keeps us going; it's what keeps us striving for the lives we deserve . . . I hope that my actions as an ability activist will leave the world more accepting and more accommodating for all people, and not just persons with disabilities.
>
> *Chaeli Mycroft, a 17-year-old disability activist from South Africa and Winner of the*
> *2011 International Children's Peace Prize (Mycroft, 2012)*

References

American Association of Persons with Disabilities. (2015, September 3). *Disability rights.* Retrieved September 2, 2015 from http://www.aapd.com/what-powers-us/disability-rights/?referrer=https://www.google.com/

Barskova, T., & Oesterreich, R. (2009). Post-traumatic growth in people living with a serious medical condition and its relations to physical and mental health: A systematic review. *Disability & Rehabilitation, 31,* 21, 1709–1733.

Bruyere, S., & Reiter, B. (2012). Disability policy and the law. In D. Maki, & V. Tarvydas, *The professional practice of rehabilitation counseling* (pp. 61–82). New York, NY: Springer Publishers.

Bureau of Labor Statistics. (2015, June 16). *Persons with a disability: Labor force characteristics 2014.* Retrieved June 16, 2015 from http://www.bls.gov/news.release/pdf/disabl.pdf

Chan, J., Chan, F., Ditchman, N., Phillips, B., & Chou, C. (2013). Evaluating Snyder's hope theory as motivational model participation and life satisfaction for individuals with spinal cord injury: A path analysis. *Rehabilitation Research, Policy, and Education, 27*(3), 171–185.

Charleton, J. (1998). *Nothing about us without us: Disability, oppression, and empowerment.* Berkeley, CA: University of California Press.

Commission on Rehabilitation Counselor Certification (CRCC). (2015, January 20). *Commission on Rehabilitation Counselor Certification.* Retrieved February 4, 2016 from http://www.crccertification.com/pages/crc_ccrc_scope_of_practice/56.php

Dembo, T., Ladieu-Leviton, G., & Wright, B. (1956). Adjustment to misfortune: A problem of social psychological rehabilitation. *Artificial Limbs, 3*(2), 4–62.

Dunn, D. (2015). *The social psychology of disability.* New York, NY: Oxford University Press.

Eddey, G., & Robey, K. (2005). Considering the culture of disability in cultural competence education. *Academic Medicine, 80*(7), 706–712.

Elliott, T., Kurylo, M., & Rivera, P. (2002). Positive growth following acquired physical disability. In C. Snyder, & S. Lopez, *Oxford handbook of positive psychology* (pp. 687–699). New York, NY: Oxford University Press.

Froh, J., & Parks, A. (2013). *Activities for teaching positive psychology.* Washington, DC: American Psychological Association.

Gostin, L. (2015). The Americans with Disabilities Act at 25: The highest expression of American values. *JAMA: Journal of American Medical Association, 313*(22), 2231–2235.

Harris, A., Thoreson, C., & Lopez, S. (2007). Integrating positive psychology into counseling. *Journal of Counseling & Development, 85,* 5–13.

Hawking, S.W. (2011). Preface. *World Report on Disability.* Geneva, Switzerland: World Health Organization and World Bank.

Hayden, S., Green, L., & Dorsett, K. (2013). Perseverance and progress: Career counseling for military personnel with traumatic brain injury. *Ideas and Research You Can Use: VISTAS 2013.* Alexandria, VA: American Counseling Association.

Heideman, E. (2015). *Inspiration porn is not okay: Activists are not impressed with feel good Super Bowl ads.* Retrieved from www.salon.com/2015/02/02/

Hill, E., & Goldstein, D. (2015). The ADA, disability, and identity. *Journal of the American Medical Association, 313*(22), 2227–2228.

Ivey, A., Ivey, M., & Zalaquett, C. (2014). *Intentional interviewing and counseling: Facilitating client development in a multicultural society.* Belmont, CA: Brooks/Cole Publishing.

Jenkins, W., Patterson, J., & Szymanski, E. (1992). Philosophical, historic, and legislative aspects of the rehabilitation counseling profession. In R. Parker, & E. Szymanski, *Rehabilitation counseling: Basics and beyond* (pp. 1–41). Austin, TX: Pro-Ed.

Joseph, S. (2009). Growth following adversity: Positive psychological perspectives on posttraumatic stress. *Psychological Topics, 2,* 335–343.

Kalpakjian, C.M. (2014). Post-traumatic growth following spinal cord injury. *The Journal of Spinal Cord Medicine, 37*(2), 218–225.

Lee, C. (2013). *Multicultural issues in counseling: New approaches to diversity (4th ed.).* Alexandria, VA: American Counseling Association.

Lewin, K. (1939). Field theory and experiment in social psychology: Concepts and methods. *American Journal of Sociology, 44,* 868–896.

Linton, S. (2006). Reassigning meaning. In L. Davis, *The disability studies reader* (pp. 161–172). New York, NY: Taylor & Francis.

Livneh, H., & Antonak, R. (2005). Psychosocial adaptation to chronic illness and disability: A primer for counselors. *Journal of Counseling and Development, 83,* 12–20.

Luse, M. (2009). The etiology of disability. In J. Stano, *Psychology of Disability* (pp. 32–69). Linn Creek, MO: Aspen Professional Services.

Maki, D., & Tarvydas, V. (2012). Rehabilitation counseling: A specialty practice of the counseling profession. In D. Maki, & V. Tarvydas, *The professional practice of rehabilitation counseling* (pp. 3–16). New York, NY: Springer Publishing Company.

Masten, A. (2001). Resilience processes in development. *American Psychologist, 56*(3), 227–238.

McCarthy, H. (2011). A modest festschrift and insider perspective on Beatrice Wright's contributions to rehabilitation theory and practice. *Rehabilitation Counseling Bulletin, 54*(2), 67–81.

McCarthy, H. (2014). Cultivating our roots and extending our branches: Appreciating and marketing rehabilitation theory and research. *Rehabilitation Counseling Bulletin, 57*(2), 67–79.

Mycroft, M. (2012, April 25). *2011 International Children's Peace Prize.* Retrieved from www.kidsrights.org

Nagler, M. (1993). *Perspectives on disability.* Palo Alto, CA: Health Markets Research.

Nosek, M. (2012). The person with a disability. In D. Maki, & V. Tarvydas, *The professional practice of rehabilitation counseling* (pp. 111–130). New York, NY: Springer Publishing Company.

Olkin, R. (2009). *What psychotherapists should know about disability.* New York, NY: The Guilford Press.

Pryor, J. (2015, June 25). *Bible verses about disability.* Retrieved July 15, 2015 from http://www.patheos.com/blogs/christiancrier/2015/06/25/top-7-bible-verses-about-disabilities/

Rand, K., & Shea, A. (2013). Optimism within the context of disability. In M. Wehmeyer, *The Oxford handbook of positive psychology and disability* (pp. 48–59). New York, NY: Oxford University Press.

Seligman, M. (2011). *Flourish.* New York, NY: Atria Paperback.

Shakespeare, T. (2006). The social model of disability. In L. Davis, *The disability studies reader* (pp. 197–204). New York, NY: Routledge.

Smedema, S., Pfaller, J., Moser, E., Tu, W., & Chan, F. (2013). Measurement structure of the trait hope factor scale in persons with spinal cord injury: A confirmatory factor analysis. *Rehabilitation Research, Policy, and Education,* 206–212.

Song, L., & Shih, C. (2014). Implementing a strengths-based model in facilitating recovery of people with psychiatric disabilities. *Journal of Social Work and Development, 24*(1,2), 29–44.

Stano, J.F. (2009). *Psychology of disability.* Linn Creek, MO: Aspen Professional Services.

Tedeschi, R., & Calhoun, L. (2004). A clinical approach to posttraumatic growth. In P. Linley, & S. Joseph, *Positive psychology in practice* (pp. 405–419). Hoboken, NJ: Wiley.

Temple University Collaborative on Community Inclusion of Individuals with Psychiatric Disabilities. (2015, September 5). *The importance of language in promoting community inclusion.* Retrieved September 5, 2015 from http://tucollaborative.org/

U.S. Holocaust Memorial Museum. (2015, September 4). *The murder of the handicapped.* Retrieved September 4, 2015 http://www.ushmm.org/outreach/en/article.php?ModuleId=10007683

Wehmeyer, M., & Shogren, K. (2014). Disability and positive psychology. In J. Teramoto, & L. Edwards, *Perspectives on the intersection of multiculturalism and positive psychology: Cross cultural advancements in positive pychology* (pp. 175–188). New York, NY: Springer.

Welch, P., & Palames, C. (2015). *A brief history of disability rights legislation in the United States.* Retrieved August 16, 2015 from http://www.udeducation.org/resources/61.html

World Health Organization. (1980). *International classification of impairment, disability, and handicaps: A manual of classification relating to the consequences of disease.* Geneva, Switzerland: Author.

World Health Organization. (2001). The International Classification of Functioning, Disability and Health (ICF). Geneva: WHO. Accessed May 31, 2016 from http://www.who.int/classifications/icf/en/

World Health Organization. (2011). *World report on disability.* Geneva, Switzerland: Author.

Wright, B.A. (1958). *Psychology and rehabilitation.* Washington, DC: American Psychological Association.

Wright, B.A. (1960). *Physical disability: A psychological approach.* New York, NY: Harper & Row Publishers.

Wright, B.A. (1983). *Physical disability: A psychosocial approach.* New York, NY: Harper & Row Publishers.

Wright, B., & Lopez, S. (2005). Widening the diagnostic focus: A case for including human strengths and environmental resources. In C. Snyder & S. Lopez, *Handbook of positive psychology* (pp. 26–44). New York, NY: Oxford University Press.

Wright, G. (1980). *Total rehabilitation.* Boston. MA: Little, Brown & Company.

Yee, S. (2011, August). *Health and health care disparities among people with disabilities.* Retrieved from www.edf.org/healthcare/Health-and-Health-Care-Disparities-Among-People-with-Disabilities.pdf

Zola, I. (1989). Toward the necessary universalizing of a disability policy. *The Millbank Quarterly, 67*(2), 401–428.

Section III

Strengths-Based Work in Different Counseling Contexts

10

The Power of Neurocounseling and Self-Regulation Skills

Lori A. Russell-Chapin

... neither is it possible to discover the more remote and deeper parts of any science, if you stand but upon the level of the same science, and ascend not to a higher science.

Sir Francis Bacon

The profession of counseling has been in existence since the beginning of time in some way or another. Perhaps it was the village shaman or a trusted mentor, but people have always reached out to others for assistance with life's complexities (Chapin & Russell-Chapin, 2014).

Living is complex. Having the skills to assist others with life's complications is a humbling and wondrous occupation. Conducting counseling for the last 30 years and teaching counseling to graduate students for 28 years have transformed my methods and beliefs about the goals of counseling.

For years I believed that the goals of counseling were to alter symptoms and change problematic thoughts and behavior. With the advances in neurobiology and neurocounseling, my counseling conceptualizations, strategies, and goals now have more depth. Currently my counseling goals are to certainly assist with symptom reduction and thought and behavioral changes, but the primary goal uses neurocounseling knowledge to help clients, clinicians, and graduate students understand the power of intrinsic self-regulation skills of individual physiology and neurobiology. This offers clients another method of developing internal locus of control in addition to counseling. With the neurocounseling tools of physiological self-regulation, many clients see their new strength and abilities as additional motivation to also be more responsible for other individual decisions. All of these self-regulation skills demonstrate another model of strengths–based work that assists clients in the implementation of living life well and holistically.

The purpose of this chapter is to teach clinicians, clients, and counseling students strength-based strategies for achieving optimal self-regulation. When functioning properly and efficiently, the brain and the body are capable of self-regulation. Due to multiple internal and external variables interacting on our system, dysregulation occurs. Major reasons for dysregulation are discussed.

In addition, a description is offered about the process of allostasis, the body's adaptive process designed to assess systemic regulation and offer feedback. Eleven methods for achieving self-regulation are illustrated through the benefits of neurocounseling, neurotherapy, diaphragmatic breathing, HRV, exercise, nutrition, mindfulness, mental imagery, skin temperature control, sleep hygiene, and neurofeedback (NRB).

A case study also shows these strength-based self-regulation strategies in a real life scenario. Emphasizing and utilizing these different self-regulation strategies teaches the value of intrinsic locus of control, personal accountability, and living life optimally.

This chapter is not exhaustive and cannot provide all the self-regulation strategies available. There are many other types of self-regulations not discussed here. For additional reading there are several indepth resources about self-regulating methods (Chapin & Russell-Chapin, 2014; Sapolsky, 2004).

Literature Review

The following literature review will define and elucidate the concepts involved in the study of the neurocounseling and self-regulation knowledge base. An example and a definition are included for: self-regulation, causes of dysregulation, neurocounseling, neurotherapy, diaphragmatic breathing, HRV, exercise, nutrition, mindfulness, mental imagery, skin temperature control, sleep hygiene, and neurofeedback.

Self-Regulation

I often tell clients that one of my tasks in counseling is to make the unconscious conscious, so there is more freedom of choice. Part of that job is to teach clients they do have some control over their physiology, emotions, and attachments. This is the task of self-regulation through the autonomic nervous system and the emotional and polyvagal systems. The vagus nerve is the longest of the twelve cranial nerves in the body extending from the brainstem to the abdomen through many organs (Porges, 2008). Eighty percent of the vagus nerve accounts for 80 percent of the parasympathetic response. Porges (2011) used the term neuroception as the unconscious ability of a human being to assess risk as safe, dangerous, and life threatening. Understanding this system helps in explaining to clients how we function in our environment and how we react.

Part of self-regulation is learning the difference between a reaction and a response. It is the use of intentionality in all aspects of living. Knowing that humans can choose to pause and respond instead of an instinctual reaction is the first step toward self-regulation in physical regulation and emotional regulation. Self-regulation teaches that humans can regulate the limbic system and the amygdala, our flight and fight reaction, by calming down the central nervous system and focusing and activating the needed parts of the brain used in practicing the self-regulation skills in this chapter, from the pre-frontal cortex to the temporal lobes (Chapin & Russell-Chapin, 2014).

Homeostasis is the concept that there is a balance or mechanism in the body that is constantly at work to achieve an optimal point of health. Criswell (1995) described the homeostatic process as an assessment from the body and mind to determine what adjustment is needed to maintain a balanced cognitive, emotional, and physical state. Sapolsky (2004) took this concept further by writing about allostasis. True balance may never actually occur but is in a process of delicate adjustment all the time. This assessment and response would require both internal changes and external behavioral adjustments. The adjustment consists of both stimulation and inhibition. During this adaptation process the brain and body use the neurotransmitter glutamate to regulate stressors in the system. Our body also has the benefit of the neurotransmitter Gaba that allows the body to turn off the stimulation or inhibit (Russell-Chapin & Jones, 2014). This constant assessment must include a neurological, somatic, autonomic nervous system and any stressors to our system (Chapin & Russell-Chapin, 2014).

Additional counseling materials addressing the importance of self-regulation are stress management and therapeutic life changes (TLC) research (Ivey, Ivey, & Zalaquett, 2014). These intentional life skills assist clients with overall wellness and physical and mental health. The "big six" TLCs validate many of the skills discussed in this chapter. Ivey et al (2014) listed the following six instructional strategies to help clients with stress management: exercise, proper sleep, social relations, nutrition, cognitive challenge, and meditation.

Causes of Dysregulation

The causes of dysregulation are many and varied. One of the biggest causes of dysregulation in the brain is just living life. Things happen from getting sick, falling off the monkey bars and hitting the head, emotional trauma, birth trauma, lack of sleep, too much sleep, abusing drugs and alcohol, not eating properly, or not exercising the mind and body. This list goes on and on. It may be different for each person.

The following Neurological Dysregulation Risk Assessment (Chapin & Russell-Chapin, 2014) is a simple and quick inventory to assist people in better understanding their own life journey into dysregulation. As a reader of this chapter, take the assessment and analyze your possible reasons for dysregulation. By customizing your risk assessment and better understanding your neurological dysregulation causes, possible interventions may be formulated to assist in goal setting for healthier living.

Neurological Dysregulation Risk Assessment

Name (or Child's Name): _____ Age: _____ Date: _____

Current Problem, Symptom or Complaint: _____

Please read each potential source of neurological dysregulation and indicate whether or not it may be a risk factor for you or your child.

    Yes   No

1. Genetic Influences: Grandparents, parents, or siblings with mental health or learning disorders (including attention deficit hyperactivity disorder), post-traumatic stress disorder, depression, generalized anxiety disorder, substance abuse, personality, or other severe psychological disorders (bipolar or schizophrenia).
2. Prenatal Exposure: Maternal distress, psychotropic medication use, alcohol or substance abuse, nicotine use, or possible exposure to environmental toxins including genetically modified foods, pesticides, petrochemicals, xenestrogens in plastics, heavy metals (lead/mercury) and fluoride, bromine, and chlorine in water.
3. Birth Complications: Forceps or vacuum delivery, oxygen loss, head injury, premature birth, difficult or prolonged labor, obstructed umbilical cord, or fetal distress.
4. Disease and High Fever: Sustained fever above 104°F due to bacterial infection, influenza, strep, meningitis, encephalitis, Reyes Syndrome, PANDAS, or other infections or disease processes.
5. Current Diagnosis: Of mental health, physical health, alcohol abuse, substance abuse, or learning disorder.
6. Poor Diet and Inadequate Exercise: Diet high in processed food, preservatives, simple carbohydrates (sugar and flour), genetically modified foods, foods treated with herbicides, pesticides and hormones, low daily water intake, high caffeine intake and lack of adequate physical exercise (20 minutes, 7 times a week).
7. Emotionally Suppressive Psychosocial Environment: Being raised or currently living in poverty, domestic violence, physical, emotional or sexual abuse, alcoholic or mentally unstable family

---

environment, emotional trauma, neglect, institutionalization, and inadequate maternal emotional availability or attachment.

8. Mild to Severe Brain Injury: Experienced one or more blows to the head from a sports injury, fall, or auto accident (with or without loss of consciousness), or episodes of open head injury, coma, or stroke.

9. Prolonged Life Distress: Most commonly due to worry about money, work, economy, family responsibilities, relationships, personal safety, and/or ill health causing sustained periods of anxiety, irritability, anger, fatigue, lack of interest, low motivation or energy, nervousness, and/or physical aches and pains.

10. Stress Related Disease: Includes heart disease, kidney disease, hypertension, obesity, diabetes, stroke, hormonal, and/or immunological disorders.

11. Prolonged Medication Use, Substance Use, or Other Addictions: Including legal or illegal drug use, substance abuse, or addiction (alcohol, drugs, nicotine, caffeine, medication, gambling, sex, spending, etc.) and overuse of screen technologies (cell phones, video games, television, computers, internet, etc.).

12. Seizure Disorders: Caused by birth complications, stroke, head trauma, infection, high fever, oxygen deprivation, and/or genetic disorders and include epilepsy, pseudo-seizures, or epileptiform seizures.

13. Chronic Pain: Related to accidents, injury, or disease processes including back pain, headache and migraine pain, neck pain, facial pain, and fibromyalgia.

14. Surgical Anesthesia, Chemotherapy, and/or Aging: Can cause mild cognitive impairment, insomnia, and depression and be related to emotional trauma, loss and grief, chronic illness, physical decline, reduced mobility, physical, social, and emotional isolation, and decreased financial security.

Scoring and Interpretation: Total Number of "Yes" Responses _____

In general, the greater the number of "yes" responses, the greater the risk of significant neurological dysregulation. However even one severe "yes" response could cause significant neurological dysregulation and result in serious mental, physical, or cognitive impairment that may benefit from individually designed neurofeedback training.

(Reprinted with permission from Chapin & Russell-Chapin, 2014, pp. 9–10.)

Neurocounseling

The term *neurocounseling* has entered into the knowledge base as recently as 2013. In an article called The Birth of the Neuro-Counselor, Montes (2013) stated, "Scientists and researchers are forging a seemingly endless stream of breakthroughs with the help of technologies that peer into the brain's structure and functions. And mental health practitioners are harnessing these discoveries through an array of new therapeutic models" (p. 33). It is out of this stream of thought that we are seeing several important shifts in our understanding of culture, health, and neurobiology, including the emergence of neurocounseling.

Neurocounseling is, by definition, an integrative understanding of the brain-behavior processes. Neurocounseling is a natural development in the counseling profession adding another dimension to the already existing counseling process. The added dimension reveals the correlations between many mental health concerns and their too often unnoticed physiological underpinnings (Russell-Chapin & Jones, 2014; Russell-Chapin & Jones, 2015).

A major component of the counseling profession's identity comes from emphasizing the strength-based practices of wellness, social justice, and developmental needs. Integrating neurocounseling into our already strong identity makes the counseling profession even stronger.

The more information and skills that clients have to engage in life, the better they can learn to utilize their physiology, thoughts, and behaviors to navigate through the difficulties of daily living. For this reason, neurocounseling is an added value to the entire counseling process, offering teachable skills to clients that may otherwise be largely inaccessible. The self-regulation skills integral to neurocounseling assist clients in regaining and maintaining the needed balance and/or allostatis that is required for healthy living. Notice, for example, in the following scenario as counselors begin to integrate neurocounseling with all the other strengths of the counseling process.

> Imagine sitting across from one of your clients for the first time. You are hearing her or his story, noting emotions, cognitions, and behaviors that play a central role in present functioning. You are developing the therapeutic relationship, empathizing, mirroring, attuning, and establishing resonance. The difference this time around is that you are also focusing on neurocounseling and how you can bridge the gap between your client's brain and behavior.

Suddenly this new emphasis opens up an entirely new territory with additional knowledge, skills, treatment, and outcome possibilities. Neurocounseling teaches clients how their physiology and brain impact behaviors and emotions. For many of our clients this new understanding, whether that is controlling skin temperature, diaphragmatic breathing, HRV, or how trauma overarouses the amygdala, assists them in better understanding how they are more than just thoughts and behaviors.

Neurocounseling immediately offers a deeper understanding of who they are and offers relief and understanding of self. Moreover, as clients learn about their own brain in a mutual process, they will be better able to regulate their own thoughts, feelings, and behaviors (Russell-Chapin & Jones, 2014).

Neurotherapy

Neurotherapy can be defined as any intervention that creates neuromodulation or a healthy change in neurons. This neurogenesis creates new neurons and pathways and more efficient connectivity in the brain. Examples of all self-regulation skills would fall under the category of neurotherapy from HRV to diaphragmatic breathing to neurofeedback. Even learning a new task or challenging the brain would be examples of neuromodulation. Any of the self-regulation tasks discussed in this chapter reflect a form of neurotherapy.

Diaphragmatic Breathing

Unless trained to breathe from our belly or diaphragm, many of us don't know how to correctly breathe, let alone breathe through the diaphragm. The diaphragm is a dome-shaped, inspiratory muscle that contracts and flattens when breathing. This muscle is located beneath the superior thoracic cavity (Marieb, 2012, p. 20). The benefit of this type of breathing is that it helps the functioning of the brain through better absorption of glucose and oxygen. In turn, this will generally improve overall daily performance and often reduce anxiety, as the body begins to relax.

Typically, normal breath rates are between 12 and 15 breaths per minute. According to Schwartz and Andrasik (2003) 2- to 5-year-old children breathe more often at about 25 to 30 breaths per minute; 5- to 12-year-old children take about 20 to 25 breaths per minute; and people older than the age of 12 breathe at 15 to 20 breaths per minute. For clients to learn the relaxation response, the breathing cycle needs to be between 4 and 6 breaths per minute.

Another way to teach this rhythmic breathing is counting slowly to five while inhaling through the nose and then exhaling to the count of five through open, pursed lips. That equates to six cycles of a 10 count for one minute. The best part of this skill is that with relaxation also comes increased skin temperature that brings on greater relaxation.

HRV

HRV is a biofeedback technique that focuses on heart rhythm feedback (beat to beat changes in heart rate) to assist with improved self-regulation (Chapin & Russell-Chapin, 2014). HRV is derived from the electrocardiogram. McCraty, Atkinson, and Tomasino (2001) conducted research through the Institute of HeartMath and found that people must learn and practice their optimal level of beat to beat variability for healthy functioning, flexibility, and adaptability. Of course negative emotions lead to increased disorder in the heart's rhythm, adversely affecting physiological and psychological health.

There are many HRV software and hardware packages on the market. Emwave is produced through the Institute of HeartMath. It uses a plethysmograph that slides into a small cuff on the index finger of the non-dominant hand or an ear sensor clip to measure HRV. Another breathing instrument is RESPeRate (InterCure, Ltd., Manchester, UK). This is the first instrument approved by the Food and Drug Administration for blood pressure control that allows clients to practice breathing while watching visual corrective feedback. Clinical trials have proven that RESPeRATE significantly reduced blood pressure without side effects when used for 15 minutes per session and three to four times per week.

Exercise

The importance of exercise has been espoused for many years. Recent books and research have begun to help people better understand the exact science behind the benefits of exercise, especially as it relates to neurobiology. Dr. John Ratey (2008; Ratey & Manning 2014) in his books on exercise and nutrition explained how exercise releases brain-derived neurotropic factors (BDNF). These cascading hormones assist the body in better learning, energy metabolism, and synaptic plasticity. BDNF are activated by glutamate which produces antioxidants and grows new brain cells. Ratey (2008) coined BDNF as the "Miracle Gro" for the brain. Ratey explained that the stress from exercise sparks brain growth. Exercise can be too harsh though, but when done correctly it strengthens the infrastructure of nerve cells against damage and disease. Ratey emphasized how healthy stress is a must for survival and growth.

Through Ratey's research, he suggested that a comprehensive exercise routine include 6 hours a week or 45 minutes to an hour a day of interval training, where the heart rate is very high for short periods of time and then returns to a lower rate for longer periods.

The most important aspect of exercise, though, is to find a sport or program that meets individual lifestyles and needs whether that be walking, Tae Kwon Do, pickleball or biking. Many people today are using wearable technology to assist in recording and maintaining a physically fit body and mind.

Nutrition

Proper nutrition has been emphasized for many decades as an essential factor toward better health. New research is being released almost daily about food, our gut, and its influence on brain dysregulation. For example, there is evidence that each person's microbiome, an ecosystem of microbes in the body, impacts many brain disorders. Research into the gut-microbiome-brain connection is gaining momentum and has implications for the treatment for anxiety and depression (Rook, Raison, & Lowry, 2012).

Even the typical American diet seems to play havoc with brain dysregulation. Many of our diets consist of simple carbohydrates, processed foods such as white bread, potatoes, pasta, and rice. Amen (2001), a brain researcher and clinician, wrote that this type of diet often makes a person feel tired, inattentive, and sluggish because blood sugars are lower than needed.

According to Amen (2001), the healthiest diet needs to consist of 8 ounces of water for cell functioning and blood flow, protein at every meal for immune functioning, complex carbohydrates such as vegetables and fruits for fiber, and some saturated and monounsaturated fats for brain and neuron health (Chapin & Russell-Chapin, 2014). Ratey and Manning (2014) theorized that our bodies have not evolved at the same pace as our industrialized sciences. Therefore, more diseases and allergies occur because the body cannot metabolize these processed foods as well as natural foods. Because of these and other factors, I encourage my clients to work with their physician and a nutritionist and/ or dietician to learn more about healthier eating.

Mindfulness

Demonstrating the benefits of mindfulness to clients is actually fun and meaningful. Siegel defined mindfulness as a specific mental practice of being "conscientious and intentional in what we do, being open and creative with possibilities or being aware of the present moment without grasping onto judgments" (Siegel, 2010, p. 1).

Taking what your clients enjoy is often the clue for what concepts or foods to first choose to illustrate the self-regulation skills of mindfulness. The use of "the mindful raisin" is always a good 5-minute starter (Williams, Teasdale, Segal, & Kabat-Zinn (2007). Touch only one raisin between your fingers, then smell the raisin and take in its aromas, next place the raisin in your mouth but do not chew it, begin to sense its taste and let the raisin tease your taste buds. Finally bite into the raisin slowly and allow its juiciness to slide down the throat. Discuss the results in the session. This small exercise on mindful intentionality teaches clients focus and activates the sensory motor cortex and the prefrontal cortex.

My favorite demonstration uses my favorite cookie, the chocolate chip cookie. Have chocolate chip cookies ready for you and your client or graduate students. First have them just hold the cookie in their hands and begin to remember what it takes to make that cookie. Think of the ingredients that went into the creation of the cookie. Ask what chemicals, heat interactions, and electricity had to occur just to make and bake that cookie. Next smell the fragrance of that delicious cookie. Describe each smell that is noticed. Then take one small bite. Let that bite sit in your mouth and feel the saliva in your mouth as it envelops your taste buds. Be sure to think of the chemistry occurring in your mouth. Begin to think about the electrical, chemical, and physical properties of the cookie as it breaks down and metabolizes into the body. Finally ask how the chocolate chip cookie tasted this time compared to the last time. A typical response is, "It was the best cookie I have ever eaten!" If life were lived more mindfully and intentionally, would it be the best ever too?

Mental Imagery

A better understanding of how brain waves work may assist clients in developing brainwave flexibility and learning to practice additional self-regulation skills. I use the mnemonic "Do Think About Brain Growth" to assist in remembering the different categories of brain waves. The D stands for delta waves that cycle from 0 to 4 Hz and represent slow waves needed for sleep. T represents theta waves cycling at 4 to 8 Hz and are often used when daydreaming and being creative. A stands for alpha waves that cycle at 8 to 12 Hz and are needed for idling and transitioning from one brain state to another. B represents the beta range from low beta of 13 to 15 to high beta of 18 to 35 Hz. Beta waves are necessary for focused attention and problem solving. The G stands for gamma waves that oscillate around 36 to 44 Hz and are needed for insight and memory retention (Russell-Chapin & Chapin, 2015).

Kershaw and Wade (2011) suggested that being able to consciously direct needed brainwaves to move up and down with presenting symptoms would be beneficial toward self-regulation. These authors encourage clients to identify needed brainwave activation and practice certain tasks for that change to occur.

For example, an imagery experience could be scripted for beta activation helping clients who are depressed, alpha activation for clients who need calm energy to resolve anxiety, and alpha theta activation for clients who need deeper reflection and recovery for problems involving addiction and emotional trauma (Chapin & Russell-Chapin, 2014).

Skin Temperature Control

Of all the self-regulation skills addressed thus far, skin temperature control is one of the easiest to teach and easiest to assess. Often clients will walk into the offices and shake hands. Immediately a sensation of their hands being cold, warm, and/or sweaty can be noticed. Skin temperature control, a form of biofeedback, teaches the client to voluntarily control peripheral skin temperature through the use of operant conditioning and a hand-held thermometer. Changing the autonomic nervous system through the vasomotor response allows the blood to flow more freely when those smooth muscles around the blood vessels become less constricted (Schwartz & Andrasik, 2003).

First a baseline temperature is taken in both hands using the index finger of the hands. Some clinicians prefer to use the non-dominant hand. An inexpensive, take home thermometer costs about one dollar. Giving it to the client is a wonderful way to encourage practice at home. Record the number and begin a relaxation exercise, mental imagery, and/or diaphragmatic breathing (Chapin & Russell-Chapin, 2014). The clinician might assist with the skin temperature elevation by eliciting an image such as, "Go to a safe place. Begin to relax and let the stressors of the day flow out your fingertips and toes."

After the exercise is finished, record the new temperature. Although there is no "normal" skin temperature, the goal for most clients is to raise the temperature to around 86°F for women and 88°F for men to achieve a state of relaxed and focused attention. Around 95°F would indicate the relaxation response and may be too relaxed for everyday tasks. Too low might be indicative of too much stress and anxiety (Lowenstein, 2002).

If raising the temperature doesn't work the first time, talk to the client about trying too hard and try again. The clinician might mention that this skill takes practice, and that it is likely the exercise didn't work due to the artificial environment of the counseling office. Once again this tactic attributes failure or setback to external factors while implying internal agency. Most of the time clients are amazed and impressed at how quickly they can raise skin temperature.

Sleep Hygiene

Understanding clients' sleep habits and sleeping patterns is one of the first pieces of the psychosocial history needed. An insomnia inventory is an excellent tool for quickly collecting this data. Sometimes clients stated they didn't sleep a wink all night. If available, using sleep monitors that track interrupted and uninterrupted sleep per night is another insightful method to gain valid information.

Another valuable strength-based intervention for sleep hygiene is to ask clients to make a list or an inventory of any exceptions to their sleep deficits. An example could be, "Tell me about a time when you got a good night's sleep. What happened to make that possible? How did you make that happen? What wasn't happening? Finally, what needs to happen to make that occur a little more often?"

Often people don't understand the necessity of quality sleep to mental health. Teaching clients about sleep hygiene is essential to the overall treatment plan. Routines for going to bed and rising at the same times, if possible; not eating a heavy meal right before bed time; exercising during the day; no or little daytime napping; no discussing of "heavy" or emotional issues right before going to bed; drinking alcohol or too much caffeine during the day and none at night are all discussed early on in the treatment (Saxon, Etten, & Perkins, 2015).

Adults need approximately 7 to 8 hours of sleep per night. Teenagers need even more. Neuroscientists have recently discovered why sleep is so important. The glial cells that often don't conduct electrical activity during the day are thriving at night, acting as "garbagemen" for our brains clearing unnecessary brain debris and toxins (Parker, 2014). When not enough sleep is obtained, too many toxins accumulate, and the brain and body don't function efficiently.

Educating clients about the pineal gland, a small cone-shaped gland that is found next to the optic nerve and in the third ventricle of the brain, is important to understand sleep hygiene (Marieb, 2012). The pineal gland produces and secretes significant amounts of the hormone melatonin. Teaching clients about screen time at night helps in comprehending why bright lights such as cell phones, television, and laptops actually tell the pineal gland to stop making melatonin. Melatonin is necessary for proper sleep. Melatonin research has shown that taking melatonin at night on a regular basis retards aging of the mitochondria as it acts as an antioxidant and a regulator of the mitochondrial bioenergetic function (Srinivasan, Spence, Pandi-Perumal, Brown, & Cardinalis, 2011).

Especially for the aging client, melatonin is produced in smaller amounts, reinforcing even more the importance of exercise and getting outside when possible. All of this information resonates with clients, and once again they realize there are some actual strategies that are in their control for making life and sleep work better.

NFB

NFB is a noninvasive intervention using a computer interface with an electroencephalogram (EEG). It is one of the self-regulation skills that requires an external resource and a neurofeedback clinician to help in the regulation and changing of the electrical activity of the brain waves.

The major tenets of NFB are twofold. The first premise is that the EEG reliably demonstrates measureable mental states. The second, and quite remarkable, fact is that these brain states can be trained and regulated (Thompson & Thompson, 2003).

The goals of neurofeedback are also twofold. The most important goal is to increase or decrease the amplitude of a certain brainwave in a particular location of the brain that may be related to a client's particular mental health symptom or behavior. The second goal of NFB is to help the overall functioning and connectivity of the neural networks between the hemispheres, within the hemispheres, and across the hemispheres (Chapin & Russell-Chapin, 2014).

Once a thorough EEG assessment, a psychosocial history, continuous performance tests, and needed paper-and-pencil inventories have been completed, a treatment plan with certain protocols at specific brain sites would commence. Utilizing the principles of classical and operant conditioning, a trained and certified neurofeedback clinician would work with the client to inhibit and reinforce dysregulated brain waves to achieve optimal functioning. Through the use of puzzles, sounds, music, and favorite movies, when the correct brain wave is being obtained by the client, a puzzle will unfold or a movie will continue. When the brain doesn't locate the right wave, then the puzzle or movie will cease until the brain is challenged enough to locate that needed threshold set by the NFB clinician.

In this case the client is training the brain to become more efficient and effective. The most meaningful statement about NFB is it helps the brain use the right brain wave for the right task and the right time (Chapin & Russell-Chapin, 2014). For example, if a person is regulated, when it is time to sleep, delta and theta waves will be ready to transition into that state. When it is time to pay attention, low beta waves will be ready to assist in focusing.

Applications of Strength-Based Self-Regulation Skills

The Case of Martha: Everyone Knows Better than Me

Martha entered into counseling two years ago with a presenting problem of anxiety. She is a 54-year-old Caucasian, married for many years, with three children. Martha works in the home and cares for her family. Her family of origin was large with 12 siblings. Martha is in the middle of her brothers and sisters. Martha stated her family was close and loving, and she remembers how sad she was when her mom went into treatment for alcoholism. Both parents died recently, and Martha continues to grieve today. Her strong Christian values and religion have helped her through many tribulations such as the death of one of her children.

Martha always arrives to counseling sessions on time, is well-dressed and fashion conscious. With the very first hand-shake, Martha was ice cold and stated she had poor circulation. Her breathing was shallow, and sometimes Martha would look away from me. As rapport was gained, Martha became compliant and receptive to goal setting, possible solutions, and homework. After three months of work, Martha confided that she has been "getting sick" approximately once or twice per week by bingeing on vegetables. I would use the word "vomit" or "throw up." Martha didn't like those words.

Martha agreed to take the Millon Clinical Multiaxial Inventory-III (MCMI-III), and her results were a dependent personality disorder with symptoms of anxiety and somaticism. These results were consistent with Martha's narratives, so our counseling goals of assertiveness, personal needs assessment, neurocounseling, and self-regulation were validated.

Three of the very first self-regulation skills Martha learned were diaphragmatic breathing, HRV, and skin temperature control. Martha's initial skin temperature was 68°F. Within one session she had raised her peripheral skin temperature to 82°F, and she was able to get her breathing in the range of six breaths per minute. Martha's responses to these self-regulation skills were enlightening, empowering, and somewhat typical. She exclaimed, "I guess I am not such a loser. You mean some of my problems are physiological? I am able to control some of these! If I can control these, I can control other things too." That day Martha left the office with a smile on her face and looking me directly in the eyes. There might have even been a little skip in her walk.

Our work was far from over. Martha was feeling less anxious but continued to binge and purge but less frequently. She began working with a physician and a nutritionist to learn more about healthy eating. We continued seeing each other on a weekly basis. Family members were still commenting on her thinness, but they were also commenting that something was different. Martha was telling family members what she needed and offering her opinions. They wanted to know what had changed. Martha finally had the courage to tell some of her family that she had been seeing a counselor, a physician, and a nutritionist. Some of her family was receptive and some thought that was just silly.

After a year of counseling, Martha had met several of her counseling goals but still reported bingeing and purging at least once every 2 weeks. We then did some imagery work with her knitting prowess and decorating skills. She envisioned a beautiful large woven basket that she placed at the front of her entryway. In this basket Martha would put only items that she cherished: special yarn and sewing materials, pictures of her family and children, a rosary, and running shoes. When Martha needed strength and extra resources, she would go to a quiet place and reflect on her strengths in that woven basket and take what she needed from the basket to finish up her day in a healthy and nonjudgmental manner. Eventually Martha even located a real basket that reminded her of her resources.

Martha saw changes in her behaviors, anxiety levels, and attitudes about herself. One day she asked if she would be a good candidate for neurofeedback. I agreed to a thorough assessment with a five-channel electroencephalogram (EEG, additional paper/pencil screenings for anxiety, depression, trauma, insomnia, the Neurological Risk Assessment, and the Test of Variable Attention. The battery of results still showed trauma at the occipital lobe (O1) and low alpha at the midsection of the scalp (Cz).

Martha decided to contract for 20 sessions of neurofeedback. Her treatment protocols were single channels of Sensory Motor Response (12 to 15 Hz) at Cz, the midsection of the scalp, and raising alpha (8 to 12 Hz) at the occipital lobe (O1). Two-channel theta and alpha synchrony was conducted at the midline at the front (Fz) and back at Pz. At the end of the 20th session we administered another five-channel EEG. The changes in her assessment were dramatic. Alpha was raised at O1 and Cz.

Martha has not binged or purged for the last 3 months. This is a behavioral change since her days in college many decades ago. The most significant behavioral changes I see in Martha are her breathing patterns and her comfort level in dealing with those around her. Martha has learned to calm her central nervous system with breathing, neurofeedback, counseling and assertiveness. She is regulating her own body and feelings and is accountable to herself. Martha is finally trusting that she is capable of making healthier decisions and often others don't know what's best for her.

Conclusion

The power of neurocounseling and teaching and practicing self-regulation are offering clients the needed skills to live life fully, often without external medications. The philosophy behind neurocounseling, tying physiology and regulation to many mental health and behavioral concerns, imparts personal freedom and responsibility and a self-respect for life.

Self-regulation skills demonstrate that the body and mind have the ability to assess themselves and the situation and choose what physiological or behavioral changes are needed to maintain or adapt to a homeostatic state. Allostasis suggests there are many internal and external changes or strategies to improve and achieve self-regulation (Chapin & Russell-Chapin, 2014).

Many of the self-regulating examples offered in this chapter are evidence based and have been researched thoroughly. The efficacy rating for neurofeedback for attention-deficit/hyperactivity disorder has ranged from a Level 3 "possibly efficacious" to a Level 5 "efficacious and specific," with randomized, blind, and controlled studies. More research is needed with all of the self-regulating techniques.

What is exciting about the self-regulating techniques discussed here is the relative ease of conducting research in a clinical population. Establishing a baseline and measuring again at the end as a post-test is an efficient and simple method of collecting data. Clients are eager for these quantitative results. It also raises individual counselor competencies for outcome measures, offering additional evidence that counseling does work.

The barriers to neurocounseling and self-regulation are the same as the strengths and implications. It takes energy and lots of time to live life well. It may be easier to have an extrinsic locus of control and let others dictate what is needed. Achieving intrinsic locus of control and self-regulation offers clients the strength-based skills needed to function independently and reliably in the hectic and chaotic existence of life.

If counselors do their jobs effectively and use many of these strength-based self-regulating techniques, perhaps counseling would not need to last as long, depending on the severity of the problems. Would we be counseling ourselves out of a job? I don't think so. Remember, life is complicated and complex. People will continue to have concerns, but teaching what we can control and what we cannot control physically and emotionally is power in itself. Armed with the power of neurocounseling and the self-regulation skills discussed in this chapter, clients have additional tools to face the hardships that life often brings, prevent some diseases, and be able to live life in a more engaged, intentional, and healthy manner.

References

Amen, D.G. (2001). *Healing of ADD*. New York, NY: Putnam.

Chapin, T. & Russell-Chapin, L. (2014). *Neurotherapy and neurofeedback: Brain-based treatments for psychological and behavioral problems.* New York, NY: Routledge.

Criswell, E. (1995). *Biofeedback and somatics*. Cotati, CA: Free Person.

Ivey, A.E., Ivey, M.B., & Zalaquett, C. (2014). *Intentional interviewing and counseling* (8th ed.). Belmont, CA: Brooks/Cole.

Kershaw, C.J., & Wade, J.W. (2011). *Brain change therapy*. New York, NY: Norton.

Lowenstein, T. (2002). *Stress and temperature*. Port Angeles, WA: Stress Market.

Marieb, E.N. (2012). *Essentials of human anatomy and physiology* (10th ed.). San Francisco, CA: Pearson.

McCraty, R., Atkinson, M., & Tomasino, D. (2001). *Science of the heart: Exploring the role of the heart in human performance.* Boulder Creek, CA: Institute of HeartMath.

Montes, S. (2013). The birth of the neuro-counselor? *Counseling Today, 56*(6), 32–40.

Parker, A. (2014, September 22). The power of sleep. *Time Magazine*. Retrieved May 23, 2016 from http://time.com/3326565/the-power-of-sleep/

Porges, S.W. (2008). The polyvagal theory: New Insights into adaptive reactions of the autonomic nervous system. *Cleveland Clinic Journal of Medicine, 75*(10), 1–5.

Porges, S.W. (2011). *The polyvagal theory*. New York, NY: Norton.

Ratey, J.J. (2008). *Spark: The revolutionary new science of exercise and the brain*. New York, NY: Little Brown.

Ratey, J.J. & Manning, R. (2014). *Go wild: Free your body and mind from the afflictions of civilization.* New York, NY: Little Brown.

Rook, G., Raison, C., & Lowry, C. (2012). Can we vaccinate against depression? *Drug Discovery Today, 17*(9–10), 451–458.

Russell-Chapin, L., & Chapin, T. (2015). Combining counseling with neurotherapy: Two successful neurofeedback case studies. *Counseling Today, 57,* 14–17.

Russell-Chapin, L., & Jones, L. (2014). Neurocounseling: Bridging brain and behavior. *Counseling Today, 56,* 20–21.

Russell-Chapin, L., & Jones, L. (2015). *Neurocounseling: Bringing the brain into clinical practice.* Retrieved May 23, 2016 from http://factbasedhealth.com/neurocounseling-bringing-brain-clinical-practice/

Sapolsky, R.M. (2004). *Why zebras don't get ulcers.* New York, NY: Holt.

Saxon, S.V., Etten, M.J., & Perkins, E.A. (2015). *Physical change & aging: A guide for the helping professions.* New York, NY: Springer Publishing Company.

Schwartz, M.S., & Andrasik, F. (2003). *Biofeedback: A practitioner's guide* (3rd ed.). New York, NY: Guilford Press.

Siegel, D.J. (2010). *The mindful therapist: A clinician's guide to mindsight and neural integration.* New York, NY: W.W. Norton.

Srinivasan, V., Spence, D.W., Pandi-Perumal, S.R., Brown, G.M., & Cardinalis, D.P. (2011). Melatonin in mitochondrial dysfunction and related disorders. *International Journal of Alzheimer's Disease, 2011,* 1–15.

Thompson, M., & Thompson, L. (2003). *The neurofeedback book.* Wheat Ridge, CO: Association for Applied Psychophysiology and Biofeedback.

Williams, M., Teasdale, J., Segal, Z., & Kabat-Zinn, J. (2007). The mindful way through depression: Freeing yourself from chronic unhappiness. New York, NY: Guilford Press.

11

Accessing Strength from Within
Music Imagery and Mandalas

Louise Dimiceli-Mitran

Everyone has inside himself . . . what shall I call it? A piece of good news!
Ugo Betti (1956)

The field of music therapy practice encompasses many treatment modalities and a full range of client populations. Within the field, the Bonny Method of Guided Imagery and Music (GIM) distinguishes itself as a reconstructive, depth-oriented psychotherapy in which specifically programmed classical music is used to generate a dynamic unfolding of inner experience (Bonny and Goldberg, 1996/2002). It is holistic, client-centered, humanistic, transpersonal, and allows for emergence of all aspects of the human experience including psychological, emotional, physical, social, and spiritual. The music adds the element of aesthetic beauty to the therapeutic process engaging the senses and thus the body as well as nonverbally activating emotional material. Inherent to the method, the music is considered a co-therapist, providing structure for exploring difficult topics, expanding the field of expression without limiting the flow, acting as a container for the experience and reflecting the client's emotions in a supportive, elegant, articulate way. It also facilitates easy movement into altered states of consciousness by providing oceanic experiences which may have life-changing properties for the individual. GIM is indicated for those who have healthy, strong egos and while it may be considered a strengths-based therapy because it allows clients to find solutions from within, it can fall short to the degree that it is inaccessible to those who lack a sufficiently strong ego for the work.

From this major music therapy model has emerged an adaptation, music imagery (MI), first pioneered by marriage and family therapist Goldberg (1994) and mental health counselor Summer (2011; both music therapists), which allows for the client experience to be safely contained and focused on a particular feeling or topic that is mutually agreed upon by therapist and client (Goldberg, 1994). Rather than the broader experience of GIM, which can facilitate a personality reconstruction, MI offers what music therapist Wheeler (1983) classified as a supportive or re-educative music therapy experience, highlighting and building on existing client strengths so the client can learn new ways of relating to the world. Therefore, it is safer for clients with weaker ego strength but still allows the benefits of an imagery-based therapy. Similarly, Saleebey (1992), an early proponent of the strengths-based perspective for social workers, defined the approach as focusing on the fact that clients are doing the best they can and doing well at the time, that they have used their capacities to survive life's pain and struggle up until now, and that change can only occur when the therapist believes in and collaborates with the client's aspirations, perceptions, and strengths. He goes on to describe the importance of embracing the worldview of the client and to meet the client where she is. This adequately describes the basic tenets of MI in that it is highly collaborative between client and therapist, highlights the client's already-existing strengths, and uses those capacities as a supportive or re-educative jumping off point to find the answers that lie within. In contrast with GIM, MI provides a more strengths-based perspective on imagery work while still making use of the transformational power of music as we will see in the case examples to follow.

Another model of music therapy which fits well into the broader strengths-based paradigm is Rolvsjord's (2010) resource-oriented approach which features client empowerment, equal collaboration between therapist and client rather than intervention, stimulation of client strengths and potential as well as linking the therapeutic process to the interaction between individual and community. The use of music is referred to here in the context of affordances and appropriations, two interconnected concepts. *Musical affordances* are the resources the music provides for client use; *appropriations* are how well the music is actually able to be used by the client. For example, a piece of music is offered as a resource for a therapeutic task; in this case, to use as a means to move into and explore the focus of the imagery experience. The appropriateness of this choice will emerge when we see, through the images that emerge, how well the client was able to make use of the music and the insights that it afforded the client.

In my private practice, MI is used as a means to break overwhelming issues into small, more workable pieces from a positive, strengths-based perspective (see the case example of Bea, presented subsequently) or as an entryway into the deeper GIM work. It is effective for those dealing with depression, anxiety, grief, trauma recovery, and bereavement. I have also used it effectively as a group intervention with cancer survivor groups at a survivorship center, for wellness groups and community experiences. It can be a gentle first step into knowing the self and trusting one's inner workings, perhaps for the first time in a world full of media and external stimulation. With a positive focus MI can reconfigure a person's opinion of themselves and help to bring an awareness of potential in a classic strengths-based way. MI builds on the potential for change that already exists in the client and can also be a path to building an inner locus of control for clients who desire relief from and insight into their unhealthy behaviors, relationships, and thought processes. Because the focus is decided upon in collaboration with the therapist, the client gains agency in the process and feels some control over what will happen in the session. The music provides a steady, dependable, and nurturing companion (Goldberg, 1994) in the journey as well as an aid to staying focused on the topic the client chooses to explore. The music can also provide what Saleebey (2009) noted as an opportunity for a different present moment and future in small ways that can have life-changing effects.

As a technique, MI accesses nonverbal and sometimes preverbal components in the psyche and thus bypasses language in a way that is unique and authentic to the client's life experience and personality. As a result, therapy seems to progress quickly. The creative aspect of listening, imaging, drawing a mandala (a drawing within a circle, Jung 1964; see case examples ahead), or writing involves the whole brain and serves as a symbolic or metaphoric bridge to the deeper consciousness. This creativity brings a "here and now" quality to the insights that emerge from the experience. Further, bringing strength to the forefront of awareness often provides an invaluable change of perspective, created on the mandala paper and with the ability to be viewed with some distance as a representation of the client's psyche. Employing these creative elements can boost self-esteem and move the therapeutic process along in a satisfying way for both client and therapist. Clients are often surprised and delighted by what their psyche has to offer through this type of strengths-based inner exploration.

Elements of the Music Imagery Session and Procedure

The components of MI, diagrammed in Fig. 11.1, are the prelude, music listening, which includes the induction (spoken over the music) and drawing or writing (during the music), and processing.

MI creates a contained pathway through the psyche, represented here by the grey box. Moving left to right: During the check-in, or prelude, a focus is collaboratively decided on and clarified by the therapist and client. As the music begins the therapist provides the induction spoken over the music. The therapist then instructs the client to draw or write while the music continues until the drawing or writing is finished. The session finishes with verbal processing of the drawing/writing and the client's experience throughout (Dimiceli-Mitran, 2015).

Prelude

The term *prelude* is consistent with Bonny's GIM language and reflective of the music process. During the prelude the client checks in with the therapist as in any verbal session, sharing recent events and present emotions. The material discussed is narrowed down to a strengths-based topic through a collaborative discussion between client and therapist. For example, in a supportive session, if the

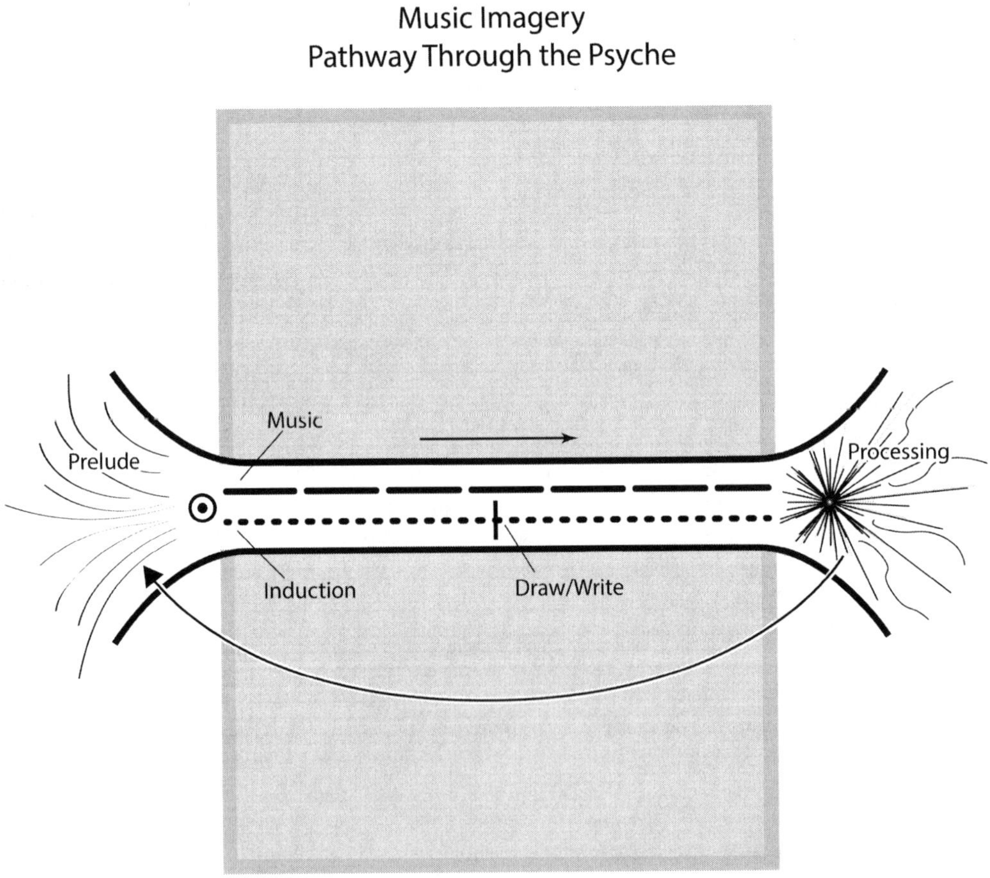

Figure 11.1 Music Imagery Session Elements

client checks in feeling upset about her mother, the focus might be on what the client feels would best help her to cope with the situation or what she needs to help her deal with it. Perhaps it would be patience, exploring a loving feeling toward her mother, or developing a safe or strong boundary. In a re-educative session, the client may want to go into, further explore, and define the difficult feelings she is experiencing. Once the focus is decided upon, the client is encouraged to specifically define and clarify its personal meaning so both she and the therapist may understand it more fully. This process also identifies the language to be used in the induction, which is mutually agreed upon.

Music Listening

Drawing/writing materials are set in the client's lap while the therapist chooses supportive music using the iso principle. The *iso principle* is defined by Burns and Woolrich (2004) as choosing music to match the prevailing current emotional state of the client; this is done while keeping in mind the nature of the focus as well. The music is started at a low enough volume for the therapist to talk over. The therapist then verbally directs the client through a brief relaxation over the music, such as

> Close your eyes and bring your attention to your breathing . . . Feel the chair supporting your body . . . and the floor under your feet . . . Now take a slow deep breath, involving your belly and then your chest . . . Take all the time you can to exhale . . . then let your breathing return to normal . . .

After the relaxation, the talkover continues with the music, using language that was mutually agreed upon to bring the client's attention to the focus. From the above example of creating a boundary, the induction might be as follows:

> Now imagine yourself creating a safe boundary . . . Notice what it is made of . . . Be aware of its qualities . . . Notice its presence around you . . . Really feel the boundary in place . . . Let yourself feel the safety . . . Be aware of how it feels . . . Let the music help you . . . Now allow an image to form of this boundary . . . Notice all you can about it . . . And now open your eyes and continue your experience on the paper.

The client begins to draw or write as the music continues. Some examples of mandalas are included later. The music is continued until the client completes the drawing/writing; the therapist continues being present and holding the space throughout.

Processing

It may be considered that the client starts processing the experience when drawing begins, but it is not unusual for images to continue development during this creative time as well. Images may also continue to develop a bit more during processing and often clients report that their insights continue for days or weeks after they leave the office. When the client is finished drawing, the therapist turns off the music and verbal processing begins. It is important that the client be considered as the expert on her imagery. Reflecting a strengths-based approach, the therapist takes care not to interpret. The client is encouraged to relate the details of the experience, what she notices and gleans from her mandala or writing, what she learned, and how she might integrate it into her life experience. The therapist may ask the client to write a title, theme, affect, and question (TTAQ), giving the experience a title, theme, main emotion (affect), and state a question if there is one. If a mandala is drawn, the therapist includes open-ended questions about the colors, shapes, and other elements of the drawing to help clients gain insight into their meaning and the meaning of the experience overall; the therapist reflects and assists the client to clarify. The client is encouraged to relate the images and learning back to what was said in the prelude as well as to previous sessions to clarify the changes that occurred during the music as well as bring awareness to strengths and personal insight that was gained from the session.

Concepts

Imagery

Imagery is a normal function of human cognition. Memories, planning for the future, and creative endeavors would all be impossible without the ability to image. It is important that the therapist be knowledgeable regarding types or styles of imagery and how to process them. Symbols and metaphors are the language of MI and it is extremely useful for the therapist to have had personal experiences with imagery and training in altered states of consciousness before entering this arena with a client. Within the modality of GIM, imagery is defined in a broad spectrum including memories, emotions, feelings, anything derived from the senses such as visual, auditory, olfactory (smell), gustatory (taste), kinesthetic, or body-based images. Images may be transpersonal (beyond normal human experience) such as the experience of flying, or spiritual in nature such as experiencing contact with a spiritual guide, animal totem, or wisdom figure. The meaning is interpreted by the client according to her personal belief system. It is common for images to reference ancient archetypes or myths as well. Goldberg (1994) included noetic images meaning that the client has a sense of knowing something that isn't gleaned any other way. These experiences are unique to each person and provide a completely client-centered focus.

Altered States of Consciousness (ASCs)

Clients often experience what can best be described as altered states of consciousness; these are common, normal occurrences in human experiences that are different than normal, waking states. Dreams, daydreams, extreme relaxation, extreme fatigue, narrowing of attention, primary process or metaphoric thinking, and the opening of experiential modes to events, stories, and actions in inner experience can all be included and fall under the category of ASCs. Other examples are meditation states, altered states brought on by the ingestion of drugs or alcohol, orgasm, grief, or bliss (Bonny, 2002). This is in contrast to many who consider imagery to be simply visualization; the range is much broader in MI where any type of imagery is accepted and expected.

Music

The music for the MI session is generally decided upon by the therapist; it is considered to be a co-therapist and accompanies the client through the inner experience. As in GIM, the music is generally chosen by the therapist who has been professionally trained to consider the musical elements including form and musical structure, use the iso principle, and intuitively sense the best option. At other times, the client may be asked to bring in music that she finds soothing to collaborate in the process. Music activates the emotions and the imagery as well as providing the potential for spiritual and transpersonal exploration; it is carefully chosen to narrow and maintain the client's focus of attention on the chosen topic or task. To this end, pieces are generally of short duration and have simple, repetitive forms with little or no development. Summer (2009) found that a single, repeated piece may produce a more focused imagery experience that can readily be applied therapeutically during processing. Short pieces can be repeated a few times during the music listening section, which can last up to 15 minutes, depending on how long the client draws or writes. This provides a nurturing environment in which the client becomes comfortable with the music and therefore can relax and explore within it. Genres may include new-age, art music, short classical selections, or classical music arrangements. The music must allow for the therapist's voice to be entrained during the talkover, with no competition between the music and the voice (Goldberg, 1994); volume is adjusted for this purpose as well. Overall, the music helps to direct the experience, provides structure through intentionally chosen musical elements, gives continuity to the inner exploration, provides an aesthetically pleasing sense of safety, and acts as a dependable, holding container for self-exploration. The general energy of the music, use of the iso principle, awareness of supporting the mutually agreed upon focus, and the therapist's intuition are all utilized in the process of music choice for the MI experience. To this end, it is important that the therapist have some training in using music for this type of personal exploration; an understanding of musical forms and personal experience as a client is invaluable and required for training. Professional training in MI and GIM is offered through programs endorsed by the Association for Music and Imagery (AMI) and information is offered through their website at www.ami-bonnymethod.org. A sensitivity to and awareness of the power of music is also important as too large a music container can bring the listener into an unsafe experience that is not therapeutic. Some examples of music are Secret Garden's *Papillon* and Handel's Largo from *Xerxes*.

The Mandala

Mandala drawing as a post-music listening exercise was introduced by Helen Bonny into GIM sessions as a result of her work and research with art therapist Joan Kellogg at the Maryland Psychiatric Institute in the early 1970s (Bonny & Kellogg, 1977/2002). Bonny was programming music for 12-hour long LSD sessions at the height of research into altered states of consciousness. Kellogg was studying psychological trends expressed in the mandalas of clients and also analyzed the mandalas of Bonny's post-music-listening clients for a research study. Bonny found that the drawing provided an opportunity for the client to create a concrete representation of nonverbal elements from their sessions and aided in the verbal processing. It also served as a bridge for the client to return to a normal state of consciousness. Mandalas became a commonly used element in Bonny's trainings and subsequently in the practice of many GIM practitioners. The creation of the mandala is not about making art; it is simply about expressing oneself in form and color. Some examples of mandalas are discussed in the following text.

Goldberg (1994) and Summer (2011) explored adaptations in psychiatric hospital and substance abuse settings as GIM is contraindicated for those with psychosis, weakened ego strength, and boundary issues. They discovered that the imaging experience could be contained in certain ways, which, besides choosing simpler music, included drawing a mandala during the music. The act of drawing could illustrate and help develop the imagery as it was being experienced while keeping the client's focus on the chosen topic. In addition, it provides an in-the-moment snapshot of the self.

Archetype and Myth

Archetypal images are characteristic in MI and are often present in the images of clients and seen in their mandalas (Ward, 2002). The concept of the archetype comes from Jungian psychology and refers to images that occur across cultures and through history that all humans recognize; they are the basic content of myths, fairytales, legends, and religions. Common examples are archetypes of the mother, father, child, hero, villain, victim, trickster, god figures, good, evil, wisdom figures, and the shadow. Others include images of oceans, suns, mountains, storms, war, birth, and death. The red heart with an arrow piercing it and the stairway to the soul in the mandalas ahead can also be considered archetypal images. It is helpful for the therapist to recognize these archetypes when they appear and bring them to the processing discussion as they often can help put personal struggles into a larger context for the client, easing the loneliness of the journey.

Case Example: Mimi

Here follows an example of a supportive MI session. "Mimi" (pseudonym) was a 66-year-old breast cancer survivor of 2.5 years at the time. After undergoing a bilateral mastectomy, this retired nurse had taken part in survivor groups and personal therapy. Mimi was struggling with negative thoughts about recurrence and suffered from high anxiety, diarrhea, and loss of appetite before physician checkups, medical tests, and around the anniversary of her diagnosis. She had also been treated with EMDR previously for post-diagnostic post-traumatic stress disorder, not uncommon after receiving news of a life-threatening illness. Mimi reported making progress with believing she was really well and showed me her number "4" pendant necklace which she wore as a reminder of her low oncotype score. The Oncotype DX is a genetic test that results in a score between 0 and 100; a low score suggests a smaller likelihood of recurrence. Mimi's score indicated only a 4% risk of recurrence; certainly a positive indicator. But she was still dealing with anxiety for a month or more before each medical appointment and currently had one scheduled soon. Mimi described her fear as an automatic response, as if a part of her shrunk when she went in for testing; she wanted to put these feelings behind her. I asked what would help her to do that; she stated she needed to nurture herself more. With encouragement to explain further, she stated that this would mean accessing her inner strength and embracing the fact that she is actually well. We agreed to make self-nurturing the focus of her MI experience. While I chose a Daniel Kobialka arrangement of Bach's *Sheep May Safely Graze* for the music, Mimi arranged herself in a comfortable sitting up position with paper and colors at the ready. This music was chosen for its gentle holding capacity, slow tempo, long phrases, the safe, simple, repetitive but still interesting structure, the spiritual reference which I knew was comfortingly familiar to Mimi, and the orchestral arrangement which added depth and a forward movement to the experience. In addition, this arrangement had a slower tempo than the original hymn and I knew this would create a calming container to draw Mimi into the experience and keep her focused. I started the music, verbally guided her through a short relaxation with a deep breath, and then into the induction, which highlighted the chosen focus of nurturing herself and feeling her inner strength. The induction was completed by directing Mimi to allow an image to form, which would represent this nurturing for her, and then continue the experience on the paper. The music continued as she drew. Figure 11.2 is the mandala that emerged.

On the back, Mimi wrote, "I believe I'm well, I believe I'm healthy. Nothing is going to happen, I'm protected, I'm beloved. Wrong Program, I'm onto it." She explained that this was a view of the bow from the top of a riverboat on the Nile River in Egypt. As it moved through the blue water the green boat was parting the white (outlined in blue) lotus flowers and green leaves seen in the upper right of the mandala; Mimi said she could smell the wonderful lotus fragrance during the music. The green hand was an actual memory from being on the boat on a vacation; it was a talisman and she

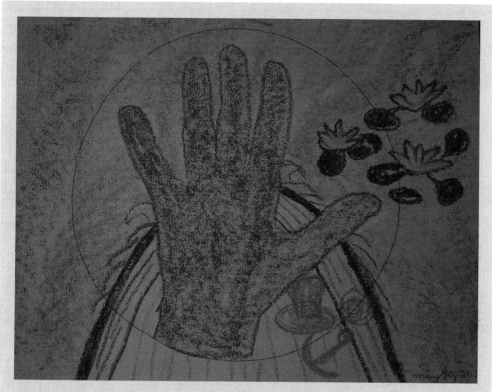

Figure 11.2 I'm well

could feel it protecting her from harm. Adding to her feeling of safety was the grey anchor which represented a grounded feeling and the stanchion (also grey) which holds the rope to tie up the boat when needed; both drawn in the lower right. As we processed the experience, I asked Mimi what self-nurturing techniques she had used before. She stated her intentions to nurture herself using massage, swaying, tapping (EFT), hugging, wearing her "4" necklace and her crucifix for protection, and using aromatherapy to ground herself. She felt this would help decrease her anxiety before medical appointments. In a strengths-based manner, I also helped Mimi to see that she already knew how to nurture herself, that this was a strength she could own and take advantage of more often. By focusing on what she could do to help herself she reaffirmed her strengths and created an image she could practically use to create safety for herself. Mimi had succeeded in shifting her focus from fear to a real plan that empowered her to act on her own behalf. When the solutions originate from within, they hold more power and give the client agency to follow through with them. It is also clear that the music chosen for Mimi's MI experience afforded her the opportunity to appropriate the music for her benefit as a therapeutic tool as in Rolvsjord's model, thus illustrating the strengths-based use of the music.

Case Example: Bea

This will describe a series of MI experiences and mandalas from session 8 of 12 with a 32-year-old Caucasian female that we will call Bea. She had come to Chicago for a 9-month work opportunity that was also serving as a trial separation from her husband of seven years who was still in her home state. Bea entered therapy for help dealing with the separation, her indecision about continuing the marriage, feelings of anxiety, loneliness, and issues with her supervisor at work. She described her father as a drug dealer who was physically and emotionally abusive; she was put into treatment as a 14-year-old after experiencing behavioral issues in school and then running away from home. After that her dad "shut her off," and Bea described feeling abandoned by him. She wanted to work creatively with music and in a transpersonal modality after having experienced couples' therapy, verbal treatment as an adolescent, and some somatic, transpersonal therapy before moving here. Bea had some strengths-based self-care practices in place; she meditated, did yoga regularly, and had an active spiritual life.

In previous imagery sessions, consisting of both GIM and MI, Bea had worked with anger toward her now aging father and come to a place of forgiveness, realizing he was powerless over her now and experiencing the beginnings of reconciliation at a recent family gathering back home. She had begun to ask for what she needed at work after hurtful criticism from her supervisor had triggered feelings of abandonment. Bea had sessions dedicated to developing already-existing strengths she could easily put into use such as creating safety for herself, feeling her power, and creating boundaries. She excitedly shared that her husband had begun making plans to move to Chicago to be with her. The first three mandalas represent re-educative MI experiences in that the focus was an exploration of difficult or conflicting emotions while the fourth is an example of a supportive experience because of the more positive focus.

Checking in for her eighth session, Bea was very upset. Her husband had called the night before to say he didn't want to move to Chicago, didn't want to get back together, and didn't love her anymore. She expressed shock, sadness, and grief and was also overwhelmed with questions about her now unknown future. She felt that now when she was finally ready to love him he didn't want her. I asked Bea if she was ready to focus on and allow her feelings of sadness and grief while listening to the music and she agreed. To the Yo-Yo Ma version of Marconi's *Gabriel's Oboe*, Bea was directed to breathe and allow her intense feelings while listening the music. She stated she was seeing an image of a flower blooming which represented new beginning, like a death and rebirth. She was then encouraged to continue this experience on the paper.

Bea's mandala was of a blue lotus flower; the petals were lightly filled in with aqua and pale blue. The flower was enclosed in bright yellow at the top and black at the bottom, representing her anger. The lotus represented death and rebirth. In her image the lotus was open but when she started to draw the flower closed which brought up her anger. She gave it a title, *Trapped, No Freedom*, adding that she felt closed inside the lotus. (See Figure 11.3.)

Figure 11.3 Trapped, No Freedom

After brief processing consisting of my questions to Bea about how she related to the colors and the function of the yellow at the top and black at the bottom, Bea was really feeling her anger and agreed to be with it in the music. To support and match her anger, *Mars*, from Holst's *Planets*, was chosen to provide a safe environment in which Bea could explore an emotion that she had earlier described as not allowed in her family milieu. As *Mars* began to play, a short induction was given for her to allow her anger to be felt and to explore it with the help of the music. Figure 11.4 depicts her mandala titled *Love Knocked Out* in which the black arrow shows the anger directed at her husband's bright-red heart. She stated she "hit him in the heart where he hit me." Bea stated that the red lines coming out from the heart were her love energy getting knocked out of him; that she was removing it. While processing, she noticed the fissure in the heart looked like a sideways "M," her husband's first initial, outlined in a darker red. The feelings coming up for her at this point were sadness, guilt, and that perhaps her love wasn't enough for him.

Figure 11.4 Love Knocked Out

As Bea spoke more about it, she expressed her intention to accept that this was really happening; her marriage was over, and she needed to allow herself to feel the pain saying, "I don't want to keep it in anymore." She also stated that the pressure she'd been feeling in her head was gone. Following Bea's lead, we decided the next focus was allowing the pain to be felt and to explore not holding it in. I chose Paart's *Spiegel im Spiegel* for its slow, meditative tempo, holding tension, and stark simplicity, which allowed space for the feeling to be explored. This is setting a re-educative function with both the music and the induction, while using the iso principle to match her affect with the music. After a breath and a short induction which encouraged her to let an image form, Bea began to draw.

Bea's mandala illustrates her experience in the music (see Figure 11.5). She imagined herself feeling overwhelming loneliness in her chest and heart in a room with no

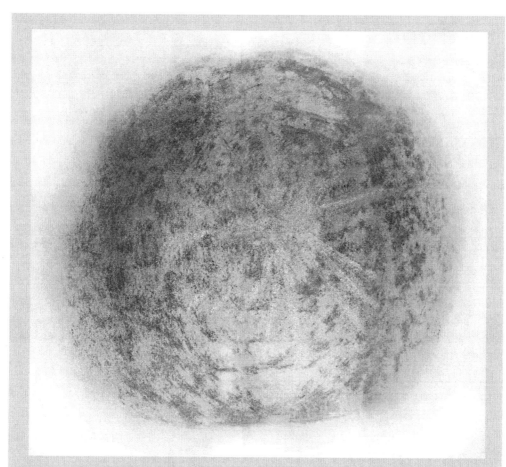

Figure 11.5 Lonely Star

windows, represented by the blues and aquas distributed throughout the drawing. She then saw a bright yellow star, radiating yellow light outwards from the middle with a message that her heart would get bigger. It stood out from and was overcoming the blue (sadness) preventing it from taking over all her space. In the light, there was possibility and freedom to be her own person. Bea then wanted to explore being her own person. After a deep breath with no music she began to draw her final mandala for the session. It is this therapist's belief that Bea requested no music so she could experience the freedom completely with no sound or input other than her self. I supported her strengths-based decision, of course.

Figure 11.6 depicts a stairway. The bottom stair is dark blue, heavy with sadness. As the stairs are ascended, the color gradually becomes lighter with green and then yellow coming in until the gold mirror is shown reflecting freedom at the top. The mirror has a thick line of yellow gold at the left and the mirror has pale blue representing the freedom. Bea stated it was less of an incline than she thought and loved how much

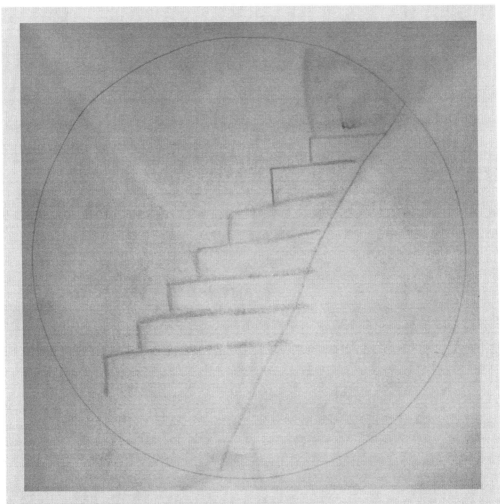

Figure 11.6 Freedom Mirror

space there was on either side of the stairs representing that she didn't know what would happen. She finally expressed a feeling of gratitude to her soon-to-be ex, "M," for the opportunity to go out on her own and experience her freedom. Bea's affect at the end of the session reflected a dramatic change from the upset demeanor she presented as she checked in; she was calm and relaxed as we briefly reviewed her mandalas. I had her review the emotional ground she had covered.

This series, done in a 2-hour session, shows the client-centered emotional journey that brought Bea from a place of sadness and grief through acknowledgement and expression of anger to acceptance of her situation. She finally moved into a feeling of gratitude for her journey and then opened to what the future could hold. The music supported her through each step as she decided what to focus on next. She was encouraged to feel the power of each emotion with the support of the music; the music afforded her the opportunity to move into and through the intense emotions. Bea was able to access her already-existing strength through the unique images that expressed her journey. She found the way through her emotions, even those that overwhelmed her, by breaking them down into smaller, more manageable pieces and navigating through each one with guidance from the music, the therapist, and her own images.

Conclusion

As illustrated here, MI focuses on acknowledging and building on the already-existing strengths of the client which brings it easily under the strengths-based umbrella. The use of MI allows a client to utilize the transformational power of music in a way that supports her style of working with her own language, gain insight into behaviors and feelings, create a vocabulary of personal symbols and metaphors that are honored and shared with the therapist, and experience appreciation for her authentic self. With more collaborative work comes more investment in the therapeutic process and, research tells us, better results.

The payoff for the therapist is facilitating sessions that involve exciting therapeutic growth as well as employing elements of creativity and aesthetic beauty as part of each session. Besides choosing the most useful music, the most difficult aspect of strengths-based MI work for the therapist may be letting go of pathology-based thinking and learning to truly follow the client through her emotions, listening and reflecting to collaboratively choose the right focus, and trusting the wisdom of the psyche with the music to bring the client what is needed. If the therapist was never allowed to express strong emotions in his family culture, opening the space to allow it for the client may be a difficult task indeed. Being aware of countertransference and practicing a non-judgmental approach toward client images and mandala-making is as imperative as a simple talkover using the client's words only. Being comfortable highlighting strengths and not playing the "expert" on imagery interpretation are also important.

As illustrated in the case examples above, clients can move through difficult emotions in a strengths-based way using music and mandalas with grace and speed by accessing their creative imaginations and owning their inner world. Formulating an induction and narrating it over the music is an art form of its own; it creates an intimate, safe setting for clients to open up to their inner selves and witness their own resilience. Perhaps in honoring and expanding the consciousness of each client, one by one we can expand the consciousness of the world.

References

Betti, U. (1956). *Three plays by Ugo Betti: The Queen and the Rebels, The Burnt Flower-Bed and Summertime*. New York: Grove Press, p. 151.

Bonny, H.L. (2002). Music and consciousness. In L. Summer (Ed.), *Music consciousness: The evolution of guided imagery and music* (pp. 78–92). Gilsum, NH: Barcelona Publishers. (Original work published 1975)

Bonny, H.L., & Goldberg, F.S. (2002). New directions in the Bonny method of guided imagery and music (GIM). In L. Summer (Ed.), *Music consciousness: The evolution of guided imagery and music* (pp. 263–268). Gilsum, NH: Barcelona Publishers. (Original work published 1996)

Bonny, H.L., & Kellogg, J. (2002). Guided imagery and music (GIM) and the mandala: A case study illustrating an integration of music and art therapies. In L. Summer (Ed.), *Music consciousness: The evolution of guided imagery and music* (pp. 205–230). Gilsum, NH: Barcelona Publishers. (Original work published 1977)

Burns, D., & Woolrich, J. (2004). The Bonny method of guided imagery and music. In A. Darrow (Ed.), *Introduction to approaches in music therapy* (pp. 53–62). Silver Spring, MD: American Music Therapy Association.

Dimiceli-Mitran, L. (2015). Focus on wellness: Using music imagery (MI) in cancer survivor groups. In D. Grocke & T. Moe (Eds.), *Guided imagery & music (GIM) and music imagery methods for individual and group therapy* (pp. 231–242). London, UK: Jessica Kingsley Publishing.

Goldberg, F.S. (1994) The Bonny method of guided imagery and music (GIM) as individual and group treatment in a short-term psychiatric hospital. *Journal of the Association for Music and Imagery, 3,* 19–33.

Jung, C.G. (1964). *A man and his symbols.* New York, NY: Dell Publishing.

Rolvsjord, R. (2010). *Resource-oriented music therapy in mental health care.* University Park, IL: Barcelona Publishers.

Rowling, J.K. (1997). *Harry Potter and the Sorcerer's Stone.* New York, NY: Arthur A. Levine Books.

Saleebey, D. (Ed.). (2009). *The strengths perspective in social work practice.* Boston, MA: Pearson Education.

Summer, L. (2009). *Client perspectives on the music in guided imagery and music (GIM).* [Doctoral dissertation]. Copenhagen, Denmark: Aalborg University. Retrieved November 9, 2015 from www. http://vbn.aau.dk/files/112202270/6467_lisa_summer_thesis.pdf.

Summer, L. (2011). Music therapy and depression: Uncovering resources in music and imagery. In A. Meadows (Ed.), *Developments in music therapy practice: Case study perspectives* (pp. 486–498). Gilsum, NH: Barcelona Publishers.

Ward, K.M. (2002). A Jungian orientation to the Bonny method. In K. Bruscia & D. Grocke (Eds.), *Guided imagery and music: The Bonny method and beyond* (pp. 207–224). Gilsum, NH: Barcelona Publishers.

Wheeler, B. (1983). A psychotherapeutic classification of music therapy practices: A continuum of procedures. *Music therapy perspectives, 1,* 8–12.

12

Resourcing the Body

Moving within Strengths to Actualize Potential

Jessica Young

If you cannot find it in your own body, where will you go in search of it?

The Upanishads

The remarkable resiliency of individuals who have experienced chronic homelessness, severe mental illness, extensive trauma, and substance use led me to working within a strengths-based model. In many ways, it felt very natural for me as my dance and movement therapy (DMT) training was influenced by a humanistic, person-centered approach. Coupled with working in an agency that embraced a harm reduction, trauma informed philosophy of care, I was immersed in strengths-based work. Rather than focusing on perceived deficits, diagnosis, symptoms, and what was unchangeable, I found myself reflecting on how and what led people to tolerate, move with, and push through to the other side of their difficulties. My curiosity led to rich discoveries of playful humor, seeds of hope, a desire for human connection, a powerful spirit, and extraordinary resourcefulness and ingenuity. My job was to simply dust off, re-vitalize, and help harness these strengths towards enhanced well-being. I considered the whole person—body, mind, and spirit—and the dance between us, as together my clients and I identified even the smallest of accomplishments and created new pathways and expanded potentials from the rich resources present within their bodies and our creative collaboration.

A strengths-based approach seamlessly supports working from this holistic perspective where the primary resource is the body, and the creative dance serves as the catalyst for change. As human beings, we need and want to be loved and validated. I found this to be especially vital for highly marginalized populations. I use a strengths-based approach, because when I see and recognize the beauty, attributes, and unique qualities that individuals carry within them, I find that they more readily engage in the therapeutic movement relationship with me where spontaneity and imagination are cultivated and lead to shifts in movement and positive change. In my experience, a strengths-based approach supports the transcendental nature of movement and the creative process. Allowing clients to guide the process of therapy, truly honoring their pace, trusting that the solutions reside within them, and reflecting those solutions back to them through movement is a powerful experience to witness.

This chapter aims to explicate how specific dance/movement therapy (DMT) techniques, such as mirroring, and processes, like empathic attunement, offer a unique inroad to working therapeutically with client strengths, beginning with their bodies and movement manifestations. Rooted in humanism, DMT inherently incorporates many strengths-based ideas; yet it is not often explicitly described from such a paradigm. This chapter will guide the reader through a DMT group, based on the work of Marian Chace. Specifically, the four core concepts of a Chacian methodology, including the therapeutic movement relationship, body action, symbolism, and rhythmic group activity, will be discussed as a means of highlighting the strengths-based nature of the work. It will go on to describe how a strengths-based approach to DMT includes, first and foremost, what resources are present for an individual on a body/movement level, bringing to the foreground one's movement preferences and strengths. It will examine how to further develop such movement as a means of expanding one's repertoire, which in turn offers a broad array of solutions to enhance one's overall well-being, health, and vitality. Anecdotal examples will be drawn upon from my clinical work in a community mental health setting and a psychosocial rehabilitation program for adults who experienced chronic homelessness, severe mental illness, trauma, and substance use.

Chace's Four Core Concepts

Chace, often considered the mother of dance/movement therapy, worked within a methodology (Levy, 1992; Sandel, Chaiklin, & Lohn, 1993) that aligns with many strengths-based concepts. Chace's work has been classified into four major areas that capture the principles of her approach to DMT: the therapeutic movement relationship, body action, symbolism, and rhythmic group activity (Chaiklin & Schmais, 1993). Chace primarily conducted group sessions, although DMT is an effective modality in working with individuals, couples, and families (American Dance Therapy Association [ADTA], 2016). Her work is influenced by Harry Stack Sullivan's teachings of the verbal and non-verbal interpersonal relationship (Schmais, 2004; Shelley, 1993), whereby empathically attuning—or reflecting back physical and emotional expressions in an empathic manner (Sandel, 1993; Schmais, 2004)—to individuals provides "uncritical and undemanding social approval" (Schmais, 2004, p. 127). In turn, the individual demonstrates increased awareness and acceptance of self, which allows for further curiosity and exploration of one's creative and unique aspects (Schmais, 2004).

Therapeutic Movement Relationship

The therapeutic movement relationship (Chaiklin & Schmais, 1993, Fischman, 2009) provides a container—or a supportive, non-judgmental, safe space of shared presence—for creative collaboration that supports growth and healing, which is continually informed by movement observation and assessment (Young, 2015). Dance/movement therapists objectively describe and organize their movement observations into a meaningful assessment that is based upon what is already present for the client (Levy, 1992), using Rudolf Laban's taxonomy of movement (Bartenieff & Lewis, 1980; Laban, 1980). Chaiklin and Schmais (1993) described how Chace emphasized that the therapeutic process begins immediately upon greeting and assessing the clients at the door, by empathically reflecting and responding to their verbal and non-verbal communication during which all movement expression, feelings, and behaviors are acknowledged, valued, and validated.

Whereas immediately engaging the client may seem like an obvious first step, Rapp and Goscha (2012) go as far as stating that it is "indispensable and critical" (p. 83) to the beginning of a therapeutic relationship in a strengths-based model. Yet, I have found that it is often overlooked or minimized, resulting in a missed opportunity to fully see and feel a client. For example, when I worked in a psychosocial rehabilitation (PSR) program with those who were homeless and living with a chronic and severe mental illness, I was intentional about giving my full attention to each individual from a place of presence within myself, as I warmly welcomed each person into the program as soon as the doors opened. I often introduced the use of touch through a handshake or hand on the shoulder.

I acknowledged each person by name, made eye contact, and verbally and non-verbally communicated that I was genuinely glad to see each individual, grateful that each person decided to come to the program, and inquired about their well-being, all while empathically attuning to them. Including the intentional use of my body in the engagement process, while connecting and responding to individuals through their movement, is one way of demonstrating a genuine therapeutic relationship that Rapp and Goscha (2012) identify in a strengths-based model.

Over time, I experienced a shift in the culture of arriving to the PSR program. Instead of everyone piling in through the door with little awareness of their own presence, surroundings, and relationships that they were entering into, there was greater acknowledgement of how they were feeling in the moment and increased connection to staff and peers. This was demonstrated through greater eye contact, brighter affect, and engagement in conversations. This also afforded an opportunity to give someone more immediate and individualized attention if needed, resulting in a smoother transition into the day. When working with a highly marginalized population who is ignored, not seen, avoided, and even despised, the power of seeing them, welcoming them, and validating them for who they are and all that they bring to the moment as another human being should not be underestimated. It also serves as an opportunity to bring intentionality to the resilience of clients as they make the choice to return to the program for another day rather than simply moving through a monotonous routine. This offers a sense of meaning and purpose instrumental to a strengths-based therapeutic relationship (Rapp & Goscha, 2012; Smith, 2006). It also highlights an aspect of Padesky and Mooney's (2012) resilience model within their strengths-based cognitive behavioral therapy approach wherein "strengths necessary for resilience can be found within recurring activities" (p. 288).

Empathic attunement (Schmais, 2004) extends beyond the initial greeting and is carried throughout the therapeutic movement relationship. It entails incorporating the emotional content of the individual's movement behavior into the verbal and non-verbal response of the dance/movement therapist, resulting in an empathic reflection that is also kinesthetic in nature (Chaiklin & Schmais, 1993). Thus, kinesthetic empathy (Fischman, 2009; Tortora, 2006) is born out of observing and embodying the movement of another with awareness towards one's own "emotional bodily reactions" (Tortora, 2006, p. 234). Participating in another's experience through movement provides kinesthetic and emotional understanding, which fosters mutuality (Tortora, 2006). In turn, "trust and a sense of self emerge—both within the self and as reflected in the other" (Tortora, 2006, p. 235).

One technique that supports the development of kinesthetic empathy is mirroring. Rapp and Goscha (2012) identified mirroring as a component of strengths-based work wherein the therapist verbally reflects back positive attributes and strengths of the client. In DMT, mirroring entails reflecting another's movement, which encapsulates more than simply mimicking. It is a form of empathic reflection, which involves entering into the movement experience of another. This entails understanding what, where, and how others move by attending to qualities such as muscle tension, rhythm, and emotional expression (Chaiklin & Schmais, 1993). The dance/movement therapist mirrors the organization of the body, spatial configurations of movement, shaping qualities, and dynamic qualities related to the motion factors of flow, space, weight, and time (Bartenieff & Lewis, 1980; Laban, 1980). For dance/movement therapists, understanding the felt experience of another through their movement is the inroad to understanding the lived experience of their clients, a necessary component of a strengths-based approach (Rapp & Goscha, 2012).

As individuals both see their movement mirrored by another and are given time and space to sense and feel it within their own bodies, a "self-affirming atmosphere" (Sandel, 1993, p. 103) is created where clients can begin to identify, acknowledge, and claim their movement as they witness it being empathically reflected by the dance/movement therapist and other group members. In other words, mirroring reflects and validates the individual and their movement, including stillness, in the present moment of their bodies. Dance/movement therapists guide individuals to discover the strengths that already reside within them by cultivating awareness of their movement repertoire and how it has aided them in their functional, expressive, communicative, relational, and behavioral ways of being in the world. Granted, individuals may not like what they see when a dance/movement therapist reflects their movement. It can be difficult to see how one's movement repertoire may be constricted, limiting, and even result in harm to oneself or others. However, opportunities to feel accepted, validated, and understood arise when dance/movement therapists kinesthetically attune to these movements. A strengths-based approach to DMT recognizes the value and purpose of all movement that comprises individuals' repertoires as the seeds of the solution from which the creative process germinates to grow those strengths into an expanded repertoire.

For example, in a typical Chace group, which is conducted in a circle, the dance/movement therapist invites participants to introduce themselves through movement and/or words, and this is reflected back by the dance/movement therapist and other group members. In the PSR program, this was an opportunity to validate the participants' presence and cultivate awareness of self and other through mobilizing what was already within the individual. What resulted over time was that individuals developed what came to be known as their signature movement, which they tended to call upon during each session as a means of introducing themselves. In addition to providing a sense of pride and ownership that each member had something to offer to the group, this allowed for those who were not in attendance to still be recognized and honored when the group introduced that person's movement. What resulted was a stronger awareness of and connection to others in the community. In describing how the counseling psychology field contributed to a strengths-based approach, Smith (2006) discussed the protective factors that arise from bonding within a community and the healing aspects afforded by cultural rituals. Similarly, movement rituals, as described above, within the culture of a community day program can provide a sense of belonging and a context for healing, which is fostered by a sense of safety and solidarity.

A fundamental aspect to my personal strengths-based approach to DMT is my use of humor, hope, and encouragement within the therapeutic movement relationship. I often tell my students to expect that their clients can reach goals that may seem unreachable. To be clear, I do not mean that unrealistic goals should be established for individuals. I mean that if we believe in our clients, then they will succeed, and often in unexpected ways. In facilitating a women's group in a PSR program, we would regularly go on community outings. On our way to the van, I engaged in playful movement and dialogue with the group members about who was going to drive, knowing full well that I was the only one who could drive. As the weeks went on, one individual, who initially shied away from the thought of driving, began to state that she would drive. One week, she caught the keys when I tossed them her way. The next week she unlocked the door. Through a series of progressive steps each week, she ultimately sat in the driver's seat and started the van. Although she never ended up driving the van, her optimism and confidence level soared, and she expressed joy and delight. These strengths transferred over into her daily life, as she ended up leaving the program to help care for the younger generation in her family. This is an example of how DMT can extend beyond the group and the milieu and into the community where our stories unfold through movement. It also illustrates how strengths, such as confidence, can be realized through the action oriented approach of DMT (Fischman, 2009; Sandel, Chaiklin, & Lohn, 1993), where each achievement along the way is reinforced with "hope-inducing behaviors" (Rapp & Goscha, 2012, p. 75).

Body Action

Following the check in and introduction of a Chace group is the warm-up. Central to the warm-up is body action, another core concept of Chace's methodology. Activating the body invites both stimulation and relaxation from which greater emotional expression can be accessed (Chaiklin & Schmais, 1993). A strengths-based dance/movement therapist facilitates such activation by keenly observing, mirroring, and verbally reflecting back the nature of the movement that is already taking place. This process invites further movement exploration, and the shifts that individuals make are reflected back to them. "The therapist makes moment-to-moment choices, affirming those patients' movements that will lead to healthier functioning" (Chaiklin & Schmais, 1993, p. 88). An intervention might sound something like, "I see Jake quickly tapping his foot. How can we warm up our feet? Margaret is circling her foot and Jane is gently shaking her foot. Notice how many different ways you can move your feet." Mirroring accompanies this verbal reflection offering individuals an opportunity to see their movement reflected back to them and hear a description of it. This facilitates an expansion of their repertoire as they try on the movements of others, making adaptations along the way. The dance/movement therapist guides the warm-up by inviting qualities of movement in one part of the body to travel to other parts of the body. "What happens when we move the shaking from our feet into our knees?" This process continues until each part of the body has been activated, often culminating in full-bodied movement.

What may appear as a simple warm-up upon first glance is really an opportunity to acknowledge and validate individuals for the movements that they share with the group while simultaneously inviting experimentation with new or different movements that evolve out of what was initially presented. As a result, body awareness increases, movement strengths are recognized, and change is introduced through both fleeting and intentional shifts in movement. The very nature of engaging people in body action emphasizes their resources and movement capabilities rather than what is absent or problematic in their movement. At the end of a group, individuals often commented on being surprised about how they were able to move. Activating the body from a place of strength motivates change, and when witnessed and reflected by others, this motivation is reinforced.

The development of a theme, related to a shared human experience, is built upon individuals' movement expression that comes forward during the warm-up. Within this process, dance/movement therapists guide the expansion of individuals' movement repertoire in a variety of ways, including exaggeration. For example, the dance/movement therapist might invite even quicker movement to help provide clarity and intention around it, as well as the accompanying affective state while meeting the group in a familiar quality. The dance/movement therapist can then guide the group in incrementally fluctuating towards the polarity of slower movement through a movement dialogue that is informed by the therapist's ability to kinesthetically attune to the group, respond to their movement expression, and encourage a spontaneous and continuous rhythmic interaction resulting in theme development (Chaiklin & Schmais, 1993).

Smith (2006) described how strengths often develop out of polarities, such as the development from physical prowess to wisdom with age. Dance/movement therapists invite and explore movement polarities as related to the dynamic, spatial, and shaping qualities in different parts of the body (Bartenieff & Lewis, 1980; Laban, 1980), and mirror them back to the individuals as a means of reinforcing new movement behaviors, which offer alternative ways of relating and coping (Chaiklin & Schmais, 1993). The goal is to find a balance between the polarities and to be able to intentionally access them when required. For example, I worked with a woman who experienced years of severe domestic violence while raising a family. Her movement was tender, and she kept her limbs close to her body, extending them only slightly into the space around her. Together, we moved in a gentle manner, taking up little space, and the woman identified how moving in this way allowed her to protect herself and care for her children. Moving from strengths that emerged out of survival skills as well as her "relational and nurturing strength" (Smith, 2006, p. 30), we began to explore safety and stability within her own body as she took up more space while increasing her use of weight through grounding movements. The theme became one of empowerment and learning to love herself as she loved her children.

Dance/movement therapists also employ props to facilitate the activation of individuals' movement potential. For example, in a PSR group, one individual was describing how he was unable to problem solve or actively work towards his goals. His movements could be described as passive, disconnected from his core, and unarticulated. I invited him to stand in the middle of the group, and the group members and I playfully tangled him up in a large stretch band. He responded by asking what he was supposed to do. I stated that it was up to him, and he identified that he wanted to get untangled from the stretch band. The group affirmed his decision. Similarly, he had to figure out how to do this on his own. After a moment of expressed helplessness, he found ways to move his body through the stretch band and ultimately free himself to his own delight and that of the group. This was followed by verbally processing what he actually did to problem solve and achieve his goal in addition to discussing, further reflecting, and exploring how his movements supported his ability to untangle himself, and ultimately how he could transfer these skills to his daily life. Through activating different body parts with increased articulation and differentiation, connecting to his weight, and using directness, he discovered creative ways of moving to disentangle himself. This example illustrates how placing change into action through the present moment experience of the body can build confidence and self-efficacy, which in turn reinforces positive change and emotional strengths such as perseverance and optimism.

Role-play can also serve as a means of activating the body in new and unfamiliar ways. For example, in a DMT group for adults with mental illness and substance abuse, an individual in the preparation/determination stage of change (Prochaska, DiClemente, & Norcross, 1992) was expressing how difficult it was for him to not succumb to peer pressure. I invited the group to role-play going over to his house with the intention of using substances with him. In fact, when the group arrived and knocked on his door, the client let them into his home. I then invited an individual who was in the action stage of change (Prochaska, DiClemente, & Norcross, 1992) to play the role of the client who was being tempted by his friends to use drugs. As the group of friends approached the house, but before they had a chance to knock on the door, the client left the actual group room. He left with such directness, quickness, and strength, that the entire group, myself included, was left a bit stunned. The group then discussed how the different movement qualities used by the two individuals supported opposing responses to triggers. This led to further discussion on various ways to handle such a situation that would support one's recovery process, and the individual who inspired this intervention began to identify ways that might work for him.

Symbolism

Another way of exploring different movement qualities and emotional expression is through the use of symbolism. Symbolism in strengths–based counseling is highlighted through the use of ritual therapy (Crockett & Prosek, 2013), the Medicine Wheel (Sundlie, 2009), and art therapy (Wilkinson & Chilton, 2013). Symbolic expression through dance/movement can serve as a means of externalizing one's subjective experience and providing a universal human understanding (Schmais, 1985). The release itself can be healing when received with empathic support and acceptance. Symbolic movement can offer a safe means of expressing conflict, repressed feelings, unconscious thoughts, and difficult emotions (Levy, 1992). For example, when I conducted a site visit for an intern working with a boy in a therapeutic day school who had a difficult time identifying emotions and engaged in disruptive and aggressive behaviors and movements, our dance led the boy to pose. When I asked what he was, he stated he was a weeping willow. When I asked how the tree felt, he said, "Sad." Time allowed us to briefly explore this feeling of sadness and the shift to softer movement qualities. If I were to have continued working with this individual, we could have gone on to explore the different parts of the tree and the qualities of each part as well as the gestalt of the tree through his embodiment of the tree and any sensations, thoughts, and emotions related to this symbolic exploration.

Symbolism through body action can also be used to provide an opportunity to illustrate positive character traits. During one PSR group, when I reflected the group's movement and asked the members what images came to mind from the movement, a theme of becoming different animals emerged. As people began to move like various animals, I invited them to also add sounds, embody one another's movements, and to interact with one another. During verbal processing, members shared what it felt like to be their identified animal. Responses included friendly like a cocker spaniel, strong like an ape, funny like a monkey, coy like a cat, free like a bird, slippery like a snake, courageous like a lion, and quiet like a mouse. We discussed how these qualities support their recovery, what it was like to try on different qualities, and how to negotiate interacting with others who had similar or different qualities.

Props can also be used as symbols to help externalize thoughts and feelings as a way to safely identify and process them. This aligns with the narrative theory technique of externalizing problems, allowing individuals to separate themselves from the problem such that solutions can be more readily recognized (White, 2002). In one PSR group, a member was describing how he almost did not come to group because he did not want to burden the group with his problems as related to his depression. To affirm the strengths that he enacted by coming to the group, I handed him a large number of beanbags to represent his depression. I then invited him to hand one beanbag to each member of the group. He was left with a small handful of beanbags. We then processed the different sensations in his body that he experienced as he offered up his beanbags as well as related thoughts and feelings. He identified feeling lighter with a greater sense of ease and relief. He recognized how if he were to have stayed at home in bed, he would still be carrying the magnitude of his depression, and how choosing to come to the group and share his feelings resulted in him feeling less depressed. In addition, his depression now felt more manageable such that he was able to effectively use his coping skills. I also checked in with how the group members felt receiving just a small part of his depression. They shared how it was not difficult at all to receive one beanbag of depression. Instead, they felt good about being able to help him, and afterward they were able to let go of the beanbag, as they had no real attachment to it. This example illustrates how this individual was able to externalize his depression, actively fight against it, and feel empowered to continue to engage in his recovery (White, 2002).

Rhythmic Group Activity

In addition to the core concepts of the therapeutic movement relationship, body action, and symbolism, a Chace approach includes the power of rhythmic group activity as a means of organizing individuals' behaviors while creating a sense of unity. Expressing feelings through a shared rhythm provides a greater sense of safety and strength, which further fuels the creative process and paves the way for change (Chaiklin & Schmais, 1993). This rhythm can be found and developed from the breath; heart beat; simple repetitive body action, such as the tapping of a foot or clapping; or in larger full-bodied dancing. Music, the playing of percussive instruments, singing, the use of voice, or the movement itself can support this rhythm.

Facilitating rhythmic group activity often begins when dance/movement therapists non-verbally and/or verbally reflect a rhythm that they hear or see from an individual in the group, such as snapping, stomping of the feet, or swaying of the arms. This is followed by an invitation to the other group members to notice the rhythm of their movement and what it is like to try on different rhythms that they are hearing and seeing. This often leads to a shared group rhythm, bringing cohesiveness to the group. The dynamics of the shared rhythm can then be further explored in the creative realm by changing the measure, tempo, and strength. In addition, the rhythm can travel to different parts of the body and through space. Further exploration might include a call and response in dyads, small groups, or between an individual and the larger group. The dance/movement therapist invites images, feelings, and thoughts that emerge from the rhythm exploration to come forward from the individuals as a means of deepening the co-creative process.

The dance/movement therapist will often empower the group to decide how to bring the rhythm to a close or support the natural quieting of it. In some instances, a return to one's unique rhythm might be encouraged to facilitate fortifying the connection between the individual and the collective. Verbal processing can focus on a number of things depending on what was created and how it was created, as well as the goals of the group and the individuals. It often includes identifying the positive qualities of each individual's rhythm and examining how adjustments impact the group's rhythm. The group also has an opportunity to discuss what they appreciate about the different individuals and collective rhythms, reflecting on their inner/outer experience of beginning with self, connecting with others, and bringing that experience back to self.

Props can also be used to support rhythmic group activity. In one PSR group, the energy level was very low. Observing the minimal movements of the group—shallow breathing, and disengaged, ungrounded bodies, while sensing in my own body a lack of motivation to actively move and a desire to remain sitting—I introduced a ball into the group. It was about the size of a large beach ball with greater weight and bounce to it. I began by simply inviting the group to pass the ball to the person next to them. The group members did so with gentle movements and little eye contact. I then invited them to pass the ball to someone who was not next to them and to state that person's name. As a result, the use of eye contact increased and the ball was rolled with a greater use of force. On their own accord, the group members began experimenting with different ways of passing the ball, including throwing, bouncing, rolling, and walking it over to someone. Soon everyone was standing and interspersing other movement such as spinning with the ball, rolling it backward through their legs, or tossing it under a leg. A game ensued in which the group members established the objective and rules. Everyone fully participated, the collective energy rose, affects brightened, moods shifted from lethargic and depressed to energized and playful, there was an increased awareness of self and other, and improved communication and teamwork skills emerged. During verbal processing, I asked the group to identify what shifted for them from the beginning to the end of group, affirmed the changes that they made, and asked them to consider how they might transfer the strengths and skills that they exhibited during group to their everyday lives. One woman identified how she felt "stimulated and alive" by the group. She went on to describe how her antipsychotic medications left her feeling numb and how she found it helpful to come to the group and move with others.

DMT Strengths: Body, Movement, and the Creative Process

Wisdom of the Body

Dance/movement therapy draws upon the wisdom of the body, its expressive movement, and the creative process of dance to cultivate emotional, cognitive, social, and spiritual health, well-being, and healing (ADTA, 2016). Smith (2006) identified 10 categories of strength, culled from a review of strengths-based literature. She began by discussing wisdom. Dance/movement therapists nurture the innate wisdom of the body. Movement is our first form of communication and our bodies often reveal the truth of our experiences. Therefore, dance/movement therapists help individuals reconcile the discrepancy between their verbal and non-verbal communication while increasing awareness of their bodies and learning to listen, trust, and respond to what their bodies are experiencing. This is one reason why warming up the body is such an important aspect of dance/movement therapy. During the warm-up, the musculature is activated and tension is released, which allows defense structures to decrease and emotional content to more readily arise (Levy, 1992). Thus, the body is often a vulnerable landscape to work with, and it is precisely out of this vulnerability where individuals' strengths emerge.

DMT is based on the premise that the body and mind are inextricably interrelated (ADTA, 2016). This was evidenced as the practice emerged in the 1940s when Chace worked at St. Elizabeth's Hospital with WWII veterans who were experiencing symptoms of what we now know as post-traumatic stress disorder and those with chronic and severe mental illness. She was able to create groups that promoted safety and trust where individuals were able to find verbal and non-verbal ways to communicate, express their feelings, and discover ways towards healing (Shelley, 1993). This body/ mind connection is now substantiated by the field of interpersonal neurobiology brought to the forefront by Siegel (2012), who defined *the mind* as "an embodied and relational process that regulates the flow and energy of information" (p. 2). In other words, our feelings and thoughts are necessarily shaped by our interactions with others and made visible through our body movement. Thus, shifting our movement can in turn shift our emotions, thoughts, and behaviors: "When attention is brought to movement, the brain creates new connections and possibilities at an incredibly rapid rate" (Baniel, 2012, p. 48).

Movement as Communication

Dance/movement therapy recognizes that we are all moving beings from the sucking of our thumb in utero to our last breath. A fundamental tenet of DMT is that "dance is communication and thus fulfills a basic human need" (Chaiklin & Schmais, 1993, p. 77). Early movement patterns that allow us to get our biological and relational needs met, take in new information, and cope with our environments lay the foundation for how we live and move in our bodies as we interact with the world and develop our sense of self (Amighi, Loman, Lewis, & Sossin, 1999). A strengths-based dance/ movement therapist notices, reflects, and validates individuals' movements while inviting them to discover the meaning of their movement. Dance/movement therapists continuously observe and assess individuals' movements throughout a session while also listening to their own bodies' responses to inform their non-verbal and verbal interventions.

Due to the continual presence of movement, it is impossible to not participate in a DMT session if present in the room. This includes those who have very limited movement, such as those who are catatonic (Levy, 1992) or dying (Dillenbeck & Hammond-Meiers, 2009). In such cases, the work often relies on attuning to the individual's breath, using touch, and being in the shared presence of another. In examining the practice of dance/movement therapy with individuals in the end stages of life, Dillenbeck and Hammond-Meiers (2009) stated, "Supporting an individual to attend to the body from a place of stillness enables movement to be witnessed at microscopic levels" (p. 109).

Shelley (1993) described how Chace illuminated the presence of movement in the room when she acknowledged the participation of those who were not engaging in the activity of the group. She accomplished this by attuning to and reflecting the subtle movements that emerged as a result of the change in the musculature of their bodies in response to what they observed and heard in the group. This acceptance of their current level of participation affords such individuals a feeling of connection to the group, so that they can more actively participate when they are ready (Shelley, 1993): "By engaging participants on whatever level they were able and willing to participate, Chace provided the opportunity to gradually develop new confidence in communicating and expressing oneself" (Shelley, 1993, p. 28). One could argue that Chace recognized what has come to be known as the Stages of Change (Prochaska, DiClemente, & Norcross, 1992) and used motivational interviewing principles (Miller & Rollnick, 2013) through the modality of movement and the medium of the body within the context of the therapeutic movement relationship (Brown, 2009).

Throughout the therapeutic process, Chace emphasized working with "'the healthy parts' of the personality" (Chaiklin & Schmais, 1993, p. 85), wherein all movement interventions are directly derived from the individuals' movements. For example, when working with an individual who was extremely depressed, I observed a very enclosed, sunken posture, flat affect, and neutral use of muscle tension. I felt deflated within my own torso and invited the individual to bring awareness to his breath as I breathed with him. Gradually, we began to increase the depth of the breath resulting in a subtle growing and shrinking rhythmic action of the body, an enlivened use of flow in his movement, and a greater ability to move out of his internal world and into connection with me. Through joining him in movement similar in form to his, I empathically reflected the essence of his depression as manifested through his body, while highlighting the access he already had to his breath. Reflecting the slight shifts in his movement, affective expression, and engagement in the therapeutic movement relationship reinforced actualization of his movement potential in the moment, which would be further developed throughout our sessions.

Dance/movement therapists engage in a movement dialogue with their clients wherein they reflect, amplify, and expand upon individuals' movements to cultivate awareness of how they experience the world through their bodies. A strengths-based approach to dance/movement therapy recognizes first and foremost what resources are present for individuals on a body/movement level. The movement dialogue begins from this place and a dance is co-created through which individuals expand their movement repertoire, affording them greater access to different ways of relating to self and others while constructively coping with their environment in satisfying, effective, and positive ways.

Movement preferences often emerge during the warm-up of a Chace group (Chaiklin & Schmais, 1993). The dance/movement therapist facilitates increasing awareness of these preferences and affirms them as strengths, which can be resourced with greater intentionality once they have been identified and further explored through movement and accompanying sensations, images, feelings, and thoughts. For example, I prefer to move with quickness and directness, which often serves me well. However, there are situations in which it would be more beneficial for me to take more time and consider more perspectives before moving forward. Fortunately, unlike other animals that rely on instinct for survival, humans can bring consciousness to their movement dynamics and expand their movement vocabulary to enrich their means of movement expression and functionality available to them, known as humane effort (Laban, 1980; Levy, 1992). Thus, humane effort allows us to optimize our ability to cope with the environment even under adverse conditions (Laban, 1980). Smith (2006) described how adapting to our environment through a wide array of coping skills can be viewed as a strength, and dance/movement therapists bring this to fruition through fostering an endless range of movement possibilities that reside within us.

Smith (2006) also described how environments can enable the development of strengths and provide restorative qualities. In strengths-based DMT practice, the environment or landscape of the body can be accessed as a source of strength and recuperation. When moving in a changed manner, recuperation can be found within one's preferred movement qualities. For example, in an attempt to slow down my need for a response from my multi focused children, I may recuperate in my preferred effort qualities of quick and direct movement by doing the dishes. Laban's theory of exertion/ recuperation posits that recuperation does not translate to a lack of movement, rather a shift in the movement as related to what part of the body is moving, where it is moving in space, or the dynamic qualities of the movement (Bartenieff & Lewis, 1980). Movements often have a natural pattern of recuperation, such as the upward rebound of the fingers when typing. Recuperation allows for a re-enlivening of the movement and a replenishing of resources. Thus, increasing awareness of individuals' preferred movement qualities and channeling those qualities into constructive behaviors has the potential to offer a fertile resource for recuperation. This recuperation can serve as a protective factor enabling individuals to increase their resiliency, a stage in Smith's (2006) strengths-based model.

The Creative Process of the Movement Narrative

Dance/movement therapy is built upon and elicits strengths of courage and creativity. Smith (2006) described creativity as extending beyond new ways of thinking to also include the arts. Dance/movement therapists co-create a dance with individuals through a shared creative process, which is fueled by improvisation, spontaneity, and subjective originality (Wengrower, 2009); each is considered a strength in its own right. The creative process of dance allows individuals to experiment with new ways of moving, by listening and responding to the body, that offer possibilities for change, new perspectives, and fresh experiences. For example, in working with a woman who described feeling suffocated in her relationships and stuck in this place, I invited her to lie down on the floor and I gently placed a pillow on her. After a pause, she asked what she was supposed to do next. I stated that it was her choice in how she wanted to respond. She sat up and handed the pillow to me. I repeated the same action of covering her with it. We went back and forth in this fashion a few times until she grabbed the pillow and sat on it with increasing pressure and directness. Calling upon her emotional strength of perseverance (Smith, 2006), she placed change into action through her body movement. This resulted in greater confidence and self-efficacy in the moment, which ultimately served to reinforce this positive change. Her kinesthetic narrative had changed and she diversified her movement qualities to support this change.

In describing non-verbal narratives as action stories, Serlin (2007) stated how a "healing movement pattern will have a clear beginning, middle, and end" (p. 326), which unfolds organically on the basis of wisdom of the body. Individuals are empowered to create new meaning through engaging in a spontaneous and creative movement dialogue that is informed by diverse bodily experiences (Ylönen & Cantell, 2009). In the preceding example, the movement text shifted. The individual bridged her inner sensation of feeling suffocated to an outer form of sitting on the pillow. The action itself was solution oriented and contains meaning. The individual discovered a new way of being and relating to others through movement that brought clarity to sensations, images, thoughts, feelings, and intentions (Serlin, 2007). The dance/movement therapist can further elicit meaning making from action through reflecting the movement, noticing what the movement shift feels like in their own body and verbally processing with individuals the meaning that they ascribe to the movement, such that meaning is not imposed by others. Serlin (2007) described this process of making meaning out of movement as kinesthetic imagining, which emerges out of sensations of muscular movement giving rise to "associated feelings, thoughts, and meanings which show up as embodied images" (p. 328) that ultimately create a dance story.

Conclusion

We are continuously experiencing and relating to the world around us first and foremost through our sensorimotor abilities. Our bodies house an infinite number of movement possibilities to support the ongoing process of actualizing our full potential in all domains of our lives. Dance/movement therapists participate in a co-creative movement process with individuals to facilitate increasing awareness of their movement strengths and preferences from which new ways of moving and being are explored. As new possibilities and perspectives emerge through the creative process of dance, individuals' movement repertoires expand, providing a wealth of options for how to cope with their environment as they relate to self and others. Chace's four core concepts of the therapeutic movement relationship, body action, symbolism, and rhythmic group activity permeate the work of dance/movement therapists and provide mechanisms for an integrative, synergistic relationship between DMT and strengths-based counseling.

References

American Dance Therapy Association (ADTA). (2016). *About dance/movement therapy.* Retrieved May 20, 2016 from www.adta.org/About_DMT/

Amighi, J.K., Loman, S., Lewis, P., & Sossin, K.M. (1999). *The meaning of movement: Developmental and clinical perspectives of the Kestenberg Movement Profile.* New York, NY: Routledge.

Baniel, A. (2012). *Kids beyond limits: Breakthrough results for children with autism, Asperger's, brain damage, ADHD, and undiagnosed developmental delays.* New York, NY: Penguin Books.

Bartenieff, I., & Lewis, D. (1980). *Body movement: Coping with the environment*. New York, NY: Gordon and Breach.

Brown, C. (2009). Moving into action: A case study of dance/movement therapy with the dually diagnosed in a methadone treatment program. In S.L. Brook (Ed.), *The use of creative therapies with chemical dependency issues* (pp. 187–203). Springfield, IL: Charles C. Thomas.

Chaiklin, S., & Schmais, C. (1993). The Chace approach to dance therapy. In S. Sandel, S. Chaiklin, & A. Lohn (Eds.), *Foundations of dance/movement therapy: The life and work of Marian Chace* (pp. 20–43). Columbia, MD: Marian Chace Memorial Fund of the American Dance Therapy Association.

Crockett, S.A., & Prosek, E. (2013, October). Promoting cognitive, emotional, and spiritual client change: The infusion of solution-focused counseling and ritual therapy. *Counseling and Values, 58*, 237–253. doi:10.1002/j.2161–007X.2013.00036.x

Dillenbeck, M., & Hammond-Meiers, J.A. (2009). Death and dying: Implications for dance/movement therapy. *American Journal of Dance Therapy, 31*, 95–121. doi:10.1007/s10465–009–9074–2

Fischman, D. (2009). Therapeutic relationships and kinesthetic empathy. In S. Chaiklin, & H. Wengrower (Eds.), *The art and science of dance/movement therapy: Life is dance* (pp. 13–32). New York, NY: Routledge.

Laban, R. (1980). *The mastery of movement* (L. Ullmann, 4th rev. & enl. ed.). Plymouth, UK: Northcote House. (Reprinted from *The mastery of movement on the stage*, by R. Laban, 1950, London, UK: MacDonald & Evans.)

Lama Zopa Rinpoche. (2001). *The Upanishads. Teachings from the Vajrasattva Retreat*. Lincoln, MA: Lama Yeshe Wisdom Archive.

Levy, F.J. (1992). *Dance movement therapy: A healing art* (rev. ed.). Reston, VA: American Alliance for Health, Physical Education, Recreation and Dance.

Miller, W.R., & Rollnick, S. (2013). *Motivational interviewing: Helping people for change* (3rd ed.). New York, NY: Guilford Press.

Padesky, C.A., & Mooney, K.A. (2012). Strengths-based cognitive-behavioral therapy: A four-step model to build resistance. *Clinical Psychology and Psychotherapy, 19*, 283–290. doi:10.1002/cpp.1795

Prochaska, J.O., DiClemente, C.C., & Norcross, J.C. (1992). In search of how people change: Applications to addictive behaviors. *American Psychologist, 47*, 1102–1114.

Rapp, C.A., & Goscha, R.J. (2012). *The strengths model: A recovery-oriented approach to mental health services* (3rd ed.). New York, NY: Oxford University Press.

Sandel, S.L. (1993). The process of empathic reflection in dance therapy. In S. Sandel, S. Chaiklin, & A. Lohn (Eds.), *Foundations of dance/movement therapy: The life and work of Marian Chace* (pp. 20–43). Columbia, MD: Marian Chace Memorial Fund of the American Dance Therapy Association.

Sandel, S.L., Chaiklin, S., & Lohn, A. (Eds.). (1993). *Foundations of dance/movement therapy: The life and work of Marian Chace*. Columbia, MD: Marian Chace Memorial Fund of the American Dance Therapy Association.

Schmais, C. (1985). Healing processes in group dance therapy. *American Journal of Dance Therapy, 8*, 17–36. doi:10.1007/BF02251439

Schmais, C. (2004). *The journey of a dance therapy teacher: Capturing the essence of Chace*. Columbia, MD: Marian Chace Foundation of the American Dance Therapy Association.

Serlin, I.A. (2007). Action stories. In S. Krippner, M. Bova, & L. Gray (Eds.), *Healing stories: The use of narrative in counseling and psychotherapy* (pp. 325–336). San Juan, Puerto Rico: Puente Publications.

Shelley, S. (1993). Marian Chace: Her later years. In S. Sandel, S. Chaiklin, & A. Lohn (Eds.), *Foundations of dance/movement therapy: The life and work of Marian Chace* (pp. 20–43). Columbia, MD: Marian Chace Memorial Fund of the American Dance Therapy Association.

Siegel, D.J. (2012). *The developing mind: How relationships and the brain interact to shape who we are* (2nd ed.). New York, NY: Guilford Press.

Smith, E.J. (2006). The strengths-based counseling model. *The Counseling Psychologist, 34*, 13–79. doi:10.1177/0011000005277018

Sundlie, M. (2009). Social work counseling using the Medicine Wheel. *Rural Social Work and Community Practice, 14*(2), 18–28.

Tortora, S. (2006). *The dancing dialogue: Using the communicative power of movement with young children*. Baltimore, MD: Paul H. Brookes.

Wengrower, H. (2009). The creative–artistic process in dance/movement therapy. In S. Chaiklin, & H. Wengrower (Eds.), *The art and science of dance/movement therapy: Life is dance* (pp. 13–32). New York, NY: Routledge.

White, V.E. (2002). Developing counseling objectives and empowering clients: A strength-based intervention. *Journal of Mental Health Counseling, 24,* 270–279.

Wilkinson, R.A., & Chilton, G. (2013). Positive art therapy: Linking positive psychology to art therapy theory, practice, and research. *Art Therapy: Journal of the American Art Therapy Association, 30,* 4–11.

Ylönen, M.E., & Cantell, M.H. (2009). Kinaesthetic narratives: Interpretations for children's dance movement therapy process. *Body, Movement and Dance in Psychotherapy: An International Journal for Theory, Research, and Practice, 4*(3), 215–230. doi:10.1080/17432970903259683

Young, J.L. (2015, October 22–25). *The therapeutic movement relationship in dance/movement therapy: A phenomenological study.* Paper presented at the American Dance Therapy Association 50th Annual Conference, San Diego, CA.

13

Equine-Assisted Psychotherapy

Applying Strengths-Based Solutions in an Arena for Change

Sandra L. Kakacek

> The horse is a mirror to your soul. Sometimes you might not like what you see. Sometimes you will.
>
> Buck Brannaman (reputed horse whisperer)

Solution-focused brief therapy (SFBT) is a primary strengths-based therapy, begun by social worker and family therapist Steve de Shazer and his partner, social worker Insoo Kim Berg, from the Milwaukee Brief Family Therapy Center. Solutions are created from the conversations between therapist and client, wherein the clinician asks the client for exceptions to his or her presenting issue- or problem-saturated stories and through a number of other techniques. The focus and purpose of the model is to seek change and is an empowering theoretical perspective that encompasses ascertaining helpful resources that clients have implemented from their working knowledge of life issues. SFBT is different from other models, such as problem-based models, in one major aspect: The goal is to help the client identify what has worked in the past, not by viewing the issue or problem from how it may have evolved, but rather by seeking exceptions to when the issue was not present. SFBT focuses on the present and future. What is also an important consideration of this strengths-based model is that it is evidence-based, thus making it a prime model accepted for treatments and insurance reimbursement (Franklin, Trepper, McCollum, & Gingerich, 2011).

Problem-based models, such as those espoused by the Mental Research Institute in the 1960s and 70s, formulated brief therapy to provide short-term work with clients by examining their language, purposes of behaviors and actions, and remediating the problems. The SFBT model evolved from many of the tenets of problem-based therapy, except with a positive view. De Shazer's (1985) principal premise of "Problem talk creates problems. Solution talk creates solutions" guides the model. For example, consider a client who is riddled with anxiety about attempting to write a paper for school. SFBT would help the client examine how, when, or where the anxiety evolved and possibly create a paradoxical intervention to continue the worrying for a specific time, with the solution being the client realization of how much time was consumed. This strengths-based model would ascertain what the client does when not worrying, when success occurred prior, and how the worry may be useful. One of the core beliefs is that the negativity serves the client in a positive manner. Helping the client reframe provides strengths the client can add to their repertoire for solutions. For example, consider the client who worries. Asking the client how the worry is helpful generally initiates a response of,

"It is not!" Asking the client to consider when it was useful to worry about getting papers done often results in responses such as, "When the worry kept nagging at me, I finally got it finished."

SFBT credence is that the client is the expert about his or her life, thus the therapist's primary function is to aid the client by providing a framework that is embedded with positive co-constructive solutions. The steps that provide the formulation are designed to use language that is positive. The techniques specifically focus on (a) assessing prior solutions, (b) the here and now and future-centered rather than past-centered, (c) embedding and adding compliments to clients' efforts, (d) clients using more of what has been successful, and (e) helping co-create goals that are linguistically positive (de Shazer, 1985). This focus is intended to help clients think about their internal resources as solutions.

Questions such as, "When was the most recent time when this (goal/desired outcome) happened?" The imperative use of language continues with questions such as, "What is a small sign of change?" as well as asking scaling questions such as, "From 1 to 10, where is the issue/problem now and where would you like it to be?" SFBT also creates and embeds compliments with clients such as, "How did you get through that so well?" Perhaps the most useful technique is called the *miracle question*. The inquiry has a "purpose to shift the conversation quickly and easily into the future when the problems [that brought the client to therapy] are gone" (de Shazer, 2000). Questioning "what needs to be different" seeks to help the client develop a goal. Strengths-based positive words are aimed at the overall creation of solutions as possibilities. Metaphorical tools and attending to how the client uses language and helping them replace negative with positive creates change. For example, the metaphor of the glass being half full is a much more powerful embedding linguistic tool for change than the glass being half empty. Or consider "remembering something" rather than "don't forget," or the opposite of fear/worry is calmness and confidence. The powerful use of positive language is key to the strengths-based solutions in a relatively new treatment modality.

Equine-Assisted Psychotherapy

Equine-assisted psychotherapy (EAP) is designed to be effective in a brief therapy model. The application of metaphorical properties includes the equine's behaviors as well as the client's verbal and nonverbal behaviors. Strengths-based models, such as SFBT, accomplish the goal to help clients co-create solutions.

SFBT for EAP provides the structure necessary for the therapist with the tools to assess the client's strengths. Metaphorical questions related to the client's interactions in relation to the equine behaviors assist the client in discovering their perceptions of what occurs with the equine. For example, a client enters the arena and is asked to approach an equine. The equine backs up as the client approaches. Asking the client what is happening with the equine, the responses will be directly related to the client's internal perceptions. "He backed up because he does not like me" or "I think he wants me to come closer," for example.

EAP, with a strengths-based model, provides a backdrop that is designed to be interactive and experiential and begins with the smells and sounds of a barn. Coupled with this are large animals. Equines are very unique due to their size and power. Even though they are big, people of all ages are often drawn to them. Equines are herd animals of prey, therefore they are reactive to the sounds, views, and emotions around them.

This characteristic of equines provides the opportunity for mirroring feelings of clients. For example, if a client is anxious and wringing their hands, the equine may be moving and darting in the field or standing still with eyes and head moving side-to-side. Equines react to people in the here and now. The saying "Don't let the equine know you are afraid because they will be also" accurately describes the relationship equines can have with humans. The opposite can also be equally powerful.

Each session is designed to provide an experiential, hands-on activity that helps the client create solutions. Tasks of intermingling with equines are noted by the counselor. It is the meaning or interpretations that clients give to the interactions with the equines that provide information to the counselor to help clients change behavior. Using a strengths-based approach grounded in brief therapy and solution focus (Berg & de Shazer, 1993), EAP provides the venue for change.

This chapter discusses a brief review of the literature regarding the evolution and effectiveness of EAP. The types of clients benefitting from this SFBT strengths-based approach will be examined. The organization of a treatment plan will be presented that encompasses (a) the effectiveness of EAP, (b) clients benefiting from EAP, (c) designing the semi-structured activities for the sessions, and (d) four key properties of change. The chapter reviews four clinical cases: a child with severe anxiety, an at-risk oppositional defiant youth, an adult with Asperger syndrome, and a couple with a pending divorce and depression. Additionally, the chapter concludes with the recommendations and challenges for practioners.

Evolution of EAP

The foundation of EAP is rooted in the past during eras whereby animals, such as dogs, cats, birds, and so forth, were utilized as "pets" and noted to create changes in people's emotions in a positive manner. Egyptians, Greeks, Romans, and others utilized animals therapeutically (Pitts, 2005; Kruger, Trachtenberg, & Serpell, 2004). According to Parshall (2003), the earliest known anecdotal case utilizing animals for treatment of mental health disorders was in England in 1699. Noted specifically were interactions with cats, dogs, even rats, which brought about a relief of depressive symptoms (Parshall, 2003).

Another key case for animal-assisted therapy (AAT) was noted in the late 1940s with returning World War II veterans. Specifically, dogs were used to help returning soldiers ameliorate emotions for what we would now call post-traumatic stress disorder (Parshall, 2003). The next important case representation of using animals to assist in mental health was noted by Boris Levinson, a clinical psychologist, who in 1961 shared a case from his practice. At an American Psychological Association conference in New York, Levinson described the facts of a session in 1953 that was a complete accident of fortune. The doctor was working with an autistic child who was, at the time, nonverbal. Inexplicably, the doctor's dog pushed the therapy office door open and walked up to the child, who began to became animated and spoke for the first time (Morrison, 2007; Parshall, 2003). This incident led to the beginning of research studies, conducted by Levinson of how animals, specifically dogs, can be used as therapeutic tools (Levinson & Mallon, 1997). Levinson's research that Freud had also used his dog in therapy was reportedly discussed as well.

Following Levinson's work, the North American Handicapped Riding Association (NAHRA) was established in 1969 with the purpose of providing services for the physically and/or mentally disabled by implementing a team approach called *hippotherapy* (NAHRA, n.d.). NAHRA is now known as the Professional Association of Therapeutic Horsemanship International (PATH Intl.). The intended outcome of the therapy is to provide multiple remediation such as speech and language, occupational, and physical therapy to increase neurological functioning. The child is placed atop an equine and there are two assistants who walk along, one on each side. Another person leads the equine. The primary purposes of hippotherapy are to provide growth and development for neuro-muscular difficulties and/or increase receptive and expressive language skills. Research has begun to note that not only do children gain muscle control and communication skills, but they also exhibit improved self-esteem (De Guitis, 2003; Glasow, 2006).

Equine-Facilitated Therapy (EFT) grew out of the hippotherapy field. EFT was designed to help children with learning challenges acquire riding skills with support. Research (Ewing, MacDonald, Taylor, & Bowers, 2007) also reports increased self-esteem and improved academic skills. The results of actually having one's body engaged in a sensory motor activity, for example, helps realign organizational skills. The movement of riding literally moves one's body side to side and the vestibular movement becomes a pathway for helping riders concentrate and focus. Academically, the result is increased attention.

Vaulting is another faction that was developed by NAHRA. Vaulting is described as conducting gymnastics off the back of an equine. Studies of vaulting have also noted increased self-awareness and self-esteem in clients (Vidrine, Owen-Smith, & Faulkner, 2002). Eventually, the use of equines as a means of support and increased mental health led to the evolution of formalized therapy with the use of equines, EAP, in 1999 (Frewin & Gardiner, 2005; Taylor, 2002).

The term equine-assisted psychotherapy (EAP) was coined by Greg Kersten, founder of the first organized certification group, named Equine-Assisted Growth and Learning Association (EAGALA) in the late 1990s. Kersten grew up on a farm with many equines and noted, after the loss of his father, that the equines on his farm became important to him as emotional support. Kersten reportedly began to spend more time with equines and less with people. He began to notice the equines' nonverbal interactions in the herd. The use of equines without riding was a unique premise which filled Kersten with awe. He began to study their communicative behaviors. Specifically, Kersten noted that the equines seemed to detect and respond to emotions. He stated that the time he spent with the equines was emotionally healing as well as providing a glimpse into the empowerment of the animals (Kersten & Thomas, 1999).

The use of equines for emotional growth is noteworthy as equines are predisposed to either flight or fight within the herd. One of the more therapeutic behaviors of equines includes mirroring the experiences of humans (McCormick & McCormick, 1997). For example, if a client is angry, the equine will often take off running. If the client is sad, the equine is often observed hanging its head. These interactions help create a therapeutic moment for the client. The therapist observes and can ask, "What do you think is happening that the equine's head is lower?" Kersten utilized his learning about the therapeutic encounters between equine and human while working with incarcerated individuals. He introduced a program using equines within a judicial system. Inmates interacted by grooming and even conducting some organized activities, but did not ride. Again, the interactions were therapeutic.

Years later, Kersten partnered with social worker Lynn Thomas, and the EAGALA came to fruition in 1999. The organization certifies both clinicians and equine specialists by providing training in EAP and equine-assisted learning. To date, Kersten has started another certification, Observation and Knowledge (OK). The effectiveness of EAP has grown and there are numerous people implementing programs for all areas of mental health disorders (Kakacek, 2010a, 2010b, 2014; Kruger & Serpell, 2006; Trotter, 2006).

Effectiveness of EAP

EAP, though relatively new as a legitimized treatment modality, continues to grow as a new therapeutic strengths-based treatment. Studies have been generated by mental health professionals with a variety of applications. Results indicate positive changes in the lessening of mental health symptomology and disorders (Kakacek, 2009; Kruger & Serpell, 2006; Holmes, Goodwin, Redhead, & Goymour, 2012; Trotter, 2006). Decreased depression, increased focus, decreased anxiety, and increase of positive self-esteem are a few of the results from EAP.

Clients Benefitting from EAP

The variety of clients benefitting from EAP traverses all diversity areas (age, gender, sexual orientation, religion, education, disability, and socioeconomic status). The youngest client on record has been documented at three years old, and the oldest in their 80s. The preponderance of EAP has no boundaries in terms of the presenting issues of various clients (Holmes et al., 2012; Kakacek, 2009; Kruger & Serpell, 2006; Trotter, 2006).

The majority of mental health issues also can gain from this treatment. Eating disorders, depression, anxiety, body dysphasia, post-traumatic stress disorder, sexual abuse, physical abuse, substance abuse, Asperger syndrome, and so forth are some of the most common mental health issues treated using equines therapeutically. Additionally, transitional issues, divorces, growth and development, and team building benefit as well. The overall benefit for clients is based on their goals and desired outcomes (Holmes et al., 2012; Kakacek, 2009; Kruger & Serpell, 2006; Trotter, 2006). The equine is certainly a partner in the change process, as is the therapist who attends to clients' needs while also listening to their language and observing the behaviors of the equine.

Process of Change

The overall theoretical presence in EAP is strengths-based. SFBT is used by this author. The process of change contains (1) the elements of organizing a session, which includes a unique environmental setting and choosing an equine; (2) assessing the client's physical and emotional needs for working with equines; (3) designing the semi-structured activities; and (4) implementing the four key properties of change (Kakacek & Ottens, 2008, 2010a, 2010b, 2014).

Organizing the Session

Sessions begin with a collaborative decision as to whether to begin inside the indoor arena or outside paddock or arena. The decision is dependent on goals and desired outcomes of the client. A brief question of asking "What brought you here today?" begins the strengths-based solution model. During an initial session, the formalities of opening a session are replete with observational data for the therapist, as the client(s) is given a tour of the facility inside the arena and then to the stalls inside and/or equines outside. A brief introduction of the equines is made. Any equine history, however, is omitted at this time. Due to the experiential nature of EAP, it is key that clients make their own discoveries or label the equines as deemed important to the client. For example, working with incarcerated juveniles, the group is very quick to state who is, in their perception, the "toughest equine or leader." Experiential work is paramount for significant metaphorical change to occur. For example, one client chose an equine that he identified as "sad" and discussed thinking the equine liked him because they might be alike. He further identified the sadness asking if the equine had been "beaten." This resulted in his revealing the same in his life. Then the equine history was disclosed. In this example, the equine had been rescued by animal rights activists and had a history of being whipped by its previous handlers. In the client's view, the identification with an equine with a shared history began the process of change, as resiliency became a theme.

During EAP, brief discussions often ensue with clients revolving around choosing an equine(s) to work with for the session. Equines available are those that have relationships with humans and each other. Like humans, equines exhibit different behaviors based on their needs. For example, if one day a particular equine appears to be more in need of physical space due to behaviors such as "kicking out," that equine is not among those able to be used that day. Interestingly, the discussion of isolation often comes about when a client chooses an equine that, for all purposes, is "off-limits" for various reasons. Separation issues may indeed become the entire session, as a client may process the metaphorical aspect of the equine being apart as they describe their own feelings.

Assessing Physical and Emotional Needs

When considering the issue of physical safety, both the equine and the client need to be taken into account. As a therapist with equine experience, physical safety when working with equines is paramount at the beginning of a session. Clients are asked what part of the equine they might need to be aware of for safety. The word *safety* is used as a strengths-based term rather than negative wording such as "watch out for or get hurt." The discussions are often full of revealing information as to how the client perceives their own environment for safety. The demonstration also peruses the client's nonverbal stance with the equine. Do they have boundaries? Do they watch their feet? Are they aware of the equines' nonverbals? Likewise, the client's behaviors are noteworthy in that the equine must be respected as well. Following a brief discussion and demonstration with the equine, therapy continues.

Assessing the client's emotional needs revolves around talking about what brought the client to therapy as well as exploring their goals. Checking the nonverbals with the equine also leads to assessing the client's emotional barometer. The client's proximity to the equine and the touch, as well as the equine's response, are full of quiet, subtle nonverbal messages from both. Using an SFBT model, the counselor can talk about what the client's internal resources have been for prior problem resolution. This interaction often paves the way for the semi-structured activity to take place. For example, a client, Jane, once shared wanting to feel more confident in developing friendships in high school. She specifically and repeatedly talked about how "scary" walking in the hallways was because she was fearful people would not speak to her. We talked about times when this was not the case, and she was able to have the confident feeling she desired. This all occurred while she was confidently petting an equine, who was looking at her and not moving.

Semi-Structured Activities

Semi-structured activities in EAP are uniquely designed to utilize their clients' strengths to achieve their goals. The activities can be as simple as watching a herd or an equine or brushing. Activities can include props such as poles, cones, or ropes and can occur inside or outside the arena. The aforementioned client, Jane, was working with an older mare who was generally quiet, although sometimes her arthritis made it difficult for her to move (and the client did not know this fact). The client was instructed to take the props into the arena and construct a path similar to a hallway in school. Poles were carefully placed and a bend was made in the path. Jane was then instructed to move the mare through the path. The client cautiously took the rope and began to walk. Quite predictably, the mare started to walk and when she came to the bend, she stopped. At this point, the client began to shed tears. By asking "What do you think the mare needs most right now? What works for you?" the client opened up and was able to search for prior times of success in school. Processing positive language, Jane was able to extrapolate what she tells herself to be successful. Jane began to give the mare positives, "You can do this! You are fine!" and the mare walked around the bend.

Four Key Properties of Change

Metaphorical constructs are the primary mechanism utilized for change (Kersten & Thomas, 1999; Irwin & Weber, 2001; Lyddon, Clay, & Sparks, 2001; Karol, 2007; Kakacek 2009, 2010a, 2010b, 2014; Kakacek & Ottens, 2008). Four prime target areas in EAP facilitate metaphor: (a) using metaphors to explain an equine's behavior ("What is the equine running away from?"), (b) analogous language to discuss props or tools ("What does the halter mean to the equine and what is your halter in life?"), (c) clients relating life lessons learned ("What does it mean that you walked to get the equine over the obstacle?"), and (d) clients inferring lessons learned in coping ("When we work through our obstacles, we succeed."; Kakacek & Ottens, 2008, p. 19).

Equine Behaviors

Metaphors used to discuss the equine's behaviors can lead to a rich exchange between the client and therapist. Referencing the client in the path and asking what happened with the equine or simply asking what is going on with the mare, opened the discussion with the aforementioned client to talk about the mare being afraid and shy. Next, asking "Is that how it is for you?" developed a commonality of the two and bridged an intervention solution for the client.

Analogous Language

The props used in equine-assisted therapy can also lead to solution tools. The client, when queried about the bend in the path, reported that was where her locker was located at school (the turn in the hallway) and where the fear grew. Coupled with the notion of a locker was the fear of the mare to move as well. Asking "What is the bend to the mare and what is your bend?" resulted in the client sharing about her locker and relating to the fears of the equine as well. The use of isomorphisms was a tool to help the client use the equine as a "mirror" of her emotions.

Additionally, the simple haltering of the equine and attaching a rope can lead to a full session in the experiential components. For example, the previously discussed client, Jane, put the halter on in such a way that worked to attach a rope and also was not "the correct way." The focus in EAP is not helping the client accomplish a task; rather it is the client experiencing their own success. The strengths-based model focuses on the client's perceptions and the therapist continually reframes and compliments the client in even the smallest of tasks. This basic component of EAP also helps the client "think out of the box," as there are no wrong or right ways to complete tasks. Rather it is about the process. Helping the client talk about how they decided where to put the halter on the equine is data for understanding how the client makes decisions. For example, this client placed the halter on "backward" and was frustrated because the client felt it was "wrong." This led to the client talking more about other times she felt she had done something wrong and how the school anxiety had manifested.

Relating Life Lessons

Through her time with the mare, Jane was able to explore feelings of inadequacy in attempting to make friends in the school. She related the haltering to the struggle to walk in the hallways and make eye contact with peers. The client then practiced walking the mare through her "hallway" in the arena. This occurred while the client told the mare, "It is okay and you are safe. Nothing is scary here."

Coping Lessons

The client was able to leave the session with a new goal of remembering how she was able to de-escalate the equine's "anxiety" by being positive. Thus, Jane worked on transferring the practice skill to the actual school hallway. The role playing, albeit isomorphic, was paramount for change. She reported in a subsequent session to being able to walk calmly and look at one peer. As she continued to practice the skills learned in the arena, new coping skills emerged and were validated.

Case One: Sue

The client, an eight-year-old, presented with anxiety and was described by her parents as having difficulty with excessive worrying. The worries had been present for about four years and impacted her daily functioning. The triggers to her anxieties were unknown. The session was outside with two miniature equines or "minis," both of which were mares. One mare was dark brown and one was white in color. Interestingly, the minis, like the client and accompanying parent, were mother and daughter. This became an important fact when processing at the end of the session.

The session began with Sue choosing to work with the dark mini, Grace. The client chose her by stating, "She seems lonely and a little nervous," (the mare was mirroring the client). I asked, "Is that like you today?" The client responded, nodding *yes*, and then in a hushed tone shared about issues at school with a friend. She indicated that she worried about the friendship and not knowing how to communicate that with the friend. I asked, "On a scale from 1 to 10, where is your worry?" Using scaling to assess, she responded, "Eight." Grace had walked up to the client, which the client attributed to Grace liking her and feeling safe, even though she was afraid. I asked the client if she thought Grace needed some help. She responded with a resounding "Yes!"

Next, I asked her to use the props nearby to build something that might represent Grace's fears. The client carefully took two poles and made a jump with cones at the ends. There were two mud puddles, and the client cautiously built the obstacle up to the puddles. I asked her to move Grace over, around, or under the obstacles. The goal was to help her uncover her own way to get "over" fear or worry. She carefully put a halter on Grace; although it was done incorrectly, that does not matter in EAP. It is the process of problem solving that adds to the richness of the experience and keeping with a strengths-based model. While figuring out the halter, the client asked her mother once to help, and the mother told the client she was "fine."

After the halter was on, the client attached a lead rope and with encouraging words to Grace, began to move her toward the obstacle. Meanwhile, Grace's daughter, Snowy, began to follow the client and Grace. I asked the client what Snowy was doing and the client responded, "Oh, she wants to have help, too, but she has to wait and be patient. I can only help Grace now." The pair approached the obstacle, and the client, still encouraging verbally, also began to nonverbally pat Grace as they walked. The client chose to have Grace walk over the obstacle. In doing so, Grace's back legs touched the pole while going over it. The client was very verbal telling Grace she had to do it (walking over the obstacle) until she did it "just right." The walking continued for another ten minutes with Grace still knocking her back legs on the pole. During this time, Snowy had walked away from the obstacles.

I reflected that doing this perfectly was important to the client. The client nodded "*Yes*," quite emphatically. Using isomorphism I asked, "What do you think Grace thinks?" The client replied, "That she needs to keep working and will get it right." Establishing a goal for the session I asked, "What else might she need to accomplish the goal?" The client replied, "I just have to tell her she is doing good all the way." The client's internal needs were revealed. Thus, the client increased positive comments and the mare finally did walk over the pole without touching it. I asked, "Are you finished with the goal?" The client replied, "Grace is, but maybe Snowy should do it, too." Snowy was not haltered and had no lead rope, and amazingly just walked up and stepped over. Immediately afterward, Grace walked up to the client's mother and just stood beside her.

Processing began with inquiring what the client thought the rope and halter meant to Grace. She replied it was a way to "help and guide her." Extrapolating the experience with the client, I asked, "What guides you?" The client stated that her parent was her guide. More processing followed and then the discussion turned to the obstacles:

Therapist: *Tell me about the obstacle you built. What do the poles mean?*
Client: *A way for Grace to get over her fear of new things.*
Therapist: *I noticed you were telling her she was doing good and touching her when you were walking her. You were also smiling. What do you do to get over new things?* [Exception to the rule.]
Client: *I tell myself I will be okay. Mother tells me too. Mostly I just try, but get really scared.*
Therapist: *I wonder what you were thinking to do with Grace to help her.*
Client: *That she could do it and needed to do it without thinking too much.*
Therapist: *Did it work for her?*
Client: *Yes, but only after many times trying.*
Therapist: *And you helped her try every time. You believed in her.* [Complimenting the client.]
Client: *Yes, but she needed to do it right.*
Therapist: *So you have a part, too, that keeps trying. And does that lessen your fears?*
Client: *Yes! Like Grace.*
Therapist: *If you were to give Grace a secret message to remember it is "ok to try," what would you tell her?* [Metaphor to explain equine behavior.]
Client: *It's ok to try and sometimes bumping a little is ok.*
Therapist: *I am wondering what would happen with the same message if you were able to tell yourself that inside, right now.*
Client: *Ok. I can do that.*
Therapist: *Tell yourself that as you go over the poles.*

The session concluded with the client working with Snowy and Grace together. The client laughed and even jumped the puddles with the mini equines. To remind her of her strengths, I cut off a little of Grace's tail for the client to keep in her pocket when she felt she needed to be brave. In the following sessions we continued to work on strengthening her confidence and self-esteem. The client worked with bigger equines, cleaned hoofs, and brushed the equines all over their bodies. She was able to take control, literally, of a "bossy" male (gelding) pony. This was in response to the issue with the friend that she initially presented. Upon learning that Grace was the mother, the client's parent also walked away with new information to be helpful in the home environment. There was a renewed effort to focus more on what the client could do. We concluded the session with a scaling question and the fear and worry had dropped to a "Four." We also reframed the words *fear* and *worry* to "can do it." Focusing on strengths that the client can accomplish using equines as therapeutic tools and enriching the experiences with rich metaphoric extrapolations is inherent in SFBT.

Case Two: Jim

EAP is an excellent model for at-risk adolescents. For eight years I had the pleasure of working with groups of incarcerated youth on a weekly basis. The power of the interactions and the use of strengths-based counseling has been rewarding. A study conducted early in the treatment indicated that recidivism rates were lower when at-risk youth participated using the equines (Kakacek, 2009).

The mere size of the equines and the power displayed has always impacted the youth by engaging their respect and cooperation with the animals. Sessions were something the group looked forward to attending. The creation of the obstacles weekly fit dynamics and needs that the staff from the center described weekly as well. All the boys that attended the EAP sessions exhibited some changes in behaviors. As with all counseling and readiness for change, some clients exhibit change more than others. One youth, in particular, was able to develop keen insight about himself and his needs to strengthen his future.

The group had been attending for ten sessions. One youth was getting ready to be discharged home and thus leave the group. These times were always emotional for the boys as they had come to identify with an equine with which they attributed similarities. The youth described in this final session came to the group with a history of involvement with gangs and drugs. During Jim's last session, rather than have the boys create their obstacles, I directed them to build a community by making a box on the ground with poles. At the same time, as typical in sessions, the equines, representative of substance abusers, are free to engage with the youth. The boys indicated they were ready to begin and they were instructed to stay within their community boundary. The community now held distractions and danger for the equines. They were also told that the four equines needed to "stay clean and avoid entering the community." Slowly, buckets of grain and a few piles of hay were added to the "community." Jim took control of the exercise and helped direct his group members to work at not letting the equines get "high" or "steal food." He, in particular, was speaking in a gentle quiet voice to the equines to "follow the rules" [strengths-based]. Eventually he indicated that each member should do their part and toss the food out of the community. "We have to keep this clean now. We have worked hard," he said [inferring lessons learned].

Processing with Jim after the session, I asked what the grain and hay represented to him. Much as he said during the exercise, he indicated that those items represented drugs to him. I then queried, "What part of this exercise will be useful to you when you exit?" (A small embedded command that, indeed, it would be useful as well as strengths-based future.) Jim said he realized how hard his mother tried to help him (with the same gentleness) and that he needed to stay away from peers who were part of the problems and move toward positive role models. Then we discussed his strengths:

Therapist:	What will you take away from equine therapy?
Client:	That I can make good decisions and I can stay in school. I want to go to college. [Extrapolating changes with equines for own life.]
Therapist:	Suppose tomorrow morning you wake up and life is just the way you want. What will you be saying, doing, and feeling? [Miracle question.]

> Client: *That I am smart, staying in school, and feeling proud that I know how to deal with feelings now.*

The last time I heard about this youth, he was in school and working hard to accomplish his goals. The client reported the following:

> If people are having problems in their lives, they should go to equine therapy to get in touch with their inner selves and to relieve stress. Once they leave there, they'll have smiles on their faces. Most dudes like to be tough, but on the inside, an equine opens up one's weakness and brings out the softness.

Case Three: Bob

An adult with Asperger syndrome, age 62, came to EAP to learn how to improve relationships with people in general. The client reported he was no longer in a relationship and wanted to figure out how his previous diagnosis of Asperger syndrome could be managed. The first day, Bob chose to work with a short stout equine called a Haflinger. The client indicated having owned equines in the past and riding horses.

The client hesitantly and methodically haltered the equine, touching the gelding only when absolutely necessary. Bob attached the rope to the halter and began to walk with the equine from one paddock to another. While walking, we discussed the parts of an equine to be aware for safety. The client also began to talk about how he believed Asperger syndrome is displayed in people by noticing that they (those diagnosed with Asperger syndrome) "just think differently." Bob went on to explain that he did not conceptually understand terms such as love or friendship. The client also spoke about how co-workers would say "hello," and Bob did not understand what the client was to do in such cases.

The client appeared frustrated verbally and was not aware of the equine's behavior at this time. The equine moved into the client's space, bumping into him. Bob jumped back and said, "I get it! I need to be aware of people in my space and say something! Like hello! Did you make the equine do that to me? This is really amazing!" [Using metaphors to explain horse behavior and relating life's lessons learned.]

The process continued and we discussed how he could begin to notice others and respond. This was a tremendous learning experience for the client. The equine, according to the client, helped him understand that people, like the equine, expected an interaction and would be "pushy" if it was not reciprocal [metaphor to explain equine behavior]. This event began the growth and development for the client as a metaphor for change. He was eager to use the equine again and eventually developed a relationship with the animal. One day, while the client was processing his "feelings," he began to laugh and reached out to pet the equine. This seemingly simple gesture and acknowledgement of laughter led the client to self-discoveries of a variety of emotions. [Client infers lessons learned.] Then I asked a miracle question: "I am wondering if after a good sleep tonight, you wake up in the morning and something is new and the frustration is replaced with new thinking, what might those thoughts be?" Bob replied, laughing, "That I can know what laughter is and how to know a little more about how to be with people, like I did Buddy [the equine]!" [Client inferring lessons learned and future positive goal.]

Case Four: Mike

Counseling couples is always a delightful, intriguing experience for me. The dynamics are so rich, and I enjoy the prospect of helping client couples uncover their strengths. Sometimes didactic or office visits are not as impactful or strengths-based. Thus, I choose to use the environment of a field full of equines to help clients search for their strengths.

This was particularly true for a client who was recently separated from his partner. The client was struggling with depressive symptoms and wanted to be able to communicate with his partner in an effective manner. The prior session in the traditional office setting did not yield a positive outcome, as the symptoms continued and no change was noted by the client.

Mike came to the session at the stable and indicated no equine experience except one whereby he took a ride on an equine and had difficulty stopping or controlling the animal. Already, I had a metaphor about how the client had seemingly "no control" with the partner that had left. I chose not to dialogue about the metaphor, as I wanted the session to flow without interruptions, and quite frankly, with a view of equines grazing in a field, I knew more interactions would be plentiful.

Mike and I walked into the field. I asked him what he needed the most today and he replied, "To figure out how to communicate better with my partner." As we walked into the field with four mares, three fillies, a pony gelding, and a very old gelding who stood away from all the other equines, I instructed the client to choose an equine with which to develop a relationship. The client, having no awareness of the equines, chose a mare that almost never approaches people. The client began by asking, "What do I do?" I responded by directing the client to do whatever he thinks will help him and the equine today. The client replied that he wanted to have the equine come to him. The client then began yelling at the equine to "Come here!" The equine looked at the client briefly and trotted away. The client, walking fast with his hands on his hips and using an adamant voice, attempted a few more times. Noticing the frustration, I asked, "How's it going?" to which he replied, "She doesn't like me!" I asked the client what he thought the equine did to indicate dislike for him, and what he would do next. He responded by stating the equine was just like his partner—walking off and not listening. [Metaphors to explain horse behavior and describe the problem.] I asked the client to think about a time when his partner walked toward him, and to specifically recall what he was doing, saying, and feeling. [Searching for exceptions to the problem and using the equine for analogous language.] The client said, "Well, I will try a different way."

The client quietly, with hands at his sides, gently spoke to the mare. As he slowly approached, the mare came towards him and he was even able to touch her. The change in the client's demeanor was rewarded by the mare through this experience. The client became teary-eyed when he stated he knew what would work with his partner. We spent the rest of the session processing the strengths of the client and practiced these in the field. I know that most work comes between sessions, and the following is a letter from Mike a few days later:

> Interesting experience and very eye-opening. I learned a lot about myself today and perhaps help me to be able to love and respect my partner in a whole new way. At least I discovered that I never learned or knew. Met a bunch of very smart and intuitive equines. My favorites are Rashada and Hercules.
>
> At first, when I approached Rashada, she ran away. I learned that with a change in the tone of my voice she accepted me! However, that did not last. She was closer to me but when I spoke in that tone she walked away. By opening myself up, not speaking and being patient in my approach she again let me come close. Wow, things change quick!
>
> I realize by taking it easier and with more patience I was able to approach old man [equine]. By being in my partner's face and not having any patience in many situations, I was pushing my partner away. Trying to pacify my own emotions with things will happen. 53 years of not having patience and always trying to fix. I understand, but I am scared, I do not want to continue to be the "old man." Makes me think about Casey [equine]. Why was he alone? He was wise with his choice of area to munch. Was he just comfortable with himself? Or did he just need some "space"? Why was the crazy male equine [Barry] given such a hard time by the females? Was he impatient and wanted everything his way? And then learned quickly it does not work that way? Why didn't I closely watch out for the piles of crap? Why? Why wasn't I scared of the equines? Last time I was near an equine, I was hurt??? How was I able to let an equine nuzzle up to my chest and why did she? [Metaphors about equine behavior, client relating lessons learned and inferred.]

Mike has continued working on the positive strengths-based outcomes from the session with the equines. He was able to modify communication to explicitly walk with quiet intention. Mike is able to have a positive outcome with his partner now.

Summary of Cases and Strengths-Based Model Applications

Each case briefly described both SFBT model techniques and the four prime areas for change used with the clients. Each session was a tiny glimpse into how using equines is a wonderful tool. Sessions are full of numerous interactions that are the foundation of growth for clients. The aforementioned pondering journal is an excellent example of how a client processes the experience with equine-assisted psychotherapy.

Clients' changes using strengths-based models are an outcome of the positives that occur with the use of the metaphorical constructs and the use of equines. The clients are more externally focused on the equine, and thus both verbal and nonverbal expressions flow freely. The solutions or mere interactions are a powerful tool for clients, from simply brushing an animal to moving the animal through an obstacle.

Recommendations for Practitioners

The field of EAP continues to grow and is exciting to practice! I still use my traditional office and always have the option of using equines. Insurance covers EAP, when billed as mental health therapy. I have found that most clients prefer to use the equines at some juncture, if not for all sessions.

When considering a practice in EAP, I recommend professionals have some equine experience. I began having an equine-experienced person with me. Now I have extra people with equine experience when I am conducting a large group or family sessions. It is advisable to have an extra set of eyes making sure the equines and people are physically safe. I also attend to the emotional safety of people during those times. In the above cases, I worked alone for three of the cases. I have conducted sessions with groups of 20 for supervision and did have two assistants in the field, one with equine experience and the other, like me, having both equine and a clinical mental health license.

Summary

Philosophically, I have always gravitated toward strengths-based counseling interventions. When combining EAP and strengths-based strategies, understanding the questioning skills of SFBT is key for successful sessions. Also, having experience with paralanguage is paramount to a successful session. Practicing nonverbal language is essential as well as observing the nuances in equines. Finally, learning how to extrapolate the metaphors for change is crucial and, for me as a clinician, the most enjoyable aspect. It is essential to pay attention to your co-therapist (the equine) and share some joy that comes with being a part of the change process. Happy Trails!

References

Berg, I.K., & de Shazer, S. (1993). Making numbers talk: Language in therapy. In S. Friedman (Ed.), *The new language of change: Constructive collaboration in psychotherapy*. New York, NY: Guilford Press.

Brannaman, B (2012). *An Afternoon with Buck* (video interview). Retrieved May 26, 2016 from https://www.youtube.com/watch?v=FMSm3gmZVp4

De Gutis, D.L. (2003). Hippotherapy aids children with sensory and motor issues. *Exceptional Child, 33*, 55–57.

de Shazer, S. (1985). *Keys to brief solutions in brief therapy*. New York, NY: W.W. Norton.

de Shazer, S. (2000). What is solution-focused-therapy? Retrieved May 27, 2016 from http://www.solutionfocused.net/what-is-solution-focused-therapy/

Ewing, C., MacDonald, P., Taylor, M., & Bowers, M.J. (2007). Equine-facilitated learning for youths with severe emotional disorders: a quantitative and qualitative study. *Child Youth Care Forum, 36*, 59–72. doi: 10.1007/s10566-006-9031-x

Franklin, C., Trepper, T.S., McCollum, E.E., & Gingerich, W.J. (Eds.) (2011). *Solution-focused brief therapy: A handbook of evidence-based practice*. New York, NY: Oxford University Press.

Frewin, K., & Gardiner, B. (2005). New age or old sage? A review of equine assisted psychotherapy. *Journal of Counseling Psychology, 6*, 13–17.

Glasow, B.L. (2006). *Semantics—to be exuberant or to be correct*. American Hippotherapy Association. Retrieved from May 10, 2015 http:///www.americanhippotherapyasscoaition.org/aha_hpot_A-semantics.htm.

Holmes, C.M.P., Goodwin, D., Redhead, E.S., & Goymour, K.L. (2012). *Child and Adolescent Social Work Journal, 29*, 111–122. DOI 10:1007/s10560–011–0251-z.

Irwin, C., & Weber, B. (2001). *Equines don't lie: What equines teach us about our natural capacity for awareness, confidence, courage, and trust*. New York, NY: Marlowe.

Kakacek, S.L. (2009). An arena for change. VISTAS Online American Counseling Association.

Kakacek, S.L. (2010a). Success stories with challenging clients. *Counseling Today, 53,* 34.

Kakacek, S.L. (2010b). An arena for change. An overview of equine-assisted psychotherapy. *Illinois Counselor, 2,* 28–29.

Kakacek, S.L. (2014). Mini equines in action. *Illinois Counseling Contact Newsletter, 74,* 8.

Kakacek, S.L. & Ottens, A.J. (2008). An arena for success: Exploring equine-assisted psychotherapy. *Michigan Journal of Counseling: Research, Theory and Practice, 35,* 14–23.

Karol, J. (2007). Applying a traditional individual psychotherapy model to equine-facilitated psychotherapy (EFP): Theory and method. *Clinical Child Psychology and Psychiatry, 12,* 77–89.

Kersten, G., & Thomas, L. (1999). *Equine assisted psychotherapy and learning training manual Level I.* Santaquin, UT: EAGALA, Inc.

Kruger, K.A., & Serpell, J. (2006). Animal-assisted interventions in mental health: Definitions and theoretical foundations. In A. Fine (Ed.), *Handbook on animal-assisted therapy: Theoretical foundations and guidelines for practice* (2nd ed.). New York, NY: Academic Press.

Kruger, K.A., Trachtenberg, S.W., & Serpell, J. (2004). Can animals help humans heal? Animal-assisted interventions in adolescent mental health. *Symposium at the Center for the Intervention of Animals and Society* (pp. 1–37). University of Pennsylvania Press.

Levinson, B.M., & Mallon, G.P. (1997). *Pet-oriented psychotherapy* (2nd ed.). Springfield, IL: Charles C. Thomas.

Lyddon, W.J., Clay, A.L., & Sparks, C.L. (2001). Metaphor and change in counseling. *Journal of Counseling and Development, 79,* 269–274.

McCormick, A., & McCormick, A. (1997). *Equine sense and the human heart.* Deerfield Beach, FL: Health Communications, Inc.

Morrison, M.L. (2007). Health benefits of animal-assisted interventions. *Complementary Health Practice Review, 12,* 51–62.

NARHA. (n.d.). *What is equine facilitated mental health association?* Retrieved February 4, 2008 from http://www.narha.org?SscEFMHA/WhatIsEFMHA.asp.

Parshall, D.P. (2003). Research and reflection: Animal-assisted therapy in mental health settings. *Counseling and Values, 48,* 47–56.

Pitts, J.L. (2005). Why animal assisted therapy is important for children and youth. *Exceptional Parent, 35,* 38–39.

Taylor, S.M. (2002) Equine facilitated psychotherapy: An emerging field. [Unpublished master's thesis.] Colchester, VT: Department of Psychology, Saint Michael's College.

Trotter, K.S. (2006, March 30–April 4). *The efficacy of equine assisted group counseling with at-risk children and adolescents.* Paper presented at the American Counseling Association National Conference, Kansas City, MO.

Vidrine, M.D., Owen-Smith, P., & Faulkner, P. (2002). Equine-facilitated group psychotherapy: Applications for therapeutic vaulting. *Issues in Mental Health Nursing, 23,* 587–603.

14

Positive Psychology in Counseling

Integrating Sport as a Framework for Performance Enhancement

Teresa B. Fletcher and Susan Hurley

> I now think that the topic of positive psychology is well-being, that the gold standard for measuring well-being is flourishing, and that the goal of positive psychology is to increase flourishing.
>
> Martin E.P. Seligman

Counseling is hard work. Helping professionals, by the very nature of their work, are consistently surrounded by individuals experiencing discomfort, stress, and trauma and who need us to be at our best to offer support, encouragement, relief, and the necessary insight and skills to overcome a wide array of obstacles. We strive to provide unconditional positive regard, validation, hope, and oftentimes humor, perspective, and wisdom. We incorporate creativity and finesse in developing and delivering treatment strategies for each client in the most effective way in order to have the greatest impact for change. Helping professionals have a responsibility to be at their best for every client, every session, every day, which can take a toll on our own quest for balance and well-being. As a gymnast uses core strength to provide balance for difficult skills, a counselor uses positive psychology as a core value to achieve balance in the profession and happiness in life.

A strengths-based counselor essentially develops a habit of finding the good. This disposition is incorporated intrapersonally, interpersonally, and then permeates outwardly to inspire others. A strengths-based counselor will exude a positive energy that can be infectious and thereby make an environment a better place to be. This approach differs from a medical model where counselors are trained to identify problematic behaviors, make diagnoses of mental illness, and encourage clients to highlight everything in their lives that makes them miserable. Unfortunately, our standard education models reflect this mentality by pointing out mistakes that need remediation rather than praising strengths (Edwards, 2012). If we continue to use traditional methods, we will continue to struggle with depleted energy, stress, and burnout. In fact, we could even say we would be doing our clients a disservice by not adopting a more positive approach to our practice. It is with this in mind that we have written a chapter just for counselors.

Counseling is a performance-based construct. We are not unlike surgeons in that we need to be sharp in executing delicate maneuvers to ensure we have done our best for clients to relieve pain and suffering and instill hope for a better life. In other words, we develop and execute a specific set of skills and likewise our work can be compared to the performance of medical professionals, artists, educators, and athletes. Therefore, it may be worthwhile for many of us in the counseling field to glean expertise from the more specialized field of performance psychology to enhance best practices. Counselors can benefit from integrating concepts from professions where excellence in performance is expected, explored, and evaluated.

The pursuit of excellence is most notable within the realm of sport and athlete performance. There is a parallel between athlete training and performance and counselor training and performance, particularly as it applies to skill development, maintaining a mind-body connection, cultivating endurance and stamina, and attaining a "flow" state for optimal functioning. Simply stated, flow can be characterized as consciousness or "a psychological state in which the person simultaneously feels cognitively efficient, motivated and happy" (Moneta & Csikszentmihalyi, 1996, p. 277). Further, both athletes and counselors integrate similar concepts for reaching a "flow experience," particularly in high-pressure situations consistently over the course of their careers.

Counselors can find themselves operating amidst stress and chaos and can often face difficulties that are exceptional and unique. Even a minimal review of the literature pertaining to counselor development would reveal that the context for these challenges is varied and broad. Positive psychology, informed by the work of Seligman and Csikszentmihalyi (2000), provides a strengths-based approach to optimal performance as well as developing and maintaining psychological well-being and good work-life balance (Seligman, 2011). The field of positive psychology at the subjective level is about valued subjective experiences: well-being, contentment, and satisfaction (in the past); hope and optimism (for the future); and flow and happiness (in the present). (See Seligman & Csikszentmihalyi, 2000.)

For the purposes of this chapter, performance factors shared by athletes and counselors are identified with regard to positive traits, relationships, and groups/institutions in addition to positive subjective experiences (Park & Peterson, 2008). The positive psychology framework posits that if these signature strengths are nurtured in a healthy way, individuals operate at their best and thereby live and represent the psychological good life (Seligman, 2002, 2011). Additionally, sport performance and counseling performance can be seen in the same light. Parallels are made by presenting concepts related to "peak" athletic performance and psychological skills training and applying them to the counseling process in order to create a "flow" experience. Once optimal experience is achieved, the goal is to replicate that experience and maintain well-being and life balance for long-term happiness and a thriving career.

Literature Review

Life can be hard. People have more resources, opportunities, and choices to make than ever before and while this can be refreshing, it can also be overwhelming. Life also comes with the unknown and unpredictable, exciting, disappointing, or more likely a combination of everything. Through life experience, individuals work towards balancing new versus old, risk versus reward, variability versus stability, or flexibility versus austerity. We identify what we want and, in a perfect world, there is a clear path to achieve goals. However, life is not perfect and we must also balance the challenges we choose with the skills necessary to reap the benefits and rewards. A mismatch can result in stress and, over time, a stress-filled life can lead to burnout.

Burnout is a term used in many professions with the same end result. For example in sports, burnout is described as the physical, emotional, and social withdrawal from a sport that once was considered enjoyable. The withdrawal is characterized by emotional and physical exhaustion, a reduced sense of accomplishment, and a devaluation of the sport in general. It is associated with chronic stress including an imbalance in what is expected physically, psychologically, and socially (Gould & Whitely, 2009). For example, an athlete may experience physical fatigue, emotional exhaustion, and miss spending time with family and friends, but forthcoming competitions conflict with taking much needed time away from training. An athlete begins to devalue the activity and stops caring about the sport (Weinberg & Gould, 2011). Oftentimes, an athlete can experience burnout, inevitably causing them to leave what has become an emotionally stressful environment in search of something more satisfying and meaningful.

Counselors can experience burnout similarly in that the demands of the job need to be balanced with the skills necessary to be successful. In other words, empathy, compassion, and caring are qualities that help counselors be effective in their work with individuals, however, these same qualities, when not balanced with self-care, may lead to a state of burnout. As counselors we take on the responsibility of providing care to our clients. Unfortunately, many times we do this at the expense of our own personal wellness (Sangganjanavanich & Balkin, 2013). Failure to monitor our personal self-care can lead to negative consequences for the counselor, the client, and eventually the profession as a whole. For example, if we enter a session exhausted or with negative energy, clients may leave the session dissatisfied with the counselor, and possibly lose hope for the counseling process and profession. In establishing a healthy lifestyle, we must recognize and monitor symptoms of burnout and develop strategies for self-care and overall wellness.

Indicators of Burnout

The term burnout in counseling was first recognized in the 1970s (Pines & Maslach, 1978) and similar to the definition of sports burnout, research in counselor burnout defines it as a psychological syndrome characterized by emotional exhaustion, depersonalization, lack of personal accomplishment, and feeling ineffective with clients (Maslach, 2003; Maslach, Schaufeli, & Leiter, 2001). Shoptaw, Stein, and Rawson (2000) describe counselor burnout as the three dimensional aspects of emotional exhaustion, depersonalization, and a lack of personal accomplishment. Emotional exhaustion leads to an inability to feel compassion for our clients, which includes a lack of interest and a loss of energy. It is the inability to attach to the emotional needs of our client, becoming overly critical in the evaluation of self, and a lack of a sense of personal accomplishment. Burnout affects counselors both emotionally and physically and includes symptoms such as feeling tired or exhausted, being overly anxious, depression, and feeling helpless, and can lead to substance abuse. We may become more cynical, pessimistic, or sarcastic as we work with or discuss clients, or as we think about working with more challenging clients.

It is difficult to recognize burnout in ourselves as it is happening. As we begin to look at symptoms, it could simply be that we find the work we are doing is no longer interesting. We start to complain that the client is not making progress or we find that the original passion is gone and counseling clients has simply become extremely dissatisfying (Skovholt, 2012). Similarly to athletes, once counselors reach this level of burnout, they are at risk to leave the profession in search of other more satisfying careers.

Findings in numerous studies indicate that counselors suffering from burnout are more likely to have stress-related illnesses, experience depression and anxiety, and have low self-worth (Shoptaw, Stein, & Rawson, 2000). Several studies found that physical ailments like headaches, insomnia, gastrointestinal issues, and cold/flu viruses are more likely to occur when counselors are experiencing burnout (Armstrong, 1979; Barner, 1982; Beck & Gargiulo, 1983). Burnout also interferes with the ability to function at work on a day-to-day basis as indicated by absenteeism, poor work performance, and more interpersonal conflicts leading to termination or voluntarily leaving the job and, eventually if untreated, the field of counseling entirely (Oser, Biebel, Pullen, & Harp, 2013). They are more likely to develop negative attitudes towards clients or have a sense of relief when a client does not keep an appointment. Counselors who show a lack of continuity in the care they provide to their clients have been positively linked to clients prematurely withdrawing from treatment (McKay, 2009; Schaefer, Ingudomnukul, Harris, & Cronkite, 2005; McCaul & Svikis, 1991; Bowen & Twemlow, 1978).

Several studies on burnout have concluded that in order for counselors to effectively serve their clients they must keep in mind the need to attend to their own personal wellness (Myers & Sweeney, 2005; Myers, Sweeney, & Witmer, 2000; Rosenberg & Pace, 2006). Skovholt (2012) suggests that we must have energy in order to give it away. To hold on to a high level of energy counselors must learn to balance work with personal life and continue to work on a personal self-care plan that will enhance our well-being and in turn move us towards career satisfaction and away from burnout (Richards, Campenni, & Muse-Burke, 2010). There are very few empirical studies that examine the contribution of training in order to reduce the occurrences of burnout and secondary trauma among counseling therapists (Ben-Porat & Itzhaky, 2011). In addition to the lack of research on reducing burnout, there does not appear to be a clear definition of self-care. For the purposes of this chapter, the concepts of self-care and wellness are explored in building a connection towards a positive psychology framework.

Self-Care

Counselors tend to focus their efforts more on the clients than on themselves when it comes to the concept of wellness. However, mindfulness training can effectively help counselors reduce stress and increase self-compassion (Shapiro, Astin, Bishop, & Cordova, 2005), deal with negative emotions, increase clarity of thought, increase capacity for more meaningful self-reflection and self-understanding (Schure, Christopher, & Christopher, 2008). Further, when we are aware of our self-care needs and are able to meet those needs in a healthy way, we thrive and so do our clients (i.e., Stanley et al. 2006).

Components of self-care include (a) physical, (b) spiritual, (c) psychological support, and (d) personal counseling (Richards, Campenni, & Muse-Burke, 2010). O'Halloran & Linton (2000) recommend that counselors should consider preventative self-care strategies. Health care professionals advocate for exercise or some other physical activity several days a week. Physical activity has been shown to reduce symptoms of anxiety and depression (Callaghan, 2004), increase the quality of life, and help people cope with the day-to-day stress in life (Anderson, King, Stewart, Camacho, & Rejeski, 2005). Exercise plays a strong role in helping people obtain wellness and healthy lifestyles because of its physical and psychological benefits (Okonski, 2003).

As counselors contemplate a positive self-care rejuvenation plan, spirituality may play a key role directing them back to a more positive sense of their own mental health (Wong, 2011). As part of a qualitative study, counselors reported that not only does spirituality promote a strong quality of life, but that it leads to a positive sense of self-awareness (Hamilton & Jackson, 1998). One example of how spirituality can be useful in promoting well-being included counselors in training and loving kindness meditation. Loving kindness was originally a Buddhist concept described as unconditional love and an ability to accept all parts of oneself. Researchers Boellinghaus, Jones, and Hutton (2013) incorporated a course in loving kindness meditation (LKM) as part of the training process. The results indicated that students found the LKM course advantageous by allowing them to become more aware of their own thoughts, feelings, and how they related to other people. They believed that this provided them with more insight into their own vulnerabilities while involved in difficult clinical work which allowed them to be more accepting, compassionate, and caring towards themselves as well as others. Although this article was specifically looking at LKM, it is representative of how spirituality can be beneficial, and the conclusion supports the need for training counselors in self-awareness and self-care.

A strong support system is crucial to being an effective and healthy counselor both from a personal and professional perspective. Self-awareness is integral in not only understanding symptoms, but also identifying strengths and recognizing what is needed and how to practice psychological self-care. Through experience, insight, and support, counselors learn when to reduce client load, when to take a vacation, when to spend time alone, with friends and family, or engage in community activities. It is important to cultivate relationships with family, friends, spouses, and significant others (Coster & Schwebel, 1997; Rupert, Stevanovic, Hartman, Bryant, & Miller, 2012) to separate that sense of self as a counselor from the sense of personal self beyond the role of the counselor. When healthy, we honor what we do well and accept limitations such as knowing when to consult with colleagues regarding a difficult client and when to make a referral. Psychological self-care includes the willingness to seek personal counseling when one is feeling distressed or impaired (Norcross, Bike, & Evans, 2009).

Having an objective perspective is helpful in monitoring boundaries and limitations while developing healthy strategies for balance (Macran, Stiles, & Smith, 1999; Pope & Keith-Spiegel, 2008).

Wellness

The concept of wellness originally began in the physical health sciences to identify a more holistic method examining human functioning in pursuit of excellence (Hettler, 1984). In counseling, wellness is defined as "A way of life oriented toward optimal health and well-being, in which body, mind and spirit are integrated by the individual to live life more fully within the human and natural community. Ideally, it is the optimum state of health and well-being that each individual is capable of achieving" (Myers et al., 2000, p. 252). Early research on wellness included a theoretical model, or the *wheel of wellness* (Sweeney & Witmer, 1991; Witmer & Sweeney, 1992; Myers et al., 2000) and later the *indivisible self*, which is an evidence-based model of wellness (Hattie, Myers, & Sweeney, 2004; Myers & Sweeney, 2005).

Wellness can be described as a strengths-based approach to mental health care (Smith, 2001) and has been linked to the positive psychology movement (Myers & Sweeney, 2004). However, when we consider the comparison between general well-being and the concept of excellence in performance, it seems more is needed. An analogy might be useful in explaining the difference; wellness is to surviving as being "in the zone" is to thriving. Additionally, these constructs associated with a "flow" state may be wide-ranging thus allowing the freedom and flexibility to identify and enhance a variation of strengths as needed based on context. In comparing the training and strengths of successful athletes to the preparation and traits of effective counselors, we explore the adaptability of using a positive psychology framework relative to positive individual traits, relationships, groups and institutions, and positive subjective experiences (Park & Peterson, 2008).

Positive Individual Traits

To be successful, individuals need to be accurate in the assessment of their assets and limitations in order to expedite change and growth and improve performance. As William Glasser states, "[therapy] . . . will be successful when they are able to give up denying the world and recognize that reality not only exists, but that they must fulfill their needs within its framework" (Glasser, 1965, p. 6). In other words, not everyone can be an Olympic champion or a brilliant clinician, but we can strive to give the best performance in any given situation and be honest in our appraisals.

Positive attributes, or signature strengths, should not be confused with talent. Talent can be described as innate, non-moral, and relatively automatic where strengths tend to be acquired, moral, and a choice that requires time, effort, and determination to develop (Seligman, 2002). The idea of talent development has gained attention from researchers and authors of books such as *Outliers* (Gladwell, 2011) and *Talent is Overrated* (Colvin, 2010). The theme of each of these books is that it takes a combination of positive individual traits in order to optimize the talent. Michael Jordan was a talented basketball player in that he had tremendous skill and knowledge of the game. But what makes him an icon was his ability to execute the right skills at the right time and in the right way so that he and his teammates were able to reach peak performance at critical times . . . over and over again.

The same is true in the counseling profession. Mental health professionals may show a talent for counseling and may be described as a good listener, empathic, or have good communication skills. However, what contributes to a counselor's success and ultimately clients' well-being is the ability to be creative in the process of implementing the right intervention, at the right time and in the right way. When the process of counseling is considered "performance," as in the sport context, it is not surprising that many individual traits overlap in terms of success, happiness, or feeling like we are prosperous. The following traits are identified to demonstrate parallels between athlete and counseling performance, which include self-awareness, initiative and motivation, resilience, openness and flexibility, managing emotions, and passion and joy.

Self-Awareness

Self-awareness can be defined as a state of being conscious of one's thoughts, feelings, beliefs, behaviors, and attitudes, and knowing how these factors are shaped by important aspects of one's developmental and social history (Gergen, 1991). The ability to have insight as well as hindsight and foresight is key to performance by identifying strengths and limitations accurately and thereby taking personal responsibility to make adjustments to training. Similarly, self-awareness is critical in counseling in order to understand how we influence the counseling process and how clients may perceive us. Mindfulness meditation, by Jon Kabat-Zinn (2005), is just one example how individuals can work towards self-awareness and psychological well-being.

Initiative and Motivation

In the sport world, athletes maneuver through a tedious process of goal setting to include outcome, performance, and process goals. An outcome goal might be to win a race or medal, whereas a performance goal highlights a standard of achievement such as reducing the time in a race or increase a free-throw percentage. A process goal identifies a need for improvement of a specific skill such as improving the accuracy of a tee shot in golf. Goals have to be realistic yet challenging and athletes develop strategies to meet and/or exceed their goals. Furthermore, in order to achieve "flow," athletes balance challenge with skill level to prevent boredom and/or apathy (Jackson & Csikszentmihalyi, 1999; Csikszentmihalyi & Csikszentmihalyi, 1988). Motivation, both intrinsic and extrinsic, may fluctuate and requires consistent monitoring and modifying to excel over a long period of time.

By the same token, counselors possess the ability to show initiative by accepting a diverse clientele and engage in lifelong learning through training and continuing education to increase their breadth and depth of knowledge. Counselors are encouraged to seek and utilize resources such as consultation and supervision for inspiration and to enhance creativity. Motivation revolves around seeing hope and instilling hopefulness in clients. The strength of the counseling profession lies in the counselors' ability to be intrinsically motivated to have a positive impact on their clients.

Resilience

In sport, the resilience is known as "mental toughness" or the ability to accept strong criticism and setbacks without competing less effectively. A mentally tough athlete does not become easily upset when losing or competing poorly, does not need excessive praise or encouragement, and recovers quickly from mistakes (Miller, 2001). Facing adversity becomes the norm in the world of sport. Athletes must perform under stressful conditions and learn to cope with pain and injury. The process of learning a skill, such as hitting a baseball or serving a volleyball, begins with failure; but through practice, patience, persistence, and commitment, mastery can be accomplished. Successful athletes become accustomed to working through adverse conditions, try to predict obstacles and make plans on how to overcome them, and some even find a way to thrive under the pressure to meet or exceed expectations.

Counselors often face similar adversity when working with complicated client issues. Many clients experience anguish and sorrow and may suffer from chronic mental illness, traumatic life events, substance abuse, poor coping skills, minimal resources, limited cognitive functioning, physical limitations, and often a combination of challenges. Clients are not always open to change; yet they provide an opportunity for counselors to develop new and creative strategies while exercising patience and developing persistence. Resilient counselors will maintain a positive attitude and an open mind. If there is something we don't know, we learn it. If an intervention doesn't work, we try something else. When we can't help our clients, we find someone who can. We want clients to leave a session feeling better than when they arrived and live better in-between. We find joy in the challenge and when we need a break, we take one. We identify positive effort while learning from experiences to sustain hopefulness. When we're feeling down, we can read *Learned Optimism* and get back on track (Seligman, 2006).

Openness and Flexibility

In the world of sport, this concept can be described as "coachability," or the willingness to accept and use feedback and adjust to coaching decisions or technique changes. When an athlete is considered coachable, he or she is cooperative and engages in making appropriate changes to enhance both personal and team performance. Prochaska's transtheoretical model of behavior change is one example of identifying openness by evaluating stage of change, precontemplation, contemplation, preparation, action or maintenance, can be informative when attempting to initiate change (Prochaska, Norcross, & DiClemente, 2007). For instance, an athlete operating in the contemplation stage may appear "uncoachable" however may simply lack information or need technical assistance. A stage-matching approach can be used to identify the stage and initiate appropriate interventions.

Counselors-in-training in particular may experience cognitive dissonance when first introduced to diverse ways of thinking, values, beliefs, and attitudes that are different from their own. In the counseling field, we emphasize the importance of being "comfortable with discomfort" stressing the notion that being flexible and open to new ideas will prevent bias and judgment from entering into the relationship and contribute to an evolving worldview. The book *Who Moved My Cheese?* by Spencer Johnson (1998) exemplifies the different ways individuals may perceive change. Although not explicitly stated in the book, flexibility can be a matter of survival for many based on the need to adapt to environmental change.

Likewise, Outward Bound (2007) identifies the *circles of comfort*, which include the comfort, stretch, and panic zones to describe the experience of taking risks. Individuals learn and grow when they are in the stretch zone, but periodically retreat to the comfort zone to renew and rejuvenate. When individuals can experience the panic zone in a deliberate and controlled way, they can gain experience with emotional regulation and learn to cope with less anxiety. As they learn effective coping skills, panic subsides contributing to a more positive subjective experience and thus becoming flexible and more open to new opportunities for growth.

Managing Emotions

The ability to manage emotions will be a determining factor in success, particularly at the higher levels of competition. Athletes, through experience, identify an individual zone of optimal functioning (IZOF), a model that focuses on describing, predicting, explaining, and regulating performance-related psychobiosocial states affecting performance (Hanin, 2000). For example, some athletes may need to get "psyched up" and will listen to specific music, or team captains or coaches may give motivational speeches designed to bring positive energy to start competition. With other sports, such as rifle shooting or golf, athletes must work to lower heart rate and remain calm in order to achieve an optimal state. The management of emotions becomes critical in achieving peak performance and excellence consistently regardless of pressure, circumstances, or a changing environment (Clark, 2011; Seligman, 2011). Successful athletes develop the ability to manage emotions, block out distractions, and stay focused on the task.

In the counseling profession, the relationship between emotions and success has received a great deal of attention over the last 20 years, since the publication of *Emotional Intelligence* by Daniel Goleman (1995). The premise behind emotional intelligence is the ability to recognize emotions in self and others, identify cognitions that contribute to emotions or vice versa, understand the source and meaning of the emotions, and manage those emotions given a particular situation (Mayer, Salovey, & Caruso, 1997). A quote from Aristotle (n.d.) captures the concept:

> Anybody can become angry—that is easy, but to be angry with the right person and to the right degree and at the right time and for the right purpose, and in the right way—that is not within everybody's power and is not easy.

This quote embodies the impact emotions can play on the ability to function and prosper in a given situation. Similar to athletes preparing for competition, counselors can take time to prepare for clients by bringing positive energy to sessions with enthusiasm, determination, compassion, and optimism to contribute to a therapeutic environment. We provide skill and expertise in identifying emotions and work with clients to become more proficient in managing their lives and experience more positive emotional states.

Passion and Joy

"The only way to do great work, is to love what you do" (Steve Jobs; Stanford University, 2005). Successful athletes find joy in the process of training, competition, and the challenge of finding out just how good they can be and how long they can be that good. They find joy in working with other professionals who share their passion and most importantly they get a sense of accomplishment and satisfaction. When athletes begin to feel stagnant or a loss of passion, many will create new goals, implement new training programs, or even change sports.

As stated previously, counselors take risks when failing to monitor signs of burnout and neglect self-care, which can erode their enthusiasm over time. Similar to athletes, counselors can seek new opportunities to keep it fresh and stimulate their passion. Some helping professionals may take on a different client population, modify their area of specialty, learn new approaches, or even change their environment. Counselors can nurture their passion in order to maintain motivation and joy to stay effective and thrive throughout a long and satisfying career (Seligman, 2002; Seligman, 2011).

Positive Relationships

Sport teams can be interactive, which requires team members to work together (i.e., soccer, basketball, ice hockey), coactive, which requires less team interaction to achieve goals (i.e., swimming, tennis, golf), or both (i.e., baseball or softball where playing defense may require teamwork, but batting is individual). The relationships between and among teammates can greatly influence performance outcome as well as performance satisfaction. Further, having positive relationships with coaches, medical and support staff can also be influential in determining the quality of an experience. As noted in the aforementioned section on positive traits, counseling performance is parallel to sport performance. Counselors establish mutual respect and rapport with clients and rely on co-workers and colleagues as well as family and friends for support. Nurturing healthy relationships while censoring the flow of negative energy is the key to success, happiness, and the ability to flourish. Virtues that contribute to positive relationships are listed below.

Trust

Successful teams create a culture of excellence, which tends to be based on the positive interactions and attitudes of its members. The ability to trust and be trusted is a key factor in working well together. Ice hockey is a good example of how trust can impact performance as well as performance satisfaction. The game of hockey is based on time and space because movement on the ice is fast and unscripted. Players anticipate movement from teammates and trust them to move to open areas quickly to make a play. When this happens and plays are made, a sense of satisfaction and accomplishment is established and momentum can develop to eventually result in a goal. If players have to stop and look to see if their teammates are moving, opportunities are lost, which can lead to frustration, disappointment, and becoming disenchanted with teammates. Similarly, athletes take personal responsibility to develop as a trustworthy teammate and player. The player-coach relationship also is based on trust. Trust involves a shared commitment and effort in working towards team goals and being in a mutually trusting environment contributes to optimal team functioning.

Likewise, in counseling trust is a cornerstone in the client-counselor relationship. Counselors and clients work together much like a team to contribute to positive outcomes. In order to be effective, counselors have to develop a trust for the process, their training and expertise, and surround themselves with other counselors who are trustworthy. Building relationships with strengths-based supervisors, mentors, and colleagues can assist clinicians in reaching peak performance in counseling sessions and throughout their careers (Edwards, 2012).

Impact of Self on Others

When working as a team, particularly with interactive sports, players develop an awareness of how their attitudes, behaviors, and performance can impact team development and functioning. Players who work towards being supportive and encouraging, maintaining emotional control, and operating within their roles can have a healthy and productive impact on how the team works together. Thus, teams can operate at an optimal level and gain more satisfaction in the process of training and competing together.

Being aware of how actions and words can impact how clients perceive the counselor can greatly impact the counseling process. Developing "finesse" in delivering an insight or implementing a directive in counseling will contribute to the client not only "hearing" what is being said without defensiveness, but also maximize the chances that the client will make a necessary change. During supervision sessions, I often ask students, "Without editing, what do you think the client needs to hear?" Once they figure out the clear message, then we work on the elegance of the delivery, "What is the best way to say that so the client is most likely to receive that message?" Counselors can learn how to have a positive impact on clients by sharpening these skills so they become more automatic and instinctive.

Communication and Social Intelligence

Participating in sport is helpful for building communication skills. Athletes' intrapersonal dialogue, or positive self-talk, can maintain focus on a task, bring about positive change when learning new skills, or enhance proficiency in competition as well as maintain composure during critical, clutch, or high-pressure situations. Interpersonal communication, both verbal and nonverbal, will allow teammates to work more effectively together when progressing through developmental stages and performing complicated tasks or sequences. Coaches in particular can enhance player development by paying attention to communication styles, nonverbal messages, and creating a safe environment for athletes to be able to express themselves to become mature and confident individuals and athletes.

During counselor training, counselors learn to pay attention to both verbal and nonverbal communication styles, from intrapersonal and interpersonal perspectives. Positive internal dialogue going into a session can contribute to mindfulness, transitioning from one client to the next, and creating and maintaining a positive flow state. Counselors use tone, inflection, body language and make word choices to effectively communicate to clients. In doing so, counselors hope to maximize client understanding thereby creating an ideal environment for the change process. In fact, counseling theorists such as Jay Haley began their careers in communication (Sluzki, 2007).

Self-control or internal locus of control

Athletes tend to perform better when they possess an internal locus of control. Turning attention towards developing their own positive attitude, thoughts, behaviors, and team role can contribute to positive expectancies. Athletes, along with everyone else, can experience frustration when they attempt to focus on the behavior of others such as teammates, coaches, referees, or officials and opponents. Further, developing the ability to ignore or disregard external negativity can be beneficial in achieving and maintaining a positive flow state (Seligman, 2011).

William Glasser (1984) developed his control theory as a response to observing client distress and conflict based on their perception of control. Counseling professionals can encourage clients to direct positive energy towards what is within their ability to control while learning to manage external stimuli. Counselors can be empowered by the ability to recognize choices and exercise control in initiating and responding to external events (Glasser, 1998). When making choices of when and how to interact within a context, counselors can work towards maintaining composure and controlling impulses in order to achieve overall well-being. The ability to develop and maintain an internal locus of control can include the virtue of self-discipline. In Seligman's most recent book, *Flourish: A Visionary New Understanding of Happiness and Well-being* (2011), he describes the concept of "GRIT", which can be considered a combination of extreme traits that include self-discipline, persistence, and passion. Grittiness has been identified by researchers as a strength within the context of what leads to success and happiness.

Positive relationships can enhance performance, in sport, within the counseling setting, and in life. Learning how to develop healthy relationships and interact with others can contribute to overall happiness and life satisfaction. Further, these positive relationships can influence overall performance in sport and counseling as well as enhance the environments in which both athletes and counselors live and work.

Positive Groups and Institutions

Developing positive attributes and nurturing healthy relationships can be beneficial in creating a robust environment. Living and working with individuals who are encouraging and supportive can be motivating and contribute to an enhanced work ethic, productivity, and an overall sense of satisfaction and happiness. The Buddhist concept of universal responsibility can be helpful in conceptualizing how individuals can create a positive milieu. The Dalai Lama often talks about universal responsibility as showing empathy and compassion towards others and being mindful of how individual behaviors affect the immediate community as well as the global environment. When we focus on creating a positive environment a natural consequence is that we will thereby be fulfilling our own needs to reach our goals (Dalai Lama, 2008). In doing so, we develop a better balance when we find a conflict between meeting our own individual needs and those of others. Athletes and counseling professionals influence their environment by their attitude, behavior, and interactions with others.

Climate

Both coaches and athletes can develop leadership skills to shape the team climate in positive ways. The ability to listen and observe can lead to the identification of strengths in others; recognizing and honoring the strengths of others contributes to a positive and productive team climate. Wayne Gretzky is known as being one of the greatest hockey players of all time. However, what made him great initially was his ability to find his teammates and deliver the puck to assist in their goal scoring. By focusing on the team goal of outscoring opponents, he was valued and respected as a leader. In turn, his teammates also learned from him and reciprocated with a commitment to the "we" instead of the "me."

In the counseling profession, a positive climate is one of unconditional positive regard and being nonjudgmental. Carl Rogers, a pioneer in the counseling field, emphasized a safe and supportive environment for interacting with clients to promote self-exploration, healing, and growth. Additionally, Rogers, along with countless other great leaders, has carried this concept to bring attention to human rights and promote world peace. By modeling through genuineness and understanding, we become leaders by example for clients to follow and emulate (Rogers, 1961).

Tolerance

Tolerance most likely is not in the sport psychology literature, however, when observing interactions between and among athletes and coaches, there are differences of opinion and style of play. Coaches have an agenda that includes what skills need to be introduced or developed, how athletes and teams should be trained, and the best way to utilize strengths of the athletes within the framework and limitations of the institution. Decisions are made based on what is in the best interest of the team or organization and can often conflict with individual needs and goals. Tolerance comes into play in order to develop a collaborative plan so that meeting one need does not result in the sacrifice of another. Frustration tolerance can include the ability to recognize a frustrating situation and engage in problem solving. An environment based on the concept of *equifinality*, or the ability to reach the same goal in multiple ways, can be useful in building tolerance and encouraging openness to new experiences.

Counselor training revolves around the notion that in order to be effective, counselors must develop tolerance for anything and everything that is different. Counselors work towards identifying beliefs and values, respecting those of our clients, and working towards the greater goal of client well-being while maintaining respect for differences. Distress tolerance has been a recent construct with the introduction of dialectic and behavior therapy (Linehan, 1993). Some clients are limited in their ability to manage even the slightest adversity and can become debilitated during a crisis or catastrophe. As a result, counselors encourage clients to put minor setbacks in perspective while building resilience and healthy coping skills and promoting a more optimistic worldview.

Norms

Within the world of athletics, each sport has its own language, desired skills and attributes, and culture. Within each sport and team, norms are established either intentionally or unintentionally as a means of shaping a standard behavior and level of play. Coaches and leaders can positively reinforce attributes such as punctuality, preparedness, effort, selflessness, encouragement, or optimism in order to create a positive team environment. One example of an optimal environment was created by NBA coach Phil Jackson, who has won more championships than any other coach in the history of professional sports. He strengthened his players, Michael Jordan in particular, who was known for his work ethic and commitment to the team goals. As a result of Jackson's leadership, his teams adopted those desired traits and conformed to training standards to create successful teams and organizations (Jackson & Delehanty, 2006; Jackson & Delehanty, 2014).

Counselors contribute to establishing positive and productive norms when interacting in groups and by providing leadership in agencies or organizations as well as the profession. In group counseling, norms create a sense of safety and security so clients are able to explore, gain insight, and make progress towards individual goals. Counselors contribute to a healthy work environment by utilizing positive traits to influence norms.

Coping Skills

Living and working in a stressful environment creates the need to develop a vast array of coping skills. Participating in sport creates the opportunity to learn and refine certain coping skills. Time management and staying organized can relieve stress and pressure from outside sources such as school or work. Athletes develop interpersonal or social skills, and conflict resolution techniques to relate to others and work through differences. They learn to identify and analyze problems and work towards finding creative solutions. They learn to reframe adversity as an opportunity for growth and use that adversity as motivation to strive to reach their goals. Oftentimes, athletes take time away from their sport to rest, reflect, and rejuvenate. The ability to identify needs, both physical and mental and find a way to meet those needs, will promote better life balance, particularly in the long term. Athletes who use their coping skills to enhance their performance tend to have a positive impact on the team and constructively contribute to the betterment of the institution and the greater good.

Effective counselors can identify when to seek counseling and consulting services in order to maintain a healthy demeanor in both personal and professional environments. Mindfulness and relaxation are commonly used tools to cope with stress while promoting insight, self-awareness, and self-care. Counselors can learn to be assertive in order to express thoughts and concerns or ask for what they need. Counselors can benefit and then become role models for resourcefulness in building support systems based on areas of interest or positive emotions and relationships experienced while engaging in certain activities. One individual may enjoy working with animals and volunteer at a rescue shelter while another may need to join a recreational hockey league.

Using positive traits and creating healthy relationships contribute to the creation of a positive team experience or work environment. Further, identifying with groups or institutions that promote positive experiences and contribute to the development of overall optimism is ideal. Focus and concentration on finding the good and making decisions with favorable outcomes can contribute to confidence and task mastery. As a result, both athletes and counselors develop positive subjective experiences and are more likely to experience the flow state.

Positive Subjective Experiences

Focus and Concentration

Athletes learn to intentionally direct focus and attention to achieve task mastery and what is known as "game sense" (i.e., ice awareness, court sense) or "sport IQ" (i.e., a soccer brain or basketball IQ). When first learning a skill such as dribbling a basketball or stickhandling, focus is narrow and internally directed such as making contact with the ball or monitoring wrist movement to direct the stick in making contact with the puck. As athletes develop and skills can be executed automatically, attention becomes more external and broad such as finding teammates, reading opponents' body language, or analyzing game situations. Ultimately, through successful experiences, athletes can anticipate movements, implement strategies, and make decisions almost effortlessly, thereby creating flow states.

The parallel between athlete and counselor performance is noticeable when simplifying how skills are learned, practiced, and later mastered. In the beginning as novice counselors are learning new skills, they tend to focus on what they are thinking, their body language, or what they need to say to clients. As they develop their skills, they can turn their full attention towards their clients and listening to the message, hearing and interpreting the source and meaning, and developing intervention and treatment strategies that are designed to meet the unique needs of that particular client in that specific space and time. As counselor educators, our role is to challenge and support students in evolving from a narrow, internal perspective to an external focus that is multidimensional, broad, and in some cases global.

Decision Making

Neuroscientists and researchers are making great strides in understanding the brain and how decisions are made as evidenced by popular psychology books such as *Blink* (Gladwell, 2007), *How We Decide* (Lehrer, 2009), or *On Second Thought* (Herbert, 2010). These authors attempted to update the public on the complexity of the brain and how it may influence everyday behavior to prevent illness and disease and promote health and well-being. In the world of sport, there are a variety of professionals who have influence on athlete decision making including coaches, medical personnel, nutritionists, strength and conditioning experts, and sport psychology consultants. The quality of decisions can be directly related to the quality of the information coming in and the credibility of the messenger. Athletes have to sort through an overwhelming amount of information, and when they are outside of training and competition, they have the ability to use their skills and resources to sort through it to inform good decisions. During competition, however, athletes are limited in the amount of information they receive, and therefore must only focus on the right information at the right time. Athletes have to make decisions that potentially impact playing time, career opportunities, or even their livelihood; pass or shoot, take a risk or play it safe. They learn to identify key pieces of information and use visualization and imagery to work through scenarios and sharpen focus to refine decision making and optimizing the chances of a successful outcome.

Counselors operate similarly during a counseling session. Counselors bring into the session a wealth of information gained from graduate school, continuing education, literary resources, and general life experience. Sorting through the theories, models, approaches, case studies, and prior counseling experience to fully and accurately conceptualize clients and develop appropriate interventions can be overwhelming: the question is whether to use silence or give feedback, cognitive-behavioral or solution-focused. Similarly, counselors narrow their focus on significant components of both verbal and nonverbal communication to inform decision making. Through success and failure, lessons learned and sharing the struggle, counselors evolve their skills to become more secure in their knowledge, fluid in their delivery, and passionate for their craft.

Confidence

In sport, the concept of developing confident athletes is multidimensional. Having confidence influences an athlete's ability to control emotions, facilitate positive self-talk and focus, set challenging goals, increase motivation and effort, and maintain momentum. Likewise, mastery of skills, previous successes, physical and mental preparation, positive social support and leadership, and environmental comfort are contributing factors to building confidence in sport and life.

The counseling profession does not address confidence directly, however, entering into a counseling session as a confident clinician can bring hope to a client. Confident counselors present with a sense of calm and can appear more empathic, genuine, and relatable. Professional counselors trust in the process and believe that no matter what client issues arise, they have the tools and resources that they need and the skills to use them.

Life Balance and Psychological Well-Being

Building a culture of excellence is on the forefront of work in the field of sport psychology. Identifying and capitalizing on athletes' natural assets and developing strategies to strengthen weaker areas of performance seems only sensible. Likewise, to classify counseling as a performance-based construct would be prudent. During counselor training, we identify positive attributes as a framework to build upon while providing supportive relationships and creating a healthy environment for a positive subjective experience.

However, to strive towards authentic happiness, knowledge of work–life discord can assist in determining where conflicts exist and which strengths and skills to incorporate into everyday living. Establishing a favorable work–life balance has become more of a challenge in recent decades (Aryee, Srinivas, & Tan, 2005; Stevanovic & Rupert, 2009; Yang, Chen, Choi, & Zou, 2000) with the global increase of women in the workforce and dual-earner and single-parent households (Korabik, Lero, & Whitehead, 2008). These economic shifts require adjustments in parenting as well as household and partner responsibilities for both men and women (Higgins, Duxbury, & Lyons, 2010). Parents are making decisions so each can become actively involved in work or career, family roles, and child rearing (Duckworth & Buzzanell, 2009). This conflict between professional and personal responsibilities may result in feeling overloaded, overwhelmed, and stressed, hence the need for life balance.

Unfortunately, researchers tend to focus on negative predictors of work–life conflict rather than positive influences of work–life balance (e.g., Allen et al., 2012; Rupert et al., 2012). In all fairness, positive and negative emotions can occur during stressful experiences (Folkman, 2008), however, positive emotions are critical in the prevention of negative subjective experiences (Fredrickson, 1998). One study exemplifies how positive psychology in the workplace can facilitate employee work–life balance. Supervisors in a Fortune 500 company qualitatively expressed that schedule changes and flexibility were the most requested work–life accommodations from employees (Lauzun, Morganson, Major, & Green, 2010). When an organization is open and supportive (positive environment), supervisors (positive relationships) can make accommodations for employees to feel empowered and important (positive traits) and create positive subjective experiences. Positive psychology can contribute to satisfactory life balance and overall well-being and happiness.

An application of this positive psychology framework is depicted in Figure 14.1 and applied within the following case study. We assess subjective experiences through inquiry and assessment. Strengths and weaknesses are identified, prioritized and we initiate intrapersonal strengths building. Healthy and problematic relationships as well as productive or challenging environments are assessed to inform solution-focused intervention strategies. The interplay among traits, relationships, and environment is helpful in determining priorities and sequencing sessions and interventions.

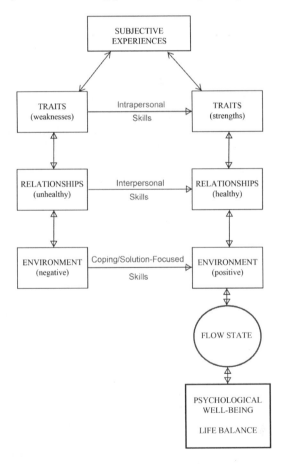

Figure 14.1 Positive Psychology Framework

The following case study is used to demonstrate the application of a strengths-based approach to enhance counselor performance. As the counselor, Laura interacted with her client with frustration and a sense of hopelessness. She admitted she was feeling disheartened with a particular client and ineffective as a counselor in general. Through strengths-based supervision, we realized the more traditional approaches of showing positive regard and using behavior modification were insufficient and lack of progress was taking its toll on Laura's confidence. Over a period of time these types of emotions can erode the counselor's ability to function effectively and can lead to burnout. Similarly, Laura began to despair and disregarded all of her positive contributions and was overwhelmed by her perceived failures. In supervision a positive, strengths-based approach was incorporated in an effort to help her feel more productive and rebuild her confidence. As a result of integrating positive psychology, she left our supervision session with a renewed sense of accomplishment, which carried forward with other clients and in her own sense of self.

Case Study: Laura

Background

Laura is a master's level student in her third year of study in a clinical mental health counseling program at a major university. She is an excellent student and has been described by her faculty members as a "natural" and as having "good instincts." As with athletes, counselors with good instincts and natural ability have a good place to start but that alone will not sustain them for the long run. Laura's practicum and first internship were developmentally uneventful. She expressed that she was happy to be working in a school/home-based program providing mental health counseling to children. However, in her final semester of internship her supervisor noticed a change of tone in the audio tapings of her sessions with a specific client. It was clear that there was a power struggle going on between the client and Laura. Her voice sounded strained and Laura expressed feeling ineffective with her client. This case study will work through the process from a counseling performance strengths-based approach as to how the supervisor was able to help Laura address her symptoms of burnout and move forward with her client.

Positive individual traits

Laura's decision to work with children comes from a very positive, strengths-based direction. Self-awareness is a strength for Laura as she has given a great deal of thought to the direction she has chosen. Laura worked with children throughout high school, providing babysitting services in the community and at her church. After her first psychology class in college she seemed to identify a career path to follow where she might combine her passion to work with children and psychology by becoming a counselor. She states that she enjoys working with children because they have a sense of humor, are creative and resilient.

She has been an excellent student and has taken to heart all that she has learned in the course of her studies to become a licensed professional counselor. She receives positive feedback on her evaluations from her site supervisors. Currently, Laura is in her last semester of graduate school and working with children who have behavioral disorders. This program is community-based and works closely with participating schools to provide behavioral modification to elementary aged students. They work with parents and teachers as well, in order to provide a consistent model and expectation for the students. Laura has been described by her faculty and site supervisors as insightful in her process of engaging and working with children and parents. She is very aware of her thoughts and beliefs, and has shown great confidence and initiative when approaching her clients to provide them with counseling, psycho-education, and even consequences when necessary. As her faculty supervisor I have found Laura to always be open to feedback and flexible in trying new things in her counseling process.

Positive relationships

Laura has strong positive relationships with her site supervisor and co-workers. She has also created strong relationships with the students in her internship class. She trusts the support she is being offered and reacts to that support in a very positive way. She has found throughout the course of her internship that she can seek advice from her site and faculty supervisor as well as her fellow students when she has questions or concerns about a client.

Laura sets good boundaries generally. A concern for her would have been that her identified strong need to work with children might interfere in her ability to set good boundaries around her ability to avoid becoming overly involved with her clients, however, she was clearly able to separate herself from her clients even with all the special needs they have had. When the client presented a strong need for support, Laura was able to empathize rather than over react.

Burnout

When Laura contacted me she was feeling depleted regarding her work with a particular 10-year-old client. Laura had been working with the client for approximately 8 months and indicated the client had been particularly challenging. She said that though some of the client's more severe behaviors, like stealing and property destruction, had subsided, she was still disrespectful towards authority figures, often lied about her actions, and still did not take responsibility for her behavior. The client's mother was diagnosed with severe anxiety/panic attacks, and as a result was fairly disengaged at home. Laura believed that every effort to teach the child to change her inappropriate behaviors and to develop more productive, healthy, positive behaviors would go out the window as they were not reinforced in the home.

As her faculty supervisor, I was able to hear changes in Laura's approach first on audio tapes she provided for supervision. It was clear that the client wanted control of each session and was only semi-cooperative with the counselor. When the client became disrespectful during her session and began to throw a tantrum it was apparent Laura's voice sounded tired and strained. However, because she is such a strong counselor it was very clear that she was going to maintain control of the session and hold her boundaries with the client. Laura immediately and calmly acknowledged the client's frustration and told her she would give her a few seconds to stretch a little and recompose herself in order to complete the session.

During supervision, Laura stated about this session, "I struggled with how to appropriately confront her avoidant behavior when she began to complain of the stomach ache, which was very dramatic; rolling around on the floor, crying, refusing to make eye contact or look at me, and using aggressive body language."

Laura's instincts as a counselor continued to maintain the appropriate boundaries she needed in order to work with this client. She showed great strength as a counselor intern and managed this client through the tantrum. I approached my supervision with her from a strengths-based position by communicating to her how much I was impressed by her ability to wait out the client's poor behavior and at the same time not give in to her manipulation to play a game, have a snack, or terminate the session early. She never raised her voice to the client, nor did she ever sound overly stern or angry. She calmly explained to the client what she would or would not do and why. She very clearly attempted to identify the positive things that had happened during the session prior to the client's meltdown and drew positive parallels to the client's strengths which she did not appear to recognize or even accept as positives about herself.

I then offered some constructive suggestion that she might try in order to continue the positive work she was doing with the client including the possibility of seeing the client a little more often for shorter intervals, and not being too concrete in her process as a counselor. In other words not always coming to the session with a concrete plan or task for the client to accomplish. I recommended that Laura work with her client to help her identify her strengths and the things she does well in order to build a base to change the inappropriate behaviors. Laura responded with a very positive attitude, feeling less discouraged by the client and more empowered by her ability to continue working with her.

Conclusion

Incorporating positive psychology into counseling sessions can be viewed as a win–win scenario. Clients can benefit from acknowledging individual strengths, surrounding themselves with healthy relationships, and contributing to building and maintaining positive environments in which to function and thrive. At the same time, clients can address shortcomings in a non-threatening manner while learning and honing life skills such as problem solving, communication, assertiveness, and coping.

Counseling professionals can benefit from building positive psychology into their professional orientation as well as their own life philosophy. Focusing on strengths allows clinicians a starting point from which to build a solid foundation of counseling skills. A strengths-based approach to counseling can further contribute to addressing shortcomings, developing confidence, and providing hope that a better future is accessible for both counselors and clients regardless of the presenting issue. Counselors in turn can use a positive framework to achieve peak performance within counseling sessions, to prevent burnout in a high stress field and maintain a healthy life balance.

References

Allen, T.D., Johnson, R.C., Saboe, K.N., Cho, E., Dumani, S., & Evans, S. (2012). Dispositional variables and work-family conflict: A meta-analysis. *Journal of Vocation Behavior, 63,* 17−26. http://doi.org/dfpn8w

Anderson, R.T., King, A., Stewart, A.L., Camacho, F., & Rejaski, W.J. (2005). Physical activity counseling in primary care and patient well-being. *Annals of Behavior Modification, 30,* 146−154.

Aristotle. (n.d.). BrainyQuote.com. Retrieved May 1, 2016 from http://www.brainyquote.com/quotes/quotes/a/aristotle132211.html

Armstrong, K.L. (1979). How to avoid burnout: A study of the relationship between burnout and worker, organizational and management characteristics in eleven child abuse and neglect projects. *Child abuse and neglect, 3,* 145−149.

Aryee, S., Srinivas, E.S., & Tan, H.H. (2005). Rhythms of life: Antecedents and outcomes of work-family balance in employed parents. *Journal of Applied Psychology, 90,* 132−146.

Barner, A.E. (1982). Do teachers like to teach? *The Pointer, 27,* 5−7.

Beck, C.L., & Gargiulo, R.M. (1983). Burnout in teachers of retarded and nonretarded children. *Journal of Educational Research, 76,* 169−173.

Ben-Porat, A., & Itzhaky, H. (2011). The contribution of training and supervision to perceived role competence, secondary traumatization, and burnout among domestic violence therapists. *The Clinical Supervisor, 30,* 95−108.

Boellinghas, I., Jones, F., & Hutton, J. (2013). Cultivating self-care and compassion in psychological therapists in training: The experience of practicing loving-kindness meditation. *Training and Education in Professional Psychology, 7,* 267−277.

Bowen, W.T. & Twemlow, S.W. (1978). Implications of staff absence for effective treatment. *Social Casework, 59,* 305−308.

Callaghan, P. (2004). Exercise: A neglected intervention in mental health care? *Journal of Psychiatric and Mental Health Nursing, 11,* 476−483.

Clark, T. (2011). *Nerve: Poise under pressure, serenity under stress, and the brave new science of fear and cool.* New York, NY: Little Brown and Company.

Colvin, G. (2010). *Talent is overrated: What really separates world-class performers from everybody else.* New York, NY: Penguin.

Coster, J.S., & Schwebel, M. (1997). Well-functioning in professional psychologists. *Professional Psychology: Research and Practice, 28,* 3−13.

Csikszentmihalyi. M., & Csikszentmihalyi, I.S. (1988). *Optimal experience: Psychological studies of flow in consciousness.* New York, NY: Cambridge University Press.

Dalai Lama. (2008, May 22). *Universal responsibility in the modern world.* Retrieved from http://www.dalailama.com/messages/transcripts/universal-responsibility-modern-world

Duckworth, J.D., & Buzzanell, P.M. (2009). Constructing work−life balance and fatherhood: Men's framing of the meanings of both work and family. *Communication Studies, 60,* 558−573.

Edwards, J.K. (2012). *Strengths-based supervision in clinical practice.* Thousand Oaks, CA: Sage.

Folkman, S. (2008). The case for positive emotions in the stress process. *Anxiety, Stress & Coping: An International Journal, 21,* 3−14. http://doi.org/dq4qvdj

Fredrickson, B.L. (1998). What good are positive emotions? *Review of General Psychology, 2,* 300−319. http://doi.org/bkc3tg

Gergen, K.J. (1991). *The saturated self, dilemmas of identity in contemporary life.* New York, NY: Basic Books.

Gladwell, M. (2007). *Blink: The power of thinking without thinking.* New York, NY: Back Bay.

Gladwell, M. (2011). *Outliers: The story of success.* New York, NY: Back Bay.

Glasser, W. (1965). *Reality therapy: A new approach to psychiatry.* New York, NY: Harper & Row.

Glasser, W. (1984). *Control theory: A new explanation of how we control our lives.* New York, NY: Harper & Row.

Glasser, W. (1998). *Choice theory: A new psychology of personal freedom.* New York, NY: Harper & Row.

Goleman, D. (1995). *Emotional intelligence: Why it can matter more than IQ.* New York, NY: Bantam Books.

Gould, D., & Whitely, M. (2009). Sources of consequences of athletic burnout among college athletes. *Journal of Intercollegiate Athletics, 2,* 16−30.

Hamilton, D.M., & Jackson, M.H. (1998). Spiritual development: Paths and processes. *Journal of Instructional Psychology, 25,* 262−271.

Hanin, Y.L. (2000). Individual zones of optimal functioning (IZOF) model: Emotion-performance relationships in sport. In Y.L. Hanin (Ed.), *Emotions in sport*. Champaign, IL: Human Kinetics.

Hattie, J.A., Myers, J.E., & Sweeney, T.J. (2004). A factor structure of wellness: Theory, assessment, analysis, and practice. *Journal of Counseling & Development, 82*, 354–365.

Herbert, W. (2010). *On second thought: Outsmarting your mind's hard-wired habits.* New York, NY: Crown.

Hettler, W. (1984). Wellness: Encouraging a lifetime pursuit of excellence. *Health Values: Achieving High Level Wellness, 8*, 13–17.

Higgins, C.A., Duxbury, L.E., & Lyons, S.T. (2010). Coping with overload and stress: Men and women in dual-earner families. *Journal of Marriage and Family, 72*, 847–859. doi:10.1111/j.1741–3737.2010.00734

Jackson, P., & Delehanty, H. (2006). *Sacred hoops: Spiritual lessons of a hardwood warrior.* New York, NY: Hyperion.

Jackson, P., & Delehanty, H. (2014). *Eleven rings: The soul of success.* New York, NY: Hyperion.

Jackson, S.A., & Csikszentmihalyi, M. (1999). *Flow in sports: The keys to optimal experiences and performances.* Champaign, IL: Human Kinetics.

Johnson, S. (1998). *Who moved my cheese? An amazing way to deal with change in your work and in your life.* New York, NY: G.P. Putman's Sons.

Kabat-Zinn, J. (2005). *Guided mindfulness meditation: A complete guided mindfulness medication program from Jon Kabat-Zinn.* Louisville, CO: Sounds True.

Korabik, K., Lero, D.S., & Whitehead, D.L. (Eds.). (2008). *Handbook of work-family integration.* London, England: Elsevier.

Lauzun, H.M., Morganson, V.J., Major, D.A., & Green, A.P. (2010). Seeking work–life balance: Employees' requests, supervisors' responses, and organizational barriers. *The Psychologist-Manager Journal, 13*, 184–205.

Lehrer, J. (2009). *How we decide.* New York, NY: Houghton Mifflin Harcourt.

Linehan, M. (1993). Skills training manual for treating borderline personality disorder. New York, NY: Guilford Press.

Macran, S., Stiles, W.B., & Smith, J.A. (1999). How does personal therapy affect therapists' practice? *Journal of Counseling Psychology, 46*, 419–431.

Maslach, C., (2003). Job burnout: New directions in research and intervention. *Current Directions in Psychological Science, 12*, 189–192.

Maslach, C., Schaufeli, W.B., & Leiter, M.P. (2001). Job burnout. *Annual Review of Psychology, 52*, 397–422.

Mayer, J.D., Salovey, P., & Caruso, D.R. (1997). What is emotional intelligence? In P. Salovey, & D. Sluyter (Eds.), *Emotional development and emotional intelligence: Implications for educators* (pp. 3–31). New York, NY: Basic Books.

McCaul, M. & Svikis, D., (1991). Improving client compliance in outpatient treatment: Counselor-targeted interventions, as cited in Oser, C.B., Biebel, E.P., Pullen, E., & Harp, K.L.H., (2013). Causes, consequences, and prevention of burnout amount substance abuse treatment counselors: A rural versus urban comparison. *Journal of Psychoactive Drugs, 45*(1), 17–27.

McKay, J.R. (2009). Continuing care research: What we have learned where we are going. *Journal of Substance Abuse Treatment, 36*, 131–145.

Miller, S.L. (2001). *Hockey tough: A winning mental game.* Champaign, IL: Human Kinetics.

Moneta, G.B., & Csikszentmihalyi, M. (1996). The effect of perceived challenges and skills on the quality of subjective experience. *Journal of Personality, 64*, 274–310. DOI: 10.1111/j.1467–6494.1996.tb00512.x

Myers, J.E., Sweeney, T.J., & Witmer, J.M. (2000). The wheel of wellness counseling for wellness: A holistic model for treatment planning. *Journal of Counseling and Development, 78*, 251–266.

Myers, J.E., & Sweeney, T.J. (2004). The indivisible self: An evidence-based model of wellness. *The Journal of Individual Psychology, 60*, 234–244.

Myers, J.E. & Sweeney, T.J. (2005). *Counseling for wellness: Theory, research and practice.* Alexandria, VA: American Counseling Association.

Norcross, J.C., Bike, D.H., & Evans, K.L. (2009). A therapist's therapist: A replication extension 20 years later. *Psychotherapy Theory, Research, Practice, Training, 46*, 32–41. DOI: 10.1037/a0015140

O'Halloran, T.M., & Linton, J.M. (2000). Stress on the job: Self-care resources for counselors. *Journal of Mental Health Counseling, 22*, 354–365.

Okonski, V. O. (2003). Exercise as a counseling intervention. *Journal of Mental Health Counseling, 25*(1), 45–56.

Oser, C.B., Biebel, E.P., Pullen, E., & Harp, K. (2013). Causes, consequences, and prevention of burnout among substance abuse treatment counselors: A rural versus urban comparison. *Journal of Psychoactive Drugs, 45*, 17–27.

Outward Bound. (2007). *Leadership the outward bound way: Becoming a better leader in the workplace, in the wilderness, and in your community.* Retrieved November 7, 2015 from http://books.google.com/books/about/Leadership_the_Outward_Bound_Way.html?id=PvcqSQ1A6_IC

Park, N., & Peterson, C. (2008). Positive psychology and character strengths: Application to strengths-based school counseling. *Professional School Counseling, 12,* 85−92.

Pines, A., & Maslach, C. (1978). Characteristics of staff burnout in mental health settings. *Hospital & Community Psychiatry, 29,* 233−237.

Pope, K.S., & Keith-Spiegel, P. (2008). A practical approach to boundaries in psychotherapy: Making decisions, bypassing blunders and mending fences. *Journal of Clinical Psychology, 64,* 638−652. DOI: 10.1002/jclp.20477

Prochaska, J.O., Norcross, J., & DiClemente, C. (2007). *Changing for good: A revolutionary six-stage program for overcoming bad habits and moving your life positively forward.* New York, NY: HarperCollins.

Richards, K. C., Campenni, C. E., & Muse-Burke, J. L. (2010). Self-care and well-being in mental health profession-als: The mediating effects of self-awareness and mindfulness. *Journal of Mental Health Counseling, 32*(3), 247−264.

Rogers, C.R. (1961). *On becoming a person.* Boston, MA: Houghton Mifflin.

Rosenberg, T., & Pace, M. (2006). Burnout among mental health professionals: Special considerations for the marriage and family therapist. *Journal of Marital and Family Therapy, 32,* 87−99.

Rupert, P.A., Stevanovic, P., Hartman, E.R.T., Bryant, F.B., & Miller, A. (2012). Predicting work-family conflict and life satisfaction among psychologists. *Professional Psychology: Research and Practice, 43,* 341−348.

Sangganjanavanich, V.F., & Balkin, R.S. (2013). Burnout and job satisfaction among counselor educators. *Journal of Humanistic Counseling, 52,* 67−79. DOI: 10.1002/j.2161−1939.2013.00033.x

Schaefer, J.A., Ingudomnukul, E., Harris, A.H., & Cronkite, R.C. (2005). Continuity of care practices and sub-stance use disorder patients' engagement in continuing care. *Medical Care, 43,* 1234−1241.

Schure, M.B., Christopher, J., & Christopher, S. (2008). Mind-body medicine and the art of self-care: Teaching mindfulness to counseling students through yoga, meditation, and Quigong. *Journal of Counseling & Develop-ment, 86,* 47−56.

Seligman, M.E.P. (2002). *Authentic happiness: Using the new positive psychology to realize your potential for lasting fulfill-ment.* New York, NY: Simon & Schuster.

Seligman, M.E.P. (2006). *Learned optimism: How to change your mind and your life.* New York, NY: Simon & Schuster.

Seligman, M.E.P. (2011). *Flourish: A visionary new understanding of happiness and well-being.* New York, NY: Simon & Schuster.

Seligman, M.E.P. & Csikszentmihalyi, M. (2000). Positive psychology: An introduction. *American Psychologist, 61,* 774−788.

Shapiro, S.L., Astin, J.A., Bishop, S.R., & Cordova, M. (2005). Mindfulness-based stress reduction for health care professionals: Results from a randomized trial. *International Journal of Stress Management, 12,* 62−67.

Shoptaw, S., Stein, J.A., & Rawson, R.A. (2000). Burnout in substance abuse counselors: Impact of environment, attitudes and clients with HIV. *Journal of Substance Abuse Treatment, 19,* 117−126.

Skovholt, T.M. (2012). The counselor's resilient self. *Turkish Psychological Counseling and Guidance Journal, 38,* 137−146.

Sluzki, C.E. (2007). A tribute to Jay Haley (1923−2007). *Journal of Family Therapy, 29,* 97−99.

Smith, H. (2001). Professional identity for counselors. In D.C. Locke, J.E. Myers, & E.H. Herr (Eds.), *The hand-book of counseling* (pp. 569−580). Thousand Oaks, CA: Sage Publications.

Stanford University. (2005, June 12). *Steve Jobs' 2005 Stanford commencement address.* Retrieved January 15, 2016 from http://youtube/UF8uR6Z6KLc

Stanley, S., Reitzel, L.R., Wingate, L.R., Cukrowicz, K.C., Lima, E.N., & Joiner, T.E. (2006). Mindfulness: A primrose path for therapists using manualized treatments? *Journal of Cognitive Psychotherapy, 20,* 327−335.

Stevanovic, P., & Rupert, P.A. (2009). Work-family spillover and life satisfaction among professional psycholo-gists. *Professional Psychology: Research and Practice, 40,* 62−68.

Sweeney, T.J., & Witmer, J.M. (1991). Beyond social interest: Striving toward optimum health and wellness. *Indi-vidual Psychology, 47,* 527−540.

Weinberg, R.S., & Gould, D. (2011). *Foundations of sport and exercise psychology* (5th ed.). Champaign, IL: Human Kinetics.

Witmer, J.M., & Sweeney, T.J. (1992). A holistic model for wellness and prevention over the lifespan. *Journal of Counseling & Development, 71,* 140−148.

Wong, P.T.P. (2011). Positive psychology 2.0: Towards a balanced interactive model of good life. *Canadian Psychol-ogy, 52,* 69−81.

Yang, N., Chen, C.C., Choi, J., & Zou, Y. (2000). Sources of work-family conflict: A Sino-U.S. comparison of the effects of work and family demands. *Academy of Management Journal, 43,* 113−123.

15
Strengths-Based Practice of Clinical Sport Psychology

Michele Kerulis

Athletes are known for being driven, strong, and committed to their goals. It takes perseverance to give maximum effort on a daily basis (sometimes multiple times a day) in practices and games. Athletes experience heartbreaking losses and exhilarating wins; it is clear that successful athletes have stellar physical strength. What is less visible is the mental toughness that transforms good athletes into phenomenal athletes. Clinical sport psychology practiced from a strengths-based perspective helps athletes use their assets to move past setbacks and enhance their existing talents. Clinical sport psychology is a multidisciplinary field with the purpose of promoting athletic success through psychological skills training while monitoring emotional wellness.

History of Sport Psychology

The history of American sport psychology can be traced back to the 1800s and has connections in kinesiology, physical education, and psychology (Gill, 1995; McCullagh, 1995; Weinberg & Gould, 2011). Weinberg & Gould (2011) categorized the history of sport psychology into six periods (the Early Years, Griffith Era, Preparation for the Future, Establishment of Academic Sport Psychology, Multidisciplinary Science and Practice in Sport and Exercise Psychology, Contemporary Sport and Exercise Psychology), which ranged from 1895 to 2000. Weinberg and Gould explained that the first research study in sport psychology took place in 1897 during the Early Years Period (1895–1920) by Norman Triplett (Indiana University) who examined motivation in cyclists. In 1918 Coleman Griffith, known as the father of American sport psychology, developed the first laboratory in sport psychology at University of Illinois. The Griffith Period (1921–1938) was rich with classic texts and groundbreaking research. Next, the Preparation for the Future Period (1939–1965) led to scholarly study and academic programs including studying motor learning in physical education and kinesiology. The Establishment of Academic Sport Psychology (1966–1977) gave way to sport psychology as an area within kinesiology. This is also the era where consultants like Bruce Ogilvie began working with athletes and teams. In fact, Ogilvie is known as the father of American applied sport psychology. During the Multidisciplinary Science and Practice Period (1978–2000) the field grew in terms of disciplines, professional associations, and scholarly journals. The United States Olympic Committee developed a Sport Psychology Advisory Board in 1980 and hired their first full time sport psychologist in 1985. In addition, two strong professional associations were established. The Association for the Advancement of Applied Sport Psychology (formerly AAASP, now called AASP, Association for

Applied Sport Psychology) was launched in 1986 (John Silva was the first president) and American Psychological Association's Division 47 Sport Psychology (now called Society for Sport, Exercise, & Performance Psychology) was created in 1987 with William Morgan as the first president. This period was also known for a focus on exercise psychology as a research area and additional interest in the psychological aspect of sport in addition to sport sciences like kinesiology. AAASP also developed guidelines for the status of Certified Consultant in 1991. The final period, the Contemporary Period (2000–present), continues to focus on graduate training, wellness and health, and applied experiences. In 2003, American Psychological Association (APA) endorsed sport psychology as an area of practice and Division 47 developed proficiencies such as holding a doctorate in psychology with a focus on treating athletes, knowledge of the culture of athletics, and awareness of the organizational structure of athletics (APA, 2015). The field continues to evolve and practitioners work to develop best practices in sport psychology.

Professionals who Provide Sport Psychology Services

Many terms have been used to describe professionals who provide sport psychology services including sport psychologist, athletic/sport counselor, sport psychology consultant, mental trainer, and mental coach. A variety of educational and field experiences are required to ethically practice sport psychology. The American Counseling Association (ACA; 2014) and AASP both state that practitioners must practice within their areas of competency including educational coursework, experience, and supervision. The practice of clinical sport psychology requires both a clinical license (legal criteria determined by each state) and formal education and training in sport psychology. Performance enhancement consulting, also known as mental skills training, can be performed by professionals who are not clinically licensed and who have formal education and training in sport psychology. Professionals in the field of sport psychology work with groups, individuals, teams, and coaches.

Sport Psychologist: Holds a doctorate degree in an area of psychology and has specific clinical training with a general population as well as with athletes. Sport psychologists are licensed to practice and must abide by federal and state psychology and mental health laws. Sport psychologists provide services including psychometric testing, counseling, and performance enhancement.

Athletic/Sport Counselor: Holds a doctorate or master's degree in an area of counseling and has specific clinical training with a general population as well as with athletes. Athletic/sport counselors are licensed to practice and must abide by federal and state counseling and mental health laws. Athletic/sport counselors provide services including psychometric testing, counseling, and performance enhancement.

Sport Psychology Consultant / Mental Trainer / Mental Coach / Performance Enhancement Consultant: Holds a doctorate or master's degree in Sport Psychology, Kinesiology, or other sport science. Sport Psychology degrees are typically earned within Kinesiology or Physical Education departments of universities and do not include clinical training. This group of professionals has specific knowledge of body mechanics and the influence that the mind has on the body and movement, and provides psychoeducation to athletes with the goal of increasing success during performances.

Certification

Although each of the educational routes listed above differs, one commonality designed to develop competence among professionals in sport psychology is AASP's Certified Consultant (CC-AASP) credential (AASP, 2015). As mentioned earlier, the credential was developed in 1991 and as of this writing is under review and requirements to earn the credential will be updated in the future.

The current requirements to become certified are listed on the AASP website (appliedsportpsych. org) and include a doctorate or master's degree in an area related to sport sciences or psychology, membership in the association, and an agreement to practice according to AASP's ethical guidelines. In addition, 12 competency areas and formal mentoring experience (monitored by a current CC-AASP) are required. This process allows new professionals to learn while they are in the field as they are guided by more experienced professionals. Mentoring is different than supervision in that mentors do not hold legal responsibility for their mentees' clients whereas clinical supervisors do have legal responsibility for their supervisees' clients. Specific educational content areas that are required are as follows:

C1: Professional Ethics and Standards, C2: Sport Psychology, C3: Biomechanical and/or Physiological Bases of Sport, C4: Historical, Philosophical, Social, or Motor Behavior Bases of Sport, C5: Psychopathology and its Assessment, C6: Counseling Skills, C7: Skills/Techniques/Analysis Within Sport or Exercise and Related Experiences Such as Coaching (this includes experiences, not a specific course), C8: Research Design, Statistics, and Test & Measures, C9: Biological Bases of Behavior, C10: Cognitive-Affective Bases of Behavior, C11: Social Bases of Behavior, C12: Individual Behavior.

The Intersection of Strengths-Based Practice and Sport Psychology

Strengths-based practice has been an integral part of sport psychology. When I talk with a client, I listen for themes of resilience and strength. Strengths are also identified from standardized assessments (discussed in the next section). I also identify areas for growth (also known as deficits). The strengths-based perspective in sport psychology does not deny the presence of deficits. Rather, sport psychology assumes the client possesses strengths to mitigate perceived deficits and increase desired outcomes.

Strengths fall into several categories: cognitive, mental, emotional, social, and physical. Assessment results are interpreted through a strengths-based lens and applied as needed. Most important to note is that strengths and resiliency are at the heart of sport psychology.

The Practice of Sport Psychology

This section describes my practice of sport psychology from the point of inquiry to termination. I believe in developing a solid relationship with clients and understanding presenting issues from their point of view. I utilize a semi-structured interview, assessments, and collaboration to create an action plan. It is vital to ensure that athletes understand the limits of confidentiality, the process of treatment, and the cooperation that is necessary for successful goal attainment.

The Inquiry

Sport psychology is unique in that services are not always provided in a traditional office setting. Sessions can take place on the field, while traveling with a team, and in a variety of other athletic settings. Counselors who work with athletes must be aware of the unique circumstances that arise due to the nature and culture of athletics and must have a full understanding of the ACA (2014) and AASP (Association for Applied Sport Psychology, n.d.) codes of ethics. Issues related to confidentiality and third party involvement must be explored before agreeing to work with an athlete or team. When I receive a call from someone inquiring about sessions I first ask about the age of the client to determine if parent/guardian consent is needed. I next learn about the client's sport history and identify the presenting concern. Once I hear about the concern I make a judgment about the nature of the case (clinical or performance enhancement) and schedule an intake session.

The Intake

The intake session is a time used to begin conceptualizing the case and understanding the client's presenting concern. It is also where I start to look for client strengths. There are times when clients identify a specific concern as primary, such as decreased motivation for sports, and the clinician recognizes a clinical disorder, like an eating disorder, as a primary issue. In these cases, it is important for the clinician and client to work together to acknowledge the issues both parties have identified and create a plan of action that will address multiple issues in effective ways. This plan will identify client strengths that will ultimately result in collaborative effort to enhance overall performance.

I begin intake sessions with a discussion about informed consent and potential for the release of information. At times athletes will want their coaches involved in sessions and at other times they will not want coach involvement. Once I am certain that the athlete understands the nature of confidentiality and the limits to confidentiality I move to a semi-structured strengths-based interview that includes a mental health assessment (Whiston, 2013) including a Mental Status Exam (MSE), Sport Clinical Intake Protocol (SCIP; Taylor & Schneider, 1992), and Wellness Plan (Kerulis, 2011). The semi-structured format allows me to gather important information like mental health history, highlights and disappointments in the sports career, and physical health and nutrition, while at the same time allowing for flexibility for the client to provide additional information that the client believes is key information. Woven into this narrative are the athlete's internal and external strengths. When I gather mental health history, in addition to asking about areas for growth, I gather information about areas of strength. I want to know how the client defines highlights and the circumstances surrounding previous successes. These circumstances include nutrition, rest/sleep, social supports, and training outcomes, for example. These strengths-based practices form a foundation upon which we can build a solid working relationship.

This is also an important time to examine the client's athletic identity, or degree to which he or she identifies self in the athletic role; degree of athletic identity has a direct impact on identity foreclosure and how open the client may be to change (Despres, Bradym, & McGowan, 2008; Kerulis, 2012). In addition, higher levels of athletic identity indicate more difficulty dealing with adversity (Cieslak, 2004). I look for strengths that are applicable to other areas of the client's life. This is a strengths-based roadmap that will inform future work with the client. A great tool to use in the intake session to develop a baseline of psychological skills is Lysek's (2014) Nine Mental Skills of Successful Athletes-High Definition (9MSSA-HD) which assesses athletes' mental skills in multiple areas that can be measured and taught with the goal of improving performance. The 9MSSA-HD has two forms: one specifically for individual athletes and one designed for athletes who play team sports. The nine areas examined include attitude, motivation, goals, people skills, self-talk, imagery, anxiety, dealing with emotions, and concentration.

The intake session provides me with a picture of the athlete as a person within and outside of sports and provides a direction for treatment. Additionally, I have gained a blueprint of the client's strengths. The conclusion of the intake is a discussion about what the client and I see as strengths-based starting points for goals and we agree upon a list of issues that were uncovered during the discussion.

Psychological Skills Training Program

After I have taken time to conceptualize the case based on the intake and any collaborating information (from guardians, parents, coaches, trainers) I begin to formulate a plan of action. A psychological skills training program is an intervention plan used commonly in sport psychology (Edwards & Steyn, 2008) and is based on defining evidence-based psychoeducational techniques (goal setting, imagery, relaxation, cognitive behavioral interventions, etc.) that are utilized with the intent of increasing athletes' strengths and decreasing deficits. I use an easy-to-follow format to help athletes understand the process and easily follow their progress. The first step is identifying the presenting concerns (agreed upon by the athlete and clinician) and internal/external strengths, conceptualize the case (the clinician's perspective of the factors involved with the concerns), identify, define, and justify interventions (provide explanation of interventions in layman's terms and provide justification of why they can be effective in this case), schedule session agenda (create a flexible plan that provides the athlete with education, practice, and homework about the interventions), and ongoing check-ins (ensure that the athlete understands the interventions and learns to implement them outside of sessions).

Psychological skills training programs can be sport-specific and designed for individual athletes and teams. They are developed with the clinician's conceptualization in mind and after determining if the client presents with a sport-performance issue or a clinical issue. Gardner and Moore (2004) recommend a multi-level classification system to determine how to proceed with sessions. Their four classification systems include performance development (athletic performance enhancement and a desire to improve athletic performance), performance dysfunction (previous levels of success are not being met due to developmental, transitional, or psychological barriers), performance impairment (clear clinical issues are present with dysfunctional behaviors and decreased psychological well-being), and performance termination (reaction to sport-career termination due to voluntary or involuntary factors). Each classification has recommended interventions. Gardner and Moore recommend utilizing psychological skills training as a primary intervention for athletes who present with performance development issues and counseling as the primary intervention (with psychological skills training secondary) for athletes who present within the other three classifications. Once a classification is determined I begin working with the athletes to highlight their strengths with the goal of decreasing deficits related to the presenting concern. Regardless of classification, client strengths inform and direct treatment planning and case conceptualization.

Sport Psychology Case Example: Sally

The Inquiry

(Specific aspects of this case and client have been modified to protect confidentiality.)

My clients are mainly word of mouth and tend to contact me via e-mail or telephone. I have found that having a strong social media presence that falls within ethical guidelines has been helpful to enhance public awareness of the practice of sport psychology (Kerulis & Cheadle, 2015).

I was contacted via e-mail by a minor client's mother after she read my blog post called *Young Athletes & Parental Involvement* (Tapak & Kerulis, 2014). The mother, Sarah, wrote that her 13-year-old daughter, Sally, an elite gymnast, was interested in sport psychology services. Sarah and I had a phone call in which I discussed informed consent for a minor, my modality of working with children and their families, and the process of treatment. During the conversation I explained that I follow legal mental health guidelines, which include privacy protection outlined in the Health Insurance Portability and Accountability Act (HIPPA; 1996) and practice according to the ACA (2014) and AASP (n.d.) codes of ethics. Establishing a safe, trusting, and ethical space with Sally was the beginning of a strengths-based sport psychology relationship. Sarah stated that Sally would voluntarily attend sessions and was looking forward to learning how to strengthen her sport psychology skills. Sarah identified the presenting issue as Sally's desire to increase focus during competitions and reduce negative self-talk.

The Intake

Sally attended the intake session with her mother and father (Sam). I explained that because Sally was 13, in addition to parental consent, she was asked to also sign all informed consent and release forms. When working with a minor I explain that the content of the session belongs to the minor (confidentiality) and that I encourage the minor to provide a verbal summary of the session to the parents at the end of our meetings with the purpose of (1) verifying that the client understands what we talked about in session, and (2) developing communication skills with the parents. I emphasized the fact that the client determines what is included in the summary before we invite the parents back into the session to conclude the meeting. The purpose of this is to empower the minor client and to develop and strengthen the therapeutic relationship. All parties agreed to this arrangement and felt confident that Sally had the ability to determine what information she would keep private and what information she would share.

Sam and Sarah were present for the beginning of the intake when we discussed developmental milestones, physical health, family counseling history, and sport injuries. The parents confirmed that Sally met all developmental milestones and was in good health with medical clearance to participate in sports. She had not had a serious sport-related injury and the family had no previous history of counseling. At this point the parents left the room and I conducted the rest of the intake with Sally. Sally described her current level of functioning within multiple domains (family, school, and social) as positive and she felt like she had support in these areas. Sally stated that she had a wonderful relationship with her parents and that, as an only child, she felt that her parents devoted a great amount of their attention to her and she felt loved. Sally denied use of substances, had an unremarkable MSE, and denied risky and dangerous behaviors. She confirmed that she had a group of best friends at school and was not involved in a romantic relationship. Sally's family did not practice a specific religion and stated that her family had spiritual beliefs that involved appreciation of community and community service. Sally's eating and sleeping were normal and she had a nutritional plan that supported the energy required to participate in elite gymnastics. Her coping strategies for distress included talking with her parents, friends, and her coaches. Her life goals included going to the Olympics and earning a college degree so that she could become a teacher.

Sally described her athletic history in a positive way (clearly she had gained a strengths-based identity from her athletic experiences). She stated that she had been in gymnastics since the age of four and had always enjoyed participating in sports. She was especially talented in both uneven bars and parallel bars. Sally said that the highlight of her gymnastics career was performing an advanced skill (completing three giants in a row on the uneven bars) and mastering her landing. She stated that the low point of her gymnastics career was attempting to complete the three giants and falling, which resulted in a minor sprain in her shoulder. The sprain did not have lasting effects and Sally enthusiastically returned to gymnastics when she received medical clearance.

Sally admitted that her parents had always been supportive of her gymnastics career and that she was currently second-guessing her commitment to the sport. Sally also said that her current coaches were very supportive and encouraging. She mentioned that her coaches recommended that she seek sport psychology services to address her "level of distraction and lack of focus in practice." I asked Sally about her statement about wanting to perform in the Olympics and her questioning her commitment to gymnastics. She stated that she was confused about this contradiction and wanted to understand how her dream to be an Olympic athlete was suddenly under question. She admitted that she felt distracted during practice with thoughts of "what if . . ." which would spiral into negative statements to herself. Sally explained that she felt excited for competitions because she loved gymnastics but also felt anxious because she didn't know if it would be her last meet due to her contemplation of retiring from gymnastics. She said that she wanted to talk to someone to help her make up her mind.

Identify the Concern(s)

After listening to Sally's statements and examining the information in the intake I determined that she did not have a clinical diagnosis and that she fell between Gardner and Moore's (2004) performance development and performance termination phases. Sarah identified Sally's issues as the need to increase focus during competitions and decrease negative self-talk, Sally said her presenting concern was focus, negative self-talk, and career termination, and I determined her concerns as overall sub-clinical anxiety regarding an uncertain future in gymnastics, negative self-talk, and identity development. Sally had high athletic identity which left her at risk of anxiety and a grief period if she chose to end her gymnastics career. Together, Sally and I created a list that summarized these points and developed a summary of the conversation. Sally was not comfortable talking to her parents about her thoughts of career termination because she did not want to disappoint them. During the intake Sally's parents mentioned that all they desired was Sally's happiness. I encouraged Sally to think about talking with them in the future about her concerns and respected her wishes to maintain confidentiality with this issue. Sally agreed that she would think about talking with her parents and appreciated our commitment to confidentiality. The summary Sally provided for her parents included the following:

1. Decrease negative-self talk during competitions and practice
2. Increase focus during competitions and practice
3. Schedule fun activities outside of gymnastics

Sally provided an age-appropriate summary of the intake for her parents, who supported the three points we identified for sport psychology session goals. They agreed to attend weekly sessions while these issues were addressed.

Case Conceptualization

Sally is a healthy teenager who is approaching a developmental milestone. According to Erikson (1968) she is in the identify vs. role confusion stage. This is the stage during which Sally will examine her roles, consider her future, and try to understand who she is as a person. My role with her is to help her understand that she has the inner ability (strengths) to navigate this phase and normalize the conflictual feelings related to her role as a gymnast.

Sally has a common dilemma faced by elite athletes—should she continue participating in the sport in which she has engaged for nearly ten years or should she retire as an athlete and move forward with other roles? This question can result in feelings of anxiety, guilt, confusion, and self-doubt. Sally has the talent to reach her goal to compete in the Olympics yet she has the desire to participate in non-sport age-appropriate activities with her friends. She has ideas of what she wants to do later in life (go to college and become a teacher) yet her high athletic identity puts her at risk of a difficult transition out of gymnastics.

The goals of strengths-based sport psychology were to reduce overall anxiety and increase confidence by helping Sally explore her options related to gymnastics participation, developing open lines of communication with her parents so that she has support in navigating this decision, and working on mental toughness through sport psychology skills training. Addressing these issues will help Sally have a safe space to process her thoughts and feelings about her current life circumstances and will result in the ability to maintain focus while she is at practice and at meets. Sally will be encouraged to allow her parents to help her with the decision-making process as this is a major life decision that will affect multiple areas of Sally's life and future. She is a motivated and open client who appreciates the support of her family and understands that she is in transition.

Identify, Define, and Justify Interventions

Sally is a client who falls between Gardner and Moore's (2004) performance development and performance termination phases for which general cocounseling and psychological skills training is recommended. Our sessions focused on helping Sally gain confidence in her decision making which reduced her overall feelings of anxiety and increase focus at practice. We will also work on her communication skills and examine why she feels the need to withhold her struggle about whether or not to stay in gymnastics. Her parents are a major support system in her life and want to take the steps necessary to enhance Sally's happiness.

Sally's anxiety manifested itself through cognitive rumination as she thought about the "What ifs . . ." regarding her situation. She mentioned minimal physiological experiences related to anxiety which may be the result of having exquisite body-awareness that is necessary for a gymnast. Her lack of focus in practice was a direct result of her anxiety and rumination. One technique that was helpful for her, based in cognitive behavioral therapy (Beck, 2011) involves thought stopping and utilizing cue words to increase focus. This technique came in handy when Sally was about to perform as it helped quiet her mind and increase her focus for competition. This was also a buffer to help her reduce likelihood of physical injury due to lack of focus.

Another technique to utilize was enhancing Sally's already existing communication skills. She was very open with her parents about most things but was hesitant to talk with them about her thoughts about retiring from gymnastics. My task was to highlight Sally's past successes at communicating with her parents and encourage her to allow her parents to help her through this stage in life. Sally was open to recommendations but did not want to disappoint her parents due to the amount of time and money they have invested into her gymnastics career. Her parents have emphasized the point that they know she is distracted but are not sure why. They are willing to support her and want her to be happy. Therefore, I helped Sally utilize her past experiences of support from her parents and apply them to her presenting dilemma.

Finally, I encouraged Sally and her family to schedule non-sport-based extracurricular activities to help Sally develop a more balanced schedule. At the time of intake she spent most of her time at school and in gymnastics (practice or meets) and had very little time to enjoy socializing with her friends or spend quality time with family. I recommended utilizing a family calendar to notate fun-time and to designate specific dates that Sally will have to socialize with her friends.

Schedule Session Agendas

Sally participated in eight weeks of 60-minute sport psychology sessions during which we addressed her presenting concerns. Length of participation in sport psychology sessions varies among athletes and depends on many individualized factors. Each week we reviewed how she assessed the presenting issues (self-talk, level of focus, fun activities, and communication) and created a plan to practice her skills during the week. We worked on Sally's communication skills and she decided to reveal her thoughts about ending her career in gymnastics to her parents in Week 4. Her parents were very receptive to her and planned to support her through the decision-making process. Sally continued to make progress throughout the sessions regarding reducing negative self-talk and increasing focus. She did not make a decision about her gymnastics career when we terminated but did feel an increased sense of confidence in her ability to allow her parents to help her with the decision. She agreed to return to sessions if she felt the need for additional consultation regarding her future.

Week 1: Intake
Week 2: Review Communication and Self-Talk
Week 3: Examine Focus and Career Termination
Week 4: Revisit Communication and Cue-Words
Week 5: Advanced practice of Self-Talk, Cue-Words, Focus
Week 6: Evaluate Confidence in Talking with Parents
Week 7: Assess Advancements in Sessions
Week 8: Celebration of Advancements and Termination

Recommendations for Future Practice

The future of sport psychology is evolving as the field continues to grow and develop. A strengths-based approach has been and continues to be an integral component of sport psychology. The field is at an exciting place where we must analyze the demands of applied fieldwork with the rigor of academic training. In 2012 founding AAASP President John Silva organized the *Coalition for the Advancement of Graduate Education and Training in the Practice of Sport Psychology* with the goal of developing common educational training and experiences that lead to competent applied practice. Unlike other professions, sport psychology does not have a standardized common educational core. The *Voluntary Graduate Program Recognition: A Competency-Based Self-Study Guide for Sport Psychology*, work group of the Coalition voiced a concern:

> Despite several decades of practice in sport psychology in the United States, no agreed upon standards or guidelines exist for the education and training of graduate students who desire to practice sport psychology. Virtually all graduate programs in helping professions (e.g., psychology, counseling, athletic training) have some form of program accreditation designed to establish and maintain standards for graduate education and practice. [A voluntary self-study can help] promote high quality programs that provide comprehensive course and practicum opportunities through a critical mass of qualified faculty serving as mentors and supervisors. (Cohen et al., 2014)

Another group of the Coalition, the *Gold Standards for Sport Psychology Graduate Practice Programs* (Van Raatle et al., 2014), developed recommendations for the future of training sport psychology professionals based on the Coalition's (Silva et al., 2013) three training pathways (master's level licensed counselor, doctoral level licensed psychologist, CC-AASP). The Gold Standards group put forward five goals and competencies: knowledge base in sport psychology, scientific inquiry and critical thinking, ethical and social responsibility in a diverse world, communication, and professional development. The goals encompass classroom experiences, field training, and supervision to help new professionals develop the unique skill set that is required to ethically practice sport psychology. The Coalition is in the process of encouraging existing graduate training programs to consider participating in a self-study that examines their current curriculum and field experiences, and comparing how they relate to the Gold Standards group's recommendations. The Coalition is also in the process of soliciting support from state boards to develop a legally protected title of sport psychology.

The goals of the Coalition are large and require several systems to cooperate and keep the wellbeing of sport psychology clients in mind. By continuing to increase the rigor of graduate training and field experiences the field of sport psychology will maintain growth in a healthy direction. Standardization of educational training and field experiences can result in well-rounded professionals who have the ability to help athletes and exercisers reach their goals, work through life transitions, and further themselves as individuals in a complicated world.

References

American Counseling Association. (2014). ACA Code of Ethics. Alexandria, VA: Author. Retrieved June 7, 2016 from http://www.counseling.org/resources/aca-code-of-ethics.pdf
American Psychological Association. (2015). APA sport psychology proficiency. Retrieved June 7, 2016 from http://www.apadivisions.org/division-47/about/sport-proficiency/index.aspx
Association for Applied Sport Psychology. (2015). Become a certified consultant. Retrieved June 7, 2016 from http://www.appliedsportpsych.org/certified-consultants/become-a-certified-consultant/
Association for Applied Sport Psychology. (n.d.). Ethics code: AASP principles and standards. Retrieved June 7, 2016 from http://www.appliedsportpsych.org/about/ethics/ethics-code/

Beck, J.B. (2011). *Cognitive behavior therapy* (2nd ed.). New York, NY: Guilford Press.

Cieslak, T.J. (2004). *Describing and measuring the athletic identity construct: Scale development and validation.* [Unpublished doctoral dissertation.] Retrieved June 7, 2016 from https://etd.ohiolink.edu/rws_etd/document/get/osu1091219903/inline

Cohen, A., Aoyagi, M., Bryant, L., Cranney, A., Finch, L., Petrie, T., . . . & Watson, J. (2014). *A competency-based self-study guide for sport psychology.* [Unpublished manuscript.]

Despres, J., Bradym, F., & McGowan, A.S. (2008). Understanding the culture of the student-athlete: Implications for college counselors. *The Journal of Humanistic Counseling, Education, and Development, 47,* 200–211.

Edwards. D.J., & Steyn, B.J.M. (2008). Sport psychological skills training and psychological well-being. *South African Journal for Research in Sport, Physical Education, and Recreation, 30,* 15–28.

Erikson, E. (1968). *Identity: Youth and crisis.* New York, NY: Norton.

Gardner, F.L., & Moore, Z.E. (2004). The multi-level classification system for sport psychology (MCS-SP). *The Sport Psychologist, 18,* 89–109.

Gill, D.L. (1995). Women's place in the history of sport psychology. *The Sport Psychologist, 9,* 418–433.

Health Insurance Portability and Accountability Act. (1996). Retrieved June 7, 2016 from https://www.cms.gov/Regulations-and-Guidance/HIPAA-Administrative-Simplification/HIPAAGenInfo/downloads/hipaalaw.pdf

Kerulis, M.C. (2011). *Personality characteristics of mixed martial artists: Counselor application for wellness.* [Doctoral dissertation.] DeKalb, IL: Northern Illinois University.

Kerulis, M. (2012). Aiding student-athletes with identity development. *Journal of Counseling in Illinois, 2*(1), 39–51.

Kerulis, M. & Cheadle, C. (2015). Are you online? Leveraging social media. In J. Taylor (Ed.), *Practice development in sport & performance psychology.* Morgantown, WV: Fitness Information Technology.

Lysek, J.J. (2014). *Nine mental skills for successful athletes.* Beachwood, OH: Ohio Center for Sport Psychology.

McCullagh, P. (1995). Sport psychology: A historical perspective. *The Sport Psychologist, 9,* 363–365.

Silva, J. et. al (2013). *Coalition for the Advancement of Graduate Education and Training in the Practice of Sport Psychology.* [Unpublished manuscript.]

Tapak, A., & Kerulis, M. (2014). *Choose wellness.* Retrieved June 7, 2016 from http://michelekerulis.blogspot.com/

Taylor, J., & Schneider, B.A. (1992). The sport-clinical intake protocol: A comprehensive interviewing instrument for applied sport psychology. *Professional Psychology Research and Practice, 23,* 318–325.

Van Raatle, J., Kerulis, M., Galli, N., Kamphoff, C., Poczwardowski, A., Butcher-Poffley, L., . . . & Statler, T. (2014). *Coalition for the Advancement of Graduate Education and Training in the Practice of Sport Psychology: Gold Standards for sport psychology graduate practice programs.* [Unpublished manuscript.]

Weinberg, R.S., & Gould, D. (2011). *Foundations of sport and exercise psychology* (5th ed). Champaign, IL: Human Kinetics.

Whiston, S.C. (2013). *Principles and applications of assessment in counseling* (4th ed.). Belmont, CA: Brooks/Cole.

16

Positive Psychology

History and Practice as a Strengths-Based Model

Jeffrey K. Edwards

But the Lord said to Samuel, "Do not look on his appearance or on the height of his stature, because I have rejected him; for the Lord does not see as mortals see; they look on the outward appearance, but the Lord looks on the heart."

1 Samuel 16.7

As has been noted elsewhere throughout this book, the history of psychology, social work, and counseling is replete with practitioner leaders that disagreed with the medically modeled view of clinical work that looks for problems alone. Modern day social work theorists (Rapp, 2011; Saleebey, 2009, 2012) developed ideas about a strengths-based model. Saleebey (2009) stated that "practicing from a strengths perspective means this—*everything* you do as a social worker will be predicated in some way, on helping to discover and embellish, explore and exploit clients' strengths and resources. . ." (p. 1). Abraham Maslow, Carl Rogers, and Albert Bandura who cared little for pathologizing their clients' ills found more interesting methods of working with the clients that came to be healed. Indeed, those other nonpathological methods were, no doubt, also less iatrogenic (Boisvert & Faust, 2002). Indeed, psychology's emphasis on wellness and strengths seemed to have been center stage up until the late 1940s, when out of necessity our forefathers shifted to treatment of "diseases" for those coming back from a war (Seligman, 2002).

Positive psychology as we know it today was first mentioned in former American Psychological Association (APA) President Martin Seligman's inaugural address (1998). Later Seligman and colleague Csikszentmihalyi (2000) wrote an article for the *American Psychologist* called "Positive Psychology: An Introduction." In Seligman's (2001) commentary on the National Institute for Mental Health's priorities for prevention research, he wrote that the use of protective factors was actually a subset of what he called "positive psychology" (p. 1). Thus began the movement of positive psychology and its next generation, positive therapy. Csikszentmihalyi described a chance meeting he had with Seligman as they both vacationed with their families on the big island of Hawaii: "For the rest of our stay, at breakfast, lunch, and dinner, we exchanged ideas as to what we thought the future of psychology ought to be" (Csikszentmihalyi & Nakamura, 2011). It was evident that both Csikszentmihalyi and Seligman not only understood how the turn in psychology had happened after WWII as large dollars came pouring into the field for both treatments of psychological problems and research to find answers to these problems. They both were, at the time of their vacation meeting, unhappy with the state of the field. "After more than three decades as a psychologist, however, I had become dissatisfied with much of what I was teaching my graduate students. Most of the research, and the conceptual framework that generated it, seemed artificial . . ." (Csikszentmihalyi, 2011, p. 4).

The positive psychology movement has since exploded into a well-oiled research effort with well over 70 books published. At last count, a google scholar search found that there were thousands of juried articles, most with scientific evidence to show their worth. The field has also become a part of mainstream psychology departments with more than 36 universities having departments with at least two faculty members, and 67 departments having at least one faculty member teaching positive psychology in some form or another. While writing and editing this book, it became evident that our title "strengths-based" could also include the title of *positive psychology*, as many of our authors chose to include positive psychology as part of their scholarship and methods in their chapters. In fact, Seligman (2011) gave a nod by suggesting that their Global Assessment Tool they use with the military is strength-based. The solution-focused therapy, narrative therapy, and more traditional strength-based models of social worker Reynolds' (1932) and later Saleebey (2006), Rapp & Gosha's (2006) foundational ideas, mostly in extra innings of editing, have been nudged quite a bit by Seligman and his cadre of colleagues from all walks of life. It is growing by leaps and bounds. Of interest is also a study by Kolodinsky et al. (2014), which illustrates the use of positive psychology in counselor education, that indicates that almost 80% (79.5%) strongly agreed or disagreed with the statement that "future CACREP standards should integrate positive psychology research" (p. 9).

This chapter introduces those who are interested in the parallel world of positive psychology. This is the second time I have attempted to write about positive psychology in the framework of being strengths-based; the first attempt being Chapter 5 in *Strengths-Based Clinical Supervision Primer: From the Roots of Psychology* (Edwards, 2013). I must admit that my knowledge of positive psychology is not as strong as I wish it were. The proliferation of information and trainings in universities has exponentially expanded. This work is but a taste of what is out there; I encourage the interested to pursue this very well-researched model and the more traditional models in earnest. Where possible, your own education can take you to places where you least expect to go, coming out far better as a clinician and an educator.

The Draw to an Alternative Model

I was first drawn to positive psychology while teaching a class on community counseling wherein I introduced students to the concept of *prevention*. Seligman's (2001) article in the APA journal *Prevention and Treatment* slighted the National Institute for Mental Health's (NIMH) lack of attention to protective factors in a world that talked a lot about risk factors instead. He suggests that it is a creature of the disease model, accepting uncritically the discontinuity of the mental "disorders." He goes on to say that the NIMH pays lip service to those protective factors that he claims give our clients their preventive effects. If that was not enough, he also points to the lack of intellectual challenge that would push away any quality science in the field. Boy, I wish I had written those reflective words. Let me repeat the claim with Seligman's (2001) own words: "[I]t is intellectually routine, making it less likely that first-rate science will be attracted to our field" (p. 2). I punctuate this notion because science becomes the *cercueil clou d'importance* for all of the positive psychology literature to overcome traditional psychotherapy and pathology seeking. One only has to look at the recent rejection of the *DSM-IV* to see that his prophecy has become a reality.

As a big believer in the family counseling's darlings like narrative and solution-focused work, I was beginning to believe this was something to which I should pay attention. In his three-page critique of the NIMH's love affair with problem-focused models and pathology elevation, he has two additional killer statements that I have resonated with for years—way back to my early days in working with folks in need.

> The disease model makes a strong assumption about the nature of the mental disorders: that they are discontinuous from "subclinical states." It is astonishing to me that this assumption remains NIMH gospel after 40 years of relevant research, in which almost no compelling evidence for discontinuity appears, and evidence for continuity abounds (Seligman, 2001, p. 2).

What drove me to a state of both tears and laughter was that I had just given a lecture/discussion about the *DSM-IV* that Seligman was speaking about and the interesting quote at the beginning of the large volume that stated the following:

> In DSM-IV there is no assumption that each category of mental disorders is a completely discrete entity with absolute boundaries dividing it from other mental disorders or from no mental disorder. There is also no assumption that all individuals described as having the same mental disorder are alike in all important ways" (APA, 2000, p. xxxi).

Seligman, despite the forces of the status quo, was on to something. One of my favorite Seligman thoughts is that we should not spend as much time "fixing" our weaknesses, as we do on finding and building what he calls our "signature strengths" (Seligman, 2002, p. 13). After studying the nonpathological assumptive models that came out of the family therapy literature, here was a well respected man stating something very similar but in a much more straightforward manner. And he included a twist. Rather than looking all over for problems, Seligman was suggesting that we look for strengths. The question is this: How are signature strengths different from what people do well naturally?

In their book *Character Strengths and Virtues: A Handbook and Classification*, Peterson and Seligman (2004) put forth 5 virtues and 24 signature strengths that define core concepts of what they believe is the most important link to living a good life. In order, the virtues are as follows: Wisdom and Knowledge, Courage, Justice, Temperance, and Transcendence. This 644-page book (without back pages and references) began the study and forth putting of what can be seen as the other side of the more traditional *Diagnostic and Statistical Manual* of pathologies. Neal Mayerson, a psychologist and entrepreneur, who with Seligman was concerned with the over use of a problem-focused way of understanding human behavior and who was interested in developing an alternative that allows for the classification and study of virtues and strengths, began the delving into strengths and virtues in a serious way. "The classification of strengths presented in this book is intended to reclaim the study of character and virtue as legitimate topics of psychological inquiry and informed societal discourse" (Peterson & Seligman, 2004, p. 3).

The various inventories that have been used over the years since the beginning of positive psychology can be found on the University of Pennsylvania "Authentic Happiness" website (see https://www.authentichappiness.sas.upenn.edu/), along with the Values in Action (VIA) Institute on Character (see https://www.viacharacter.org/www/). They have amassed a very large sample of people who have taken the various inventories, from the population of people all over the globe. I have taken their many inventories several times, and found that they led me to a fascinating addition to my life. I found some of my signature strengths to be in areas I considered, but had passed by due to a life headed in other directions.

But I am getting a bit ahead of myself here. The beginning of positive psychology that so quickly became one of the most prominent strengths-based models started way back with Seligman's (1975) work on *learned helplessness*, which he changed to *learned optimism* (Seligman, 1991, 1996). During his student days in the doctoral program of psychology, he and a few colleagues began to do experiments with dogs, inflicting random electrical shocks to condition them. They found, quite contrary to previous thinking of B.F. Skinner, that the dogs developed what they called *learned help-lessness* (Seligman & Maier,1967). From there, Seligman (2002) went on to write *Authentic Happiness*, an amazing book that outlined both what he believed at that point and a wonderful set of ideas and challenges that helped move his ever-evolving work to a place of prominence among many scholars and clinicians. By this time, positive psychology had reached its own as a scientific tour de force giving challenge to the normal views of mental health clinical work and the use of evidence-based models. Seligman (2005) suggested that one of the problems with evidence-based models lies within the fact that they line up with the criteria of the problem-saturated diagnostic manuals that we all use for clinical work. Both the *Diagnostic and Statistical Manual* and evidence-based work miss the larger elements of human resiliency, family, and friendly support and a tie to spiritual beliefs of hope, meaning, and a notion that there is a greater force in the universe than in the individual. The quest for a quick medically oriented solution (i.e., pharmaceuticals) runs the risk of encouraging clinicians to focus only on techniques that are focused on problems and designed to "fix" individuals that fit into *DSM* categories. As such, our mental health system is locked into problem saturation and, to an extent, an iatrogenic system. Seligman's (2011) latest book, *Flourish: A Visionary New Understanding of Happiness and Well-Being*, presents not only a change of direction from his focus on happiness as the center to his new thinking about how humans can have better lives. He also forages with positive psychology into the military as a way of helping change the costly and problem focus of that system and a whole set of very interesting research on the cost of negativity and the hope of optimism in medicine. One of the strengths that Seligman brings to his work is the steadfast notion of scholarship and research and the willingness to change course when necessary. His book *Flourish* is an example of that, as he tells of his move away from simple happiness to a life that fits where people are in their lives. As an avid reader of Seligman's work, I read with great interest this newer work during a yearly vacation with extended family. While my family was out boating, I was on the dock reading about this change. My daughter, wife, and nephew had to force me into the speedboat, dragging me away from my reading. I do not want to ruin your own reading, but my interest in what he calls the "new gold standard"—*flourishing*—is described as living within an optimal range of human functioning, one that connotes goodness, generativity, growth, and resilience (Fredrickson & Losada, 2005). Flourishing is the opposite of both pathology and languishing, which are usually described as living a life that feels both hollow and empty. According to Seligman (2001), a life of flourishing contains certain elements that he calls PERMA, a mnemonic for the following: Positive emotions, Engagement, Relationships, Meaning, and Achievement. Although these elements have as of yet to be validated, there is work in that direction, and it enhances and builds on his work significantly.

The Force Is with Them

To focus on Seligman alone in this field would do him a disservice. His call to change the field of psychology came while he was the president of the American Psychological Association in 1998. His tenure affected and brought along many likeminded others who were also distressed about the negativity that was primary in the field. His work with Csikszentmihalyi, known for his work with flow as well as the beginning of positive psychology (1990, 2011; Seligman & Csikszentmihalyi, 2000), and Peterson (2006; Peterson & Seligman, 2004) developed a primary hold on the efficacy of positive psychology. The setting of a solid program at the University of Pennsylvania, The Master of Applied Positive Psychology (MAPP) under the leadership of Seligman, became the first educational program dedicated to the study of and training in positive psychology. Positive psychology was blossoming. The flood of articles and books on positive psychology began in earnest. The scope and thrust of positive psychology is large, and I suggest that the interested reader begin with those works I include in this chapter. Clearly, however, a solid study would include much more than is provided here.

Treatments or Teaching?

For those of you that have never spent any time reading or thinking about positive psychology, the manner in which the "techniques" are given will seem very different. You are most likely used to having a client, or clients, come to see you in your office, and you ask questions, make interesting and thought provoking statements, reflect on what your client(s) say, and even perhaps dispute what they tell you at times. The models we all learn can be person-centered, cognitive behavioral, or a family-systems model. In fact, it could be any of the supposed thousands of ways a clinician and client might engage in work to deal with the presenting problems of the client(s) (Feltham, 1997). They all expect the clinician to begin the session, describing a usual 50-minute hour, helping the client describe the presenting problem with other interesting information as supporting causes, and then apply one of the many models to the process. Variations of this come in different settings, from group counseling, multiple family groups, and the most common, individual therapy. Some protocols may even prescribe homework assignments or in-session enactments. They all have in common the notion that the therapeutic process is something that the clinician presents and that the client or clients will be receptive, or, heaven forbid, be resistant to. The traditional clinical work is aimed at problems, or pathology, with the intent to change that to something less problematic. Some look to the treatment to produce change through insight, others from cognitive restructuring, and many rely on behavioral change due to practice, and changing how they react. Change is difficult, after all, but it is inevitable.

Positive psychology uses education, and other techniques, to effect change. But the biggest difference is its objective. Rather than treating mental illness or problems of clients, positive psychology aims to help clients have a satisfactory life. But before you diehard mental health folks turn the page, you need to know that more recent work by the positive psychology team has also come up with a solid scientific way to change trauma from post-traumatic stress syndrome to post-traumatic growth (Seligman, 2011; Elliot, Kurylo, & Rivera, 2005). Not only that, but the medical benefits of such simple but interesting discernments are evident, such as how forgiveness can actually benefit a person with respect to decreased anxiety and stress, lower blood pressure, and stronger heart health, among others is important. (McCullough & van Oyen Witvliet, 2005; Zheng, Fehr, Tai, Narayanan, & Gelfand, 2014). There can be a lowering of depression with many of the different protocols of positive psychology, such as acts of gratitude, and taking part in similar group training such as has been done with the Penn Resiliency Program (PRP). This program, a component of MAPP, is an evidence-based program where optimism and resiliency are taught.

> PRP promotes optimism by teaching students to think more realistically and flexibly about the problems they encounter. PRP also teaches assertiveness, creative brainstorming, decision making, relaxation, and several other coping skills. PRP is the most widely researched depression prevention program in the world. (Seligman, 2011)

Most interesting to me, in the combatting and preventing of depression, one of the leading mental health problems, is the 2011 report by eight of the leading experts in understanding and treating depression. Together they discussed and wrote an article for *Clinical Psychology* (Forgeard et al., 2011). Conclusions, from these eminent researcher/practitioners, including Seligman, pointed to the learned helplessness, that he began his career with. Of course, the best way of treating this debilitating problem is through the training of learned optimism, which they suggested is the most relevant component of learned helplessness as a basic process involved in the development of depression.

Positive psychology has many scientifically relevant ways of working to help humans live more effective and flourishing lives. I want to talk about three of the many well-researched techniques I teach during the many workshops and trainings on strengths-based work I have given over the years. The first is called *the best of the best*, the second is *savoring*, and the third, that has wonderful science behind it, is *the act of gratitude*. One of those that I use in my workshops, that I will not talk about here, demonstrates the use of programs like PRP, the notion of changing post-traumatic stress disorder (PTSD) to post-traumatic growth. It is an amazing feat of cognitive changes in a group educational setting, and invokes a simple idea that research has shown how those going into the military are very familiar with the concept of PTSD, whereas only a small percentage have ever heard of the amazing power every human being has, that of resilience. I will leave this one to your own reading with the hopes that you will purchase the book *Flourish* and be awed by the power of positive psychology's simple yet very powerful ideas.

Three clinical change models

I have begun to start my workshops with two pre understandings I present, that seem to help participants move away from what used to be a flood of negative comments that are based on their previous notions about clinical work and our field in general. We have been, as my former mentor Froma Walsh has stated in her groundbreaking book *Normal Family Process* (2003), subjugated by the medical model, training our students to look for deficits and problems. The first early understanding is that we are all stuck with the perceptual sets we have seemed to have inherited. I have discussed this in Chapter 1, as well as the next Chapter 17. We are enslaved it seems to a way of thinking and believing that guides us through the worldviews we embrace and believe. This means that new and different ideas are hard to swallow. The second is a gift we all received from pioneering philosopher of science Thomas Kuhn. His revolutionary book (Kuhn, 2000), *The Structure of Scientific Revolutions*, introduced the notion that all science goes thorough the natural change from what he calls normal science to new science as we look for and find new ways of looking at, and understanding, that which we study and use in our fields. These paradigm shifts can cause dilemmas for those of us who believe in the truth of our ideas, methods, and theories. Kuhn maintained that "When scientists must choose between competing theories, two men fully committed to the same list of criteria for choice may nevertheless reach different conclusions" (1977, p. 320). I use these two supports before I move on to the information I am providing, and it has seemed to help give support to the newer ideas I present.

The Best of the Best

I learned about this interesting way of presenting the notion of strengths from a book Chris Peterson (2006) wrote. Soon after I read about it, I adapted my own story to it, so that I could relevantly address the issue of the power of positive stories. This is always given (at least the way I use it) as a story within a story.

My workshops begin with a tale about my coming home from Pittsburg, after attending the annual American Counseling Association as the president of the Illinois branch—the Illinois Counseling Association. I got on the plane with Seligman's book *Happiness* clutched tightly in my hand, and quickly found my seat. The plane had rows of two seats on each side; I had asked for the aisle seat for easy access. In the window seat sat an interesting looking rugged young man, a few years my junior. I nodded hello to the passenger in the window seat, sat down, and opened the book to the current page, beginning to pick up reading where I had left off. The gentleman in the window seat said,

"Hi, I'm Tom. You are headed to Chicago, do you live there?"
I nodded that I did and went back to what I hoped might be a quiet flight where I could read a
    few chapters.
"What were you doing in Pittsburgh?" Tom asked.
"I was at a conference!" I retorted.

"What sort of conference?" my inquisitive row mate asked.

"It was a counseling conference!!" I said trying to mumble.

Tom was having none of this silence, I could tell. How might I extract myself from a lengthy conversation, I thought.

"Oh, are you a counselor?" he asked. "I sure could use one!!"

"Really," I said, trying not to *sound interested*.

And then it began. The stories of his family, a daughter who was problematic, a wife who did not understand him at all, the potential for a divorce, and the fact that he was a cop who was told by his commander to take some time off because he was very stressed and it was hurting his work in the field. Oh my. Well, I made a deal with Tom, I said that I was really interested in getting through a few of the chapters in the book I wanted to read, but I would be glad to listen to his story on the last leg of the trip, if he would do two things for me . . . let me read for a while, and prepare a list of things he liked about his family and the relationships that they had that worked. I would even give him an opinion, if he liked. He agreed, the rest of the trip was quiet, and Tom and I struck up an interesting conversation during the last half hour of our trip. He said later that he had never given pause to think about the parts of his family life that went well and that perhaps, after I suggested it, he might find a good "shrink" to help fix his family and even perhaps some of his own "stuff." He seemed happy enough that someone had taken him and his problems seriously . . . even though he had come up with nice things to say about his family.

I was struck by the fact that this stranger was more than willing to tell me about all the horrible things going on with his family, if I had let him. Also, that with a bit of guidance, he was able to change the course of what could have been a giant bitch session about his family, which might reinforce his position about his family life.

This is the first story, embedded in the two stories. And it illustrates the idea about how we are so problem focused and also how quickly we can help to change the narrative. Next, I tell my own story. It goes like this:

I have two sons and a daughter. I am in my second marriage, with the two sons coming to live with my second wife and me when they were preteens. Their mother was desperately ill, and the boys had to come and live with my wife Betsy and me a few months after we were married. Betsy is a saint. I'm not. The boys were what you might expect, given the issues with their mother and the fact that they were still unhappy about the fact that their mother and I had divorced 5 years earlier. We had some very difficult times—times that now are far behind us but that were rough years for us all. Through it all, Betsy was very helpful and cared for both sons. She even bought them letterman sweaters, as they were both, by this time, doing well in sports. We helped them through their teens, provided them with what we could when they went off to college, and also had a girl child born to us while all of this was going on. A few years after they graduated, my youngest son came to us saying that he and his girlfriend of several years wanted to get married. He asked us if we could help with the rehearsal dinner and some of the other needs. Our daughter was about four at this time, and he said that she was to be the flower girl. Life had settled down, but life was not totally back to normal. The boys had come and gone a few times in the typical launching and bouncing back home that we saw a lot happening in families back then. I was glad, frankly, that my son was going to get married, and I was hopeful it would light up his life and give him a push to settle down.

The wedding went off without a hitch, and the reception was lots of fun. I told my son that I had never seen him so happy. He said, "Of course . . . I have my whole family together here . . ." Then the dance began. My new daughter-in-law and son began to dance the wedding dance, and then she went and found her dad and began to dance with him. My son walked across the dance floor and asked his mother to dance too. About midway through the dance, my son escorted his mom back to the sidelines where everyone was watching, gave her a hug, turned around, and walked to his stepmother and asked her to finish the dance with him. She did, people were amazed, and I was crying as were many relatives who had been with us during a lot of the usual teen angst and problems. My son had shown us all the best of the best for that time, and we all knew that life was somehow knitted back together in love.

I have told this story at least a dozen times in classes and workshops, and every time people shed tears . . . including me. The story, of course, tells us that life, even when difficult, can be changed and that there are positive parts of life we sometimes do not expect. They come about because of very deep emotions and love. We are conditioned for some reason to talk more about the problems in life than we do about the wonderful best-of-the-best times. I have found, or have opened up, to many more best of the bests since then.

The story is not over there, of course. I then have students get into pairs and tell each other their own best-of-the-best stories. Sometimes they cry, sometimes they laugh, but they all come away with a better notion that life is not only about problems, but also it is about good times, wonderful times, when we can celebrate what goes well in our lives.

Savoring

Another of the several positive psychology techniques I have used in classes and workshops is the idea of savoring. I first learned about savoring, perhaps, from my grandmother Bea, who was always suggesting to my cousins and me that we should take our time, enjoy the moment and the flavor of the food, and savor the moment. What was a small child to do but to pretend that I was doing what Gramma suggested then bolt out the door with my cousins and across the street to the park to play on the monkey bars and slide. I did not give it a second thought until I reached later adulthood. Reading Kabat-Zinn's (2009) book *Full Catastrophe Living: Using the Wisdom of Your Body and Mind to Face Stress, Pain, and Illness* continued my quest to expand my understanding of new and novel ways of helping the human dilemmas. One of the interesting tactics he suggested is the use of a raisin, which I will get into in a bit. The idea, of course, is to help us scattered and overactive humans savor what we do in life. It works.

Later, I put Kabat-Zinn's ideas together with an interesting article by Positive Psychologist Fred Bryant (2003), who has shown that the capacity to savor is connected with our perceived control over positive emotions. To this end, Bryant developed an inventory to explore and measure beliefs about savoring behaviors. This work connects the ability of perception of savoring with the personal beliefs of individuals. The issue and relevance of perceptual sets and how they are encoded in the mind is discussed in both Chapters 1 and 17 of this book.

In any case, the issue of savoring is pertinent to helping enjoyment become an important part of clinical work, including individual sessions as well as clinical supervision.

The event

I have used the technique of savoring both in group situations as well as one on one clinical supervision. I always begin with the raisin exercise, handing out a box of raisins and asking that the participants take two raisins from the box and place one of them in their mouth. They are asked not to chew, but as expected and anticipated, some of the group or individuals have already begun to chew the raisin. With a bit of fun and banter regarding their desire to just "get on with it," the task takes on a more fun venture rather than a "what is this silly thing about"? I then ask them once again to take a raisin out of the box, place it into their mouth, and using their tongue, feel around, explore the texture of the raisin, and then the feel of it in their mouth. We move on to having them taste it without biting, then biting and exploring the flavor, and finally swallowing the chewed raisin. There is then a processing of the event, and exploring their feelings and experiences that leads to a discussion of our ability to take our time, and enjoy, and what seems to either get in the way of that, or how they can control that enjoyment. Next, we together move to the next part of the event, and they are asked to think of a very pleasant time in their lives, and to begin to savor that time. Instructions are given slowly regarding taking their time, what feelings come about from that savoring, what the time line of their own savoring is, et cetera. I have found that during a supervision session where a supervisee comes in and has a case he or she is working with in which he or she has had trouble of one sort or another, I can use this situation with savoring to turn their negative "I messed this one up" attitude around. I ask him or her to think of a time when he or she had a good session, be it a few minutes or longer, and close his or her eyes and savor that good session and all that transpired. Then I ask him or her to think about applying anything they can think of from that good session to the one that was not as good and spend time savoring how it might come out in all of the many ways. I have seen dramatic changes from one perceptual set of thinking to a more hopeful, optimistic perceptual set.

Our ability to move our perceptual sets from one that is not so well perceived to another that has better outcome potentials all because of their ability to savor a time when things went well, is a learned optimism behavior.

My very first time doing a clinical workshop at an association convention was specifically changed from a scary "I cannot do this" attitude to a winning presentation. After confessing my fear, my dissertation chair suggested to me to think of a time when I was in front of a class for a presentation, one that was successful, and to remember that when I was in front of a large crowd of professionals. I savored that good time, and the workshop was a success. I will forever be grateful to Dr. Robert "Bob" Nejedlo for knowing how to help me savor the best and apply it to the next time I lead a workshop.

Gratitude: A Daily Event

Who in the world would ever think to start a discussion about gratitude by delving into the vicissitudes of evolution? But Seligman (2011) does so and nicely points out the weaknesses of such self-serving notions the likes of which come from Richard Dawkins' (1990) *The Selfish Gene*. Gratitude, and the altruism that it springs from, fails to account for the many explanations of altruistic and other-serving activities. Altruism abides in the mentorship of students where no thanks are expected, in the calm and intentional covering of grenades by senior-level and regulars in the service in order to protect their comrades, and, the most dependable of all, during the crashing of the World Trade Center where first responders unselfishly charged into certain doom to protect and save others. According to the research of social science that includes positive psychology, the gratitude that is not required or expected provides benefits for the one speaking the gratitude and not usually to the one who has been the helper. Social resiliency maintains a needed cohesion of the group. To express one's gratitude to another includes a tricky social event, where the one expressing the gratitude may vacillate between gushing thanks and praise for the one who has been of help, whereas the one receiving the gratitude might want to avoid or down play the need for words of praise. It can be uncomfortable for both, I have found. The work and research of Emmons and Shelton (2005) goes deep into the meaning and research regarding gratitude, noting that "although intuitively compelling, many of the general claims concerning the power of a grateful lifestyle are speculative or empirically untestable" (p. 459). Not wanting to be ungrateful, it seems that the social principle of the act of gratitude can be difficult for both parties, even though it can seem like the right thing to do. Years after I had received my doctorate and secured a job, I found myself in a situation where one of my mentors, Dr. Bob Nejedlo, and I were in the same place at the same time. I thanked him again for all of the help he had provided me, and in an almost stern manner he said, "You have told me this a few times before, and it is not necessary to show your appreciation any more." Context seems an important factor indeed. Yet the sparseness of research continues to point to the fact that giving gratitude is helpful to both the giver and the receiver. There is enough information to begin making specific claims to the potential benefits of a grateful life.

> One can draw a significant conclusion from these studies, in our estimation, in that grateful individuals are not naively optimistic nor are they under some illusion that suffering and pain are nonexistent. Rather, these persons have consciously taken control by choosing to extract benefits from adversity, with one of the major benefits being the perception of life as a gift. Grateful people may have more psychic maneuverability than the ungrateful, enabling them to be less defenses and more open to life (Emmons & Shelton, 2005).

The gratitude exercise is a wonderful beginning for folks who want to work on themselves as a way of understanding how it can be of benefit to their clients. I have taught this in every workshop and several classes over the last 5 years. The interest in gratitude as a viable way of living life began with my parents, of course. Many of the sayings that came from my gramma to my mother were about gratitude. It was a way of remaining strong during several very difficult times in their lives and followed their religious lives, I am sure. While beginning my study of positive psychology, I came across a Ted Talk featuring positive psychologist Shawn Achor (2011), and I began to use it in the beginning of my own talks, as a way of introducing ideas that I would later go over during the workshop presentation. I recommend this Ted Talk to you (see https://www.ted.com/talks/shawn_achor_the_happy_secret_to_better_work?language=en).

One can give out great stats and research on counseling models, but to have a fun and interesting video is a wonderful way of engaging your audience. The most pertinent aspect of Achor's discussion of gratitude is that it shows that a specific manner of behavior change fits with what we know about behavioral changes that occur as a result of repeated behaviors. In this case, it is explicitly stated that a set of repeated gratitudes—three a day for 21 days to be exact—will retrain the brain to be more open and happy in many areas. Achor calls it the *happiness advantage* and links it to many positive benefits, including more resiliency, productivity, and less burnout on the job. The claim, hooked to being more grateful among other things, is that one will also begin to scan the environment and life for more positives. I was down with that, so I tried it, and found it to be absolutely true. What I also found to be true is that like dieting, deciding to exercise, or any of those behavioral changes, it is also easy to let go of them and reverse the good work if one begins to forget to follow the pattern and begin a downward spiral back. Routine and staying with it is the real key.

Next, after showing the video, I talk about the benefits, and have the audience close their eyes and think of someone to whom they feel grateful. Imagining the person and then writing in a letter what one might say is a great way of embedding this concept. But Achor's suggestion of doing so three times a day works well too, and I used it on Facebook for a long time. It does not have to be hooked to a person all the time; also, it can be connected to events or places—almost anything to which one feels grateful. The important thing is to begin looking for and being grateful to these people or events on a regular basis—making it a normal part of one's life. I am always grateful for my wife and my friends. The point is to make it known to them or the world that you have found the involvement meaningful in your life.

As I was doing one of my workshops, a young woman who was a former student of mine raised her hand and asked if she might claim who she was grateful for right there and then. I said, "OK," and she began to describe how I had been helpful to her in her career and that she had never told me how much I had meant to her. She asked if she might give me a hug, and in front of almost 70 people she showed her gratitude to a professor she now said had been helpful to her and her life. I was very pleased to receive this gratitude, and she was overjoyed that she could finally express it. I think we both benefited from this experience. I can look back on that time as a moment when someone whom I had not only taught, but apparently had been a help to, publicly appreciated that, and she was able to finally say the words she must have been holding on to for a few years. Professors teach many students over the course of their careers; mine was 28 years. It is rare, although appreciated, when a student provides that feedback, especially when heartfelt and, yes, public. I suspect that this student received as much benefit for having said this as I did in receiving. It certainly adds to a social bonding of a society, regardless of what Richard Dawkins hypothesizes. Though a professor expects little in return for being a good professor, the event does add to the humanity of altruistic behavior. It knits us together in a very meaningful way.

What I have given you within this chapter is a taste of what positive psychology is about, where it came from, and what it can do. I am hopeful that, given the amount of discussion regarding positive psychology in this volume, those of you who know a little may choose, after reading this chapter, to check out some of the work from those others who have been in the fold of positive psychology in a serious and steady manner. The continual changing tides in our field—be it mental health or something else—are an interesting and ever evolving forum. As mentioned earlier in this chapter, the paradigm shifts are always evident (Kuhn, 2000). I am always fascinated by the idea that where we are today in terms of the field is not where we will be a year from now, or for sure, a decade from now. One can only hope that we will have moved on to a more positive view of human behavior, meaning, and management. And if you so choose, you too can be a part of this changing view.

References

Achor, S. (2011). *The happy secret to better work.* [Ted Talk.] Retrieved from https://www.ted.com/talks/shawn_achor_the_happy_secret_to_better_work/transcript?language=en

American Psychiatric Association. (2000). Diagnostic and statistical manual of mental disorders: DSM-IV-TR. Washington, DC: American Psychiatric Association (p. xxxi).

Boisvert, C., & Faust, D. (2002). Iatrogenic symptoms in psychotherapy: A theoretical exploration of the potential impact of labels, language, and belief systems. *American Journal of Psychotherapy, 56,* 244–259.

Bryant, F.B. (2003). Savoring Beliefs Inventory: A scale for measuring beliefs about savoring. *Journal of Mental Health, 12,* 175–196.

Csikszentmihalyi, M. (1990). *Flow: The psychology of optimal experience.* New York, NY: Harper & Row.

Csikszentmihalyi, M., & Nakamura, J. (2011). Positive psychology: Where did it come from, where is it going? In K. Sheldon, T.B. Kashdan, & M.F. Steger (Eds.), *Designing positive psychology: Taking stock and moving forward.* Oxford, UK: Oxford University Press.

Dawkins, R. (1990). *The selfish gene* (2nd ed.). New York, NY: Oxford University Press.

Edwards, J.K. (2013). *Strengths-based supervision in clinical practice.* Thousand Oaks, CA: Sage Publications.

Elliot, T.R., Kurylo, M., & Rivera, P. (2005). Positive growth following acquired physical disabilities. In C.R. Snyder & S.J. Lopez (Eds.), *Handbook of positive psychology* (pp. 687–699). Oxford, UK: Oxford University Press.

Emmons, R.A., & Shelton, C.M. (2005). Gratitude and the science of positive psychology. In C.R. Snyder & S.J. Lopez (Eds.), *Handbook of positive psychology* (pp. 459–471). Oxford, UK: Oxford University Press.

Feltham, C. (1997). *Which psychotherapy? Leading exponents explain their differences.* Thousand Oaks, CA: Sage Publications.

Forgeard, M.J. C, Haigh, E.A.P., Beck, A.T., Davidson, R.J., Henn, F.A., Maier, S.F., . . . Seligman, M.E.P. (2011). Beyond depression: Toward a process-based approach to research, diagnosis, and treatment. *Clinical Psychology, 18,* 275–299.

Fredrickson, B.L., & Losada, M.F. (2005). Positive affect and complex dynamics of human flourishing. *American Psychologist, 60,* 678–686.

Kabat-Zinn, J. (2009). *Full catastrophe living: Using the wisdom of your body and mind to face stress, pain, and illness.* New York, NY: Delta.

Kolodinsky, P., Englar-Carlson, M., Montopoli, G., Edgerly, B., Dubner, D., Horn, R., & Draves, P. (2014). *Positive psychology in counselor education: An exploration of counselor educators' opinions.* Alexandria, VA: American Counseling Association.

Kuhn, T. (1977). *The essential tension: Selected studies in scientific tradition and change.* Chicago, IL: University of Chicago Press.

Kuhn, T. (2000). *The structure of scientific revolutions.* Chicago, IL: University of Chicago Press.

McCullough, M.E., & van Oyen Witviliet, C. (2005). The psychology of forgiveness. In C.R. Snyder & S.J. Lopez (Eds.), *Handbook of positive psychology* (pp. 446–458). Oxford, UK: Oxford University Press.

Peterson, C. (2006). *A primer in positive psychology.* New York, NY: Oxford University Press.

Peterson, C., & Seligman, M.E.P. (2004). *Character strengths and virtues.* New York, NY: Oxford University Press.

Rapp, C.A. (2011). *The strengths model: A recovery-oriented approach to mental health services.* New York, NY: Oxford University Press.

Reynolds, B.C. (1932). *An experiment in short-contact interviewing.* New York, NY: Taylor & Francis.

Saleebey, D. (2009). (Ed.). *The strengths perspective in social work practice.* (5th ed.). New York, NY: Pearson.

Saleebey, D. (2012). *The strengths perspective in social work practice.* London, UK: Longman Pub Group.

Seligman, M.E.P. (1975). *Helplessness: On depression, development, and death.* San Francisco, CA: W.H. Freeman.

Seligman, M.E.P. (1991). *Learned optimism: How to change your mind and your life.* New York, NY: Albert Knopf.

Seligman, M.E.P. (1993). *What you can change and what you can't: The complete guide to successful self-improvement.* New York, NY: Albert Knopf.

Seligman, M.E.P. (1996). *The optimistic child: Proven program to safeguard children from depression & build lifelong resilience.* New York, NY: Houghton Mifflin.

Seligman, M.E.P. (1999). Inaugural Address; In Gerald Kocher, *The APA 1998 Annual Report,* Washington, DC: American Psychologist, (537–568).

Seligman, M.E.P. (2001). Comment on "priorities for prevention research at NIMH." *Prevention and Treatment, 4,* 24.

Seligman, M.E.P. (2002). *Authentic happiness: Using the new positive psychology to realize your potential for lasting fulfillment.* New York, NY: Free Press.

Seligman, M.E.P. (2005). Positive psychology, positive prevention, and positive therapy. In C.R. Snyder & S.J. Lopez (Eds.), *Handbook of positive psychology* (pp. 3–9). Oxford, UK: Oxford University Press.

Seligman, M.E.P. (2011). *Flourish: A visionary new understanding of happiness and well-being.* New York, NY: Free Press.

Seligman, M.E.P., & Csikszentmihalyi, M. (2000). Positive psychology: An introduction. *American Psychologist, 55,* 5–14.

Seligman, M.E.P., & Maier, S.F. (1967). Failure to escape traumatic shock. *Journal of Experimental Psychology, 74,* 1–9.

Walsh, F. (Ed.). (2003). *Normal family process: Growing diversity and complexity.* New York, NY: Guilford Press.

Zheng, X., Fehr, R., Tai, K., Narayanan, J., & Gelfand, M.J. (2014). The unburdening effects of forgiveness: Effects on slant perception and jumping height. *Social Psychological & Personality Science, 5,* 1–8.

Section IV
Training and Education

17

Strengths-Based Clinical Supervision

An Examination of How it Works

Jeffrey K. Edwards

> We all blossom in the presence of one who sees the good in us and who can coax the best out of us.
>
> Desmond Tutu (p.143)

A Circuitous Orientation to Strengths-Based Clinical Supervision

I have been excited by news from the *Harvard Business Review* (*HBR*) for years. My wife is a wonderful high-level manager of operations at a very large company, and she reads it on line all the time. Me, when I am wandering through grocery stores or the lonely bookstores that are still around, I grab the *HBR* when it looks like there is information I might adapt to the clinical world. I have quoted information from it over the years, both in chapters and in lectures. Somehow, some of those folks in mental health, and there are only a few, do not like the crossover references, whereas others do not seem to mind. Many of their articles are about leadership, and I think of those of us who have attained the status of a supervisor as being a leader. There are many kinds of leadership ideas but the ones I have gravitated to are those that are either about servant leadership (i.e., Greenleaf & Spears, 2002) or strengths-based (Rath & Conchie, 2008). Several days ago while checking out at the local Whole Foods, I spied my old friend, the *HBR*'s OnPoint, with a front title that said "Be a Better Boss: How to Bring Out the Best in Your People" (OnPoint, 2015). It sounded like something I would really like, so when I opened it up while waiting in line, I was thrilled to see that there were two articles right up my alley, and that would fit the chapter I was writing for our book. The first was about the simple but powerful word *together* that I will discuss briefly, and the other was about an old friend I have researched and written about before, the Pygmalion effect. I write about that later in this chapter under the heading "Supervising with Compassion Rather than for Compliance."

Together

I look for motivators all the time. There was a big one right there in the current *HBR* titled, "Managers Can Motivate Employees with One Word," by Heidi Grant Halvorson (2015). I have cited this author before, and I have one of her books, so she has tremendous referent power for me. The word is *together* and there is solid research that Grant Halvorson quotes which mystifies me because I'm thinking that we do not use it enough in our field of supervision. I have my own ideas about why this powerful word is left out, but the information shows that

> ...the word "together" is a powerful social cue to the brain. In and of itself, it seems to serve as a kind of relatedness reward, signaling that you belong, that you are connected, and that people you can trust are working with you toward the same goal. (Grant Halvorson, 2015, p. 15)

The word *together* can be a wonderful tool for helping our supervisees trust the process and us during a time that is potentially worrisome. Talking about cases that are problematic can leave the supervisee feeling vulnerable as they talk it out with us. When we invoke this magical word, we are both in the discourse jointly. We share in our discussion of what to do, without one of us being in charge and all-knowing. It even may lower that anxiety that normally comes about with a flood of responses from the hypothalamus to activate the sympathetic nervous system, and the adrenal-cortical system, beginning the fight or flight response.

Throughout this chapter I give you other researched information that, when used congruently and genuinely, can make your supervision not only strengths-based, but also even more effective than it might be already.

Situating My Beginnings

I first became aware of strengths-based supervision over 25 years ago, when I was contracting for my supervision of supervision in order to receive the American Association for Marriage and Family Therapy's (AAMFT's) Approved Supervision Designation. AAMFT had the supervisory training and credentialing long before any of the other associations, and during my doctoral training I realized I might need this credential to supervise students wherever I might land a job. My search stopped at Northern Illinois University's Family Therapy Studies program where Dr. Tony Heath directed the program. As it turned out, Dr. Heath was the AAMFT national organization's chair of supervisory training at that time—lucky me. During our first time together, as I nervously began my interview, I shared my story of having crossed eyes at a young age, finally learning to read in the fourth grade, failing eighth grade, being told by my guidance counselor (now called *school counselor*) that I should follow a course of vocational studies because college was not on the cards for me; I was marginalizing by "experts." Yet, amazingly, I did go to college, and after that, got into graduate school for a masters in science in counseling psychology. Call it grace or perseverance, but finally I ended up a new doc student wanting to be an approved supervisor. Tony listened patiently as I laid out my woeful problem-saturated story and then said oh so slowly, "So, I'm curious; how would any of that stop you from being a great supervisor?"

Now, in one short sentence Dr. Heath had dispelled my fears and set the bar higher for me than I had ever expected. I would gain my doctorate in counseling, and become an AAMFT approved supervisor. Perhaps I could even teach graduate-level classes. A short strengths-based conversation gave me confidence in my quest to become someone who others (and myself) had said I could never be. Language really does construct reality. I wanted to be like Tony, and help those who like me had what he called an imposter syndrome. He assured me that most everyone who reached for the starry heavens felt that way at one time or another. He normalized it for me saying that those who had the imposter syndrome and admitted it were probably better off than those who pretended, or who fooled themselves into thinking that they know it all. Supervision is about a relationship I was told—a trusting relationship. Making relationships work is not about being one-up on those with whom you want to relate. So, humility and the willingness to show my imperfect side, to be a real human being that makes mistakes and who does not claim to know it all, would make me a far better mentor/supervisor and guide for our field. If I played to my own strengths, and not work to hide my weaknesses—my faults and problems—I could be on a better road to transparency and genuineness. It made good sense to me.

I had been trained early on in my career with the psychodynamic therapy model, and later person-centered, and finally family systems therapy. I learned solution-focused (de Shazer & Berg, 1997) and narrative therapies (White & Epston, 1990), all of which seemed to bypass looking for problems, and went straight to encouraging and building strengths. I was amazed at how quickly someone could change their position or point of view regarding what they saw as problematic. All of these changes without digging in the dirt of "causation," that according to Bertrand Russell (1953) does not exist.

The usual mental health model we all had learned, of assessing a problem and forming a treatment that the client was to work on, are deeply embedded in our training. The early clinicians, psychiatrists with medical training, simply began to use the medical models, to work with what they assumed were pure psychological or psychiatric problems. Now, we know that our clients come to us with bio-psycho-socio-cultural-familial-spiritual and dare I add political constructs. There is most often more than one factor negatively influencing our being that brings us to a place where we seek outside help. Clinicians and people in general think of these issues as pathology, or maladaptation. They can, how-ever, be seen as a grouping of perceptual sets that influence thinking and thus behavior. Rather than brain chemistry or conditions, they are mindsets influenced by the part of the brain called the nar-rative, or more technically the thalamocortical network (Siegel, 2007). It is this part of the mind that processes all of the information within our brains about the correct way to think, our beliefs, and our perceptual sets. Siegel goes on to say that our narrative brain actually enslaves us to think and believe all that we have encoded in the thalamocortical network. This network has the purpose of making decisions about life easier to act upon. The information is encoded through life events and learning, no matter if it is factual or old outdated data, or even old wives' tales. Our beliefs about religion, politics, courtesies, and social behavior have been encoded, and it takes a lot of informational input to counter some of these sets. Sets can be helpful, and the set can be wrong. Sets can become what is called "confirmational data or bias" (opinions), as the set confirm and conform to our beliefs without our checking to make sure the belief is correct. They can also block out new, more correct information.

What I am beginning to see in training and studies is that the effects of working with a person's strengths, rather than their construed problems (sets), can be a quicker, less problem-focused way of working with clients, be they clinical or supervisory. In addition to the quickness of these models of change is the interesting information about what are called *iatrogenic problems*, which are problems that arise from being in some sort of treatment. I know that there is a great risk of patients in the doc-tor's office, or a hospital clinic, "catching" a disease or virus just from being in proximity of someone else who has that virus. The same has been found to be true of psychological issues, especially the use of problem-focused language, diagnosis for instance (Boisvert & Faust, 2002). I suggest that the strengths-based language is less apt to provide a negative consequence, or as I now know, a negative set. This is not to say that there aren't some drastic problems out there, but the majority of those coming to us for help are usually not pure biological problems. They are mind constructs—mind perceptual sets that cause difficulties. This is also accurate when I talk about what can happen dur-ing supervision. The nature of our usual medically modeled system is for supervisees to come in and talk about the problems they are having with their clients. Strengths-based supervision changes this clinical supervision set. I might begin a supervision session by asking what they think they did well in their recent clinical work, or what they liked about it. Questions such as these can be followed up by asking what they wish they had done differently, or more of, rather than pursuing the problems they perceive they had in a particular session.

As a new assistant professor in a counseling program, I was charged with clinical supervision of sections of both mental health and couple and family counseling students, and it was during this time I became keenly aware of the potential of working with students' strengths, rather than dwelling on what they might be doing wrong in their work. When working in a supervision class for masters students, I spend time demonstrating different techniques using the students as clients, with either real or made-up scenarios, and then have them practice those skills so that they will become more proficient. I remember working with a woman who, during a role play, talked about being childless. She said she felt as if she was missing something, even though she rattled off many reasons why it wasn't a problem. But family and friends had "socially constructed" this problem for her by asking about it, and insisting that it must cause her great pain. I suggested that perhaps being childfree was something that might have many benefits. I could tell I had connected with her with this reframe, as her eyes got brighter, and she sat up taller in her chair as she mulled over what I had just said. "Yes, I think that is a far better way to think about it," she said, and I too began to think I had done our most serious work, all with one sentence . . . just as had Tony Heath. How is this strengths-based? Well, I did not have to go working with what some might see as problematic issues that this woman "had." My supervisee had a second-order change.[1] She had a change in cognition that shifted the way she perceived her situation, and all of her perceptions and thoughts moved on in life with little or no regrets regardless of what her family and friends might think. The socially constructed view or set that family and friends had subtly implanted in her head during their discussions, even though they thought they were helpful comments, would no longer work to cause her pain, regret, or anguish.

The constructivist movement in family therapy and counseling programs where these ideas were spreading began to change how some professors as well as our protégé students began to understand and think differently. Two of my more fun published works as an assistant and associate professor were articles I wrote with two of my masters students, Julie Milne and Jill Murchie (Milne, Edwards, & Murchie, 2001), and another with my colleague Mei Whei Chen (Edwards & Chen, 1999). In both articles I invoked the strengths-based models of postmodernity and social constructivism relative to the times. Both articles used ideas I had learned from my two mentors. So, from early on in my academic career, I have been interested in, and practice, a form of strengths-based work. And I must say that this early work, although it was not done purposely, began to change me as a clinician and as a person. I began to believe in myself more . . . a kind of "future pull" was apparent to me.

Side Effects

Back in June of 2014, I was asked to present a workshop on strengths-based clinical supervision to the site supervisors of a rather large Illinois university. They invited site supervisors from their clinical programs, PsyDs, masters in marriage and family therapy, and their counselor education program. About 60 or more site supervisors of every ilk came to hear me talk about something I have taught for 15 years, both locally and nationally. I have also published on this topic (Edwards & Chen, 1999; Edwards, 2012). The site supervisors engaged with me around the various ideas I presented and watched a video of me supervising a woman who was really stuck clinically and personally on a case she presented. At the end of the not-nearly-enough 2.5 hours of training, there were a few differing opinions on what I had presented. I expected that. It gave us concepts to discuss and unpack. Afterward there were many supervisors who approached me offering compliments for my ideas. Several weeks later, when I received the aggregate of feedback, I was pleased to see mostly positive comments regarding the presentation. There were also two very mean-spirited comments stating that my presentation was the worst they had ever seen and that the video of supervision was useless and not a good example of supervision of any kind. Interestingly enough, the same video has always received great feedback from scores of other professionals, and the supervisee whose work I showed in the video said it was extremely helpful to her. What all of this proved to me is that the same old song about who knows what works best in both clinical work as well as clinical supervision is alive and well. Also, that the guilds that are competing for space and supremacy have different ideas based on their running metaphors for clinical practice correctness. I still wonder, with over 400 models of clinical practice (Edwards & Heath, 2007; Smith, Glass, & Miller, 1986; Stiles, Shapiro, & Elliot, 1986) and a couple of dozen models of clinical supervision, how anyone can claim first place. It is as if the old well-known notion of Supreme Court Justice Potter Stewart's characterization of pornography that "I know it when I see it" might also apply to our various ways of understanding truth. So much for objectivity and true scientific knowledge of what is best.

The issues some folks have with strengths-based supervision land right beside those who have difficulty understanding or using strengths-based clinical work. Clinicians in general have been trained to look for problems first, with the notion that as clinicians I can then help those I am working with find alternative modes of behaving or thinking. This is a hierarchical stance that places clinicians as experts, and can disempower clients. Working with strengths rather than problems—looking for what is working already and encouraging more of that—rather than addressing the problems one has and trying to make changes seems cockeyed to some. Our models of mental health clinical work have usually trained us to be problem-focused, giving us a mindset that can reject strengths work. In her book *Normal Family Process*, Froma Walsh (2003a) argued that the work of clinicians was taken over by the medical model in which clinicians are trained to look for deficits and problems rather than resiliencies. This is a natural thought process, as we search for what is called confirmational data or bias—the tendency for us to search for and recall information that helps bolster our already "known" beliefs about something. We have been taught through media assumptions about therapy that we have taken in, and believe. This set is usually based on opinions that have been stated and used over and over again, without actual fact finding. All one has to do is watch the various opinions of our politicians and one can understand how confirmational bias works. Even when evidence regarding one group's understandings is incorrect, they will find competing albeit perhaps incorrect facts to refute their opponents' opinions. Unfortunately, like fingers on one's hand, everyone has many opinions that are nothing more than confirmational data or bias. I will go into why scientifically and biologically this occurs later on in this chapter, but for now, just know that the more emotionally charged the issue is, the more people tend to use confirmational data. We hate to be wrong, and will cling to our preconceived ideas. However, there is overwhelming evidence that looking for and encouraging strengths works very well, while dwelling on problems can also at times cause iatrogenic problems (Boisvert & Faust, 2002). Positive psychology (Seligman, Steen, Park, & Peterson, 2005) as well as both narrative therapy (Nichols, 2013) and solution-focused therapy (Franklin, Trepper, Gingerich, & McCollum, 2012) have evidence—scientifically researched and proven evidence that it works. But then so does much of problem-focused models of clinical work (Norcross, 2011). I go into why we believe the evidence of working with strengths is a stronger way of helping those I work with throughout this chapter.

Muddles of Models of Clinical Supervision

We learn from other models of supervision that came before. We take them for granted as the best and true way to supervise, but they can have the effect of causing great harm, or provide solid clinical supervision. A few years ago, I was teaching a doctoral class on clinical supervision. I like to demonstrate the model I use and explain how it works and why I use it. I contextualize it and situate it as the model I am most comfortable with, but, in the context of the class, the students also learn other models. After demonstrating my own version of strengths-based supervision, there are lots of questions. Some of the students really liked the model, others wondered at its lack of specifying to supervisees what to do with their clients, while helping them find their own unique way. A few weeks later one of the students asked if she could discuss a problem in class that related to her own site supervisor and how this student felt disempowered rather than empowered. The student was in a counseling psychology program, and her site supervisor was a clinical psychologist. Now there are not that many differences between the two types of psychologists, but there are enough to cause this student angst. In their supervision, the supervisor suggested that the issue was that she, the student, should use a clinical psych model and abandon her training as a counseling psychologist. She wondered what to do, because as a student, she feared a bad review in her internship if she disagreed. I was a bit flabbergasted and suggested that she just have a conversation about the issue with folks with slightly different models of clinical work. The class, to a person, took up her dilemma as one that they all face in their training.

Ethically, I have concerns about a supervisor making suggestions like the one presented in class. It borders on that portion appearing in every guild's ethics code regarding the right to self-determination. Also, there is not a shred of evidence that the use of clinical psychology concepts is any better than that of counseling psychology. In fact, there has never been to my knowledge any research that shows definitively that one guild's practices are better than others'. Just on general principles, the notion that a whole class of students are afraid to discuss these kind of issues with their site supervisors for fear of reprisal on grades or continued placement is an ethical problem all unto itself. It is wrong, and certainly not in the interest of engendering trust in the supervisory relationship.

Generally, our fields took our models of clinical supervision from the medical world. Surgeons train with the watch one, do one, teach one model. After years of training, and learning through books, the surgeon in training then may work on cadavers and simulated experiences. Then during their intern years, they work under direction of a licensed and skilled mentor surgeon. During this process the mentor/trainer surgeon describes the process several times as the intern watches the procedures closely, then may assist, and then solos while the mentor watches. Finally, after some time, the intern may teach the procedure to a group of fledgling surgeons. In our field of mental health, there have been several additions to this medical model that add to the understanding of clinical supervision. Bernard (1979, 1997) pinpointed areas that need to be addressed during supervision. She mentions process skills, conceptualization skills, and personalization skills as well as three spheres of influence the supervisor can use: training, consultation, and counseling. Supervisors who are aware of when and how to use these will be more helpful during the supervision sessions. Stoltenberg and Delworth enlightened us with the concept that clinicians go through developmental stages as do supervisors, as they learn their various tasks.

> This developmental process is organic rather than static. One is never stuck in one stage, but may be working at issues in several of our arbitrary descriptions of development. In fact, the transformation from one's experiences are expected, or hoped to be changed into meaningful information. (Edwards, 2012, p. 44)

One of the more important concepts, to my mind, is the issue of parallel process, and isomorphs. While the notion of parallel process has been explained more in the literature and training among most of the professions, the concept of isomorphs seems to belong to the couple and family practitioners. *Isomorphs* are described as a sameness of form or part of a system (Liddle & Saba, 1983, 1985). Although parallel process is a description of an event that happens and has connections to the psychodynamic school, isomorphs have been described and used in supervision to help supervisors become aware of events that are happening with sameness in multiple parts of the system. A client family may be having difficulties coming up with how to discipline or provide change expectations for a child, the clinician working with the family may be having the same sort difficulty helping the family to make changes, and the supervisor could be having the same sort of dilemma with her supervisee. Parallel process sees the events as part of individual behavior being repeated, while isomorphs recognize the interconnectedness of the system . . . extended family, family, clinician, and supervisor. Knowing that and seeing it as a replication of the system's connectedness allows the supervisor to extricate himself or herself and provide a difference that makes a change. Understanding isomorphs allows for a static process to change by making changes that matter. Repeating the same patterns over and over again, and not providing some difference, does nothing.

Anyone who has taught a complicated process to others will recognize the skill and understanding it takes to teach the process well. Teaching can also make the process one's own as the trainer is able to articulate step by step what needs to happen, potential pitfalls, and a process from beginning to end. The same process of learning has been used in mental health clinical training. Unlike the medical experiences, human beings and their mental health is a multilayered process of understanding, and paying attention to a client whose bio-psycho-socio-cultural-familial-spiritual-political being is what has created the need for change I call counseling or psychotherapy. What the trainer or, in our case, supervisor has learned to pay attention to in his or her own experiences will also be transmitted to the supervisee. Depending on the training one receives from their clinical organizational guild, their university, or even the agency where one interns, the clinical expectations and protocols can vary greatly. The transmission of "facts" regarding how to ply one's trade, the importance of empathy, or cognition, et cetera, will isomorphically be passed on from supervisor, to supervisee, to client. In many cases, an agency where the intern is learning to practice their skills under supervision could have their own beliefs and practices (Edwards, 2012). Some agencies are practicing an individual focused model, while others might insist on family work, or group work, or an eclectic version of many different models, modalities, and practices. Within the modalities there might also be multiple varieties of practice. Some training might use a Bowenian frame of family therapy, while another might use a different model. For instance, training in clinical psychology from one university or agency internship, regardless of core guild values of clinical psychology, may receive variations of training in any of the modalities depending on the professor or agency supervisor. There is no guarantee the a student in agency A, will provide similar training in individual therapy, family, or group work, as it is dependent on the supervisor's or professors own training and beliefs. It will also be dependent on values and methods of each individual faculty or site supervisors and their favorite modalities of clinical work. If agency B believes in using only Family Therapy for every client, or Cognitive Behavioral Therapy, then that is what the students will learn and most likely use in their own work (Edwards & Heath, 2007).

In the last two decades, there have been a plethora of new methods and models of counseling/ psychotherapy. When the book on Mental Health Services was published back in 2008, Edwards and Heath (2008) wrote that there were well over 260 models of counseling and psychotherapy and that most people seeking help had only a vague idea of what to expect. The desire of academics and clinicians in the field to try out and proselytize their new methods has increased that number every year since, whereas the *Diagnostic and Statistical Manual* (*DSM*) model printed by psychiatry and mandated by managed care and big pharma much of the time attempts to hold us to a standard that is unrealistic.

> In the *DSM–IV* there is no assumption that each category of mental disorder is a completely discrete entity with absolute boundaries dividing it from other mental disorders or from no mental disorder. There is also no assumption that all individuals described as having the same mental disorder are alike in all important ways. (American Psychiatric Association, 2000, p. *xxxi*)

The latest edition of the *DSM* of the American Psychiatric Association has been rejected by the National Institute of Mental Health for using research they call "bad science" (Lane, 2013). The medical model that much of our mandated treatment is predicated on is actually based on problem-focused perspective. This model looks for what is wrong, attempts to diagnose and then provide either a fix or a remediation that is designed and provided by the clinician in a top-down manner. Seligman, the founder of positive psychology, states that mental health professionals have consistently overlooked positive traits of personality, and argues that the highest levels of life satisfaction come from building and using one's signature strengths (Seligman, 2002). He points out that the usual vehicle for diagnosing, the *DSM* in its several iterations, is directly lined up with evidence-based work that is deficit- and problem-focused, leaving out large parts of human strengths and wellness.

Strengths-based work of any kind is 180 degrees away from the thinking and behaving that most of us have been taught to use in our practice, but does that mean it doesn't work well? In this chapter, I discuss my ideas of a strengths-based model of supervision and hook it to the sciences that I believe make it work. I will also discuss how it is different from other models and why I choose to use strengths-based supervision over other methods or as part of an integrated approach.

Strengths-Based Supervision and How It Works

As you wander through this book you will find several different views about how to work from a strengths-based perspective. Over the past few decades strengths-based ideas and strengths-based clinical supervision, specifically, have become more mainstream. As noted in the earlier chapters, social workers begun the strengths-based practices (Rapp, 1997; Saleebey, 2002) and lately this has been taken up in the field of clinical supervision by social worker Ben-Zion Cohen (1999), family therapist, and counseling psychologists Edwards and Chen (1999), Edwards (2012), and positive psychologists Wade and Jones (2014). Each of these clinicians take their own place in the current understanding of supervision, with varying methods and theory constructs. But I want to discuss the premises I rely on during a strengths-based supervision and thus what I consider makes strengths-based processes work.

Working Premise One—Moving Away From a Problem-Focused World

Working from a strengths-based perspective to me means that I almost totally abandon discussing anything that might bring a problem-focus to the conversation. I say "almost" because our culture has a problem-and-fix zeitgeist. A zeitgeist lasts for a period of time when an idea is widespread during that place and time and space—even if it is not a truth or fact. Even in physical medicine, practices change, methods and notions of how to be helpful evolve as we find what we surmise works best. Our clients and supervisees come to the table looking for answers to the issues or conditions they see as problematic. Media and our training have helped to condition the clients and supervisees I see into the medically modeled belief that in order to help and have positive change in one's life or practice, investigating what has gone wrong, and then fixing it is the most efficient way. This problem-focused model is based on the notion of diagnosis and assessment, followed by remediation and correction of the problem. As Walsh (2003a) has commented, we have bought into the medical model. Our roots go back to the days of medical men working closely with patients, superimposing their understanding of what creates problems for humans on to a singular within-the-body-or-mind problem that needs to be changed. So, if what you have been taught is a problem-focused, pathologically oriented way of thinking it is natural to think that what a strengths-based clinician will present or do with their clients, be they clinical or supervisor clients, is incorrect. This medical model, although it has many holes, has worked well up until now. And of course there is a great deal of evidence to show that our perceptual sets—what I have learned and believe to be true and right—are locked up in the thalamocortical networks of our brain (Siegel, 2007, p. 45). Those clinicians who have been trained to understand and diagnose problems "within" a person, and later within a system, will look for, and most likely "find," areas that are problematic and need fixing. Clients will benefit, according to this model, from change or remediation. The notion that something is "wrong" or has been wrong will linger, however, giving possible rise to iatrogenic issues later.

Another part of this change in thinking has to do with the idea of being at risk. While I might talk about those I work with, especially children, as being "at risk," one of the best operative changes is that our internal systems may begin to see our clients/supervisees as "at potential" due to this change in perception (Bermeo, 2009). Our sets work better when we have the ability to see the person we are working with as a capable and willing collaborator. I do love Saleebey's (2008) manifesto he used for social workers and believe it should be part of anyone who works from a strengths-based model, that:

> practicing from a strengths perspective means this—*everything* you do as a social worker will be predicated in some way on helping to discover and embellish, explore, and exploit clients' strengths and resources in service of assisting them to achieve their goals, realize their dreams, and shed the irons of their own inhibitions and misgivings and society's domination. (2008, p. 1)

A very simple explanation and technique to provide the conditions that Saleebey (2009) suggested, and that anyone can use, has to do with the functions of the parasympathetic and sympathetic nervous systems. I talked briefly about this above. We know that the sympathetic nervous system has the ability and function when aroused to increase the flight or fight response as it controls "perceived" threats. Because it is a part of the autonomic nervous system, it happens automatically. The parasympathetic nervous system is a controller of what makes the body and the brain relax. Homeostasis is controlled here, again, to "perceived" conditions of safety. Research that Boyatzis, Smith, Van Oosten, and Woolford (2013) describe suggests that subjects who are being evaluated show signs of stress when provided with negative evaluations first. Providing positive talk about their growth and productivity early in the session can change this. I then could add to the conversation, "I have some ideas that might help in this case. Would you like to hear them?" (An invitation to work together.) I might even add, "These ideas may be counter to what you are thinking, and I can tell you my thinking about it, if you believe it might help. The ideas have worked for me in similar situations, and that might be the case here. You could also add your own ideas to mine, or reject them if you believe they are ill advised in your situation."

> Resonant relationships, in which people feel in sync with each other about their shared purpose (i.e., vision, mission, and values), their shared caring for each other (i.e., compassion), tuning into and paying attention to yourself and others (i.e., mindfulness), and being playful stimulate the neuroendocrine system called the parasympathetic nervous system. (Boyatzis, Smith, Van Oosten, & Woolford, 2013, p. 19)

I believe that some supervisors who are eager to help start off by attempting to provide their own correction to the case or situation that is being discussed. It has been my experience, now validated by research, that the relationship between supervisor and supervisee is dependent on working to have a powerful and positive relationship that is collaborative, genuine, and shows care for each other that is more like a mentor relationship than a one-up hierarchical situation. One begins every session with a check in regarding how each of the participants is doing that day. I always begin sessions with the phrase "What would you like to get from our time together today? What might you hope to have done by the end of our work today?" It is a nice collaborative set of statements that also suggests that we are doing this together and that we are equal partners in this endeavor. It does not mean, however, that the supervisee has more ideas or knowledge about the clinical work, but it does indicate that as a supervisor, I recognize that the supervisee—my co-visee, if you will—has ideas that are good, and has knowledge about the process and their client that I recognize as important. After all they have been through a lot of clinical education by this time, and I would hope that they had some good ideas from all that training—that it was money I spent. What I do is only adding in a collaborative way to their understanding of how to be the best they can be. I believe that they have an important understanding of their clients that I am only privy to through this dialogue.

Supervising with compassion rather than for compliance

This means that supervisors need to change their modus operandi from one of being in charge and all-knowing to someone who talks to their supervisees about what is important in their lives and work. Also as important is to provide steady co-construction of case solutions upon which supervisees (I called them *co-visees* before in Edwards and Chen, 1999) want suggestions and discussion. I should engage them by also talking about their own personal visions, how to protect themselves from burnout, asking, and talking about load balance along with having outside interests. Our conversations should also include those professional conversations, about ethics, and joining guild associations where they can develop strong relationships with other like-minded clinicians. All of this will create clinicians that are professionals, who are also persons that are thinking, positive individuals. I am someone who listens for areas where I can gently correct them by providing discussions about how I think and listen to how they think also. I should listen to them because I care about them. I want our supervisees to feel our care and concern and to respond to them in kind to their own clients. We have been handcuffed by our beliefs that I must maintain a strong professional distance from those with whom I work. That may be necessary for clinical clients, but I contend that it is different when one supervises other clinicians. The most important part of supervision is to help provide clinician efficacy . . . the belief of a clinician that they know and understand how to work with clients in a reasonable way. It is our belief that part of the supervisory experience works better when it is more like a mentoring one. "Mentoring at its best is a path where informal transmission of knowledge, as well as introduction into a higher level of involvement in the chosen field and the support to succeed occurs during a sustained period of time" (Edwards, 2011). In addition, this relationship as supervisor can also be seen as one of leadership. I take Covey's (2005) instruction that, simply put—at its most elemental and practical level—leadership is communicating to people their worth and potential so clearly that they come to see it in themselves.

If supervising for compassion is supposed to help a supervisee get better, how does a supervisor provide key feedback that also improves their competency? There are lots of measures that can help, such as self-assessment is the best feedback when done in a collaborative and compassionate manner. If the research is correct, developing a positive relationship where the supervisee feels supported allows them to actually open up and discuss their strengths. I want a relationship where I ask questions without engendering fear of being chastised, downgraded on final grades or pay scale, or looking foolishly incompetent in front of their supervisor. Talking about your own mistakes also normalizes the notion that we all make mistakes sometimes, along with talking about the actual growth curve in any new endeavor. Starting off with a discussion about their failures and problems is a sure way to create a tension where they will be worried about how you are evaluating them. Counseling self-efficacy and the personal agency that goes with it are key to both basic and strengths-based clinical supervision principles (Edwards, 2012).

Clinicians learn to have agency every time they have a mastery experience in the field and their site supervisor notices. Supervisors who are aware of a new counselor making it through a session without stalling, or who asks the right questions, or comments when they smile when they leave will have a mastery experience. Each time puts more experience in their clinical knowledge bank. Clinicians gain agency when they watch their supervisor actually do a live clinical session, and know that they can replicate a technique or skill they watched (Edwards, 2012).

Strengths-based supervision is being an encourager of the supervisee's personal and clinical strengths and that should isomorphically carry over to the work they do with their own clients. First and foremost, supervisors must remember that they are in a co-constructing situation, where the supervisee has personal experience with their clients. Supervisors have perceptual sets that will need to be acknowledged, they will work with their supervisee far better when they feel included and validated, and that opening phrases from the supervisor will make a large difference in how the session goes. The issue of compliance is something that most supervisors take very seriously. And they should when there are questions of ethics. However, the question usually is compliance to what? What model or method? What part is wrong and according to whom? What ethic have they disobeyed and how might this impropriety be discussed in a compassionate way so that there is learning, not judgment and fear? Most supervisors are wonderful, kind, and very well meaning souls. In my 40-some-year career, I have had six or eight supervisors. Most were great however one was off the mark, and one was downright mean. In the many workshops on clinical supervision I have provided, I always ask for a show of hands of those who have ever had bad supervision. Lots of hands go up. Then when I ask about good supervision the number of hands is not quite the same, indicating that what the perception of supervisors is not what we might expect. Comments range from "not so hot supervision", to "are more involved in themselves," "spending more time with issues other than case consultation", "not being available when needed", and "insisting that the supervisee does clinical work their way", rather than helping the supervisee come up with their own ideas. I have heard from prominent clinicians in other fields who come back for an advanced degree how their own experience is put down, rather than using it as a gentle way to scaffold new information or techniques. After 10 years as a masters'-level clinician I sought out specific training that was to be an add on to my already pretty good skills, and the trainer said, "I am going to teach you how to give the correct way of providing services." Nothing shows disrespect like trying to take away what someone already has and suggesting that their skills are no good. It's a downright "gotcha moment."

I worked with a very seasoned and nationally known music therapist once. She had decided to add to the clinical training she had, deciding to get the training that state licensure requires, and applied at a doctoral program in clinical psychology. During the orientation one of the faculty asked what everyone's previous training was, and when she told her about her years as a music therapist, she was publicly bashed about the skills she already had. "Here, I will provide you with 'real' clinical skills, and teach you to be a real clinician," the professor said. How arrogant a statement this was to someone who already knew a great deal! An easier way to join and gain confidence with language of compassion would be to say that she would learn even more skills that would match and extend her already good proficiency. Scaffolding in education can be any variety of technique that moves a student toward even stronger understanding of a subject without trashing what they already know. It's an add on, not a takeaway and replacement strategy. Had that faculty member taken a compassionate stance, our music therapist might have become a wonderful clinical psychologist who used music as a sound vehicle to help her clients even more.

Finally, I want to focus your attention once again on the concept of the Pygmalion effect. I have written and lectured about this phenomenon before, but I was delighted recently when I found it discussed in the *HBR's OnPoint* (2015). This well-known but not often discussed component of relational conduct makes it clear that our expectations—our personal sets—about people we are involved with as a leader, supervisor, and now manager, have significant outcomes. The Pygmalion effect has been demonstrated to have successful outcomes, both in the classroom (Rosenthal, 2002) and for organizations (Cooperrider, 2000). According to Rosenthal (2002), evidence shows that educators who have positively constructed views of their students have more successful students, and leaders who have positive views of their organization have successful outcomes within that realm. Our socially constructed perceptual sets affect our views, thus how we then act toward them in supervision or directing clinical work of any kind, with a positive view enhancing our sets, and negative sets providing a negative view (Cooperrider, 2000; Edwards, 2012). It is important that we check our views of those we work with at the door, and again and again, as those sets are very hard to get away from.

The problem-focused model is changing

As outlined in Chapter 1, from the beginnings of strengths-based work beginning with social work, through the early to current psychologists and family therapists, positive psychology and positive therapy movements, and the use of the neurocounseling (see Chapter 10 by Russell-Chapin in this book) that everyone seems to understand, but perhaps may not always agree with specific way of working with people's wellness, and strengths. The issue of how to help our clients and supervisors flourish in a world that is complicated and multilayered with truths and understandings has, like other models, evolved. As positive psychologist Mihaly Csikszentmihalyi has stated,

> The claim is that when a successful change is introduced into society, those involved in it see that change as their own doing—their actions made history. But after a generation or two, the change has become so much a part of everyday life that people see it as part of nature—like the weather, or the shape of the ground on which they live. (Csikszenthmihalyi & Nakamura, 2011, p. 4)

So too has been the state of strengths-based work of all kinds. The history of working from a strengths-based model is important to understand, but so are the multiple ways that it has spread across the fields of mental health, teaching, and leadership.

Working Premise Two—Reality Is Socially Constructed

According to Anderson et al. (2008), the meanings we assign to the world are not our private inventions. They do not originate in minds cut away from others; instead, they are created within our history of relationships, from our early childhood to our most recent conversations. Our beliefs and models of the world—our worldview—provide the grounding of the clinical work we do and are dependent on our perceptual sets. These beliefs are informed by our learning in our family of origin, our cultural relativism, the biological conditions we are given, the spirituality or lack of same we own, the training and education we have had, the psychological world we live in, and the social and political situations we have including the guilds to which we belong. Compression of all these can be considered our worldview. Once again, and as mentioned elsewhere in this book, note that all of this information is encoded into our thalamocortical network that then functions as a filter, permitting in information that fits with our worldview and pushing aside information that seems to make no sense, and is at odds with that which we already believe to be true. This understanding, now authenticated by brain science (Siegel, 2007), has been around for quite some time, as in epistemology (or how we know what we know), from the study of learning and understanding. What all of this means is that "truth" of almost anything is shaped by many factors. Thus, a problem-focused model will be embedded within the thalamocortical networks in the brain by these factors, and create those perceptual sets that keep us from believing or viewing other ways of thinking. Siegel (2007) indicates that this phenomenon "enslaves" our beliefs, because the system, for purpose of conservation of time and action, sends out messages that negate alternative views. If a clinician has a belief that a certain behavior is caused by, say, a problem within a childlike oppositional defiant disorder, and another clinician who has been trained to see problems as being a family system, they will have competing beliefs as methods of addressing change for the problem. According to Kuhn (1977), "When scientists must choose between competing theories, two [scientists] fully committed to the same list of criteria for choice may nevertheless reach different conclusions" (p. 324). This is also evident in many areas of our lives like politics and religion. Many of these belief systems become hardened perceptual sets that inform us of appropriate behaviors, thinking, and such. They are encoded by the information presented to us beginning at young ages by our family, culture, and education. Republicans believe that their way of thinking makes the most sense, as do Tea Party Republicans, as will Democrats. Religious beliefs are also encoded into our neural network from an early age, and unless something happens along the way to change those perceptual sets, they stick with us, varying only slightly as we grow. They may also be introduced to slight variations or exceptional circumstances along the way that interrupt those patterns of beliefs. The perceptual sets make sense to us as a way of being in relationship with the world we know. As two persons come together they begin to have a discussion about worldviews that affects their own perceptual sets that in turn informs them of how to understand reality.

So, what is it that I believe encompasses a strengths-based model? What is my own worldview of how to be helpful to a supervisee? Primarily, I believe that what I do with supervisees is isomorphic; it is part of a language system that creates and enhances how I view the world, from ourselves, to our supervisees, to the client, and perhaps from clients to their own system of language, and the behavior that is a product of all that. We are socially constructionist beings. But as Anderson et al. (2008) pointed out, these meanings do not stand alone, but depend on others understanding us and affirming that what we have said is understood, but also that the words make sense even if not agreed with. "Meaning is born in the act of affirmation. If I speak to another, and there is no response we are left to wonder whether or not our words are heard . . . when there is some form of 'yes, I understand'" we then feel heard (Anderson et al., 2008, p. 34). So we must listen to our supervisee without judgment and convey that I do understand them and why what they are doing with their clients makes sense to them from their point of view. Only then might we add or suggest other courses of action. It is respectful. It also means that we need to work on our self, using all the strengths-based ideas at our disposal to be the best, optimistic, congruent, and authentic person we can be. That alone will model a strengths-based perspective for those we work with. We make mistakes, but attempt to rectify them, and we work diligently to be true to our own beliefs knowing full well that our views are ours alone, and others' views may be diametrically opposed to ours. Understanding others' views and the how and why of those views will open up dialogue and acceptance.

Working Premise Three—Modern Psychology

I am a fan of the modern psychological ideas that contribute to the strengths-based ideal. I believe that resiliency and the many ideas from positive psychology apply very well to what I use in clinical supervision. Resiliency is an amazing concept that Anne Masten and colleagues first investigated (Masten, Best, & Garmezy, 1990) and that looked at this process she would later call *ordinary magic* (Masten, 2001, p. 1). This adaptation process provides what can be successful outcomes to challenging and/or threatening circumstances. Their primary investigation found that children who fare well or recover successfully usually have a positive relationship with a carrying person. In addition, adversity is also buffered during this relationship and resilient process when they also have the ability to engage well with people, and areas where they are competent already, and have a perceived value of themselves previously. "Resiliency appears to be a common phenomenon arising from ordinary human adaptive processes" (Masten, 2001, p. 1; Masten, 2015). No wonder she calls it ordinary magic.

Two other scholars who delved into resilience are Dr. Froma Walsh, who extended the concept to understanding and work with families (Walsh, 1996, 1998, 2003a, 2003b, 2006) and Dr. Martin Seligman whose work helped devise a protocol that helps military personnel that are involved in treatment for PTSD and who had potential to change to post-traumatic growth. Walsh has made a point that working with people from a resiliency perspective is not really a technique, but is an attitude (F. Walsh, personal communication, January, 19, 2013). If it is not so special because every person has the potential to access resiliency, and it is not about techniques or special ways of working with clients—in our case supervisees—what does it take to work from a position of resiliency? My answer comes from listening to others who are practicing from a strengths-based philosophy. It is not a series of techniques, and it actually is aligned with Saleebey's (2009) ideas that have been quoted several times in this book. Along with this, I have learned from my friends and co-authors of this book. Andy Young has introduced me to what he calls *the ways of being*, and no one does this better than Andy. He suggests that one must be benevolently curious, self-reflective, speculative rather than definitive, sincerely complimentary, and context focused.

Case Study

Teddi was a first year doc student, who volunteered to help me demonstrate strengths-based supervision during a class I was teaching. I had told Teddi that she could either make something up or discuss a real clinical situation she wanted to talk about. She chose the real situation.

Jeff: Well, I am pleased and honored that you want to discuss something with me that is foremost in your head today.

Teddi: No problem, I am used to it. We have practiced both in our master's program and here in the doc program. No sweat at . . . they all know me anyway.

Jeff: Okay, then Teddi I would like to begin . . . what do you think you might want to get out of this time we spend together? How would you like this time to be helpful at the end?

Teddi: Well, I have this case that is giving me nightmares . . . the kid in the family . . .

Jeff: Are you doing family work?

Teddi: Yes, and the kid . . . a girl. She is 15 and a bit of a loner . . . she does not want to go to school, or out with friends or anything. The parents are really worried. She used to be completely different; outgoing, she was in a youth group as a leader. Everyone seemed to like her.

Jeff: So, what have you done so far with this family . . . and for how long? It seems like a very sudden change.

Teddi: Well, it was a case that had been in the agency for a few months and the previous worker—she was a doc intern . . . she completed her internship and I inherited the family.

Jeff: And you have been with them for . . .

Teddi: A few months now . . . three weeks. And John, my site supervisor, sat in with me for the first two sessions and helped with the transition. The family does not know what to do. I'm not sure I do either.

Jeff: So what shall we work on together, what do you want to talk about?

Teddi: I want to know what you think I should do. Give me some suggestions please.

Jeff: Okay, what have you been working on in your sessions?

Teddi: Well, we are really just getting to know each other. I have been talking with the parents about what might have triggered this change, and I have spent some time with Chelsey . . . that's her name, Chelsey. She cannot remember a time, or at least she says she can't remember a time that might have caused this change. What do you think?

Jeff: I'm not sure. The case is yours, and you know them better than I do . . .

Teddi: Ya, maybe.

Jeff: Well, I have a thought and a question. Want to hear them?

(I always get a mandate to speak about their work—permissions are important, I believe.)

Teddi: Yes, please.

Jeff: I wonder if there are times when you are talking with the parents, or with Chelsey, when you really feel like you are getting somewhere. And what is that somewhere, when it happens? And I am really interested in how the parents got Chelsey to come to therapy . . . if she is so lost and alone, or whatever. I mean, I would think that would have been a major accomplishment.

(I use expectant and positive language here. "When it happens" rather than "if" it happens. Teddi is free to disagree, but I am expecting that it does.)

Teddi: I am not sure about that "somewhere." We are talking about the change, and mom started to cry, and then Chelsey began to cry too. I liked the realness of that moment, and felt close to them and the problem. It had real meaning and . . . depth to something.

Jeff: I wonder what it all meant to them . . . how did dad react?

Teddi: He had tears in his eyes, but not like Chelsey or mom. I guess I could have asked them what was going on. I was just sort of in the moment and didn't want to distract them.

Jeff: Wow, Teddi, I think that might have been a good idea. Great insight!! As you think about that moment now, what are you thinking . . . what are you feeling?

(Praise always helps, and hooking it to a current feeling helps also.)

Teddi: I am wishing that I had the forethought back then to ask. I think I missed something.

Jeff: I think you learned something . . . and that something was your own. Neat!! What might help you to access that sort of technique in the future . . . and remember, it's just a technique. The relation is far more important, or at least that is what the clinical research tells us.

Teddi: Really, oh ya.

Jeff: So the family has been real with you, and cried in front of you, and somehow mom and dad, and Chelsey are still coming—that is something very positive.

Jeff: Think of a time or two when you were able to use a technique like this, or you said something and they really responded, sort of like back there but one you don't often think about using, and a time you remembered to use it, and it worked very well? Think about it for a minute or two and then tell me when you have it in your head and how it happened and felt.

(I am about to use a positive psychology technique called savoring, *and it is a great way of helping clinicians of all sorts see their own strengths, as well as how to access and "set" it in clinical context.)*

Teddi: Okay, do you want me to tell you about it?

Jeff: Not right away. I want you to close your eyes, and just savor what you did, how it all felt, and how the outcome was alive and good for the client or clients you were working with.

Teddi: Okay, I have it.

Jeff: Now think about how that worked for you—remember using that technique . . . what brought it to your thinking? Sit with that for a few minutes.

(I want this remembrance to be savored and enjoyed, so the set can sink in.)

Teddi: It feels good, and like something I can remember. I know how to do that . . . relax in the sessions.

Jeff: I like that, you come up with good ideas. Now, you asked me to give you some ideas about what to do. Do you still want to hear my ideas?

Teddi: Sure, that might help.

Jeff: You should remember, however, that even though I have some good ideas, they may not be as good as some that you come up with. My ideas have worked with families in similar situations, but there are always differences. No two families are the same, and I might say things differently than you do, and that is great. You got to be you, 'cause I am already taken.

(Lots more happened, but let's jump to the end.)

Teddi: Funny, Dr. E.

Jeff: So now, I would like you to tell me how this supervision session was for you. Did you get what you wanted, or are there some things you might have wanted from me that you did not get? I want feedback from you, so that if we were to have a next session I can sort of tailor make it for you. Research from an old colleague of mine, Scott Miller and his group have good evidence that checking in at the end of sessions is an excellent way of us staying on track with where we both want to go, and end up. It works equally well with clients.

I like to drop information like my last sentence to give them something to chew on, in addition to providing a context for what I do at the session's ending. It just hangs there for them to take in, and some ask about it more. So I move on to discuss a few ideas I had. Simple ones, but the focus was always on helping Teddi become a better clinician by trusting her own ideas, and using them. If I were to have a perception that Teddi is off track, I would check in to see how it is going, what might give her that perception, and how she would know if she is on track or off track. I might also check in to suggest she also check in with the family to see if they agree with her perception of success. The research by Miller, Hubble, and Duncan (2007) tells us that the check in with folks you are working with at the end of the session provides valuable information that can keep you on track. I end sessions almost the same way I begin. What is it you as a supervisee want to work on, and how was the session and what might we have done together that would have made the session even better (or better)? Many of us have the same old sayings we use over again when similar situations come up. Like teaching, I use the same jokes, the same grabber sayings, the same style of saying things. We also use sets, and improvise on them too. Teddi went on to learn a lot more, and she graduated and had a practice as well as teaching some. And like me with Dr. Tony Heath, she remembers the way I treated her in this session.

One of my favorite sayings has been attributed to Carl W. Buehner as well as Maya Angelou— "I've learned that people will forget what you said, people will forget what you did, but people will never forget how you made them feel." I think this counts here.

Case Study

Shane was a master's-level professional who sought me out to complete the hours he needed for his clinical license. He had gone through the master's program where 26 years earlier I had interned as a doc student. I have two or three points I want to provide in this chapter. The first is about iatrogenic symptoms that can arise in clinical conversations . . . both with clients and with supervisees. It has been validated that the use of language and how it can produce negative consequences. As a supervisor we should always be checking ourselves, and working at changing the negative narrative sets . . . that is why it can be difficult as that network keeps sending us a "check it again or dump-it input, information does not match with existing data" message. So it was with Shane. The second point is that resiliency comes easiest when the person has had positive input from their family of origin or a significant other adult (Masten, 2001) that builds on efficacy and believes in the person's ability to become what they want to be. Finally, the issue of helping a supervisee to become all that he or she believes they can be seems to fit very well with all that I know about strengths-based supervision.

Jeff: So, Shane, how would you like to use our time together today? What might we talk about together so you know that our time has been helpful?

Shane: I have a few cases I might use . . . cases where I fell just horribly short of the mark.

Jeff: Humm, I am always interested in clinicians who feel this way—that perceive their work as not good enough. I wonder . . .

Shane: It's more than just a perception. I am thinking that I am in the wrong business. I just want to either understand what I can do to get better as a counselor, or get the heck out of the field.

Jeff: Well, I am certainly interested in how you are feeling and what factors are telling you that you aren't any good . . . I also want to hear about any times you feel like you might have made an impact . . . built a beginning relationship with your clients too. NO one is downright horrible all the time. What is telling you about both the good and the horrible?

(I want to introduce the concept of normalcy in all of life . . . no one is one way all the time, yet we all suffer at times from the imposter syndrome, or are haunted by old stories about ourselves . . . old narratives.)

Jeff: I am impressed with your willingness to even talk about this issue . . . lots of clinicians I have known over my many years make huge mistakes, and want to just sweep them under the rug. How is it that you are different than that . . . what helps you want to work on this self-perception?

Shane: I want to know . . . should I stay in this field, or move on? Several people have told me that I am not cut out for this job. I'm too judgmental, too worried about what people . . . friends and clients—about what they think of me. My previous supervisor at the site I was interning at told me that this was a job that I probably shouldn't be doing.

(Now, there are folks who are just not cut out for this type of work, but I have not experienced anything horrible with Shane in our first few sessions. This is the first time this issue has come up, so I want to know . . . Why now!!)

Jeff: So tell me about the last few days . . . I want to know what you think you have done well, and what you think you wish you had done differently? Again, we are always a combination of good stuff and stuff that needs adjusting. What one thing needs adjusting? Then we will also talk about anything you have done that seemed okay. Okay?

(Adjusting is a lot different than horrible. Language creates our reality, our perceptual sets are created by all the narratives in our head, and creates the behaviors that result.)

Shane: Okay, that sounds fair . . . but you will tell me if I am not cut out for this, right?

Jeff: I think we will both know together in a few weeks if your perceptions are correct, or if they are pushing you around . . . if that is the case, then you can learn to push back and change, fair enough?

Shane: Okay.

I went on to talk about both sides of this dilemma, he had learned in his classes about the use of narrative therapy, and had been interested, but never used them before. Most of all, he liked the way I began to talk about his work, as well as a history of his problem-saturated sets. I also introduced him to positive psychology ideas that fit with the concepts of flourishing. He liked the idea that a great life is one where you don't just survive or get by, but a life where you and those you love flourish.

And to really flourish, one must be very resilient in life. It became a goal to work on, and an opening for us to share as we both worked together at self-improvement as a genuine ongoing part of our lives. So, his work with me became more of a strengths-based assessment of how he can begin to change the narratives he was living by, he talked about his family some, and I encouraged him to find a strengths-based clinician he could work with. His mood changed, and the iatrogenic issues seemed to begin melting away. Our work on supervision began to take a different direction as he worked on his own issues within the context of his own clinical work with clients. He began and reported he felt good about working with clients' strengths. Again, my elements were not only those of Saleebey's (2009) but included understanding of a series of ideas that influence Andy Young's ways of being. Both for me, and for Shane.

Conclusions

Strengths-based clinical supervision moves away from the typical medically modeled motifs that examine supervisees' mistakes in order for the supervisor to correct them. Instead, strengths-based work assumes the premises and practices of strengths-based clinical models. We look for opportunities to see our supervisees' strengths and positive helpful work. We encourage them to look for times when they like the work they are doing, and are able to recreate those times in their clinical relationships. We encourage their growth, and ability to be independent in their own work. All of the aforementioned ideas are similar to a great deal of ordinary clinical supervision. However, we work to enhance a new perceptual set that has an optimistic outlook on life and works to find supervisee's strengths, rather than having a negative problem-focus. As Seligman and his crew show, optimistic views on life provide better relationships in life. Optimism also provides a better chance to overcome depression, and illnesses, and a longer happier life. I would surmise that there would be better counselor efficacy for our supervisees. That means a far more realistic and positive worldview that can isomorphically be transferred to clients. When some one embraces a strengths-finding life, they also become heliotropic (Cooperrider, Sorensen, Whitney, & Yaeger, 2000). Like the sunflowers that follow the sun every day because that is a primary source of life for them, strengths-based living also searches and finds those parts of our lives and of others that enhance and provide better living. Human beings search, find, and need the life giving energy that is human strengths.

To reiterate the core of this chapter, let us consider the following as the major ways of thinking about and considering these life sources for flourishing. First of all, the philosophies that enhance and allow for a relative change in our thinking are the philosophies that move away from a more modernist view to a postmodern way of thinking. Strengths-based work and ideology are based on specific premises.

Life Forces Look for Life—We Are Heliotropic

First and foremost is that to begin the quest that is strengths means that one is forever changed. Our models of treating mental or emotional problems does not need to be hooked to the medical model of diagnosis of problems and having a hierarchical guide or clinician that knows more about the client's problems and treatment than does the client. In fact, once smitten by the strengths-based way of thinking, one tends to look for and find more of the life giving forces that helps to lift us and those we have contact with all around. It is like the sunflower that is on the cover of this book that follows the sun to take in those life giving forces it seeks and finds all around. And so it can be with us. It is with all of those around. Life is experienced as good, and acknowledgement of the issues in life is seen as temporal rather than permanent. This is a primary sense of those who are optimistic. We can live through and with our disabilities and frailties in life.

Compassion Rather than Compliance Is Manifest

There is an acknowledgement that we have newer, more relevant viewpoints that fit with what we know to be true in brain functions. We have embraced the postmodern, social constructivist, and positive psychology that are built on propositions that are different than the old metaphors that were based on fixing bodily problems like broken legs or herniated disks. Instead we have recognized the functions of the narrative part of the brain that provides us with perceptual sets that align with the bio-psycho-socio-cultural-familial-political inputs we have absorbed. We recognize the multiplicity of life, accepting that we have differences, and compassion is more effective than compliance with someone else's expectations. I also recognize that this is difficult for some people to accept.

The Ways of Being Can Transcend

The ways of being are being benevolently curious, being self-reflective, providing a speculative rather than definitive discussion, providing sincere compliments, and being context focused.

Concepts that Help Provide Our Belief in Others' Strengths

We know that the Pygmalion effect can produce great changes in our recursive interactions with those with whom we relate. Also, we acknowledged that Saleebey's (2009) ideas that we work to find and increase strengths in all those with whom we are interacting, along with the notion that seeing people as being "at potential," and believing in human resiliencies changes our cultural beliefs that there is an innate original sin, or sins of the fathers that we are playing out generation after generation. If life looks for life, we are made as competent, healthy creatures that desire good lives and positive relationships with those in community.

Collaboration Works

We acknowledge that the word *together* is a positive force in bringing us together from different places to find common ground and that asking our colleagues and clients of every kind to join us by asking what would you like to get from our time together today? How might we work in concert?

Our Tools Are Not beyond Our Ways

We are indebted to the makers of strengths-based models, such as solution oriented therapy, narrative therapy, and positive psychology, but are not chained to them. We expect that there will be and have been additional models that will help us continue to learn and become more proficient in what we believe to be a stronger model of interacting with other human beings. We look forward to finding other means also to flourish and live good lives. We are currently exploring both mindfulness as well as neurocounseling as means to help those who need strengthening in their finding life, as well as ourselves. We look forward to work with our supervisees' strengths in ways that produce more and more results knowing that the ones we use may someday be looked on as charming and no longer normal science (Kuhn, 1977). The ushering in of the postmodern philosophies gave rise to the deconstruction of the usual interpretations of culture and all it holds true. Positivism gives way to postpositivism, where science must finally agree that this entire field can no longer be viewed as separate or independent of the human influence. Objectivity is not a solid truth. Our views of understanding life, viewing human dualism of good and bad, are social constructions, and therefore we can rearrange our perceptual sets to finding and appreciating our strengths. One constant, however, is that the crux of our strengths-based work is to work on ourselves. We have found that the basic tenets of strengths-based work will keep us open and working on "who I am." So, lets begin.

Note

1. Second-order change involves a change in the rules of the system and thus in the system itself (Becvar and Becvar, 2012, p. 294).

References

American Psychiatric Association. (2000). Diagnostic and statistical manual of mental disorders: DSM-IV-TR. Washington, DC: American Psychiatric Association (p. xxxi).

Anderson, H., Cooperrider, D., Gergen, K., Gergen, M., McNamee, S., . . . Whitney, D. (2008). *The appreciative organization.* Chagrin Falls, OH: Taos Institute Publications.

Becvar, D.S., & Becvar, R.J. (2012). *Family therapy: A systemic integration.* (8th ed.). New York, NY: Pearson.

Bermeo, C.A. (2009, March). *Developing a climate of access, equity and excellence in education for all students.* Keynote address presented at the meeting of American Counseling Association, Charlotte, NC.

Bernard, J. M. (1979). Supervisor training: A discrimination model. *Counselor Education and Supervision, 19,* 60–68.

Bernard, J. M. (1997). The Discrimination Model. In C. E. Watkins, Jr. (Ed.), *Handbook of psychotherapy supervision* (pp. 310–327). New York, NY: Wiley.

Becvar, D. S., & Becvar, R. J. (2012). *Family therapy: A systemic integration.* (8th ed.). New York, NY: Pearson.

Boisvert, C., & Faust, D. (2002). Iatrogenic symptoms in psychotherapy: A theoretical exploration of the potential impact of labels, language, and belief systems. *American Journal of Psychotherapy, 56,* 244–259.

Boyatzis, R.E., Smith, M.L., Van Oosten, E., & Woolford, L. (2013). Developing resonant leaders through emotional intelligence, vision and coaching. *Organizational Dynamics, 42,* 17–24.

Cohen, B.-Z. (1999). Intervention and supervision in strengths-based social work practice. *Family in Society: The Journal of Contemporary Social Services, 80,* 460–466.

Cooperrider, D.L. (2000). Positive image, positive action: The affirmative basis of organization. In D.L. Cooperrider, P. Sorensen, D. Whitney, & T. Yaeger (Eds.) *Appreciative inquiry: Rethinking human organization toward a positive theory of change* (pp. 29–54). Champaign, IL: Stipes.

Cooperrider, D., Sorensen, P.F., Whitney, D., & Yaeger, T.F. (Eds.) (2000). *Appreciative Inquiry: Rethinking Human Organization toward a Positive Theory of Change.* Champaign, IL: Stipes.

Covey, S.R. (2005). *The 8th habit: From effectiveness to greatness.* Philadelphia, PA: Running Press Miniature Editions.

de Shazer, S., & Berg, I.K. (1997). What works? Remarks on research aspects of solution-focused brief therapy. *Journal of Family, 19,* 121–124.

Edwards, J.K. (2011). Mentoring: What it is and what it can be. *The Illinois Counselor, 3,* 14–15.

Edwards, J.K. (2012). *Strengths-based supervision in clinical practice.* Thousand Oaks, CA: Sage Publications.

Edwards, J.K., & Chen, M.W. (1999). Strength-based supervision: Frameworks, current practice and future directions: A Wu-Wei method. *The Family Journal, 7,* 349–357.

Edwards, J.K., & Heath, A.W. (2007). *A consumer's guide to mental health services: Unveiling the mysteries and secrets of psychotherapy.* Binghamton, NY: Haworth Press.

Franklin, C., Trepper, T.S., Gingerich, W.J., & McCollum, E.E. (2012). *Solution-focused brief therapy: A handbook of evidence-based practice.* New York, NY: Oxford University Press.

Greenleaf, R.K, & Spears, L.C. (Eds.). (2002). *Servant leadership: A journey into the nature of legitimate power and greatness.* Mahwah, NJ: Paulist Press.

Halvorson, H.G. (2015). Managers Can Motivate Employees with One Word. Watertown MA: On Point, *Harvard Business Review.* Retrieved on May 18, 2016 from https://hbr.org/2014/08/managers-can-motivate-employees-with-one-word/

Kuhn, T. (1977). *The essential tension: Selected studies in scientific tradition and change.* Chicago, IL: University of Chicago Press.

Lane, C. (2013). *The NIMH withdraws support for DSM-5.* Retrieved May 4, 2015 from https://www.psychology today.com/blog/side-effects/201305/the-nimh-withdraws-support-dsm-5

Liddle, H.A., & Saba, G.W. (1983). On context replication: The isomorphic relationship of training and therapy. *Journal of Strategic & Systemic Therapies, 2,* 3−11.

Liddle, H.A., & Saba, G.W. (1985). The isomorphic nature of training and therapy: Epistemological foundation for a structural-strategic training paradigm. In J. Schwartzman (Ed.), *Families and other systems: The macrosystemic context of family therapy* (pp. 27−47). New York, NY: Guilford Press.

Masten, A.S. (2001). Ordinary magic: Resilience processes in development. *American Psychologist, 56,* 227−238.

Masten, A.S. (2015). *Ordinary magic: Resilience in development.* New York, NY: Guilford Press.

Masten, A.S., Best, K.M., & Garmezy, N. (1990). Resilience and development: Contributions from the study of children who overcome adversity. *Development and psychopathology, 2,* 425−444.

Miller, S., Hubble, M., & Duncan, B. (2007, November/December). Supershrinks. *Psychotherapy Networker, 56,* 27−35.

Milne, J., Edwards, J.K., & Murchie, J. (2001). Family treatment of oppositional defiant disorder: Changing views and strength-based approaches. *The Family Journal, 9,* 17−28.

Nichols, M. P. (2013). *Family therapy: Concepts and methods* (10th ed.). Boston, MA: Pearson.

Norcross, J.C. (2011). *Psychotherapy relationships that work: Evidence-based responsiveness* (2nd ed.). New York, NY: Oxford University Press.

OnPoint, (2015), *Be a Better Boss,* Harvard Business Review, Watertown, MA: Harvard Business Publishing.

Rapp, C. (1997). *The strengths model: Case management with people suffering from severe and persistent mental illness.* New York, NY: Oxford University Press.

Rath, T., & Conchie, B. (2008). *Strengths-based leadership.* Washington, DC: Gallup Press.

Rosenthal, R. (2002). The Pygmalion effect and its mediating mechanisms. In J. Aronson (Ed), *Improving academic achivement: Impact of psychological factors on education* (pp. 26–35). Walhjam, MA: Academic Press.

Russell, B. (1953). On the notion of cause, with applications to the free-will problem. In H. Feigl & M. Brodbeck (Eds.), *Readings in the philosophy of science.* (pp. 182−197). New York, NY: Appleton-Century-Crofts.

Saleebey, D. (2002). *The strengths perspective in social work practice* (3rd ed.). Toronto, Ontario, Canada: Allyn & Bacon.

Saleebey, D. (2008). *The strengths perspective in social work practice* (5th ed.). Toronto, Ontario, Canada: Allyn & Bacon.

Seligman, M.E.P. (2002). *Authentic happiness: Using the new positive psychology to realize your potential for lasting fulfillment.* New York, NY: Free Press.

Seligman, M.E.P. (2011). *Flourish: A visionary new understanding of happiness and well-being.* New York, NY: Free Press.

Seligman, M.E.P., Steen, T.A., Park, N., & Peterson, C. (2005). Positive psychology progress: Empirical validation of interventions. *American Psychologist, 60,* 410−421.

Siegel, D.J. (2007). *The mindful brain: Reflections and attunement in the cultivation of well-being.* New York, NY: W.W. Norton & Company.

Smith M., Glass, G., & Miller, T. (1980). The Benefits of Psychotherapy. Baltimore, MD: John Hopkins University Press.

Stiles, W. B., Shapiro, D.A., & Elliot, R. (1986). Are all psychotherapies equal? *American Psychologist,* 41, 165–180.

Stoltenberg, C. D., & Delworth, U. (1987). *Supervising counselors and therapists: A developmental approach.* San Francisco, CA: Jossey-Bass.

Tutu, D. (1984). Hope and Suffering: Sermons and Speeches, Grand Rapids, MI, USA. : W.B. Eerdmans (p. 143).

Wade, J., & Jones, J. (2014). Strength-based clinical supervision: A positive psychology approach to clinical training. New York, NY: Springer.

Walsh, F. (1996). Family resiliency: A concept and its application. *Family Process, 35,* 261−282.

Walsh, F. (1998). *Strengthening family resilience.* New York, NY: Guilford Press.

Walsh, F. (2003a). Clinical views of family normality, health, and dysfunction: From deficit to strengths perspective. In F. Walsh (Ed.), *Normal family process: Growing diversity and complexity.* New York, NY: Guilford Press.

Walsh, F. (2003b). Family resilience: A framework for clinical practice. *Family Process, 42,* 1−18.

Walsh, F. (2006). *Strengthening family resiliency* (2nd ed.). New York, NY: Guilford Press.

White, M., & Epston, D. (1990). *Narrative means to therapeutic ends.* New York, NY: W.W. Norton.

18

Reflecting Processes in Counselor Training

Iterating Socially Constructed Strengths-Based Learnings within and Beyond the Classroom

David Kleist, Jane Coe Smith, and Katie Kostohryz

Maybe our talk will bring ideas that could be useful for your conversation.

Tom Andersen

We were asked to begin our chapter with a discussion on what we consider to be a strengths-based approach and its utility. To be congruent with Tom Andersen's (1991a) conceptualization of reflecting processes, which we will discuss below, we find it best to have each of us share our personal definitions. After completing our chapter, we again will revisit this question to see if our conceptualizations have changed. As we enter our chapter, please entertain our current understanding of strengths-based work:

David: For myself, a strengths-based approach is related to Tom Andersen's perspective on keeping people in conversation by allowing them to maintain their integrity, allowing openness for new awareness, growth, and change to be the ultimate purpose. Andersen's ideas are connected to Goolishian and Anderson's (1988) view of clinicians as master conversationalists whose goal is to facilitate conversation long enough for problems to dissolve. In this way, my goal is to keep students and supervisees in conversation long enough to find their way to asset- or strength-oriented self-understandings. To facilitate such conversations I have found value in Andersen's emphasis on respecting students/supervisees' sense of integrity. I find supporting students/supervisees' development in this way integrates seamlessly into my overall social constructionist view of learning as a co-constructed process of meaning that truly is without end. If I can facilitate students' understanding of their own strengths, or assets, I trust that when they leave the classroom or supervisory meeting their increased awareness will act as seeds for further growth that will take place in the students' own time and pace.

Jane: For me, situating learning and action within a strengths-based approach stems from the idea of well-being. While well-being has broad and varied meaning it includes aspects of living a preferred life, positive and fulfilling life experiences, resiliency through adversity, and the knowledge, skills, and attitudes associated with mental and physical well-being. That is in contrast to a focus on "what not to do" or identifying and focusing on the problems and the contributing factors to life going awry. Synonyms for strength may include fortitude, resilience, spirit, strength of character, courage, and pluck.

Seligman (2011a) outlined a theory of well-being that is underpinned with attention to human character strengths. In working collaboratively with emerging and practicing counselors, reflecting on and expressing character strengths as they promote well-being, contributes to both personal and professional development. This means situating learning in a context of thoughts, feelings, and actions that promote well-being, meeting challenges with positive actions, experiencing self-efficacy, and learning and teaching strategies of resilience.

A strengths-based approach is preferred as it situates personal and professional development in a context that privileges learning in the realm of the desired outcome—positive and meaningful life experiences and relationships. I believe that helping self and others to learn about and experience positive well-being, preferred living, and what contributes to and maintains well-being is a more efficient and effective strategy to get to that outcome.

Katie: Strengths-based work allows counselor educators to focus on the ability and potential of students as opposed to deficits or problems in their learning. This approach teaches students how to cultivate strengths within themselves, clients, colleagues, families, and other members of the community, university, and schools. Building a trusting, collaborative classroom environment is essential. Relationships are fostered both in and out of the classroom as strengths-based work promotes collaboration and positive connections intra- and interpersonally. To me, this modality does not include a PowerPoint or traditional lecture where knowledge is imparted from the expert to the novice. Instead, strengths-based work encourages students and counselor educators to take risks and be vulnerable together. There is also a commitment to wellness and hope. Counselor educators, students, and clients have the capacity to learn, grow, and change and the systems we reside in are seen as resourceful and capable.

Reflective Processing toward Strengths-Based Counselor Education

Our efforts to emphasize strengths in our roles as counselor educators have involved the use of Tom Andersen's (1991a) reflecting processes and the Values in Action (VIA) Classification of Strengths (Peterson & Seligman, 2004). All three of us have utilized reflecting teams (Andersen, 1987) and/or the reflecting process in numerous didactic classes and clinical experiences. However, Katie has made some considerable gains in integrating a greater strengths-based focus in her use of the reflecting process in an individual counseling theory course as well as a testing course. Jane, though having added strength to her use of reflecting teams in a similar family and couple theory class, has recently emphasized increasing reflective awareness of students' character strength development in a number of her courses. What follows is a brief overview of the reflective process of Tom Andersen with attention on its use in counselor education described via a case example of the reflective process in action in a counselor education class. We then move on to describing character strength work (Peterson & Park, 2009; Peterson & Seligman, 2004), and its usage in counselor education through another case example.

Reflecting Processes: a Brief Overview

The seeds were planted for a rogue wave of change back in 1984 when Tom Andersen (1987) decided to simply try something different, something more transparent, more authentic with a family seeking relational help. He literally provided a window into hearing and seeing the consultation team's thoughts and ideas related to their family; the reflecting team was born. While conducting a family session with the consultation team he decided to take a therapeutic break. But instead of leaving the family alone for him to consult with the observing team out of earshot of the family, Andersen decided to simply switch the lights and audio on for the observing team to share their thoughts while he and the family listened, together. The idea of reflexivity was not new, and reflective practice had already found its way into the field of education (Schön, 1983) but Tom Andersen's mindful attention to novelty facilitated its prominence in the field of family therapy, and clinical counseling work overall. The history and use of reflecting teams, and reflecting processes (Andersen, 1991a, b) in therapeutic contexts has been well documented in the 30 plus years since its inception (e.g., mental health settings [Eubanks, 2002; Lax, 1989; Shilts, Rudes, & Madigan, 1993], medical facilities [Griffith, Griffith, & Slovik, 1990; Seikkula et al., 1995; Watson & Lee, 1993], schools [Swim, 1995]). Please see Andersen (1987), Chang (2010), Kleist (1999), Pender and Stinchfield (2012), and/or Willott, Hatton, and Oyebode (2012) for an overview of the integration of reflecting teams into clinical practice and related research.

Reflective Processes: Winding Its Way into Clinical Training

Andersen (1991a, 1991b, 1992, 1995) had moved beyond speaking directly to reflecting teams and more to the underlying reflecting process, because it is the process, and not the mere team, that holds therapeutic power and influence. The reflective process embraces the importance of being present, not only in, but to the conversation as a means to increase understanding. For Andersen (e.g., 1987, 1991, 1995), being in conversation with another provides access to that person's effort to communicate meaning. The evolution of the reflective process' utility has shifted solely from direct clinical practice to finding ways for integration into educational contexts. Professionals in counselor education, psychology, as well as nursing have all recently explored ways reflecting processes can enhance students' conceptual development and clinical skills.

Most frequently, educators and supervisors have utilized the reflecting process to enhance clinical skill development (Cox, Bañez, Hawley, & Mostade, 2003; Maggio, 2014; Harrawood, Parmanand, & Wilde, 2011; Hawley, 2006; James, MacCormack, Korol, & Lee, 1996; McGovern & Harmsworth, 2010; Kleist & Hill, 2003; Landis & Young, 1994; Reichelt & Skjerve, 2013). Within these educational contexts the emphasis has been on integration of reflecting processes into teaching couple and family counseling/therapy (Harrawood et al., 2011; Landis & Young, 1994; MacCormack et al., 1996; McGovern & Harmsworth, 2010; Shilts, Rudes, & Madigan, 1993). Harrawood et al. (2001) integrated reflecting teams into a family theory course in a master's program in counseling while examining the role of emotion within experiential activities via a phenomenological study. Students rotated across the following roles: counselor, role played family, reflecting team member, and observing team member. Students reported feeling heightened anxiety when a member of the reflecting team as they had to be more attentive, and knowledgeable, of the utilized theory in order to comment on theory integration with the role-played client. Students reported learning the most from participation as a reflecting team member versus the other roles. MacCormack et al. (1996) utilized reflecting teams in a doctoral level clinical psychology program within their family therapy practicum in developmental fashion. As a means to hone and prepare doctoral practicum students for eventual direct clinical work with families they first participated as reflecting team members until clinical skill conceptualization was developed enough to prompt direct work with families. Students expressed greater involvement as a result of the active nature of reflecting teams and increased self-confidence. Once on the other side of the mirror, as clinicians, away from their role as observers behind the one-way mirror, practicum students felt the reflecting team provided support, encouragement, and validation. McGovern and Harmsworth (2010) provided a wonderful example of impromptu creativity in reflective process use. During an initial class day on systemic practice in their doctoral program in clinical psychology they began with a simple family role play. Observing students had been instructed to simply watch intently. Faculty were so moved by the students' attentiveness they thought of engaging in a traditional reflecting team but had concerns conversation would get too theoretical, too expert-oriented, too early in class. Instead, observing team members were instructed to stand next to the family member whose story they felt most connected to, for whatever reason. Then, one by one, the observing members shared their experience of connection with the particular family member. Once completed, the role play family spoke of the experience of hearing the observing team members' sense of connection. Students highly valued the experiential activity as a means to illuminate theoretical constructs. Landis and Young (1994, along with Shilts et al. [1993]), utilized the reflecting team in similar ways. Both integrated reflecting teams into the process of learning basic, master's-level couple and family counseling skills, in which students had the opportunity to role play as a counselor, and observe such role plays as a reflecting team member. As with McGovern and Harmsworth, students in Shilts et al. (1993) provided positive feedback, indicating that the reflecting team process gave them encouragement, validation of feelings, and enhanced confidence in sharing their own ideas. Given that the origins of reflective practice began in the context of clinical work with families, it makes sense that its initial use in an educational setting would also be in classes focused on couples and family work. However, other educators have found additional venues for its integration into clinical training.

Though systems thinking, with a postmodern twist, is at the core of reflective practice in couple and family clinical training, relational learning is congruent with applications to group work (Cox et al., 2003), basic skills training (Hawley, 2006; Maggio, 2014), and supervision (Kleist & Hill, 2003; Reichelt & Skjerve, 2013). Cox et al. (2003) utilized reflective teams in the development of master's-level counselors' group work skills. Students divided into two groups, one serving as the group in counseling, the other as the reflecting team. Two formats were utilized: one in a group theory and technique class in which the two groups switched roles over the course of a semester, and in an introductory group process class in which the two groups did not change over the course of the semester. Similar to the preceding examples, students in these groups received feedback more easily, valued multi-perspectives, and particularly relevant for group training, the reflective process allowed them to take on a meta-perspective to their own group process.

Basic skills training in counseling, at the master's level in the counseling profession (Hawley, 2006), and the doctoral level for clinical psychology (Maggio, 2014), commonly takes place in role play formats with peers serving as clients. For Hawley (2006), reflecting teams were infused into a basic counseling skills class in a master's program in counseling. Students would rotate across three roles: counselor, client, and reflecting team member throughout the semester. As the counselor and client worked, reflecting team members observed from behind a one-way mirror. Each practice session would have a time where the reflecting team would switch with the counselor–client pair to give comment on the developing skills of the student in the role of counselor. Students benefitted from participation as a reflecting team member as they felt more involved, given their responsibility to provide comment on the counselor's use of basic counseling skills. Students in the counselor role also benefitted from hearing reflecting team members' comments as it increased internal awareness of how they were embodying the counselor role. Maggio (2014) integrated reflecting teams into a similar context (i.e., students acting in the roles of clinician, client, and reflecting team member) but in a doctoral level clinical psychology practicum. Two aspects of her integration stand out as additions to Hawley's (2006) use of reflecting teams in basic skills training. First, in addition to clinician skill development, the team's reflections paid particular attention to understanding the client's experience in session. Second, she utilized Andersen's (1997) "post-therapy interviews" (which she reconceptualized as "post-therapy trialogues") in which the instructor interviews both the counselor and client at the end of the semester with a team of students acting as the reflecting team. Counselor and client are asked to process the experience of being counselor and client with particular focus on helpful/unhelpful ways of intervening across the semester-long counselor process. The reflecting team would comment on this processing, followed up with the instructor, counselor, and client processing team comments for final learning gleaned from the semester-long practicum. Students were strongly impacted by the ability to better understand client perspectives after being members of a reflecting team and hearing the comments of the reflecting team across the semester.

In addition to skills training that occurs in courses, the climax of skills development is integrating counseling skills with real clients, in real community/school settings. In this context reflecting teams have been integrated into triadic supervision of a community-based practicum (Kleist & Hill, 2003) as well as a doctoral level group supervision of a community-based practicum in clinical psychology (Reichelt & Skjerve, 2013). After the Council for Accreditation of Counseling and Related Educational Programs (CACREP) approved the use of triadic supervision (two supervisees paired with a supervisor) in 2001 for clinical supervision of master's-level counseling students, I (Kleist) began to explore ways that Andersen's reflecting process could be utilized in triadic supervision. After some time conceptualizing and fine tuning what was later called the *reflective model of triadic supervision* (RMTS), I and a colleague (Kleist & Hill, 2003; see Stinchfield, Hill, & Kleist, 2007 for fuller description of the RMTS) began to implement the model into our separate supervision sessions with first practicum counseling students.

In RMTS, students would bring to supervision meetings videotaped sessions for review. One student would show the tape first and engage in traditional supervisory conversation with the supervisor. While this is occurring the other master's student would observe (silently and inconspicuously while sitting in the same room) the supervisory conversation and tape being reviewed. After 20 minutes, the supervisor would turn to the peer-as-reflecting team and engage in a reflective conversation about what they have seen and heard in the supervisor–supervisee conversation and/ or in the videotaped session that seemed noteworthy to them. While this is occurring the supervisee who just showed the videotaped session now sits silently listening to their peer and supervisor process the peer's observations. This part of the RMTS process will last no longer than ten minutes at which time the supervisor turns back to the supervisee who began with showing a videotaped session, to process what he/she has heard in the reflective conversation of their peer and supervisor and what aspects they will take away and integrate into sessions forthcoming. The process then repeats with the other supervisee now showing a video segment of a recent counseling session. Research on the RMTS (Stinchfield, Hill, & Kleist, 2010) indicated supervisees, though initially apprehensive about sharing their counseling skill development in front of a peer, valued the power shift in supervision as the traditional hierarchy dissolved as their peer feedback was as valued as the faculty supervisor's comments. A finding that stands as unique from other comments on the impact of reflective processes in counselor training was the notion of what was referred to as "shared developmental process" in which supervisees acknowledged the comfort of knowing someone else was moving through similar developmental issues, and the experience of doing so, together.

Reichelt and Skjerve (2013) have utilized reflecting teams in the provision of group supervision to doctoral level clinicians in a clinical psychology program. Students would come to group supervision and either show a videotaped session or orally present a case. The other students, acting as the reflecting team, would observe and listen to the faculty supervisor talk with the clinician on their oral case presentation or videotaped session. After some time, the reflecting team would talk among themselves about their peer's work and supervisory conversation just observed, while the presenting peer now sits in a listening position. After which, the instructor and supervisee would process the reflecting team's conversation. Though supervisors found the process somewhat useful with the presentation of multiple perspectives, some clinicians and faculty supervisors found the comments too critical and/or too directed on solving the case versus providing the supervisee with comments on furthering their clinical development. A cautionary note is given to follow Andersen's (1991a) initial guidelines for reflecting teams as a means to avoid such potential pitfalls. As Andersen stated, comments are presented tentatively, avoiding knowing too quickly, and formed as positive connotations, or imaginings versus negative or blaming in nature.

Reflecting teams, and reflective processes, clearly have a place in skill development in clinically focused mental health professions (e.g., counseling and clinical psychology). Other authors have found the reflective process as impactful for more traditional didactic classes and experiences in and beyond the mental health professions (Morrison, 2009; Sloan-Power, 2008; Tseliou, 2007). Morrison integrated reflecting teams and processes into a general nursing class focusing on understanding mental illness. Students were first given the assignment of finding social media that communicated statements/beliefs about mental illness and those individuals with mental illness. Once information was gathered, students were prompted to develop and "tell" a story of mental illness, or those with mental illness, and share with the rest their class members. At this point Morrison infuses Michael White's (1997) "outsider witness" process. Outsider witnessing is a process similar to Andersen's (1991) reflecting team, but the outsider witnesses are not mental health professionals (i.e., experts), but people important to the storyteller's life (e.g., friends, family). Class members acted as the reflecting team, or outsider witness, to the story of mental illness. Upon hearing the story of mental illness the outsider witnesses shared their responses to hearing the story and its personal meaning for them. Once shared, the original storyteller (in this case the student who gathered information on mental illness), responds to the meanings shared by the outsider witnesses. Student comments on this integrative use of reflective processes and outsider witness focused on increased awareness of others' experiences with mental illness, their own thoughts and feelings toward mental illness, and an overall greater sense of empathy and compassion. Sloan-Power (2008) investigated the use of reflecting teams as a vehicle for teaching concepts of spiritual diversity in a master's-level social work program. The author found that students felt inhibited, at times, to speak about sensitive matters such as one's own spirituality or religiosity. A modified reflecting team was used in classroom instruction, wherein students could share their thoughts and feelings in a group setting without the social expectation of being questioned on their personal beliefs. Students reported increased self-efficacy and decreased anxiety for dealing with spiritual matters in a classroom environment. Tseliou (2007) was involved in teaching an undergraduate psychology class to students in psychology and primary age teacher education programs. The focus was on teaching a class on feminism and psychotherapy. She presented a mental health case involving a woman, as shared through a detailed genogram. Class members split into small groups. Each group was told to take on the role and voice of one of the people in the woman's life. After assuming the role of a member of the woman's genogram, the instructor told the story of the woman. Students were told to listen with the ears and mindset of the person they were role playing. After the story was told, each group shared their individually constructed story for the sake of weaving together a unified voice of the member they were playing. Each group then spoke from the voice of this person. Other members listened silently, only later to share their phenomenological understanding of what it would be like to be this woman within this relational network. Tseliou (2007) reported this use of the reflecting process allowed for multiple layers of reflection, increased curiosity of students toward other people's lives, as well as their own.

Reflecting on the Evolution of Reflective Processes

The use of reflecting teams, and the underlying reflective processes, has clearly expanded beyond direct clinical use with families seeking therapy as with its initial use with Andersen (1987). Its breadth of clinical uses is extensive and it appears that the reflective process has come full circle back into the educational realm of informing the development of professional counselors, clinical psychologists, nurses, teachers, and more. As mentioned, Donald Schön (1983), with his book *The Reflective Practitioner*, helped direct those in teacher education and higher education to more fully attend to promoting students' reflective (or reflexive in some writings) thinking. What is different, due to Tom Andersen's contributions, is a method, and more formalized process for promoting such reflexivity. What also surfaces in reviewing reflecting teams', and/or processes, use in the various realms described in the preceding text, is the inherent positive and supportive context through which meaning is explored and promoted. There is an almost inherent strengths-based attitude within the process of reflecting teams (Brownlee, 2009), yet its full potential has not yet been harnessed, in our opinion. For strengths-based work to reach fuller potential and impact, intentional focus on promoting students' strengths is vital. What follows is our current understanding and practice of strengths-based pedagogy in our respective counselor education programs.

Strengths-Based Counselor Education: Possibilities

Katie will provide the first examples of strengths-based counselor education. She has found numerous ways to integrate strengths-based work into her role as counselor educator at Penn State University.

During an individual counseling theories class, a strengths-based reflecting team was used with first semester, first year master's-level students to enhance their knowledge and ability to demonstrate theoretical interventions with clients. Each week for the duration of the semester, different groups of students performed a role play of a particular theory. The reflecting team (class members not playing a role) watched the session while sitting separately from the client and counselors. The reflecting team worked to listen and develop hypotheses and suggestions for the client and counselors to consider within the theoretical orientation. The instructor then asked the reflecting team to share their observations regarding the session, including strengths of the counselors and specific theoretical interventions while the client and counselors listened.

The team members gave their observations, shared thoughts, and non-judgmentally described their experience of the session and commented on specific theoretical strengths demonstrated by the counselor. The reflecting team's purpose was to encourage the counselor toward strengths-based work with clients utilizing the specific theory. Multiple viewpoints were given by reflecting team members in order for the counselor to choose the ideas that they connect with most. Also, the team helped counselors progress their understanding of integrating theory in the role play session. After the reflection team shared, the instructor asked the clients to discuss their thoughts on the role play, the theory, and what they found useful from the observations. Last, the counselors also reflected on their experience, the theory, and the comments they were given by the reflecting team.

In Katie's second example, a reflecting team was utilized as a vehicle for teaching within a didactic classroom of combined first and second year master's-level counseling students during Tests in Counseling. In this example, she utilized a strengths-based reflective team approach when comparing and contrasting qualitative versus quantitative assessments during one three-hour class period.

Students were given the case study one week prior to class and then selected what group they wanted to be in: the family case study, the two qualitative groups, or the one quantitative assessment group. The groups divided up for the first 30 minutes to create a plan for the role play. The quantitative group utilized the Inventory of Family Protective Factors (Gardner, Huber, Steiner, Vazquez, & Savage, 2008) as the class had previously read the article for test construction. The two qualitative groups were given freedom to pick or create an assessment based on Deacon and Piercy's (2001) article identifying numerous creative family interventions. These two groups identified the counselors for the role play as well as the assessment they wanted to demonstrate in class. Meanwhile, the role play group spent time in class rehearsing the dynamics within the five-person family consisting of two primary caregivers, one adolescent, and two children.

Those not directly involved in the role play either as family members or as counselors acted as the reflecting team. The class began with the first qualitative group instructing the family to draw a picture of the family doing something. After the role play, the reflecting team identified strengths of the counselors as well as observations on the family and strengths with their assessment tool. Next, the family identified strengths of the counselors followed by their observations and insights and comments. Last, the counselors were asked to point out strengths they saw in themselves and the family as well as the assessment tool. During this time, students displayed benevolent curiosity and asked for clarification and reported noticing both strengths and differences between the assessments and theory and practice. They also asked questions such as, I wonder . . . I noticed . . . I was curious about . . . what might happen if the counselor tried this?

For the next group using the quantitative tool, the instructor attempted a different order to see how it changed the processing. The family processed first, then the counselor, and last, the reflecting team. The reflecting team allowed students to see the developmental considerations, ethics, processing strengths and challenges and logistics when utilizing quantitative versus qualitative tools with children, adolescents, and adults. Changing the order of the reflecting teams allowed students to stay engaged and not rely on the group before them to point out strengths and wonderings. We switched up the order one more time with the final qualitative assessment group using the want ads (Deacon & Piercy, 2001), as the counselors processed first, the reflecting team and then the family. The class then processed the activity as a whole. Students reported at that time and again at the end of the semester that the reflecting team role play was the most impactful class of the semester.

Our next set of examples will come from Jane. She's involved in multiple uses of strengths-based work in her role as counselor educator at Idaho State University. Jane advances the notion of strengths-based work into an area not yet promoted by use of reflecting teams nor reflective processes: character strengths.

Well-Being and Character Strengths Applied to Counselor Training

Out of the positive psychology movement, starting with the new millennium, came a burgeoning theoretical and research focus on the *positive elements of human beings—psychological assets, positive attributes, and character strengths* (Kobau et al., 2011; Peterson & Park, 2009; Peterson & Seligman, 2004). This connected well with the counseling profession, which has long-held core values of supporting prevention, optimum development, and positive functioning (Myers & Sweeney, 2007). While the fields of counseling, psychology, and social work have a long-standing relationship with the medical model of therapeutic change there has been a highly active shifting of attention to more positive and strengths-based therapeutic work. Most can agree that it is essential for emerging and practicing counselors to have knowledge and skills on using the *Diagnostic and Statistical Manual of Mental Disorders, 5th ed.* (*DSM-5*; American Psychiatric Association, 2013) due to the prevalent use of this classification system in medical and mental health practices. However, this system has long been fraught with controversy attracting a multitude of scientific and conceptual criticisms (McLaren, 2010; Welch, Klassen, Borisova, & Clothier, 2013). One philosophical criticism centers on the deficit and problem-based view of human living that is at the center of this diagnostic system. Use of diagnostic labels for mental health concerns has been shown to lead to negative attitudes and stereotypes toward people and their reported problems (Khoury, Langer, & Pagnini, 2014). According to Lopez et al. (2006) "this focus on negative aspects has occurred at the expense of identifying the strengths of individuals and their environmental resources and assisting people in their pursuit of optimal human functioning" (p. 259). This statement aligns with the strengths-based orientation of a theory of well-being postulated by Seligman (2011a) as an update to his original theory of happiness presented in *Authentic Happiness* (Seligman, 2002). The topic of well-being is situated within a highly strengths-based context. Introducing, instructing, and exploring well-being with emerging counselors is extremely relevant to any of the multiple counseling specialties (e.g., clinical mental health; marriage, couple, and family; school; student affairs) that professional counselors can be engaged with in their practice.

Ensuring that emerging and practicing counselors have a strong foundation in what constitutes and contributes to well-being allows them to personally and professionally practice within a strengths-based framework in order to effectively maximize wellness for themselves and others—the very heart of the field of professional counseling (Kaplan, Tarvydas, & Gladding, 2013) and critical to the profession's commitment to counselor wellness (Lawson & Venart, 2004; Limberg & Ohert, 2013).

As a socially constructed notion, well-being can inevitably have varied definitions, along with broad meanings and applications. However, it is hard to argue with the construct of well-being as a beneficial concept and one worthy of significant attention and focus within counselor training. Counselor training curriculums historically include a focus on developing personal awareness, personal growth, and well-being for emerging counselors. The importance of attending to personal development and well-being is well established in the counselor education arena (ACA, 2015; CACREP, 2016). The better we are, as mental health professionals, at understanding ourselves, positively addressing our own life challenges, and living a life of well-being the better we are able to assist others with those same positive ways of living.

Seligman's (2011a) theory of well-being postulates that there are five elements connected to the construct of well-being. Each of these elements can be operationalized and therefore measured, whether subjectively or objectively. The elements of well-being include *positive emotion, engagement, positive relationships, meaning,* and *accomplishment* (referred to as PERMA). Each of these elements contributes to a person's experience of well-being (Seligman, 2011a; Jayawickreme, Forgeard, & Seligman, 2012).

Earlier in the development of a positive psychology discipline, Peterson and Seligman (2004) led the development of a classification of human strengths and virtues known as the Values in Action (VIA) Classification of Strengths. This classification system includes 24 character strengths grouped under the six virtue categories of *wisdom and knowledge, courage, humanity, justice, temperance, and transcendence.* (See Appendix 18.A.) As described by Peterson and Seligman (2004), "*character strengths* are the psychological ingredients—processes or mechanisms—that define the virtues" (p. 13). The VIA Classification of Strengths was developed through extensive research of character across time, context, and culture with the belief that "good character can be cultivated" (Peterson & Seligman, 2004, p. 3). A tenet of this classification system holds that these general, positive traits have a degree of stability but can also be influenced by the individual's experiences and setting and are capable of change (Peterson and Seligman, 2004). Helping people make meaning of their character strengths can also advance the positive expression of those strengths. Character is part of what people care about doing and who they are—a way of expressing self (VIA Institute on Character, 2015).

The VIA Classification of Strengths (Peterson & Seligman, 2004) is the basis for the online VIA Inventory of Strengths (VIA-IS) used to measure an individual's character strengths profile (Peterson & Park, 2009; Peterson & Seligman, 2004). Seligman (2011a) considers the strengths and virtues of this classification and the accompanying strengths inventory to underpin the five elements of his theory of well-being. Knowledge of and practice with these personal character strengths can encourage and promote the personal and professional development of emerging counselors, connecting to their and their clients' well-being.

This character strengths classification system and strengths inventory have been shown to have cross-cultural relevance and utilization (Dahlsgaard, Peterson, & Seligman, 2005; Park, Peterson, & Seligman, 2006), along with measured validity and reliability (Niemiec, 2013; Wen-jie, Yu, Yonghong, & Xiao-qing, 2011). Research has been conducted showing positive effects on well-being and performance from becoming aware of and engaging with personal character strengths (Duan, Ho, Tang, Li, & Zhang, 2013; Gander, Proyer, Ruch, & Wyss, 2012; Linley, Nielsen, Gillett, & Biswas-Diener, 2010). Character strengths in relationship to college student academic success have also been studied (Bowers & Lopez, 2010; Lounsbury, Fisher, Levy, & Welsh, 2009).

Therefore, one beneficial component of a strengths-based counselor education curriculum (Kolodinsky et al., 2014) is to include character strengths knowledge and activities with the intention of positively influencing emerging and practicing counselors' personal and professional development. Incorporating character strengths knowledge and practices can be included in core and supplemental coursework, clinical supervision, extracurricular activities (e.g., service learning, professional advocacy, professional organizations), and continuing educational–professional development activities.

There is a long-standing tradition of including character education within a preschool through high school learning environment (Linkins, Niemiec, Gillham, & Mayerson, 2013). Historically, most character education programs have been prescriptive in nature with the content typically driven by societal and institutional standards of behavior (Linkins et al., 2013). This type of character strength education is then open to criticism of cultural, religious, or political bias (Linkins et al., 2013) or, at the very least, viewed as restrictive in its ability to be broadly applied. The intent of the VIA Strengths Classification System and VIA-IS is to reveal, elicit, and nurture (Linkins et al., 2013) the inherent strength traits of the individual student. This leads to a character education goal of describing and facilitating the calling forth of strengths-based traits (Linkins et al., 2013, Peterson & Park, 2009) that lead an individual to develop and grow in a positive direction based on a unique interpretation and application of personal character strengths.

This strengths classification system and strengths inventory can be foundational to establishing a strengths-based focus for a counselor education program or other context. These tools provide a common set of strengths and underpin a focus on well-being, positive development, and positive action. The plurality and inherency of character strengths in humans is captured with the VIA Classification of Strengths (Linkins et al., 2013; Peterson & Seligman, 2004) and the VIA-IS (Peterson & Park, 2009; Peterson & Seligman, 2004), while allowing for individual interpretation and lived-experience with these strengths. Through social constructionist teaching strategies, students can increase their understanding, connection with, and use of their own strengths and learn from others' varied interpretations and experiences. Framing the character strengths and the inventory results within social constructionist pedagogy allows for flexibility, individual and shared learning through exploring meanings, and creativity.

Applications of Character Strength Reflections for Personal and Professional Development

The following section provides suggested guidelines and examples for using character strengths as part of any counselor education program or activity, including within a doctoral cohort and a multicultural counseling course, and is based on Jane's experiences infusing character strengths into counselor education courses and supervision activities.

1) *Developing a Foundational Framework for Broad Use of Character Strengths in Counselor Education Training Activities.* Introduce the VIA Classification of Character Strengths (Peterson & Seligman, 2004) and the VIA-IS (Peterson & Park, 2009; Peterson & Seligman, 2004) at the start of a course, workshop, or counselor education program. Individuals can access and take the online VIA-IS at no cost. There are options for selecting a more in-depth results interpretation at a small cost and this could be built in to the fees for the training program or workshop. Share, review, and teach on the components of the strengths classification and inventory results.

   a. Review the components of the strengths classification system and inventory. Provide background on theoretical and research information related to these tools.

   b. When the students or participants take the VIA-IS review the results as a group allowing the students or participants to first reflect individually on these results, then share their character strength information, as desired, in smaller groups and then the large group. Reflection questions can include: *Which of your strengths do you experience as most like you? Which of your strengths do you remember expressing today—describe that action in your small group. Which strengths do you call on the most during difficult or challenging times? Which strengths have you most often expressed since starting this education program? Which strength is the easiest and most fun for you to express? Which is the most challenging and least fun to express? What influences that ease or difficulty? Which strength do you believe will serve you the best later today in your planned activities? Which strength will you likely call on frequently in this course or workshop? How do you anticipate using that strength for your benefit?*

  c.   Introduce the concept of *signature strengths* as those character strengths that are most easily expressed by an individual, come naturally, fit authentically as part of you, and results in a sense of excitement when expressed. (Note: These are generally the top four to seven strengths on an individual's VIA-IS results.) Focusing on increasing the expression of signature strengths is believed to lead to an increased sense of well-being (Peterson & Park, 2009; Peterson & Seligman, 2004; Seligman, 2011a, 2011b).

  d.   Continue connecting and applying the character strength tools and personal results to concepts of strengths-based learning, personal and professional development, along with associated knowledge, skills, and attitudes for the course or workshop topic throughout the learning context through subsequent activities (see additional ideas in subsequent text).

Counselor educators need to possess knowledge and experience with the character strengths and inventory and can gain this through accessing literature on these systems, taking online courses specific to these systems, and formally or informally integrating character strengths practices into their own personal and professional activities (VIA Institute on Character, 2015).

2)   ***Signature Character Strength Reflection and Sharing in a Classroom Setting.*** During a class or workshop, ask the students or participants to choose one character strength (preferably one of their signature strengths or a strength relevant to the learning topic (e.g., *bravery*, or other courage related strength, for the topic of assertiveness strategies; *teamwork* or *leadership* for anticipation of a group course assignment; a humanity related strength, *love, kindness,* or *social intelligence* when working in a challenging context with others). Have the student or participant reflect on their interpretation of this strength and how they view themselves expressing this strength in their life currently (in relevant personal, educational, and work contexts). Next have the students or participants merge into small groups of three to five participants and discuss the ways they have expressed the chosen character strength in one or more of the contexts they reflected on earlier. Finally, have the small group discuss ways that their expressed character strength connects to their personal or professional development or the targeted learning topic. Additional options for developing further positive expression of the individual's character strength can include a step to create a goal (e.g., strength-spotting: *I will notice myself expressing [choose strength] during [choose context or activity] and note how I felt following.*) At the end of the small group activity, invite the larger group of students to share any new understandings of their strengths as they relate to the skill or topic of study. *How will they go forward expressing this strength in their personal and professional activities? How will being mindful and intentionally noting or engaging with this strength benefit their personal and professional development?*

3)   ***Team Character Strengths for Building Doctoral Cohort Cohesiveness.*** The VIA-IS results can be configured into a team report. This allows any group of individuals to assess, understand, and use the unique configuration of character strengths in their team or group to optimize group functioning and performance (VIA Institute on Character, 2015 at http://www.viacharacter.org). The VIA Pro Team report was utilized during a course with a new cohort of counselor education and counseling doctoral students in the first semester of their program. While the course included the full contingent of doctoral students in the program, the first year doctoral cohort participated in a character strength reflection and practice project related to their own cohort's interaction and cohesiveness. Elements of this strengths-based reflecting project included the following:

  a.   The project goals included (i) establishing a strengths-based context for cohort interaction and development, (ii) learning and using a common language and strengths-based system

(VIA Classification System and VIA-IS; Peterson & Park, 2009; Peterson & Seligman, 2004) for reflecting on, conversing about, and increasing the expression of both individual and cohort-based character strengths, and (iii) positively building the cohort personal and professional bond to enhance the strength of the team for collegial interaction and professional support.

b. The doctoral cohort took the individual based VIA-IS and the results for the entire cohort from the VIA Team Pro report were presented and reviewed in a group dialogue led by the strengths facilitator. Prior to the review of team results, the individual character strength results can be reviewed in an individual dialogue with the strengths facilitator.

c. Five weeks of individual and team character strength reflection activities included *Reflective Prompts for Team-Building* provided by the strengths facilitator. Members would engage in independent or shared reflection with one or more team members if desired, and then submit a written response to the weekly prompt that would be read by all team members prior to a weekly facilitated cohort dialogue on cohort strengths. During the weekly meeting (see the following text box for plan example) the strengths facilitator would guide a cohort dialogue incorporating (i) aspects of the team character strengths results, (ii) reflection on the individual written responses to the weekly prompt, and (iii) reflective questions encouraging further application and connection with the ways that the cohort has expressed strengths throughout the week and plans for using individual and cohort strengths in the upcoming week. In addition, activities such as *strength-spotting* were presented and encouraged to assist in developing mindful-based application of character strengths in action.

d. For the final weekly meeting, the cohort was asked to develop a cohort *mission and values statement* that incorporated cohort strengths and to utilize the character strength knowledge and skills they had gained through this project to engage in developing this statement. They were encouraged to use full creativity in the development of this expression of cohort strengths. One team shared their expression of cohort strength through a video of their interaction during an experiential problem-solving exercise.

4) ***Character Strengths in a Cultural Counseling Course: Learning about Self and Others in a Strengths-Based Context.*** The ACA, the Association for Multicultural Counseling and Development (AMCD), and the Association of Lesbian, Gay, Bisexual, and Transgender Issues in Counseling (ALGBTIC) have adopted and promoted various documents of professional competencies crafted by leading professionals and task forces in the area of cultural counseling and counseling diverse populations (ACA, 2010; ALGBTIC LGBQQIA Competencies Taskforce, 2013; Ratts, Singh, Nassar-McMillan, Butler, & McCullough, 2015; Arredondo et al., 1996; Sue, Arredondo, & McDavis, 1992). These competency guidelines consistently focus on encouraging learning and growth for emerging and practicing counselors across the three aspects of (i) *beliefs and attitudes*, (ii) *knowledge*, and (iii) *skills* regarding awareness of *own* assumptions, values, and biases and understanding the worldview of *others*, especially those culturally different from ourselves. The use of character strengths for deepening the emerging and practicing counselor's cultural awareness and connection for both *self* and *others* situates this learning in a strengths-based context. The context and tools of character strength reflection and practice can build new *awareness* for an individual

- regarding values held and expressed,
- on beliefs and biases about people and the world, and
- for the ways that human strengths and differences vary in their expression.

Doctoral Cohort Character Strengths Team Building Project

Meeting 1 Facilitation Ideas

Character Strengths are related to values, principles, and virtues that are expressed through your *way of being*. They can be expressed through actions, skills, attitudes, and decision-making. They are present in both intrapersonal and interpersonal thinking, feeling, and acting components of the individual.

Relationship Building: *Acknowledge the connection and relationship that already exists with this team.*

Dialogue Goals:

1. Discuss self and self-in-group through a character strengths lens.
2. Develop an increased understanding of the dynamics of the team and contributions of the team members through a character strengths lens.

Dialogue Questions:

1. Share briefly about one way that you have acted on your character strength information (as an individual and/or a team) outside of class time. (All share)
2. Choose one of your top strengths and share with the group. (All share)

    a. How do you know that it is a top strength (other than it's on your list)?
    b. How does it represent you?
    c. In what way (actions, attitude, other) do you bring that strength to this group (either previously known or new information through this inventory)?

3. Team Review

    a. Review the Team Character Strength Snapshot from the team report results (showing all the team members' top strengths and the resulting pattern of shared and varying strengths).

       i. What virtue categories show the highest number of team signature strengths?
       ii. What other patterns do you see with the team's signature strengths?

    b. How have you seen your team express any of the character strengths under the virtue of Justice? Humanity? Courage?
    c. Review the Team Character Strength Culture from the team report results (showing the frequency that the members' top strengths are shared among the team).

       i. Which of the top 5 shared CSs stands out for you as most prevalent for your team?

Ideas for facilitated dialogue using character strengths and the VIA Pro Team report (© VIA Institute on Character, 2015, www.viacharacter.org) as a strengths-based approach for developing team cohesion and productivity. Meeting outline for introductory facilitation.

Interacting with character strengths in reflecting group activities on cultural concepts of privilege, oppression, discrimination, marginalization, and other social justice issues can assist participants in navigating these important topics, which can often be met with vulnerability and threat. Understanding, reflecting, and practicing, within the context of self and others, with virtues, such as *courage*, *humanity*, *justice*, and *transcendence*, and with character strengths, such as *curiosity*, *perspective*, *love*, *kindness*, *social intelligence*, *fairness*, *forgiveness*, *humility*, *hope*, *appreciation of beauty and excellence*, *gratitude*, and *judgment* (see Appendix 18.A). It is easy to see a deep connection with these virtues and character strengths and the sphere of cultural learning. To begin addressing a cultural concept like "historical injustices for marginalized groups of people" through reflecting on personal and community aspects of *justice* and *humanity* and *transcendence* will situate the new information and sometimes harsh reality in a context of strength, well-being, advocacy, and change. This more aspirational exploration and context allows the learner to connect with their own and others' lived experience, including challenges, inequities, biases, and trauma, and gain an increased sense of unique and shared humanity. Situating cultural learning in a strengths-based approach propels the learner through challenging self-reflection and new awareness of others supported by strengths such as *hope*, *honesty*, *creativity*, *humility*, and *humor*, which are strengths that build our sense of understanding and connection with others. This is critical to developing multicultural counseling competence with emerging and practicing counselors.

Reflecting on Our Strengths-Based Understandings

David: As I re-visit our chapter I need to add the following words to my sense of strengths-based work: preferred/intentional focus, connection, humanity. Strengths-based work is more than selecting a process that is inherently strength-oriented, as with reflecting teams and processes. For myself, I need to more consciously challenge myself to prefer, or intend, a strengths-based focus in my use of reflecting processes. Connection is brought about by the attributes of reflective processes with the potential for greater strengths-based outcomes, which only facilitates more connection and relationship with others. Humanity. A strengths-based approach values our humanity, our connection, our ability to assist in each other's development and our collective co-development as people.

Jane: In reflecting on our writing, additional elements and deeper meanings came up for me in regard to the scope of a strengths-based approach. First, the significant value of reflecting and pausing in the learning experience became apparent. In my own use of reflecting and in my role as a facilitator encouraging others to reflect and pause, I have experienced and witnessed the power of being apart from the interaction or dialogue and focusing on what is happening both internally and externally in the moment. This allows the reflector to privilege whatever is coming into their awareness, connecting mindfully with that awareness, and allowing the experience of that awareness to impact them without interference. This is in contrast to reflecting in action, where the reflector must also continue interacting while working to think about and connect with new ideas, presented information, and contrasting views. Reflecting and pausing away from the interaction, even momentarily, allows the learner to notice and connect to aspects of self and others in ways that they might otherwise have missed, thereby deepening their understanding and the meaning for them. Second, the notion of aspiration as part of the context of a strengths-based approach gave more significance to my work in this area. The idea of aspiring is connected to hope, aim, and positive ambition. While I reflected on our writing, I experienced a more ardent belief in a strengths-based approach as aspirational learning, with the power to inspire and motivate learners and educators in promoting positive development and well-being in self and others.

Katie: As I reflected on our chapter, I realize how much I value Jane and David as colleagues and friends. (I also miss working with them on a daily basis at Idaho State.) Reviewing our chapter encourages me to find more ways to incorporate strengths-based reflecting teams both inside and out the classroom. I don't think we spend enough time in faculty meetings discussing teaching strategies and ideas presented in our chapter. I'm going to attempt to use David's model of RMTS in triadic supervision this semester as well as elements of Jane's processing of VIA-IS. I also appreciate the idea of Tseliou (2007) giving voice to each part of a case study as I can see the benefits of that in my courses. One thing I left out was the role and importance of creating a supportive and collaborative program and department environment for counselor educators in order for them to build on their own strengths and resiliency. Last, I'll end with eight core areas I see in our chapter: Openness. Vulnerability. Support. Growth. Connection. Challenge. Humor. Compassion.

References

ALGBTIC LGBQQIA Competencies Taskforce. Harper, A., Finnerty, P., Martinez, M., Brace, A., Crethar, H.C., Loos, B., Harper, B., Graham, S., Singh, A., Kocet, M., Travis, M., Lambert, S., Burnes, T., Dickey, L.M., & Hammer, T.R. (2013). Association for Lesbian, Gay, Bisexual, and Transgender Issues in Counseling: Competencies for counseling with lesbian, gay, bisexual, queer, questioning, intersex, and ally individuals. *Journal of LGBT Issues in Counseling, 7,* 2–43. doi: 10.1080/15538605.2013.755444

American Counseling Association. (2010). Competencies for counseling with transgender clients. *Journal of LGBT Issues in Counseling, 4,* 135–159.

American Psychiatric Association. (2013). *Diagnostic and statistical manual of mental disorders* (5th ed.). Washington, DC: Author.

Andersen, T. (1987). The reflecting team: Dialogue and meta-dialogue in clinical work. *Family Process, 26,* 415–428.

Andersen, T. (1991a). Reflections on reflecting with families. In S. McNamee & K.J. Gergen (Eds.). *Therapy as social construction* (pp. 54–68). London, England: Sage.

Andersen, T. (1991b). *The reflecting team: Dialogues and dialogues about the dialogues.* New York, NY: W.W. Norton.

Andersen, T. (1992). Relationship, language and pre-understanding in the reflecting process. *The Australian and New Zealand Journal of Family Therapy, 13,* 87–91.

Andersen, T. (1995). Reflecting processes: Acts of informing and forming. You can borrow my eyes, but you must not take them away from me! In S. Friedman (Ed.), *The reflecting team in action* (pp. 11–37). New York, NY: Guilford Press.

Andersen, T. (1997). Researching client-therapist relationships: A collaborative study for informing therapy. *Journal of Systemic Therapies, 16*(2), 125–133.

Arredondo, P., Toporek, M.S., Brown, S., Jones, J., Locke, D.C., Sanchez, J., & Stadler, H. (1996). *Operationalization of the multicultural counseling competencies.* Alexandria, VA: Association for Multicultural Counseling and Development.

Bowers, K.M., & Lopez, S.J. (2010). Capitalizing on personal strengths in college. *Journal of College and Character, 11,* 1–11.

Brownlee, K. (2009). Review of the reflecting team process: Strengths, challenges, and clinical implications. *The Family Journal, 17,* 139–145.

Chang, J. (2010). The reflecting team: A training method for family counselors. *The Family Journal, 18,* 36–44.

Council for Accreditation of Counseling and Related Programs. (2016). *2016 CACREP standards.* Washington, DC: Author.

Cox, J.A., Bañez, L., Hawley, L.D. & Mostade, J. (2003). Use of the reflecting team process in the training of group workers. *Journal for Specialists in Group Work, 28,* 89–105.

Dahlsgaard, K., Peterson, C., & Seligman, M.E.P. (2005). Shared virtue: The convergence of valued human strengths across culture and history. *Review of General Psychology, 9,* 203–213.

Deacon, S., & Piercy, F. (2001). Qualitative methods in family evaluation: Creative assessment techniques. *The American Journal of Family Therapy, 29,* 355–373. doi:10.1080/01926180127627

Duan, W., Ho, S.M.Y., Tang, X., Li, T., & Zhang, Y. (2013). Character strength-based intervention to promote satisfaction with life in the Chinese university context. *Journal of Happiness Studies.* doi: 10.1007/s10902-013-9479-y.

Eubanks, R. (2002). The MRI reflecting team: An integrated approach. *Journal of Systemic Therapies, 21,* 10–19.

Gander, F., Proyer, R.T., Ruch, W., & Wyss, T. (2012). Strength-based positive interventions: Further evidence for their potential in enhancing well-being and alleviating depression. *Journal of Happiness Studies, 6,* 1241–1249. doi: 10.1007/s10902-012-9380-0. [Online article.] Retrieved from https://www.viacharacter.org/www/Portals/0/Relationships/Signature%20strengths%20and%208%20other%20CS%20interventions%20-%20Gander%20Proyer%20Ruch%20Wyss.pdf

Gardner, D.L., Huber, C.H., Steiner, R., Vazquez, L.A., & Savage, T.A. (2008). The development and validation of the inventory of family protective factors: A brief assessment for family counseling. *The Family Journal, 16,* 107–117. doi:10.1177/1066480708314259

Goolishian, H.A. & Anderson, H. (1988). *Menschliche Systeme. Vor welche Probleme sie uns stellen und wie wir mit ihnen arbeiten.* New York, NY: Springer Publishing.

Griffith, J.L., Griffith, M.E., & Slovik, L.S. (1990). Mind-body problems in family therapy: Contrasting first- and second-order cybernetic approaches. *Family Process, 29,* 13–28.

Harrawood, L.K., Parmanand, S. & Wilde, B., (2011). Experiencing emotion across a semester-long family role-play and reflecting team: Implications for counselor development. *Family Journal: Counseling and Therapy for Couples and Families, 19,* 198–203.

Hawley, L. (2006). Reflecting teams and microcounseling in beginning counselor training: Practice and collaboration. *Journal of Humanistic Counseling, Education, and Development, 45,* 198–207.

James, S., MacCormack, T., Korol, C., & Lee, C.M. (1996). Using reflecting teams in training psychology students in systemic therapy. *Journal of Systemic Therapies, 15,* 46–58.

Jayawickreme, E., Forgeard, M.J.C., & Seligman, M.E.P. (2012). The engine of well-being. *Review of General Psychology, 16,* 327–342.

Kaplan, D.M., Tarvydas, V.M., & Gladding, S.T. (2013). 20/20: A vision for the future of counseling: The new consensus definition of counseling. *Journal of Counseling and Development, 92,* 366–372.

Khoury, B., Langer, E.J., & Pagnini, F. (2014). The DSM: Mindful science or mindless power? A critical review. *Frontiers in Psychology: Psychology for Clinical Settings, 5,* 602. doi:103389/fpsyg.2014.00602

Kleist, D.M. (1999). Reflecting on the reflecting process: A research perspective. *The Family Journal, 7,* 270–275.

Kleist, D.M., & Hill, N.R. (2003). *The reflective model of triadic supervision.* (Unpublished manuscript.) Pocatello, ID: Department of Counseling, Idaho State University.

Kobau, R., Seligman, M.E.P., Peterson, C., Diener, E., Zack, M.M., Chapman, D., & Thompson, W. (August 2011). Mental health promotion in public health: Perspectives and strategies from positive psychology. *American Journal of Public Health, 101,* e1–e9. doi: 10.2105/AJPH.2010.300083

Kolodinsky, P., Englar-Carlson, M., Montopoli, G., Edgerly, B., Dubner, D., Horn, R., & Draves, P. (2014). *Positive psychology in counselor education: An exploration of counselor educators' opinions.* VISTAS Online, Article 15, American Counseling Association.

Landis, L.L., & Young, M.E. (1994). The reflecting team in counselor education. *Counselor Education and Supervision, 33,* 210–216.

Lawson, G., & Venart, B. (2004). *Preventing counselor impairment: Vulnerability, wellness and resilience.* VISTAS Online, Article 53, American Counseling Association, 243–246.

Lax, W.D. (1989). Systemic family therapy with young children and their families: Use of the reflecting team. *Psychotherapy and the Family, 3,* 55–73.

Limberg, D., & Ohrt, J. (2013). Wellness: American Counseling Association Practice Briefs. *The Center for Counseling Practice, Policy, and Research.* Retrieved July 21, 2016 from http://www.counseling.org/docs/practice-briefs/wellness.pdf?sfvrsn=2

Linkins, M., Niemiec, R.M., Gillham, J., & Mayerson, D. (2013). Through the lens of strength: A framework for educating the heart. *The Journal of Positive Psychology.* doi: 10.1080/17439760.2014.888581

Linley, P.A., Nielsen, K.M., Gillett, R., & Biswas-Diener, R. (2010). Using signature strengths in pursuit of goals: Effects on goal progress, need satisfaction, and well-being, and implications for coaching psychologists. *International Coaching Psychology Review, 5,* 6–15.

Lopez, S. J., Edwards, L. M., Pedrotti, J. T., Prosser, E. C., LaRue, S., Spalitto, S. V., & Ulven, J. C. (2006) Beyond the DSM-IV: Assumptions, alternatives, and alterations. *Journal of Counseling and Development, 84,* 259–267.

Lounsbury, J.W., Fisher, L.A., Levy, J.J., & Welsh, D.P. (2009). Investigation of character strengths in relation to the academic success of college students. *Individual Differences Research, 7,* 52–69.

Maggio, L.M. (2014). Privileging the client's voice in a counseling psychology doctoral program. *Journal of Systemic Therapies, 33,* 35–46.

McGovern, M., & Harmsworth, P. (2010). A taste of reflecting practice. *Journal of Family Therapy, 32,* 440–443.

McLaren, N. (2010). The DSM-V project: Bad science produces bad psychiatry. *Ethical Human Psychology and Psychiatry, 12,* 189–199.

Morrison, P.A. (2009). Using an adapted reflecting team approach to learn about mental health and illness with general nursing students: An Australian example. *International Journal of Mental Health Nursing, 18,* 18–25.

Myers, J.E., & Sweeney, T.J. (2007). *Wellness in counseling: An overview* (ACAPCD-09). Alexandria, VA: American Counseling Association.

Niemiec, R.M. (2013). VIA character strengths: Research and practice (The first 10 years). In H.H. Knoop & A. Delle Fave (Eds.), *Well-being and cultures: Perspectives on positive psychology* (pp. 11–30). New York, NY: Springer.

Park, N., Peterson, C., & Seligman, M.E.P. (2006). Character strengths in fifty-four nations and the fifty US states. *Journal of Positive Psychology, 1,* 118–129.

Pender, R.L., & Stinchfield, T.A. (2012). A reflective look at reflecting teams. *The Family Journal, 20*(2), 177–122. doi: 10.1177/1066480712438526.

Pender, R.L., & Stinchfield, T.A. (2014). Making meaning: A couple's perspective of the reflecting team process. *The Family Journal, 22,* 273–281.

Peterson, C., & Park, N. (2009). Classifying and measuring strengths of character. In S.J. Lopez & C.R. Snyder (Eds.), *Oxford handbook of positive psychology* (2nd ed., pp. 25–33). New York, NY: Oxford University Press. www.viacharacter.org

Peterson, C., & Seligman, M.E.P. (2004). *Character strengths and virtues: A handbook and classification.* New York, NY: Oxford University Press. www.viacharacter.org

Ratts, M.J., Singh, A.A., Nassar-McMillan, S., Butler, S.K., & Rafferty McCullough, J. (2015). *Multicultural and social justice counseling competencies.* Multicultural Counseling Competencies Revision Committee. Endorsed by the Association of Multicultural Counseling and Development Executive Council, a division of the American Counseling Association. Washington, DC: American Counseling Association.

Reichelt, S., & Skjerve, J. (2013). The reflecting team model used for clinical group supervision without clients present. *Journal of Marital and Family Therapy, 39,* 244–255.

Schön, D.A. (1983). *The reflective practitioner: How professionals think in action.* New York, NY: Basic Books.

Seikkula, J., Aaltonen, J., Alakare, B., Haarakangas, K., Keranen, H., & Sutela, M. (1995). Treating psychosis by means of open dialogue. In S. Friedman (Ed.), *The reflecting team in action* (pp. 62–80). New York, NY: Guilford Press.

Seligman, M.E.P. (2002). *Authentic happiness: Using the new positive psychology to realize your potential for lasting fulfillment.* New York, NY: Simon & Schuster.

Seligman, M.E.P. (2011a). *Flourish: A visionary new understanding of happiness and well-being.* New York, NY: Simon & Schuster.

Seligman, M.E.P. (2011b). Building resilience. *Harvard Business Review,* 100–106.

Shilts, L., Rudes, J., & Madigan, S. (1993). The use of a solution-focused interview with a reflecting team format: Evolving thoughts from clinical practice. *Journal of Systemic Therapies, 24,* 1–9.

Sloan-Power, E. (2008). Progressive pedagogy and diversity awareness for MSW students: An empirical reflecting team approach for teaching spirituality in the classroom. *Dissertation Abstracts International Section A: Humanities and Social Sciences, 68,* 4866.

Stinchfield, T.A., Hill, N., & Kleist, D. (2007). The reflective model of triadic supervision: Defining an emerging modality. *Counselor Education and Supervision, 46,* 172–183.

Stinchfield, T.A., Hill, N.R., & Kleist, D.M. (2010). Counselor trainees' experiences in triadic supervision: A qualitative exploration of transcendent themes. *International Journal of Advanced Counselling, 32,* 225–239.

Sue, D.W., Arredondo, P., & McDavis, R.J. (1992). Multicultural counseling competencies and standards: A call to the profession. *Journal of Counseling & Development, 70,* 477–486.

Swim, S. (1995). Reflective and collaborative voices in the school. In S. Friedman (Ed.), *The reflecting team in action* (pp. 100–118). New York, NY: Guilford Press.

Tseliou, E. (2007). 'Polyphonic dialogue' as a means for teaching systemic and social-constructionist ideas. *Journal of Family Therapy, 29,* 330–333.

VIA Institute on Character (2015) accessed May 23 2016 from http://www.viacharacter.org/www/Character-Strengths/Science-Of-Character

Watson, W.L., & Lee, D. (1993). Is there life after suicide? The systemic belief approach for "survivors" of suicide. *Archives of Psychiatric Nursing, 7,* 37–43.

Welch, S., Klassen, C., Borisova, O., & Clothier, H. (2013). The DSM-5 controversies: How should psychologists respond? *Canadian Psychology, 54,* 166–175.

Wen-jie, D., Yu, B., Yong-hong, Z., & Xiao-qing, T. (2011). Values in Action Inventory of Strengths in college students: Reliability and validity. *Chinese Journal of Clinical Psychology, 19,* 473–475.

White, M. (1997). Challenging the culture of consumption: Rites of passage and communities of acknowledgement. *Dulwich Centre Newsletter, 2/3.*

Willott, S., Hatton, T., & Oyebode, J. (2012). Reflecting team processes in family therapy: A search for research. *Journal of Family Therapy, 34,* 180–203.

Appendix 18.A

The VIA Classification of Character Strengths

1. **Wisdom and Knowledge**: Cognitive strengths that entail the acquisition and use of knowledge

    - **Creativity** [originality, ingenuity]: Thinking of novel and productive ways to conceptualize and do things; includes artistic achievement but is not limited to it
    - **Curiosity** [interest, novelty-seeking, openness to experience]: Taking an interest in ongoing experience for its own sake; finding subjects and topics fascinating; exploring and discovering
    - **Judgment** [critical thinking]: Thinking things through and examining them from all sides; not jumping to conclusions; being able to change one's mind in light of evidence; weighing all evidence fairly
    - **Love of Learning:** Mastering new skills, topics, and bodies of knowledge, whether on one's own or formally; obviously related to the strength of curiosity but goes beyond it to describe the tendency to add systematically to what one knows
    - **Perspective** [wisdom]: Being able to provide wise counsel to others; having ways of looking at the world that make sense to oneself and to other people

2. **Courage**: Emotional strengths that involve the exercise of will to accomplish goals in the face of opposition, external or internal

    - **Bravery** [valor]: Not shrinking from threat, challenge, difficulty, or pain; speaking up for what is right even if there is opposition; acting on convictions even if unpopular; includes physical bravery but is not limited to it
    - **Perseverance** [persistence, industriousness]: Finishing what one starts; persisting in a course of action in spite of obstacles; "getting it out the door"; taking pleasure in completing tasks
    - **Honesty** [authenticity, integrity]: Speaking the truth but more broadly presenting oneself in a genuine way and acting in a sincere way; being without pretense; taking responsibility for one's feelings and actions
    - **Zest** [vitality, enthusiasm, vigor, energy]: Approaching life with excitement and energy; not doing things halfway or halfheartedly; living life as an adventure; feeling alive and activated

3. **Humanity**: Interpersonal strengths that involve tending and befriending others

- **Love:** Valuing close relations with others, in particular those in which sharing and caring are reciprocated; being close to people
- **Kindness** [generosity, nurturance, care, compassion, altruistic love, "niceness"]: Doing favors and good deeds for others; helping them; taking care of them
- **Social Intelligence** [emotional intelligence, personal intelligence]: Being aware of the motives and feelings of other people and oneself; knowing what to do to fit into different social situations; knowing what makes other people tick

4. **Justice**: Civic strengths that underlie healthy community life

- **Teamwork** [citizenship, social responsibility, loyalty]: Working well as a member of a group or team; being loyal to the group; doing one's share
- **Fairness**: Treating all people the same according to notions of fairness and justice; not letting personal feelings bias decisions about others; giving everyone a fair chance
- **Leadership**: Encouraging a group of which one is a member to get things done and at the same time maintain good relations within the group; organizing group activities and seeing that they happen

5. **Temperance**: Strengths that protect against excess

- **Forgiveness**: Forgiving those who have done wrong; accepting the shortcomings of others; giving people a second chance; not being vengeful
- **Humility**: Letting one's accomplishments speak for themselves; not regarding oneself as more special than one is
- **Prudence**: Being careful about one's choices; not taking undue risks; not saying or doing things that might later be regretted
- **Self-Regulation** [self-control]: Regulating what one feels and does; being disciplined; controlling one's appetites and emotions

6. **Transcendence**: Strengths that forge connections to the larger universe and provide meaning

- **Appreciation of Beauty and Excellence** [awe, wonder, elevation]: Noticing and appreciating beauty, excellence, and/or skilled performance in various domains of life, from nature to art to mathematics to science to everyday experience
- **Gratitude**: Being aware of and thankful for the good things that happen; taking time to express thanks
- **Hope** [optimism, future-mindedness, future orientation]: Expecting the best in the future and working to achieve it; believing that a good future is something that can be brought about
- **Humor** [playfulness]: Liking to laugh and tease; bringing smiles to other people; seeing the light side; making (not necessarily telling) jokes
- **Spirituality** [faith, purpose]: Having coherent beliefs about the higher purpose and meaning of the universe; knowing where one fits within the larger scheme; having beliefs about the meaning of life that shape conduct and provide comfort

19

Strengths-Based Internship Supervision

James Ruby

Success is achieved by developing our strengths, not by eliminating our weaknesses.
Marilyn vos Savant (Jones-Smith, 2014)

Counseling students facing their clinical fieldwork training often experience significant fear and anxiety. As early as 1984, Brala (1984) discussed the potential impacts of student fears of negative evaluation of their therapeutic fieldwork. These feelings of fear or anxiety on the counseling student's part have also been shown to be linked to the client's anxiety and overall therapeutic outcomes. The potential for criticism or negative evaluation is consistent with older, more traditional supervisory models that essentially highlighted ways in which the student was making errors and placed focus on those shortcomings. Fortunately, more strengths-based models have emerged that encourage supervisors to have confidence in their students and avoid a hierarchical relationship between supervisor and student (Edwards, 2013; Edwards & Chen, 1999). This chapter highlights these postmodern approaches to engaging in clinical education and supervision.

I can attest to the significant difference that a strengths-based model of supervision can make in one's life. I have personally experienced supervision and coaching that were focused on my deficits and it was difficult to differentiate whether the feedback was intended to challenge my performance or to challenge my personhood. In other words, I was never quite sure whether the criticisms were aimed at my work or at me. As a result, I became hesitant and filled with doubt. I was not sure whether I had what it took to fulfill the role I was assigned. Ultimately, it led to me leaving the setting and feeling like a failure. I was certain that my supervisor simply chalked it up to me not having what it takes to succeed in the business. It was not until I entered an environment that focused on my strengths that I began to recognize my personal potential, feel less self-doubt, and ultimately begin to believe in myself as a competent professional. Since that time, I have focused my writing, my instructional approaches, and my clinical supervision practice on examining barriers to effective practice and how postmodern and strengths-based models might positively impact the work of the counselor and other human services professionals (Ruby, 2010).

Anyone who has survived the stress of a counseling internship can testify to the fact that the nature of the supervision significantly shapes not only the internship, but the emerging professional identity of the counselor. Obviously, the counseling intern seeks guidance and feedback from the supervisor, but often the intern also seeks personal affirmation. Therefore, it is logical to conclude that utilizing strengths-based approaches to supervision, informed by positive psychology and humanistic principles, may have a strong affirmative impact on the intern. This chapter discusses the clinical usefulness of a strengths-based supervision model with counseling interns and will suggest practical ways to integrate such an approach into a counselor education program or agency internship. Challenges to utilizing a strengths-based model are addressed.

The power of integrating a strengths-based model in supervision first came to me when working with a particularly self-critical student. This student consistently found multiple reasons to doubt her own abilities and she often predicted her own failure. She would focus on what she considered to be mistakes and missed opportunities in her clinical encounters, whether they were in role plays or in her work with clients in the internship setting. Her consistent focus on her own shortcomings often led to an increased sense of anxiety and depression. It was as if she was never able to allow herself to be "in the moment" and rest in the confidence that her training or her own natural abilities would serve her well. She would, instead, act as if she were an observer of her clinical work, judging and criticizing herself. During supervision one evening I could tell that she was particularly agitated and feeling insufficient as an intern and as a person. I asked if she could silence the inner thoughts and voices that were focusing on her perceived shortcomings and simply answer a couple of questions. I asked her, "What did you do well during your session?" and "What did you like about yourself during your session?" After a long and uncomfortable silence the intern began to cry. After composing herself a bit she was able to say, "I've never thought about that before. I'm not used to thinking that way."

Unfortunately, this intern is not alone. Many of us fall prey to defining ourselves by our deficits rather than our strengths—who we think we should be instead of who we are, what we don't have instead of what we do have. At the outset, though, I want to emphasize that I am not suggesting that counseling interns do not need guidance and corrective feedback; clearly they do. But this chapter acknowledges that the counselor's sense of self makes a significant contribution to the effectiveness of the counseling experience. As such, an internship experience that builds up rather than tears down is going to be emphasized as an important variable for improving the quality of the work of professional counselors, regardless of the setting.

In the face of increased demands for evidence-based practice in the fields of mental health and human services, clinicians, programs, and agencies are facing increasing pressure to prove or measure their worth and effectiveness (Rubin, 2013). One manner in which they have approached this task is by increasing the scrutiny of the supervisory efforts with student clinicians. Unfortunately, this has led to less than useful supervisor-student relationships. What might happen if a student was confident that her/his supervisor believed in her/him? How might that student respond to this positive atmosphere? Might s/he grow and flourish as a counselor? The premise of this chapter is that s/he will, indeed, become a better counselor and will thrive in this strengths-based atmosphere.

Literature Review

Edwards (2013), Wade and Jones (2015), and others have provided a rich review of the foundation upon which strengths-based counseling supervision is built. The counseling profession was founded on strengths-based assumptions informed by key historical figures, particularly from the humanistic and existential traditions. Carl Rogers viewed the people he worked with as organic—ever changing, ever growing toward their real whole selves (1961). Rollo May (1953) stated,

> Finding the center of strength within ourselves is the best contribution we can make to our fellow men . . . This is what our society needs—not new ideas and inventions; important as

these are, and not geniuses and supermen, but persons who can "be", that is, persons who have a center of strength within themselves. (p. 54)

Abraham Maslow (1971) is quoted as saying, ". . . I hate the medical model that they imply because the medical model suggests that the person who comes to the counselor is a sick person, beset by disease and illness, seeking a cure" (p. 51). Maslow goes on to advocate a process of growing that entails becoming the best one can be rather than fixing or remediating a person. Gerald May (1990) suggested that one "simply be how you are, completely. Better yet, just realize that you are being who you are, right now, completely" (p. 103). All of these theorists disavowed the ideas of pathological thinking, and looked for strengths within those with whom they worked. As such, supervisors are encouraged to incorporate these strengths-based assumptions when they are working with their interns. Wade and Jones (2015) refer to the *Pygmalion effect*, the notion that supervisory assumptions and beliefs about the supervisee have a subconscious impact on the supervisor's behavior toward the supervisee and the work performance of the supervisee.

The founder of modern positive psychology, Martin Seligman (2002) said, "I do not believe that you should devote overly much effort to correcting your weaknesses. Rather, I believe that the highest success in living and the deepest emotional satisfaction comes from building and using your signature strengths" (p. 13).

> What we have learned over 50 years is that the disease model does not move us closer to the prevention of these serious problems. Indeed the major strides in prevention have largely come from a perspective focused on systematically building competency, not correcting weakness . . . We need now to call for massive research on human strength and virtue. We need to ask practitioners to recognize that much of the best work they already do in the consulting room is to amplify strengths rather than repair the weaknesses of their clients. (Seligman & Csikszentmihalyi, 2000, pp. 6−7)

For Seligman (2011), happiness is the result of increasing one's sense of well-being and life satisfaction. Happiness is valuable for a number of reasons. Lyubomirsky (2007) found that happy people are half as likely to die over the same time period as others. They live longer than average, have better health habits, have lower blood pressure, have more robust immune systems, are more productive on the job, and are able to tolerate more pain. In an effort to understand how to foster happiness, Seligman defined what he called the five pillars of well-being as *positive emotion, engagement, relationships, meaning, and accomplishments* (PERMA). Each of these pillars, sometimes referred to as the *PERMA model of happiness*, is related to the supervisor-intern relationship and the supervisory experience.

If one's positive emotion is related to signature strengths, as Seligman (2011) suggests, it is logical to assume that if an intern is able to identify and build on those strengths, s/he will experience increased positive emotion. Engagement is related to being absorbed in an experience. Thus, if the intern is able to step away from observing her/himself in a counseling scenario, s/he is more likely to be able to fully engage in the experience and increase the chances of finding happiness.

Seligman's (2011) dimension of relationships refers to social connectedness. The more isolated or alone the intern feels, the less happy s/he will be, thus leading to less effective skill development. Rogers (1961) stated, "When you criticize me I intuitively dig in to defend myself. However, when you accept me like I am, I suddenly find I am willing to change" (p. 90). How might an intern feel about the relationship s/he has with the supervisor if s/he is accepted and not criticized? I suggest that the relationship would be strengthened and would therefore lead to increased happiness on the part of the intern (and likely the supervisor, too). Several years ago Heath and Tharp (1991) pointed out many important characteristics of positive psychology informed supervision, namely, (1) relationships between the supervisor and supervisee are based on mutual respect; (2) supervision and evaluation are not the same thing so don't try to do both at the same time; (3) it is best to assume that the supervisee is competent since s/he is likely hard enough on her/himself already; (4) affirm the supervisee by empowering and listening to her/him and helping her/him see what s/he is doing right; and (5) remember that the supervision experience is one between humans, not machines.

The work of the counselor is meaningful work. We strive to make a positive impact in the lives of our clients, their families, and society at large. This sense of altruism is another pillar that Seligman (2011) defines as meaning. Thus, there should be inherent happiness that comes in the work the counseling intern does because it is meaningful work. Wade and Jones (2015) suggest that the way supervisees perceive themselves and the world around them—their mindset—impacts whether the interns will exercise their strengths in meaningful work. The goal is to develop a strengths-based mindset rather than a deficit-based mindset in hopes that the intern may embrace the significance of the work that s/he is doing.

Seligman's (2011) last pillar is accomplishment. If the intern is constantly feeling defeated and incompetent, s/he is likely never going to feel a sense of achievement or that a level of mastery is ever within reach. Thus, the happiness that is acquired by learning a new skill is robbed of the clinical intern when s/he is caught in a spiral of self-doubt and self-criticism. On the other hand, positive psychological capital described as hope, resilience, optimism, and efficacy has been shown to have a positive relationship with professional satisfaction, work performance, and commitment to work related tasks (Luthans, Norman, Avolio, & Ivey, 2008).

Utilizing a strengths-based approach has been shown to create an environment where an intern's skills are engaged and challenges are presented in a positive manner (Csikszentmihalyi, 2003). In this environment, supervisors promote innovation and an enjoyable atmosphere for the intern.

The supervisor's behavior and style of supervision impact the intern's motivation (Sirota, Mischkind, & Meltzer, 2006). If the supervisor understands the intern's goals, maintains enthusiasm, and treats the intern fairly, it fosters pride in the intern's work and positive relationships with colleagues.

Applications and Techniques

Traditionally, there have been three primary functions of clinical supervision, according to Kadushin (1992): administrative, supportive, and educational. Unfortunately, the administrative function has taken on a more dominant theme. As such, the internship supervisor must find a way to build an effective strategy for fostering strengths in the face of administrative and bureaucratic demands.

Lopez (2011) argued that a strengths-based supervision model built on positive psychology foundations is characterized by determined efforts of the supervisee and the responses of a good supervisor. The good supervisor, suggested Lopez, enhances the supervisory encounter by focusing on the following guidelines:

- Ask the supervisee about positive experiences that took place
- Notice and actively mirror the supervisee's enthusiasm
- When positive experiences are mentioned, ask meaningful questions about them
- Connect the positive experiences to the supervisee's strengths.

Ledford (2011) suggested that strengths-based supervisors engage in the following tasks:

- Communicating his/her vision and commitment to strengths-based practice
- Providing opportunities for staff to learn and/or practice strengths-based techniques and interventions
- Modeling strengths-based practice with consumers
- Developing policies and procedures that support strengths-based practices

- Advocating for strengths-based practice from system partners
- Developing quality management practices that support strengths-based philosophy
- Supervising staff using strengths-based strategies. (p. 2)

Promoting a strengths-based environment requires several steps, according to Ledford (2011). It all starts with altering the focus away from primarily viewing the counseling client's deficits. This includes a discussion with the intern concerning the client's skills and strengths. As s/he is able to explore strengths within the client, s/he is then more able to explore strengths within her/himself. Next, the supervisee is encouraged to identify the personal qualities that the supervisee has that make her/him successful. And finally, when the intern needs guidance or support, it is helpful to explore ideas concerning what s/he might have done differently, not within a framework of judgment, but in hopes of encouraging future possibility.

Waskett (2006) formulated an understanding of strengths-based supervision informed by solution-focused therapy. It includes the following characteristics of supervisors:

- Seeks to be helpful to the supervisee in his or her agenda for work
- Focuses on abilities, learning, and strengths that the therapist already has
- Pragmatic—helps the therapist notice what works, their skills, abilities, creative ideas, etc. in the service of the client/patient
- Collaborates with the therapist on the agenda for work with clients/patients
- Listens constructively for the therapist's unique strengths and resources in order to aid clients and his/her practice generally
- Invites and develops the therapist's preferred future in terms of being as good a therapist as they can possibly be for clients in their working context
- Uses scales and circular questioning to note and measure progress toward the therapist's best practice
- Maintains professional, ethical boundaries of time, place, etc., as well as appropriate accountability and care for clients/patients
- Strives for best practice in supervision. (p. 10)

Scales and circular questioning, in particular, allow the supervisor to adopt a position of curiosity. Selvini Palazzoli, Boscolo, Cecchin, and Prata (1980) introduced the technique of circular questioning many years ago and it has made a significant contribution to systemic and family counseling models. Used effectively in supervision, it allows supervisees to think about their ways of thinking. Are they being overly critical or focusing on their deficits? If so, how might they adjust their thinking and focus on potential growth? This is where scales become particularly useful. How might they rate themselves in terms of their growth? What have they done to get to that point and how might they focus on the knowledge, skills, and dispositions that have allowed them to get to where they are today?

Edwards and Chen (1999) developed a strengths-based approach to supervision informed by Zen traditions called *wu-wei*. Wu-wei refers to action or non-action. The model developed by Edwards and Chen is non-directive and relies more on the natural growth tendencies of the individual. The supervisor attempts to do less talking and encourages the supervisees to give voice to their own stories and ways to address counseling client concerns.

Specific strategies encouraged by the wu-wei model include brainstorming with the supervisees, thus tapping into the supervisees' strengths and allowing the supervisees to instruct the supervisors on what went well. This provides the supervisees with significant direction over the counseling session. There is also a focus on competence, which reflects the strengths-based approach to working with clients that is assumed in the Edwards and Chen (1999) model.

Another important aspect of the wu-wei model is ensuring that supervisory language is competence-based and avoids the use of labels or diagnostic jargon. This process fosters greater respect for how clients are discussed in supervision and occasionally includes inviting clients themselves to the supervision sessions. Even if counseling clients are not able to attend the supervisory sessions, supervisees are asked to imagine that their clients are present.

Edwards and Chen (1999) encourage the supervisor to take on a "not-knowing" stance, being willing to share with the supervisee some of their own struggles in becoming a counselor. This flattened hierarchy allows for expression of doubt, open rejection of differing ideas, and an authentic give and take between the supervisor and supervisee. The wu-wei model also includes the use of reflecting teams, tag teams, role plays, and respectful and curious conversations.

Scenarios

The following scenarios will provide the reader with some examples of how strengths-based supervision might be utilized with a clinical counseling intern. These scenarios are not intended to be prescriptive in nature, but only examples of how one might integrate the previously discussed strategies into the intern supervisory process. These scenarios are based on actual supervisory experiences with interns, though all of the identifying factors of the students have been altered in order to protect their anonymity.

"Sharon"

Sharon was an intern at a family counseling agency in an affluent suburb. She had come from a blended family and was committed to helping others find ways to negotiate the challenges of family life. Sharon was assigned a case that was referred by the Department of Child and Family Services and she quickly expressed her nervousness to her supervisor. The initial intake paperwork indicated that the family was of a different ethnicity than Sharon and that a five-year-old child had been injured by his step-mother. Sharon was concerned about how her own preconceived judgments of step-mothers and her anxiety related to being a potentially judgmental counselor were side tracking her abilities to be open-minded and have confidence in her clinical decision making. Many would have seen this as an opportunity to remind Sharon of the importance of being non-judgmental or how to better incorporate multi-cultural counseling skills. While these elements are vitally important to incorporate into all counseling work, there are some unique strengths-based approaches to help Sharon deal with her anxiety and self-doubt.

In line with many of the solution-focused models, the strengths-based supervisor might have approached Sharon with questions that could help her find a more useful way of thinking, one that was not overly focused on negative outcomes. "What are your goals for your first session with this family?" "What would you like to accomplish with the family in your initial session?" "What are some of your highest hopes for your initial meeting with the family?" These questions might have shifted the intern's focus from hypothetical negative assumptions that fostered her anxiety to more positive possibilities, which are built on the assumption that good things could happen. Hearing these types of questions from the supervisor implies that s/he has positive expectations for the intern, too. Knowing that my supervisor believes that good things can happen fosters greater confidence within me, whether I am an intern or a seasoned veteran counselor.

By openly expressing expectations for positive outcomes, the pre-counseling session energy may be changed from anxiety to hope. Most of us would rather anticipate success than failure and the positive focus of a supervisor is a key factor in helping counseling interns feel hopeful in their work with clients.

"Bradley"

Bradley was an intern in a therapeutic high school setting. He was eager to blend his training in mental health counseling with his training in educational development and career exploration. The private therapeutic high school seemed like the perfect place to blend these professional interests.

Bradley was assigned a small group of four freshmen boys, with the hope that he would be able to help them improve their social skills. The goal was for them to learn to interact more respectfully and stay focused on tasks longer so that they might be able to return to their home schools. Unfortunately, after about three sessions, Bradley was feeling discouraged by what he believed was a lack of progress of the group. He was beginning to doubt himself and wondered whether or not he had what it takes to do the job.

In supervision, it might be tempting to ask Bradley what was going wrong and spend time reviewing what was not working. "What have you tried that isn't working?" "Why do you think things aren't going well?" "Have you ever thought about trying . . .?" Edwards (2013) and Wade and Jones (2015) have made it clear that interns typically have a clear sense that things are not going well and they can clearly describe what is not working in their sessions with clients. Where they often struggle is being able to describe what they are doing well or what is working, at least a little.

The strengths-based supervisor has a unique opportunity to shift the experience of the intern. Assuming that the supervisor has taken time to observe the intern, or has reviewed a recording of a counseling session, Bradley's supervisor could highlight issues like those expressed in the following inquiries. "Tell me about some of the strengths that you demonstrated in this session with your students." "I really can appreciate your clear descriptions of times when group is not going well. That is helpful information for me as your supervisor. I would also like to hear about the times when you are not experiencing those challenges." "What can you identify that is different about the times that you seem to be having success with these young men in group?"

These types of questions continue to reinforce the idea that the supervisor recognizes the intern has strengths and experiences successes. Assuming Bradley did the work of identifying his own strengths, the supervisor would provide positive reinforcement for the intern's willingness and ability to do so. The strengths-based supervisor would likely even amplify Bradley's ability to be insightful for being able to notice these things about himself and the work that he is doing in group.

Bradley might have said something along the lines of, "Those boys just aren't willing to work. They are just too resistant. They [problematic behavior] too much!" When the intern focuses on client deficits, the strengths-based supervisor might shift the focus back on what the intern is doing. In part, this is tied to the notion that the only thing the counselor is able to control is her/himself.

Asking the following kinds of questions could have helped Bradley look at his own contribution to the counseling process, thus highlighting how influential he really might be. "What kinds of things would you have liked to do with the group instead of what you did?" "Tell me about times in group when you haven't had that issue/challenge." "What do you think you might have done differently in group, knowing what you know now?" "When that [problematic behavior] is happening, what do you suppose the group is thinking/feeling?" "What do you think the group might like you to do differently?" The goal here is not to blame Bradley, but actually to help him see possibilities for different outcomes, even if he is the only one to make any changes.

But let's say Bradley really did make some significant errors and was authentically struggling in his group counseling work. How might we approach getting him the help he needs in a strengths-based manner? Providing helpful skills development feedback is an important professional and ethical mandate for clinical counseling supervisors, so a strengths-based approach does not imply that the supervisor ignores an intern's challenges.

We might ask Bradley, "How do you believe you and your group will be able to work yourselves out of this temporary impasse?" Beginning counselors can be highly self-critical, but with time and experience, most counselors learn that difficulties and unanticipated challenges naturally occur during the counseling process. We also know that clients and the counselor typically find a way to resolve these unexpected impasses. An intern simply doesn't have this perspective, yet.

Addressing these moments within the counseling session must be done with tact, respect, and in a manner that does not put the intern on the defensive, nor exaggerates her/his sense of self-criticism. So, whether after observing a counseling session or while reviewing a recorded session with Bradley, the strengths-based supervisor might ask the following questions in reference to specific moments within the group session. "What were you trying to accomplish with that question/reflection/intervention/etc.?" "Help me understand how that might have been useful to your group members or to the counseling process?" "What do you wish you could go back to and do differently?" "How do you think your group members would respond if you did that?"

One of the keys to successfully exploring an intern's strengths is in how the supervisor's questions are being articulated—word choice, tone, facial expressions during the question, etc. The goal is to ask questions that help the intern explore possibilities rather than personal limitations. Possibilities lead to hope for meaningful change.

Additionally, after the questioning is completed, it is important to wrap up any supervisory sessions with genuine positive feedback, or compliments. If these comments are tied to counseling client progress, that is all the better. The intern will be given the opportunity to connect her/his actions with client improvement. This connection bolsters confidence and increases optimism.

Group Supervision

Utilizing strengths-based approaches in group supervision can be especially powerful for all involved. The cooperative learning and mutual encouragement offered in positive group experiences can become a valuable tool to help promote intern strengths. Starling and Baker (2000) found that group supervision decreased confusion and anxiety, helped counselors clarify their client goals, and increased confidence in the group supervisees. They suggested that supervisors could incorporate strategies like having the interns share success stories of when they were able to conceptualize a counseling case effectively and effect a positive outcome.

Starling and Baker (2000) point out the importance of involving the supervision group members in outlining the requirements for the group. This would include detailed guidelines for how feedback is solicited and offered by group members. They suggest that having the intern begin by sharing what s/he is doing well is a good start. Balancing this strategy by being proactive with those who might be most critical or negative in their evaluations is also important. By building a strengths-based group supervisory process, we might begin a legacy of encouragement and optimism for future generations of clinical counseling professionals.

Agency Evaluation

The reality for those of us who have worked in many agencies is that regular personnel evaluation is a standard part of what is expected to take place. As mentioned earlier, it is also both a professional and ethical mandate. One of the common criticisms of strengths-based supervision models, though, is how to conduct meaningful evaluation while using a strengths-based paradigm. Is it possible? Is it realistic? Is it thorough?

Ledford (2011) reminds us that highlighting strengths and conducting evaluations are not mutually exclusive events. In fact, helping interns see their strengths is actually an important part of the supervisory process. Focusing on strengths creates a safe environment for the interns, where they may reflect on their self-efficacy and confidence while reinforcing what they have learned. This type of environment will also make corrective feedback more easily acceptable for the intern.

Briggs and Miller (2005) made a case for success enhancing supervision, focusing on evaluation that is based on solution-focused underpinnings. Harvey and Struzziero (2008) adapted the model and proposed a specific checklist of items to be explored with school psychologists in training. Both suggested a comprehensive approach that included honest self-evaluation of the supervisor, along with the intern.

Of course, few interns would continue to take supervision seriously if no corrective feedback were offered. The goal of the strengths-based supervisor is to provide evaluative feedback in a safe environment where the corrective comments may be viewed with positive intentions. The interns will be more willing to take the comments in and not feel incompetent based on them.

Strengths-Based Evaluation Guide

The following questions are offered as a general guide for incorporating strengths-based approaches into your own supervision practice. It is important to remember that this is a guide and not a comprehensive list of questions that addresses all of the unique needs of a given setting. It will highlight the philosophy behind a strengths-based exploration of those things an intern might keep doing and what s/he might consider doing differently in the future.

The format of the guide is intended to bring about a meaningful conversation between the intern and the supervisor. Hopefully, the questions promote a dialogue that fosters mutual learning and growth.

Counseling Intern Strengths-Based Performance Evaluation

1. Let's review your goals for your counseling internship. Tell me about those goals and what made them important to you.
2. What would you consider to be some of the strengths that you bring to your counseling internship?
3. How have your strengths helped you in achieving your goals?
4. How have you been able to utilize your strengths for your clients?
5. How have you been able to utilize your strengths for the agency/program?
6. Have there been any barriers to you being able to perform your responsibilities as a counseling intern? How would you describe those and how might we work together to address them?
7. Do you find the work you are doing to be meaningful? Why/why not?
8. Are there areas in which you think you need further growth or development? If so, how might we work together to help you progress in those areas?
9. How might your counseling clients describe the quality of your work?
10. Have there been tasks or responsibilities that you didn't expect to have to manage? If so, what do I, as your supervisor, need to know about those tasks or responsibilities?
11. What kind of methods or messages of feedback have I given you that have been helpful? Are there other ways that I might offer you useful feedback?
12. What kinds of other questions or concerns do you have for me?

As you can see, the questions above would likely foster an in depth conversation about the intern, the internship experience, the relationship between the supervisor and the intern, and perhaps much more. This rich dialogue, and the nature of the inquiries, would also help keep the intern from becoming defensive and would highlight the mutuality of the intern-supervisor relationship.

As mentioned earlier, the interview guide may be altered to fit the needs of a given setting. For instance, specific questions related to issues like frequency of sessions, number of cancellations, intern collegiality, and others may be added to enrich the evaluation for a specific context.

Final Thoughts

Charlotte Dailey (2009) wrote an essay for psychotherapy.net that describes her own anxiety as an intern when she was assigned the case of "Sam," a survivor of sexual abuse during his childhood (https://www.psychotherapy.net/article/beginning-psychotherapy). In the midst of her story, she describes multiple struggles with Sam and how these made her doubt herself and whether she was cut out for the profession. When sharing her challenges with an experienced counselor at the agency, Charlotte remembers the experienced counselor telling her, "It sounds like you did the right thing." That simple phrase made a significant change in her emerging professional identity. Charlotte was well aware of the things she was not able to do, or believed she was not able to do well. What she had forgotten to notice were the things that she did well.

All counseling interns have some knowledge, skills, and dispositions that need to be recognized in order for them to be fostered and encouraged. Supervising clinical counseling interns from a strengths-based perspective is one way we might be able to increase effectiveness and decrease anxiety in our next generation of counselors.

References

Brala, P. (1984). Effects of therapist fear of negative evaluation in supervision and supervisory focus on therapist and client anxiety and on a measure of therapy effectiveness. *Dissertation Abstracts International*. (Order No. 8325671). (303151253). Retrieved May 17 2014 from http://search.proquest.com/docview/303151253?accountid=9840.

Briggs, J. & Miller, G. (2005). Success enhancing supervision. *Journal of Family Psychotherapy, 16*, 199–222.

Csikszentmihalyi, M. (2003). *Good business: Leadership, flow, and the making of meaning*. New York, NY: Penguin Group.

Dailey, C. (2009). *A crash course in psychotherapy: Moving through anxiety and self-doubt*. Retrieved on March 15, 2015 from https://www.psychotherapy.net/article/beginning-psychotherapy

Edwards, J.K. (2013). *Strengths-based supervision in clinical practice*. Thousand Oaks, CA: Sage Publishing.

Edwards, J.K. & Chen, M.-W. (1999). Strengths-based supervision: Frameworks, current practice, and future directions : A Wu-Wei method. *The Family Journal: Counseling and Therapy for Couples and Families, 7*, 349–357. DOI: 10.1177/1066480799074005

Harvey, V. S., & Struzziero, J.A. (2008). *Professional development and supervision of school psychologists* (2nd ed.). Thousand Oaks, CA: Sage.

Heath, A. & Tharp, L. (1991, November). *What therapists say about supervision*. Paper presented at the annual conference of the American Association for Marriage and Family Therapy, Dallas, TX.

Jones-Smith, E. (2014). *Theories of counseling and psychotherapy: An integrative approach*. Thousand Oaks, CA: Sage Publications.

Kadushin, A. (1992). *Supervision in social work* (3rd ed.). New York, NY: Columbia University Press.

Ledford, R.N. (2011). *Strength-based supervision*. Retrieved on March 16, 2015 from www.elitecme.com

Lopez, S.J. (2011). *Focusing on what's right: A strengths-based workplace*. Workshop at University of Kansas Medical School, Wichita, KS.

Luthans, F., Norman, S.M., Avolio, B.J., & Ivey, J.B. (2008). The mediating role of psychological capital in the supportive organizational climate-employee performance relationship. *Journal of Organizational Behavior, 29*, 219–238.

Lyubomirsky, S. (2007). *The how of happiness: A scientific approach to getting the life you want*. New York, NY: Penguin.

Maslow, A. (1971). *The farther reaches of human nature*. New York, NY: Viking Press.

May, G. (1990). *Simply sane: The spirituality of mental health*. New York, NY: Crossroads.

May, R. (1953). *Man's search for himself*. New York, NY: W.W. Norton.

Rogers, C.R. (1961). *On becoming a person: A therapist's view of psychotherapy*. London, UK: Constable.

Rubin, A. (2013). *Statistics for evidence-based practice and evaluation* (3rd ed.). Independence, KY: Cengage Learning.

Ruby, J.R. (2010). *Barriers to practitioner research: Making research education relevant and productive*. Saarbrücken, Germany: Lambert Academic Publishing.

Seligman, M.E.P. (2002). *Authentic happiness: Using the new positive psychology to realize your potential for lasting fulfilment*. New York, NY: Free Press.

Seligman, M.E.P. (2011). *Flourish: A visionary new understanding of happiness and well-being*. New York, NY: The Free Press.

Seligman, M.E.P., & Csikszentmihalyi, M. (2000). Positive psychology: An introduction. *American Psychologist, 55*, 5–14.

Selvini Palazzoli, M., Boscolo, L., Cecchin, G., & Prata, G. (1980). Hypothesizing circularity-neutrality: Three guidelines for the conductor of the session. *Family Process, 19*, 3–12.

Sirota, D., Mischkind, L.A., & Meltzer, M.I. (2006). Stop demotivating your employees. *Harvard Management, 11*, 1–5.

Starling, P.V., & Baker, S.B. (2000). Structured peer group practicum supervision: Supervisees' perceptions of supervision theory. *Counselor Education and Supervision, 39*, 162–177.

Wade, J.C., & Jones, J.E. (2015). *Strengths-based clinical supervision: A positive psychology approach to clinical training*. New York, NY: Springer Publishing.

Waskett, C. (2006). The pluses of solution focused supervision. *Healthcare Counselling and Psychotherapy Journal, 6*, 9–11.

20

Strengths-Based Supervision

Experiences of Supervisors and Supervisees

Mary Nichter and Reade Dowda

In this chapter, we present our perception of strengths-based supervision, discuss how strengths-based supervision is influenced by positive psychology, and consider what strengths-based supervision looks like as we move from theory to practice. We investigate the shift in thinking from a deficient model to a strengths-based model of supervision as the focus of and expectations in a supervision course. Specifically, we discuss how a doctoral supervision course in a counselor education program following Council for Accreditation of Counseling and Related Educational Programs (CACREP) standards incorporates a strengths-based supervision focus. Included in the chapter are experiences of doctoral students working from a strengths-based model providing supervision to master's level practicum students. In addition, perceptions of master's level practicum students as supervisees who are receiving strengths-based supervision are presented. We close this chapter with guidelines for conducting a strengths-based supervision session and a strengths-based record and reflection form for documenting the session.

Strengths-Based Supervision

Strengths-based supervision is an approach to supervision that sets the stage for success. Specifically, success for supervisees as supervisors focus on their supervisees' innate attributes, their ability to demonstrate what they have learned as counselors-in-training, and their heartfelt desire to help others. Supervisors are poised for success, as well, as they observe their supervisees' development into autonomous skillful clinicians. Capitalizing on supervisees' strengths can be challenging for both supervisors and supervisees because the natural tendency is a gravitation toward shortcomings, lack of competence, and overall negativity. Rozin and Royzman (2001) described a negativity bias that permeates our culture. The field of psychology and mental health has not escaped the bias toward negativity that is a deficit or pathological dominance (Maddux, 2008).

Strengths-based work has roots in positive psychology, specifically influenced by Peterson and Seligman (2004) and Seligman, Rashid, and Parks (2006). Strengths-based work detours from the long-held notion that psychology and other mental health disciplines based on the medical model are aimed at healing with little or no recognition of strengths, assets, and what is working in a client's life. Strengths-based applies to multiple areas of mental health support, including counseling, social work, psychology, and supervision of these disciplines. According to Saleebey (2009),

> . . . practicing from a strengths perspective means this—"everything" you do as a social worker will be predicated in some way on helping to discover and embellish, explore and exploit clients' strengths and resources in service of assisting them to achieve their goals, realize their dreams, and shed the irons of their own inhibitions and misgivings and society's domination. (p. 1)

Social workers/family therapists Steve de Shazer and Insoo Kim Berg changed the problem-solving strategic family therapy model to one that is solution-focused. During their work at their Milwaukee Brief Family Therapy Center, they wrote many book chapters and articles, both together and separately (Berg, 1994; de Shazer, 1988, 1994). In the same postmodern vein, Australian Michael White and New Zealander David Epston introduced their narrative therapy model to the world, indicating that it is stories about our lives that create our realities. They believed that most of these narratives either contain marginalizing edits or wide gaps that leave out our times of fighting back against those stories that marginalize our strengths (White & Epston, 1990). Marginalization of strengths leads to a focus on the need for healing, which implies a disease or pathological model, with an emphasis on negative aspects, shortcomings, and failures, wherein individuals are deficient.

In contrast to the dominance of negativity and the deficit model, Seligman and Csikszentmihalyi (2000) stated that "the aim of positive psychology is to begin to catalyze a change in the focus of psychology from preoccupation only with repairing the worst things in life to also building positive qualities" (p. 5). In their article "Positive Psychology: An Introduction", Seligman and Csikszentmihalyi (2000) noted that "psychology is not just the study of pathology, weakness, and damage; it is also the study of strength and virtue. Treatment is not just fixing what is broken; it is nurturing what is best" (p. 7). In fact, some researchers argue that nurturing what is best is more beneficial than fixing what is broken. Cheavens, Strunk, Lazarus, and Goldstein (2012) concluded that cognitive-behavioral therapy (CBT) with a focus on strengths was more effective in treating depression than CBT with a focus on alleviating deficits.

Positive psychology has been conceptualized as a scientific endeavor of optimal human functioning and the illumination of the role of human strengths (Lopez et al., 2006; Rashid, 2015; Seligman & Csikszentmihalyi, 2000). Smith (2006) conceptualized and proposed a bridge between positive psychology and counseling practice and presented a strengths-based model for counseling professionals to use when working with clients. Clinicians who focus on clients' strengths and assets bring hope, optimism, and an expectation of success to clients' life circumstances. Peterson and Seligman (2004) conceptualized hope as the pathway into an optimistic future, that is, there is an expectation that clients have some control over their futures rather than feeling powerless. These same expectations with a focus on strengths leading to hope, optimism, and success can be applied to supervision of mental health providers.

Whether in counseling or supervision the strengths-based approach differs from other models in a significant way. A cornerstone of this approach is the understanding that identifying a client's or supervisee's strengths is a basic growth oriented intervention. Rashid (2015) postulated "growth happens through assessing, acknowledging, and building strengths" (p. 26). People, whether clients or supervisees, have optimized growth outcomes when strengths and assets are the focus. Rashid (2015) discussed findings of a study conducted by Scheel, Davis, and Henderson (2012) that examined therapists' use of client strengths. The results of their study added to the benefits of working from a strengths-based model in counseling. Specifically, therapists reported that working from a strengths-based model facilitated the development of trusting relationships and motivated clients by creating hope. Peterson and Seligman (2004) conceptualized hope as the pathway to an optimistic view of the future: There is an expectation that individuals have control over their futures. The belief in hope and in an individual's power and control of the future is fueled by working from each person's strengths and using those strengths to manage challenges and struggles that they may face.

How Strengths-Based Supervision Is Different

When applied to supervision, strengths-based ideas and premises look similar to strengths-based counseling. Specifically, the medical model with a focus on shortcomings does not set the framework or determine the approach of the supervisor. Supervisors who embrace the strengths-based principles encourage a supervisory relationship wherein the supervisees' confidence and expectation for success are emphasized. As perceived by the authors of this chapter, this implies that strengths-based supervision differs from other models. Other models differ from strengths-based in the following ways. Other models (e.g., developmental, process, cognitive-behavioral) emphasize either directly or indirectly:

a) Hierarchical structure
b) Focus on mistakes, weaknesses
c) Focus on what the supervisees do not know rather than what they know
d) Limited perspective that the supervisee must do things the supervisor's way
e) Status of the supervisor as an expert
f) Promotion of the idea of right and wrong

Supervising from a hierarchical structure implies that the supervisor knows and the supervisee does not know. This stance leads to an expectation that the supervisor is right and if the supervisee has ideas or practices that deviate from the supervisor's then the supervisee is wrong. One of the participants in a study conducted by Fall, Lyons, and Lewis (2003) described her experience in supervision and stated,

> I felt like a sponge. Like I didn't know anything, but needed to know everything. As a sponge, I didn't feel I could trust myself or all the learning I had just completed. I mainly listened to my supervisor and tried to do what they told me to do. (p. 15)

This may result in the assumption that in order to "do counseling right," the supervisee needs to become like the supervisor and will have to wait until the supervision session to see if he or she did counseling the right way. Supervisors who focus on mistakes and weaknesses become absorbed in problems and focus supervision on supervisee deficits. A tone of judgment, criticism, and possibly shame results as the supervisee hears more about their shortcomings and failures than their strengths and developing skills.

Although it is true that supervisors have more professional counseling experience and thereby more confidence in their clinical skills and abilities, they need not be pressured to assume the role of expert. Rather they must nurture the strengths and uniqueness of their supervisees and demonstrate confidence in the supervisee's capability to become an effective mental health professional. The supervisor is in a position of power in that he or she has the ability to influence and shape another person. According to Haynes, Corey, and Moulton (2003) the supervisory relationship by nature has a built-in power differential with the supervisor being the authority in the relationship. Strengths-based supervisors work to reduce the power differential by establishing a collaborative relationship.

What happens in the supervision room is often mirrored in the counseling room (Bernard & Goodyear, 2013). The supervisee's approach to working with a client is often influenced by the supervisor's approach to supervision. As the supervisor behaves and works with the supervisee, so will the supervisee work with the client. Therefore, if the supervisor's approach to supervision is from a deficit stance, the supervisee will carry this attitude back into the counseling room and focus on the client's shortcomings thereby working from a problem-centered approach. Edwards (2013), Lietz and Rounds (2009), and Shulman (2005) discuss the concepts of parallel process and isomorphs. Although some researchers and writers (Bernard & Goodyear, 2013; Koltz, Odegard, Feit, Provost, & Smith, 2012) pointed out the differences between parallel process and isomorphism there is agreement that there is replication or reenactment between what occurs in the supervisory relationship and the counseling relationship. In the following section, we share our respective experiences with strengths-based supervision and offer our perspectives on the benefits of this approach.

What Strengths-Based Supervision Means to Me (Dowda)

I quickly became passionate about strengths-based supervision during my doctoral program. My natural approach to supervision was strengths-based, so I was elated to hear about strengths-based supervision. Having a model of supervision that focuses on strengths meant I could use a model that fit my personality and philosophy of learning. My curiosity about and faith in strengths-based supervision was so strong that I completed my dissertation by interviewing 12 doctoral students trained in a model of strengths-based supervision to gain a better understanding and add to the dearth of literature on strengths-based supervision.

Analyzing the data validated my beliefs that focusing on strengths in supervision is beneficial to the growth and development of supervisees. My participants all agreed that strengths-based supervision edified counselors-in-training. This instruction included (a) the growth and development of the supervisee, (b) building confidence, (c) reducing anxiety, and (d) fostering independence.

I use strengths-based supervision over other models of supervision for three reasons: I provide supervision in a manner in which I would like to receive supervision. A strengths-based approach fits my personality, and I believe that strengths-based supervision has many benefits. First of all, relating to the concerns of my first supervisees was easy because I had recently completed my master's program and knew all too well the anxiety associated with providing therapy to actual clients. I remember both deficit-focused and strengths-focused supervisory experiences and labeled them as negative and positive, respectively. Like Edwards (2013), I do not remember particular supervisory interventions, but I do remember my past supervisory relationships. I use strengths-based supervision over other models because I supervise the way I would like to be supervised. When my supervisors focused on what I was doing well, I felt empowered and excited to provide therapy.

Second, focusing on strengths fits my optimistic personality. I see issues as mostly transient with resiliency as a bulwark for growth. Froma Walsh has written extensively on resiliency and she documented people do not merely bounce back, but grow from challenging situations and bounce forward (Walsh, 2002). Seligman (2011) more recently echoed this idea when he described post-traumatic stress disorder as the opportunity for post-traumatic growth. According to the Values in Action Inventory of Strengths (VIA-IS), my top two strengths are hope and perseverance. I believe these strengths are related; I persevere because I am hopeful about the future. This translates into the way I provide supervision. I am optimistic that my supervisees already have well-established strengths when they begin seeing clients and that these strengths will provide the pathway to their success as counselors. Thich Nhat Hanh (2010) explained that people have both positive and negative seeds, but we should only water the positive seeds. Strengths-based supervisors plant the seeds of expectation, growth, and success within their supervisees. When these seeds are encouraged to grow in a positive manner, supervisees flourish. At a meeting of the American Counseling Association, Bermeo (as cited in Edwards, 2013) reported strengths-based supervisors and clinicians see people as being at potential, rather than at risk.

Third, I have discovered many benefits from using a strengths-based model of supervision such as promoting a positive supervisory alliance and fostering the growth and development of supervisees.

A positive supervisory relationship was the most important aspect of my supervisory experiences, therefore, I am adamant that a positive working relationship must be established prior to the progression of supervision. Results from my dissertation supported these beliefs; all 12 of my participants affirmed strengths-based supervision to be a useful model of supervision. In fact, all participants reportedly integrated strengths-based supervision with other models of supervision. The most common reason for integrating strengths-based supervision with other models was to foster more of a focus on strengths. This focus on strengths led to the growth and development of supervisees and fostered the supervisory relationship.

What Strengths-Based Supervision Means to Me (Nichter)

As I think about my work as a professional, I discover that my approach to others—whether I'm working with students, clients, or supervisees—has always been strengths-based. I had not heard of strengths-based in the early 1970s, but early in my career, I knew that I wanted to focus on the assets of others and do my part in helping them find, own, and operate from their assets.

I began my professional career as a first grade teacher and quickly realized how impressionable the children were. I found that I could build them up or I could tear them down. As many beginning teachers do, I watched the seasoned teachers and often tried to copy them. Very soon I realized that many of them had styles of interacting with the children that did not suit me. They often shamed, embarrassed, belittled, and quickly paddled children into submission. In contrast, my style of interacting with children was to encourage, empower, and point out what they were doing well. I quickly understood that children needed to be encouraged, empowered, and to have an adult believe in them. This led to my pursuing a master's degree in school counseling, hoping that as the school counselor I could work with more students and positively influence them by believing in them, encouraging them, and being their cheerleader.

After completing my doctoral degree in marriage and family therapy, and obtaining my license as a professional counselor and approved supervisor and my license as a marriage and family therapist and board-approved supervisor, I became a counselor educator and supervisor. Just as I understood the need to empower and encourage children, I understood that adult learners are not much different. That is, they need positive feedback, encouragement, and an expression of my confidence in them as counselors-in-training and supervisors-in-training. As a faculty member teaching doctoral level supervision courses, I carry this style of encouragement into the classroom as well as when I train supervisors and oversee supervision sessions. However, the concept of strengths-based supervision took on a more concrete frame when I was asked to review the draft of the Introduction and Chapters 1 and 3 of Jeffrey Edwards' (2013) book *Strengths-Based Supervision in Clinical Practice*. As I read Dr. Edwards' words, I was so encouraged to learn about strengths-based supervision, a style that reflected my style.

Literature Review for Supervisors

Every person who aspires to become a health care professional must have supervision when he or she begins a career in the counseling field (Barnett & Molzon, 2014). Supervision is an intervention that aims to guide the next generation of health care professionals and is provided by someone with more experience to someone with less experience (Bernard & Goodyear 2013; Todd & Storm, 2014). Supervision is a major component of mental health care programs (Stoltenberg, McNeill, & Delworth, 1998). The supervisor not only guides the supervisee in all aspects of providing therapy, but also serves as a mentor and role model who aids supervisees in finding an identity in their profession (Barnett & Molzon, 2014). Counseling and counselor education programs accredited by CACREP require students to be supervised while providing therapy in their practica, internships, and while seeking their professional licensure (CACREP, 2016; Fall et al., 2003). Counselors who receive supervision report higher self-efficacy than those who do not receive supervision (Cashwell & Dooley, 2001).

While the guidelines for supervision are clearly stated, there are no specific expectations for how supervision is to be presented. The how of supervision is left to the selection of the supervisor including structure, focus, procedures, framework, model, expectations, et cetera (Dowda & Nichter, in review).

Similar to how counselors choose their model of counseling, supervisors are free to choose their model of supervision. Strengths-based supervision is a relatively new approach to conducting supervision. Edwards and Chen (1999) offered one of the earliest definitions; they explained that strengths-based supervision has been influenced by "second-order cybernetics and quantum physics, and later understood from a postmodern and languaging-systems perspective" (p. 350). Providing effective supervision is of paramount importance because every master's student is required to receive supervision in his or her counseling program and every doctoral student is required to both receive and provide supervision in his or her supervision training as part of the requirements for a CACREP accredited doctoral program (CACREP, 2016). Furthermore, people aspiring to become licensed professional counselors must also receive supervision (Bernard & Goodyear, 2013).

Review of Literature Regarding Strengths-Based Compared with Other Supervision Approaches

An extensive search of the literature yielded articles addressing strengths-based approaches to counseling (Bozic, 2013; Smith, 2006; Welfare, Farmer, & Lile, 2013; Wong, 2014), positive psychology and its influence on strengths-based approaches to counseling (Rashid, 2015; Seligman & Csikszentmihalyi, 2000), and strengths-based supervision (Cohen, 2004; Edwards & Chen, 1999; Lietz & Rounds, 2009; Wade & Jones, 2015). Other than our own research, we found no published articles about strengths-based supervision with our population of doctoral student supervisors and master's practicum student supervisees. Therefore, we will briefly discuss the literature about supervision and strengths-based supervision and follow with the results of our research focusing on the population presented in this chapter.

Traditionally, supervision has been conducted within a hierarchical structure in which the supervisor assumes the role of the expert (Edwards, 2013; Edwards & Chen, 1999). Recently, researchers have remarked that supervision is more effective if practiced within an egalitarian structure in which collaboration and strengths are emphasized (Edwards, 2013; Edwards & Chen, 1999; Fall et al., 2003; Schueller, 2009). According to Edwards and Chen (1999), emphasizing strengths of the supervisee during supervision puts a focus on "punctuating what the counselor does well rather than looking for problems" (p. 349). Cohen (2004) described an assessment of supervisees' clinical work and organized feedback themes around strengths and problems and stated that recent trends in clinical work and supervision reflect a more inclusive, less hierarchical, strengths-based framework for practice that emphasizes competence rather than shortcomings.

Our research on strengths-based supervision was designed to gather perceptions of supervisees and supervisors concerning their experience with strengths-based supervision. We created two questionnaires, one for the supervisee and one for the supervisor, which was used for recording their responses. Participants for this study were doctoral counselor education students and master's counseling students at a CACREP accredited university where the first author is a faculty member and the second author is a student in the doctoral program. The doctoral students take two supervision courses, and those doctoral students who participated in our study had recently completed the second supervision theory and practice course. As part of the requirements for the courses, doctoral students provide individual supervision of a master's level student enrolled in the practicum course. The master's students were counseling clients weekly in the university counseling clinic. The master's students had recently completed a 15-week practicum course. A total of 19 master's students and 9 doctoral students participated in the study. Participants include 1 male doctoral student, 8 female doctoral students, and 19 female master's students. Participants varied in age from 25 to 51.

The results of our study confirmed that all of the participants, supervisees and supervisors, perceived strengths-based supervision to be a positive experience. Specifically, noted was the impact of a strengths-based approach as the foundation of a supportive supervisory relationship. All supervisees acknowledged the benefits of having a supervisor who identified the supervisee's strengths and communicated confidence in the supervisee's ability to be helpful to clients. Supervisees stated that having confidence expressed by their supervisor confirmed that they were developing the skills needed to become competent mental health providers. One of the supervisees shared, "By hearing from someone that I was doing many things right, I was able to feel good about those things while giving attention to the areas in which I needed to improve." Ten of the supervisees confirmed that the experience of strengths-based supervision encouraged them to focus on the strengths of their clients. This supports the ideas of parallel process and isomorphism as discussed by Edwards (2013), Lietz and Rounds (2009), and Shulman (2005). All of the nine supervisors confirmed that working from a strengths-based model or incorporating strengths-based methods with other chosen models would definitely be their approach to supervision.

The second author of this chapter recently completed his dissertation, *Counselor Education Students' Perceptions of Strengths-Based Supervision* (Dowda, 2015). The research question that guided the study was: What are the perceptions of doctoral counselor education students relevant to their training in a model of strengths-based supervision? Twelve doctoral students were the participants for the dissertation study. The participants included 10 females and 2 males ranging in age from 26 to 55. All participants identified benefits from using a strengths-based model of supervision such as building confidence, supporting growth, and fostering a positive supervisor relationship. Eleven of the 12 participants perceived no drawbacks to using a strengths-based model of supervision. One participant identified an area of concern experienced when working from a strengths-based model: the lack of ease she felt when trying to deliver constructive feedback.

Results of the dissertation research confirmed that all 12 of the doctoral student participants supervised from a strengths-based model. Although some of the participants stated that they integrate strengths-based with other models of supervision all participants confirmed they use a strengths-based approach and confirmed advantages of focusing on supervisees' strengths. Doctoral student supervisors participating in Dowda's (2015) dissertation research asserted that strengths-based supervision was a gentler approach to supervision that fosters a trusting collaborative relationship.

Application: Strengths-Based Supervision, the Model of Choice

Seeking what methods are most effective has always been the focus of teaching, counseling, supervision, and interactions for both authors of this chapter. As soon as Dr. Edward's (2013) book *Strengths-Based Supervision in Clinical Practice* was published and available for distribution, it was adopted for the two doctoral level supervision courses taught in our CACREP accredited Counselor Education doctoral program.

For the first supervision course doctoral students take, the learning objectives aligned with CACREP standards include introducing students to various supervision models (Standard IV.A.2) and demonstrating the application of theory and skills of clinical supervision (Standard IV.B.1). To address CACREP Standard IV.A.2, students were assigned to read *Strengths-Based Supervision in Clinical Practice* (Edwards, 2013) and *Fundamentals of Clinical Supervision* (Bernard & Goodyear, 2013). Students read both textbooks and throughout the first supervision course have to provide supervision from various supervision models for their master's level practicum supervisees. The strengths and assets of the supervisee are always included as a focus of supervision regardless of the model of supervision students are practicing. However, the majority of the doctoral students in our program have been supervised from a deficit model in the past and, as we have a tendency to repeat what we have learned from our own experiences, many of the doctoral supervisors approach supervision similarly. This method points out shortcomings, missed opportunities, and approach supervision with a critical slant or a negativity bias. Therefore, the first task of faculty teaching the supervision course is to prepare supervisors for strengths-based focus and dialogue. This requires the faculty to help doctoral students understand the importance of recognizing and building upon supervisees' strengths. As the faculty and doctoral students read and discuss the textbook *Strengths-Based Supervision in Clinical Practice* (Edwards, 2013), faculty teaching the course make certain that doctoral students understand and implement the executive skills of strengths-based supervision. In addition, doctoral students are assigned to complete the online VIA-IS (http://www.viacharacter.org/Survey/). The VIA-IS is a self-assessment character survey consisting of 24 character strengths that provides a ranking of strengths on the basis of participant responses. Peterson and Seligman (2004) labeled the top five character strengths as the *signature strengths*, which are on the recommendations "to identify people's highest talents and strengths and then help them to find opportunities to use these strengths more" (p. 777).

To accomplish CACREP Standard IV.B.1, doctoral students provided individual supervision for a master's student enrolled in a supervised practicum course. During the first supervision session, which usually takes place prior to the master's students' first appointment with a client, the doctoral supervisors assigns the supervisee to complete the online VIA-IS. Supervisees are instructed to bring the results of the VIA-IS assessment to the next supervision session for discussion. Doctoral supervisors encourage supervisees to use their identified strengths to address challenges and thereby are empowered as they find solutions to their areas of concern using their self-identified strengths. Doctoral students engage in helping supervisees explore how to use their strengths and translate their strengths in meaningful ways that influence their work as clinicians.

Doctoral student supervisors request that master's level supervisees come prepared for supervision having listened to their audiotaped/videotaped sessions and note occasions during the session that focus on their strengths and successes. Supervisees are requested to share at least two strengths they noticed and to play these portions of the taped counseling session during supervision. In addition, supervisees are requested to bring up a concern or an area they would like to process with the supervisor.

Doctoral students submit a videotape of each week's supervision session along with a completed Record and Reflection Form (R & R Form), see Box 20.1.

Box 20.1 Strengths-Based Supervision Record and Reflection Form

Supervision Record and Reflection

Strengths-Based Supervision: Form III

Date:
Supervisee:
Supervision Session #:
Supervisor:

Client Initials: If client is a child add a (C) and include age of child. If client is an adult add (A). If counseling a couple add (Co). If counseling a family add (F).

Supervisee Focused Feedback

Identify the strengths of your supervisee and provide times from the supervision video where supervisee's strengths were discussed: (Strengths may have been identified by supervisee or by you, the supervisor. If identified by supervisee, how did you respond? Strengths may include understanding, counseling skills, values clarification, attitude, clinical judgment, case conceptualization, identifying client's strengths, etc).

Identify the greatest professional growth area you have observed in your supervisee as a new counselor:

How did the supervisee help clients identify their strengths? Provide times from video where this was discussed:

Supervisor Focused Feedback

What are your strengths as a supervisor? Provide times from video where you are demonstrating your strengths:

Discuss how you responded to supervisee's perceived area of concern. How did you validate your supervisee's concern? Remember that to demonstrate understanding does mean that you agree only that you have acknowledged and validated supervisee's expressed concern:

Discuss your progress and growth as a supervisor:

Each week, I (Nichter) watch the supervision videotape, review the R & R Form, and provide feedback by inserting comments within the R & R Form. In addition to learning about strengths-based supervision, doctoral students experience a strengths-based focus by receiving feedback highlighting their strengths and the successes for each week's supervision session from me as I provide supervision of supervision. For an example of a completed R & R Form with doctoral supervisor evaluation of the supervision session and my feedback to the doctoral supervisor, see Figure 20.1.

Supervision Record and Reflection
Strengths-Based Supervision
Form III

Date: 3–9–15   Supervision Session #: 5

Supervisee: Linda   Supervisor: Susan

Client Initials: If client is a child add a (C) and include age of child. If client is an adult add (A). If counseling a couple add (Co). If counseling a family add (F).

Clients this week: P.K. (C, 4 years), M.R. and P.R. (Co).

Supervisee Focused Feedback

Identify the strengths of your supervisee and provide times from the supervision video where supervisee's strengths were presented and discussed: (Strengths may have been

Figure 20.1 Completed Strengths-Based Supervision Record and Reflection Form (Supervisor's comments are underlined and faculty [Supervision of Supervision] comments are italicized.)

identified by supervisee or by you, the supervisor. If identified by supervisee, how did you respond? Strengths may include communicating empathy, counseling skills, values clarification, attitude, clinical judgment, case conceptualization, cultural awareness, identifying strengths of clients, etc.

I began the session by asking Linda what went well during her counseling sessions this week. Linda had the tape cued and played the segment (6:42 to 8:31)—a place during the session she felt she did something well with P.K., her child client. She did a great job allowing P.K. to name and define the play objects as she wanted them to be. She did not try to force the real names of objects or what they were to be used for on the client (as she did in previous sessions). I commented to Linda that she demonstrated respect for P.K. and reinforced P.K.'s control over her play. She gave P.K. space to be creative and let toys represent whatever she chose for them to represent. I also reminded Linda that she was doing a nice job of demonstrating child-centered play therapy which is the approach she selected as her guiding theory for play therapy.

Susan, very nice job of highlighting Linda's accomplishments and evidence of growth especially working from her theory of child-centered play therapy. You offered specific feedback when you acknowledged how she was working from her theory when you pointed out how she shifted from a counseling-centered to child-centered session, i.e. when Linda let P.K. take control of naming and using play objects however she wanted.

Linda reported that she didn't feel very good about the session with the couple. She cued the tape (15:20 to 16:43) to a segment where she felt she was at a loss for words. She said that she overused silence but just didn't know what to say. She said as she reviewed the tape of the session this week she considered this a missed opportunity as she could have asked M.R. (wife) to reflect back to P.R. (husband) what she heard him say and encourage wife to ask husband for accuracy of her understanding of what he means. I pointed out to Linda that self-supervision was a sign of her growth as a counselor and that this will happen throughout her career as a counselor as it does for all counselors who are mindful of their work. I explained that it is much easier to think after a session than during the session.

Susan, this was very insightful of you and encouraging to Linda. Normalizing this for Linda and letting her know that this will happen throughout her career from time to time will help her expect to learn from reflecting on her sessions and her work as a counselor. Self-supervision is certainly something we must all be mindful of as we develop in our careers and work independently.

Identify the strengths and greatest professional growth area you have observed in your supervisee as a new counselor:

Linda has grown in her ability to conceptualize and understand her client's world view. She is also becoming a better listener and this is allowing her to allow clients to lead the session rather than feeling that she must. We watched several segments of her tapes of the sessions and she commented that her clients seem to be much more actively engaged and opening up more comfortably. She is becoming more comfortable with her young client and play therapy which she was very fearful of in the beginning of practicum. She is doing a great job of trying new techniques and stretching her limits even though she doesn't feel it always works out. She takes feedback very well and implements it in the next session with client. I pointed out to Linda that based on my observations of her as a counselor-in-training her greatest strengths are her desire to help clients and learn all that she can from her clients, her peers, supervision, and the entire experience of practicum.

Figure 20.1 (Continued)

Good summary of supervisee's professional growth, Susan. As I read your comments to Linda's greatest area of strength—parallel processing comes to my mind as these comments you are noting about Linda's growth also reflect your growth as a supervisor—I am sure you observe your progress and increased comfort in the role of supervisor as you watch the tapes of your supervision sessions. I can certainly see your growth—congratulations!!

How did the supervisee help clients identify their strengths? Provide times from video where this was discussed:

Linda and I explored her perceptions of how she helps her clients identify their strengths. Linda quickly stated (42:00 to 45:13) that she feels frustrated about pointing out the couple's strengths as every time she attempted to point out their strengths as individuals and as a couple the wife quickly discounts and says things were like that at one time but not now. However, I think Linda did an excellent job of responding to the wife with her statement, "We don't lose our strengths we are just not always using them." Then she encouraged the couple to think how they might work together to bring their strengths back into the present situation. I complimented Linda on acknowledging that the couple still has their strengths—and that sometimes we just are out of touch with our strengths but we can reclaim them and use them to tackle the current challenging situation.

This was a good effort to help Linda shift from her disapproving self-evaluation to identifying the wisdom and skills in her work. Susan, this is one of your strengths as well!!

Supervisor Focused Feedback

What are your strengths as a supervisor during this session? Provide times from video where you are demonstrating your strengths:

I think one of my strengths as a supervisor is staying focused on Linda, my supervisee, rather than spending too much time on what I would have said or my thoughts about her clients. I think this has been a great growth area of me as my tendency when I started supervising was to share my perceptions about Linda's clients with her rather than understand her thoughts and case conceptualization. I would have to say that this is one of my greatest strengths and growth areas. Evidence of this strength is at 9:35, 17.53, and 47:14. Another strength I believe I have that is helpful to Linda is something I remind her of often as I must also remember myself as a counselor and certainly for beginning counselor is to avoid over-thinking about client's problems and feeling pressure to offer an insightful solution—rather I remind Linda and myself that "just being there and listening with empathy" may be the most helpful thing we can do for clients.

Very insightful and helpful feedback for Linda—normalizing the tendency to fix things for clients is something we all have struggled with at times during our work with clients. Another strength I noted around 37:30 is how respectfully and skillfully you encouraged Linda to process her thoughts about P.K., the child client. Linda acknowledges that she expects certain behaviors from children and is easily frustrated about the power struggle P.K. seems to create in play therapy session. You stated in a very respectful way that Linda consider the dynamics in creating a power struggle that two are involved in the interaction and you encouraged Linda to think of something she could do differently rather than be drawn in as often happens when P.K. seeks to exercise her power. You continue by encouraging Linda to think of what P.K. may be needing by pushing for control and power and you asked her to reflect on how the play therapy

Figure 20.1 (Continued)

space and relationship could be a safe place to experience this need. You handled this in such a supportive and encouraging way—yet, you are planting seeds for Linda to process and grow. Nice Work!!

Discuss how you responded to supervisee's perceived area of concern. How did you validate your supervisee's concern? Remember that to demonstrate understanding does mean that you agree only that you have acknowledged and validated supervisee's expressed concern:

I validated Linda's concerns relative to her meeting with P.K.'s father and the negative feedback she received from him during the meeting. She felt "dumb" because she didn't know what had happened last semester with this child and the father's feelings of anger at the previous counselor were projected onto her. Linda admitted that she was intimated by the father and began to feel angry herself. She acknowledged that her tone with him became defensive and that she let her anger show. I asked Linda to find the segment on the tape of the meeting with P.K.'s father where this occurred. When I observed the conversation on the tape where P.K.'s father is expressing anger I did not get the sense that he was directing the anger toward Linda. However, I respected how Linda perceived it even though I did not interpret it as anger toward her. I acknowledged her feelings and confirmed my understanding of the challenge we face not defending ourselves to intense emotions that clients seem to project onto us.

You did a good job helping Linda see that P.K.'s father's intense emotions flowed over onto her. A good reminder and learning experience that counselors must maintain a good boundary with clients.

Discuss your progress and growth as a supervisor:

I am finally beginning to understand my role as a supervisor and how that role is similar to yet different from counseling. I am learning how to be strengths-based within a developmental frame. I do continue to struggle at times as I want to tell Linda what to do with her clients—I reframe (most of the time) as I realize my way may not be her way and if it's not her way—then it won't work! This is the fifth week of practicing as a supervisor and while I am certainly still at the novice level, I believe I have grown in the ability to identify where my supervisee is in the developmental process of supervision in addition to helping her to purposefully highlight her strengths instead of focusing on negatives, shortcomings, and weaker areas.

Susan, I agree with you and easily observe your growth and development as a supervisor. I have noticed a significant decrease in the time you spend talking as compared to the first week of supervision. You are expecting your supervisee to bring the content for supervision and to lead where she wants to go during the conversation. You are pointing out her strengths and she is taking this idea back into her counseling sessions with clients! You are spending a lot of time reviewing the video of supervision and completing the Record and Reflection Form. You are doing a good job of reflecting on the supervisee's strengths as well as your strengths as a supervisor! Nice Work!!

Figure 20.1 (Continued)

Strengths-based supervision provides the foundation and guiding model for the doctoral students enrolled in the supervision courses. When doctoral students are enrolled in the second supervision course and are free to choose the supervision model they will use while providing supervision to a master's level practicum student most of them continue with the strengths-based model.

However, doctoral students who select other models such as the integrated developmental model (IDM) (Stoltenberg et al., 1998) or the discrimination model (Bernard, 1979) integrate a strengths-based perspective into their approach to supervision.

Supervisors need to establish climates in the supervision relationship that focus on and foster the strengths of their supervisees. What supervisees are doing well and feeling good about provides the content for supervision sessions. Theoretical and empirical literature suggest that focusing on strengths may enhance supervisee self-efficacy, and therefore may indirectly influence these other positive outcomes through their influence on counseling self-efficacy (Aasheim, 2012). It has been posited that trainees, particularly those in early stages of development, have a tendency to be self-deprecating, critical, and unsure of their own abilities, and that this tendency may have a negative impact on their competence as therapists (Gelso & Woodhouse, 2003; Stoltenberg, et al., 1998).

Case Study: From "Terrible Sessions" to "What's the Doc Program Like?" (Dowda)

One of the first counselors-in-training I ever supervised stands out as an exceptional example of the benefits of strengths-based supervision. She began our second session by describing how poorly she performed during her first night of practicum. She began our supervision session with a deficit focus and negativity bias and recited all the errors she had made in her first therapy session. Fortunately, I had already watched her video and was prepared to process a variety of strengths with her. Pointing out her strengths and eliciting others from her brought new meaning to our conversation of how she viewed her foundational counseling skills. We processed the many small victories she had with her client, and she left our session feeling much more encouraged with the assignment of bringing in one clinical success for each client to process the following week. Our sessions continued in this manner for weeks and eventually these exercises helped to create a shift in her thinking that lasted throughout the semester. She recognized that she brought many natural personality traits that were beneficial to counseling and that she had developed the skills necessary to excel in practicum and internship. She also reported reduced anxiety and increased confidence as she provided therapy. We continued to discuss areas of growth, but began each session with a small victory from each of her four clients. This particular supervisee became one of the best-performing students in her practicum class and far exceeded the minimum skill level to earn a final course grade of A. I was pleasantly surprised during our last session when she asked many questions about the doctoral program. Through our strengths-focused sessions, she found the confidence to apply to PhD programs in counselor education with the hope of educating future counselors.

When Is Strengths-Based Supervision Appropriate to Use with Supervisees?

Strengths-based supervision is appropriate to use throughout the supervisory relationship. It serves as a foundation for conducting supervision, and many supervisors integrate this approach with other models such as the integrative developmental model and the discrimination model. The focus on strengths is appropriate during the middle and ending sessions as well as in the beginning. Focusing on strengths throughout supervision reinforces the growth of supervisees and highlights their successes. Supervisees supervised from a strengths-based approach reported productive and positive supervision experiences and claimed that this approach helped to reduce their anxiety and increase their confidence (Fall et al., 2003).

Strengths-based supervision has many benefits such as building the supervisory relationship, instilling confidence, fostering independence, and reducing anxiety (Dowda, 2015). Current researchers of the arousal of the sympathetic and parasympathetic nervous systems show that focusing on a person's strengths instead of his or her faults contributes to a higher degree of agreement and goal attainment for both the clinician and client (Boyatzis & McKee, 2005). The core of what Boyatzis and colleagues (Boyatzis, Smith, Van Oosten, & Woolford, 2013) are demonstrating lies with their concept of the *positive and negative emotional attractors*. They believe that these attractors have the ability to pull individuals, couples, and whole organizations toward them. Positive emotional attraction happens when the parasympathetic nervous system is aroused. During this aroused state of the parasympathetic system, there is a focus on possibilities that include home and strength. This felt emotion works to create movement toward a desired goal. Clients see potential and possibilities of positive change. The opposite occurs when the negative emotional attractor is raised and happens when the sympathetic nervous system is aroused. The focus is then on problems, fear, and perceived weaknesses in a person, couple, team, or organization (Boyatzis et al., 2013). Focusing on negatives when talking with the group or individual potentiates the fight or flight condition and closes down the potential of looking at positives or hope. Strengths-based supervision fosters a non-judgmental working environment in which supervisees feel safe to be open and honest. We suggest that this translates into being genuine in the supervision session. People are at their best when they are truly present (Hanh, 2010). We believe counselors who are genuine and present with their clients do the best work and that these qualities are promoted by supervisors who focus on strengths.

Furthermore, supervisees receiving strengths-based supervision are often empowered to try new interventions (Dowda & Nichter, in review). Expanding one's counseling tool belt based on positive reinforcement is supported by Fredrickson's (2001) broaden and build theory. She asserted that positive emotions develop personal resources while negative emotions reduce personal resources. Applied to strengths-based supervision, supervisees develop confidence through focusing on positives which leads them to take more risks in the therapeutic session.

Strengths-based supervision is particularly appropriate to use when faced with supervisees who experience a lack of confidence or heightened anxiety. Many supervisees lack confidence (Jordan & Kelly, 2004) and this can be very detrimental when providing therapy. Focusing on strengths builds this much needed confidence. Supervisees gain increased confidence in counseling skills and in their ability to focus on the strengths of their clients when they are aware of their own strengths and have confidence in their ability to be effective as counselors (Dowda, 2015). Many supervisees also suffer from anxiety (Fall et al., 2003; Jordan & Kelly, 2004; Wade & Jones, 2015). This anxiety can be lowered significantly by focusing on what supervisees do well (Dowda, 2015). Enhancing the independence of supervisees is another benefit of focusing on strengths. Strengths-based supervision helps supervisees find their own style and learn to self-supervise by observing their own strengths on video and audio. Hearing what they do well as counselors-in-training encourages supervisees by giving them a sense of hope in their professional future. It is the goal of counselor educators as faculty teaching in graduate counseling programs to train competent, effective clinicians who are confident and ready to begin their counseling careers. Strengths-based supervision provides the framework for counselors-in-training to enter the field of counseling with confidence in their ability to make a difference. Therefore, strengths-based supervision is not only appropriate to use with supervisees throughout their training program, it is a critical component of counseling programs that are sending their graduates into the mental health field.

Challenges of Strengths-Based Supervision

Dowda (2015) interviewed 12 supervisors trained in strengths-based supervision about their perception of strengths-based supervision. The two biggest concerns expressed by the participants were

(a) adhering to the philosophy of strengths-based supervision while addressing areas of growth and (b) addressing worries that strengths-based supervision lacks necessary constructive feedback. Strengths-based supervision is often misunderstood (Dowda, 2015); it does not ignore areas of growth or lack constructive feedback but instead strengths-based supervisors address areas of growth and provide constructive feedback while maintaining a strengths focus. Our philosophy of strengths-based supervision simply echoes the same message Rashid (2015) described about psychotherapy. We are calling for more of a balance between focusing on strengths and weaknesses. We argue that supervising from a strengths focus rather than a deficit focus is more effective for the growth and development of counselors-in-training.

Finding a greater balance between focusing on strengths and weaknesses does not imply ignoring weaknesses. Supervisors, regardless of orientation, are required to oversee the performance and development of supervisees. If a supervisee is unable to competently provide counseling to clients, the supervisor is responsible for gatekeeping and remediation (American Counseling Association [ACA], 2014). Addressing areas of growth and providing appropriate interventions are essential to the growth and development of supervisees. This is particularly important when a supervisee has clients who are a danger to themselves or others. We find that we have already built a strong supervisory relationship by the time supervisees encounter challenging clients such as those experiencing suicidal ideation. Therefore, we are able to be more direct about the severity of the situation. Supervisees might experience anxiety related to providing therapy to a client in immediate danger, therefore, we often process the feelings of the supervisee and emphasize our continued support and encouragement. Supervisees have also reported that role-playing how to provide an assessment has proved beneficial.

Structure Promotes Predictability

We believe predictability is directly related to trust which is a crucial part of the supervisory relationship. Our approach to conducting strengths-based supervision is highly structured with definite goals for each session as well as the semester. We focus on establishing rapport and building the relationship during our initial sessions. Throughout our middle sessions we review audio or video segments with supervisees. These middle sessions are where we apply Vygotsky's zone of proximal development (Zaretskii, 2009) to supervision. We begin challenging supervisees to try new interventions and step outside their comfort zone with our support and encouragement.

We seek to empower and encourage our supervisees by revisiting clinical successes during the last few supervisory sessions. We find fostering hope and optimism during the last few sessions produces a more positive evolution to internship or the beginning of supervisees' careers. Our goal of the semester is for our supervisees to gain a greater understanding of their strengths and how these strengths translate into competent and effective provision of therapy. Our approach to strengths-based supervision is structured in a way that supervisees quickly gain an understanding of what to expect. This understanding of the structure of supervision fosters self-supervision (Dowda, 2015), a major goal of supervision (Todd & Storm, 2014).

Addressing Areas of Growth through a Strengths-Based Lens

"Successfully resolving problems can lead to more growth and development than a smooth journey ever could" (Wade & Jones, 2015, p. 149). Do not let the term *strengths-based* mislead you. We often focus on areas of growth within our strengths-based sessions. Misperceptions often lead to concerns about operating from a strengths-based model of supervision. The two main challenges supervisors reported from using strengths-based supervision were that it lacks constructive feedback and supervisors felt as though focusing on areas of growth meant they were deviating from the philosophy of strengths-based supervision (Dowda, 2015). It is important for faculty teaching and supervising doctoral students in the strengths-based approach help students understand that following this approach does not imply that constructive feedback for growth and development is to be overlooked.

We suggest that a trusting supervisory relationship must be established prior to offering constructive feedback to discuss areas for growth. Supervisees often begin their practicum experience with feelings of inferiority and anxiety (Fall et al., 2003) and a fear of evaluation. Johnston and Milne (2012) noted that supervisees struggled with being genuine when they perceived that they had a weak or uncomfortable relationship with their supervisors. Supervisees are less likely to become frustrated or discouraged if they feel that their supervisors believe in them. Strengths-based supervisors establish this relationship and rapport during the initial supervision sessions. A strong positive supervisory relationship is essential to productive supervision (Bernard & Goodyear, 2013; Dowda, 2015; Johnston & Milne, 2012; Nuttgens & Chang, 2013; Todd & Storm, 2014).

We are direct and provide constructive feedback through a strengths-based lens and employ two different strategies to address weaknesses. We ask supervisees to identify their own areas of growth and assist them in exploring how their strengths as identified on the VIA-IS might be used to address these areas. Supervisees are often aware of their weaknesses and open to discussing them in session. Supervisors may therefore sandwich a conversation about growths between conversations about strengths. In addition, supervisees can identify their own areas for growth by filling out a self-evaluation form and processing it with the supervisor or by verbally processing their areas of growth in supervision sessions. We find asking supervisees how they would like to improve or what they might do differently is a non-threatening way to elicit areas of growth. During the semester the master's student is supervised during practicum, the supervisors may observe their supervisees through a one-way mirror. In addition, supervisors are given the opportunity throughout the semester to try out the bug in the ear to provide immediate feedback to supervisees while they are counseling clients. Supervisors are encouraged to be open and comfortable in providing constructive feedback as well as positive feedback.

By sandwiching the area of growth or constructive feedback between two strengths, we validate the strengths and progress of the supervisee while addressing weaknesses. For example, "You are doing well establishing the therapeutic relationship with the client. I would like for you to be less tentative with your reflections. The reflections you do offer demonstrate advanced empathy and I would like to see you use this skill more."

On the rare occasion when the gentler approaches do not produce the desired growth, we take a more direct stance with the supervisee. Supervisees deserve due process and must be informed if they are in danger of failing a class or requiring remediation. The sooner supervisees know they are lacking in a particular skill, the sooner they can begin to develop that particular skill. We believe supervisors are responsible for providing appropriate time and interventions aimed at supervisee development.

Although focusing on the strengths of our supervisees is of paramount importance, areas of growth must also be addressed. Once a trusting supervisory relationship has been established, we address areas of growth for two reasons and provide corrective feedback which can be delivered in a strengths-based manner (Edwards, 2013). First of all, supervisees often know what skills are lacking and desire to better themselves; they take initiative in their own development. Second, as supervisors, we are responsible for the development and performance of our supervisees as well as the welfare of their clients (ACA, 2014; Wade & Jones, 2015).

Strengths-based supervision has been the focus of instruction and training in two doctoral supervision courses and has proven to be a model that is quite effective for both supervisors and supervisees. Currently, three cohorts of doctoral students have been trained in strengths-based supervision and have used *Strengths-Based Supervision in Clinical Practice* (Edwards, 2013) as their primary textbook. The first author of this chapter will continue teaching and modeling strengths-based supervision to doctoral students. The second author began his career as a counselor educator in the fall of 2015 and has implemented his strengths-based philosophy and practices to the counselors-in-training he teaches.

References

Aasheim, L. (2012). *Practical clinical supervision for counselors.* New York, NY: Springer.

American Counseling Association. (2014). *ACA code of ethics.* Alexandria, VA: Author.

Barnett, J.E., & Molzon, C.H. (2014). Clinical supervision of psychotherapy: Essential ethics issues for supervision and supervisees. *Journal of Clinical Psychology, 70,* 1051–1061. doi:10.1002/jclp.22126

Berg, I.K. (1994). *Family based services: A solution-focused approach.* New York, NY: Norton.

Bernard, J.M. (1979). Supervisor training: A discrimination model. *Counselor Education and Supervision, 21,* 19–30.

Bernard, J.M. & Goodyear, R.K. (2013). *Fundamentals of clinical supervision* (5th ed.). Upper Saddle River, NJ: Pearson.

Boyatzis, R.E. & McKee, A. (2005). *Resonant leadership: Renewing yourself and connecting with others through mindfulness, hope, and compassion.* Boston, MA: Harvard Business School Press.

Boyatzis, R.E., Smith, M.L., Van Oosten, E., & Woolford, L. (2013). Developing resonant leaders through emotional intelligence, vision and coaching. *Organizational Dynamics, 42,* 17–24.

Bozic, N. (2013). Developing a strength-based approach to educational psychology practice: A multiple case study. *Educational & Child Psychology, 30*(4), 18–29.

Cashwell, T.H. & Dooley, K. (2001). The impact of supervision on counselor self-efficacy. *The Clinical Supervisor, 20,* 39–47.

Cheavens, J.S., Strunk, D.R., Lazarus, S.A., & Goldstein, L.A. (2012). The compensation and capitalization models: A test of two approaches to individualizing the treatment of depression. *Behaviour Research & Therapy, 50,* 699–706. doi:10.1016/j.brat.2012.08.002

Cohen, R.I. (2004). *Clinical supervision: What to do and how to do it.* Belmont, CA: Brooks/Cole-Thomson Learning.

Council for Accreditation of Counseling and Related Educational Programs (CACREP). (2009). *2009 CACREP accreditation manual.* Alexandria, VA: Author.

de Shazer, S. (1988). *Clues: Investigating solutions in brief therapy.* New York, NY: Norton.

de Shazer, S. (1994). *Words were originally magic.* New York, NY: Norton.

Dowda, R. (2015). *Counselor education doctoral students' perceptions of using a strengths-based model of supervision.* (Unpublished doctoral dissertation). Huntsville, TX: Sam Houston State University.

Dowda, R., & Nichter, M. (in review). Supervisory focus on strengths: Perceptions of supervisors and supervisees. *Journal of Professional Counseling: Practice, Theory, and Research.*

Edwards, J.K. (2013). *Strengths-based supervision in clinical practice.* Los Angeles, CA: Sage.

Edwards, J.K., & Chen, M. (1999). Strength-based supervision: Frameworks, current practice, and future directions. *The Family Journal: Counseling and Therapy for Couples and Families, 7,* 349–357. doi: 10.1177/1066480799074005

Fall, K.A., Lyons, C., & Lewis, T. (2003). Contributions of supervisees: A strength-based element of supervision. *Journal of Professional Counseling: Practice, Theory, Research, 31,* 15–20.

Fredrickson, B. (2001). The role of positive emotions in positive psychology. *American Psychologist, 56,* 218–226. doi: 10.1037//0003–066X.56.3.2.218

Gelso, C.J., & Woodhouse, S. (2003). Toward a positive psychotherapy: Focus on human strengths. In B.W. Walsh (Ed.), *Counseling, psychology, and optimal human functioning* (pp. 171–197). Mahwah, NJ: Lawrence Erlbaum.

Hanh, T.N. (2010). *You are here: Discovering the magic of the present moment* (S.C. Kohn, Trans.). Boston, MA: Shambhala Publications.

Haynes, R., Corey, G., & Moulton, P. (2003). *Clinical supervision in the helping professions: A practical guide.* Pacific Grove, CA: Brooks/Cole.

Johnston, L.H., & Milne, D.L. (2012). How do supervisees learn during supervision? A grounded theory study of the perceived developmental process. *Cognitive Behaviour Therapist, 5,* 1–23. doi: 10.1017/S1754470X12000013

Jordan, K., & Kelly, W.E. (2004). Beginning practicum students' worries: A qualitative investigation. *Counseling & Clinical Psychology Journal, 1,* 100–105.

Koltz, R.L., Odegard, M.A., Feit, S.S., Provost, K., & Smith, T. (2012). Parallel process and isomorphism: A model for decision making in the supervisory triad. *The Family Journal: Counseling and Therapy for Couples and Families, 20,* 233–238. doi: 10.1177/1066480712448788

Lietz, C.A., & Rounds, T. (2009). Strengths-based supervision: A child welfare supervision training project. *The Clinical Supervisor, 28,* 124–140. doi:10.1080/17439760.2014.920411

Lopez, S.J., Magyar-Moe, J.L., Petersen, S.E., Ryder, J.A., Krieshok, T.S, . . . Fry, N. (2006). Counseling psychology's focus on positive aspects of human functioning. *The Counseling Psychologist, 34,* 205–227.

Maddux, J.E. (2008). Positive psychology and the illness ideology: Toward a positive clinical psychology. *Applied Psychology: An International Review, 57,* 54–70. doi: 10.1111/j1464–0597.2008.00354

Nuttgens, S., & Chang, J. (2013). Moral distress within the supervisory relationship: Implications for practice and research. *Counselor Education & Supervision, 52,* 284–296. doi:10.1002/j.1556–6978.2013.00043.x

Peterson, C., & Seligman, M.E.P. (2004). *Character strengths and virtues: A handbook and classification.* Washington, DC: American Psychological Association.

Rashid, T. (2015). Positive psychotherapy: A strength-based approach. *The Journal of Positive Psychology, 10,* 25–40.

Rozin, P., & Royzman, E.B. (2001). Negativity bias, negativity dominance, and contagion. *Personality and Social Psychology Review, 5,* 296–320.

Saleebey, D. (2009). *The strengths perspective in social work practice.* Upper Saddle River, NJ: Pearson.

Scheel, M.J., Davis, C.K., & Henderson, J.D. (2012). Therapist use of client strengths: A qualitative study of positive process. *The Counseling Psychologist, 41,* 392–427. doi: 10.1177/ 0011000012439427

Schueller, S.M. (2009). Promoting wellness: Integrating community and positive psychology. *Journal of Community Psychology, 37,* 922–937. doi:10.1002/jcop.20334

Seligman, M. E. P. (2011). *Flourish: A visionary new understanding of happiness and well-being.* NY: Simon & Schuster.

Seligman, M.E.P., & Csikszentmihalyi, J. (2000). Positive psychology: An introduction. *American Psychologist, 55,* 4–14. doi: 10.1037//0003–066X.55.1.5

Seligman, M.E.P., Rashid, T., & Parks, A.C. (2006). Positive psychology. *American Psychologist, 61,* 774–788. doi: 10.1037/0003–066X61.8.774

Shulman, L. (2005). The clinical supervisor-practitioner working alliance: A parallel process. *The Clinical Supervisor, 24,* 23–47.

Smith, E.J. (2006). The strength-based counseling model. *The Counseling Psychologist, 34,* 13–79.

Stoltenberg, C.D., McNeill, B.W., & Delworth, U. (1998). *IDM: An integrated developmental model for supervising counselors and therapists.* San Francisco, CA: Jossey-Bass.

Todd, T.C., & Storm, C.L. (2014). *The complete systemic supervisor: Context, philosophy, and pragmatics.* New York, NY: Authors Choice Press.

Wade, J.C., & Jones, J.E. (2015). *Strength-based clinical supervision: A positive psychology approach to clinical training.* New York, NY: Springer.

Walsh, F. (2002). Bouncing forward: Resilience in the aftermath of September 11. *Family Process, 41,* 34–36. doi:10.1111/j.1545–5300.2002.40102000034x

Welfare, L.E., Farmer, L.B., & Lile, J.J. (2013). Empirical evidence for the importance of conceptualizing client strengths. *Journal of Humanistic Counseling, 52,* 146–163. doi: 10.1002/j.2161–1939.2013.00039

White, M., & Epston, D. (1990). *Narrative means to therapeutic ends.* New York, NY: Norton.

Wong, Y.J. (2014). The psychology of encouragement: Theory, Research, and Application. *The Counseling Psychologist, 43,* 178–216. doi: 10:1177/0011000014545091

Zaretskii, V.K. (2009). The zone of proximal development: What Vygotsky did not have time to write. *Journal of Russian & East European Psychology, 47*(6), 70–93. doi: 10.2753/RPO1061-0405470604

21

Strengths-Based Counselor Education

One Instructor's Perspective

Julie K. West Russo

Mentors and apprentices are partners in an ancient human dance, and one of teaching's great rewards is the daily chance it gives us to get back on the dance floor. It is the dance of the spiraling generations, in which the old empower the young with their experience and the young empower the old with new life, reweaving the fabric of the human community as they touch and turn.

Parker J. Palmer

Counselor educators and supervisors play a significant role in the training of future mental healthcare professionals. It is a privilege to meet, teach, supervise, and mentor these uniquely gifted students; an honor to become part of their life stories. In this role, I have an opportunity to witness and participate in the refinement of the natural talents and encourage the passionate goals of students, the chance to contribute to the need in our society for trained and caring counselors. The role of counselor educator and supervisor is also a difficult role, one that operates in the tension between building competence and a sense of self-efficacy in the next generation of counselors and the ethical mandate that counselor educators and supervisors have to serve as gatekeepers for the profession.

The culture of academia lends itself well to gatekeeping. Students are subjected to ongoing assessment during their time in a graduate training program. Knowledge retention is tested, skills are assessed, and interpersonal behavior is observed. Deficits are identified and plans for remediation are suggested. During this process, counselor educators often assume a position of vigilance, always aware of the significant role that students will one day occupy in the lives of clients. Although the duty to protect the well-being of future clients is a sacred trust, the focus on gatekeeping can result in a rather myopic lens through which we interpret statements and behaviors. Our interactions with the students can become centered on how they should improve—what they should not do. These deficit-based exchanges between educator and student do little to inspire confidence or a sense of self-efficacy. In effect, the gatekeeping mindset, if not held in check, can serve to diminish the value of the natural talents and strengths that drew the student toward the profession. As such, it is important that counselor educators incorporate into their approach principles and practices that affirm, encourage, and empower the students in their care.

In this chapter, I discuss a strengths-based approach to working with master's level students in a counselor education program. Incorporating a strengths-based approach with students into the important gatekeeping role involves acknowledging areas for growth and concern but also keeping a focus on the unique strengths that each student brings into their professional training program.

Strengths-Based Counselor Education

Counselor educators and supervisors prepare and equip the next generation of professionals for the important work of walking alongside those who struggle with life challenges. Training future counselors for this important work requires educators and supervisors to be vigilant about the character of individuals that we endorse for the field. Counselor educators are expected to conduct counselor training programs in an ethical manner and serve as gatekeepers for the profession, working to allow only those well-suited for the profession to enter into it (American Counseling Association [ACA], 2014; Council for Accreditation of Counseling and Related Educational Programs [CACREP], 2009). Consequently, there are "gates" along the way—assessment protocols put in place to protect future clients from counselors who might not provide appropriate services.

Counselor educators also have an obligation to nurture the growth and development of their students as they progress through the counseling training programs (Myers, Mobley, & Booth, 2003). As they enter graduate school, students frequently experience increased levels of anxiety as they face not only the pressures of the academic requirements but the professional and personal demands of the role of counselor (Bowman, Bowman, & DeLucia, 1990). During this time, counselor educators are called on to provide significant and varied roles, often with minimal training in how to most effectively serve the multiple needs of a diverse population of adult learners (Edwards, 2013). Attention must be paid not only to what we teach, but to how we teach it.

Historically, the two paradigms that have significantly formed our approach to counselor education are modernism and constructivism, with the predominant model falling into the category of modernism (McAuliffe & Eriksen, 2000). Modernists posit that an objective reality exists and that scientific principles can be employed as a means by which we can discover and validate these truths. The task of the educator becomes one of organizing a framework within which to impart these truths to their students (McAuliffe & Eriksen, 2000). Students will respectfully listen, take notes, and discuss the topics as presented by the instructor. Cranton (1994) suggested that students are familiar, and comfortable, with this approach due to previous experiences in educational settings. However, it has been argued that this approach hinders ability to creatively conceptualize work with clients (Nelson & Neufeldt, 1998) and may not facilitate counselor conceptual development (Fong, 1998). In contrast to this objective view of reality, constructivists view knowledge as subjective and suggest that it varies on the basis of the mental construction of the observer (McAuliffe & Eriksen, 2000). As opposed to the use of language to impart facts, from the instructor to the student, this approach suggests that educators teach students to use language as a tool to convey their own understanding of phenomenon. While this view is noticeable in many contemporary models of counseling, it is less evident in pedagogical literature (Guiffrida, 2005). Although this model certainly allows for a more individual expression of ideas and learning, it does not necessarily affirm the unique strengths and experiences of the adult learners. McAuliffe (2011) states that a model of teacher-as-expert and student-as-receiver has increasingly been challenged as ineffective in a field that strives to produce self-authorizing professionals who must be aware of, and develop, their own individual strengths.

Over the last several years, many counselor educators have suggested that the pedagogical methods used in counselor education are in need of review and revision to best prepare counselors for the work that they will do (Hayes & Paisley, 2002; House & Sears, 2002; Guiffrida, 2005). Counselor education, like many other areas of academia, has relied primarily on a pedagogical approach that views students as receptacles for knowledge imparted to them by educators with experience in the field of counseling. This approach does little to identify, affirm, or develop the inherent talents and strengths of the student. Rather, it creates an atmosphere where the approach, and perspective, of the instructor is presented as the goal toward which students should strive, a journey in which deficits must be overcome. Paradoxically, we teach our students to focus on the unique experiences and strengths of future clients. A strengths-based approach with adult learners looks for "the best of the best" in our students (Chickering & Reisser, 1993), values their natural talents and unique learning styles, seeks not only to train but also to affirm and empower them, and approaches the process in a collaborative manner (Granello & Hazler, 1998).

Strengths-based education is not a new approach to teaching, rather it is a return to what was proven to contribute to student confidence nearly 100 years ago (Lopez & Louis, 2009). It is an approach focused on identifying, recognizing, and affirming the strengths of students as a means by which students can be motivated to achieve and excel. Dewey (1938) stated his belief that "the purpose of education is to allow each individual to come into full possession of his or her personal power" (p. 10), a principle that is at the foundation of a strengths-based approach to educating our students. This approach to education focuses on the positive experiences and strengths of a student and is a move away from the conventional deficit-based model, an approach that focuses on problems and shortcomings. Currently, strengths-based approaches to education are being used with promising results on hundreds of campuses in the United States and Canada (Lopez & Luis, 2009). This philosophical approach to counselor education begins with the review of applications for admission and continues on through the important tasks of advising, teaching, and supervising.

A Strengths-Based Approach: the Practices

In an address on the need for educational reform, B.F. Skinner once commented that "[c]ollege teaching is the only profession for which there is no professional training. Would-be doctors go to medical school, would-be lawyers go to law schools, and would-be engineers go to institutes of technology, but would-be teachers just start teaching" (as cited in Edwards, 2013, p. 76). This quote accurately describes my experience and that of several of my colleagues; we were students who became clinicians and then, one day, we stood in front of a classroom full of students who were looking to us to deliver the primary components of their training experience. Despite the critical nature of this instructional role in the lives of counselor educators, it has been found that there has been a noticeable lack of attention to, and variety in, pedagogical training experiences for doctoral students (Magnuson, Shaw, Tubin, & Norem, 2004).

How then does excellence in counselor education develop? It might happen in a variety of ways. Increasingly, doctoral programs have recognized the importance of teaching the skills of teaching (CACREP, 2009, Section IV.C.2). Mentors emerge within the field to provide guidance to new faculty members, books are written with practical suggestions and sage advice, and students offer valuable feedback on their experience in classrooms. However, while techniques can be acquired and sharpened over time and through experience, excellence emerges out of attending to each activity in which we engage with an awareness of the impact of our words and actions on our students. As counselor educators, this important role that we play in the lives of our students begins at the point of admission to our programs and continues on through advising, teaching, and supervising. The strength of the relationships we develop with them begins with a focus on the strengths of each individual, both student and educator.

A strengths-based educator views every aspect of his or her role as one in which positive individual characteristics and human strengths of students will be identified, emphasized, and developed in ways that serve to empower students and help them to flourish in the classroom rather than merely survive the semester (Liesveld & Miller, 2005). It is a view that emphasizes the assumption that every student has resources that can, and should, be developed in many areas of life (Anderson, 2000; Saleebey, 2001). In academia, this requires intentionality on the part of the instructor to note strengths not measured by the data we frequently rely on to demonstrate "success," such as high exam scores.

Admissions: Considering the Applicant's Strengths

An application for admission to graduate school typically passes through many hands before it is sent to a specific program director. Assessments have been made about sufficiency of undergraduate course work and grade point averages. Graduate Record Examination or Miller Analogies Test scores are reviewed and assessed, financial aid considerations have been discussed, and letters of recommendation have been received and reviewed. In other words, a determination has been made that an individual has met the basic requirements for admission. What has not been determined is whether or not this decision is a wise one for the student or for the field of study. The area left to review is the natural talents, the strengths, of the applicant.

In the early days of my role as reviewer of applicants to our program, I found myself wondering about the best way to assess for success in our program and in the field of counseling. What are the criteria that we look for in an individual who desires to be a counselor? How can we know if he or she will be well-suited to the work? Are we inherently designed to do some jobs well or is it better to view life experience as preparing us for future success? Research tells us that there are certain traits and personality characteristics that do contribute to success in counseling, such as open-mindedness, acceptance of diverse viewpoints, sensitivity, empathy, genuineness, and emotional stability (Pope, 1996; Scheffler, 1984). These characteristics are difficult to teach to those who do not already possess them. They are unique talents that are innate to certain individuals that can, with awareness and intentionality, be developed into strengths. These contributors toward success are demonstrated in ways other than "hard data" in an application for admission to the program. Although items like grade point average (GPA) or an entrance exam score are useful for predicting future academic success, we know that counseling is foundationally relational; the professional must possess and demonstrate strengths related to earning trust, forming relationships, and empowering clients (Corey, 2005).

One way to assess for characteristics that will contribute to success in a field is to look for applicant characteristics, or strengths, that are demonstrated through successful experiences over time. A review of prior work and volunteer activities might reveal a pattern of seeking out opportunities to provide assistance to those in need. Service awards often reflect the willingness of the applicant to go beyond what is required and provide leadership and excellence in service. Rich information about applicant strengths is also found in the responses to essays, in the narratives offered by the applicants themselves on the applications, and in the faculty interview process. Individuals who are considering entering a counselor education program, or who have recently matriculated, are often asked about what kind of work they hope to be doing in the future and how they decided to pursue this type of work as a career. There is often reference to a sense of purpose, a feeling that this is the career that the student has been "called" to pursue. While the responses vary in unique and interesting ways, there are two common themes that emerge.

The first common theme that I have noticed in the responses of applicants involves stories of personally overcoming major life challenges, such as addiction, abuse, a broken family, or an eating disorder. Individuals who focus on these stories often include in the narrative testimonies about the positive influence of a counselor in their lives. They have a desire to give back, to pay it forward, and to be that professional in the lives of others who experience struggles of a similar nature. A second theme that commonly emerges in applicant responses is the presence of a desire, a longing to "help others" with life challenges that has existed over the course of their lives and has manifested itself in many areas of their lives. These individuals have typically been "sought out" by others as one who is naturally empathic, nonjudgmental, and a source of wise counsel. Job histories, volunteer activities, and special interest organization involvements listed on applications or résumés often reflect participation in people-helping endeavors. Letters of recommendation typically emphasize the natural giftedness of the individual in the area of interpersonal relations. In each of these common applicant themes, strengths are apparent that can and should be considered in the application process.

Case in Point: Toni

At the time of her application to the MA in Mental Health Counseling program, Toni was 44 years old. She had recently completed her BA in an adult education program and was working as an administrative assistant for a pharmaceutical company. She had been widowed when her children were young and took her present job to provide for them. Now that her children were grown and had left the home, Toni began to think of her own future as possibly having options. While she was happy with her friends, her involvement in her church, and her home, she realized that her job was a source of discontent. Her pastor suggested that she pursue training as a professional counselor.

At first glance, Toni's admission for application was not strong. Her GPA reflected acceptable work for her program but it was at the lower end of what we hope to see in our applicants. Her entrance exam score was consistent with her ranking in the area of grades. Financial aid would be available to her, primarily through loans, but the cost of the degree would be significant for her. In other words, a review of this applicant "by the numbers" was not encouraging. However, what was missing from the hard data were the key strengths of this applicant.

The responses Toni provided to the essay questions on her application for admission were powerful and told the story of an individual who had been able to persevere, overcome obstacles, and maintain both integrity and also hope throughout her life. Her answers contained insight, discernment, humor, and wisdom; she conveyed both confidence and also humility. The letters of reference for this applicant were among the strongest that I have read. Each contained detailed stories of Toni's positive impact on the lives of others through caring interactions and relationship. Each reference mentioned natural attributes such as empathy, compassion, wisdom, discernment, ability to work with diverse others, and dependability.

For Toni, the final step in the decision process was the interview, a time during which I was able to hear the story of how her strengths and hopes for the future influenced her decision to apply to our program. At the conclusion of our time together, it was apparent that Toni possessed natural strengths that could contribute significantly to an effective and rewarding career in counseling. Discussing these strengths was affirming for her and allowed for us to enter into a discussion about how she could draw on these strengths to manage the potential stressors of the rigorous training program that lay ahead.

Advising: Collaborating on Strengths

Research has shown that effective faculty advising is a crucial element of graduate student satisfaction, academic success, and student retention (Schlosser, Knox, Moskovitz, & Hill, 2003). Over the course of their educational program, students are exposed to a number of faculty members and adjunct faculty. Although these instructors may become familiar with students, it is not possible to know each one of them well enough to attend to developmental needs. Instead, the faculty advisor can become the consistent person throughout a student's enrollment who can provide guidance, offer suggestions, encourage and support, and ultimately help a student to thrive through the identification and development of unique strengths.

Individuals at the beginning of graduate school often experience feelings of anxiety about a decision of this magnitude, a decision that requires a commitment of significant time and money in the pursuit of the degree. For assistance with this wide range of feelings, students often turn to faculty members in their educational programs for confirmation of their decision and support during their journey. In the field of mental health counseling, this means that students look to counselor educators.

Historically, academic advisors have utilized one of two approaches to the task of academic advising: prescriptive advising or developmental advising. In prescriptive advising, the student is viewed as a more passive recipient of information (Crookston, 1972). The student-advisee brings questions to the academic advisor who, in turn, provides authority-based answers to those questions. Developmental advising focuses more on an ongoing relationship between faculty advisors and students, integrating a student's academic and professional goals with personal goals (Wong, Selke, & Thomas, 1995). Strengths-based advising is not incongruent with developmental models and does not ignore the value of prescribing as needed. Rather, it incorporates a focus on the natural strengths and talents that students possess. Strengths-based advising is used to build both confidence and motivation, by increasing a student's awareness of their strengths so that they can further develop the competencies that will help them reach their goals (Schreiner & Anderson, 2005). The focus of the strengths of the student in advising creates the opportunity for advisor and advisee to collaborate in the exploration of the issue at hand, the definition of the optimal outcomes, and the review of occasions in the past when the student has successfully addressed similar concerns. We look for the "best of the best" in the past as we attempt to recreate that flow in the present.

This role of academic advisor came with my promotion from part-time to full-time faculty. At the beginning of my first full-time academic year, I received a list of existing and incoming students assigned to me. Shortly thereafter, I began to receive requests from students for appointments. I received no formal training in advising. I anticipated that I would listen empathically to the issues presented by the students and then provide answers or suggestions to them. This was the way that I had experienced advising as a graduate student.

As I reflected on my early advising appointments, I realized that those appointments provided little lasting assistance. According to customary models of advising, graduate-level students would be seen as competent, mature individuals who have selected a career path and meet with advisors primarily in attempts to resolve ambivalence about semester scheduling options. I was not advising as much as I was confirming selections that they had already made. Occasionally a student was experiencing frustration in a particular class or stress due to the demands of the program. Yet even in these situations the advising experiences felt to me as though significant opportunities were being missed. I was looking at the situation as one in which a problem existed so that I could help the student by solving it for them. I realized that I had fallen into a pattern of deficit-based advising, built on an assumption, foundational in much of higher education, that deficit remediation is the most effect strategy for helping students to complete a degree. However, it seemed to me that this approach was unlikely to result in serving my students well. I wanted students to leave the meetings with me not simply feeling as though a particular challenge had been heard and addressed but rather feeling more confident in their own abilities to address the current and also future challenges. The solution for me was a shift to a strengths-based approach to advising.

Case in Point: Tim

Tim was a 50-something, second-career student in our program who requested an advising appointment with me to discuss his doubts about continuing with the degree. Tim was in his first semester, struggling with course expectations, and doubting his ability to successfully complete the program. Our meeting began with Tim presenting the evidence for his concerns. He had prepared a chart of his courses, the grades he had received on submitted assignments, the tasks yet to be done, and the scores he anticipated he would receive on future items. As I reviewed the documentation that he had prepared, it was easy to see why Tim felt discouraged. His initial scores were low. If this was, in fact, a predictor of future scores, Tim would not pass at least two of his courses. Tim stated that he felt overwhelmed and inadequate. His conclusion: Learning was not one of his strengths.

Prior to strategizing with Tim around upcoming papers and exams, I asked him to tell me about his life prior to returning to school, with special attention given to successes that he experienced and times that he felt good about accomplishments. Tim's expression shifted to one of confidence as he went on to tell me about extraordinary accomplishments in his career in sales, his rewarding relationships with customers and employees, his solid marriage to his high school sweetheart, and his role as head of the family after his father's passing. Tim had taken on significant life challenges over the years, assessed and navigated obstacles, and successfully balanced multiple life roles. Tim had strengths that he utilized well in overcoming past challenges. The task ahead of us that day was to help Tim see how those same strengths could be applied to his current situation. Shifting to this mindset, Tim was able to see the parallels between current and past challenges and talk about how to employ strategies that had worked for him in the past. He was also empowered through remembering, and describing, his history of success. Equipped with a renewed sense of self-efficacy, Tim was able to view current challenges in a new way. We worked together to identify strategies used in past successes to plan for present challenges.

Tim's situation was not unique. Students who enter the program after years, or decades, away from formal education often struggle to acclimate themselves to the culture of academia. They see other (often younger) students around them who appear to be doing well "naturally" and they assume that they do not have what it takes to succeed in academia. What they often fail to consider is that their history of perseverance and success in managing life obstacles is one of the key strengths that can make them an effective and empathic counselor. Strengths are best recognized, affirmed, and developed in relationship. The counselor educator role of advising, and mentoring, is an excellent opportunity to provide a student with this type of relationship.

Teaching: Constructing a Course

The task that is often seen as most significant for counselor educators, at least in terms of the time allotted to it, is that of teaching courses. Indeed, research has found that counselor education faculty spends more time teaching than on scholarship or service activities (Davis, Levitt, McGlothlin, & Hill, 2006). The classroom is generally viewed as our opportunity to focus on important areas of our field and attempt to equip our students well. It is also the area where most beginning professional educators have the least amount of experience and the least amount of formal training in how to effectively "teach" others (Barrio Minton, Myers, & Morganfield, 2012; Barrio Minton, Wachter-Morris, & Yaites, 2014).

A strengths-based approach to teaching is understood better as a philosophy than as a theory—a way of being with students rather than being above them. It is a perspective built on the assumption that every individual has natural resources, or talents, which can contribute toward achieving success in life (Anderson, 2000) and an approach that is characterized by efforts to label "what is right" within people, reduce a hierarchical structure, and facilitate collaboration in classrooms where significant differences in natural abilities always exist (Buckingham, 2007). In the preparation of the course syllabus, materials for time in class, and methods of assessment, instructors consider the strengths and life experiences of the students as valuable resources. To "educate" literally means to "draw out" or "to bring forth." As such, strengths-based educators approach teaching with a desire to draw out the strengths that exist in students, noticing and affirming these times, and seeking to build on them.

Syllabi

The development of a course syllabus is the best time to begin considering ways in which students can be motivated and empowered (Cox, 2013). While instructors generally allot significant time and attention to what is communicated in syllabi, it is also important to attend to how it is communicated. Harnish et al. (2011) encouraged educators to create a "warm" syllabus that "provides a sense of belonging and community . . . and removes unnecessary and unhelpful barriers between instructors and students, making the classroom a comfortable and safe place for discovery" (p. 23). Descriptions of the required papers and projects in a course provide an opportunity to demonstrate a value for the unique strengths of the students, offering opportunities for natural abilities to be recognized and developed through means other than exams.

The first meeting of the class is generally the time during which the final version of a course syllabus is presented to the students. This is the time during which we, as educators, invite students into the process. The manner in which it is done is important. Syllabi that are presented as rigid and rule-bound contracts, with emphasis on penalties for absenteeism, late submissions, and plagiarism, set a tone quite different from a presentation done with warmth, humor, and passion for the subject matter. Matejka and Kurke (1994) suggested that the review of the syllabus include brief, meaningful activities related to course requirements to encourage early engagement and enthusiasm in students. In contrast with the more common instructor-delivery-of-requirements approach, this method invites student participation, collaboration, and emotional involvement.

Lectures

While teaching involves several components, the primary focus for many novice instructors (and some seasoned veterans) is the lecture. This is the time when educators become "the sage on the stage," orally communicating the important information for each class meeting. The word *lecture* is derived from the Latin word *lectus*, which means "to read." Although we certainly strive to do more than read a lecture in our counseling classes, the point is that it is difficult to encourage student engagement and recognize the strengths that they bring to the classroom if the focus remains on the lecturer. A teacher-centered environment does not invite students into the learning process or produce the type of affirmation that researchers across academic levels have found to be linked to student learning (Dorman & Fraser, 2009; Meyers, 2009). Although the lecture is a time-honored and time-efficient approach to the didactic part of what we do, it is important that it is learner-centered rather than teacher-centered (Savickas, 2013). In order to identify, affirm, and develop the unique strengths of our students, it is necessary to collaborate with our students in the process of learning.

To create a collaborative classroom environment, researchers suggest that optimal learning happens when educators discover and honor the way that their students actually learn (Ambrose, Bridges, DiPietro, Lovett, & Norman, 2010; Bain, 2004). Jane Vella, an expert in the area of adult education, issued the following statement as a challenge to teachers of adults: "You probably teach very well without recognizing that, often, the more teaching, the less learning. Our job is not to cover a set of course materials, but to engage adults in effective and significant learning" (as cited in McAuliffe & Eriksen, 2011, p. 3). Edwards (2013) suggested that on the continuum-based view of educational approaches ranging from pedagogy (teacher driven) to andragogy (student driven or self-driven), the andragogical approach should be considered in the education of counselors and counselor supervisors (pp. 76–77). In the related educational field of social work education, Polloio and Macgowan (as cited in Edwards, 2013) argued for an andragogical approach, stating that "the learner is an adult, and is capable of participating in the educational process, rather than a more passive learning approach" (p. 77). A key distinction between pedagogy and andragogy is that pedagogy rarely takes into consideration the valuable life experiences that students bring into the classroom, which are critical factors in adult learning (Young & Hundley, 2013). Indeed, research has demonstrated that adults prefer a more active role in their education rather than the more traditional role of passive recipient (Knox, 1986).

Strengths-based education suggests a different approach to an instructor's presence with students, a recognition that each individual brings into the classroom unique strengths, variable styles of learning, and valuable life experiences. As such, educators shift from the role of instructor as teacher to the role of instructor as facilitator, utilizing class discussions and experiential activities as a means by which learning happens and student strengths can be identified, affirmed, and developed.

Case in Point: the Summer Experiment

A few years ago, I was asked to teach a summer section of Multicultural Issues in Counseling in a modified, intensive format. Typically this format would include three weekends (Friday and Saturday) over the course of the summer. My experience with the 2-day weekend format was that students tended to grow tired (or bored) with 2 solid days of class, so I requested permission to "flip" the classroom and reduce the face-to-face time required. I had been doing some research on the flipped classroom and was drawn to the logic of the approach.

When viewed in the terms of Bloom's taxonomy (Bloom et al., 1956), a flipped classroom approach means that the students are doing the lower levels of cognitive work (gaining knowledge and comprehension) by completing the reading prior to the class time, and using time in class to focus on the higher levels of cognitive work (application, analysis, synthesis, evaluation, and creation). This is a "flip" from the more traditional model, where "first exposure" typically is delivered through an instructor's lecture and assimilation of knowledge through subsequent assignments. This approach seemed well suited to our students, individuals who have demonstrated the capability of acquiring and assimilating new information in prior life tasks. The flipped classroom is also well suited to an intensive format.

After a few weeks of agonizing over how to accomplish course objectives in significantly reduced face-to-face time, I realized that I was approaching it as though I were the only one bringing information to the class. I had slipped into a deficit-based approach. I was not considering the valuable life experiences and wisdom that the students would bring into the equation. After that important realization, planning went smoothly. Reading was assigned ahead of time, lectures were replaced with discussions, and research papers were replaced with an assortment of experiential and outside-of-class activities.

During the first meeting of the class on campus, I realized that the strengths-based approach to teaching is a natural fit with the flipped classroom. The lecture diminishes in importance when students have completed, and contemplated, the reading in advance. I abandoned my typical position at the head of the class and sat in a large circle with the students. Although a portion of our time together was spent clarifying concepts presented in the reading, the majority of it was spent discussing reactions to the material, life experiences that influenced our reactions, and both practical and professional applications of what we had learned. The strengths of the students emerged through interpersonal interactions. Their life stories received positive attention, interest, and affirmation.

Despite some initial anxiety and concern on my part due to the reduced face time, this course was a resounding success. The focus was removed from me as presenter and on to my students as both learners and also information providers. As we interacted around the important topics of culture and diversity, each student was able to teach the group about their own life experience and about what they had learned in outside-of-class activities. Thoughts were discussed and debated, challenges were acknowledged, and differences in worldviews were recognized and explored. The strengths of each individual and each culture represented were afforded the opportunity to be seen and heard.

Assessment

A final important piece of teaching is the need for educators to assess whether learning has taken place. Although the future work of counseling is fundamentally interpersonal, the training program is significantly exam driven. Admission to the program requires an acceptable score on a graduate entrance exam, courses require acceptable scores on mid-term and final exams, comprehensive exams require a passing score, and, ultimately, students must pass the National Counselor Exam to work in the field. In sum, exams are a necessary component of courses in our program because they are a fundamental component of the license that will enable our students to work in their chosen field. However, with students for whom exams are not reflective of their primary strengths, assessment of competence that is based primarily on these scores creates feelings of discouragement and personal doubt. In essence, the strengths that have the potential to make these students effective counselors are not recognized.

As we consider individual traits that we know to be critical in the field of counseling, how do we best acknowledge and celebrate these strengths? How do we assess for empathy, compassion, wisdom, or discernment? How do we support and encourage students who do not earn high marks in exams but excel in relational skills? A strengths-based approach to counselor education acknowledges the role played by exams but seeks to expand on the assessment process through the identification, affirmation, and development of strengths not easily assessed in the exam process. This can occur through intentional course design that provides a variety of assignments in which students can demonstrate, and be recognized for, their unique strengths. Anderson and Krathwohl (2001) suggested that advanced cognitive abilities can be assessed through essays or oral presentations and self-reflections. Another essential avenue for acknowledging students' strengths is through positive feedback (Wiggins, 2012), both in the forms of instructor-to-student and student-to-student (Petty, 2006). In each case, strengths are acknowledged and affirmed through oral and written feedback. Students are provided with positive reinforcement in areas of natural ability, thereby increasing a sense of self-efficacy in all areas of endeavor.

Strengths-Based Counselor Educators

To work most effectively with the strengths of students, educators must be operating out of their own strengths rather than attempting to emulate the approach of colleagues who appear to be "doing it right." While mentoring is valuable in the early years of teaching, it does not necessarily facilitate the identification of one's own unique talents and gifts. We cannot teach authentically with someone else's strengths. A strengths-based approach to teaching creates educators who intentionally seek to discover their own talents; they are instructors who develop and apply their own strengths as they simultaneously work to help students identify and apply their strengths in the process of learning.

Embracing Our Own Strengths

The first course that I taught in our program was Addictions Counseling, an area of clinical experience and competence for me. Although I was comfortable with the clinical work, I had less confidence in my ability to teach others how to do it. In an effort to "see how it was done," I decided that it would be helpful to sit in on the class as it was being taught by one of my colleagues. I admired this colleague; students enjoyed him. What better way to learn than to have an effective method modeled, right? That was my hope. The result of that experience was an increase in my anxiety and a decrease in my level of confidence that I would be an effective instructor for this course. Each time that I sat in on one of my colleague's classes, I found myself thinking, "I could not have presented the topic that way" or "I would not have been able to use that example" or "That isn't my style of relating to students." Rather than emerging from that experience with ideas and motivation, I left feeling inadequate and deficient.

How do we discover our strengths? How do we help our students identify theirs? There are several measures that can be used to identify positive individual qualities. Perhaps the most widely used assessment is the Clifton StrengthsFinder, an instrument developed by Gallup (Rath, 2007). The StrengthsFinder (https://www.gallupstrengthscenter.com/) is an Internet-based measure that assesses 34 possible talent themes and provides respondents with personal feedback on their 5 most dominant clusters of talent. Since 1998, the Clifton StrengthsFinder has been used as a talent/strength identification tool in development programs in academic institutions, faith-based organizations, major businesses, and other organizations. For these purposes, the measure has adequate internal consistency, stability, validity, and cross-cultural applicability (Asplund, Lopez, Hodges, & Harter, 2007).

Case in Point: Finding My Strengths

In their book *Teach with Your Strengths*, Liesveld and Miller (2005) discuss the various StrengthsFinder themes as they would relate to the work of educators. As I read about the sections on my top five identified strengths, I began to understand how they worked together to create an approach that was effective for me. I also began to understand how these themes were sometimes not congruent with the educator that I had once attempted to be by modeling my approach after colleagues. When I took the StrengthsFinder assessment, my top five strengths themes were identified as follows:

1. The theme of *intellection* is associated with individuals who are characterized by a tendency to examine their own thought processes and appreciate intellectual discussions. This is a strength that I have been able to utilize in the development of presentations, assignments, and activities for the courses that I teach. I enjoy thinking and often spend time reflecting on lectures after class has ended. I make note of what worked well and also attempt to modify what did not.
2. The theme of *input* pertains to a desire to know more, a tendency to identify subjects of interest and accumulate information about those subjects. Teaching in higher education allows for an area of specialization. It is not necessary for me to be an expert on all courses offered. I enjoy the opportunity that this provides for me to spend time learning more about the topics that I teach and am passionate about.
3. The theme of *maximizer* is described as a focus on the stories and strengths of others in an effort to stimulate growth. This is a foundational piece of a strengths-based approach. Advising meetings provide opportunities to discover and discuss unique talents, papers present opportunities to include encouraging and affirming comments, and classrooms become safe places for sharing life stories and experiences.
4. The theme of *deliberative* is described as a tendency to cautiously make decisions and anticipate obstacles. This is a necessary component in the planning stages with students, the selection of field work sites, and the supervision of counselor interns. This tendency toward caution is also an important piece of the gatekeeping role.
5. The final theme, that of *learner*, represents a desire to learn and an enjoyment of the process of learning. This theme, combined with the other four themes, best helps me understand why I so deeply enjoy the work that I do. I learn by giving

> myself permission to spend a great deal of time thinking about the work that I do, by focusing on the topics that most interest me, through hearing, considering, and valuing the stories and strengths of students, and by being cautious and intentional in the decisions that I make about the manner in which I spend my time and energy.
>
> It is important to note that there is no value assigned to the themes identified in the Clifton StrengthsFinder. It is not an assessment designed to identify whether or not you are "talented enough" or "have the right strengths" for a specific profession. Each strength has equal merit. The value of identifying one's strengths is the opportunity to use those strengths well in your chosen profession, to build on the strengths and rely on them to handle areas that appear to require strengths that you do not naturally possess.

Articulating the Application of Our Strengths

As educators, an important piece of our professional journey is the discovery of our own truths about teaching, that is, our personal beliefs about how best to educate and empower our students. Although many of these beliefs are ones we hold in common with our colleagues, others are reflective of our discipline and of who we are as individuals. Teaching philosophy statements provide an opportunity for educators to reflect on, and articulate, their own beliefs about teaching, beliefs that develop out of unique strengths and personal experiences. In writing about the importance of this process, Brookfield (2006) suggested that many faculty ignored their own beliefs, stating that "[m]any of us are so cowed by the presumed wisdom of authorities in our field that we dismiss our private understandings as fantasies until an expert legitimizes them by voicing them" (as quoted in West, Bubenzer, & Gimenez Hinkle, 2013, p. 5). However, we do life best when we identify, develop, and affirm who we have been uniquely created to be. Our teaching philosophy statements should reflect and celebrate our strengths.

A strengths-based teaching philosophy statement highlights the belief that not only the educator, but also each student, possesses unique strengths that, when developed, will contribute to a rich and rewarding life. We see our role as collaborators in the discovery, development, and discussion of those strengths. We are curious, compassionate, and collegial. We lecture but we begin by listening to our students and learning about their strengths through their stories of success. We attend to gatekeeping but not without grace.

Final Thoughts: the Lasting Influences of Strengths-Based Mentors

I am a counselor educator. I enjoy what I do and cannot imagine doing anything else. With that said, teaching was never part of my career plan. Rather, my first experience as an educator was the result of a spur-of-the-moment decision to teach as an adjunct. However, subsequent to signing the contract, I realized something quite significant about my decision: I did not actually know how to teach a class! I found myself wishing that I had paid a little more attention to how my former professors had succeeded in making learning enjoyable for me.

After 2 years of teaching as an adjunct, I realized that I had stumbled upon a job that I enjoyed a great deal. I wondered about the possibility of a career as an educator. Positive student feedback had been a necessary but not sufficient motivator for me to make a career shift of this magnitude. I made the decision at that point to return to school in a program that would result in a doctorate in education with a focus in counselor education and supervision. I reasoned that, within the first few courses, I would either be affirmed in this new career path or I would realize that it was better left as a part-time experience.

The initial courses in my doctoral program were enjoyable. This was not a surprise to me. I feel comfortable and competent in academic environments. However, I was no more or less persuaded about a decision to move from the role of adjunct to professional educator. My primary fear at that time was that my abilities would fail me at some point, that I did not actually possess the natural abilities required to succeed in teaching. My ambivalence was resolved through the influence of Jeff Edwards, a counselor educator solidly grounded in a strengths-based approach to teaching. Over time, Jeff was able to help me see that I did, in fact, have the strengths necessary to succeed in the program and become an effective counselor educator. He taught me that I did not need to be naturally talented in all areas; I only needed to use the talents that I did naturally possess to overcome challenges along the way. Jeff's consistent focus on my strengths, and what I did well, allowed for me to gain the confidence and sense of self-efficacy that was necessary for me to succeed. I gained far more than an increase in knowledge and skills, and a degree, from my doctoral program. I gained the awareness that students often need instructors who will help them identify and develop their strengths so that they can not only do their future work better but also thrive in the process.

I have also learned some important lessons in my experience as a counselor educator. One of the most significant has been that learning in the classroom is a collaborative endeavor. It is not merely the end result of effective content delivery. Each semester, I collaborate with my students in an effort to create a classroom experience where content is delivered, discussed, debated, and developed. To accomplish this, I have learned that I must be aware of the strengths of the students in the class and interact with them in a way that best utilizes both their strengths and also my strengths. The students that I work with are in our program for a relatively brief period of time. When they leave, they will begin the important work of walking with clients through times of stress, doubt, discouragement, and feelings of loss. It is my hope that these new counselors will remember what it felt like to have their own strengths identified, affirmed, and developed so that they can pass this along to their clients as part of the work that is done. This, I believe, is the self-perpetuating gift of a strengths-based approach to education.

References

Ambrose, S.A., Bridges, M.W., DiPietro, M., Lovett, M.C., & Norman, M.K. (2010). *How learning works: 7 research-based principles for smart teaching*. San Francisco, CA: Jossey-Bass.

American Counseling Association. (2014). *ACA code of ethics*. Retrieved January 4, 2015 from http://www.counseling.org/docs/ethics/2014-aca-code-of-ethics.pdf

Anderson, E.C. (2000, February). *Affirming students' strengths in the critical years*. Paper presented at the National Conference on the First Year Experience, Columbia, SC.

Anderson, L.W., & Krathwohl, D.R. (2001). *A taxonomy for learning, teaching, and assessing*. New York, NY: David McKay.

Asplund, J., Lopez, S.J., Hodges, T., & Harter, J. (2007). *The Clifton StrengthsFinder 2.0 technical report: Development and validation*. Washington, DC: The Gallup Organization.

Bain, K. (2004). *What the best college teachers do*. Cambridge, MA: Harvard University Press.

Barrio Minton, C.A., Myers, J.E., & Morganfield, M.G. (2012). *Meeting the 2013 standard: An initial look at the demand for counselor educators*. Retrieved January 4, 2015 from http://www.acesonline.net/meeting-the-2013-standard-an-initial-look-at-the-demand-for-counselor-educators/

Barrio Minton, C.A., Wachter-Morris, C.A., & Yaites, L.D. (2014). Pedagogy in counselor education: A 10-year content analysis of journals. *Counselor Education and Supervision, 53,* 162–177.

Bloom, B., Englehart, M. Furst, E., Hill, W., & Krathwohl, D. (1956). *Taxonomy of educational objectives: The classification of educational goals. Handbook I: Cognitive domain.* New York, Toronto: Longmans, Green.

Bowman, R.L., Bowman, V.E., & DeLucia, J.L. (1990). Mentoring in a graduate counseling program: Students helping students. *Counselor Education and Supervision, 30,* 58–65.

Brookfield, S.D. (2006). *The skillful teacher: On technique, trust, and responsiveness in the classroom* (2nd ed.). San Francisco, CA: Jossey-Bass.

Buckingham, K. (2007). *Go put your strengths to work.* New York, NY: Free Press.

Chickering, A.W., & Reisser, L. (1993). *Education and identity.* San Francisco, CA: Jossey-Bass.

Corey, G. (2005). *Theory and practice of counseling and psychotherapy* (7th ed.). Pacific Grove, CA: Brooks/Cole.

Council for Accreditation of Counseling and Related Educational Programs. (2009). *2009 CACREP accreditation manual.* Alexandria, VA: Author.

Cox, J.A. (2013). Creating a syllabus and course anticipation: Early engagement of students. In West, J.D., Bubenzer, D.L., Cox, J.A., & McGlothlin, J.M. (Eds.), *Teaching in counselor education: Engaging students in learning* (pp. 13–24). San Francisco, CA: Jossey-Bass.

Cranton, P. (1994). *Understanding and promoting transformative learning.* San Francisco, CA: Jossey-Bass.

Crookston, B.B. (1972). A developmental view of academic advising as teaching. *Journal of College Student Personnel, 13,* 12–17.

Davis, T.E., Levitt, D.H., McGlothlin, J.M., & Hill, N.R. (2006). Perceived expectations related to promotion and tenure: A national survey of CACREP program liaisons. *Counselor Education and Supervision, 46,* 146–156.

Dewey, J. (1938). *Experience in education.* New York, NY: Collier.

Dorman, J.P., & Fraser, B.J. (2009). Psychological environment and affective outcomes in technology-rich classrooms: Testing a causal model. *Social Psychology of Education, 12,* 77–99. doi: 10.1007/s11218-008-9069-8

Edwards, J.K. (2013). *Strengths-based supervision in clinical practice.* Thousand Oaks, CA: Sage.

Fong, M.L. (1998). Considerations of a counseling pedagogy. *Counselor Education and Supervision, 38,* 106–112.

Granello, D.H., & Hazler, R.J. (1998). A developmental rationale for curriculum order and teaching styles in counselor education programs. *Counselor Education and Supervision, 38,* 89–102.

Guiffrida, D.A. (2005). The emergence model: An alternative pedagogy for facilitating self-reflection and theoretical fit in counseling students. *Counselor Education & Supervision, 44,* 201–213.

Harnish, R.J., O'Brien McElwee, R., Slattery, J.M., Frantz, S., Haney, M.R., Chore, C.M., & Penley, J. (2011). Creating the foundation for a warm classroom climate: Best practices in syllabus tone. *Observer, 24,* 23–27.

Hayes, R.L., & Paisley, P.O. (2002). Transforming school counselor preparation programs. *Theory Into Practice, 41,* 169–176.

House, R.M., & Sears, S.J. (2002). Preparing school counselors to be leaders and advocates: A critical need in the new millennium. *Theory Into Practice, 40,* 154–162.

Knox, A.B. (1986). *Helping adults learn.* San Francisco, CA: Jossey-Bass.

Liesveld, R., & Miller, J.A. (2005). *Teach with your strengths: How great teachers inspire their students.* New York, NY: Gallup Press.

Lopez, S.J., & Louis, M.C. (2009). The principles of strengths-based education. *Journal of College & Character, 10*(4), 1–8.

Magnuson, S., Shaw, H., Tubin, B., & Norem, K. (2004). Assistant professors of counselor education: First and second year experiences. *Journal of Professional Counseling: Practice, Theory, & Research, 32,* 3–18.

Matejka, K., & Kurke, L.G. (1994). Designing a great syllabus. *College Teaching, 42,* 115–188.

McAuliffe, G.J. (2011). Preface. In McAuliffe, G., & Eriksen, K. (Eds.), *Handbook of counselor preparation* (pp. vii–x). Thousand Oaks, CA: Sage.

McAuliffe, G., & Eriksen, K. (2000). *Preparing counselors and therapists.* Virginia Beach, VA: Donning.

Meyers, S. (2009). Do your students care whether you care about them? *College Teaching, 57,* 205–210. doi: 10.1080/87567550903218620

Myers, J.E., Mobley, A.K., & Booth, C.S. (2003). Wellness of counseling students: Practicing what we preach. *Counselor Education and Supervision, 42,* 264–274.

Nelson, M.L., & Neufeldt, S.A. (1998). The pedagogy of counseling: A critical examination. *Counselor Education & Supervision, 38,* 70–88.

Palmer, P.J. (1998). *The courage to teach.* San Francisco, CA: Jossey-Bass.

Petty, G. (2006). *Evidence-based teaching.* Gloucestershire, England: Nelson Thornes.

Pope, V.T. (1996). Stable personality characteristics of effective counselors: The Counselor Characteristic Inventory (Doctoral dissertation, Idaho State University). *Dissertation Abstracts International, 57,* 1503.

Rath, T. (2007). Strengths finder 2.0. New York: Gallup Press.

Saleebey, D. (2001). *Human behavior and social environments: A biopsychosocial approach.* New York, NY: Columbia University Press.

Savickas, M.L. (2013). Preparing and presenting lectures that exemplify the ideals of counselor education. In West, J.D., Bubenzer, D.L., Cox, J.A., & McGlothlin, J.M. (Eds.), *Teaching in counselor education: Engaging students in learning.* San Francisco, CA: Jossey-Bass.

Scheffler, L.W. (1984). *Help thy neighbor.* New York, NY: Grove Press.

Schlosser, L., Knox, S., Moskovitz, A.R., & Hill, C.E. (2003). A qualitative examination of graduate advising relationships: The advisee perspective. *Journal of Counseling Psychology, 50,* 178–188.

Schreiner, L.A., & Anderson, E. (2005). Strengths-based advising: A new lens for higher education. *NACADA Journal, 25*(2), 20–29.

West, J.D., Bubenzer, D.L., & Gimenez Hinkle, M.S. (2013). Considering and articulating one's beliefs about teaching. In West, J.D., Bubenzer, D.L., Cox, J.A., & McGlothlin, J.M. (Eds.), *Teaching in counselor education: Engaging students in learning* (pp. 1–11). San Francisco, CA: Jossey-Bass.

Wiggins, G. (2012). Seven keys to effective feedback. *Educational Leadership, 1,* 10–16.

Wong, T.D., Selke, M.J., & Thomas, M.L. (1995). Advisement in graduate education: The graduate dean's perspective. *NASPA Journal, 32,* 287–292.

Young, M.E., & Hundley, G. (2013). Connecting experiential education and reflection in the counselor education classroom. In West, J.D., Bubenzer, D.L., Cox, J.A., & McGlothlin, J.M. (Eds.), *Teaching in counselor education: Engaging students in learning* (pp. 51–66). Alexandria, VA: Association for Counselor Education and Supervision.

22

Strength in Numbers

Strengths-Based Group Counseling

Duane A. Halbur and Holly J. Nikels

Some people love to decipher puzzles, solve crosswords, play video games, fix broken items, and engage in activities such as orienteering or survivalist pursuits. From an objective point of view, it may seem that humans enjoy spending time in problems. The joy in problem solving might be due to the fact that, for many, solving a problem just feels good. It can be financially rewarding or may bring a troubled relationship to a more intimate status. However, in relationship-based fields, such as teaching, leadership, coaching, and counseling, it is common practice to talk about the problem and focus on what is missing. Although this serves an intellectual purpose, it often thwarts success and reduces the potential for new thinking. Strengths-based approaches are now being embraced in these fields bringing successful, quick, and empowering change to those involved (Burkus, 2011; Edwards, 2012; Lopez & Louis, 2009; Wade & Jones, 2015; Wong, 2006).

Typically, clients come to counseling to understand and solve problems. They have "failed" in attempts to talk with and garner sufficient advice or support from friends, family members, and even themselves to alleviate their distress. It only makes sense then, as they move to professionals for guidance, that the focus of counseling is problem solving. Clients and counselors often spend a great amount of therapeutic time and mental energy focusing on the client's challenges and their sufferings. However, strengths-based counseling approaches are an effective approach to helping clients find meaningful and quick change to their lives (Wong, 2006). With significant roots in positive psychology and emerging as a late parallel to solution-focused therapy, strengths-based counseling helps clients focus on solutions and their own unique assets. This allows the therapy to not be weighed down focusing on perceived failures, losses, and mental illness. Instead, strengths-based counseling helps clients become empowered through embracing what skills, strengths, and assets they have currently.

Traditionally, strengths-based approaches have been utilized more in individual counseling as opposed to the group therapy setting. The dearth of research in this area is a reflection of this reality. However, strengths-based work has shown great promise through diverse fields such as leadership (Rath & Chonchie, 2009; Burkus, 2011), teaching (Lopez & Louis, 2009), and individual counseling (Wong, 2006). Although less utilized, strengths-based counseling is also effectively utilized within group counseling settings (Galassi, Griffin, & Akos, 2008; Proudlock & Wellman, 2011). As mental illness and environmentally based stressors continue to rise, so does the need for the availability of therapeutic resources. Additionally, as generational changes in economic success show a decline, the fields of counseling and allied professionals are asked to offer more affordable, yet effective, therapeutic interventions. Group counseling is one such way. Group counseling is not often the first choice of assistance sought by an individual facing a personal, social, or mental health concern. However, many clients will benefit from group therapy more than individual counseling (Corey, Corey, & Corey, 2010; Gladding, 2003; Yalom, 1995). In groups, there are opportunities for change and heightened focus on relationships that are not feasible in a traditional one-on-one counseling session. Chen and Rybak (2004) posited that "interpersonal dynamics affect the essence of who we are; it is through interpersonal dynamics that we come to discover and understand the various facets of ourselves and to unlock psychological blocks that may hinder our growth" (p. 2). This is indeed offered through group counseling.

Support for Strengths-Based Group Counseling

The emotional healing that occurs in group therapy is often credited as a new modality stemming from around the turn of the 20th century. This historic time showed a reduction in medically pre-scribed solutions for mental health illnesses to a boon of "talk therapy" solutions. However, the active discussing of daily struggles and storytelling at the root of therapeutic groups likely dates back at least 5,000 years. The universal experiences shared by our ancestors were done so not in isolation but in the communal activities of tribe, clan, or extended family coming together. Groups continue to receive recognition as a powerful way to connect.

Much more recent is the approach spawning from positive psychology and solution-focused therapies to make groups brief and strengths-based in their application (Wong, 2006). Although this could seem as almost less humanistic than the more spontaneous gatherings of old, it is meaningful in addressing the realities of life in the 21st century. Time and empowerment are the commodities of today.

Strengths-based counseling challenges counselors to make a shift in thinking from more tradi-tional problem-based therapies toward more contemporary positively focused therapy. This is a sig-nificant change from many of the formalized therapies and techniques of recent history. The therapist looks for assets in areas of the client's life such as strengths, successes, beliefs, and strategies (Padesky & Mooney, 2012). There are several models that specifically define the progression of therapy and expected stages within a strengths-based approach (Wong, 2006) and many others that identify the development of a group (Corey, Corey, & Corey, 2010; Gazda, 1989; Gladding, 2003; Tuckman & Jensen, 1977; Yalom, 1995). The merging of these two avenues of application and research serves as a basis for effectively using strengths-based group therapies.

Although there is emerging research that specifically addresses strengths-based interventions, most of the tenants are attributed to the related work of solution-focused brief therapy (de Shazer, 1985). Solution-focused approaches have shown effectiveness in many populations, such as those with intel-lectual disabilities (Roeden, Maaskant, & Curfs, 2014), adolescents and children (Travell, 2013), mul-ticultural settings (Meyer & Cottone, 2013), domestic violence within families (Stith, McCollum, & Rosen, 2011), and building hope (Reiter, 2010).

Solution-focused therapies commonly embrace several key ideas that serve as a foundation for successful therapy (de Shazer, 1985). It is a future-focused approach whereby clients serve as the experts of their own lives and healing (Proudlock & Wellman, 2011). A first step important to solution-focused therapies includes assessing what clients are already doing that contributes to their current problem. When this is realized, clients have the opportunity to make immediate change. Additionally, it becomes important to acknowledge the belief that knowing where the client wants to go makes getting there easier. As a teleological approach, focused on only the presenting goal, this method is an ideal therapeutic intervention for brief issues (de Shazer, 1985; Proudlock & Wellman, 2011). Finally, a common practice, which becomes the foundation of strengths-based approaches, is assessing strengths. Through acknowledging and utilizing clients' strengths, therapy can focus on what resources the client has at his or her disposal. To further these processes, solution-focused approaches offer a myriad of techniques that have become commonplace in counselors' and therapists' practice leading to such strengths-based interventions as "the miracle question," strengths assessments, and scaling questions (Lloyd & Dallos, 2006).

Strengths-based approaches embrace the spirit of solution-focused work yet avoid spending significant time looking at the problem. From this lens, it is more important to focus on using what clients already possess to change the landscape of their lives. Their personal strengths (such as confidence or intellectual ability) as well as their successes (such as resilience through a past situation or overcoming a personal crisis successfully) move to rocketing clients through their personal, present calamities.

Strengths-Based Group Counseling at Work

There are several paramount models that offer assistance to the counselor applying strengths-based counseling (Padesky & Mooney, 2012; Wong, 2006). It is important to note that for successful application of a strengths-based approach, it is best to make a philosophical or paradigm shift that helps the practitioner begin to think in a way that can promote change through embracing client assets instead of focusing specifically on problems. Helping clients identify their strengths and promoting other group members to do the same functions to help clients acknowledge and embrace their personal strengths. At the most basic level of therapeutic thought, practitioners need to change their stance from one of a doctor alleviating symptoms to a detective finding strengths.

Strengths-based counseling is not a comprehensive theoretical orientation of counseling. It lacks a developmental theory (although it may be argued that its developmental understanding is based in positive psychology), a traditional view of psychopathology, and a framework for conceptualizing diagnosis. Unlike many approaches, strengths-based counseling does not rely on the therapist to teach clients any new skills, but instead assists them in finding the assets they already have (Padesky & Mooney, 2012). Consequently, it does not exclude the practitioner from utilizing a formalized theoretical approach such as cognitive-behavioral, humanistic, or psychodynamic. However, the seminal group work model proposed by Yalom (1975), which is an atheoretical model of group work, can serve as one means to successfully conceptualize and apply strengths-based counseling.

Yalom's (1975, 1995) group approach, like strengths-based counseling, promotes less of a specific set of techniques and skills while relying more on the facilitator's use of the immediate experience of clients and group members. In developing a solid group therapy approach, Yalom (1975, 1995) was successful in developing a comprehensive model of therapy that is separate from specific theories of counseling or psychotherapy schools of thought. Therefore, a humanistic counselor as well as a behavioral therapist can understand and intervene in group therapy. As this approach is compatible to other theories and therapies, it serves well as a framework upon which to place strengths-based counseling.

There are many techniques, skills, and interventions available to group counselors and therapists. However, in promoting change there are two main roles group counselors perform. These roles, identified by Yalom (1975), are the *technical expert* and *model participant*. The work that therapists perform within the group setting can be summarized by these two roles.

Technical Expert and Strengths-Based Counseling

The technical expert is the first role identified by Yalom (1975, 1995) and is the one with which most counselors have the greatest training, experience, and, likely, comfort. The technical expert role serves to assist in the development of norms that promote change and safety in the group through eliciting specific responses, directing the group members through group changes, and providing details as to how the group or its specific members should behave. Group counseling skills are proposed by a variety of sources typically found in most counselors' repertoire. These include, but are not limited to, facilitating, initiating, goal setting, giving advice, suggesting, protecting, fanning, linking, blocking, and self-disclosure (Corey, Corey, & Corey, 2010).

Within a strengths-based approach, the fundamental skills utilized by the facilitator allow for members to identify and embrace their already existing assets. For example, a recent group member shared, "I found I was able to be assertive this week with my supervisor." As a facilitator acting as a strengths-based technical expert, the group skill of fanning was used to ask, "Who else in this group has an example of a time they were assertive this week?" This opened the group up to explore their individual assets in a similar way to the eliciting statement about assertiveness. In this case, the outcomes were better than expected. Although only one group member was able to share an "assertive example," several members shared personal assets that they were either proud of or viewed as a success. For example, one client shared she did not say "yes" to her children's demands (and incessant begging) for candy as they were leaving a local grocery store. This was an important success as she had been struggling with being enmeshed with her children and often meeting too many of their wants.

There are frequent opportunities for counselors to serve as the technical expert when facilitating various types of groups. However, a distinction in a strengths-based approach is that therapists must often take on an investigative, curious style as they search for assets or successes the members have but are not able to yet see in themselves. The therapist's job requires finding the potential within clients that is accessible although presently lacking awareness.

Model Participant and Strengths-Based Counseling

The previously described role of technical expert promotes the counselor taking charge of the group in a traditional way. In this role, the facilitator is using directives, questions, and advice to take charge and help the group members explore their strengths. However, this is not the only way to invite group members to explore their own assets. The stance of model participant challenges therapists to share their own feelings, experiences, or cognitions in such a way that is personal from their own phenomenological views. The facilitators, in essence, join the group but also attempt to be as near perfect a member as possible (Yalom, 1975, 1995).

Of course, this is not always an easy task, but it is one in which the subtleties displayed will direct the group to act and perform in a way similar to the facilitator, emulating the therapist's style. In the previous example, the therapists do a traditional fanning skill asking, "Who else in this group has an example of a time they were assertive this week?" As a model participant, however, the facilitator might say, "Assertiveness is hard for me, too. But this last week, I was able to stand up for a fellow colleague at a team meeting, and I felt courageous." In the model participant stance, the counselor behaves in the manner he or she believes will most likely encourage the group members to identify and focus on their own skills, successes, and assets. This is particularly helpful when the group seems to have little energy. It can provide the momentum to revive the group or thrust the group forward through the process of asset exploration.

Strength in Factors

Strengths-based counseling and group work serve as adjunctive concepts that help therapeutic change to occur. In Yalom's (1975) seminal work, he and his researchers set out to define, conceptualize, and track how therapeutic changes occur in group therapy. From this, 12 factors were identified of high importance to the subjective meaningfulness that group members shared regarding their group experience (Yalom, 1975). The intent in investigating and discovering these factors was to help facilitators be more effective in their role and to serve as a guidepost for successful groups (Yalom, 1975).

In later writings, Yalom defined these 12 factors as eleven (see Yalom, 1995; Yalom & Leszcz, 2005). It is believed that facilitators should explore and understand these factors, as they constitute one way to describe the "magic" and the power of a group. Not only do these factors serve to describe group processes, but they also help facilitators know when and how to exert their own influence on a therapy group (Yalom, 1995). Although these factors are only one way to view and conceptualize therapeutic groups, these 12 standardized therapeutic factors or curative factors have received the greatest attention when compared with other models (Lovett & Lovett, 1991; MacDevitt & Sanislow, 1987; Saiger, 1996).

While defining the entirety of a group member's experience is a large task, defining these factors assists in the process. The factors stand in isolation as definable, reliable constructs. However, there is significant overlapping of the factors' representativeness of group processes. For example, a critical group incident may serve to "install hope" in a group member and at the same time serve to build group "cohesiveness"—two of the therapeutic factors. The therapeutic factors provide clinicians and researchers a language with which to discuss and conceptualize the group process. These factors first served as a way to describe the complicated interplay within the progression of any particular group. These factors were identified as follows:

1. Altruism
2. Group cohesiveness
3. Universality
4. Interpersonal learning–input
5. Interpersonal learning–output
6. Guidance
7. Catharsis
8. Identification
9. Family reenactment (recapitulation of the primary family group)
10. Self-understanding
11. Installation of hope
12. Existential factors (Yalom, 1995, pp. 73–79).

To develop an effective strengths-based group, the facilitator utilizes the roles of technical expert and model participant to promote these factors as the group moves forward to the solid working stages. Although there are various written theories on the terminology and specific occurrences at each stage (Gazda, 1989; Gladding, 2003; Tuckman & Jensen, 1977; Yalom, 1995), Yalom's stage conceptualization fits well in a strengths-based approach because of the congruency with most counselors, as the model can be utilized with any theoretical approach. The commonality among these stage theories centers on progression from an initial stage of ambiguity toward a working stage of the group, where members have the greatest discourse in a safe environment. As such, this is where the greatest therapeutic change can occur. The varied therapeutic factors may differ between members in the group, as each factor may be effective for the individuals in different ways and times. Some may need installation of hope, others advice, and still others catharsis. Consequently, a keen therapist will attempt to promote as many of the factors as possible remembering that "[t]herapists and their clients differ in their views about important therapeutic factors" (Yalom & Leszcz, 2005, p. 108). Although the 12 therapeutic factors have some basic face validity, a short description of each in a strengths-based paradigm is warranted.

Altruism is the first curative factor listed (Yalom, 1995). The factor of altruism explains the human experience in which it feels good to give. In a strengths-based approach, the facilitator helps to role model and invite members to do subtle acts of kindness toward one another. In therapeutic groups, this is most often observed as members giving each other advice, compliments, and feedback.

Typically, members do not follow the advice of their fellow group participants, however, receiving advice is a gift and to offer advice feels good as it stirs up feelings of individual usefulness—a desired strength. For example, in one support group, two members seemed less engaged and rather bored at times. The other members of the group, however, seemed to move forward without them. A different, very active member, that we will call Katarina, was sharing her struggles in moving forward emotionally due to the death of her sister. She shared that she did not think she had the ability to move forward. When there was a chance to intervene, we asked the "silent members" (Aiden and Marissa) if they had any reactions to share with her. Aiden, reluctant to share, but confident in his message, shared that he heard her share several stories of her life in which she overcame struggles, including a past divorce, and that she relied on her strong circle of support. In this situation, Aiden was pulled into the role of being altruistic, serving in a curative manner. We later learned this was a defining incident for his growth in the therapeutic group. At the same time, Katarina received a gift, a reminder of her social preparedness and support system. This reminded us as the facilitators of the power in peers in finding strengths within each other.

Group cohesiveness is a vital component to a strengths-based therapy group (Yalom, 1995). Group cohesiveness is often considered the most important therapeutic component of group work and is typically described as the "attractiveness" of the group by its members (Yalom, 1995). This is highly significant, as it allows members to feel safe, disclose, and take as well as receive feedback. A group that is cohesive gives members a sense of pride in self, the group, and their autonomous choice to seek and receive help.

Although cohesiveness may not necessarily provide members with a greater understanding or acceptance of their own personal strengths, this curative factor promotes an environment where strengths are shared. Cohesive groups have trust among members, a freedom to interact, and an authenticity in which members have the courage to identify others' strengths and accept the feedback of others.

Universality contributes to therapeutic gains in that it is beneficial for others to feel understood (Yalom, 1995). Universality is a powerful therapeutic condition that is not typically offered in individual counseling. Feelings of universality are in problem-saturated approaches and therapies best described by the cliché "misery loves company." However, universality is also seen in human traditions of coming together to celebrate achievements (such as graduations, ceremonies, and other public acts of recognition). In a strengths-based approach, it is a vital component of helping recognize others' resilience and the assets they have in common. In a group setting, if cohesiveness is present, a sense of universality is elicited simply by the therapist inviting the group members to go around and identify one talent or positive characteristic they possess.

For example, when Katarina was given feedback by Aiden, the group closed by asking members to identify what strengths they heard others share that they believed they too held. Most of the members had little struggle in accomplishing this task. This intervention was designed to encourage the discovery of universal strengths held by the members. In the subsequent meeting, members would be asked to share a strength that was mentioned in the previous group that they found was a part of their week. For example, Marissa, the silent member who was becoming much more active, shared in the initial check-in of group that she had displayed confidence (a theme in the previous session and a characteristic she often felt she lacked) by beginning to apply for higher level positions within her company.

Interpersonal learning-input and *interpersonal learning-output* are actually two curative factors that so closely intertwine, it is pragmatic to describe them together (Yalom, 1995; Yalom & Leszcz, 2005). Within a strengths-based model, these have great importance as they summarize the significance of the social assets members share with or in the group process. They also acknowledge the potential for the group to help individuals share their true self. In a group with good rapport, members will inevitably share their personalities as well as their strengths and weaknesses (Yalom, 1995). In strengths-based counseling it becomes vital to recognize strengths while reducing the narrative dialogue of problems.

For example, in a substance abuse group in which one of the members (Jeremy) was struggling to open up in the group we learned he was also struggling with participation in his 12-step group. At the beginning of one group meeting, members were asked what they were finding to be their personal resources they were bringing to recovery. One rather vocal member (Sarah) shared that she could not think of anything except for her willingness to try and change. However, the next to speak was Jeremy. He shared that he had only been able to speak at his 12-step group by "repeating" similar information as Sarah. He utilized her as a role model to help himself become more active in his outside groups. Of course, this was very helpful to Jeremy. However, Sarah shared she learned a powerful lesson as she was able to share that she often downplayed her own strengths in her social interactions with others. In learning this, she was able to be more cognizant of this tendency both within and outside the group.

Guidance (advice giving) is the process of members helping each other by sharing information with each other (Yalom, 1995). The facilitator's involvement in this process is important; however, advice that comes from group members is typically received in a more favorable light. Information in a strengths-based approach helps members to teach each other lessons typically learned outside of the group experience.

Advice or guidance given can be very subtle, such as a member saying, "Keep your chin up." However, it may emerge in more direct routes such as a group member telling another he "should start praying every day." Each individual within the group has the potential to learn and explore a personal, internal strength that she or he may possess. For example, in the substance abuse therapy group, a member realized that he tended to stay sober whenever he felt he was serving others. He shared his internal strength with another member saying, "I have an easier time staying sober when I am in the service of others. Perhaps you should find a way to give back more; perhaps you could volunteer."

Catharsis describes the venting or spewing of emotions or the feeling of release that comes after expressing one's feelings and/or pain (Yalom, 1995). Most commonly there is a belief, promoted through the work of Sigmund Freud (as cited in Corey, Corey, & Corey, 2010), that acts of harmless anger or venting of sadness through crying will reduce or eliminate these emotions. However, there is a body of research suggesting that acting out anger and extreme displays of sadness may actually lead to greater energy surrounding these emotions; although, it still may be therapeutic to do so (Bushman, 2002). Strengths-based counseling focuses less on emotions that need purging or thwarting and more on emotions (such as joy and laughter) that should be fostered. Building energy behind positive emotions is an inherent goal of strengths-based group counseling.

Applying the concept of catharsis to a strengths-based approach is rather common sense. A facilitator, acting in the role of technical expert, may actually call upon members to show a greater display of emotion (Yalom & Leszcz, 2005). The facilitator may elicit laughter or tears by retelling experiences shared in the group that may invoke strong, meaningful emotions. More simply, as in a group that had become slightly macabre, we called upon Shahidi and colleagues' (2011) research of the positives of laugh therapy, that is, we asked (or more truthfully, told) the members to laugh. Although staring, blank eyes were the reactions of most members, we then informed them "to fake laugh, if you cannot real laugh." By the end of this cathartic experience most members were authentically laughing.

Identification within a strengths-based approach encourages the facilitator and members alike to find those strengths and assets that they share with others but previously have not allowed to be recognized (Yalom, 1995). People often run the risk of forgetting or repressing the basic strengths they possess. It is not uncommon that these strengths were once known but have been lost in the client's current awareness. This is especially true within the midst of crisis or personal loss. The power of the group allows members to be reminded of their own assets, skills, and talents or to practice new characteristics they see in others they would like to emulate.

For example, in a group with high-school students that struggled socially, one member shared that during the previous week he was able to have small talk with a waiter at a restaurant (a homework assignment he was given). After hearing this, another member spoke up saying, "That is something I can do!" She displayed the power of the curative factor of identification. We often have a tendency to forget those resources we have and can draw upon easily. In a strengths-based group, the members have the opportunity to see where others draw their strength and to identify strengths they have in common.

Family reenactment (also called *recapitulation of the primary family group*) is a creative therapeutic factor that provides great opportunity for members to move through emotional pains of the past in a supportive environment (Yalom, 1995; Yalom & Leszcz, 2005). This allows new strengths and assets to emerge where they were once absent or no longer in conscious realization. The group, with its trust and support, serves as a practice ground for individual members to engage contemporary skills they possess to solve past problems. Thus, they bring their strengths to the forefront.

This therapeutic factor typically arises at the urging of the counselor serving in the role of technical expert. The facilitator calls upon a member, or a few, to act out or verbally play an early family or childhood experience that continues to cause pain, fear, trauma, or sadness. Commonly when this is done, the member who has the primary focus will attempt to move through the roleplay utilizing skills that they have today, but did not at the time of the event. This is an insight we hope they gain, thus bringing their current strengths into the forefront of their awareness.

In a group mostly comprised of individuals with anxiety disorders as a primary diagnosis, one of the members continued with a common theme surrounding her childhood often sharing a discourse like, "I knew that was wrong, I should have told her that." The member, who had suffered childhood sexual abuse from her mother, was perplexed as to why she was not able to tell her mother "no." It was pointed out that as a child she did not have that strength, that she was nearly powerless and an innocent victim. When asked what skills she has today that would have been helpful as a young child, she replied, "all of them." Thus implying that as a child she had yet to develop confidence and the ability to confront a cherished adult. Through this reenactment she was able to begin to move forward at a greater pace, realizing that the strengths she had today could serve her in her contemporary world. Although beginning the process of healing her childhood trauma was important, perhaps just as significant was the transfer of learning that occurred. She was able to realize her strengths and use them to trudge through current problems and conflicts she was experiencing.

Self-understanding is the therapeutic process of insight (Yalom, 1995). Gaining insight is often experienced as an "ah ha" moment in life. Often when individuals are suffering, they have only understanding of their emotional distress and not a realization of the solutions that are before them or the strengths they personally possess. For example, they may forget that the problems they have moved through in the past were not solved by luck or chance, but through the efforts and skills they put forth and utilized.

Groups include a myriad of worldviews and perspectives that can help a struggling individual find an obscured solution or even an obvious answer to a current dilemma. While steeping in misery, it is often difficult to see what solutions an individual has at his or her disposal. The members of the group, as well as the facilitators, can all help one another gain insight. For some individuals, knowing "why" they think, feel, or act in a certain way promotes healing.

Installation of hope is the group phenomenon that occurs as members begin to believe that there is "light at the end of the tunnel" and that their present situation will not be forever and is indeed temporary (Yalom, 1995). This curative factor is seen daily in common occurrences, such as in visits to the doctor for an illness or infection. When an individual is given a medication for his or her ills, it often takes time for the medicine to be effective. However, many individuals often feel better after they begin taking it, thinking, "I will get better now." Similarly, hope is vital for therapy to be effective. Yalom and Leszcz (2005) expressed the importance of this concept when they stated, "Until the individual acquires hope and the motivation to engage in treatment, no progress will be made" (p. 109).

Hope is consistently offered to those who are struggling, ill, or having a personal crisis. Neighbors, family, friends, and even co-workers may share such slogans and clichés as "it will get better," "you will be a stronger person after this," and "this too shall pass." These inspirational statements bring hope to individuals, and we know that hope helps people heal in physical, mental, and even spiritual dimensions (Hobbs & Baker, 2012). This process, which occurs outside of an individual counseling session, can run rampant in a therapy group. The group itself may serve as a therapeutic control, letting participants know that their mere attendance and activity within the group can give them strength outside of it. In addition, it is that group members see others further in their own healing process as a source of strength, inspiration, and hope as a source of strength, inspiration, and hope.

Finally, *existential factors* are an important curative concept in the process of group therapy that can frequently be dismissed in a strengths-based approach (Yalom, 1995). This lack of focus likely occurs as the existential factors are often considered to be the "doom and gloom" of group psychotherapy, with the focus on the concepts of life being temporary and essentially unfair. We challenge this notion and ask practitioners to consider the possibility that the existential factors provide opportunities to discover the ways in which individual group members use their unique situations and assets to face life on the terms offered and pursue a meaningful existence.

The existential factors may help members to deal with the temporality of life because, like group, life also inevitably ends (Yalom & Leszcz, 2005). Although the amplitude of group ending and life ending are extremely different, they both promote a similar affective response. A rather poignant example that we saw occur in a long-term group was when one of the facilitators was going to be leaving, due to an employment change, before the group was set to end. When he shared this with the group, some members shared minor sadness, others offered congratulations to his future endeavors, and some seemed relatively unaffected. However, after his announcement, one group member (Jean) became curt with him. This was surprising, as she was a group member who had worked with him for a long time and had previously sought his attention and guidance. In the second to last session he had with the group, Jean was crying a great deal. When the counselor probed as to the reason, Jean seemed to have little insight. However, she did disclose that her father was dying. She stated she had not shared it with the group because it was due to terminal disease and there was "nothing to do but accept it."

Jean learned a powerful lesson that day and in the group sessions that followed. Accepting losses and grief when she had no control over what was happening to her became her goal. She saw the facilitator, similar to her father, leaving her and moving on to a place she could not follow. Over the next few weeks, this curative factor surfaced several times. Other members of the group also began to reflect upon how they come to terms with losses and find their personal strengths in accepting life on its terms, even when it is unfair and/or undesirable. Some members found courage, or hope or faith was helping them through their struggles and it was possible to utilize these assets in other areas of their lives. The existential curative factor helped many members identify their strengths while observing the role modeling of others as they dealt with issues of death, accountability, and acceptance.

Strength in Numbers

Strengths-based group counseling asks the clinician to consider shifting from a traditional problem-based counseling approach to one that focuses on helping clients identify and embrace personal assets, talents, and successes. Group therapy is an excellent modality for this positive process as peers and facilitators can identify the individual assets of specific members. Individuals are given new perspectives, and often the group offers meaningful insights. This consensual validation occurs as one individual of the group has a personal self-description of, for example, "weakness," whereas several members view this individual as strong. The consensual validation of others sharing their differing perspectives offers the member the opportunity to change. Consequently, the group, with the strength of many voices, may raise the individual through a description as "strong." As the group progresses and provides feedback, the individual has to make the decision as to either hold tight to a previous view (weakness) or accept consensual feedback (strength). In strengths-based group counseling there are multiple opportunities for members to realize personal assets and/or others to reflect existing strengths that may have previously gone unnoticed.

There are many models of how to provide group therapy and how to predict the stages that a healthy counseling group may experience (Gazda, 1989; Gladding, 2003; Tuckman & Jensen, 1977; Yalom, 1995). When promoting a strengths-based approach Yalom's seminal work (Yalom, 1975, 1995; Yalom & Leszcz, 2005) supports an atheoretical approach to conducting and facilitating strengths-based groups. This work highlights that the group therapist's interventions can be primarily described in the two vital roles the facilitator conducts. One role, the technical expert, is displayed when the facilitator directly influences the group. This more commonly used role in contemporary therapy includes asking direct questions, giving advice or encouragement, linking, fanning, teaching, or facilitating feedback loops.

An additional role, the model participant, likely impacts and influences the group in a much different way. The facilitator "acts" as he or she would expect other members in a healthy therapeutic group in the working stage. It is through this role that facilitators may authentically share how they feel, share an insight they have gained from the group, or model responsibility of how they have thought, behaved, or felt during the group. The primary goal of these roles is to promote the 12 therapeutic factors that are considered the curative components of any therapy group (Yalom, 1995). In a strengths-based group, these factors may be even more essential as they focus on healing, finding strength, and personal development. Again, the curative factors are as follows:

1. Altruism
2. Group cohesiveness
3. Universality
4. Interpersonal learning-input
5. Interpersonal learning-output
6. Guidance
7. Catharsis
8. Identification
9. Family reenactment (recapitulation of the primary family group)
10. Self-understanding
11. Installation of hope
12. Existential factors (Yalom, 1995, pp. 73–79).

By promoting each of these factors in a strengths-based group approach, members will progress both individually and collectively, thus bringing about positive change. It is important to provide an opportunity for each of the factors to emerge "like diners in a cafeteria, group members will choose their personalized menu of therapeutic factors, depending on such factors as their needs, their social skills, and their character structure" (Yalom & Leszcz, 2005, p. 77).

Group counseling has long been recognized as a way to support and solve people through challenges presented by life. The modality of talking in a group is therapeutic and has a history that predates formalized fields of inquiry. Finding support from others is a meaningful and effective way to bring about change. As a professional field, group therapy is an efficient and effective means to help people grow and develop through their emotional distress, life transitions, and even mental illness. Group counseling, preferred by many insurance companies (due to the reduction in cost), and potentially more therapeutic than individual counseling (due to curative factors), is likely underutilized in the counseling field. Strengths-based approaches offer an avenue to bring to the surface the assets that already exist in clients. It allows for a humanistic endeavor to engage clients in a diverse world pulling in their potential instead of soaking in their distress.

Some final thoughts as a reminder to the group facilitators and/or therapists hoping to move toward being more strengths-based in their work: Yalom and Leszcz (2005) offered these words of wisdom:

> The leader may, by offering a model of nonjudgmental acceptance and appreciation of others' strengths as well as their problem areas, help shape a group that is health oriented. If, on the other hand, leaders conceptualize their role as that of a detective of psychopathology, the group members will follow suit. (p. 125)

References

Berg, K.B. (2003). *Children's solution work.* New York, NY: W.W. Norton.

Burkus, D. (2011). Building the strong organization: Exploring the role of organizational design in strengths-based leadership. *Journal of Strategic Leadership, 3,* 54–66.

Bushman, B.J. (2002). Does venting anger feed or extinguish the flame? Catharsis, rumination, distraction, anger, and aggressive responding. *Personality and Social Psychology Bulletin, 28,* 724–731.

Chen, M., & Rybak, C.J. (2003). *Group leadership skills: Interpersonal process in group counseling and therapy.* Belmont, CA: Brooks/Cole.

Corey, M.S., Corey, G., & Corey, C. (2010). *Groups: Process and practice.* Boston, MA: Brooks/Cole.

de Shazer, S. (1985). *Keys to solution in brief therapy.* New York, NY: W.W. Norton.

Edwards, J.K. (2012). *Strengths-based supervision in clinical practice.* Thousand Oaks, CA: Sage.

Galassi, J.P., Griffin, D., & Akos, P. (2008). Strengths-based school counseling and the ASCA National Model. *Professional school counseling, 12,* 176–181.

Gazda, G. (1989). *Group counseling: A developmental approach* (4th ed.). Boston, MA: Allyn & Bacon.

Gladding, S.T. (2003). *Group work: A counseling specialty* (4th ed.). New York, NY: Macmillan.

Hobbs, M., & Baker, M. (2012). Hope for recovery—how clinicians may facilitate this in their work. *Journal of Mental Health, 21,* 144–153. doi:10.3109/09638237.2011.648345

Lloyd, H., & Dallos, R. (2006). Solution-focused brief therapy with families who have a child with intellectual disabilities: A description of the content of initial sessions and processes. *Clinical Child Psychology and Psychiatry, 11,* 367–386.

Lopez, S.J., & Louis, M.C. (2009). The principles of strengths-based education. *Journal of College & Character, X*(4), 2–8.

Lovett, L., & Lovett, J. (1991). Group therapeutic factors on an alcohol in-patient unit. *British Journal of Psychiatry, 159,* 365–370.

MacDevitt, J., & Sanislow, C. (1987). Curative factors in offenders' groups. *Small Group Behavior, 18,* 72–81.

Meyer, D.D., & Cottone, R.R. (2013). Solution-focused therapy as a culturally acknowledging approach with American Indians. *Journal of Multicultural Counseling And Development, 41,* 47–55. doi:10.1002/j.2161-1912.2013.00026

Padesky, C.P., & Mooney, K.A. (2012). Strengths-based cognitive-behavioural therapy: A four-step model to build resilience. *Clinical Psychology and Psychotherapy, 19,* 283–290. doi: 10.1002/cpp.1795

Proudlock, S., & Wellman, N. (2011). Solution focused groups: The results look promising. *Counselling Psychology Review, 26*(3), 45–54.

Rath, T., & Conchie, B. (2009). *Strength based leadership: Great leaders, teams, and why people follow.* New York, NY: Gallup Press.

Reiter, M.D. (2010). Hope and expectancy in solution-focused brief therapy. *Journal of Family Psychotherapy, 21,* 132–148. doi:10.1080/08975353.2010.483653

Roeden, J.M., Maaskant, M.A., & Curfs, L.G. (2014). Processes and effects of Solution-Focused Brief Therapy in people with intellectual disabilities: A controlled study. *Journal of Intellectual Disability Research, 58,* 307–320. doi:10.1111/jir.12038

Saiger, G.M. (1996). Some thoughts on the existential lens in group psychotherapy. *Group, 20,* 113–130.

Shahidi, M., Mojtahed, A., Modabbernia, A., Mohammad Mojtahed, M., Shafiabady, A., Delavar, A., & Honari, H. (2011). Laughter Yoga versus group exercise program in elderly depressed women: a randomized controlled trial. *Journal of Geriatric Psychiatry, 26,* 332–337. doi:10.1002/gps.2545

Stith, S.M., McCollum, E.E., & Rosen, K.H. (2011). *Couples therapy for domestic violence: Finding safe solutions.* Washington, DC: American Psychological Association. doi:10.1037/12329–003

Travell, C. (2013). Review of working with children and teenagers using solution focused approaches: Enabling children to overcome challenges and achieve their potential. *Emotional & Behavioural Difficulties, 18,* 345–347. doi:10.1080/13632752.2012.683552

Tuckman, B.W., & Jensen, M.S. (1977). Stages of small group development revisited. *Organization Studies, 2,* 419–427.

Wade, J., & Jones, J. (2015). *Strengths-based clinical supervision: A positive psychology approach to clinical training.* New York, NY: Springer.

Wong, J.Y. (2006). Strength-centered therapy: A social constructionist, virtues-based psychotherapy. *Psychotherapy, 43,* 133–146.

Yalom, I.D. (1975). *The theory and practice of group psychotherapy.* New York, NY: Basic Books.

Yalom, I.D. (1995). *The theory and practice of group psychotherapy* (4th ed.). New York, NY: Basic Books.

Yalom, I.D., & Leszcz, M. (2005). *Theory and practice of group psychotherapy* (5th ed.). New York, NY: Basic Books.

23

Finding Common Factors

Andy Young, James Ruby, Duane A. Halbur,
Holly J. Nikels, and Jeffrey K. Edwards

The claim is that when a successful change is introduced into society, those involved in it see that change as their own doing—their actions made history. But after a generation or two, the change has become so much a part of everyday life that people see it as part of nature—like the weather, or the shape of the ground on which they live.

Mihaly Csikszentmihalyi and Jeanne Nakamura

What is strengths-based clinical work in the 21st century? Will it survive, will it scatter and become something else, or will the pathology driven mental health paradigm persist and push strengths work away again? In Chapter 2 of this book, Kelly and Gates presented a useful interdisciplinary historical account of strengths-based clinical work. As has been noted throughout this work, psychologists, counselors, marriage and family therapists, and recently positive psychologies have taken to using the name of *strengths-based*. It is evident to us that the push for a different sort of clinical effort has had its ups and downs.

One of the dilemmas that we ran into while we worked on this book was an overwhelming desire to find common factors. We wanted to know what the elements are that when put into clinical work of one kind or another make it strengths-based. Are they those specific first phases of a group effort in social work that make it special? Can they then lay claim to their work as the only basis for strengths-based work? Where do the works of early psychologists, prior to the significant changes that occurred because of war veterans returning from WWII, get placed in the strengths-based movement? How about the changes attributed to a postmodern influence in the marriage/couple and family field? The authors of solution-focused (de Shazer & Berg, 1995) and narrative work (White & Epston, 1990) were social workers, after all! Even though their preferred placements seem to be in marriage and family therapy, their guild and formative training came from social work. Then the powerhouse of positive psychology that takes no prisoners in this ruckus with the traditional models has many ways of helping change occur for the better. What lies ahead in the new frontier are neurocounseling endeavors to help clients find ways of self-regulation and mindful meditation that have helped anxiety sufferers and hastened a quicker entry back with post-traumatic growth for returning veterans, both of which are discussed in this book. What is significant is that many of these strengths-searching models meet the criteria of evidence-based or science-based work.

The Process

With the push to strengthen the mental health field (Kennedy, 2015), and the continued search for ways to expand both service delivery and therapeutic models by clinicians and academics alike, our aim was to find common factors that seem to be the stalwart means to health within the strengths-based models. In so doing, we began by contacting several of our colleagues whom we knew to be proactive agents within this movement both as academic trainers and as practitioners. The 19 clinically oriented chapters within this volume represent this modest slice of the many writers and practitioners using strengths-based work around the world. There are also 4 chapters that are ancillary: an introduction, an historical setting, a stab at the burgeoning work in positive psychology, and the final chapter that codes and analyzes the ideas culled from those 19 clinical chapters. Our authors' use and interest in this work included a breadth of settings within which they worked. They were selected for their diversity: for instance, clinical populations such as sexual abuse and substance abuse survivors; school counseling; lesbian, gay, bisexual, trans, queer (LGBTQ), et cetera; different strengths-based modalities (i.e., equine therapy, movement and dance therapy, music therapy, etc.); and, finally, training with several different modalities (i.e., in classroom settings with reflectivity, clinical supervision of master's-level as well as doctoral training) and also what makes strengths-based approaches work technically. The authors were provided with a simple rubric at the beginning of the writing project, with the expectation that they would follow through with the requirements (see Table 23.1).

The rubric also had the expectation that authors could use it in any manner they believed would make their work easier both for themselves and for the reader. We expected to have to data mine these chapters for codes, mainly in the beginning of the chapters or somewhere prominent where authors were supposed to explain their concepts of strengths-based work, as well as in their case studies and their final thoughts. We found areas to code throughout, however, but mainly in the areas we expected.

As the chapters came in, our three-editor team provided suggestions to improve the readability of the ideas in text or to clarify meanings and ideas, and then the chapter was sent back for potential changes. In several cases copyediting was included, with an attempt to save the core meaning of those chapters. Every chapter was read and edited by at least two of the three editors, in a roundabout manner that provided a consistency of the common purpose of the book. Every chapter experienced

Table 23.1 Authors' Rubric

---

1. Introduction: Your perception of what is strengths-based (SB) work. How do you differentiate it from other models? Why do you use SB in this particular modality over other methods or as part of an integrated approach? Why with your particular population?
2. Literature review: What does the literature say regarding using SB use with your population versus other models?

   This section should be brief and applicable for specialty.

3. Your Application of the SB technique: how to? What do you do that makes it SB? Other considerations you might have to add.
4. Where appropriate, please provide one to two case studies that demonstrate your use of SB work with your particular population.
5. Wrap up and implications of using SB with your population: How do you know it works? How do you get paid for your work, if you do? How does it fit into a managed care or similar framework? What are the benefits? What is the payoff? What are the barriers to this approach?
6. Final thoughts?

---

comments, suggestions, and challenges, and to our delight authors' comments back indicated that editorial comments made their work stronger.

The three-person editing team plus one worked to discover the codes, and then began to identify some basic themes within them. Four members of the team met for a day long process of reading chapters and making codes. As we looked over the chapters, we discussed where each of the codes fit as well as how they were either similar or different. These codes where then placed into a table (see Table 23.2) that helped in commenting on them. Finally, an independent member of the team was a final reader to assure that we had covered all of the aspects of the work, reassuring that our eyes had not missed, or added information to the final claim of core common factors.

Table 23.2 Major Strengths-Based Concepts Common Factors

Category	Associated concept
1 Way of being (Listed in order of most frequently coded)	• Authentic in modeling through life • Self-reflective • Proficient in relationship strengths • Client strength-centered • Hopeful • Benevolently curious • Non-hierarchical • An advocate at system level • Creative and playful • Self-disclosing • Disavowing of problem mindset • Context-focused
2 Core concept	• Strengths exist in everyone • Strengths precede intervention • Strengths, resources, and adversities are contextual • Strengths constitute resilience against adversity • Strengths-based work is empowering • Strengths-based work is future-focused • Strengths-based work is pragmatic • Strengths-based work has a Pygmalion effect
3 Collaboration	• Empowerment • Clinical decision making • Clinician transparency • Broad collaborations
4 Models	Progenitorial models • Positive psychology • Solution-focused therapy • Narrative therapy • Social constructionism • Strengths-based social work • Client-centered therapy Descendant models • Cass's strengths-oriented model • Collaborative change model • Family resilience models • Motivational interviewing

(Continued)

Table 23.2 (Continued)

Category	Associated concept
	• P-SAEF (peer supervision model) • Recovery movement • Strengths-based affirmative advocacy • Strengths-finder themes model Integrated models
	• ASCA National Model • Attachment-based trauma work • Bonny method of guided imagery • Caplan's consultee-centered model • Dance-movement therapy • Equine-assisted psychotherapy • Minority stress theory
5 Renouncing a pathology bias	• Departure from problem-based thinking • Reasons for departure from deficit model • Culture and power • Renouncing traditional treatment models • Renouncing diagnostic language and labels • Renouncing hierarchy and expert stance
6 Delivery method	• Interpersonal therapeutic methods • Advocacy methods • Family and community support • Utilizing what already exists • Using the word *together* • Providing a positive comment early on in conversations

In searching for common factors, we chose to use a quasi-qualitative method of data gathering, coding, and analysis, first with open codes we already believed fit and in vivo codes of words, events, or expressions we believed fit the idea of strengths-based work. From these 19 chapters, there were 578 codes, many with overlapping contexts and meanings. These codes were then placed into general categories or axial codes we all agreed upon as central to the practice of strengths-based work. Because we were looking for common factors rather than developing a theory, this work lacks precision in the scientific sense. It is our hope and belief, however, that this end chapter will provide some cohesiveness or a road map, if you will, to the exponentially expanding pasture that contains strengths-based work.

Ways of Being

As the idea of this volume first began to germinate among us, we had a strong, although not yet articulated, sense that one of the most salient features of strengths-based clinical work is that it has more to do with being than doing or is more about personhood than clinical behaviors. Though we did not make this distinction explicit to the authors we invited into the project, it became clear as we began reviewing their submitted materials that such a distinction was rather ubiquitous among our colleagues. This sentiment is perhaps best articulated by Russo (Chapter 21) in her assertion that strengths-based work is better understood as a philosophy or way of being rather than as a theory per se. Marmé takes this differentiation even further, suggesting that infusing the strengths-based philosophy need not necessarily involve implementing interventions that are explicitly strengths-oriented (Chapter 9). In other words, it is about the person of the clinician more than the interventions utilized.

In this vein, as we began coding the information within this volume, we looked for every refer-ence regarding what it means for the various authors to be strengths-based rather than what it means to simply do strengths-based work. Twelve common ways of being were distilled and are listed in Table 23.2 in order of their frequency across the volume. Within this cross-reference, a portrait of the strengths-based practitioner begins to emerge.

By far, the two most frequently identified traits were for clinicians to be authentic in modeling a strengths-based life and to be self-reflective. Interestingly, among all of the 12, these 2 dominant ways of being may be seen as the most emblematic of the broader picture of one's life rather than of, simply, one's professional identity or who one is in the therapy office. The other ten can be more easily seen as specific to the therapeutic relationship. Certainly these two traits reflect well-established characteristics embodied by most clinicians trained in the foundational work of Carl Rogers and others. Genuineness, authenticity, and an integrated self come to mind. In some ways, one doesn't need to go any further than Rogers to understand and employ the strengths-based nature of these traits. As Mason Buford-Howell, Kelly, and Whitnell point out in Chapter 6, however, even seasoned clinicians can lose sight of these principles, and it is worth noticing how our theoretical roots laid a foundation we can return to and build upon. In many ways, becoming strengths-based is not a departure from, but rather a deepening of those foundational roots. Young (Chapter 12), for exam-ple, brings authentic modeling and self-reflection into her body-based work, creating a place of pres-ence within herself and listening to her own body response as a therapist. Similarly, Ruby notes in Chapter 19 how these traits are reflected even in how we articulate questions through word choice, tone, and facial expression.

The next most common trait was that of being proficient in relationship strengths. Again, we shouldn't be surprised to see this identified across the spectrum of seasoned clinicians assembled in this volume. As we would expect, for example, most authors cited optimism as an important trait. Others included mindfulness, creativity, resilience, engagement, patience, and compassion. Both Young and Dimiceli-Mitran (Chapters 12 and 11, respectively) offer examples of using these traits in a shared presence, holding the space with the client. Such examples, again, challenge us to move beyond our traditionally held notions of therapeutic interchange.

While the first three ways of being are clearly focused on the clinician, as we move to the remain-ing traits we begin to see the shift toward a client-specific focus. The fourth most frequently cited trait that we found was that of being client strength-centered. Although this term bears resemblance to the more familiar (if not more general) term *client-centered*, we intend to differentiate the two significantly in that a tenacious dedication to focusing on a client's assets to the exclusion of their deficits is para-mount to strengths-based work. As Nikels and Halbur point out, even when perception suggests the client is presently lacking, it is important the clinician attend to their potential (Chapter 22).

Being hopeful, benevolently curious, and non-hierarchical follow in sequential order. Perhaps these could have been integrated into the previously mentioned ways of being. However, their level of frequency throughout the text suggests they may deserve more highlighted mention. Benevolent curiosity and a non-hierarchical stance may be seen as interrelated. Curiosity, by definition, implies a lack of concrete knowing, which in turn sets the stage for a flattened hierarchy. The not-knowing stance of solution-focused therapy, as highlighted by Ruby in Chapter 19, encapsulates these ways of being. Marmé (Chapter 9) similarly refers to a non-shaming response that can be employed in response to client setbacks.

Although the next trait—being an advocate at the system level—may seem like more of a role than a way of being, we felt it was pervasive enough throughout the chapters to warrant inclusion in this list. Understanding advocacy as a way of being rather than a task or role invites clinicians to infuse the philosophy of advocacy more holistically into one's identity. Several authors identified their work as not just advocating for their clients when necessary, but also being an advocate throughout their clinical work. As Beck suggests, advocating for the strengths of the marginalized challenges the status quo and places one in the position of being a trailblazer, or visionary of change (Chapter 8). Perhaps no one makes this point more crystalline than Barrett and Stone Fish when they assert that strengths-based work creates a "refuge from contextual variables that dehumanize" (Chapter 3).

Creativity and playfulness, including the use of humor, emerged throughout the chapters. As did the use of self-disclosure, disavowing oneself from the traditional problem-based mindset, and being context-focused. In some ways, though these traits recurred throughout the volume, they may be less comfortable than others for some clinicians. Halbur and Nikels (Chapter 22) noted that at minimum, strengths-based work represents more of a paradigm shift for clinicians than they often realize. Dimiceli-Mitran even adds that disavowing the pathology bias may be the most difficult aspect of strengths-based work (Chapter 11). Self-disclosure may be the most controversial of these ways of being and certainly should remain the topic of inquiry and debate regarding ethics. Nevertheless, as with many of the traits that make up the emerging portrait of the strengths-based practitioner, we must become and remain willing to take the risk of stepping outside of our comfort zones in order to situate our professions within the portrait brought forth in these ways of being.

Core Concepts

Next, we combed the chapters seeking to find those concepts that seemed most universal in supporting a strengths-based belief system among professionals. As we coded each author's conceptualizations into general groupings, eight core concepts emerged, as listed in Table 23.2. Although these may not be exhaustive, they appear to represent some of the most essential principles that strengths-based clinicians appeal to in their work.

The most primary concept by far is the belief that innate strengths exist in everyone, regardless of the clinical issue bringing someone in for therapy. Barrett and Stone Fish (Chapter 3) suggest that client strengths are the very cornerstone of healing. This assertion alone challenges an entire legacy of traditional beliefs, as well as a subsequent library of clinical materials, regarding what it means to help someone change. Seeing our clients as "at promise" rather than "at risk," as Thomas, Massengale, and Odunewu suggest (Chapter 5), allows us to recognize their signature strengths (Ruby, Chapter 19) as unique strengths representing the best of the best within the person (Russo, Chapter 21).

Several authors inferred that these innate strengths precede any clinical intervention. This represents our second core concept of strengths-based work. Following in the vein of Thomas, Massengale, and Odunewu (Chapter 5), if the clinician moves forward from the assumption that successes already exist and that people have good intentions, the therapeutic process can embrace those already existing assets (Halbur & Nikels, Chapter 22) and further call forth such traits (Kleist, Kostohryz, & Coe Smith, Chapter 18). To Kleist and colleagues' point, the important distinction here is this idea of calling forth, or uncovering (Young, Chapter 4) those assets, which were there all along rather than the instillation of strengths from a position of external expert.

The authors of this volume are almost unanimous in identifying the importance of context within the strengths-based framework. Contextual factors are influential to identifying not only strengths, but also resources and even adversities. Such contexts may be sociopolitical (Thomas, Massengale, & Odunewu, Chapter 5), cultural (Mason et al., Chapter 6), communal (Barrett and Stone Fish, Chapter 3), and intrapersonal (Young, Chapter 4) in nature. Mason and others describe the importance of celebrating culture-specific assets such as family bonds, biculturalism, and bilingualism (Chapter 6). As Ruby, Barrett and colleagues demonstrate, social networks and community are fertile grounds for assessing both resources and vulnerabilities. Examples of contextual adversities are found in Davis and Young's (Chapters 7 and 4, respectively) attention to countering, if not eliminating, social injustices and public stigma.

With regard to adversity, many of the authors examined the relationship between innate strengths, resilience, and adversity. Davis, for example, posits that families rise above the ashes when engaged in strengths-based work (Chapter 7), whereas Thomas and colleagues describe resilience as positive adaptation to adversity (Chapter 5). Young (Chapter 12) goes so far as to say that strengths often develop out of polarities. For skeptics of the strengths-based mindset, what should be clear is that we do not promote the denial of adversity or vulnerability but rather the integration of these antagonists of change into our contextual approach.

As seen throughout the text and across the chapters, strengths-based work empowers a client's right to construct meaning (Marmé, Chapter 9), sense of mattering (Mason et al., Chapter 6), and ability to flourish (Russo, Chapter 21). It is a future-focused approach (Halbur & Nikels, Chapter 22) that initiates a legacy of optimism for the future (Ruby, Chapter 19) and a foundation of skills that can be drawn upon in the future (Mason et al., Chapter 6). It is pragmatic in its inclination toward usefulness (Ruby, Chapter 19) rather than insight. Where the strengths orientation opens one up to insight, the purpose remains pragmatic, primarily geared toward allowing access to draw upon one's own assets (Russo, Chapter 21).

Last, regarding core concepts of strengths-based work, the Pygmalion effect in which higher expectations lead to increased performance outcomes is seen throughout the strengths landscape. Young (Chapter 12) describes how the self-affirming, hope-inducing nature of strengths-based work leads to an expanded repertoire of strengths. She postulates that if the clinician believes in the client, success will often occur in unexpected ways. Similarly, Thomas and colleagues suggest that focusing on positives has a snowball effect (Chapter 5).

Collaboration

One core concept was found to be so ubiquitous throughout the various chapters and central to strengths-based thinking that we thought it deserving of its own code in our analysis—the concept of collaboration. As Marmé succinctly puts it in Chapter 9, strengths-based work is collaborative at its heart. Or, as Davis suggests in Chapter 7, collaborating with clients allows strengths and resilience to emerge. As we coded the concept of collaboration throughout this volume, four distinct principles came forward: collaboration as empowerment, collaborative clinical decision making, clinician transparency, and building broad collaborations.

As Young notes in Chapter 4, recognizing an individual's autonomy is empowering by definition. Thus, working collaboratively and flattening clinical hierarchy (Ruby, Chapter 19) is inherently empowering.

One clear way that strengths-oriented clinicians bear out the principle of collaboration was noted by several authors as acknowledging the client as an active member of the treatment team (Barrett & Stone Fish, Chapter 3). Specifically, this is done largely by collaborating with the client in making decisions regarding the course of treatment (Dimiceli-Mitran, Chapter 11; Kakacek, Chapter 13; Russo, Chapter 21). This includes mutually agreeing on the larger blueprint of treatment (Barrett & Stone Fish, Chapter 3), the focus of a particular therapy session (Dimiceli-Mitran, Chapter 11; Kakacek, Chapter 13), and identifying specific strategies for change (Russo, Chapter 21).

Another central aspect to strengths-based collaboration appears to be transparency on the part of the clinician. This involves acknowledging one's strengths as a clinician (Barrett & Stone Fish, Chapter 3) and countering therapist omnipotence through appropriate self-disclosure (Young, Chapter 4). As Mason and colleagues note (Chapter 6), this also involves modeling optimism and other strengths-based traits. Authentic, transparent collaboration as exemplified in Kleist and colleagues' reflecting team work (Chapter 18) and Ruby's description of honest supervisor self-evaluation (Chapter 19) often follow in the wake of effective self-disclosure (Beck, Chapter 8).

Yet we also find that collaboration is not limited to the therapeutic relationship. Several authors note the value of broad collaborations, including peer-to-peer partnerships (Mason et al., Chapter 6), bringing those whom Barrett and colleagues call "Angels" into the therapeutic process (Chapter 3), and fostering a collaborative worldview among clients that they will likely carry with them into the community (Halbur & Nikels, Chapter 22).

Models

Constructing strengths-based work as a unitary model inherently draws lines in the sand. Though boundary distinctions are, at times, useful and necessary, more often than not they are restrictive, exclusionary, and isolating. Our goal in circumventing the quest for a unified clinical model in favor of exploring a broader strengths-based orientation is to avoid such limitations through finding common ground and cumulative assets across disciplines and specialties. Clinicians come to this orientation along varied and unique paths and from a diverse number of previous theoretical orientations. As we reviewed the clinical models that are referenced throughout the chapters of this volume, we found three general pathways in which they intersect with the strengths-based philosophy.

The first group, *progenitorial models*, consists of those which have set the stage for the strengths orientation to materialize. In essence, they are the parents without whom strengths-based work could not exist. When giving in to the temptation of disciplinary territorialism, these are the models with which clinicians of various strains may stake claims of first arrival or highest purity of principle. We find such battles less useful than focusing on the well of cumulative assets that all can draw from across disciplines. By far, the progenitorial model most frequently mentioned by the authors was positive psychology, followed closely by those models falling under the general grouping of postmodern, constructivist theories (solution-focused therapy, narrative therapy, and other systems-based models), and strengths-based social work theory. Interestingly, these three overarching parental categories appear to align squarely with the three disciplines within which our varied authors find their roots: psychology, professional counseling (including marriage/family counseling), and social work. Although unique pioneers of strengths-based work can be found in each of these disciplines, what is clear is that no single discipline can claim singularity of origin over the strengths-based orientation. In the same vein as we see in many cultural traditions such as language, music, culinary arts, or even the spice trade, the effects of interactional cross-pollination over time can both obfuscate origins and potentiate usefulness. What we see in the new world of strengths-oriented work are clinicians drawing from a rich blend of ideas and skills, more uniform in application, perhaps, than in origin.

The second general group of models we distilled from our authors consists of the *descendant models*, or those that have been subsequently birthed out of the strengths movement. The origin of these has been largely contingent upon the previous emergence of strengths-based theories and models. These appear to be the sort of models that come forward when clinicians well versed in the strengths orientation further develop its application toward a specific population or clinical issue. In this way, these models tend to be more narrow and specific in focus yet, as with today's strengths-based clinicians, they often employ concepts from more than one progenitorial model. Examples of these strengths-based offspring include Cass's strength model in working with LGBTQ youth (Beck, Chapter 8), Barrett and Stone Fishes' collaborative change model (Barrett & Stone Fish, Chapter 3), family resilience models (Thomas et al., Chapter 5), motivational interviewing, Wachter, Minton, and Clemens' P-SAEF peer supervision model for school counselors (Mason et al., Chapter 6), the recovery movement (Young, Chapter 4), strengths-based affirmative advocacy (Beck, Chapter 8), and the strengths-finder themes model (Russo, Chapter 21).

A third group is made up of several models that appear on some level to be incongruent with the strengths orientation, yet clinicians are successfully, if at times surprisingly, integrating them with their own adherence to strengths-based principles. We are referring to this group as *integrated models*. They are not contingent upon the strengths orientation, nor vice versa. Yet neither are they as contradictory or exclusive to the strengths orientation as some clinicians may have once thought.

In this way, the use of strengths-based concepts within these seemingly divergent models may represent more of a challenge to one's strongly held affection for a particular progenitorial theory. In all cases, they are established models unto themselves, in which dynamic clinicians are infusing strengths-based work in novel ways, without prejudice or ideologically self-imposed limitations. It is these thoughtful clinicians who remind us that in disavowing the pathology bias we must not throw the baby out with the bath water. Examples from this group include the ASCA National Model (Mason et al., Chapter 6), attachment-based trauma work (Barrett & Stone Fish, Chapter 3), the Bonny method of guided imagery (Dimiceli-Mitran, Chapter 11), Caplan's consultee-centered model (Davis, Chapter 7), equine-assisted psychotherapy (Kakacek, Chapter 13), and minority stress theory (Beck, Chapter 8).

Renouncing a Pathology Bias

By far, one of the most defining characteristics of the strengths-based paradigm is its departure from problem-based thinking or a pathology bias. Although the pathways to the strengths perspective have occurred across multiple disciplines, including psychology, social work, professional counseling, and school counseling, this push back against an older, traditional, problem-focused theory is present within them all. At its most basic, this is about focusing on strengths rather than deficits, toward the development of assets (Mason et al., Chapter 6), or as Marmé puts it in Chapter 9, enhancing positive states rather than minimizing negative ones. Beck even demonstrates this push back at the systemic level, calling for the showcasing of inclusive practices rather than simply speaking out against inhibitive policies (Chapter 8).

Illuminating the motivation of various authors toward the use of the strengths orientation will both remind the reader of the pragmatic nature of strengths-based practice and highlight the reasons for a departure away from the deficit model. According to our authors, the pathology bias obscures competence (Young, Chapter 4), diminishes autonomy (Mason et al., Chapter 6), inhibits solution finding (Mason et al., Chapter 6), creates tension and worry (Edwards, Chapter 16), is iatrogenic (Edwards, Nikels, & Young, Chapter 16), and robs the individual of learning a new skill (Ruby, Chapter 19).

But the problem of focusing on problems runs deeper. As Thomas and colleagues (Chapter 5) point out, culturally diverse clients have historically been seen as deficient and, as Barrett and Stone Fish (Chapter 3) note, minority status has been pathologized and marginalized. However, strengths-based work represents an important shift away from this, accounting for cultural contexts and influences as not being deviant (Thomas et al., Chapter 5) but ripe with crucial assets (Mason et al., Chapter 6).

Departing from the pathology bias for many clinicians has meant departing from traditional treatment models within their field of specialty. Young (Chapter 4) describes the ineffectiveness of traditional alcohol and drug treatment. Mason and colleagues (Chapter 6), Kleist and colleagues (Chapter 18), and others discuss moving away from the medical models in pursuit of the positivity of a strengths approach. As Ruby (Chapter 19) notes, many attributes consistent with traditional models of both treatment and clinical supervision, such as criticism, highlighting errors and shortcomings— most of which clients and interns already know about themselves—don't move the process closer to the prevention of problems.

Several authors specified the shift away from diagnostic language and labels. Young (Chapter 4) notes the ways in which naming through diagnosis becomes one's identity, while Marmé (Chapter 9) suggests that such labeling or "digging in the dirt of causation" (Edwards, Nikels, & Young, Chapter 16) often becomes self-defeating. What is favored is the acknowledgment, as Barrett and Stone Fish (Chapter 3) suggest, that cycles of growth are not failures but natural, evolving processes.

Delivery Methods

Among the delivery methods noted by authors throughout this volume, we see traces of the clinical models, including those that constitute progenitorial models, descendant models, and integrated models. A broad array of interpersonal techniques are included, such as matching the client's ambivalence (A. Young, Chapter 4), finding exceptions to the problem (Thomas et al., Chapter 5), expressive arts techniques (Dimiceli-Mitran, Chapter 11; Chapin, Chapter 10; J. Young, Chapter 12), and self-regulation skills (Chapin, Chapter 10).

Significant attention is also paid to advocacy methods at the family, school, community, and cultural level. Thomas and colleagues (Chapter 5) refer to the clinician in this case as a cultural broker. This also involves promoting self-advocacy and collaborating toward social justice (Beck, Chapter 8). Similarly to the importance placed on advocacy, many authors stress the use of strategies to recognize and build upon family, community, educational, religious, and cultural support systems within the strengths-based framework. Whether in reference to support, advocacy, or interpersonal therapeutic skills, several authors appeal to the importance of utilizing those resources that already exist within the client and his or her environment.

Two specifically different models that fit within the role of delivery are discussed by Edwards (Chapter 17) and include the use of voice and timing in providing thoughtful ideas to clients, especially in clinical supervision. The autonomic nervous system includes the parasympathetic and sympathetic systems. The parasympathetic provides a calming effect while the sympathetic provides a flight or fight response. The first note has to do with the use of the work "together" that has demonstrated that the use of that word brings people into the fold. It has also been demonstrated that opening conversations with a calming and joining manner lowers the chances of upset. Language and timing matter.

Conclusions

In their book *Angels Fear*, Gregory Bateson and daughter Mary Catherine Bateson (2004) talked specifically, yet metaphorically, about advances in systems theory, and more. It was systems theory first, especially those words that came from the Batesonian thoughts of how ideas, the humanities, and the natural sciences have common properties, that captured the thinking of more than one of us on this team. Those parts of the system were, as Bateson believed, interconnected, interrelated, and interdependent (Bateson, 1979; 1972/2000). That concept moved some of us to begin making changes in the way we thought about mental health work. This book and this chapter share an interconnected view of what has come to be called *strengths-based clinical work*. It was a natural evolution of the different guilds and their respective models to find commonality and appreciation for something other than continued problem-seeking efforts. All through this book one will find examples of clinicians and scholars who refute that way of thinking and working. Strengths-based models appear to have blossomed for a second time in our collective fields. They, like the many thousands of refugees streaming into both Europe and the Americas, will have a heavy cultural exchange with the current way of behaving by adding to and changing worldviews and making alterations that will frustrate some and will appeal to others. The current view of mental health will remain but will be much different too. The number of people who now use a variation—a way of being, if you will—of strengths-based ideas have to more than nudge traditional notions. With Kuhn (1962) and his paradigm-shifting sciences, the change started in the training of many clinicians from all the guilds, including social workers (Reynolds, 1932; Saleebey, 2009, 2012), psychologists (Rogers, 1961; Maslow, 1971), and family therapists (de Shazer & Berg, 1995; White & Epston, 1990), and has only added to and cross-pollinated each guild, affecting their way of thinking. We postulate from our work here that the scholarship of each of these guilds was hardly ever read by members of the other guilds, and yet they all began to refute the notion of the medical model being the only way of working with those in need. As we reviewed Table 23.2, it occurred to some of us that we might add an additional column to the table comprising commonly understood and taught models from the typical medical model. It would, no doubt, have a very different series of codes and ways of being with clients. Do it yourself and see if we aren't correct.

What is crystal clear to us is that it really has, as suspected, little to do with models, progenitorial or descendant. It does, however, have to do with our view of the world and of people. Strengths-based people look for and believe that all people have a core of strengths that they have available to them. Strengths-based people make a choice to look for the good in their clients, rejecting the notion that the manner in which we work with people has to do with our snubbing the negativity that is so inherent in our culture and in many other cultures as well. We do not deny that there are bad things in the world or that some people are outright evil, we just make choices to look for what is life affirming, that is what is heliotropic in life as a way of living our lives and of being in relationships with others. The medical model is a great way to work with and understand how to diagnose and cure physical problems. But when it comes to human beings, or even dogs, cats, and horses—living breathing creatures that have relationships with others—working with their strengths seems to work very well. We are all interconnected, as are the various, extant models from any of the guilds, as will be those that are to come.

As has been said before in our first chapter, Dr. Froma Walsh argued that the work of clinicians has been taken over by the medical model in which clinicians are trained to look for deficits and problems rather than for resiliencies. Positive psychology/positive therapy founder Dr. Martin Seligman (2002) believes that mental health professionals have been trained to look at weaknesses rather than strengths and to overlook positive traits of personality. We have bought into the idea of problems and have become hooked on medications that are pushed on us and funded by lobbying pharmaceutical companies. According to the Center for Responsive Politics, using the U.S. Senate Office of Public Records data, companies give out $178,863,490 annually to ensure that their products are front and center in the mental health industry.

Those models—over 400 now—no matter how well they work, are only theories. Human strength comes from our kindness and our belief in each other; everything else is but a metaphor for a theoretical idea waiting to be proven wrong. As Mary Catherine Bateson (Bateson & Bateson, 2004) said, and I paraphrase, "What is a meta for?"

References

Bateson, G. (1979). *Mind and nature: A necessary unity: Advances in systems theory, complexity, and the human sciences.* New York, NY: Hampton Press.

Bateson, G. (2000). *Steps to an ecology of mind: Collected essays in anthropology, psychiatry, evolution, and epistemology.* Chicago, IL: University of Chicago Press. (Original work published 1972)

Bateson, G., & Bateson, M.C. (2004). *Angels fear: Towards an epistemology of the sacred.* Chicago, IL: University of Chicago Press.

Csikszentmihalyi, M., & Nakamura, J. (2011). Positive psychology: Where did it come from, where is it going? In K. Sheldon, T.B. Kashdan, & M.F. Steger (Eds.), *Designing positive psychology: Taking stock and moving forward* (p. 4). New York, NY: Oxford University Press.

de Shazer, S. & Berg, I.K. (1995). The brief therapy tradition. In J.H. Weakland & W.A. Ray (Eds.), *Propagations: Thirty years of influence from the mental research institute* (pp. 249–252). Binghamton, NY: The Haworth Press.

Kennedy, P. (2015). Patrick Kennedy On Drug Addiction and Abuse, Brook Baldwin, CNN Tonight. [Television broadcast] October 21, 2015. Retrieved May 23, 2016 from http://www.cnn.com/videos/tv/2015/10/22/patrick-kennedy-mental-health-interview-ctn.cnn/video/playlists/the-kennedys/

Kuhn, T.S. (1962). *The structure of scientific revolutions.* Chicago, IL: University of Chicago Press.

Maslow, A. (1971). *The farther reaches of human nature.* New York, NY: The Viking Press.

Reynolds, B.C. (1932). *An experiment in short-contact interviewing.* New York, NY: Taylor & Francis.

Rogers, C.R. (1961). *On becoming a person: A therapist's view of psychotherapy.* London, England: Constable.

Saleebey, D. (Ed.). (2009). *The strengths perspective in social work practice* (5th ed). New York, NY: Pearson.

Saleebey, D. (Ed.). (2012). *The strengths perspective in social work practice.* London, UK: Longman Pub Group.

Seligman, Martin E.P. (2002). *Authentic happiness: Using the new positive psychology to realize your potential for lasting fulfillment.* New York, NY: Free Press.

White, M., & Epston, D. (1990). *Narrative means to therapeutic ends.* New York, NY: W.W. Norton.

Index

Date Due
